HONDA CIVIC & CR-V
2001-06 REPAIR MANUAL

CHILTON'S

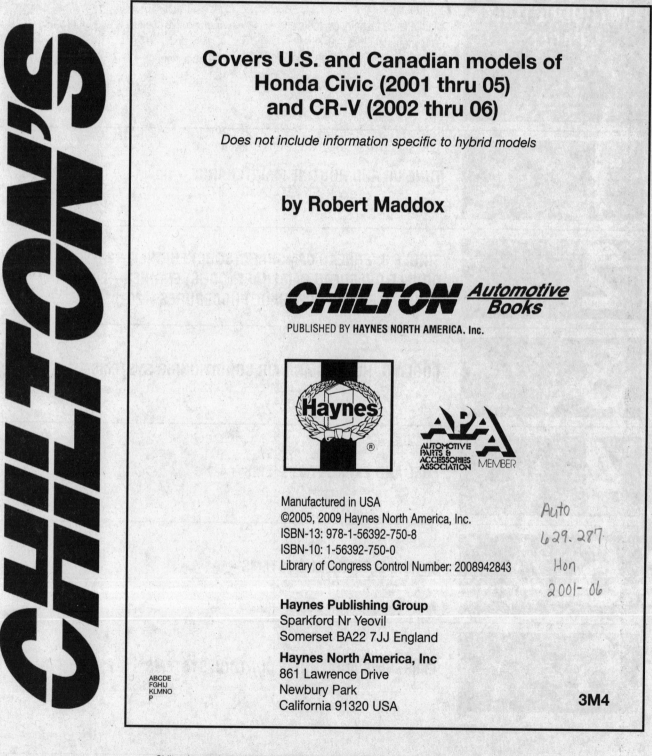

**Covers U.S. and Canadian models of
Honda Civic (2001 thru 05)
and CR-V (2002 thru 06)**

Does not include information specific to hybrid models

by Robert Maddox

CHILTON *Automotive Books*

PUBLISHED BY **HAYNES NORTH AMERICA. Inc.**

Haynes

A|P|A
AUTOMOTIVE
PARTS &
ACCESSORIES
ASSOCIATION MEMBER

Manufactured in USA
©2005, 2009 Haynes North America, Inc.
ISBN-13: 978-1-56392-750-8
ISBN-10: 1-56392-750-0
Library of Congress Control Number: 2008942843

Haynes Publishing Group
Sparkford Nr Yeovil
Somerset BA22 7JJ England

Haynes North America, Inc
861 Lawrence Drive
Newbury Park
California 91320 USA

ABCDE
FGHIJ
KLMNO
P

3M4

Contents

1
TUNE-UP AND ROUTINE MAINTENANCE – 1-1

2
SINGLE OVERHEAD CAMSHAFT (SOHC) ENGINES – 2A-1
DOUBLE OVERHEAD CAMSHAFT (DOHC) ENGINES – 2B-1
GENERAL ENGINE OVERHAUL PROCEDURES – 2C-1

3
COOLING, HEATING AND AIR CONDITIONING SYSTEMS – 3-1

4
FUEL AND EXHAUST SYSTEMS – 4-1

5
ENGINE ELECTRICAL SYSTEMS – 5-1

6
EMISSIONS AND ENGINE CONTROL SYSTEMS – 6-1

Photographer and mechanic with a 2003 Honda Civic

ACKNOWLEDGEMENTS

Wiring diagrams provided exclusively for Haynes North America, Inc. by Valley Forge Technical Information Systems. Technical writers who contributed to this project include Mike Stubblefield and John Wegmann.

While every attempt is made to ensure that the information in this manual is correct, no liability can be accepted by the authors or publishers for loss, damage or injury caused by any errors in, or omissions from, the information given.

About this manual

ITS PURPOSE

The purpose of this manual is to help you get the best value from your vehicle. It can do so in several ways. It can help you decide what work must be done, even if you choose to have it done by a dealer service department or a repair shop; it provides information and procedures for routine maintenance and servicing; and it offers diagnostic and repair procedures to follow when trouble occurs.

We hope you use the manual to tackle the work yourself. For many simpler jobs, doing it yourself may be quicker than arranging an appointment to get the vehicle into a shop and making the trips to leave it and pick it up. More importantly, a lot of money can be saved by avoiding the expense the shop must pass on to you to cover its labor and overhead costs. An added benefit is the sense of satisfaction and accomplishment that you feel after doing the job yourself.

USING THE MANUAL

The manual is divided into Chapters. Each Chapter is divided into numbered Sections. Each Section consists of consecutively numbered paragraphs.

At the beginning of each numbered Section you will be referred to any illustrations which apply to the procedures in that Section. The reference numbers used in illustration captions pinpoint the pertinent Section and the Step within that Section. That is, illustration 3.2 means the illustration refers to Section 3 and Step (or paragraph) 2 within that Section.

Procedures, once described in the text, are not normally repeated. When it's necessary to refer to another Chapter, the reference will be given as Chapter and Section number. Cross references given without use of the word "Chapter" apply to Sections and/or paragraphs in the same Chapter. For example, "see Section 8" means in the same Chapter.

References to the left or right side of the vehicle assume you are sitting in the driver's seat, facing forward.

Even though we have prepared this manual with extreme care, neither the publisher nor the author can accept responsibility for any errors in, or omissions from, the information given.

➡NOTE

A *Note* provides information necessary to properly complete a procedure or information which will make the procedure easier to understand.

✳✳ CAUTION

A *Caution* provides a special procedure or special steps which must be taken while completing the procedure where the Caution is found. Not heeding a Caution can result in damage to the assembly being worked on.

✳✳ WARNING

A *Warning* provides a special procedure or special steps which must be taken while completing the procedure where the Warning is found. Not heeding a Warning can result in personal injury.

Introduction to the Honda Civic and CR-V

Civic models are available in two-door coupe, hatchback and four-door sedan body styles. CR-V models are available in a four-door SUV body style only.

The transversely mounted inline four-cylinder engine used in these models is equipped with electronic fuel injection.

The engine drives the front wheels through either a five-speed manual transaxle, four-speed automatic transaxle or a Continuously Variable Transaxle (CVT) via independent driveaxles. On 4WD CR-V models, power is transmitted to the rear wheels (automatically) through a transfer case, driveshaft, differential and independent driveaxles, when the front wheels begin to lose traction.

Independent suspension, featuring coil spring/shock absorber units, is used on all four wheels. The power-assisted rack-and-pinion steering unit is mounted behind the engine.

The brakes are disc at the front and either discs or drums at the rear, with power assist standard. An Anti-lock Braking System (ABS) is available on most models.

Vehicle Identification numbers

Modifications are a continuing and unpublicized process in vehicle manufacturing. Since spare parts manuals and lists are compiled on a numerical basis, the individual vehicle numbers are essential to correctly identify the component required.

VEHICLE IDENTIFICATION NUMBER (VIN)

This very important identification number is stamped on a plate attached to the dashboard inside the windshield on the driver's side of the vehicle (see illustration). It can also be found on the certification label located on the driver's side door post. The VIN also appears on the Vehicle Certificate of Title and Registration. It contains information such as where and when the vehicle was manufactured, the model year and the body style.

On the models covered by this manual the model year codes* are:

1	2001
2	2002
3	2003
4	2004
5	2005
6	2006

* The model year code is the tenth character in the VIN.

CERTIFICATION LABEL

The certification label is attached to the driver's door post (see illustration). The plate contains the name of the manufacturer, the month and year of production, the Gross Vehicle Weight Rating (GVWR), the Gross Axle Weight Rating (GAWR) and the certification statement.

ENGINE IDENTIFICATION NUMBERS

The engine serial number can be found on the front side of the engine (see illustration).

The vehicle certification label is located on the end of the driver's door

The Vehicle Identification Number (VIN) is located on a plate on top of the dash (visible through the windshield)

The engine number can be found stamped on the side of the engine block

Buying parts

Replacement parts are available from many sources, which generally fall into one of two categories - authorized dealer parts departments and independent retail auto parts stores. Our advice concerning these parts is as follows:

Retail auto parts stores: Good auto parts stores will stock frequently needed components which wear out relatively fast, such as clutch components, exhaust systems, brake parts, tune-up parts, etc. These stores often supply new or reconditioned parts on an exchange basis, which can save a considerable amount of money. Discount auto parts stores are often very good places to buy materials and parts needed for general vehicle maintenance such as oil, grease, filters, spark plugs, belts, touch-up paint, bulbs, etc. They also usually sell tools and general accessories, have convenient hours, charge lower prices and can often be found not far from home.

Authorized dealer parts department: This is the best source for parts which are unique to the vehicle and not generally available elsewhere (such as major engine parts, transmission parts, trim pieces, etc.).

Warranty information: If the vehicle is still covered under warranty, be sure that any replacement parts purchased - regardless of the source - do not invalidate the warranty!

To be sure of obtaining the correct parts, have engine and chassis numbers available and, if possible, take the old parts along for positive identification.

Maintenance techniques, tools and working facilities

MAINTENANCE TECHNIQUES

There are a number of techniques involved in maintenance and repair that will be referred to throughout this manual. Application of these techniques will enable the home mechanic to be more efficient, better organized and capable of performing the various tasks properly, which will ensure that the repair job is thorough and complete.

Fasteners

Fasteners are nuts, bolts, studs and screws used to hold two or more parts together. There are a few things to keep in mind when working with fasteners. Almost all of them use a locking device of some type, either a lockwasher, locknut, locking tab or thread adhesive. All threaded fasteners should be clean and straight, with undamaged threads and undamaged corners on the hex head where the wrench fits. Develop the habit of replacing all damaged nuts and bolts with new ones. Special locknuts with nylon or fiber inserts can only be used once. If they are removed, they lose their locking ability and must be replaced with new ones.

Rusted nuts and bolts should be treated with a penetrating fluid to ease removal and prevent breakage. Some mechanics use turpentine in a spout-type oil can, which works quite well. After applying the rust penetrant, let it work for a few minutes before trying to loosen the nut or bolt. Badly rusted fasteners may have to be chiseled or sawed off or removed with a special nut breaker, available at tool stores.

If a bolt or stud breaks off in an assembly, it can be drilled and removed with a special tool commonly available for this purpose. Most automotive machine shops can perform this task, as well as other repair procedures, such as the repair of threaded holes that have been stripped out.

Flat washers and lockwashers, when removed from an assembly, should always be replaced exactly as removed. Replace any damaged washers with new ones. Never use a lockwasher on any soft metal surface (such as aluminum), thin sheet metal or plastic.

Fastener sizes

For a number of reasons, automobile manufacturers are making wider and wider use of metric fasteners. Therefore, it is important to be able to tell the difference between standard (sometimes called U.S. or SAE) and metric hardware, since they cannot be interchanged.

All bolts, whether standard or metric, are sized according to diameter, thread pitch and length. For example, a standard 1/2 - 13 x 1 bolt is 1/2 inch in diameter, has 13 threads per inch and is 1 inch long. An M12 - 1.75 x 25 metric bolt is 12 mm in diameter, has a thread pitch of 1.75 mm (the distance between threads) and is 25 mm long. The two bolts are nearly identical, and easily confused, but they are not interchangeable.

In addition to the differences in diameter, thread pitch and length, metric and standard bolts can also be distinguished by examining the bolt heads. To begin with, the distance across the flats on a standard bolt head is measured in inches, while the same dimension on a metric bolt is sized in millimeters (the same is true for nuts). As a result, a standard wrench should not be used on a metric bolt and a metric wrench should not be used on a standard bolt. Also, most standard bolts have slashes radiating out from the center of the head to denote the grade or strength of the bolt, which is an indication of the amount of torque that can be applied to it. The greater the number of slashes, the greater the strength of the bolt. Grades 0 through 5 are commonly used on automobiles. Metric bolts have a property class (grade) number, rather than a slash, molded into their heads to indicate bolt strength. In this case, the higher the number, the stronger the bolt. Property class numbers 8.8, 9.8 and 10.9 are commonly used on automobiles.

Strength markings can also be used to distinguish standard hex nuts from metric hex nuts. Many standard nuts have dots stamped into one side, while metric nuts are marked with a number. The greater the number of dots, or the higher the number, the greater the strength of the nut.

Metric studs are also marked on their ends according to property class (grade). Larger studs are numbered (the same as metric bolts), while smaller studs carry a geometric code to denote grade.

It should be noted that many fasteners, especially Grades 0 through 2, have no distinguishing marks on them. When such is the case, the only way to determine whether it is standard or metric is to measure the thread pitch or compare it to a known fastener of the same size.

Standard fasteners are often referred to as SAE, as opposed to metric. However, it should be noted that SAE technically refers to a non-metric fine thread fastener only. Coarse thread non-metric fasteners are referred to as USS sizes.

Since fasteners of the same size (both standard and metric) may have different strength ratings, be sure to reinstall any bolts, studs or nuts removed from your vehicle in their original locations. Also, when replacing a fastener with a new one, make sure that the new one has a strength rating equal to or greater than the original.

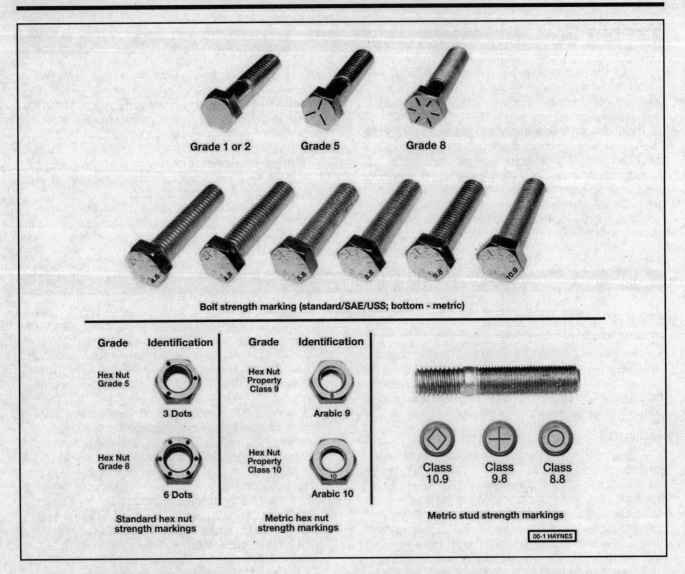

Grade 1 or 2   Grade 5   Grade 8

Bolt strength marking (standard/SAE/USS; bottom - metric)

Grade	Identification
Hex Nut Grade 5	3 Dots
Hex Nut Grade 8	6 Dots

Standard hex nut strength markings

Grade	Identification
Hex Nut Property Class 9	Arabic 9
Hex Nut Property Class 10	Arabic 10

Metric hex nut strength markings

Class 10.9   Class 9.8   Class 8.8

Metric stud strength markings

00-1 HAYNES

Tightening sequences and procedures

Most threaded fasteners should be tightened to a specific torque value (torque is the twisting force applied to a threaded component such as a nut or bolt). Overtightening the fastener can weaken it and cause it to break, while undertightening can cause it to eventually come loose. Bolts, screws and studs, depending on the material they are made of and their thread diameters, have specific torque values, many of which are noted in the Specifications at the end of each Chapter. Be sure to follow the torque recommendations closely. For fasteners not assigned a specific torque, a general torque value chart is presented here as a guide. These torque values are for dry (unlubricated) fasteners threaded into steel or cast iron (not aluminum). As was previously mentioned, the size and grade of a fastener determine the amount of torque that can safely be applied to it. The figures listed here are approximate for Grade 2 and Grade 3 fasteners. Higher grades can tolerate higher torque values.

Fasteners laid out in a pattern, such as cylinder head bolts, oil pan bolts, differential cover bolts, etc., must be loosened or tightened in sequence to avoid warping the component. This sequence will normally be shown in the appropriate Chapter. If a specific pattern is not given, the following procedures can be used to prevent warping.

Initially, the bolts or nuts should be assembled finger-tight only. Next, they should be tightened one full turn each, in a criss-cross or diagonal pattern. After each one has been tightened one full turn, return to the first one and tighten them all one-half turn, following the same pattern. Finally, tighten each of them one-quarter turn at a time until each fastener has been tightened to the proper torque. To loosen and remove the fasteners, the procedure would be reversed.

Component disassembly

Component disassembly should be done with care and purpose to help ensure that the parts go back together properly. Always keep track of the sequence in which parts are removed. Make note of special characteristics or marks on parts that can be installed more than one way, such as a grooved thrust washer on a shaft. It is a good idea to lay the disassembled parts out on a clean surface in the order that they were removed. It may also be helpful to make sketches or take instant photos of components before removal.

When removing fasteners from a component, keep track of their locations. Sometimes threading a bolt back in a part, or putting the washers and nut back on a stud, can prevent mix-ups later. If nuts and bolts cannot be returned to their original locations, they should be kept in a compartmented box or a series of small boxes. A cupcake or muffin tin is ideal for this purpose, since each cavity can hold the bolts and nuts from a particular area (i.e. oil pan bolts, valve cover bolts, engine mount bolts, etc.). A pan of this type is especially helpful when

Metric thread sizes

	Ft-lbs	Nm
M-6	6 to 9	9 to 12
M-8	14 to 21	19 to 28
M-10	28 to 40	38 to 54
M-12	50 to 71	68 to 96
M-14	80 to 140	109 to 154

Pipe thread sizes

1/8	5 to 8	7 to 10
1/4	12 to 18	17 to 24
3/8	22 to 33	30 to 44
1/2	25 to 35	34 to 47

U.S. thread sizes

1/4 - 20	6 to 9	9 to 12
5/16 - 18	12 to 18	17 to 24
5/16 - 24	14 to 20	19 to 27
3/8 - 16	22 to 32	30 to 43
3/8 - 24	27 to 38	37 to 51
7/16 - 14	40 to 55	55 to 74
7/16 - 20	40 to 60	55 to 81
1/2 - 13	55 to 80	75 to 108

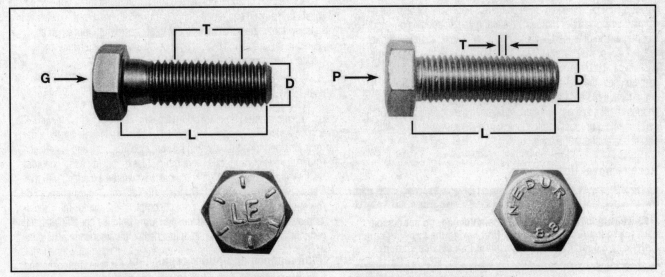

Standard (SAE and USS) bolt dimensions/grade marks

G   Grade marks (bolt strength)
L   Length (in inches)
T   Thread pitch (number of threads per inch)
D   Nominal diameter (in inches)

Metric bolt dimensions/grade marks

P   Property class (bolt strength)
L   Length (in millimeters)
T   Thread pitch (distance between threads in millimeters)
D   Diameter

working on assemblies with very small parts, such as the carburetor, alternator, valve train or interior dash and trim pieces. The cavities can be marked with paint or tape to identify the contents.

Whenever wiring looms, harnesses or connectors are separated, it is a good idea to identify the two halves with numbered pieces of masking tape so they can be easily reconnected.

Gasket sealing surfaces

Throughout any vehicle, gaskets are used to seal the mating surfaces between two parts and keep lubricants, fluids, vacuum or pressure contained in an assembly.

Many times these gaskets are coated with a liquid or paste-type gasket sealing compound before assembly. Age, heat and pressure can sometimes cause the two parts to stick together so tightly that they are very difficult to separate. Often, the assembly can be loosened by striking it with a soft-face hammer near the mating surfaces. A regular hammer can be used if a block of wood is placed between the hammer and the part. Do not hammer on cast parts or parts that could be easily damaged. With any particularly stubborn part, always recheck to make sure that every fastener has been removed.

Avoid using a screwdriver or bar to pry apart an assembly, as they can easily mar the gasket sealing surfaces of the parts, which must remain smooth. If prying is absolutely necessary, use an old broom handle, but keep in mind that extra clean up will be necessary if the wood splinters.

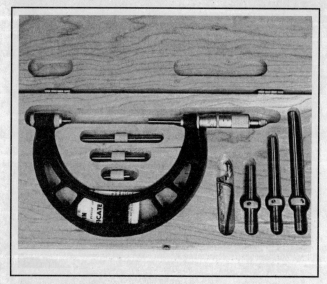

Micrometer set

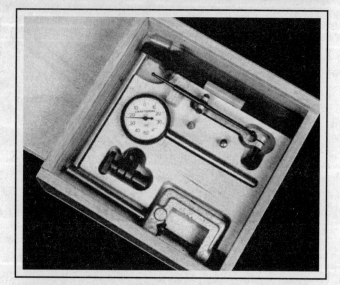

Dial indicator set

After the parts are separated, the old gasket must be carefully scraped off and the gasket surfaces cleaned. Stubborn gasket material can be soaked with rust penetrant or treated with a special chemical to soften it so it can be easily scraped off. A scraper can be fashioned from a piece of copper tubing by flattening and sharpening one end. Copper is recommended because it is usually softer than the surfaces to be scraped, which reduces the chance of gouging the part. Some gaskets can be removed with a wire brush, but regardless of the method used, the mating surfaces must be left clean and smooth. If for some reason the gasket surface is gouged, then a gasket sealer thick enough to fill scratches will have to be used during reassembly of the components. For most applications, a non-drying (or semi-drying) gasket sealer should be used.

Hose removal tips

❋❋ WARNING:

If the vehicle is equipped with air conditioning, do not disconnect any of the A/C hoses without first having the system depressurized by a dealer service department or a service station.

Hose removal precautions closely parallel gasket removal precautions. Avoid scratching or gouging the surface that the hose mates against or the connection may leak. This is especially true for radiator hoses. Because of various chemical reactions, the rubber in hoses can bond itself to the metal spigot that the hose fits over. To remove a hose, first loosen the hose clamps that secure it to the spigot. Then, with slip-joint pliers, grab the hose at the clamp and rotate it around the spigot. Work it back and forth until it is completely free, then pull it off. Silicone or other lubricants will ease removal if they can be applied between the hose and the outside of the spigot. Apply the same lubricant to the inside of the hose and the outside of the spigot to simplify installation.

As a last resort (and if the hose is to be replaced with a new one anyway), the rubber can be slit with a knife and the hose peeled from the spigot. If this must be done, be careful that the metal connection is not damaged.

If a hose clamp is broken or damaged, do not reuse it. Wire-type clamps usually weaken with age, so it is a good idea to replace them with screw-type clamps whenever a hose is removed.

TOOLS

A selection of good tools is a basic requirement for anyone who plans to maintain and repair his or her own vehicle. For the owner who has few tools, the initial investment might seem high, but when compared to the spiraling costs of professional auto maintenance and repair, it is a wise one.

To help the owner decide which tools are needed to perform the tasks detailed in this manual, the following tool lists are offered: *Maintenance and minor repair, Repair/overhaul* and *Special*.

The newcomer to practical mechanics should start off with the *maintenance and minor repair* tool kit, which is adequate for the simpler jobs performed on a vehicle. Then, as confidence and experience grow, the owner can tackle more difficult tasks, buying additional tools as they are needed. Eventually the basic kit will be expanded into the *repair and overhaul* tool set. Over a period of time, the experienced do-it-yourselfer will assemble a tool set complete enough for most repair and overhaul procedures and will add tools from the special category when it is felt that the expense is justified by the frequency of use.

Maintenance and minor repair tool kit

The tools in this list should be considered the minimum required for performance of routine maintenance, servicing and minor repair work. We recommend the purchase of combination wrenches (box-end and open-end combined in one wrench). While more expensive than open end wrenches, they offer the advantages of both types of wrench.

Combination wrench set (1/4-inch to 1 inch or 6 mm to 19 mm)
Adjustable wrench, 8 inch
Spark plug wrench with rubber insert
Spark plug gap adjusting tool
Feeler gauge set
Brake bleeder wrench
Standard screwdriver (5/16-inch x 6 inch)
Phillips screwdriver (No. 2 x 6 inch)
Combination pliers - 6 inch
Hacksaw and assortment of blades
Tire pressure gauge
Grease gun
Oil can
Fine emery cloth

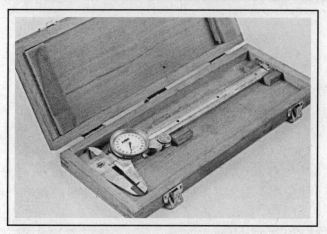

Dial caliper

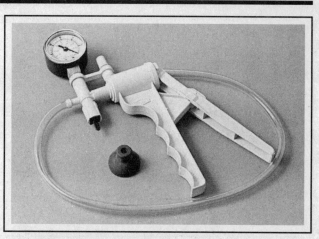

Hand-operated vacuum pump

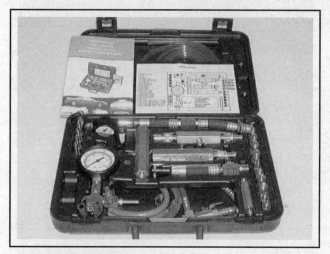

Fuel pressure gauge set

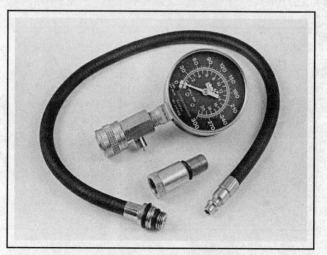

Compression gauge with spark plug hole adapter

Wire brush
Battery post and cable cleaning tool
Oil filter wrench
Funnel (medium size)
Safety goggles
Jackstands (2)
Drain pan

➡**Note: If basic tune-ups are going to be part of routine maintenance, it will be necessary to purchase a good quality stroboscopic timing light and combination tachometer/dwell meter.
Although they are included in the list of special tools, it is mentioned here because they are absolutely necessary for tuning
most vehicles properly.**

Repair and overhaul tool set

These tools are essential for anyone who plans to perform major
repairs and are in addition to those in the maintenance and minor
repair tool kit. Included is a comprehensive set of sockets which,
though expensive, are invaluable because of their versatility, especially
when various extensions and drives are available. We recommend the
1/2-inch drive over the 3/8-inch drive. Although the larger drive is
bulky and more expensive, it has the capacity of accepting a very wide
range of large sockets. Ideally, however, the mechanic should have a
3/8-inch drive set and a 1/2-inch drive set.

Socket set(s)

Reversible ratchet
Extension - 10 inch
Universal joint
Torque wrench (same size drive as sockets)
Ball peen hammer - 8 ounce
Soft-face hammer (plastic/rubber)
Standard screwdriver (1/4-inch x 6 inch)
Standard screwdriver (stubby - 5/16-inch)
Phillips screwdriver (No. 3 x 8 inch)
Phillips screwdriver (stubby - No. 2)
Pliers - vise grip
Pliers - lineman's
Pliers - needle nose
Pliers - snap-ring (internal and external)
Cold chisel - 1/2-inch
Scribe
Scraper (made from flattened copper tubing)
Centerpunch
Pin punches (1/16, 1/8, 3/16-inch)
Steel rule/straightedge - 12 inch
Allen wrench set (1/8 to 3/8-inch or 4 mm to 10 mm)
A selection of files
Wire brush (large)
Jackstands (second set)
Jack (scissor or hydraulic type)

Damper/steering wheel puller

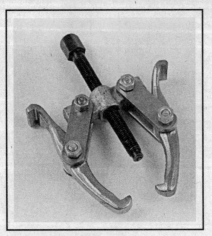

General purpose puller

Hydraulic lifter removal tool

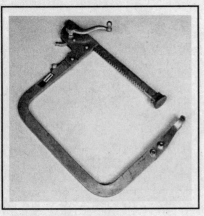

Valve spring compressor

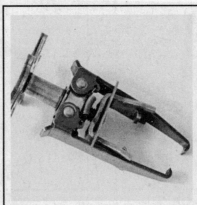

Valve spring compressor

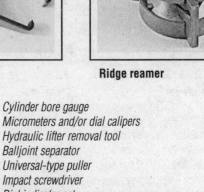

Ridge reamer

➡**Note: Another tool which is often useful is an electric drill with a chuck capacity of 3/8-inch and a set of good quality drill bits.**

Special tools

The tools in this list include those which are not used regularly, are expensive to buy, or which need to be used in accordance with their manufacturer's instructions. Unless these tools will be used frequently, it is not very economical to purchase many of them. A consideration would be to split the cost and use between yourself and a friend or friends. In addition, most of these tools can be obtained from a tool rental shop on a temporary basis.

This list primarily contains only those tools and instruments widely available to the public, and not those special tools produced by the vehicle manufacturer for distribution to dealer service departments. Occasionally, references to the manufacturer's special tools are included in the text of this manual. Generally, an alternative method of doing the job without the special tool is offered. However, sometimes there is no alternative to their use. Where this is the case, and the tool cannot be purchased or borrowed, the work should be turned over to the dealer service department or an automotive repair shop.

Valve spring compressor
Piston ring groove cleaning tool
Piston ring compressor
Piston ring installation tool
Cylinder compression gauge
Cylinder ridge reamer
Cylinder surfacing hone

Cylinder bore gauge
Micrometers and/or dial calipers
Hydraulic lifter removal tool
Balljoint separator
Universal-type puller
Impact screwdriver
Dial indicator set
Stroboscopic timing light (inductive pick-up)
Hand operated vacuum/pressure pump
Tachometer/dwell meter
Universal electrical multimeter
Cable hoist
Brake spring removal and installation tools
Floor jack

Buying tools

For the do-it-yourselfer who is just starting to get involved in vehicle maintenance and repair, there are a number of options available when purchasing tools. If maintenance and minor repair is the extent of the work to be done, the purchase of individual tools is satisfactory. If, on the other hand, extensive work is planned, it would be a good idea to purchase a modest tool set from one of the large retail chain stores. A set can usually be bought at a substantial savings over the individual tool prices, and they often come with a tool box. As additional tools are needed, add-on sets, individual tools and a larger tool box can be purchased to expand the tool selection. Building a tool set gradually

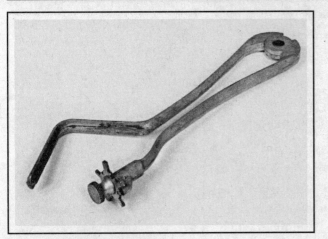

Piston ring groove cleaning tool

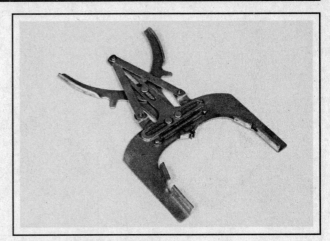

Ring removal/installation tool

Ring compressor

Cylinder hone

Brake hold-down spring tool

allows the cost of the tools to be spread over a longer period of time and gives the mechanic the freedom to choose only those tools that will actually be used.

Tool stores will often be the only source of some of the special tools that are needed, but regardless of where tools are bought, try to avoid cheap ones, especially when buying screwdrivers and sockets, because they won't last very long. The expense involved in replacing cheap tools will eventually be greater than the initial cost of quality tools.

Care and maintenance of tools

Good tools are expensive, so it makes sense to treat them with respect. Keep them clean and in usable condition and store them properly when not in use. Always wipe off any dirt, grease or metal chips before putting them away. Never leave tools lying around in the work area. Upon completion of a job, always check closely under the hood for tools that may have been left there so they won't get lost during a test drive.

Some tools, such as screwdrivers, pliers, wrenches and sockets, can be hung on a panel mounted on the garage or workshop wall, while others should be kept in a tool box or tray. Measuring instruments, gauges, meters, etc. must be carefully stored where they cannot be damaged by weather or impact from other tools.

When tools are used with care and stored properly, they will last a very long time. Even with the best of care, though, tools will wear out if used frequently. When a tool is damaged or worn out, replace it. Subsequent jobs will be safer and more enjoyable if you do.

HOW TO REPAIR DAMAGED THREADS

Sometimes, the internal threads of a nut or bolt hole can become stripped, usually from overtightening. Stripping threads is an all-too-common occurrence, especially when working with aluminum parts, because aluminum is so soft that it easily strips out.

Usually, external or internal threads are only partially stripped. After they've been cleaned up with a tap or die, they'll still work. Sometimes, however, threads are badly damaged. When this happens, you've got three choices:

1) *Drill and tap the hole to the next suitable oversize and install a larger diameter bolt, screw or stud.*

2) *Drill and tap the hole to accept a threaded plug, then drill and tap the plug to the original screw size. You can also buy a plug already threaded to the original size. Then you simply drill a hole to the specified size, then run the threaded plug into the hole with a bolt and jam nut. Once the plug is fully seated, remove the jam nut and bolt.*

3) *The third method uses a patented thread repair kit like Heli-Coil or Slimsert. These easy-to-use kits are designed to repair damaged threads in straight-through holes and blind holes. Both are available as kits which can handle a variety of sizes and thread patterns. Drill the hole, then tap it with the special included tap. Install the Heli-Coil and the hole is back to its original diameter and thread pitch.*

Regardless of which method you use, be sure to proceed calmly

Torque angle gauge

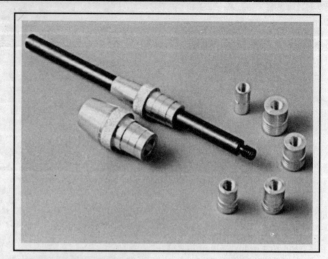

Clutch plate alignment tool

and carefully. A little impatience or carelessness during one of these relatively simple procedures can ruin your whole day's work and cost you a bundle if you wreck an expensive part.

WORKING FACILITIES

Not to be overlooked when discussing tools is the workshop. If anything more than routine maintenance is to be carried out, some sort of suitable work area is essential.

It is understood, and appreciated, that many home mechanics do not have a good workshop or garage available, and end up removing an engine or doing major repairs outside. It is recommended, however, that the overhaul or repair be completed under the cover of a roof.

A clean, flat workbench or table of comfortable working height is an absolute necessity. The workbench should be equipped with a vise that has a jaw opening of at least four inches.

As mentioned previously, some clean, dry storage space is also required for tools, as well as the lubricants, fluids, cleaning solvents, etc. which soon become necessary.

Sometimes waste oil and fluids, drained from the engine or cooling system during normal maintenance or repairs, present a disposal problem. To avoid pouring them on the ground or into a sewage system, pour the used fluids into large containers, seal them with caps and take them to an authorized disposal site or recycling center. Plastic jugs, such as old antifreeze containers, are ideal for this purpose.

Always keep a supply of old newspapers and clean rags available. Old towels are excellent for mopping up spills. Many mechanics use rolls of paper towels for most work because they are readily available

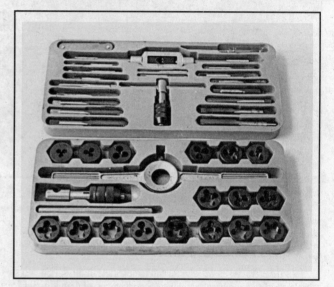

Tap and die set

and disposable. To help keep the area under the vehicle clean, a large cardboard box can be cut open and flattened to protect the garage or shop floor.

Whenever working over a painted surface, such as when leaning over a fender to service something under the hood, always cover it with an old blanket or bedspread to protect the finish. Vinyl covered pads, made especially for this purpose, are available at auto parts stores.

Jacking and towing

JACKING

The jack supplied with the vehicle should only be used for raising the vehicle for changing a tire or placing jackstands under the frame.

✳✳ WARNING:

Never crawl under the vehicle or start the engine when the jack is being used as the only means of support.

All vehicles are supplied with a scissors-type jack. When jacking the vehicle, it should be engaged with the notch in the rocker panel flange (see illustration).

The vehicle should be on level ground with the wheels blocked and the transmission in Park. Pry off the hub cap (if equipped) using the tapered end of the lug wrench. Loosen the lug nuts one-half turn and leave them in place until the wheel is raised off the ground.

Place the jack under the side of the vehicle in the indicated position. Use the supplied wrench to turn the jackscrew clockwise until the wheel is raised off the ground. Remove the lug nuts, pull off the wheel and install the spare.

With the beveled side in, install the lug nuts and tighten them until snug. Lower the vehicle by turning the jackscrew counterclockwise. Remove the jack and tighten the nuts in a diagonal pattern to the torque listed in the Chapter 1 Specifications. If a torque wrench is not available, have the torque checked by a service station as soon as possible. Install the hubcap by placing it in position and using the heel of your hand or a rubber mallet to seat it.

TOWING

Civic and 2WD CR-V models

As a general rule, the vehicle should be towed with the front (drive) wheels off the ground (the best method is to have the vehicle placed on a flat-bed tow truck). If they can't be raised, place them on a dolly. The ignition key must be in the OFF position, since the steering lock mechanism isn't strong enough to hold the front wheels straight while towing.

The jack fits over the rocker panel flange (there are two jacking points on each side of the vehicle)

Vehicles equipped with an automatic transaxle can be towed from the front with all four wheels on the ground, provided that speeds don't exceed 35 mph and the distance is not over 50 miles. Before towing, check the transmission fluid level (see Chapter 1). If the level is below the HOT line on the dipstick, add fluid or use a towing dolly. Additionally, perform the following steps:

a) Release the parking brake
b) Start the engine
c) Move the transaxle gear selector into D4, then to Neutral
d) Turn off the engine
e) Place the ignition key in the OFF (not the LOCK position).

✳✳ CAUTION:

Never tow a vehicle with an automatic transaxle from the rear with the front wheels on the ground.

4WD CR-V models

The preferred method for towing these models is on a flat-bed tow truck. Tow trucks that use wheel-lift or sling-type equipment cannot be used. These models can be towed with all four wheels on the ground, provided that the proper towing equipment is used, towing speed does not exceed 65 miles per hour, and the ignition key is turned to the accessory position (with all accessories turned off so the battery doesn't go dead). Additionally, before towing, the following procedure must be performed, or the transaxle will be severely damaged:

a) Start the engine
b) Depress the brake pedal and move the shift lever through all of the gear positions
c) Move the shift lever to the D position, then to the Neutral position
d) Release the parking brake
e) Turn the engine off, but leave the ignition key in the accessory position (with all accessories turned off)

This procedure must be performed at the beginning of each towing day, and every 300 miles, or damage to the transaxle will occur.

✳✳ CAUTION:

Towing a 4WD CR-V with one end of the vehicle raised will cause damage to the 4WD system.

All models

When towing a vehicle equipped with a manual transaxle or Continuously Variable Transaxle with all four wheels on the ground, be sure to place the shift lever in neutral and release the parking brake.

Equipment specifically designed for towing should be used. It should be attached to the main structural members of the vehicle, not the bumpers or brackets.

Safety is a major consideration when towing and all applicable state and local laws must be obeyed. A safety chain system must be used at all times. Remember that power steering and power brakes will not work with the engine off.

Booster battery (jump) starting

Observe the following precautions when using a booster battery to start a vehicle:

a) Before connecting the booster battery, make sure the ignition switch is in the Off position.

b) Turn off the lights, heater and other electrical loads.

c) Your eyes should be shielded. Safety goggles are a good idea.

d) Make sure the booster battery is the same voltage as the dead one in the vehicle.

e) The two vehicles MUST NOT TOUCH each other.

f) Make sure the transmission is in Park.

g) If the booster battery is not a maintenance-free type, remove the vent caps and lay a cloth over the vent holes.

Connect the red jumper cable to the positive (+) terminals of each battery.

Connect one end of the black cable to the negative (-) terminal of the booster battery. The other end of this cable should be connected to a good ground on the engine block (see illustration). Make sure the cable will not come into contact with the fan, drivebelts or other moving parts of the engine.

Start the engine using the booster battery, then, with the engine running at idle speed, disconnect the jumper cables in the reverse order of connection.

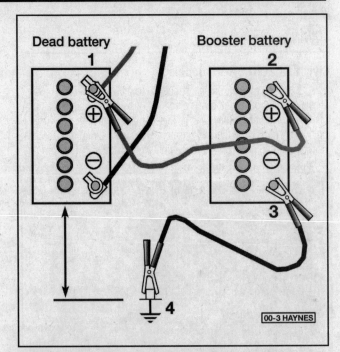

Make the booster battery cable connections in the numerical order shown (note that the negative cable of the booster battery is NOT attached to the negative terminal of the dead battery)

Conversion factors

Length (distance)

Inches (in)	X	25.4	= Millimeters (mm)	X 0.0394	= Inches (in)
Feet (ft)	X	0.305	= Meters (m)	X 3.281	= Feet (ft)
Miles	X	1.609	= Kilometers (km)	X 0.621	= Miles

Volume (capacity)

Cubic inches (cu in; in³)	X	16.387	= Cubic centimeters (cc; cm³)	X 0.061	= Cubic inches (cu in; in³)
Imperial pints (Imp pt)	X	0.568	= Liters (l)	X 1.76	= Imperial pints (Imp pt)
Imperial quarts (Imp qt)	X	1.137	= Liters (l)	X 0.88	= Imperial quarts (Imp qt)
Imperial quarts (Imp qt)	X	1.201	= US quarts (US qt)	X 0.833	= Imperial quarts (Imp qt)
US quarts (US qt)	X	0.946	= Liters (l)	X 1.057	= US quarts (US qt)
Imperial gallons (Imp gal)	X	4.546	= Liters (l)	X 0.22	= Imperial gallons (Imp gal)
Imperial gallons (Imp gal)	X	1.201	= US gallons (US gal)	X 0.833	= Imperial gallons (Imp gal)
US gallons (US gal)	X	3.785	= Liters (l)	X 0.264	= US gallons (US gal)

Mass (weight)

Ounces (oz)	X	28.35	= Grams (g)	X 0.035	= Ounces (oz)
Pounds (lb)	X	0.454	= Kilograms (kg)	X 2.205	= Pounds (lb)

Force

Ounces-force (ozf; oz)	X	0.278	= Newtons (N)	X 3.6	= Ounces-force (ozf; oz)
Pounds-force (lbf; lb)	X	4.448	= Newtons (N)	X 0.225	= Pounds-force (lbf; lb)
Newtons (N)	X	0.1	= Kilograms-force (kgf; kg)	X 9.81	= Newtons (N)

Pressure

Pounds-force per square inch (psi; lbf/in²; lb/in²)	X	0.070	= Kilograms-force per square centimeter (kgf/cm²; kg/cm²)	X 14.223	= Pounds-force per square inch (psi; lbf/in²; lb/in²)
Pounds-force per square inch (psi; lbf/in²; lb/in²)	X	0.068	= Atmospheres (atm)	X 14.696	= Pounds-force per square inch (psi; lbf/in²; lb/in²)
Pounds-force per square inch (psi; lbf/in²; lb/in²)	X	0.069	= Bars	X 14.5	= Pounds-force per square inch (psi; lbf/in²; lb/in²)
Pounds-force per square inch (psi; lbf/in²; lb/in²)	X	6.895	= Kilopascals (kPa)	X 0.145	= Pounds-force per square inch (psi; lbf/in²; lb/in²)
Kilopascals (kPa)	X	0.01	= Kilograms-force per square centimeter (kgf/cm²; kg/cm²)	X 98.1	= Kilopascals (kPa)

Torque (moment of force)

Pounds-force inches (lbf in; lb in)	X	1.152	= Kilograms-force centimeter (kgf cm; kg cm)	X 0.868	= Pounds-force inches (lbf in; lb in)
Pounds-force inches (lbf in; lb in)	X	0.113	= Newton meters (Nm)	X 8.85	= Pounds-force inches (lbf in; lb in)
Pounds-force inches (lbf in; lb in)	X	0.083	= Pounds-force feet (lbf ft; lb ft)	X 12	= Pounds-force inches (lbf in; lb in)
Pounds-force feet (lbf ft; lb ft)	X	0.138	= Kilograms-force meters (kgf m; kg m)	X 7.233	= Pounds-force feet (lbf ft; lb ft)
Pounds-force feet (lbf ft; lb ft)	X	1.356	= Newton meters (Nm)	X 0.738	= Pounds-force feet (lbf ft; lb ft)
Newton meters (Nm)	X	0.102	= Kilograms-force meters (kgf m; kg m)	X 9.804	= Newton meters (Nm)

Vacuum

Inches mercury (in. Hg)	X	3.377	= Kilopascals (kPa)	X 0.2961	= Inches mercury
Inches mercury (in. Hg)	X	25.4	= Millimeters mercury (mm Hg)	X 0.0394	= Inches mercury

Power

Horsepower (hp)	X	745.7	= Watts (W)	X 0.0013	= Horsepower (hp)

Velocity (speed)

Miles per hour (miles/hr; mph)	X	1.609	= Kilometers per hour (km/hr; kph)	X 0.621	= Miles per hour (miles/hr; mph)

Fuel consumption*

Miles per gallon, Imperial (mpg)	X	0.354	= Kilometers per liter (km/l)	X 2.825	= Miles per gallon, Imperial (mpg)
Miles per gallon, US (mpg)	X	0.425	= Kilometers per liter (km/l)	X 2.352	= Miles per gallon, US (mpg)

Temperature

Degrees Fahrenheit = (°C x 1.8) + 32

Degrees Celsius (Degrees Centigrade; °C) = (°F - 32) x 0.56

FRACTION/DECIMAL/MILLIMETER EQUIVALENTS

DECIMALS to MILLIMETERS

Decimal	mm	Decimal	mm
0.001	0.0254	0.500	12.7000
0.002	0.0508	0.510	12.9540
0.003	0.0762	0.520	13.2080
0.004	0.1016	0.530	13.4620
0.005	0.1270	0.540	13.7160
0.006	0.1524	0.550	13.9700
0.007	0.1778	0.560	14.2240
0.008	0.2032	0.570	14.4780
0.009	0.2286	0.580	14.7320
		0.590	14.9860
0.010	0.2540		
0.020	0.5080		
0.030	0.7620		
0.040	1.0160	0.600	15.2400
0.050	1.2700	0.610	15.4940
0.060	1.5240	0.620	15.7480
0.070	1.7780	0.630	16.0020
0.080	2.0320	0.640	16.2560
0.090	2.2860	0.650	16.5100
		0.660	16.7640
0.100	2.5400	0.670	17.0180
0.110	2.7940	0.680	17.2720
0.120	3.0480	0.690	17.5260
0.130	3.3020		
0.140	3.5560		
0.150	3.8100		
0.160	4.0640	0.700	17.7800
0.170	4.3180	0.710	18.0340
0.180	4.5720	0.720	18.2880
0.190	4.8260	0.730	18.5420
		0.740	18.7960
0.200	5.0800	0.750	19.0500
0.210	5.3340	0.760	19.3040
0.220	5.5880	0.770	19.5580
0.230	5.8420	0.780	19.8120
0.240	6.0960	0.790	20.0660
0.250	6.3500		
0.260	6.6040		
0.270	6.8580	0.800	20.3200
0.280	7.1120	0.810	20.5740
0.290	7.3660	0.820	21.8280
		0.830	21.0820
0.300	7.6200	0.840	21.3360
0.310	7.8740	0.850	21.5900
0.320	8.1280	0.860	21.8440
0.330	8.3820	0.870	22.0980
0.340	8.6360	0.880	22.3520
0.350	8.8900	0.890	22.6060
0.360	9.1440		
0.370	9.3980		
0.380	9.6520		
0.390	9.9060	0.900	22.8600
0.400	10.1600	0.910	23.1140
0.410	10.4140	0.920	23.3680
0.420	10.6680	0.930	23.6220
0.430	10.9220	0.940	23.8760
0.440	11.1760	0.950	24.1300
0.450	11.4300	0.960	24.3840
0.460	11.6840	0.970	24.6380
0.470	11.9380	0.980	24.8920
0.480	12.1920	0.990	25.1460
0.490	12.4460	1.000	25.4000

FRACTIONS to DECIMALS to MILLIMETERS

Fraction	Decimal	mm	Fraction	Decimal	mm
1/64	0.0156	0.3969	33/64	0.5156	13.0969
1/32	0.0312	0.7938	17/32	0.5312	13.4938
3/64	0.0469	1.1906	35/64	0.5469	13.8906
1/16	0.0625	1.5875	9/16	0.5625	14.2875
5/64	0.0781	1.9844	37/64	0.5781	14.6844
3/32	0.0938	2.3812	19/32	0.5938	15.0812
7/64	0.1094	2.7781	39/64	0.6094	15.4781
1/8	0.1250	3.1750	5/8	0.6250	15.8750
9/64	0.1406	3.5719	41/64	0.6406	16.2719
5/32	0.1562	3.9688	21/32	0.6562	16.6688
11/64	0.1719	4.3656	43/64	0.6719	17.0656
3/16	0.1875	4.7625	11/16	0.6875	17.4625
13/64	0.2031	5.1594	45/64	0.7031	17.8594
7/32	0.2188	5.5562	23/32	0.7188	18.2562
15/64	0.2344	5.9531	47/64	0.7344	18.6531
1/4	0.2500	6.3500	3/4	0.7500	19.0500
17/64	0.2656	6.7469	49/64	0.7656	19.4469
9/32	0.2812	7.1438	25/32	0.7812	19.8438
19/64	0.2969	7.5406	51/64	0.7969	20.2406
5/16	0.3125	7.9375	13/16	0.8125	20.6375
21/64	0.3281	8.3344	53/64	0.8281	21.0344
11/32	0.3438	8.7312	27/32	0.8438	21.4312
23/64	0.3594	9.1281	55/64	0.8594	21.8281
3/8	0.3750	9.5250	7/8	0.8750	22.2250
25/64	0.3906	9.9219	57/64	0.8906	22.6219
13/32	0.4062	10.3188	29/32	0.9062	23.0188
27/64	0.4219	10.7156	59/64	0.9219	23.4156
7/16	0.4375	11.1125	15/16	0.9375	23.8125
29/64	0.4531	11.5094	61/64	0.9531	24.2094
15/32	0.4688	11.9062	31/32	0.9688	24.6062
31/64	0.4844	12.3031	63/64	0.9844	25.0031
1/2	0.5000	12.7000	1	1.0000	25.4000

Automotive chemicals and lubricants

A number of automotive chemicals and lubricants are available for use during vehicle maintenance and repair. They include a wide variety of products ranging from cleaning solvents and degreasers to lubricants and protective sprays for rubber, plastic and vinyl.

CLEANERS

Carburetor cleaner and choke cleaner is a strong solvent for gum, varnish and carbon. Most carburetor cleaners leave a dry-type lubricant film which will not harden or gum up. Because of this film it is not recommended for use on electrical components.

Brake system cleaner is used to remove brake dust, grease and brake fluid from the brake system, where clean surfaces are absolutely necessary. It leaves no residue and often eliminates brake squeal caused by contaminants.

Electrical cleaner removes oxidation, corrosion and carbon deposits from electrical contacts, restoring full current flow. It can also be used to clean spark plugs, carburetor jets, voltage regulators and other parts where an oil-free surface is desired.

Demoisturants remove water and moisture from electrical components such as alternators, voltage regulators, electrical connectors and fuse blocks. They are non-conductive and non-corrosive.

Degreasers are heavy-duty solvents used to remove grease from the outside of the engine and from chassis components. They can be sprayed or brushed on and, depending on the type, are rinsed off either with water or solvent.

LUBRICANTS

Motor oil is the lubricant formulated for use in engines. It normally contains a wide variety of additives to prevent corrosion and reduce foaming and wear. Motor oil comes in various weights (viscosity ratings) from 0 to 50. The recommended weight of the oil depends on the season, temperature and the demands on the engine. Light oil is used in cold climates and under light load conditions. Heavy oil is used in hot climates and where high loads are encountered. Multi-viscosity oils are designed to have characteristics of both light and heavy oils and are available in a number of weights from 0W-20 to 20W-50.

Gear oil is designed to be used in differentials, manual transmissions and other areas where high-temperature lubrication is required.

Chassis and wheel bearing grease is a heavy grease used where increased loads and friction are encountered, such as for wheel bearings, balljoints, tie-rod ends and universal joints.

High-temperature wheel bearing grease is designed to withstand the extreme temperatures encountered by wheel bearings in disc brake equipped vehicles. It usually contains molybdenum disulfide (moly), which is a dry-type lubricant.

White grease is a heavy grease for metal-to-metal applications where water is a problem. White grease stays soft under both low and high temperatures (usually from -100 to +190-degrees F), and will not wash off or dilute in the presence of water.

Assembly lube is a special extreme pressure lubricant, usually containing moly, used to lubricate high-load parts (such as main and rod bearings and cam lobes) for initial start-up of a new engine. The assembly lube lubricates the parts without being squeezed out or washed away until the engine oiling system begins to function.

Silicone lubricants are used to protect rubber, plastic, vinyl and nylon parts.

Graphite lubricants are used where oils cannot be used due to contamination problems, such as in locks. The dry graphite will lubricate metal parts while remaining uncontaminated by dirt, water, oil or acids. It is electrically conductive and will not foul electrical contacts in locks such as the ignition switch.

Moly penetrants loosen and lubricate frozen, rusted and corroded fasteners and prevent future rusting or freezing.

Heat-sink grease is a special electrically non-conductive grease that is used for mounting electronic ignition modules where it is essential that heat is transferred away from the module.

SEALANTS

RTV sealant is one of the most widely used gasket compounds. Made from silicone, RTV is air curing, it seals, bonds, waterproofs, fills surface irregularities, remains flexible, doesn't shrink, is relatively easy to remove, and is used as a supplementary sealer with almost all low and medium temperature gaskets.

Anaerobic sealant is much like RTV in that it can be used either to seal gaskets or to form gaskets by itself. It remains flexible, is solvent resistant and fills surface imperfections. The difference between an anaerobic sealant and an RTV-type sealant is in the curing. RTV cures when exposed to air, while an anaerobic sealant cures only in the absence of air. This means that an anaerobic sealant cures only after the assembly of parts, sealing them together.

Thread and pipe sealant is used for sealing hydraulic and pneumatic fittings and vacuum lines. It is usually made from a Teflon compound, and comes in a spray, a paint-on liquid and as a wrap-around tape.

CHEMICALS

Anti-seize compound prevents seizing, galling, cold welding, rust and corrosion in fasteners. High-temperature anti-seize, usually made with copper and graphite lubricants, is used for exhaust system and exhaust manifold bolts.

Anaerobic locking compounds are used to keep fasteners from vibrating or working loose and cure only after installation, in the absence of air. Medium strength locking compound is used for small nuts, bolts and screws that may be removed later. High-strength locking compound is for large nuts, bolts and studs which aren't removed on a regular basis.

Oil additives range from viscosity index improvers to chemical treatments that claim to reduce internal engine friction. It should be noted that most oil manufacturers caution against using additives with their oils.

Gas additives perform several functions, depending on their chemical makeup. They usually contain solvents that help dissolve gum and varnish that build up on carburetor, fuel injection and intake parts. They also serve to break down carbon deposits that form on the inside surfaces of the combustion chambers. Some additives contain upper cylinder lubricants for valves and piston rings, and others contain chemicals to remove condensation from the gas tank.

MISCELLANEOUS

Brake fluid is specially formulated hydraulic fluid that can withstand the heat and pressure encountered in brake systems. Care must be taken so this fluid does not come in contact with painted surfaces or plastics. An opened container should always be resealed to prevent contamination by water or dirt.

Weatherstrip adhesive is used to bond weatherstripping around doors, windows and trunk lids. It is sometimes used to attach trim pieces.

Undercoating is a petroleum-based, tar-like substance that is designed to protect metal surfaces on the underside of the vehicle from corrosion. It also acts as a sound-deadening agent by insulating the bottom of the vehicle.

Waxes and polishes are used to help protect painted and plated surfaces from the weather. Different types of paint may require the use of different types of wax and polish. Some polishes utilize a chemical or abrasive cleaner to help remove the top layer of oxidized (dull) paint on older vehicles. In recent years many non-wax polishes that contain a wide variety of chemicals such as polymers and silicones have been introduced. These non-wax polishes are usually easier to apply and last longer than conventional waxes and polishes.

Safety first!

Regardless of how enthusiastic you may be about getting on with the job at hand, take the time to ensure that your safety is not jeopardized. A moment's lack of attention can result in an accident, as can failure to observe certain simple safety precautions. The possibility of an accident will always exist, and the following points should not be considered a comprehensive list of all dangers. Rather, they are intended to make you aware of the risks and to encourage a safety conscious approach to all work you carry out on your vehicle.

ESSENTIAL DOS AND DON'TS

DON'T rely on a jack when working under the vehicle. Always use approved jackstands to support the weight of the vehicle and place them under the recommended lift or support points.

DON'T attempt to loosen extremely tight fasteners (i.e. wheel lug nuts) while the vehicle is on a jack - it may fall.

DON'T start the engine without first making sure that the transmission is in Neutral (or Park where applicable) and the parking brake is set.

DON'T remove the radiator cap from a hot cooling system - let it cool or cover it with a cloth and release the pressure gradually.

DON'T attempt to drain the engine oil until you are sure it has cooled to the point that it will not burn you.

DON'T touch any part of the engine or exhaust system until it has cooled sufficiently to avoid burns.

DON'T siphon toxic liquids such as gasoline, antifreeze and brake fluid by mouth, or allow them to remain on your skin.

DON'T inhale brake lining dust - it is potentially hazardous (see Asbestos below).

DON'T allow spilled oil or grease to remain on the floor - wipe it up before someone slips on it.

DON'T use loose fitting wrenches or other tools which may slip and cause injury.

DON'T push on wrenches when loosening or tightening nuts or bolts. Always try to pull the wrench toward you. If the situation calls for pushing the wrench away, push with an open hand to avoid scraped knuckles if the wrench should slip.

DON'T attempt to lift a heavy component alone - get someone to help you.

DON'T rush or take unsafe shortcuts to finish a job.

DON'T allow children or animals in or around the vehicle while you are working on it.

DO wear eye protection when using power tools such as a drill, sander, bench grinder, etc. and when working under a vehicle.

DO keep loose clothing and long hair well out of the way of moving parts.

DO make sure that any hoist used has a safe working load rating adequate for the job.

DO get someone to check on you periodically when working alone on a vehicle.

DO carry out work in a logical sequence and make sure that everything is correctly assembled and tightened.

DO keep chemicals and fluids tightly capped and out of the reach of children and pets.

DO remember that your vehicle's safety affects that of yourself and others. If in doubt on any point, get professional advice.

STEERING, SUSPENSION AND BRAKES

These systems are essential to driving safety, so make sure you have a qualified shop or individual check your work. Also, compressed suspension springs can cause injury if released suddenly - be sure to use a spring compressor.

AIRBAGS

Airbags are explosive devices that can CAUSE injury if they deploy while you're working on the vehicle. Follow the manufacturer's instructions to disable the airbag whenever you're working in the vicinity of airbag components.

ASBESTOS

Certain friction, insulating, sealing, and other products - such as brake linings, brake bands, clutch linings, torque converters, gaskets, etc. - may contain asbestos or other hazardous friction material. Extreme care must be taken to avoid inhalation of dust from such products, since it is hazardous to health. If in doubt, assume that they do contain asbestos.

FIRE

Remember at all times that gasoline is highly flammable. Never smoke or have any kind of open flame around when working on a vehicle. But the risk does not end there. A spark caused by an electrical short circuit, by two metal surfaces contacting each other, or even by static electricity built up in your body under certain conditions, can ignite gasoline vapors, which in a confined space are highly explosive. Do not, under any circumstances, use gasoline for cleaning parts. Use an approved safety solvent.

Always disconnect the battery ground (-) cable at the battery before working on any part of the fuel system or electrical system. Never risk spilling fuel on a hot engine or exhaust component. It is strongly recommended that a fire extinguisher suitable for use on fuel and electrical fires be kept handy in the garage or workshop at all times. Never try to extinguish a fuel or electrical fire with water.

FUMES

Certain fumes are highly toxic and can quickly cause unconsciousness and even death if inhaled to any extent. Gasoline vapor falls into this category, as do the vapors from some cleaning solvents. Any draining or pouring of such volatile fluids should be done in a well ventilated area.

When using cleaning fluids and solvents, read the instructions on the container carefully. Never use materials from unmarked containers.

Never run the engine in an enclosed space, such as a garage. Exhaust fumes contain carbon monoxide, which is extremely poisonous. If you need to run the engine, always do so in the open air, or at least have the rear of the vehicle outside the work area.

THE BATTERY

Never create a spark or allow a bare light bulb near a battery. They normally give off a certain amount of hydrogen gas, which is highly explosive.

Always disconnect the battery ground (-) cable at the battery before working on the fuel or electrical systems.

If possible, loosen the filler caps or cover when charging the battery from an external source (this does not apply to sealed or maintenance-free batteries). Do not charge at an excessive rate or the battery may burst.

Take care when adding water to a non maintenance-free battery and when carrying a battery. The electrolyte, even when diluted, is very corrosive and should not be allowed to contact clothing or skin.

Always wear eye protection when cleaning the battery to prevent the caustic deposits from entering your eyes.

HOUSEHOLD CURRENT

When using an electric power tool, inspection light, etc., which operates on household current, always make sure that the tool is correctly connected to its plug and that, where necessary, it is properly grounded. Do not use such items in damp conditions and, again, do not create a spark or apply excessive heat in the vicinity of fuel or fuel vapor.

SECONDARY IGNITION SYSTEM VOLTAGE

A severe electric shock can result from touching certain parts of the ignition system (such as the spark plug wires) when the engine is running or being cranked, particularly if components are damp or the insulation is defective. In the case of an electronic ignition system, the secondary system voltage is much higher and could prove fatal.

HYDROFLUORIC ACID

This extremely corrosive acid is formed when certain types of synthetic rubber, found in some O-rings, oil seals, fuel hoses, etc. are exposed to temperatures above 750-degrees F (400-degrees C). The rubber changes into a charred or sticky substance containing the acid. Once formed, the acid remains dangerous for years. If it gets onto the skin, it may be necessary to amputate the limb concerned.

When dealing with a vehicle which has suffered a fire, or with components salvaged from such a vehicle, wear protective gloves and discard them after use.

Troubleshooting

CONTENTS

This section provides an easy reference guide to the more common problems which may occur during the operation of your vehicle. These problems and their possible causes are grouped under headings denoting various components or systems, such as Engine, Cooling system, etc. They also refer you to the chapter and/or section which deals with the problem.

Remember that successful troubleshooting is not a mysterious art practiced only by professional mechanics. It is simply the result of the right knowledge combined with an intelligent, systematic approach to the problem. Always work by a process of elimination, starting with the simplest solution and working through to the most cornplex - and never overlook the obvious. Anyone can run the gas tank dry or leave the lights on overnight, so don't assume that you are exempt from such oversights.

Finally, always establish a clear idea of why a problem has occurred and take steps to ensure that it doesn't happen again. If the electrical system fails because of a poor connection, check the other connections in the system to make sure that they don't fail as well. If a particular fuse continues to blow, find out why - don't just replace one fuse after another. Remember, failure of a small component can often be indicative of potential failure or incorrect functioning of a more important component or system.

ENGINE

1 Engine will not rotate when attempting to start

1   Battery terminal connections loose or corroded (Chapter 1).
2   Battery discharged or faulty (Chapter 1).
3   Automatic transaxle/Continuously Variable Transaxle (CVT) not completely engaged in Park (Chapter 7) or clutch not completely depressed (Chapter 8).
4   Broken, loose or disconnected wiring in the starting circuit (Chapters 5 and 12).
5   Starter motor pinion jammed in flywheel ring gear (Chapter 5).
6   Starter solenoid faulty (Chapter 5).
7   Starter motor faulty (Chapter 5).
8   Ignition switch faulty (Chapter 12).
9   Starter pinion or flywheel teeth worn or broken (Chapter 5).

2 Engine rotates but will not start

1   Fuel tank empty.
2   Battery discharged (engine rotates slowly) (Chapter 5).
3   Battery terminal connections loose or corroded (Chapter 1).
4   Leaking fuel injector(s), faulty fuel pump, pressure regulator, etc. (Chapter 4).
5   Fuel not reaching fuel rail (Chapter 4).
6   Ignition components damp or damaged (Chapter 5).
7   Worn, faulty or incorrectly gapped spark plugs (Chapter 1).
8   Broken, loose or disconnected wiring in the starting circuit (Chapter 5).
9   Broken, loose or disconnected wires at the ignition coil or faulty coil (Chapter 5).

3 Engine hard to start when cold

1   Battery discharged or low (Chapter 1).
2   Malfunctioning fuel system (Chapter 4).
3   Injector(s) leaking (Chapter 4).

4 Engine hard to start when hot

1   Air filter clogged (Chapter 1).
2   Fuel not reaching the fuel injection system (Chapter 4).
3   Corroded battery connections, especially ground (Chapter 1).

5 Starter motor noisy or excessively rough in engagement

1   Pinion or flywheel gear teeth worn or broken (Chapter 5).
2   Starter motor mounting bolts loose or missing (Chapter 5).

6 Engine starts but stops immediately

1   Loose or faulty electrical connections at coil or alternator (Chapter 5).
2   Insufficient fuel reaching the fuel injector(s) (Chapters 1 and 4).
3   Vacuum leak at the gasket between the intake manifold and throttle body (Chapters 1 and 4).

7 Oil puddle under engine

1   Oil pan gasket and/or oil pan drain bolt washer leaking (Chapter 2).
2   Oil pressure sending unit leaking (Chapter 2).
3   Cylinder head covers leaking (Chapter 2).
4   Engine oil seals leaking (Chapter 2).

8 Engine lopes while idling or idles erratically

1   Vacuum leakage (Chapters 2 and 4).
2   Air filter clogged (Chapter 1).
3   Fuel pump not delivering sufficient fuel to the fuel injection system (Chapter 4).
4   Leaking head gasket (Chapter 2).
5   Timing belt and/or pulleys worn (Chapter 2).
6   Camshaft lobes worn (Chapter 2).

9 Engine misses at idle speed

1   Spark plugs worn or not gapped properly (Chapter 1).
2   Vacuum leaks (Chapter 1).
3   Uneven or low compression (Chapter 2).
4   Fault in the fuel injection or engine control system (Chapters 4 and 6).

10 Engine misses throughout driving speed range

1   Fuel filter clogged and/or impurities in the fuel system (Chapter 1).
2   Low fuel pressure (Chapter 4).
3   Faulty or incorrectly gapped spark plugs (Chapter 1).
4   Faulty emission system components (Chapter 6).
5   Low or uneven cylinder compression pressures (Chapter 2).
6   Weak or faulty ignition system (Chapter 5).
7   Vacuum leak in fuel injection system, intake manifold, air control valve or vacuum hoses (Chapter 4).

11 Engine stumbles on acceleration

1   Spark plugs fouled (Chapter 1).
2   Fuel injection system faulty (Chapter 4).
3   Fuel filter clogged (Chapters 1 and 4).
4   Intake manifold air leak (Chapters 2 and 4).

12 Engine surges while holding accelerator steady

1 Intake air leak (Chapter 4).
2 Fuel pump faulty (Chapter 4).
3 Loose fuel injector wire harness connectors (Chapter 4).
4 Defective ECU or information sensor (Chapter 6).

13 Engine stalls

1 Fuel filter clogged and/or water and impurities in the fuel system (Chapters 1 and 4).
2 Faulty emissions system components (Chapter 6).
3 Faulty or incorrectly gapped spark plugs (Chapter 1).
4 Vacuum leak in the fuel injection system, intake manifold or vacuum hoses (Chapters 2 and 4).
5 Valve clearances incorrectly set (Chapter 1).

14 Engine lacks power

1 Faulty or incorrectly gapped spark plugs (Chapter 1).
2 Faulty fuel injection system (Chapter 4).
3 Faulty coil (Chapter 5).
4 Brakes binding (Chapter 9).
5 Automatic transaxle/Continuously Variable Transaxle (CVT) fluid level incorrect (Chapter 1).
6 Clutch slipping (Chapter 8).
7 Fuel filter clogged and/or impurities in the fuel system (Chapters 1 and 4).
8 Emission control system not functioning properly (Chapter 6).
9 Catalytic converter plugged (Chapter 6).
10 Low or uneven cylinder compression pressures (Chapter 2).
11 Obstructed exhaust system (Chapter 4).

15 Engine backfires

1 Emission control system not functioning properly (Chapter 6).
2 Faulty secondary ignition system (cracked spark plug insulator, faulty coil, (Chapters 1 and 5).
3 Fuel injection system malfunctioning (Chapter 4).
4 Vacuum leak at fuel injector(s), intake manifold, air control valve or vacuum hoses (Chapters 2 and 4).
5 Valve clearances incorrectly set and/or valves sticking (Chapter 1).

16 Pinging or knocking engine sounds during acceleration or uphill

1 Incorrect grade of fuel.
2 Fuel injection system faulty (Chapter 4).
3 Improper or damaged spark plugs or wires (Chapter 1).
4 Vacuum leak (Chapters 2 and 4).
5 Knock sensor malfunctioning (Chapter 6).

17 Engine runs with oil pressure light on

1 Low oil level (Chapter 1).
2 Short in wiring circuit (Chapter 12).
3 Faulty oil pressure sender (Chapter 2).
4 Worn engine bearings and/or oil pump (Chapter 2).

18 Engine diesels (continues to run) after switching off

1 Idle speed too high (Chapter 6).
2 Excessive engine operating temperature (Chapter 3).

ENGINE ELECTRICAL SYSTEM

19 Battery will not hold a charge

1 Alternator drivebelt defective or not adjusted properly (Chapter 1).
2 Battery electrolyte level low (Chapter 1).
3 Battery terminals loose or corroded (Chapter 1).
4 Alternator not charging properly (Chapter 5).
5 Loose, broken or faulty wiring in the charging circuit (Chapter 5).
6 Short in vehicle wiring (Chapter 12).
7 Internally defective battery (Chapters 1 and 5).

20 Alternator light fails to go out

1 Faulty alternator or charging circuit (Chapter 5).
2 Alternator drivebelt defective or out of adjustment (Chapter 1).
3 Alternator voltage regulator inoperative (Chapter 5).

21 Alternator light fails to come on when key is turned on

1 Warning light bulb defective (Chapter 12).
2 Fault in the printed circuit, dash wiring or bulb holder (Chapter 12).

FUEL SYSTEM

22 Excessive fuel consumption

1 Dirty or clogged air filter element (Chapter 1).
2 Emissions system not functioning properly (Chapter 6).
3 Faulty fuel injection system (Chapter 4).
4 Low tire pressure or incorrect tire size (Chapter 1).

23 Fuel leakage and/or fuel odor

1 Leaking fuel line (Chapters 1 and 4).
2 Tank overfilled.
3 Evaporative canister defective (Chapters 1 and 6).
4 Faulty fuel injection system (Chapter 4).

COOLING SYSTEM

24 Overheating

1 Insufficient coolant in system (Chapter 1).
2 Radiator core blocked or grille restricted (Chapter 3).
3 Thermostat faulty (Chapter 3).
4 Cooling fan switch faulty (Chapter 3).
5 Electric coolant fan blades broken or cracked (Chapter 3).
6 Radiator cap not maintaining proper pressure (Chapter 3).

25 Overcooling

1 Faulty thermostat (Chapter 3).
2 Inaccurate temperature gauge sending unit (Chapter 3)

26 External coolant leakage

1 Deteriorated/damaged hoses; loose clamps (Chapters 1 and 3).
2 Water pump defective (Chapter 3).
3 Leakage from radiator core or coolant reservoir bottle (Chapter 3).
4 Engine drain or water jacket core plugs leaking (Chapter 2).

27 Internal coolant leakage

1 Leaking cylinder head gasket (Chapter 2).
2 Cracked cylinder bore or cylinder head (Chapter 2).

28 Coolant loss

1 Too much coolant in system (Chapter 1).
2 Coolant boiling away because of overheating (Chapter 3).
3 Internal or external leakage (Chapter 3).
4 Faulty radiator cap (Chapter 3).

29 Poor coolant circulation

1 Inoperative water pump (Chapter 3).
2 Restriction in cooling system (Chapters 1 and 3).
3 Thermostat sticking (Chapter 3).

CLUTCH

30 Pedal travels to floor - no pressure or very little resistance

1 No fluid in reservoir (Chapter 1)
2 Faulty clutch master cylinder, release cylinder or hydraulic line (Chapter 8).
3 Broken release bearing or fork (Chapter 8).

31 Unable to select gears

1 Faulty transaxle (Chapter 7).
2 Faulty clutch disc (Chapter 8).
3 Release lever and bearing not assembled properly (Chapter 8).
4 Faulty pressure plate (Chapter 8).
5 Pressure plate-to-flywheel bolts loose (Chapter 8).

32 Clutch slips (engine speed increases with no increase in vehicle speed)

1 Clutch plate worn (Chapter 8).
2 Clutch plate is oil soaked by leaking rear main seal (Chapter 8).
3 Clutch plate not seated. It may take 30 or 40 normal starts for a new one to seat.
4 Warped pressure plate or flywheel (Chapter 8).
5 Weak diaphragm spring (Chapter 8).
6 Clutch plate overheated. Allow to cool.

33 Grabbing (chattering) as clutch is engaged

1 Oil on clutch plate lining, burned or glazed facings (Chapter 8).
2 Worn or loose engine or transaxle mounts (Chapters 2 and 7).
3 Worn splines on clutch plate hub (Chapter 8).
4 Warped pressure plate or flywheel (Chapter 8).
5 Burned or smeared resin on flywheel or pressure plate (Chapter 8).

34 Transaxle rattling (clicking)

1 Release lever loose (Chapter 8).
2 Clutch plate damper spring failure (Chapter 8).
3 Low engine idle speed (Chapter 1).

35 Noise in clutch area

1 Fork shaft improperly installed (Chapter 8).
2 Faulty bearing (Chapter 8).

36 Clutch pedal stays on floor

1 Faulty clutch master or release cylinder (Chapter 8).
2 Broken release bearing or fork (Chapter 8).

37 High pedal effort

1 Piston binding in bore of clutch master or release cylinder (Chapter 8).
2 Pressure plate faulty (Chapter 8).

MANUAL TRANSAXLE

38 Knocking noise at low speeds

1 Worn driveaxle constant velocity (CV) joints (Chapter 8).
2 Worn driveaxle bore in differential case (Chapter 7A).*

39 Noise most pronounced when turning

Differential gear noise (Chapter 7A).*

40 Clunk on acceleration or deceleration

1 Loose engine or transaxle mounts (Chapters 2 and 7A).
2 Worn differential pinion shaft in case.*
3 Worn driveaxle bore in differential case (Chapter 7A).*
4 Worn or damaged driveaxle inboard CV joints (Chapter 8).

41 Clicking noise in turns

Worn or damaged outboard CV joint (Chapter 8).

42 Vibration

1 Rough wheel bearing (Chapters 1 and 10).
2 Damaged driveaxle (Chapter 8).
3 Out of round tires (Chapter 1).
4 Tire out of balance (Chapters 1 and 10).
5 Worn CV joint (Chapter 8).

43 Noisy in neutral with engine running

1 Damaged input gear bearing (Chapter 7A).*
2 Damaged clutch release bearing (Chapter 8).

44 Noisy in one particular gear

1 Damaged or worn constant mesh gears (Chapter 7A).*
2 Damaged or worn synchronizers (Chapter 7A).*
3 Bent reverse fork (Chapter 7A).*
4 Damaged fourth speed gear or output gear (Chapter 7A).*
5 Worn or damaged reverse idler gear or idler bushing (Chapter 7A).*

45   Noisy in all gears

1   Insufficient lubricant (Chapter 7A).
2   Damaged or worn bearings (Chapter 7A).*
3   Worn or damaged input gear shaft and/or output gear shaft (Chapter 7A).*

46   Slips out of gear

1   Worn or improperly adjusted linkage (Chapter 7A).
2   Transaxle loose on engine (Chapter 7A).
3   Shift linkage does not work freely, binds (Chapter 7A).
4   Input gear bearing retainer broken or loose (Chapter 7A).*
5   Worn shift fork (Chapter 7A).*

47   Leaks lubricant

1   Driveaxle oil seals worn (Chapter 7).
2   Excessive amount of lubricant in transaxle (Chapters 1 and 7A).
3   Loose or broken input gear shaft bearing retainer (Chapter 7A).*
4   Input gear bearing retainer O-ring and/or lip seal damaged (Chapter 7A).*

48   Locked in gear

Lock pin or interlock pin missing (Chapter 7A).*

* Although the corrective action necessary to remedy the symptoms described is beyond the scope of the home mechanic, the above information should be helpful in isolating the cause of the condition so that the owner can communicate clearly with a professional mechanic.

AUTOMATIC TRANSAXLE/CONTINUOUSLY VARIABLE TRANSAXLE (CVT)

➡**Note: Due to the complexity of the automatic transaxle/Continuously Variable Transaxle (CVT), it is difficult for the home mechanic to properly diagnose and service this component. For problems other than the following, the vehicle should be taken to a dealer or transmission shop.**

49   Fluid leakage

1   Automatic transmission fluid is a deep red color. Fluid leaks should not be confused with engine oil, which can easily be blown onto the transaxle by air flow.
2   To pinpoint a leak, first remove all built-up dirt and grime from the transaxle housing with degreasing agents and/or steam cleaning. Then drive the vehicle at low speeds so air flow will not blow the leak far from its source. Raise the vehicle and determine where the leak is coming from. Common areas of leakage are:
   a) *Pan (Chapters 1 and 7)*
   b) *Dipstick tube (Chapters 1 and 7)*
   c) *Transaxle oil lines (Chapter 7)*
   d) *Speed sensor (Chapter 7)*

50   Transaxle fluid brown or has a burned smell

Transaxle fluid burned (Chapter 1).

51   General shift mechanism problems

1   Chapter 7 deals with checking and adjusting the shift linkage on automatic transaxles. Common problems which may be attributed to poorly adjusted linkage are:
   a) *Engine starting in gears other than Park or Neutral.*
   b) *Indicator on shifter pointing to a gear other than the one actually being used.*
   c) *Vehicle moves when in Park.*
2   Refer to Chapter 7B for the shift linkage adjustment procedure.

52   Engine will start in gears other than Park or Neutral

Transmission range switch malfunctioning (Chapter 6).

53   Transaxle slips, shifts roughly, is noisy or has no drive in forward or reverse gears

There are many probable causes for the above problems, but the home mechanic should be concerned with only one possibility - fluid level. Before taking the vehicle to a repair shop, check the level and condition of the fluid as described in Chapter 1. Correct the fluid level as necessary or change the fluid and filter if needed. If the problem persists, have a professional diagnose the cause.

DRIVEAXLES

54   Knock or clunk when accelerating after coasting

Worn or damaged CV joint. Check for cut or damaged boots (Chapter 1). Repair as necessary (Chapter 8).

55   Clicking noise in turns

Worn or damaged outer CV joint. Check for cut or damaged boots (Chapter 1).

56   Shudder or vibration during acceleration

1   Worn or damaged CV joints (Chapter 8).
2   Sticking inboard CV joint assembly (Chapter 8).

57   Vibration at highway speeds

1   Out-of-balance front wheels and/or tires (Chapters 1 and 10).
2   Out-of-round front tires (Chapters 1 and 10).
3   Worn CV joint(s) (Chapter 8).

BRAKES

➡**Note: Before assuming that a brake problem exists, make sure that:**
   a) *The tires are in good condition and properly inflated (Chapter 1).*
   b) *The front end alignment is correct (Chapter 10).*
   c) *The vehicle is not loaded with weight in an unequal manner.*

58   Vehicle pulls to one side during braking

1   Incorrect tire pressures (Chapter 1).
2   Front end out of alignment (have the front end aligned).

3 Front, or rear, tires not matched to one another.
4 Restricted brake lines or hoses (Chapter 9).
5 Malfunctioning drum brake or caliper assembly (Chapter 9).
6 Loose suspension parts (Chapter 10).
7 Loose calipers (Chapter 9).
8 Excessive wear of brake shoe or pad material or disc/drum on one side.

59 Noise (high-pitched squeal when the brakes are applied)

1 Disc brake pads worn out. Replace pads with new ones immediately (Chapter 9).
2 Drum brake shoes worn out. Replace the shoes immediately (Chapter 9).

60 Brake roughness or chatter (pedal pulsates)

1 Excessive brake disc lateral runout or brake drum out-of-round (Chapter 9).
2 Parallelism of disc not within specifications (Chapter 9).
3 Uneven pad wear caused by caliper not sliding due to improper clearance or dirt (Chapter 9).
4 Defective brake disc (Chapter 9).

61 Excessive brake pedal effort required to stop vehicle

1 Malfunctioning power brake booster (Chapter 9).
2 Partial system failure (Chapter 9).
3 Excessively worn pads or shoes (Chapter 9).
4 Piston in caliper or wheel cylinder stuck or sluggish (Chapter 9).
5 Brake pads or shoes contaminated with oil or grease (Chapter 9).
6 New pads or shoes installed and not yet seated. It will take a while for the new material to seat against the disc or drum.

62 Excessive brake pedal travel

1 Partial brake system failure (Chapter 9).
2 Insufficient fluid in master cylinder (Chapters 1 and 9).
3 Air trapped in system (Chapters 1 and 9).

63 Dragging brakes

1 Incorrect adjustment of brake light switch (Chapter 9).
2 Master cylinder pistons not returning correctly (Chapter 9).
3 Restricted brakes lines or hoses (Chapters 1 and 9).
4 Incorrect parking brake adjustment (Chapter 9).

64 Grabbing or uneven braking action

1 Malfunction of proportioning valve (Chapter 9).
2 Malfunction of power brake booster unit (Chapter 9).
3 Binding brake pedal mechanism (Chapter 9).

65 Brake pedal feels spongy when depressed

1 Air in hydraulic lines (Chapter 9).
2 Master cylinder mounting bolts loose (Chapter 9).
3 Master cylinder defective (Chapter 9).

66 Brake pedal travels to the floor with little resistance

1 Little or no fluid in the master cylinder reservoir caused by leaking caliper piston(s) (Chapter 9).
2 Loose, damaged or disconnected brake lines (Chapter 9).

67 Parking brake does not hold

Parking brake improperly adjusted (Chapter 9).

SUSPENSION AND STEERING SYSTEMS

➡**Note: Before attempting to diagnose the suspension and steering systems, perform the following preliminary checks:**

a) *Tires for wrong pressure and uneven wear.*
b) *Steering universal joints from the column to the steering gear for loose connectors or wear.*
c) *Front and rear suspension and the steering gear assembly for loose or damaged parts.*
d) *Out-of-round or out-of-balance tires, bent rims and loose and/or rough wheel bearings.*

68 Vehicle pulls to one side

1 Mismatched or uneven tires (Chapter 10).
2 Broken or sagging springs (Chapter 10).
3 Wheel alignment (Chapter 10).
4 Front brakes dragging (Chapter 9).

69 Abnormal or excessive tire wear

1 Wheel alignment (Chapter 10).
2 Sagging or broken springs (Chapter 10).
3 Tire out of balance (Chapter 10).
4 Worn shock absorber (Chapter 10).
5 Overloaded vehicle.
6 Tires not rotated regularly.

70 Wheel makes a thumping noise

1 Blister or bump on tire (Chapter 10).
2 Improper shock absorber/coil spring action (Chapter 10).

71 Shimmy, shake or vibration

1 Tire or wheel out-of-balance or out-of-round (Chapter 10).
2 Loose or worn wheel bearings (Chapter 10).
3 Worn tie-rod ends (Chapter 10).
4 Worn balljoints (Chapter 10).
5 Excessive wheel runout (Chapter 10).
6 Blister or bump on tire (Chapter 10).

72 Hard steering

1 Lack of lubrication at balljoints and tie-rod ends (Chapter 10).
2 Front wheel alignment (Chapter 10).
3 Low tire pressure(s) (Chapters 10).

73 Poor returnability of steering to center

1 Lack of lubrication at balljoints and tie-rod ends (Chapter 1).
2 Binding in balljoints (Chapter 10).
3 Binding in steering column (Chapter 10).
4 Lack of lubricant in steering gear assembly (Chapter 10).
5 Front wheel alignment (Chapter 10).

74 Abnormal noise at the front end

1 Lack of lubrication at balljoints and tie-rod ends (Chapter 1).

2   Damaged shock absorber/coil spring mount (Chapter 10).
3   Worn control arm bushings or tie-rod ends (Chapter 10).
4   Loose stabilizer bar (Chapter 10).
5   Loose wheel nuts (Chapter 1).
6   Loose suspension bolts (Chapter 10)

75   Wander or poor steering stability

1   Mismatched or uneven tires (Chapter 10).
2   Lack of lubrication at balljoints and tie-rod ends (Chapter 1).
3   Worn shock absorber/coil spring assemblies (Chapter 10).
4   Loose stabilizer bar (Chapter 10).
5   Broken or sagging springs (Chapter 10).
6   Wheels out of alignment (Chapter 10).

76   Erratic steering when braking

1   Front hub bearings worn (Chapter 10).
2   Broken or sagging springs (Chapter 10).
3   Leaking wheel cylinder or caliper (Chapter 10).
4   Warped discs or drums (Chapter 10).

77   Excessive pitching and/or rolling around corners or during braking

1   Loose stabilizer bar (Chapter 10).
2   Worn shock absorbers or mounts (Chapter 10).
3   Broken or sagging springs (Chapter 10).
4   Overloaded vehicle.

78   Suspension bottoms

1   Overloaded vehicle.
2   Worn shock absorbers (Chapter 10).
3   Incorrect, broken or sagging springs (Chapter 10).

79   Cupped tires

1   Front wheel or rear wheel alignment (Chapter 10).

2   Worn shock absorbers (Chapter 10).
3   Wheel bearings worn (Chapter 10).
4   Excessive tire or wheel runout (Chapter 10).
5   Worn balljoints (Chapter 10).

80   Excessive tire wear on outside edge

1   Inflation pressures incorrect (Chapter 1).
2   Excessive speed in turns.
3   Front end alignment incorrect (excessive toe-in). Have professionally aligned.
4   Suspension arm bent or twisted (Chapter 10).

81   Excessive tire wear on inside edge

1   Inflation pressures incorrect (Chapter 1).
2   Front end alignment incorrect (toe-out). Have professionally aligned.
3   Loose or damaged steering or suspension components (Chapter 10).

82   Tire tread worn in one place

1   Tires out of balance.
2   Damaged or buckled wheel. Inspect and replace if necessary.
3   Defective tire (Chapter 1).

83   Excessive play or looseness in steering system

1   Front hub bearing(s) worn (Chapter 10).
2   Tie-rod end loose (Chapter 10).
3   Steering gear loose or worn (Chapter 10).
4   Worn or loose steering intermediate shaft (Chapter 10).

84   Rattling or clicking noise in steering gear

1   Steering gear loose (Chapter 10).
2   Steering gear defective (Chapter 10).

Notes

Section

Reference to other Chapters

CHECK ENGINE light on - See Chapter 6

1

TUNE-UP AND ROUTINE MAINTENANCE

Engine compartment layout (Coupe/Sedan)

1	Air filter housing	4	Engine oil filler cap	6	Power steering fluid
2	Brake fluid reservoir	5	Windshield washer fluid		reservoir
3	Engine oil dipstick		reservoir	7	Radiator cap

8	Coolant reservoir
9	Battery
10	Underhood fuse/relay block

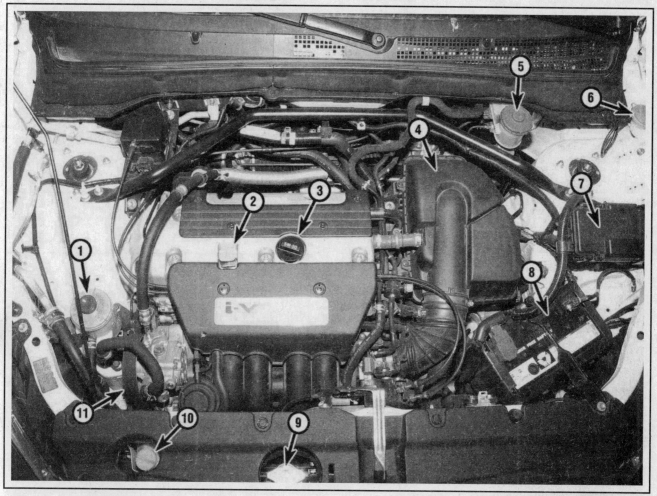

Engine compartment layout (CR-V)

1	Power steering fluid reservoir	5	Brake fluid reservoir	9	Radiator cap
2	Engine oil dipstick	6	Windshield washer fluid reservoir	10	Coolant reservoir
3	Engine oil filler cap	7	Underhood fuse/relay block	11	Drivebelt
4	Air filter housing	8	Battery		

1 Maintenance schedule

The maintenance intervals in this manual are provided with the assumption that you, not the dealer, will be doing the work. These are the minimum maintenance intervals recommended by the factory for vehicles that are driven daily. If you wish to keep your vehicle in peak condition at all times, you may wish to perform some of these procedures even more often. Because frequent maintenance enhances the efficiency, performance and resale value of your car, we encourage you to do so. If you drive in dusty areas, tow a trailer, idle or drive at low speeds for extended periods or drive for short distances (less than four miles) in below freezing temperatures, shorter intervals are also recommended.

When your vehicle is new, follow the maintenance schedule to the letter, record the maintenance performed in your owners manual and keep all receipts to protect the new vehicle warranty. In many cases, the initial maintenance check is done at no cost to the owner.

EVERY 250 MILES (400 KM) OR WEEKLY, WHICHEVER COMES FIRST

Check the engine oil level (Section 4)
Check the engine coolant level (Section 4)
Check the windshield washer fluid level (Section 4)
Check the brake fluid level (Section 4)
Check the power steering fluid level (Section 4)
Check the automatic transaxle fluid level (Section 4)
Check the tires and tire pressures (Section 5)
Check the operation of all lights
Check the horn operation

EVERY 3000 MILES (4800 KM) OR 3 MONTHS, WHICHEVER COMES FIRST

All items listed above plus:
Change the engine oil and oil filter (Section 6)

EVERY 7500 MILES (12,000 KM) OR 6 MONTHS, WHICHEVER COMES FIRST

All items listed above plus:
Inspect (and replace, if necessary) the windshield wiper blades (Section 7)
Check and service the battery (Section 8)
Check the cooling system (Section 9)
Rotate the tires (Section 10)
Check the seat belts (Section 11)
Inspect the brake system (Section 12)

EVERY 15,000 MILES (24,000 KM) OR 12 MONTHS, WHICHEVER COMES FIRST

All items listed above plus:
Inspect the suspension, steering components and driveaxle boots (Section 13)*

Inspect and replace, if necessary, all underhood hoses (Section 14)
Replace the air filter (Section 15)*
Replace the interior ventilation filter (Section 16)
Inspect the fuel system (Section 17)
Check the exhaust system (Section 18)

EVERY 30,000 (48,000 KM) MILES OR 24 MONTHS, WHICHEVER COMES FIRST

All items listed above plus:
Check and adjust, if necessary, the engine drivebelts (Section 19)
Replace the brake fluid (Section 20)
Check (and replace, if necessary) the spark plugs (conventional, non-platinum or iridium type) (Section 24)

EVERY 60,000 MILES (96,000 KM) OR 36 MONTHS

Service the cooling system (drain, flush and refill) (Section 21)

EVERY 90,000 MILES (145,000 KM) OR 60 MONTHS

Change the rear differential lubricant (Section 22)

EVERY 110,000 MILES (176,000 KM) OR 36 MONTHS, WHICHEVER COMES FIRST

Valve clearance check and adjustment (only if noisy) (see Section 23)
Replace the spark plugs (platinum or iridium type) (Section 24)
Replace the timing belt, and inspect the auto tensioner and water pump (see Chapter 2A or 2B and Chapter 3)

EVERY 120,000 MILES (192,000 KM) OR 72 MONTHS, WHICHEVER COMES FIRST

Change the automatic transaxle fluid (Section 25)**
Change the manual transaxle fluid (Section 26)***

*This item is affected by "severe" operating conditions as described below. If your vehicle is operated under "severe" conditions, perform all maintenance indicated with a * at 5000 mile/6 month intervals. Severe conditions are indicated if you mainly operate your vehicle under one or more of the following conditions:

Operating in dusty areas
Towing a trailer
Idling for extended periods and/or low speed operation
Operating when outside temperatures remain below freezing and when most trips are less than five miles

**If operated under one or more of the following conditions, change the automatic transaxle fluid every 30,000 miles.

***If operated under one or more of the following conditions, change the manual transaxle fluid every 60,000 miles.

In heavy city traffic where the outside temperature regularly reaches 90-degrees F (32-degrees C) or higher
In hilly or mountainous terrain

2 Introduction

This Chapter is designed to help the home mechanic maintain the Civic and CR-V with the goals of maximum performance, economy, safety and reliability in mind.

Included is a master maintenance schedule, followed by procedures dealing specifically with each item on the schedule. Visual checks, adjustments, component replacement and other helpful items are included. Refer to the accompanying illustrations of the engine compartment and the underside of the vehicle for the locations of various components.

Servicing the vehicle, in accordance with the mileage/time maintenance schedule and the step-by-step procedures will result in a planned maintenance program that should produce a long and reliable service life. Keep in mind that it is a comprehensive plan, so maintaining some items but not others at the specified intervals will not produce the same results.

As you service the vehicle, you will discover that many of the procedures can - and should - be grouped together because of the nature of the particular procedure you're performing or because of the close proximity of two otherwise unrelated components to one another.

For example, if the vehicle is raised for chassis lubrication, you should inspect the exhaust, suspension, steering and fuel systems while you're under the vehicle. When you're rotating the tires, it makes good sense to check the brakes since the wheels are already removed. Finally, let's suppose you have to borrow or rent a torque wrench. Even if you only need it to tighten the spark plugs, you might as well check the torque of as many critical fasteners as time allows.

The first step in this maintenance program is to prepare yourself before the actual work begins. Read through all the procedures you're planning to do, then gather up all the parts and tools needed. If it looks like you might run into problems during a particular job, seek advice from a mechanic or an experienced do-it-yourselfer.

OWNER'S MANUAL AND VECI LABEL INFORMATION

Your vehicle owner's manual was written for your year and model and contains very specific information on component locations, specifications, fuse ratings, part numbers, etc. The Owner's Manual is an important resource for the do-it-yourselfer to have; if one was not supplied with your vehicle, it can generally be ordered from a dealer parts department.

Among other important information, the Vehicle Emissions Control Information (VECI) label contains specifications and procedures for applicable tune-up adjustments and, in some instances, spark plugs (see Chapter 6 for more information on the VECI label). The information on this label is the exact maintenance data recommended by the manufacturer. This data often varies by intended operating altitude, local emissions regulations, month of manufacture, etc.

This Chapter contains procedural details, safety information and more ambitious maintenance intervals than you might find in manufacturer's literature. However, you may also find procedures or specifications in your Owner's Manual or VECI label that differ with what's printed here. In these cases, the Owner's Manual or VECI label can be considered correct, since it is specific to your particular vehicle.

3 Tune-up general information

The term tune-up is used in this manual to represent a combination of individual operations rather than one specific procedure.

If, from the time the vehicle is new, the routine maintenance schedule is followed closely and frequent checks are made of fluid levels and high wear items, as suggested throughout this manual, the engine will be kept in relatively good running condition and the need for additional work will be minimized.

More likely than not, however, there will be times when the engine is running poorly due to lack of regular maintenance. This is even more likely if a used vehicle, which has not received regular and frequent maintenance checks, is purchased. In such cases, an engine tune-up will be needed outside of the regular routine maintenance intervals.

The first step in any tune-up or diagnostic procedure to help correct a poor running engine is a cylinder compression check. A compression check (see Chapter 2C) will help determine the condition of internal engine components and should be used as a guide for tune-up and repair procedures. If, for instance, a compression check indicates serious internal engine wear, a conventional tune-up will not improve the performance of the engine and would be a waste of time and money. Because of its importance, the compression check should be done by someone with the right equipment and the knowledge to use it properly.

The following procedures are those most often needed to bring a generally poor running engine back into a proper state of tune.

MINOR TUNE-UP

Check all engine related fluids (Section 4)
Clean, inspect and test the battery (Section 8)
Check the cooling system (Section 9)
Check all underhood hoses (Section 14)
Check the air filter (Section 15)
Check and adjust the drivebelts (Section 19)

MAJOR TUNE-UP

All items listed under minor tune-up, plus . . .

Replace the air filter (Section 15)
Check the fuel system (Section 17)
Replace the spark plugs (Section 24)

4   Fluid level checks (every 250 miles [400km] or weekly)

1   Fluids are an essential part of the lubrication, cooling, brake, clutch and other systems. Because these fluids gradually become depleted and/or contaminated during normal operation of the vehicle, they must be periodically replenished. See *Recommended lubricants and fluids* and *Capacities* at the end of this Chapter before adding fluid to any of the following components.

➡Note: The vehicle must be on level ground before fluid levels can be checked.

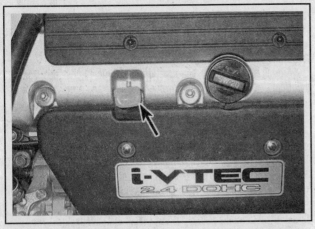

4.2a On DOHC engines the oil dipstick is located on the front side of the engine

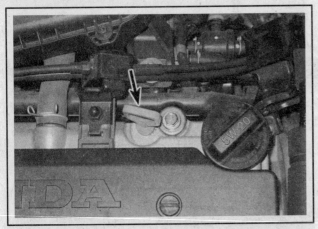

4.2b On SOHC engines the oil dipstick is located on the left side of the engine

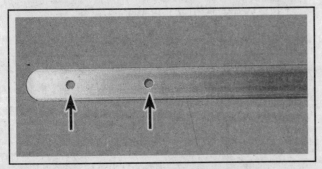

4.4 The oil level should be between the two holes in the dipstick

ENGINE OIL

◆ **Refer to illustrations 4.2a, 4.2b, 4.4 and 4.6**

2   The engine oil level is checked with a dipstick located on top of the valve cover (see illustrations). The dipstick extends through a metal tube from which it protrudes down into the engine oil pan.

3   The oil level should be checked before the vehicle has been driven, or about 5 minutes after the engine has been shut off. If the oil is checked immediately after driving the vehicle, some of the oil will remain in the upper engine components, producing an inaccurate reading on the dipstick.

4   Pull the dipstick from the tube and wipe all the oil from the end with a clean rag or paper towel. Insert the clean dipstick all the way back into its metal tube and pull it out again. Observe the oil at the end of the dipstick. At its highest point, the level should be between the upper and lower holes (see illustration).

5   It takes one quart of oil to raise the level from the lower hole to the upper hole on the dipstick. Do not allow the level to drop below the lower hole or oil starvation may cause engine damage. Conversely, overfilling the engine (adding oil above the upper hole) may cause oil fouled spark plugs, oil leaks or oil seal failures.

6   Remove the threaded cap from the valve cover to add oil (see illustration). Use a funnel to prevent spills. After adding the oil, install the filler cap hand tight. Start the engine and look carefully for any small leaks around the oil filter or drain plug. Stop the engine and check the oil level again after it has had sufficient time to drain from the upper block and cylinder head galleys.

7   Checking the oil level is an important preventive maintenance step. A continually dropping oil level indicates oil leakage through damaged seals, from loose connections, or past worn rings or valve guides. If the oil looks milky in color or has water droplets in it, a cylinder head gasket may be blown or the oil cooler could be leaking. The engine should be checked immediately. The condition of the oil should also be checked. Each time you check the oil level, slide your thumb and index finger up the dipstick before wiping off the oil. If you see small dirt or metal particles clinging to the dipstick, the oil should be changed (see Section 6).

4.6 The oil filler cap is located on the valve cover - always make sure the area around the opening is clean before unscrewing the cap to prevent dirt from contaminating the engine (DOHC engine shown)

ENGINE COOLANT

▶ **Refer to illustration 4.9**

❈❈ WARNING:

Do not allow antifreeze to come in contact with your skin or painted surfaces of the vehicle. Flush contaminated areas immediately with plenty of water. Don't store new coolant or leave old coolant lying around where it's accessible to children or pets - they're attracted by its sweet smell. Ingestion of even a small amount of coolant can be fatal! Wipe up garage floor and drip pan spills immediately. Keep antifreeze containers covered and repair cooling system leaks as soon as they're noticed.

8   All vehicles covered by this manual are equipped with a pressurized coolant recovery system. A coolant reservoir, located on the right side of the engine compartment, is connected by a hose to the base of the radiator filler neck. If the coolant overheats, it can escape through the pressurized filler cap, then through the connecting hose into the reservoir. As the engine cools, the coolant is automatically drawn back into the cooling system to maintain the correct level.

9   The coolant level in the reservoir should be checked regularly. It must be between the MAX and MIN lines on the tank. The level will vary with the temperature of the engine. When the engine is cold, the coolant level should be at or slightly above the MIN mark on the tank. Once the engine has warmed up, the level should be at or near the MAX mark. If it isn't, allow the fluid in the tank to cool, then remove the cap from the reservoir (see illustration) and add coolant to bring the level up to the MAX line.

❈❈ WARNING:

Do not remove the radiator cap to check the coolant level when the engine is warm! Use only the recommended coolant and water in the mixture ratio listed in this Chapter's Specifications. Do not use supplemental inhibitors or additives. If only a small amount of coolant is required to bring the system up to the proper level, water can be used. However, repeated additions of water will dilute the recommended antifreeze and water solution. In order to maintain the proper ratio of antifreeze and water, it is advisable to top up the coolant level with the correct mixture.

10 If the coolant level drops within a short time after replenishment, there may be a leak in the system. Inspect the radiator, hoses, engine coolant filler cap, drain plugs and water pump. If no leak is evident, have the radiator cap pressure tested.

❈❈ WARNING:

Never remove the radiator cap or the coolant reservoir cap when the engine is running or has just been shut down, because the cooling system is hot. Escaping steam and scalding liquid could cause serious injury.

11 If it is necessary to open the radiator cap, wait until the system has cooled completely, then wrap a thick cloth around the cap and turn it to the first stop. If any steam escapes, wait until the system has cooled further, then remove the cap.

12 When checking the coolant level, always note its condition. It should be relatively clear. If it is brown or rust colored, the system should be drained, flushed and refilled. Even if the coolant appears to be normal, the corrosion inhibitors wear out with use, so it must be replaced at the specified intervals.

13 Do not allow antifreeze to come in contact with your skin or painted surfaces of the vehicle. Flush contacted areas immediately with plenty of water.

WINDSHIELD WASHER FLUID

▶ **Refer to illustration 4.14**

14 Fluid for the windshield washer system is stored in a plastic reservoir which is located at the right front corner of the engine compartment on Hatchback models, and is located on the left side of the engine compartment on Coupe, Sedan and CR-V models (see illustration). In milder climates, plain water can be used to top up the reservoir, but the reservoir should be kept no more than 2/3 full to allow for expansion should the water freeze. In colder climates, the use of a specially designed windshield washer fluid, available at your dealer and any auto parts store, will help lower the freezing point of the fluid. Mix the solution with water in accordance with the manufacturer's directions on the container. Do not use regular antifreeze. It will damage the vehicle's paint.

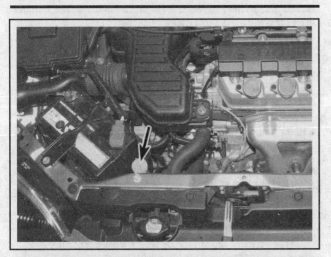

4.9 The cooling system reservoir is located on the right side of the engine compartment (Sedan model shown)

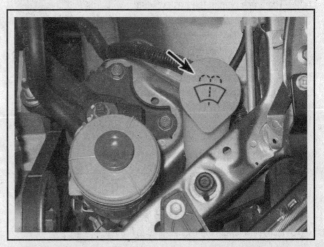

4.14 Fluid for the windshield washer system is stored in this plastic reservoir

4.16 The brake fluid level should be kept at the MAX mark on the translucent plastic reservoir

4.26 The power steering fluid reservoir is translucent so the fluid level can be checked without removing the cap - keep the fluid between the two lines

BRAKE FLUID

▶ **Refer to illustration 4.16**

15 The brake master cylinder is located on the driver's side of the engine compartment firewall.

16 The level should be maintained at the MAX mark on the reservoir (see illustration).

17 If additional fluid is necessary to bring the level up, use a rag to clean all dirt off the top of the reservoir. If any foreign matter enters the master cylinder when the cap is removed, blockage in the brake system lines can occur. Also, make sure all painted surfaces around the master cylinder are covered, since brake fluid will ruin paint. Carefully pour new, clean brake fluid into the master cylinder. Be careful not to spill the fluid on painted surfaces. Be sure the specified fluid is used; mixing different types of brake fluid can cause damage to the system. See *Recommended lubricants and fluids* at the end of this Chapter or your owner's manual.

18 At this time the fluid and the master cylinder can be inspected for contamination. If deposits, dirt particles or water droplets are seen in the fluid, the system should be drained and refilled with fresh fluid (see Section 20).

19 Reinstall the master cylinder cap.

20 The brake fluid in the master cylinder will drop slightly as the brake shoes or pads at each wheel wear down during normal operation. If the master cylinder requires repeated replenishing to keep the level up, it's an indication of leaks in the brake system, which should be corrected immediately. Check all brake lines and connections, along with the wheel cylinders and booster (see Chapter 9 for more information).

21 If you discover that the reservoir is empty or nearly empty, the brake system should be filled, bled (see Chapter 9) and checked for leaks.

POWER STEERING FLUID

▶ **Refer to illustration 4.26**

22 Check the power steering fluid level periodically to avoid steering system problems, such as damage to the pump.

❋ CAUTION:

DO NOT hold the steering wheel against either stop (extreme left or right turn) for more than five seconds. If you do, the power steering pump could be damaged.

23 The power steering reservoir is located at the right side of the engine compartment on CR-V models, and on the left side of the engine compartment on Coupe and Sedan models. The reservoir has LOWER LEVEL and UPPER LEVEL fluid level marks on the side. The fluid level can be seen without removing the reservoir cap.

24 Park the vehicle on level ground and apply the parking brake.

25 Run the engine until it has reached normal operating temperature. With the engine at idle, turn the steering wheel back and forth about 10 times to get any air out of the steering system. Shut the engine off with the wheels in the straight-ahead position.

26 Note the fluid level on the side of the reservoir. It should be between the two marks (see illustration).

27 Add small amounts of fluid until the level is correct.

❋ CAUTION:

Do not overfill the reservoir. If too much fluid is added, remove the excess with a clean syringe or suction pump.

28 Check the power steering hoses and connections for leaks and wear.

AUTOMATIC TRANSAXLE FLUID

▶ **Refer to illustrations 4.32a, 4.32b and 4.32c**

29 The level of the automatic transaxle fluid should be carefully maintained. Low fluid level can lead to slipping or loss of drive, while overfilling can cause foaming, loss of fluid and transaxle damage.

30 The transaxle fluid level should only be checked when the transaxle is hot (at its normal operating temperature). If the vehicle has just been driven over 10 miles (15 miles in a frigid climate), and the fluid temperature is 160 to 175-degrees F, the transaxle is hot.

4.32a The automatic transaxle dipstick is located on the right side of the engine compartment on Coupe and Sedan models . . .

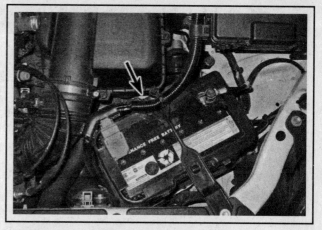

4.32b . . . and on the left side on CR-V models

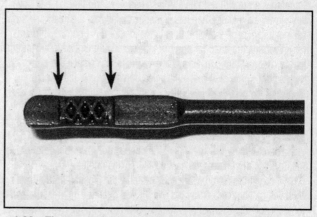

4.32c The automatic transaxle fluid level should be in the cross-hatched area on the dipstick

✳ CAUTION:

If the vehicle has just been driven for a long time at high speed or in city traffic in hot weather, or if it has been pulling a trailer, an accurate fluid level reading cannot be obtained. Allow the fluid to cool down for about 30 minutes.

31 If the vehicle has not just been driven, park the vehicle on level ground, set the parking brake and start the engine. While the engine is idling, depress the brake pedal and move the selector lever through all the gear ranges, beginning and ending in Park.

32 With the engine still idling, remove the dipstick from its tube. Check the level of the fluid on the dipstick and note its condition (see illustrations).

33 Wipe the fluid from the dipstick with a clean rag and reinsert it back into the filler tube until the cap seats.

34 Pull the dipstick out again and note the fluid level. The fluid level should be in the operating temperature range (between the upper and lower mark). If the level is at the low side of either range, add the specified automatic transmission fluid through the dipstick tube with a funnel.

35 Add just enough of the recommended fluid to fill the transaxle to the proper level. It takes about one pint to raise the level from the low mark to the high mark when the fluid is hot, so add the fluid a little at a time and keep checking the level until it is correct.

36 The condition of the fluid should also be checked along with the level. If the fluid at the end of the dipstick is black or a dark reddish brown color, or if it emits a burned smell, the fluid should be changed (see Section 25). If you are in doubt about the condition of the fluid, purchase some new fluid and compare the two for color and smell.

MANUAL TRANSAXLE FLUID

➡**Note: It isn't necessary to check this lubricant weekly; every 3000 miles (4800 km) or 3 months will be adequate.**

37 The manual transaxle does not have a dipstick. To check the fluid

level, raise the vehicle and support it securely on jackstands. On the transaxle housing, remove the fluid fill plug. If the lubricant level is correct, it should be up to the lower edge of the hole.

38 If the transaxle needs more lubricant (if the level is not up to the hole), use a syringe or a gear oil pump to add more. Stop filling the transaxle when the lubricant begins to run out the hole.

39 Install the plug and tighten it securely. Drive the vehicle a short distance, then check for leaks.

REAR DIFFERENTIAL FLUID (CR-V)

➡**Note: It isn't necessary to check this lubricant weekly; every 3000 miles (4800 km) or 3 months will be adequate.**

40 To check the fluid level, raise the vehicle and support it securely on jackstands. On the axle housing, remove the check/fill plug. If the lubricant level is correct, it should be up to the lower edge of the hole.

41 If the differential needs more lubricant (if the level is not up to the hole), use a syringe or a gear oil pump to add more. Stop filling the differential when the lubricant begins to run out the hole.

42 Install the plug and tighten it securely. Drive the vehicle a short distance, then check for leaks.

5   Tire and tire pressure checks (every 250 miles [400 km] or weekly)

▶ **Refer to illustrations 5.2, 5.3, 5.4a, 5.4b**

1   Periodic inspection of the tires may spare you from the inconvenience of being stranded with a flat tire. It can also provide you with vital information regarding possible problems in the steering and suspension systems before major damage occurs.

2   Normal tread wear can be monitored with a simple, inexpensive device known as a tread depth indicator (see illustration). When the tread depth reaches the specified minimum, replace the tire(s).

3   Note any abnormal tread wear (see illustration). Tread pattern irregularities such as cupping, flat spots and more wear on one side than the other are indications of front end alignment and/or balance problems. If any of these conditions are noted, take the vehicle to a tire shop or service station to correct the problem.

4   Look closely for cuts, punctures and embedded nails or tacks. Sometimes a tire will hold its air pressure for a short time or leak down very slowly even after a nail has embedded itself into the tread. If a slow leak persists, check the valve core to make sure it is tight (see illustration). Examine the tread for an object that may have embedded itself into the tire or for a "plug" that may have begun to leak (radial tire punctures are repaired with a plug that is installed in a puncture). If a puncture is suspected, it can be easily verified by spraying a solution of soapy water onto the puncture area (see illustration). The soapy solution will bubble if there is a leak. Unless the puncture is inordinately large, a tire shop or gas station can usually repair the punctured tire.

5   Carefully inspect the inner side of each tire for evidence of brake fluid leakage. If you see any, inspect the brakes immediately.

6   Correct tire air pressure adds miles to the lifespan of the tires, improves mileage and enhances overall ride quality. Tire pressure cannot be accurately estimated by looking at a tire, particularly if it is a

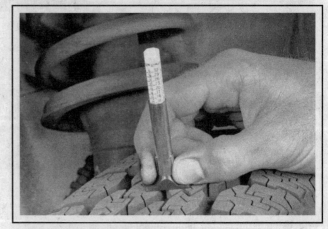

5.2 A tire tread depth indicator should be used to monitor tire wear - they are available at auto parts stores and service stations and cost very little

radial. A tire pressure gauge is therefore essential. Keep an accurate gauge in the glovebox. The pressure gauges fitted to the nozzles of air hoses at gas stations are often inaccurate.

7   Always check tire pressure when the tires are cold. "Cold," in this case, means the vehicle has not been driven over a mile in the three hours preceding a tire pressure check. A pressure rise of four to eight pounds is not uncommon once the tires are warm.

8   Unscrew the valve cap protruding from the wheel or hubcap and push the gauge firmly onto the valve (see illustration). Note the reading on the gauge and compare this figure to the recommended tire pres-

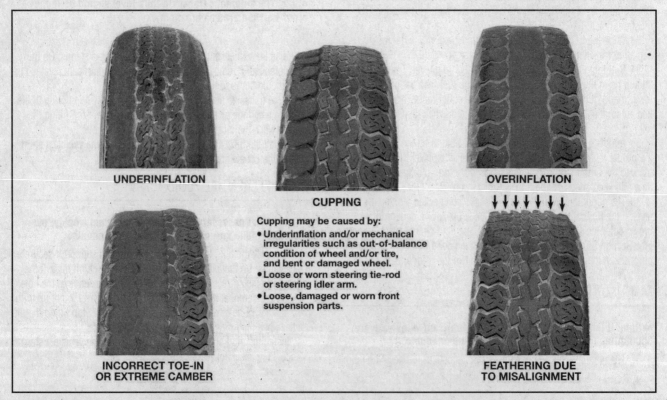

UNDERINFLATION

CUPPING

OVERINFLATION

Cupping may be caused by:
- Underinflation and/or mechanical irregularities such as out-of-balance condition of wheel and/or tire, and bent or damaged wheel.
- Loose or worn steering tie-rod or steering idler arm.
- Loose, damaged or worn front suspension parts.

INCORRECT TOE-IN
OR EXTREME CAMBER

FEATHERING DUE
TO MISALIGNMENT

5.3 This chart will help you determine the condition of your tires, the probable cause(s) of abnormal wear and the corrective action necessary

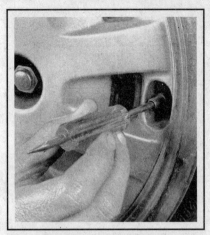

5.4a If a tire loses air on a steady basis, check the valve core first to make sure it's snug (special inexpensive wrenches are commonly available at auto parts stores

5.4b If the valve core is tight, raise the corner of the vehicle with the low tire and spray a soapy water solution onto the tread as the tire is turned slowly - slow leaks will cause small bubbles to appear

5.8 To extend the life of your tires, check the air pressure at least once a week with an accurate gauge (don't forget the spare!)

sure shown on the tire placard on the left door jamb. Be sure to reinstall the valve cap to keep dirt and moisture out of the valve stem mechanism. Check all four tires and, if necessary, add enough air to bring them up to the recommended pressure levels.

9   Don't forget to keep the spare tire inflated to the specified pressure (consult your owner's manual). Note that the air pressure specified for the compact spare is significantly higher than the pressure of the regular tires.

6   Engine oil and oil filter change (every 3000 miles [4800 km] or 3 months)

▶ **Refer to illustrations 6.2, 6.7, 6.12 and 6.14**

➡**Note: While the vehicle is raised, be sure to check the manual transaxle fluid level (if equipped) and if you have a 4WD CR-V model, the rear differential fluid level.**

1   Frequent oil changes are the best preventive maintenance the home mechanic can give the engine, because aging oil becomes

diluted and contaminated, which leads to premature engine wear.

2   Make sure you have all the necessary tools before you begin this procedure (see illustration). You should also have plenty of rags or newspapers handy for mopping up any spills.

3   Access to the underside of the vehicle is greatly improved if the vehicle can be lifted on a hoist, driven onto ramps or supported by jackstands.

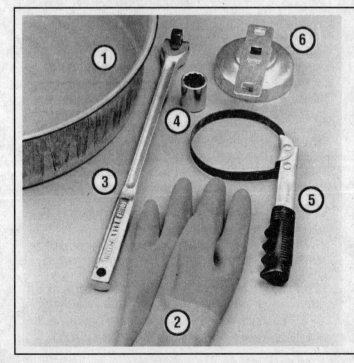

6.2 These tools are required when changing the engine oil and filter

1   *Drain pan* - It should be fairly shallow in depth, but wide in order to prevent spills
2   *Rubber gloves* - When removing the drain plug and filter, it is inevitable that you will get oil on your hands (the gloves will prevent burns)
3   *Breaker bar* - Sometimes the oil drain plug is pretty tight and a long breaker bar is needed to loosen it
4   *Socket* - To be used with the breaker bar or a ratchet (must be the correct size to fit the drain plug)
5   *Filter wrench* - This is a metal band-type wrench, which requires clearance around the filter to be effective
6   *Filter wrench* - This type fits on the bottom of the filter and can be turned with a ratchet or beaker bar (different size wrenches are available for different types of filters)

6.7 Use a proper size box-end wrench or socket to remove the oil drain plug and avoid rounding it off

6.12 Use an oil filter wrench to remove the filter

6.14 Lubricate the oil filter gasket with clean engine oil before installing the filter on the engine

✳✳ WARNING:

Do not work under a vehicle which is supported only by a bumper, hydraulic or scissors-type jack.

4   If this is your first oil change, get under the vehicle and familiarize yourself with the locations of the oil drain plug and the oil filter. The engine and exhaust components will be warm during the actual work, so try to anticipate any potential problems before the engine and accessories are hot.

5   Park the vehicle on a level spot. Start the engine and allow it to reach its normal operating temperature. Warm oil and sludge will flow out more easily. Turn off the engine when it's warmed up. Remove the filler cap from the valve cover.

6   Raise the vehicle and support it securely on jackstands.

✳✳ WARNING:

Never get beneath the vehicle when it is supported only by a jack. The jack provided with your vehicle is designed solely for raising the vehicle to remove and replace the wheels. Always use jackstands to support the vehicle when it becomes necessary to place your body underneath the vehicle.

7   Being careful not to touch the hot exhaust components, place the drain pan under the drain plug in the bottom of the pan and remove the plug (see illustration). You may want to wear gloves while unscrewing the plug the final few turns if the engine is hot.

8   Allow the old oil to drain into the pan. It may be necessary to move the pan farther under the engine as the oil flow slows to a trickle. Inspect the old oil for the presence of metal shavings and chips.

9   After all the oil has drained, wipe off the drain plug with a clean rag. Even minute metal particles clinging to the plug would immediately contaminate the new oil.

10   Clean the area around the drain plug opening, reinstall the plug and tighten it securely, but do not strip the threads.

11   Move the drain pan into position under the oil filter.

12   Loosen the oil filter (see illustration) by turning it counterclockwise with an oil filter wrench. Once the filter is loose, use your hands to unscrew it from the block. Keep the open end pointing up to prevent the oil inside the filter from spilling out.

✳✳ WARNING:

The exhaust system may still be hot, so be careful.

13   With a clean rag, wipe off the mounting surface on the block. If a residue of old oil is allowed to remain, it will smoke when the block is heated up. Also make sure that none of the old gasket remains stuck to the mounting surface. It can be removed with a scraper if necessary.

14   Compare the old filter with the new one to make sure they are the same type. Smear some clean engine oil on the rubber gasket of the new filter (see illustration).

15   Attach the new filter to the engine, following the tightening directions printed on the filter canister or packing box. Most filter manufacturers recommend against using a filter wrench due to the possibility of overtightening and damaging the seal.

16   Remove all tools, rags, etc. from under the vehicle, being careful not to spill the oil in the drain pan, then lower the vehicle.

17   Add new oil to the engine through the oil filler cap in the valve cover. Use a funnel, if necessary, to prevent oil from spilling onto the top of the engine. Pour three quarts of fresh oil into the engine. Wait a few minutes to allow the oil to drain into the pan, then check the level on the oil dipstick (see Section 4). If the oil level is at or near the upper hole on the dipstick, install the filler cap hand tight, start the engine and allow the new oil to circulate.

18   Allow the engine to run for about a minute. While the engine is running, look under the vehicle and check for leaks at the oil pan drain plug and around the oil filter. If either is leaking, stop the engine and tighten the plug or filter.

19   Wait a few minutes to allow the oil to trickle down into the pan, then recheck the level on the dipstick and, if necessary, add enough oil to bring the level to the upper hole.

20   During the first few trips after an oil change, make it a point to check frequently for leaks and proper oil level.

21   The old oil drained from the engine cannot be reused in its present state and should be disposed of. Check with your local auto parts store, disposal facility or environmental agency to see if they will accept the oil for recycling. After the oil has cooled it can be drained into a container (capped plastic jugs, topped bottles, milk cartons, etc.) for transport to one of these disposal sites. Don't dispose of the oil by pouring it on the ground or down a drain!

7 Windshield wiper blade inspection and replacement (every 7500 miles [12,000 km] or 6 months)

▶ **Refer to illustrations 7.5a and 7.5b**

1   The windshield wiper and blade assembly should be inspected periodically for damage, loose components and cracked or worn blade elements.

2   Road film can build up on the wiper blades and affect their efficiency, so they should be washed regularly with a mild detergent solution.

3   The action of the wiping mechanism can loosen bolts, nuts and fasteners, so they should be checked and tightened, as necessary, at the same time the wiper blades are checked.

4   If the wiper blade elements are cracked, worn or warped, or no longer clean adequately, they should be replaced with new ones.

5   Lift the arm assembly away from the glass for clearance, press on the release lever, then slide the wiper blade assembly out of the hook at the end of the arm (see illustrations).

6   Attach the new wiper to the arm. Connection can be confirmed by an audible click.

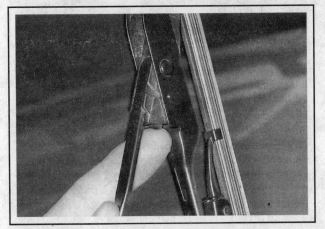

7.5a To release the blade holder, pull up on the release tab . . .

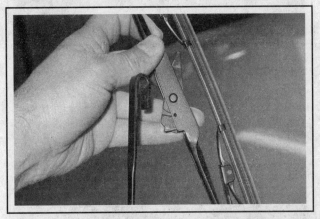

7.5b . . . and pull the wiper blade in the direction of the windshield to separate it from the arm

8 Battery check, maintenance and charging (every 7500 miles [12,000 km] or 6 months)

▶ **Refer to illustrations 8.1, 8.6a, 8.6b, 8.7a, 8.7b and 8.8**

❋❋ WARNING:

Certain precautions must be followed when checking and servicing the battery. Hydrogen gas, which is highly flammable, is always present in the battery cells, so keep lighted tobacco and all other open flames and sparks away from the battery. The electrolyte inside the battery is actually diluted sulfuric acid, which will cause injury if splashed on your skin or in your eyes. It will also ruin clothes and painted surfaces. When removing the battery cables, always detach the negative cable first and hook it up last!

1   A routine preventive maintenance program for the battery in your

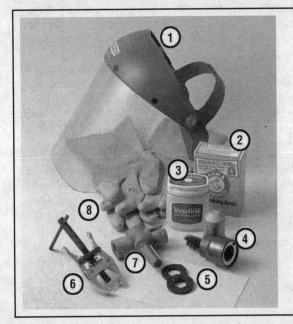

8.1 Tools and materials required for battery maintenance

1   *Face shield/safety goggles* - When removing corrosion with a brush, the acidic particles can easily fly up into your eyes

2   *Baking soda* - A solution of baking soda and water can be used to neutralize corrosion

3   *Petroleum jelly* - A layer of this on the battery posts will help prevent corrosion

4   *Battery post/cable cleaner* - This wire brush cleaning tool will remove all traces of corrosion from the battery posts and cable clamps

5   *Treated felt washers* - Placing one of these on each post, directly under the cable clamps, will help prevent corrosion

6   *Puller* - Sometimes the cable clamps are very difficult to pull off the posts, even after the nut/bolt has been completely loosened. This tool pulls the clamp straight up and off the post without damage

7   *Battery post/cable cleaner* - Here is another cleaning tool which is a slightly different version of number 4 above, but it does the same thing

8   *Rubber gloves* - Another safety item to consider when servicing the battery; remember that's acid inside the battery

8.6a Battery terminal corrosion usually appears as light, fluffy powder

8.6b Removing a cable from the battery post with a wrench - sometimes a pair of special battery pliers are required for this procedure if corrosion has caused deterioration of the nut hex (always remove the ground (-) cable first and hook it up last!)

vehicle is the only way to ensure quick and reliable starts. But before performing any battery maintenance, make sure that you have the proper equipment necessary to work safely around the battery (see illustration).

2   There are also several precautions that should be taken whenever

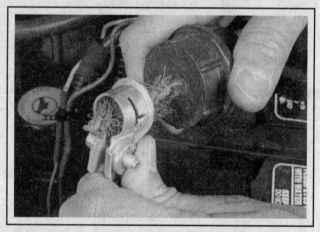

8.7a When cleaning the cable clamps, all corrosion must be removed (the inside of the clamp is tapered to match the taper on the post, so don't remove too much material)

8.7b Regardless of the type of tool used to clean the battery posts, a clean, shiny surface should be the result

battery maintenance is performed. Before servicing the battery, always turn the engine and all accessories off and disconnect the cable from the negative terminal of the battery (see Chapter 5, Section 1).

3   The battery produces hydrogen gas, which is both flammable and explosive. Never create a spark, smoke or light a match around the battery. Always charge the battery in a ventilated area.

4   Electrolyte contains poisonous and corrosive sulfuric acid. Do not allow it to get in your eyes, on your skin on your clothes. Never ingest it. Wear protective safety glasses when working near the battery. Keep children away from the battery.

5   Note the external condition of the battery. If the positive terminal and cable clamp on your vehicle's battery is equipped with a rubber protector, make sure that it's not torn or damaged. It should completely cover the terminal. Look for any corroded or loose connections, cracks in the case or cover or loose hold-down clamps. Also check the entire length of each cable for cracks and frayed conductors.

6   If corrosion, which looks like white, fluffy deposits (see illustration) is evident, particularly around the terminals, the battery should be removed for cleaning. Loosen the cable clamp bolts with a wrench, being careful to remove the ground cable first, and slide them off the terminals (see illustration). Then disconnect the hold-down clamp bolt and nut, remove the clamp and lift the battery from the engine compartment.

7   Clean the cable clamps thoroughly with a battery brush or a terminal cleaner and a solution of warm water and baking soda (see illustration). Wash the terminals and the top of the battery case with the same solution but make sure that the solution doesn't get into the battery. When cleaning the cables, terminals and battery top, wear safety goggles and rubber gloves to prevent any solution from coming in contact with your eyes or hands. Wear old clothes too - even diluted, sulfuric acid splashed onto clothes will burn holes in them. If the terminals have been extensively corroded, clean them up with a terminal cleaner (see illustration). Thoroughly wash all cleaned areas with plain water.

8   Make sure that the battery tray is in good condition and the hold-down clamp fasteners are tight. If the battery is removed from the tray, make sure no parts remain in the bottom of the tray when the battery is reinstalled. When reinstalling the hold-down clamp bolts, do not overtighten them.

9   Information on removing and installing the battery can be found

in Chapter 5. If you disconnected the cable(s) from the negative and/or positive battery terminals, see Chapter 5, Section 1. Information on jump starting can be found at the front of this manual.

10 Corrosion on the hold-down components, battery case and surrounding areas can be removed with a solution of water and baking soda. Thoroughly rinse all cleaned areas with plain water.

11 Any metal parts of the vehicle damaged by corrosion should be covered with a zinc-based primer, then painted.

CHARGING

✳✳ WARNING:

When batteries are being charged, hydrogen gas, which is very explosive and flammable, is produced. Do not smoke or allow open flames near a charging or a recently charged battery. Wear eye protection when near the battery during charging. Also, make sure the charger is unplugged before connecting or disconnecting the battery from the charger.

12 Slow-rate charging is the best way to restore a battery that's discharged to the point where it will not start the engine. It's also a good way to maintain the battery charge in a vehicle that's only driven a few miles between starts. Maintaining the battery charge is particularly important in the winter when the battery must work harder to start the engine and electrical accessories that drain the battery are in greater use.

13 It's best to use a one or two-amp battery charger (sometimes called a "trickle" charger). They are the safest and put the least strain on the battery. They are also the least expensive. For a faster charge, you can use a higher amperage charger, but don't use one rated more than 1/10th the amp/hour rating of the battery. Rapid boost charges that claim to restore the power of the battery in one to two hours are hardest on the battery and can damage batteries not in good condition. This type of charging should only be used in emergency situations.

14 The average time necessary to charge a battery should be listed in the instructions that come with the charger. As a general rule, a trickle charger will charge a battery in 12 to 16 hours.

9   Cooling system check (every 7500 miles [12,000 km] or 6 months)

▶ **Refer to illustration 9.4**

1 Many major engine failures can be attributed to a faulty cooling system. The cooling system also cools the transaxle fluid and thus plays an important role in prolonging transaxle life.

2 The cooling system should be checked with the engine cold. Do this before the vehicle is driven for the day or after the engine has been shut off for at least three hours.

3 Remove the radiator cap by turning it to the left until it reaches a stop. If you hear a hissing sound (indicating there is still pressure in the system), wait until it stops. Now press down on the cap with the palm of your hand and continue turning to the left until the cap can be removed. Thoroughly clean the cap, inside and out, with clean water. Also clean the filler neck on the radiator. All traces of corrosion should be removed. The coolant inside the radiator should be relatively transparent. If it's rust colored, the system should be drained and refilled (see Section 21). If the coolant level isn't up to the top, add additional antifreeze/coolant mixture (see Section 4).

4 Carefully check the large upper and lower radiator hoses along with the smaller diameter heater hoses which run from the engine to the firewall. Inspect each hose along its entire length, replacing any hose which is cracked, swollen or shows signs of deterioration. Cracks may become more apparent if the hose is squeezed (see illustration). Regardless of condition, it's a good idea to replace hoses with new ones every two years.

5 Make sure that all hose connections are tight. A leak in the cooling system will usually show up as white or rust colored deposits on the areas adjoining the leak. If wire-type clamps are used at the ends of the hoses, it may be a good idea to replace them with more secure screw-type clamps.

6 Use compressed air or a soft brush to remove bugs, leaves, etc. from the front of the radiator or air conditioning condenser. Be careful not to damage the delicate cooling fins or cut yourself on them.

7 Every other inspection, or at the first indication of cooling system problems, have the cap and system pressure tested. If you don't have a pressure tester, most gas stations and repair shops will do this for a minimal charge.

Check for a chafed area that could fail prematurely.

Check for a soft area indicating the hose has deteriorated inside.

Overtightening the clamp on a hardened hose will damage the hose and cause a leak.

Check each hose for swelling and oil-soaked ends. Cracks and breaks can be located by squeezing the hose.

9.4 Hoses, like drivebelts, have a habit of failing at the worst possible time - to prevent the inconvenience of a blown radiator or heater hose, inspect them carefully as shown here

10 Tire rotation (every 7500 miles [12,000 km] or 6 months)

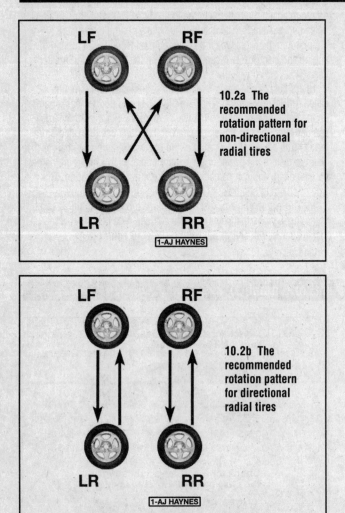

10.2a The recommended rotation pattern for non-directional radial tires

10.2b The recommended rotation pattern for directional radial tires

▶ **Refer to illustrations 10.2a and 10.2b**

1   The tires should be rotated at the specified intervals and whenever uneven wear is noticed. Since the vehicle will be raised and the tires removed anyway, check the brakes (see Section 12) at this time.

2   Radial tires must be rotated in a specific pattern (see illustrations). Most models are equipped with non-directional tires, but some models may have directional tires, which have a different rotation pattern. When rotating tires, examine the sidewalls. Directional tires have arrows on the sidewall that indicate the direction they must turn, and a set of these tires includes two left-side tires and two right-side tires. The left and right side tires must not be rotated to the other side.

3   Refer to the information in *Jacking and towing* at the front of this manual for the proper procedures to follow when raising the vehicle and changing a tire. If the brakes are to be checked, do not apply the parking brake as stated. Make sure the tires are blocked to prevent the vehicle from rolling.

4   Preferably, the entire vehicle should be raised at the same time. This can be done on a hoist or by jacking up each corner and then lowering the vehicle onto jackstands placed under the frame rails. Always use four jackstands and make sure the vehicle is firmly supported.

5   After rotation, check and adjust the tire pressures as necessary and be sure to check the lug nut tightness. Ideally, lug nuts should be tightened to the torque listed in this Chapter's Specifications with a torque wrench, and rechecked after 25 miles of driving.

6   For further information on the wheels and tires, refer to Chapter 10.

11 Seat belt check (every 7500 miles [12,000 km] or 6 months)

1   Check seat belts, buckles, latch plates and guide loops for obvious damage and signs of wear.

2   See if the seat belt reminder light comes on when the key is turned to the Run or Start position. A chime should also sound. On passive restraint systems, the shoulder belt should move into position in the A-pillar.

3   The seat belts are designed to lock up during a sudden stop or impact, yet allow free movement during normal driving. Make sure the retractors return the belt against your chest while driving and rewind the belt fully when the buckle is unlatched.

4   If any of the above checks reveal problems with the seat belt system, replace parts as necessary.

12 Brake system check (every 7500 miles [12,000 km] or 6 months)

⁂ WARNING:

The dust created by the brake system is harmful to your health. Never blow it out with compressed air and don't inhale any of it. An approved filtering mask should be worn when working on the brakes. Do not, under any circumstances, use petroleum-based solvents to clean brake parts. Use brake system cleaner only!

➡Note: For detailed photographs of the brake system, refer to Chapter 9.

1   In addition to the specified intervals, the brakes should be inspected every time the wheels are removed or whenever a defect is suspected.

2   Any of the following symptoms could indicate a potential brake system defect: The vehicle pulls to one side when the brake pedal is depressed; the brakes make squealing or dragging noises when applied; brake pedal travel is excessive; the pedal pulsates; or brake fluid leaks, usually onto the inside of the tire or wheel.

12.6 You'll find an inspection hole like this in each caliper - placing a ruler across the hole should enable you to determine the thickness of the remaining material on the inner pad

DISC BRAKES

▶ Refer to illustration 12.6

3   Disc brakes can be visually checked without removing any parts except the wheels. Remove the hub caps (if applicable) and loosen the wheel lug nuts a quarter turn each.

4   Raise the vehicle and place it securely on jackstands.

✳ WARNING:

Never work under a vehicle that is supported only by a jack!

5   Remove the wheels. Now visible is the disc brake caliper which contains the pads. There is an outer brake pad and an inner pad. Both must be checked for wear.

6   Measure the thickness of the outer pad at each end of the caliper and the inner pad through the inspection hole in the caliper body (see illustration). Compare the measurement with the limit given in this Chapter's Specifications; if any brake pad thickness is less than specified, then all brake pads must be replaced (see Chapter 9).

7   If you're in doubt as to the exact pad thickness or quality, remove them for measurement and further inspection (see Chapter 9).

8   Check the disc for score marks, wear and burned spots. If any of these conditions exist, the disc should be removed for servicing or replacement (see Chapter 9).

9   Before installing the wheels, check all the brake lines and hoses for damage, wear, deformation, cracks, corrosion, leakage, bends and twists, particularly in the vicinity of the rubber hoses and calipers.

10   Install the wheels, lower the vehicle and tighten the wheel lug nuts to the torque given in this Chapter's Specifications.

DRUM BRAKES

▶ Refer to illustrations 12.14 and 12.16

11   On models with rear drum brakes, make sure the parking brake is off then tap on the outside of the drum with a rubber mallet to loosen it.

12   Remove the brake drums. If the drum still won't come off, refer to Chapter 9

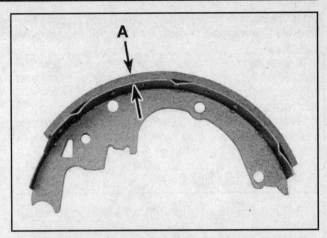

12.14 If the lining is bonded to the brake shoe, measure the lining thickness from the outer surface to the metal shoe; if the lining is riveted to the shoe, measure from the lining outer surface to the rivet head

13   With the drums removed, carefully clean the brake assembly with brake system cleaner.

✳ WARNING:

Don't blow the dust out with compressed air and don't inhale any of it (it is harmful to your health).

14   Note the thickness of the lining material on both front and rear brake shoes (see illustration). Compare the measurement with the limit given in this Chapter's Specifications; if any lining thickness is less than specified, then all of the brake shoes must be replaced (see Chapter 9). The shoes should also be replaced if they're cracked, glazed (shiny areas), or covered with brake fluid.

15   Make sure all the brake assembly springs are connected and in good condition.

16   Check the brake components for signs of fluid leakage. With your finger or a small screwdriver, carefully pry back the rubber cups on the wheel cylinder located at the top of the brake shoes (see illustration). Any leakage here is an indication that the wheel cylinders should be replaced immediately (see Chapter 9). Also, check all hoses and connections for signs of leakage.

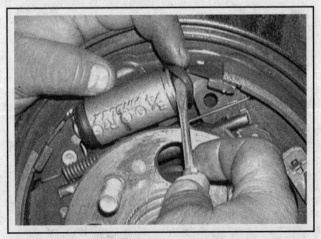

12.16 Carefully peel back the wheel cylinder boot and check for leaking fluid, indicating that the cylinder must be replaced

17 Wipe the inside of the drum with a clean rag and denatured alcohol or brake cleaner. Again, be careful not to breathe the dangerous brake dust.

18 Check the inside of the drum for cracks, score marks, deep scratches and "hard spots" which will appear as small discolored areas. If imperfections cannot be removed with fine emery cloth, the drum must be taken to an automotive machine shop for resurfacing.

19 Repeat the procedure for the remaining wheel. If the inspection reveals that all parts are in good condition, reinstall the brake drums, install the wheels and lower the vehicle to the ground.

BRAKE BOOSTER CHECK

20 Sit in the driver's seat and perform the following sequence of tests.

21 With the brake fully depressed, start the engine - the pedal should move down a little when the engine starts.

22 With the engine running, depress the brake pedal several times - the travel distance should not change.

23 Depress the brake, stop the engine and hold the pedal in for about 30 seconds - the pedal should neither sink nor rise.

24 Restart the engine, run it for about a minute and turn it off. Then firmly depress the brake several times - the pedal travel should decrease with each application.

25 If your brakes do not operate as described, the brake booster has failed. Refer to Chapter 9 for the replacement procedure.

PARKING BRAKE

26 Slowly pull up on the parking brake and count the number of clicks you hear until the handle is up as far as it will go. The adjustment is correct if you hear the specified number of clicks (see this Chapter's Specifications). If you hear more or fewer clicks, it's time to adjust the parking brake (see Chapter 9).

27 An alternative method of checking the parking brake is to park the vehicle on a steep hill with the parking brake set and the transmission in Neutral. If the parking brake cannot prevent the vehicle from rolling, it is in need of adjustment (see Chapter 9).

---

13 Steering, suspension and driveaxle boot check (every 15,000 miles [24,000 km] or 12 months)

➡**Note: For detailed illustrations of the steering and suspension components, refer to Chapter 10.**

WITH THE WHEELS ON THE GROUND

▶ **Refer to illustration 13.4**

1 With the vehicle stopped and the front wheels pointed straight ahead, rock the steering wheel gently back and forth. If freeplay is excessive, a front wheel bearing, steering shaft universal joint or lower arm balljoint is worn or the steering gear is out of adjustment or broken. Refer to Chapter 10 for the appropriate repair procedure.

2 Other symptoms, such as excessive vehicle body movement over rough roads, swaying (leaning) around corners and binding as the steering wheel is turned, may indicate faulty steering and/or suspension components.

3 Check the shock absorbers by pushing down and releasing the vehicle several times at each corner. If the vehicle does not come back

to a level position within one or two bounces, the shocks/struts are worn and must be replaced. When bouncing the vehicle up and down, listen for squeaks and noises from the suspension components.

4 Check the struts and shock absorbers for evidence of fluid leakage (see illustration). A light film of fluid is no cause for concern. Make sure that any fluid noted is from the shocks and not from some other source. If leakage is noted, replace the shocks as a set.

5 Check the shocks to be sure they are securely mounted and undamaged. Check the upper mounts for damage and wear. If damage or wear is noted, replace the shocks as a set (front and rear).

6 If the shocks must be replaced, refer to Chapter 10 for the procedure.

UNDER THE VEHICLE

▶ **Refer to illustrations 13.10 and 13.11**

7 Raise the vehicle with a floor jack and support it securely on jackstands. See *Jacking and towing* at the front of this book for the proper jacking points.

8 Check the tires for irregular wear patterns and proper inflation. See Section 5 in this Chapter for information regarding tire wear and Chapter 10 for information on hub bearing replacement.

9 Inspect the universal joint between the steering shaft and the steering gear housing. Check the steering gear housing for lubricant leakage. Make sure that the dust seals and boots are not damaged and that the boot clamps are not loose. Check the steering linkage for looseness or damage. Check the tie-rod ends for excessive play. Look for loose bolts, broken or disconnected parts and deteriorated rubber bushings on all suspension and steering components. While an assistant turns the steering wheel from side to side, check the steering components for free movement, chafing and binding. If the steering components do not seem to be reacting with the movement of the steering wheel, try to determine where the slack is located.

10 Check the balljoints for wear by trying to move each control arm up and down with a pry bar (see illustration) to ensure that its balljoint has no play. If any balljoint does have play, replace it. See Chapter 10

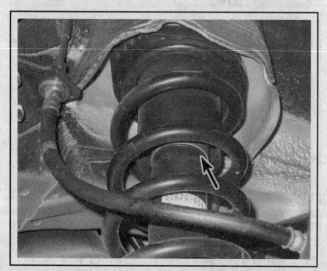

13.4 Check the shocks for leakage at the indicated area

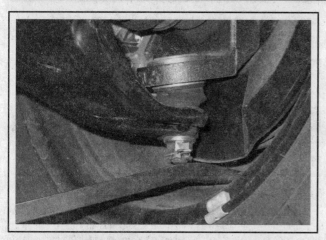

13.10 To check the balljoint for wear, try to pry the control arm up and down to make sure there is no play in the balljoint (if there is, replace it)

13.11 Check the balljoint boot for damage

for the balljoint replacement procedure.

11 Inspect the balljoint boots for damage and leaking grease (see illustration). Replace the balljoints with new ones if they are damaged (see Chapter 10).

12 At the rear of the vehicle, inspect the suspension arm bushings for deterioration. Additional information on suspension components can be found in Chapter 10.

DRIVEAXLE BOOT CHECK

▶ **Refer to illustration 13.14**

→**Note: For detailed illustrations of the driveaxles, refer to Chapter 8.**

13 The driveaxle boots are very important because they prevent dirt, water and foreign material from entering and damaging the constant velocity (CV) joints. Oil and grease can cause the boot material to deteriorate prematurely, so it's a good idea to wash the boots with soap and water. Because it constantly pivots back and forth following the steering action of the front hub, the outer CV boot wears out sooner and should

13.14 Flex the driveaxle boots by hand to check for cracks and/or leaking grease

be inspected regularly.

14 Inspect the boots for tears and cracks as well as loose clamps (see illustration). If there is any evidence of cracks or leaking lubricant, they must be replaced as described in Chapter 8.

14 Underhood hose check and replacement (every 15,000 miles [24,000 km] or 12 months)

✷✷ WARNING:

Replacement of air conditioning hoses must be left to a dealer service department or air conditioning shop that has the equipment to depressurize the system safely. Never remove air conditioning components or hoses until the system has been depressurized.

GENERAL

1 High temperatures under the hood can cause deterioration of the rubber and plastic hoses used for engine, accessory and emission systems operation. Periodic inspection should be made for cracks, loose clamps, material hardening and leaks.

2 Information specific to the cooling system hoses can be found in Section 9.

3 Most (but not all) hoses are secured to the fittings with clamps. Where clamps are used, check to be sure they haven't lost their tension, allowing the hose to leak. If clamps aren't used, make sure the hose has not expanded and/or hardened where it slips over the fitting, allowing it to leak.

PCV SYSTEM HOSE

4 To reduce hydrocarbon emissions, crankcase blow-by gas is vented through the PCV valve in the rocker arm cover to the intake manifold via a rubber hose on most models. The blow-by gases mix with incoming air in the intake manifold before being burned in the combustion chambers.

5 Check the PCV hose for cracks, leaks and other damage. Disconnect it from the valve cover and the intake manifold and check the inside for obstructions. If it's clogged, clean it out with solvent. See Chapter 6 for check and replacement.

VACUUM HOSES

6 It's quite common for vacuum hoses, especially those in the emissions system, to be color coded or identified by colored stripes molded into them. Various systems require hoses with different wall thickness, collapse resistance and temperature resistance. When replacing hoses, be sure the new ones are made of the same material.

7 Often the only effective way to check a hose is to remove it completely from the vehicle. If more than one hose is removed, be sure to label the hoses and fittings to ensure correct installation.

8 When checking vacuum hoses, be sure to include any plastic T-fittings in the check. Inspect the fittings for cracks and the hose where it fits over each fitting for distortion, which could cause leakage.

9 A small piece of vacuum hose (1/4-inch inside diameter) can be used as a stethoscope to detect vacuum leaks. Hold one end of the hose to your ear and probe around vacuum hoses and fittings, listening for the "hissing" sound characteristic of a vacuum leak.

✳✳ WARNING:

When probing with the vacuum hose stethoscope, be careful not to come into contact with moving engine components such as drivebelts, the cooling fan, etc.

FUEL HOSE

✳✳ WARNING:

Gasoline is flammable, so take extra precautions when you work on any part of the fuel system. Don't smoke or allow open flames or bare light bulbs near the work area, and don't work in a garage where a gas-type appliance (such as a water heater or clothes dryer) is present. Since fuel is carcinogenic, wear latex gloves when there's a possibility of being exposed to fuel, and, if you spill any fuel on your skin, rinse it off immediately with soap and water. Mop up any spills immediately and do not store fuel-soaked rags where they could ignite. The fuel system is under constant pressure, so, if any fuel lines are to be disconnected, the fuel pressure in the system must be relieved first

(see Chapter 4 for more information). When you perform any kind of work on the fuel system, wear safety glasses and have a Class B type fire extinguisher on hand.

10 The fuel lines are usually under pressure, so if any fuel lines are to be disconnected be prepared to catch spilled fuel.

✳✳ WARNING:

Your vehicle is equipped with fuel injection and you must relieve the fuel system pressure before servicing the fuel lines.

Refer to Chapter 4 for the fuel system pressure relief procedure.

11 Check all flexible fuel lines for deterioration and chafing. Check especially for cracks in areas where the hose bends and just before fittings, such as where a hose attaches to the fuel pump, fuel filter and fuel injection unit.

12 When replacing a hose, use only hose that is specifically designed for your fuel injection system.

13 Spring-type clamps are sometimes used on fuel return or vapor lines. These clamps often lose their tension over a period of time, and can be "sprung" during removal. Replace all spring-type clamps with screw clamps whenever a hose is replaced. Some fuel lines use spring-lock type couplings, which require a special tool to disconnect. See Chapter 4 for more information on this type of coupling.

METAL LINES

14 Sections of metal line are often used for fuel line between the fuel pump and the fuel injection unit. Check carefully to make sure the line isn't bent, crimped or cracked.

15 If a section of metal fuel line must be replaced, use seamless steel tubing only, since copper and aluminum tubing do not have the strength necessary to withstand vibration caused by the engine.

16 Check the metal brake lines where they enter the master cylinder and brake proportioning unit (if used) for cracks in the lines and loose fittings. Any sign of brake fluid leakage calls for an immediate thorough inspection of the brake system.

15 Air filter replacement (every 15,000 miles [24,000 km] or 12 months)

♦ **Refer to illustration 15.1**

1 The air filter is located inside a housing inside of the engine compartment. To remove the air filter, loosen the clamp securing the inlet tube to the air filter cover, remove the screws securing the two halves of the air filter housing together, then separate the cover halves and remove the air filter element (see illustration).

2 Inspect the outer surface of the filter element. If it is dirty, replace it. If it is only moderately dusty, it can be reused by blowing it clean from the back to the front surface with compressed air. Because it is a pleated paper type filter, it cannot be washed or oiled. If it cannot be cleaned satisfactorily with compressed air, discard and replace it. While the cover is off, be careful not to drop anything down into the housing.

✳✳ CAUTION:

Never drive the vehicle with the air cleaner removed. Excessive engine wear could result and backfiring could even cause a fire under the hood.

3 Wipe out the inside of the air cleaner housing.

4 Place the new filter into the air cleaner housing, making sure it seats properly.

5 Installation of the housing is the reverse of removal.

15.1 Pull the cover out of the way and remove the element

16 Interior ventilation filter replacement (every 15,000 miles [24,000 km] or 12 months)

▶ Refer to illustrations 16.2, 16.3 and 16.4

1   These models are equipped with an air filtering element in the air conditioning system, located in a housing next to the evaporator, under the right side of the instrument panel.

2   Release the glovebox stops, then lower the glove box and let it hang (see illustration).

3   Release the tab and remove the filter door (see illustration).

4   Remove the filter from the air evaporator housing (see illustration).

5   Installation is the reverse of the removal procedure.

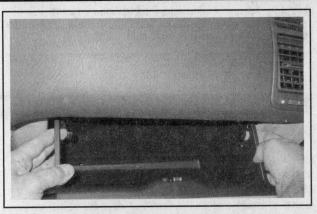

16.2 Release the glovebox stops and lower the box

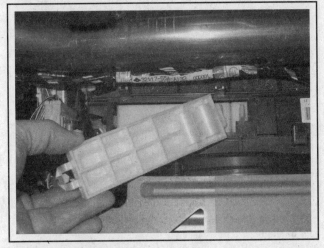

16.3 Open the filter door . . .

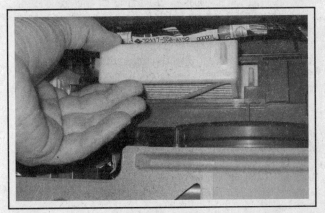

16.4 . . . then pull the filter element from the housing

17 Fuel system check (every 15,000 miles [24,000 km] or 12 months)

✳✳ WARNING:

Gasoline is flammable, so take extra precautions when you work on any part of the fuel system. Don't smoke or allow open flames or bare light bulbs near the work area, and don't work in a garage where a gas-type appliance (such as a water heater or clothes dryer) is present. Since fuel is carcinogenic, wear latex gloves when there's a possibility of being exposed to fuel, and, if you spill any fuel on your skin, rinse it off immediately with soap and water. Mop up any spills immediately and do not store fuel-soaked rags where they could ignite. When you perform any kind of work on the fuel system, wear safety glasses and have a Class B type fire extinguisher on hand. The fuel system is under constant pressure, so, before any lines are disconnected, the fuel system pressure must be relieved (see Chapter 4).

1   If you smell gasoline while driving or after the vehicle has been sitting in the sun, inspect the fuel system immediately.

2   Remove the fuel filler cap and inspect if for damage and corrosion. The gasket should have an unbroken sealing imprint. If the gasket is damaged or corroded, install a new cap.

3   Inspect the fuel feed line for cracks. Make sure that the connections between the fuel lines and the fuel injection system are secure and dry.

✳✳ WARNING:

Your vehicle is fuel injected, so you must relieve the fuel system pressure before servicing fuel system components. The fuel system pressure relief procedure is outlined in Chapter 4.

4   Since some components of the fuel system - the fuel tank and the fuel lines, for example - are underneath the vehicle, they can be inspected more easily with the vehicle raised on a hoist. If that's not possible, raise the vehicle and support it on jackstands.

5   With the vehicle raised and safely supported, inspect the gas tank and filler neck for punctures, cracks and other damage. The connection between the filler neck and the tank is particularly critical. Sometimes a rubber filler neck will leak because of loose clamps or deteriorated rubber. Inspect all fuel tank mounting brackets and straps to be sure that the tank is securely attached to the vehicle.

⁜⁜ WARNING:

Do not, under any circumstances, try to repair a fuel tank (except rubber components); the fuel tanks in these vehicles are made of plastic and must be replaced if damaged.

6   Carefully check all hoses and lines leading away from the fuel tank. Check for loose connections, deteriorated hoses, crimped lines and other damage. Repair or replace damaged sections as necessary (see Chapter 4).

18   Exhaust system check (every 15,000 miles [24,000 km] or 12 months)

▶ **Refer to illustration 18.2**

1   With the engine cold (at least three hours after the vehicle has been driven), check the complete exhaust system from the engine to the end of the tailpipe. Ideally, the inspection should be done with the vehicle on a hoist to permit unrestricted access. If a hoist isn't available, raise the vehicle and support it securely on jackstands.

2   Check the exhaust pipes and connections for evidence of leaks, severe corrosion and damage. Make sure that all brackets and hangers are in good condition and tight (see illustration).

3   At the same time, inspect the underside of the body for holes, corrosion, open seams, etc. which may allow exhaust gases to enter the passenger compartment. Seal all body openings with silicone or body putty.

4   Rattles and other noises can often be traced to the exhaust system, especially the mounts and hangers. Try to move the pipes, muffler and catalytic converter. If the components can come in contact with the body or suspension parts, secure the exhaust system with new mounts.

5   Check the running condition of the engine by inspecting inside the end of the tailpipe. The exhaust deposits here are an indication of engine state-of-tune. If the pipe is black and sooty or coated with white deposits, the engine may need a tune-up, including a thorough fuel system inspection and adjustment.

18.2   Be sure to check each exhaust system rubber hanger for damage

19   Drivebelt check, adjustment and replacement (every 30,000 miles [48,000 km] or 24 months)

⁜⁜ WARNING:

The electric cooling fan(s) on these models can activate at any time the ignition switch is in the ON position. Make sure the ignition is OFF when working in the vicinity of the fan(s).

CHECK

▶ **Refer to illustrations 19.1, 19.3 and 19.4**

1   The drivebelts are located at the front of the engine and play an important role in the operation of the vehicle and its components. Due to their function and material makeup, the belts are prone to failure after a period of time and should be inspected and adjusted periodically to prevent major damage. On CR-V and Hatchback models no adjustment is necessary because they are equipped with an automatic drivebelt tensioner. If the wear indicator has moved beyond the specified range, replace the drivebelt (see illustration).

2   The number of belts used on a particular vehicle depends on the accessories installed. Drivebelts are used to turn the alternator, power steering pump, water pump (CR-V and Hatchback models), and air conditioning compressor. Depending on the pulley arrangement, more than one of these components may be driven by a single belt.

19.1   Details of the drivebelt tensioner (CR-V and Hatchback models)

1   Maximum length (belt worn out)

2   Belt length indicator

3   With the engine turned off, open the hood and locate the drivebelts at the front of the engine. Use a flashlight to carefully check each belt. Check for a severed core, separation of the adhesive rubber on

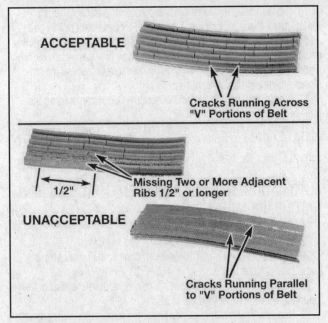

ACCEPTABLE

Cracks Running Across "V" Portions of Belt

1/2"

Missing Two or More Adjacent Ribs 1/2" or longer

UNACCEPTABLE

Cracks Running Parallel to "V" Portions of Belt

19.3 Here are some of the more common problems associated with drivebelts (check the belts very carefully to prevent an untimely breakdown)

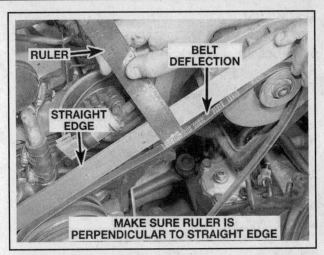

RULER   BELT DEFLECTION

STRAIGHT EDGE

MAKE SURE RULER IS PERPENDICULAR TO STRAIGHT EDGE

19.4 Measure the drivebelt deflection with a straightedge and ruler - make sure the ruler is perpendicular to the straightedge

both sides of the core and for core separation from the belt side. Inspect the ribs for separation from the adhesive rubber and for cracking or separation of the ribs, torn or worn ribs or cracks in the inner ridges of the ribs (see illustration). Also check for fraying and glazing, which gives the belt a shiny appearance. Inspect both sides of the belt by twisting the belt to check the underside. Use your fingers to feel the belt where you can't see it. If any of the above conditions are evident, replace the belt(s).

4   On Coupe and Sedan models the tension of each belt is checked by pushing on it at a distance halfway between the pulleys. Apply about 10 pounds of force with your thumb and see how much the belt moves down (deflects). Measure the deflection with a ruler (see illustration) and compare your results to the deflection limits listed in this Chapter's Specifications.

ADJUSTMENT (COUPE AND SEDAN MODELS)

Power steering belt

▶ **Refer to illustration 19.5**

5   Loosen the power steering pump mounting bolt nut and locknut, then turn the adjuster bolt to set the belt tension (see illustration). When you have obtained the desired tension, tighten the pump fasteners securely.

Alternator/air conditioning compressor belt

▶ **Refer to illustration 19.6**

6   Loosen the alternator upper mounting bolt and nut, then loosen the adjuster bracket lock bolt and lower mounting bolt. Turn the adjuster bolt to set the belt tension (see illustration). When you have obtained the desired tension, tighten the fasteners securely.

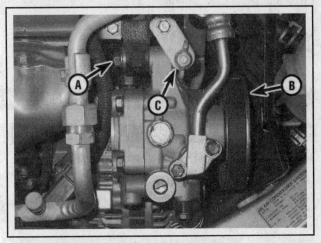

19.5 Power steering pump adjustment details

A)   Pump locknut
B)   Pump mounting bolt/nut (not visible in this photo)
C)   Adjusting bolt

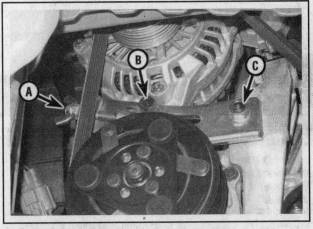

19.6 Alternator/air conditioning compressor belt adjustment details

A)   Adjusting bolt   C)   Bracket mounting bolt
B)   Lock bolt

REPLACEMENT

Coupe and Sedan models

Power steering belt

7 Follow Step 5 for drivebelt adjustment, but slip the belt off the pulleys and remove it.

8 When installing the belt, make sure the belt is centered on the pulleys.

9 Adjust the drivebelt as described in Step 5.

Alternator/air conditioning compressor belt

10 Remove the power steering pump drivebelt (see Step 5).

11 Follow Step 6 for drivebelt adjustment, but slip the belt off the pulleys and remove it.

12 When installing the belt, make sure the belt is centered on the pulleys.

13 Adjust the drivebelt as described in Step 6.

14 Install the power steering pump drivebelt.

CR-V and Hatchback models

15 Apply the parking brake, loosen the right (passenger's side) front wheel lug nuts, raise the front of the vehicle and support it securely on jackstands. Remove the wheel, then remove the splash shield.

16 The automatic tensioner must be released to allow drivebelt replacement. Place a wrench or a socket on the tensioner pulley bolt and rotate it clockwise until the belt can be removed. Remove the belt and slowly release the tensioner. Install the new belt then rotate the tensioner clockwise to allow the belt to slip over it, then release the tensioner slowly until it contacts the drivebelt.

17 When installing the belt, make sure the belt is centered on the pulleys.

18 Install the splash shield, wheel and lug nuts. Lower the vehicle and tighten the lug nuts to the torque listed in this Chapter's Specifications.

AUTOMATIC TENSIONER REPLACEMENT (CR-V AND HATCHBACK MODELS)

19 Remove the drivebelt (see Steps 15 and 16).

20 If you're working on a CR-V model, remove the power steering pump (see Chapter 10).

21 If you're working on a Hatchback model, remove the idler pulley mounting bolts, then remove the pulley.

22 Unscrew the tensioner pulley bolt, then remove the pulley mounting bolts. Remove the pulley.

23 Installation is the reverse of removal.

20 Brake fluid change (every 30,000 miles [48,000 km] or 24 months)

❋❋ WARNING:

Brake fluid can harm your eyes and damage painted surfaces, so use extreme caution when handling or pouring it. Do not use brake fluid that has been standing open or is more than one year old. Brake fluid absorbs moisture from the air. Excess moisture can cause a dangerous loss of braking effectiveness.

1 At the specified intervals, the brake fluid should be drained and replaced. Since the brake fluid may drip or splash when pouring it, place plenty of rags around the master cylinder to protect any surrounding painted surfaces.

2 Before beginning work, purchase the specified brake fluid (see *Recommended lubricants and fluids* at the end of this Chapter).

3 Remove the cap from the master cylinder reservoir.

4 Using a hand suction pump or similar device, withdraw the fluid from the master cylinder reservoir.

5 Add new fluid to the master cylinder until it rises to the base of the filler neck.

6 Bleed the brake system as described in Chapter 9 at all four brakes until new and uncontaminated fluid is expelled from the bleeder screw. Be sure to maintain the fluid level in the master cylinder as you perform the bleeding process. If you allow the master cylinder to run dry, air will enter the system.

7 Refill the master cylinder with fluid and check the operation of the brakes. The pedal should feel solid when depressed, with no sponginess.

❋❋ WARNING:

Do not operate the vehicle if you are in doubt about the effectiveness of the brake system.

21 Cooling system servicing (draining, flushing and refilling) (every 60,000 miles [96,000 km] or 36 months)

❋❋ WARNING:

Do not allow antifreeze to come in contact with your skin or painted surfaces of the vehicle. Rinse off spills immediately with plenty of water. Antifreeze is highly toxic if ingested. Never leave antifreeze lying around in an open container or in puddles on the floor; children and pets are attracted by its sweet smell and may drink it. Check with local authorities about disposing of used antifreeze. Many communities have collection centers which will see that antifreeze is disposed of safely. Never dump used antifreeze on the ground or pour it into drains.

1 Periodically, the cooling system should be drained, flushed and refilled to replenish the antifreeze mixture and prevent formation of rust and corrosion, which can impair the performance of the cooling system and cause engine damage. When the cooling system is serviced, all hoses and the radiator cap should be checked and replaced if necessary.

DRAINING

▸ **Refer to illustrations 21.3 and 21.4**

2 Apply the parking brake and block the wheels.

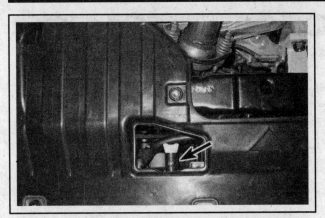

21.3 The radiator drain fitting is located at the bottom of the radiator - before opening the valve, push a short length of rubber hose onto the plastic fitting to prevent the coolant from splashing

21.4 On SOHC engines, loosen the engine block drain plug, located next to the oil filter

※※ WARNING:

If the vehicle has just been driven, wait several hours to allow the engine to cool down before beginning this procedure. Turn the heater control to maximum heat.

3 Move a large container under the radiator drain to catch the coolant. The radiator drain plug is located on the right side lower corner of the radiator (see illustration). Unscrew the drain plug until coolant starts flowing from the drain hole (a pair of pliers may be required to turn it).

4 Remove the radiator cap and allow the radiator to drain, then, move the container under the engine. If you're working on an SOHC engine, loosen the engine block drain plug and allow the coolant in the block to drain (see illustration).

5 While the coolant is draining, check the condition of the radiator hoses, heater hoses and clamps (refer to Section 9 if necessary).

6 Replace any damaged clamps or hoses. Close the drain plugs.

FLUSHING

♦ Refer to illustration 21.9

7 Once the system is completely drained, remove the thermostat from the engine (see Chapter 3), then reinstall the thermostat housing without the thermostat. This will allow the system to be thoroughly flushed.

8 Turn the heating system controls to Hot, so that the heater core will be flushed at the same time as the rest of the cooling system.

9 Disconnect the upper radiator hose from the radiator, then place a garden hose in the upper radiator inlet and flush the system until the water runs clear at the upper radiator hose (see illustration).

10 In severe cases of contamination or clogging of the radiator, remove the radiator (see Chapter 3) and have a radiator repair facility clean and repair it if necessary.

11 Many deposits can be removed by the chemical action of a cleaner available at auto parts stores. Follow the procedure outlined in the manufacturer's instructions.

➡Note: When the coolant is regularly drained and the system refilled with the correct antifreeze/water mixture, there should be no need to use chemical cleaners or descalers.

12 Remove the overflow hose from the coolant recovery reservoir. Drain the reservoir and flush it with clean water, then reconnect the hose.

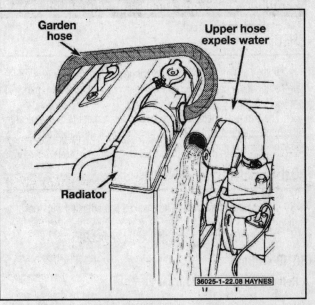

Garden hose

Upper hose expels water

Radiator

36025-1-22.08 HAYNES

21.9 With the thermostat removed, disconnect the upper radiator hose and flush the radiator and engine block with a garden hose

REFILLING

13 Reconnect the upper radiator hose and reinstall the thermostat.

14 Fill the cooling system with the proper type and mixture of antifreeze (see this Chapter's Specifications), up to the base of the radiator cap filler neck. Loosely install the radiator cap.

15 Start the engine and run it at approximately 1500 rpm until the radiator fan comes on two times. Feel the upper radiator hose - it should be warm, indicating the thermostat has opened.

16 Turn off the engine and let it cool down. Slowly remove the radiator cap and check the coolant level, adding as necessary.

※※ WARNING:

If you hear a hissing sound as you unscrew the cap, STOP. Let the engine cool down longer. Fill the coolant reservoir up to the MIN mark, if necessary.

17 Start the engine, allow it to reach normal operating temperature once again and check for leaks.

22   Rear differential lubricant change (CR-V) (every 90,000 miles [145,000 km] or 60 months)

1   This procedure should be performed after the vehicle has been driven, so the lubricant will be warm and therefore will flow out of the differential more easily.

2   Raise the vehicle and support it securely on jackstands. You'll be draining the lubricant by removing the drain plug, so move a drain pan, rags, newspapers and wrench under the vehicle. Remove the check/fill plug.

3   Remove the drain plug and allow the lubricant to drain into the pan, then clean and reinstall the drain plug. Tighten the plug securely.

4   Using a hand pump, syringe or squeeze bottle, fill the differential housing with the specified lubricant until it's level with the bottom of the fill plug hole.

5   Install the plug and tighten it securely. Drive the vehicle a short distance, then check for leaks.

6   The old oil drained from the transaxle cannot be reused in its present state and should be disposed of. Check with your local auto parts store, disposal facility or environmental agency to see if they will accept the oil for recycling. After the oil has cooled it can be drained into a container (capped plastic jugs, topped bottles, milk cartons, etc.) for transport to one of these disposal sites. Don't dispose of the oil by pouring it on the ground or down a drain!

23   Valve clearance check and adjustment (see Maintenance Schedule for service intervals)

CHECK

1   Valve clearances generally do not need adjustment unless valvetrain components have been replaced, or a valve job has been performed.

2   The simplest check for proper valve adjustment is to listen carefully to the engine running with the hood open. If the valvetrain is noisy, adjustment is necessary.

ADJUSTMENT

3   The valve clearance must be checked and adjusted with the engine cold.

4   Remove the valve cover (see Chapter 2A or 2B).

SOHC engines

▶ **Refer to illustrations 23.6 and 23.7**

5   Place the number one piston (closest to the drivebelt end of the engine) at Top Dead Center (TDC) on the compression stroke. This is accomplished by rotating the crankshaft in the normal direction of rotation (which is counterclockwise) until the white TDC mark on the crankshaft pulley aligns with the timing pointer on the lower timing belt cover and the UP mark on the camshaft sprocket is at the twelve o'clock position (see Chapter 2A).

6   With the engine in this position, the number one cylinder valve adjustment can be checked and adjusted (see illustration).

7   Start with the intake valve clearance. Insert a feeler gauge of the correct thickness (see this Chapter's Specifications) between the valve stem and the rocker arm (see illustration). Withdraw it; you should feel a slight drag. If there's no drag or a heavy drag, loosen the adjuster nut and back off the adjuster screw. Carefully tighten the adjuster screw until you can feel a slight drag on the feeler gauge as you withdraw it.

8   Hold the adjuster screw with a screwdriver (to keep it from turning) and tighten the locknut. Recheck the clearance to make sure it hasn't changed. Repeat the procedure in this Step and the previous Step on the other intake valve, then on the two exhaust valves.

9   Rotate the crankshaft pulley 180-degrees counterclockwise (the camshaft pulley will turn 90-degrees) until the number three cylinder is at TDC. With the number three cylinder at TDC, the UP mark on the camshaft sprocket will be at the nine o'clock position. Check and adjust the number three cylinder valves.

10 Rotate the crankshaft pulley 180-degrees counterclockwise until the number four cylinder is at TDC. With the number four cylinder at TDC, the UP mark on the camshaft sprocket will be pointed straight down. Check and adjust the number four cylinder valves.

11 Rotate the crankshaft pulley 180-degrees counterclockwise to bring the number two cylinder to TDC. The UP mark on the camshaft sprocket should be at the three o'clock position. Check and adjust the number two cylinder valves.

12 Install the valve cover (see Chapter 2A).

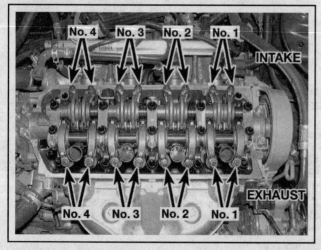

23.6 SOHC valve layout

23.7 To make sure the adjusting screw doesn't move when the locknut is tightened, use a box-end wrench and have a good grip on the screwdriver

DOHC engines

▶ **Refer to illustrations 23.14, 23.15 and 23.16**

13 Place the number one piston (closest to the drivebelt end of the engine) at Top Dead Center (TDC) on the compression stroke. This is accomplished by rotating the crankshaft in the normal direction of rotation (which is clockwise) until the white TDC mark on the crankshaft pulley aligns with the timing pointer on the lower timing belt cover, the punch marks on the camshaft sprockets should be at the twelve o'clock position and the TDC marks are aligned on both sprockets (see Chapter 2B, Section 8).

14 With the engine in this position, the number one cylinder valve adjustment can be checked and adjusted (see illustration).

15 Start with the intake valve clearance. Insert a feeler gauge of the correct thickness (see this Chapter's Specifications) between an intake camshaft lobe and the rocker arm (see illustration). Withdraw it; you should feel a slight drag. If there's no drag or a heavy drag, loosen the adjuster nut and back off the adjuster screw. Carefully tighten the adjuster screw until you can feel a slight drag on the feeler gauge as you withdraw it.

16 Hold the adjuster screw with a screwdriver (to keep it from turning) and tighten the locknut (see illustration). Recheck the clearance to make sure it hasn't changed. Repeat the procedure in this Step and the previous Step on the other intake valve, then on the two exhaust valves.

17 Rotate the crankshaft pulley 180-degrees clockwise (the camshaft pulley will turn 90-degrees) until the number three cylinder is at TDC. With the number three cylinder at TDC, the punch marks on the camshaft sprocket will be at the three o'clock position. Check and adjust the number three cylinder valves.

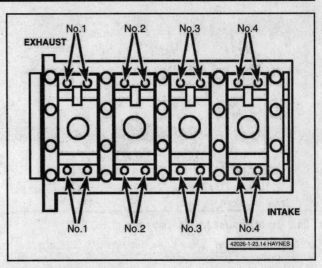

23.14 DOHC valve layout

18 Rotate the crankshaft pulley 180-degrees clockwise until the number four cylinder is at TDC. With the number four cylinder at TDC, the punch marks on the camshaft sprockets will be pointed straight down. Check and adjust the number four cylinder valves.

19 Rotate the crankshaft pulley 180-degrees clockwise to bring the number two cylinder to TDC. The punch marks on the camshaft sprockets should be at the nine o'clock position. Check and adjust the number two cylinder valves.

20 Install the valve cover (see Chapter 2A).

23.15 Insert the feeler gauge between the camshaft lobe and the rocker arm

23.16 A special tool is available to tighten the locknuts while holding the adjusting screw

24 Spark plug check and replacement (see Maintenance Schedule for service intervals)

▶ **Refer to illustrations 24.2, 24.5a, 24.5b, 24.9, 24.10, 24.11a and 24.11b**

1 The spark plugs are located in the center of the cylinder head.

2 In most cases the tools necessary for spark plug replacement include a spark plug socket which fits onto a ratchet (this special socket is padded inside to protect the porcelain insulators on the new plugs and hold them in place), various extensions and a feeler gauge to check and adjust the spark plug gap (see illustration). Since these engines are equipped with an aluminum cylinder head, a torque wrench should be used when tightening the spark plugs.

3 The best approach when replacing the spark plugs is to purchase the new spark plugs beforehand, adjust them to the proper gap and then replace each plug one at a time. When buying the new spark plugs, be sure to obtain the correct plug for your specific engine. This information can be found in the Specification Section at the end of this Chapter or in your owner's manual.

4 Allow the engine to cool completely before attempting to remove any of the plugs. During this cooling off time, each of the new spark

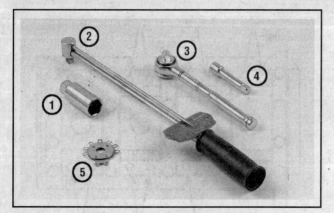

24.2 Tools required for changing spark plugs

1 **Spark plug socket** - This will have special padding inside to protect the spark plug porcelain insulator
2 **Torque wrench** - Although not mandatory, use of this tool is the best way to ensure that the plugs are tightened properly
3 **Ratchet** - Standard hand tool to fit the plug socket
4 **Extension** - Depending on model and accessories, you may need special extensions and universal joints to reach one or more of the plugs
5 **Spark plug gap gauge** - This gauge for checking the gap comes in a variety of styles. Make sure the gap for your engine is included

plugs can be inspected for defects and the gaps can be checked.

5   The gap is checked by inserting the proper thickness gauge between the electrodes at the tip of the plug (see illustrations). The gap between the electrodes should be as listed in this Chapter's Specifications or in your owner's manual.

✳✳ CAUTION:

The manufacturer recommends against adjusting the gap on platinum-tipped spark plugs; if the gap is out of specification, replace the plug.

Also, at this time check for cracks in the spark plug body (if any are found, the plug must not be used).

6   Cover the fender to prevent damage to the paint. Fender covers are available from auto parts stores but an old blanket will work just fine.

7   Remove the ignition coils (see Chapter 5).

8   If compressed air is available, use it to blow any dirt or foreign material away from the spark plug area.

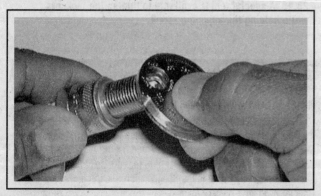

24.5b To change the gap, bend the side electrode only, using the adjuster hole in the tool, and be very careful not to crack or chip the porcelain insulator surrounding the center electrode

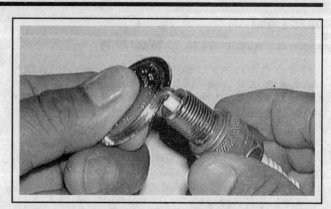

24.5a Spark plug manufacturers recommend using a tapered thickness gauge when checking the gap - slide the thin side into the gap and turn it until the gauge just fills the gap, then read the thickness on the gauge - do not force the tool into the gap or use the tapered portion to widen a gap

✳✳ WARNING:

Wear eye protection!

The idea here is to eliminate the possibility of material falling into the cylinder through the spark plug hole as the spark plug is removed.

9   Place the spark plug socket over the plug and remove it from the engine by turning it in a counterclockwise direction (see illustration).

10 Compare the spark plug this chart to get an indication of the overall running condition of the engine.

11 Apply a small amount of anti-seize compound to the spark plug threads (see illustration). Install one of the new plugs into the hole until you can no longer turn it with your fingers, then tighten it with a torque wrench (if available) or the ratchet. It is a good idea to slip a short length of rubber hose over the end of the plug to use as a tool to thread it into place (see illustration). The hose will grip the plug well enough to turn it, but will start to slip if the plug begins to cross-thread in the hole - this will prevent damaged threads and the accompanying repair costs.

12 Attach the coil to the new spark plug using a twisting motion until it is firmly seated on the end of the spark plug. Tighten the mounting bolts securely.

13 Repeat the procedure for the remaining spark plugs.

24.9 Use a ratchet and extension to remove the spark plugs

A normally worn spark plug should have light tan or gray deposits on the firing tip.

A carbon fouled plug, identified by soft, sooty, black deposits, may indicate an improperly tuned vehicle. Check the air cleaner, ignition components and engine control system.

An oil fouled spark plug indicates an engine with worn piston rings and/or bad valve seals allowing excessive oil to enter the chamber.

This spark plug has been left in the engine too long, as evidenced by the extreme gap. Plugs with such an extreme gap can cause misfiring and stumbling accompanied by a noticeable lack of power.

A physically damaged spark plug may be evidence of severe detonation in that cylinder. Watch that cylinder carefully between services, as a continued detonation will not only damage the plug, but could also damage the engine.

A bridged or almost bridged spark plug, identified by a build-up between the electrodes caused by excessive carbon or oil build-up on the plug.

24.10 Inspect the spark plug to determine engine running conditions

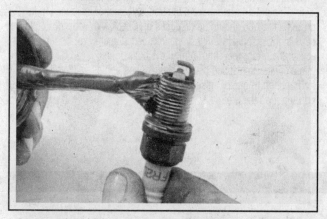

24.11a Apply a thin coat of anti-seize compound to the spark plug threads

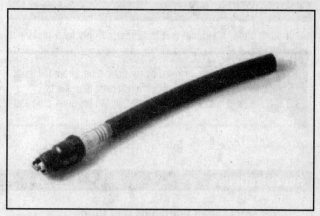

24.11b A length of snug-fitting rubber hose will save time and prevent damaged threads when installing the spark plugs

25 Automatic transaxle fluid change (every 120,000 miles [72,400 km] or 72 months)

▶ **Refer to illustration 25.6**

1   The automatic transaxle fluid should be changed at the recommended intervals.

2   Before beginning work, purchase the specified transmission fluid (see *Recommended lubricants and fluids* at the end of this Chapter).

3   Other tools necessary for this job include jackstands to support the vehicle in a raised position, wrenches, drain pan capable of holding at least four quarts, newspapers and clean rags.

4   The fluid should be drained immediately after the vehicle has been driven. Hot fluid is more effective than cold fluid at removing built up sediment.

✳ WARNING:

Fluid temperature can exceed 350-degrees F in a hot transaxle. Wear protective gloves.

5   After the vehicle has been driven to warm up the fluid, raise the front of the vehicle and support it securely on jackstands.

✳ WARNING:

Never work under a vehicle that is supported only by a jack!

6   Place the drain pan under the drain plug in the transaxle pan and remove the drain plug (see illustration). Be sure the drain pan is in position, as fluid will come out with some force. Once the fluid is drained, reinstall the drain plug securely. Measure the amount of fluid drained and write down this figure for reference when refilling.

7   Lower the vehicle.

8   With the engine off, add new fluid to the transaxle through the dipstick tube (see *Recommended lubricants and fluids* for the recommended fluid type). Begin the refill procedure by initially adding 1/3 of the amount drained. Then, with the engine running, add 1/2-pint at a time (cycling the shifter through each gear position between additions) until the level is correct on the dipstick.

9   If desired, repeat Steps 5 through 8 once to flush any contaminated fluid from the torque converter.

10 The old oil drained from the transaxle cannot be reused in its present state and should be disposed of. Check with your local auto parts store, disposal facility or environmental agency to see if they will accept the oil for recycling. After the oil has cooled it can be drained into a container (capped plastic jugs, topped bottles, milk cartons, etc.)

25.6 Location of the transaxle fluid drain plug

for transport to one of these disposal sites. Don't dispose of the oil by pouring it on the ground or down a drain!

26 Manual transaxle fluid change (every 120,000 miles [72,400 km] or 72 months)

1   Raise the vehicle and support it securely on jackstands in a level position.

✳✳ WARNING:

Never work under a vehicle that is supported only by a jack!

2   Remove the fill plug, followed by the drain plug. Drain the fluid into a suitable container capable of holding at least four quarts.

3   After the fluid has completely drained, install the drain plug and tighten it to the torque given in this Chapter's Specifications.

4   Fill the transaxle with the recommended lubricant (see *Recommended lubricants and fluids* at the end of this Chapter).

5   The old oil drained from the transaxle cannot be reused in its present state and should be disposed of. Check with your local auto parts store, disposal facility or environmental agency to see if they will accept the oil for recycling. After the oil has cooled it can be drained into a container (capped plastic jugs, topped bottles, milk cartons, etc.) for transport to one of these disposal sites. Don't dispose of the oil by pouring it on the ground or down a drain!

Specifications

Recommended lubricants and fluids

➡Note: The fluids and lubricants listed here are those recommended by the manufacturer at the time this manual was written. Vehicle manufacturers occasionally upgrade their fluid and lubricant specifications, so check with your local auto parts store for the most current recommendations.

Engine oil	
Type	API "Certified for gasoline engines"
Viscosity	SAE 5W-20
Automatic transaxle fluid	Honda ATF-Z1 or equivalent
Manual transaxle fluid	Honda manual transmission fluid (MTF or equivalent)
Rear differential fluid (CR-V)	Honda Dual Pump System Fluid or equivalent
Brake fluid type	DOT 3 brake fluid
Power steering system fluid	Honda power steering fluid or equivalent
Fuel type	Unleaded gasoline, 86 octane or higher
Engine coolant	50/50 mixture of Honda All Season Antifreeze/Coolant Type 2 or equivalent

Capacities*

Engine oil (including oil filter)
    CR-V and hatchback models   4.4 quarts (4.2 liters)
    Coupe and Sedan models
        D17A2, D17A6 engines   3.7 quarts (3.5 liters)
        D17A1 engine   3.4 quarts (3.2 liters)
Automatic transaxle fluid (drain and refill)**
    Coupe and Sedan models   2.9 quarts (2.7 liters)
    CR-V
        2WD models   3.1 quarts (2.9 liters)
        4WD models   3.3 quarts (3.1 liters)
Manual transaxle (drain and refill)
    Coupe/sedan/hatchback   1.6 quarts (1.5 liters)
    CR-V   2.0 quarts (1.9 liters)
Rear differential (CR-V)
    2002 through 2004   1.1 quarts (1.0 liters)
    2005 and later   1.5 quarts (1.4 liters)
Cooling system
    Coupe and Sedan
        Manual transaxle models   4.2 quarts (4.0 liters)
        Automatic transaxle models   4.1 quarts (3.9 liters)
    CR-V
        Manual transaxle models   5.8 quarts (5.5 liters)
        Automatic transaxle models   5.7 quarts (5.4 liters)
    Hatchback models   5.3 quarts (5.0 liters)

All capacities approximate. Add as necessary to bring to appropriate level.
**If you want to flush the converter during a fluid change, purchase twice the amount of fluid listed here.*

Valve clearances (cold engine)

2001 models

Civic
    Intake valve   0.007 to 0.009-inch (0.18 to 0.22 mm)
    Exhaust valve   0.009 to 0.011-inch (0.23 to 0.27 mm)
CR-V
    Intake valve   0.003 to 0.005-inch (0.08 to 0.12mm)
    Exhaust valve   0.006 to 0.008-inch (0.16 to 0.20 mm)

2002 and later models

Civic
    DOHC
        Intake valve   0.008 to 0.010-inch (0.21 to 0.25 mm)
        Exhaust valve   0.011 to 0.013-inch (0.28 to 0.32 mm)
    SOHC
        Intake valve   0.007 to 0.009-inch (0.18 to 0.22 mm)
        Exhaust valve   0.009 to 0.011-inch (0.23 to 0.27 mm)
        CR-V
            Intake valve   0.008 to 0.010 inch (0.21 to 0.25 mm)
            Exhaust valve   0.011 to 0.013-inch (0.28 to 0.32 mm)

Ignition system

Spark plug type and gap
    Type
        Coupe and Sedan models   NGK: PZFR6F-11 or DENSO: PKJ20CR-M11
        CR-V and hatchback models   NGK: IZFR6K-11 or DENSO: SKJ20DR-M11
    Gap   0.039 to 0.043 inch (1.0 to 1.1 mm)
Engine firing order   1-3-4-2

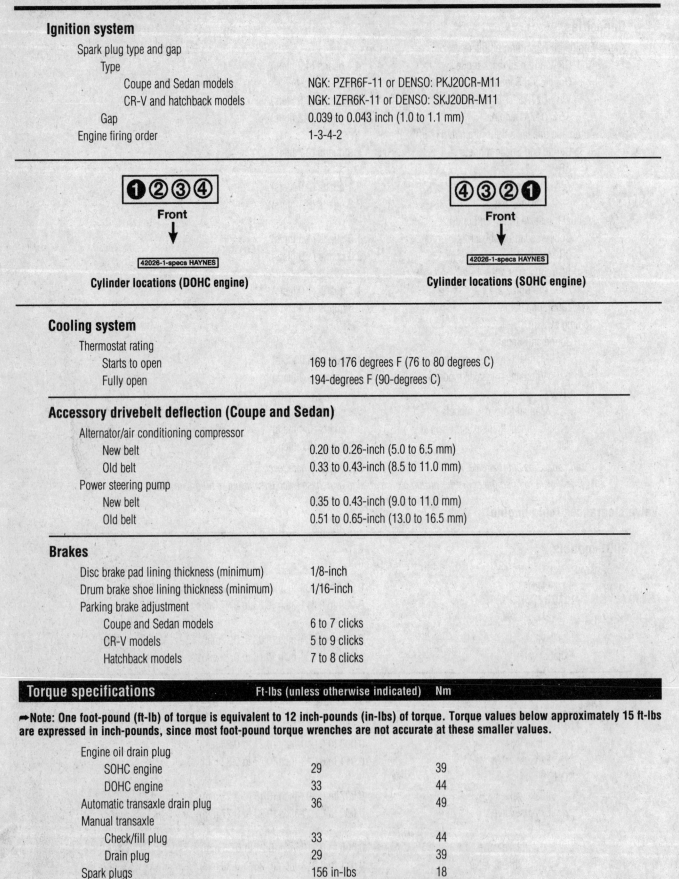

Cylinder locations (DOHC engine)   **Cylinder locations (SOHC engine)**

Cooling system

Thermostat rating
    Starts to open   169 to 176 degrees F (76 to 80 degrees C)
    Fully open   194-degrees F (90-degrees C)

Accessory drivebelt deflection (Coupe and Sedan)

Alternator/air conditioning compressor
    New belt   0.20 to 0.26-inch (5.0 to 6.5 mm)
    Old belt   0.33 to 0.43-inch (8.5 to 11.0 mm)
Power steering pump
    New belt   0.35 to 0.43-inch (9.0 to 11.0 mm)
    Old belt   0.51 to 0.65-inch (13.0 to 16.5 mm)

Brakes

Disc brake pad lining thickness (minimum)   1/8-inch
Drum brake shoe lining thickness (minimum)   1/16-inch
Parking brake adjustment
    Coupe and Sedan models   6 to 7 clicks
    CR-V models   5 to 9 clicks
    Hatchback models   7 to 8 clicks

Torque specifications	Ft-lbs (unless otherwise indicated)	Nm

➡**Note: One foot-pound (ft-lb) of torque is equivalent to 12 inch-pounds (in-lbs) of torque. Torque values below approximately 15 ft-lbs are expressed in inch-pounds, since most foot-pound torque wrenches are not accurate at these smaller values.**

	Ft-lbs	Nm
Engine oil drain plug		
SOHC engine	29	39
DOHC engine	33	44
Automatic transaxle drain plug	36	49
Manual transaxle		
Check/fill plug	33	44
Drain plug	29	39
Spark plugs	156 in-lbs	18
Wheel lug nuts	79.6	108

Section

Reference to other Chapters

2A

SINGLE OVERHEAD CAMSHAFT (SOHC) ENGINES

1 General information

This Part of Chapter 2 is devoted to in-vehicle repair procedures for the 1.7 liter, fuel injected, four cylinder engine. Three different versions of this engine have been produced by Honda for the Civic product line, all of which are covered in this Part of Chapter 2. All versions of this engine utilize a Single Overhead Camshaft (SOHC), with 4 valves per cylinder (16V). Two versions of this engine incorporate the VTEC (Variable Valve Timing and lift Electronic Control) system, which electronically alters valve timing to enhance engine performance. For more information on the VTEC system, see Section 7 of this Chapter.

Engine designations include:

D17A1   1.7L 16 valve SOHC non-VTEC 115 horsepower engine
D17A2   1.7L 16 valve SOHC VTEC 117 horsepower engine (lean burn)
D17A6   1.7L 16 valve SOHC VTEC 127 horsepower engine

The SOHC engines are lightweight in design with an aluminum alloy block (with steel cylinder liners) and an aluminum alloy cylinder head. The crankshaft rides in a single carriage unit that houses the renewable insert-type main bearings, with separate thrust bearings at the number four position assigned the task of controlling crankshaft endplay.

The pistons have two compression rings and one oil control ring. The semi-floating piston pins are press fitted into the small end of the connecting rod. The connecting rod big ends are also equipped with renewable insert-type plain bearings.

The engine is liquid-cooled, utilizing a centrifugal impeller-type pump, driven by the timing belt, to circulate coolant around the cylinders and combustion chambers and through the intake manifold.

Lubrication is handled by a rotor-type oil pump mounted on the front of the engine under the timing belt cover. It is driven directly by the crankshaft. The oil is filtered continuously by a cartridge-type filter mounted on the rear of the engine.

All information concerning engine removal and installation can be found in Part C of this Chapter.

The following repair procedures are based on the assumption that the engine is installed in the vehicle. If the engine has been removed from the vehicle and mounted on a stand, many of the steps outlined in this Part of Chapter 2 will not apply.

The Specifications included in this Part of Chapter 2 apply only to the procedures contained in this Chapter. Chapter 2C contains the Specifications necessary for certain engine block assembly procedures.

2 Repair operations possible with the engine in the vehicle

Clean the engine compartment and the exterior of the engine with some type of degreaser before any work is done. It will make the job easier and help keep dirt out of the internal areas of the engine.

Depending on the components involved, it may be helpful to remove the hood to improve access to the engine as repairs are performed (refer to Chapter 11 if necessary). Cover the fenders to prevent damage to the paint. Special pads are available, but an old bedspread or blanket will also work.

If vacuum, exhaust, oil or coolant leaks develop, indicating a need for gasket or seal replacement, the repairs can generally be made with the engine in the vehicle. The intake and exhaust manifold gaskets, oil pan gasket, crankshaft oil seals and cylinder head gasket are all accessible with the engine in place.

Exterior engine components, such as the intake and exhaust manifolds, the oil pan, the water pump, the starter motor, the alternator, the distributor and the fuel system components can be removed for repair with the engine in place.

Since the cylinder head can be removed without pulling the engine, camshaft and valve component servicing can also be accomplished with the engine in the vehicle. Replacement of the timing belt and sprockets is also possible with the engine in the vehicle.

In extreme cases caused by a lack of necessary equipment, repair or replacement of piston rings, pistons, connecting rods and rod bearings is possible with the engine in the vehicle. However, this practice is not recommended because of the cleaning and preparation work that must be done to the components involved.

3 Top Dead Center (TDC) for number one piston - locating

▶ **Refer to illustration 3.5**

➡**Note: These engines are not equipped with a distributor. Piston position must be determined by feeling for compression at the number one spark plug hole, then aligning the ignition timing marks as described in Step 5.**

1   Top Dead Center (TDC) is the highest point in the cylinder that each piston reaches as it travels up-and-down during crankshaft rotation. Each piston reaches TDC on the compression stroke and again on the exhaust stroke, but TDC generally refers to piston position on the compression stroke.

2   Positioning the piston(s) at TDC is an essential part of many other repair procedures discussed in this manual.

3   Before beginning this procedure, be sure to place the transmission in Neutral and apply the parking brake or block the rear wheels. Remove the spark plugs (see Chapter 1). Disable the fuel system (see Chapter 4, Section 2). Install a compression gauge in the spark plug

hole for cylinder no. 1.

4   In order to bring any piston to TDC, the crankshaft must be turned using one of the methods outlined below. When looking at the front (timing belt end) of the engine, normal crankshaft rotation is counterclockwise.

   a) *The preferred method is to turn the crankshaft with a socket and ratchet attached to the bolt threaded into the front of the crankshaft.*

   b) *A remote starter switch, which may save some time, can also be used. Follow the instructions included with the switch. Once the piston is close to TDC, use a socket and ratchet as described in the previous paragraph.*

   c) *If an assistant is available to turn the ignition switch to the Start position in short bursts, you can get the piston close to TDC without a remote starter switch. Make sure your assistant is out of the vehicle, away from the ignition switch, then use a socket and ratchet as described in Paragraph a) to complete the procedure.*

5   Turn the crankshaft until compression registers on the gauge, then turn it slowly until the TDC notch is aligned with the pointer on the timing belt cover (see illustration).

➡Note: There are two marks on the pulley. The white mark is for TDC, the red mark is only for setting ignition timing with a timing light.

The number one piston is now at TDC on the compression stroke.

6   After the number one piston has been positioned at TDC on the compression stroke, TDC for any of the remaining pistons can be located by turning the crankshaft in its normal direction of rotation, in 180-degree (1/2-turn) increments, and following the firing order. Divide the crankshaft pulley into two equal sections with chalk marks at each point, each indicating 180-degrees of crankshaft rotation. Rotating the engine past TDC no. 1 to the next mark will place the engine at TDC for cylinder no. 3.

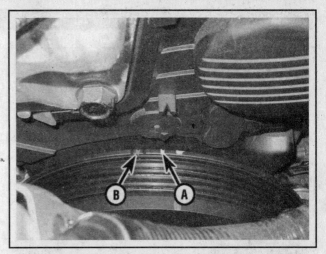

3.5 Align the white (TDC) mark (A) on the crankshaft pulley with the pointer on the timing belt cover. The red mark (B) is for the timing light

4   Valve cover - removal and installation

REMOVAL

1   Disconnect the cable from the negative terminal of the battery (see Chapter 5, Section 1).
2   Remove the ignition coils (see Chapter 5).
3   Mark and detach any hoses or wires from the throttle body or valve cover that will interfere with the removal of the valve cover.
4   Remove the engine oil dipstick (see Chapter 1).
5   Wipe off the valve cover thoroughly to prevent debris from falling onto the exposed cylinder head or camshaft/valve train assembly.
6   Remove the valve cover bolts. Follow the reverse of the tightening sequence (see illustration 4.10).
7   Carefully lift off the valve cover and gasket. If the gasket is stuck to the cylinder head, tap it with a rubber mallet to break the seal. Do not pry between the cover and cylinder head or you'll damage the gasket mating surfaces.

INSTALLATION

▶ Refer to illustrations 4.9 and 4.10

8   Remove the old gasket and clean the mating surfaces of the cylinder head and the valve cover. Clean the surfaces with a rag soaked in lacquer thinner or acetone.
9   Install a new molded rubber gasket into the groove around the valve cover perimeter. Apply beads of RTV sealant to the gasket in the indicated areas (see illustration). Also install new spark plug seals into their recesses.
10 Place the cover into position and tighten the bolts in the recommended sequence to the torque listed in this Chapter's Specifications (see illustration).
11 The remainder of installation is the reverse of removal.
12 Reconnect the battery (see Chapter 5, Section 1).

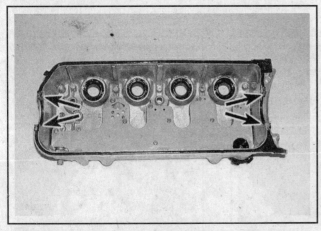

4.9 Apply a small amount of RTV sealant to the corners of the gasket

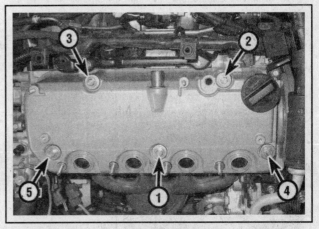

4.10 Valve cover bolt TIGHTENING sequence

5   Intake manifold - removal and installation

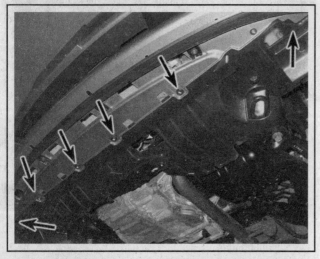

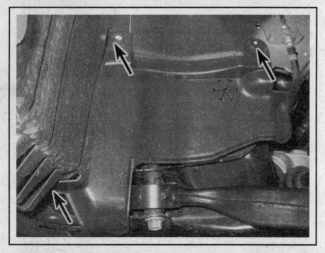

5.9a Remove the fasteners from the splash shield - center section shown

5.9b Remove the fasteners from the right side of the vehicle splash shield . . .

✳✳ WARNING 1:

Gasoline is extremely flammable, so take extra precautions when you work on any part of the fuel system. Don't smoke or allow open flames or bare light bulbs near the work area, and don't work in a garage where a gas-type appliance (such as a water heater or clothes dryer) is present. If you spill any fuel on your skin, rinse it off immediately with soap and water. When you perform any kind of work on the fuel system, wear safety glasses and have a Class B type fire extinguisher on hand.

✳✳ WARNING 2:

Wait until the engine is completely cool before beginning this procedure.

REMOVAL

▶ Refer to illustrations 5.9a, 5.9b, 5.9c, 5.10a, 5.10b and 5.12

1   Disconnect the cable from the negative terminal of the battery (see Chapter 5, Section 1).
2   Drain the cooling system (see Chapter 1).
3   Remove the intake air duct and air filter housing (see Chapter 4).
4   Clearly label and detach any vacuum lines and electrical connectors which will interfere with removal of the manifold.
5   Detach the accelerator cable from the throttle lever (see Chapter 4).
6   Disconnect any electrical connectors from the throttle body.
7   Relieve the fuel system pressure and disconnect the fuel feed and return lines at the fuel rail (see Chapter 4).
8   Raise the vehicle and support it securely on jackstands.
9   Remove the splash shield from under the engine (see illustrations).
10 Working from underneath the engine compartment, remove the brace that supports the intake manifold (see illustrations).
11 Disconnect the heater hoses from the intake manifold bracket.
12 Remove the intake manifold nuts and bolts and remove the man-

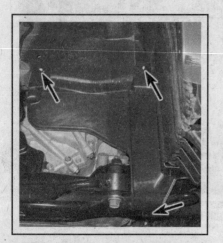

5.9c . . . and the left side of the vehicle splash shield

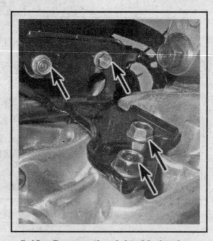

5.10a Remove the right side intake manifold brace . . .

5.10b . . . and the left side intake manifold brace

ifold from the engine (see illustration).

13 Remove the injector base and the intake manifold gasket from the cylinder head.

INSTALLATION

14 Clean the manifold fasteners with solvent and dry them with compressed air, if available.

15 Check the mating surfaces of the manifold for flatness with a precision straightedge and feeler gauges.

16 Inspect the manifold for cracks and distortion. If the manifold is cracked or warped, replace it or see if it can be resurfaced at an automotive machine shop.

17 Check carefully for any stripped or broken intake manifold bolts/studs. Replace any defective fasteners with new parts.

18 Using a scraper, remove all traces of old gasket material from the cylinder head and manifold mating surfaces. Clean the surfaces with lacquer thinner or acetone.

19 Install the intake manifold with a new gasket, then install the fasteners and tighten them to the torque listed in this Chapter's Specifications.

5.12 Location of two of the intake manifold mounting nuts on the underside of the intake manifold

20 Reconnect the battery (see Chapter 5, Section 1).

21 The remainder of installation is the reverse of removal. Refer to Chapter 1 and refill the cooling system.

6 Exhaust manifold - removal and installation

REMOVAL

▶ **Refer to illustrations 6.5, 6.6 and 6.8**

1 Disconnect the cable from the negative terminal of the battery (see Chapter 5, Section 1).

2 Raise the front of the vehicle and support it securely on jackstands.

3 Remove the splash shield from under the engine (see illustrations 5.9a, 5.9b and 5.9c).

4 Disconnect the oxygen sensor electrical connectors on D17A1 and D17A6 engines (see Chapter 6).

5 Detach the exhaust pipe from the exhaust manifold (see illustration). Apply penetrating oil to the fastener threads if they are difficult to remove.

6 Remove the heat shield from the exhaust manifold (see illustration). Be sure to soak the bolts and nuts with penetrating oil before attempting to remove them from the manifold.

7 Remove the exhaust manifold bracket, if equipped.

6.5 Remove the exhaust pipe flange bolts

8 Remove the exhaust manifold nuts (see illustration) and detach the exhaust manifold from the cylinder head.

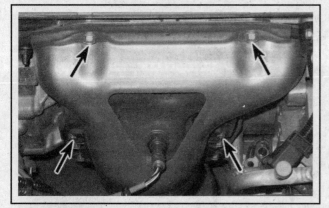

6.6 Remove the bolts retaining the heat shield to the exhaust manifold

6.8 Location of the exhaust manifold mounting nuts - non-VTEC engine shown

INSTALLATION

9 Discard the old gasket and use a scraper to clean the gasket mating surfaces on the exhaust manifold and cylinder head, then clean the surfaces with a rag soaked in lacquer thinner or acetone.

10 Place the exhaust manifold in position on the cylinder head and install new nuts. Starting at the center and working out to the ends, tighten the nuts to the torque listed in this Chapter's Specifications.

11 Install the heat shield, using new upper bolts (the two upper bolts are the exhaust manifold upper mounting bolts). Tighten the two upper bolts to the torque listed in this Chapter's Specifications. Tighten the other heat shield bolts securely.

12 Connect the exhaust pipe to the exhaust manifold, using new bolts. Tighten the bolts to the torque listed in this Chapter's Specifications.

13 The remainder of installation is the reverse of removal.

14 Reconnect the battery (see Chapter 5, Section 1).

15 Start the engine and check for exhaust leaks between the manifold and the cylinder head and between the manifold and the exhaust pipe.

7 VTEC system - description and component checks

GENERAL DESCRIPTION

1 The VTEC system is Honda's design for Variable Valve Timing and Lift Electronic Control. The VTEC lettering cast into the valve cover identifies models equipped with this system. This system incorporates camshaft technology with several different camshaft lobe profiles for various operating conditions. The rocker arms, along with the various camshaft lobe profiles, are switched during this process by a computer, a VTEC solenoid and VTEC valve. VTEC also incorporates the engine's oil system to hydraulically operate the pistons inside the rocker arm assemblies.

2 The differences between conventional engines and the VTEC system are strictly in the components and operation of the valve train.

3 The engine management computer has the ability to physically change which camshaft intake lobes are being used to operate the intake valves. The computer turns the system ON or OFF, depending on sensor input.

4 The PGM-FI engine management system relies on information from the vehicle speed sensor (vehicle speed), CKP sensor (engine speed), throttle position sensor (throttle angle), coolant temperature sensor (coolant temperature) and the MAP sensor (engine load).

5 The camshaft has two different intake valve lobe profiles (lift and duration specifications).

6 At low speeds, the secondary intake valve operates on its own camshaft lobe, which has lift and duration profiles designed specifically for the low end torque and responsiveness. The opening (valve duration) is intended to be just enough to keep atomized fuel from puddling at the valve head. This limited valve operation is designed to provide good low end torque and responsiveness, by inducing swirl in the combustion chamber from the primary intake valve, which operates with a normal profile.

7 When performance is needed, the primary and secondary rocker arms are locked together through the use of an electrically controlled hydraulic system. Hydraulically operated synchronizing pistons lock two rocker arms together. When activated, the intake valves open to the higher lift and duration of the rocker arm, which has its own camshaft lobe designed with the higher lift profile.

➡Note: Refer to the Specifications at the end of this Chapter for the exact camshaft lobe lift profiles.

COMPONENT CHECKS

➡Note: The VTEC system will require specialized diagnostic equipment to access the on-board computer to test the electrical circuits, actuators and sensors. However, there are some mechanical tests of the VTEC system that the home mechanic can perform to check for obvious and simple problems within the system. Have the VTEC system diagnosed by a dealer service department or other qualified automotive repair facility. Also, some checks and inspections of the VTEC components require removal of the rocker arm assembly (see Section 10).

VTEC solenoid valve

➡Note: Most common problems in the VTEC system are associated with the solenoid valve and its filter. Regular engine oil and filter changes are necessary for trouble-free operation of the valve.

8 The VTEC solenoid valve is located on the rear end of the cylinder head. The VTEC oil pressure switch is located in the cylinder head next to the EGR valve.

9 Remove the VTEC solenoid valve (see Chapter 6) and check the filter/O-ring for clogging. Clean and reinstall with a new O-ring. A clogged filter screen is often the cause of system problems.

Rocker arms

10 Position the number one piston at Top Dead Center (see Section 3). Remove the valve cover (see Section 4).

11 Press on the secondary intake rocker arm for cylinder number 1 to see that it moves independently of the primary intake rocker arm. Check the rockers for the other cylinders at their own TDC positions.

Synchronizing assembly

12 Once the rocker arm assemblies have been removed and disassembled (see Section 8), separate the rocker arms and synchronizing components.

VTEC components:

a) *Primary rocker arm*
b) *Secondary rocker arm*
c) *Synchronizing pistons*

13 Inspect the timing spring, making sure it's not broken or collapsed. Replace it if necessary.

14 Inspect all other parts (rocker arms and synchronizing pistons) for wear (see illustration 8.9a and 8.9b), galling, scoring or signs of overheating (bluish in color). Use your finger to push on the rocker arm pistons to check for smooth movement. Replace any parts, if necessary.

15 Reassemble each cylinder's components and wrap a rubber band around the rocker arms before trying to assemble them on the rocker shaft (see Section 8).

8   Rocker arm assembly - removal, inspection and installation

➡Note 1: The camshaft bearing caps are removed together with the rocker arm assembly. To prevent the transaxle end of the camshaft from popping up from timing belt tension after the assembly is removed, have an assistant hold the camshaft down, then reinstall the bearing cap on that end to hold it in place until reassembly (assuming the timing belt remains installed).

➡Note 2: While the camshaft bearing caps are off, inspect them, as well as the camshaft bearing journals, as described in Section 11.

REMOVAL

▶ **Refer to illustration 8.4**

1   Remove the valve cover (see Section 4).

2   Position the number one piston at Top Dead Center (see Section 3).

3   Have an assistant hold down the transaxle end of the camshaft, then loosen the camshaft bearing cap bolts 1/4-turn at a time, in the correct order, until the spring pressure is relieved. Follow the reverse of the tightening sequence (see illustration 8.12).

4   Lift the rocker arm and shaft assembly from the cylinder head (see illustration).

Oil control orifice

▶ **Refer to illustration 8.5**

5   Pull the orifice from the cylinder head (see illustration).

➡Note: VTEC engines are equipped with an O-ring on the lower section of the oil control orifice. Non-VTEC engines are not equipped with an O-ring on the oil control orifice.

INSPECTION

▶ **Refer to illustration 8.7**

6   If you wish to disassemble and inspect the rocker arm assembly, (a good idea as long as you have them off), remove the retaining bolts

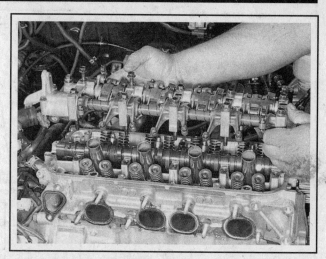

8.4 Remove the camshaft bearing caps, bolts and rocker arm assembly

and slip the rocker arms, springs, collars and bearing caps off the shafts. Mark the relationship of the shafts to the bearing caps and keep the components in order. They must be reassembled in the same positions they were removed from.

✳✳ CAUTION:

On VTEC engines, it is a good idea to bundle the intake rocker arms together with rubber bands

7   Thoroughly clean the components and inspect them for wear and damage. Check the rocker arm faces that contact the camshaft and the rocker arm tips (see illustration). Check the surfaces of the shafts that the rocker arms ride on, as well as the bearing surfaces inside the rocker arms, for scoring and excessive wear. Replace any parts that are damaged or excessively worn. Also, make sure the oil holes in the shafts are not plugged.

8   Clean the orifice so there are no obstructions and oil flows freely through the orifice.

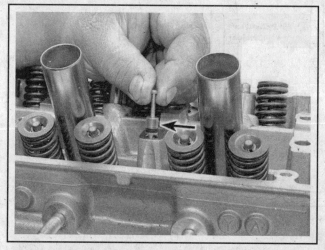

8.5 To remove the oil control orifice for cleaning, thread a machine screw into the top and pull up on the orifice

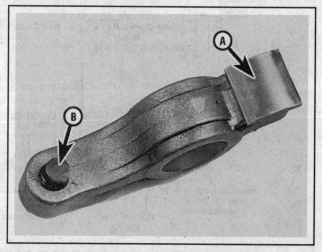

8.7 Check the contact face (A) and adjuster tip (B) for damage or wear - non-VTEC rocker arm shown

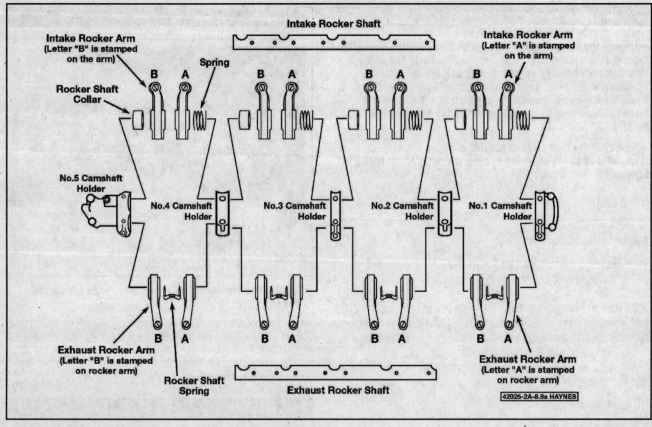

8.9a Exploded view of the rocker arms and shafts on a non-VTEC engine

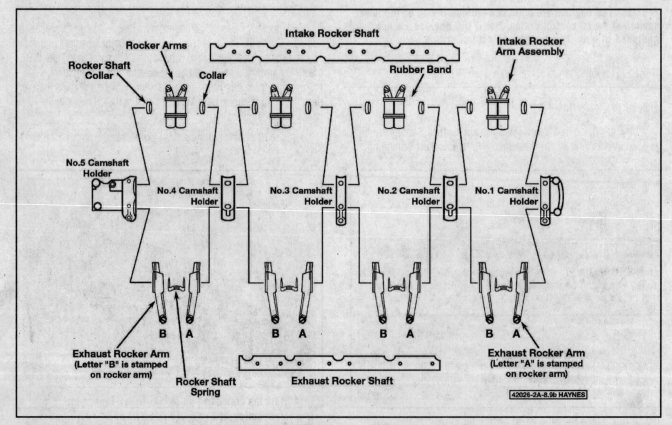

8.9b Exploded view of the rocker arms and shafts on a VTEC engine

INSTALLATION

♦ **Refer to illustrations 8.9a, 8.9b and 8.12**

9   Lubricate all components with engine assembly lubricant or engine oil and reassemble rocker arms on to the shafts. When installing the rocker arms, shafts and springs, note the markings and the difference between the left and right side components (see illustrations).

10   Replace the O-ring on the oil control orifice, then install the orifice in the cylinder head.

11   Coat the camshaft lobes and journals with camshaft installation lubricant. Apply anaerobic-type sealant to the cylinder head contact surfaces of bearing caps 1 and 5 and install the rocker arm assembly.

12   Tighten the camshaft bearing cap bolts a little at a time, in the proper sequence (see illustration) to the torque listed in this Chapter's Specifications.

13   Make sure the alignment marks on the cylinder head plug are even with the top edge of the cylinder head.

8.12 Rocker arm assembly bolt TIGHTENING sequence

14   The remainder of installation is the reverse of removal. Adjust the valve clearance, if necessary (see Chapter 1).

15   Run the engine and check for oil leaks and proper operation.

---

9   Timing belt and sprockets - removal, inspection and installation

REMOVAL

♦ **Refer to illustrations 9.13, 9.14, 9.17 and 9.19**

1   Disconnect the cable from the negative terminal of the battery (see Chapter 5, Section 1).

2   Place blocks behind the rear wheels and set the parking brake.

3   Loosen the lug nuts on the left front wheel and raise the front of the vehicle. Support the front of the vehicle securely on jackstands (see Chapter 1).

4   Remove the left front wheel and remove the splash shield from under the engine (see illustrations 5.9a, 5.9b and 5.9c). Remove the drivebelts (see Chapter 1).

5   Remove the power steering pump and position it aside, but don't disconnect the hoses (see Chapter 10).

6   Remove the alternator (see Chapter 5).

7   Remove the valve cover (see Section 4).

8   Support the engine with a floor jack. Place a wood block between the jack pad and the oil pan to avoid damaging the pan.

9   Remove the upper left engine mount bracket (see Section 17).

10   Position the number one piston at Top Dead Center (see Section 3).

❋ CAUTION:

Always rotate the crankshaft counterclockwise (viewed from the pulley end of the engine). Clockwise rotation may cause incorrect adjustment of the timing belt.

11   Disconnect the camshaft position sensor (CMP)/top dead center (TDC) sensor (see Chapter 6).

12   Remove the side engine mount bracket (see Section 17).

13   Remove the upper timing belt cover (see illustration).

14   Using a strap wrench or chain wrench to hold the crankshaft pulley stationary, loosen the crankshaft pulley bolt with a socket and breaker bar (see illustration).

9.13 Location of the timing belt upper cover mounting bolts

9.14 Hold the crankshaft pulley while you loosen the crankshaft pulley bolt - a chain wrench can be used if you first wrap a length of old drivebelt around the pulley

9.17 If you intend to reuse the belt, make an arrow to indicate the direction of rotation, and match marks to align the sprockets with the bolt

9.19 Location of the timing belt tensioner bolt (upper arrow) and crankshaft position sensor (lower arrow)

9.21 Check the belt tensioner pulley for rough operation, bearing play and freedom of movement

15 Slip the pulley off the crankshaft.

16 Remove the lower timing belt cover.

17 If you intend to reuse the timing belt, use white paint or chalk to make match marks to align the sprockets with the belt and an arrow to indicate the direction of rotation (see illustration).

18 Remove the crankshaft position sensor (CKP) (see Chapter 6).

19 Loosen the timing belt tensioner bolt (see illustration). Push on the tensioner to release the tension on the belt, then retighten the bolt. Remove the crankshaft position sensor and slip the belt off. If you're replacing the crankshaft oil seal, slip the sprocket and inner belt guide off the crankshaft (see Section 10).

20 If you're replacing the camshaft or camshaft oil seal, slip a large screwdriver through the camshaft sprocket to keep it from rotating and remove the bolt, then pull off the sprocket. Also remove the Woodruff key.

INSPECTION

▶ **Refer to illustrations 9.21 and 9.22**

21 Rotate the belt tensioner pulley by hand and move it from side-to-side, checking for play and rough rotation (see illustration). Replace it if roughness or play is detected.

22 Check the timing belt for wear (especially on the thrust side of the teeth), cracks, splits, fraying and oil contamination (see illustration). Replace the belt if any of these conditions are noted.

➡**Note: Unless the engine has very low mileage, it's common practice to replace the timing belt with a new one every time it's removed. Don't reinstall the original belt unless it's in like-new condition. Never reinstall a belt in questionable condition.**

INSTALLATION

▶ **Refer to illustrations 9.24, 9.25, 9.26 and 9.27**

23 If you removed the sprockets, reinstall them. Don't forget the Woodruff key for the camshaft sprocket and the inner belt guide for the crankshaft sprocket. Tighten the camshaft sprocket bolt to the torque listed in this Chapter's Specifications.

24 Before installing the timing belt, make sure the dot or "UP" mark on the camshaft sprocket is at the top and the two index marks are in line with the cylinder head surface (see illustration).

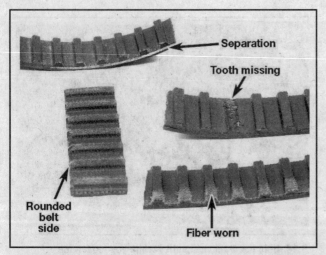

9.22 Carefully inspect the timing belt for cracked or missing teeth - wear on one side of the belt indicates sprocket misalignment problems

Separation

Tooth missing

Rounded belt side

Fiber worn

9.24 Alignment marks for the camshaft sprocket - be sure the word UP is at the twelve o'clock position. It may be necessary to use a straight-edge or ruler to align the two timing marks with the cylinder head surface

9.25 Align the mark on the crankshaft sprocket with the pointer on the oil pump

25 Temporarily reinstall the crankshaft pulley and bolt and turn the crankshaft (if it was disturbed) until the timing mark on the crankshaft sprocket and the pointer on the oil pump are aligned (see illustration).

26 Align the holes on the tensioner pulley and the tensioner base and insert a 0.12 inch (3 mm) diameter pin or drill bit into the holes (see illustration).

27 Install the timing belt tightly around the crankshaft sprocket, then around the tensioner pulley, water pump pulley and camshaft sprocket in sequence (see illustration).

28 Loosen the tensioner mounting bolt 1/2-turn (180-degrees), allowing the tensioner to tension the belt slightly.

29 Carefully turn the crankshaft counterclockwise two revolutions and recheck the timing marks and camshaft sprocket index marks for proper alignment. If the crankshaft binds or seems to hit something, do not force it, as the valves may be hitting the pistons. If this happens, valve timing is incorrect. Remove the belt and repeat the installation procedure and verify that the installation is correct.

30 Tighten the tensioner mounting bolt to the torque listed in this Chapter's Specifications and remove the pin (see illustration 9.26).

31 Reinstall the remaining parts in the reverse order of removal.

32 Refer to Chapter 1 and adjust the drivebelts.

33 Reconnect the battery (see Chapter 5, Section 1).

34 Run the engine and check for proper operation.

9.26 Align the holes on the tensioner pulley (C) and tensioner base (B), then insert a 0.12 inch (3.0 mm) diameter pin (C) into the holes - after the belt has been installed and rotated, tighten the tensioner mounting bolt (A)

9.27 Route the timing belt around the belt tensioner and water pump

10 Crankshaft pulley and front oil seal - replacement

▶ Refer to illustrations 10.2a, 10.2b, 10.3 and 10.4

1 Remove the timing belt (see Section 9).

2 Remove the crankshaft sprocket from the crankshaft, then remove the inner belt guide (see illustrations).

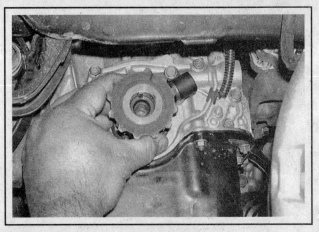

10.2a Remove the crankshaft sprocket . . .

10.2b ... and the inner belt guide - note that the concave side faces toward the engine (away from the timing belt)

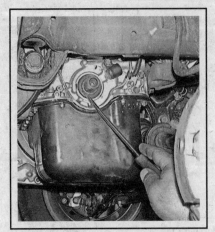

10.3 Carefully pry the oil seal out with a removal tool or a screwdriver - don't nick or scratch the crankshaft or oil pump housing or the new seal will leak

10.4 Drive in a new seal with a socket with an outside diameter slightly smaller than the outside diameter of the seal

3   Carefully pry the seal out of the oil pump housing with a seal removal tool or a screwdriver (see illustration). Don't scratch the seal bore or damage the crankshaft in the process (if the crankshaft is damaged, the new seal will end up leaking).

4   Clean the bore in the oil pump housing and coat the outer edge of the new seal with engine oil or multi-purpose grease. Using a seal driver or a socket with an outside diameter slightly smaller than the outside diameter of the seal, carefully drive the seal into place with a hammer (see illustration). If a socket is not available, a short section of a large diameter pipe will work. Check the seal after installation to be sure the spring did not pop out.

5   Install the inner belt guide and the crankshaft sprocket.

6   Install the timing belt (see Section 9).

7   Lubricate the sleeve of the crankshaft pulley with engine oil or multi-purpose grease, then install the crankshaft pulley. The remainder of installation is the reverse of removal.

➡Note: Install the inner belt guide with the concave surface facing in toward the front seal.

8   Run the engine and check for leaks.

11 Camshaft - removal, inspection and installation

ENDPLAY AND RUNOUT CHECK

▶ Refer to illustration 11.1

1   To check camshaft endplay:
   a) Install the camshaft and secure it with the caps.
   b) Mount a dial indicator on the cylinder head with the pointer resting on the camshaft nose (see illustration).
   c) Using a large screwdriver as a lever at the opposite end, move the camshaft forward-and-backward and note the dial indicator reading.
   d) Compare the reading with the endplay listed in this Chapter's Specifications.
   e) If the indicated reading is excessive, either the camshaft or the cylinder head is worn. Replace parts as necessary.
2   To check camshaft runout:
   a) Support the camshaft with a pair of V-blocks and set up a dial indicator with the plunger resting against the center bearing journal on the camshaft.
   b) Rotate the camshaft and note the indicated runout.
   c) Compare the results to the camshaft runout listed in this Chapter's Specifications.
   d) If the indicated runout exceeds the specified runout limit, replace the camshaft.

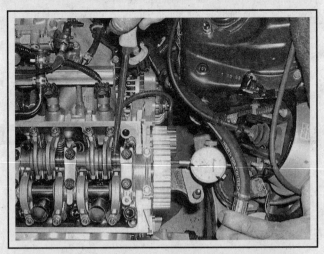

11.1 To check camshaft endplay, set a dial indicator like this, with the gauge plunger touching the nose of the camshaft

REMOVAL

▶ Refer to illustration 11.8

3   Remove the ignition coils (see Chapter 5).

11.8 Lift the camshaft from the cylinder head

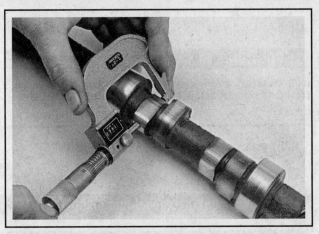

11.10 Measure the camshaft lobe heights with a micrometer

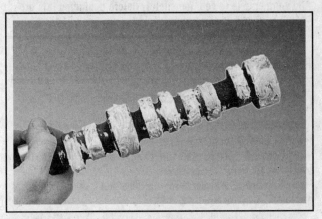

11.14 Be sure to apply camshaft assembly lubricant to the lobes and bearing journals before installing the camshaft

4   Remove the valve cover (see Section 4).

5   Set the engine at TDC for cylinder number one (see Section 3) and remove the timing belt (see Section 9).

6   If necessary, separate the sprocket from the camshaft by removing the camshaft sprocket bolt.

➡ **Note: Prevent the camshaft from turning by inserting a screwdriver through one of the holes in the sprocket.**

7   Remove the rocker arm assembly (see Section 8). If the camshaft bearing caps must be removed from the assembly and they don't have numbers on them, number them before removal. Be sure to put the marks on the same ends of all the caps to prevent incorrect orientation of the caps during installation.

8   Lift out the camshaft (see illustration), wipe it off with a clean shop towel, remove the camshaft seal and set the camshaft aside.

INSPECTION

▶ **Refer to illustration 11.10**

9   Check the camshaft bearing journals and caps for scoring and signs of wear. If they are worn, replace the cylinder head with a new or rebuilt assembly.

10   Check the cam lobes for wear:

a)   *Check the toe and ramp areas of each cam lobe for score marks and uneven wear. Also check for flaking and pitting.*

b)   *If there's wear on the toe or the ramp, replace the camshaft, but first try to find the cause of the wear. Look for abrasive substances in the oil and inspect the oil pump and oil passages for blockage. Lobe wear is usually caused by inadequate lubrication or dirty oil.*

c)   *Using a micrometer, measure the cam lobe height* (see illustration). *If the lobe wear is indicated, replace the camshaft.*

11   Inspect the rocker arms for wear, galling and pitting of the contact surfaces (see Section 8).

12   If any of the conditions described above are noted, the cylinder head is probably getting insufficient lubrication or dirty oil. Make sure you track down the cause of this problem (low oil level, low oil pump capacity, clogged oil passage, etc.) before installing a new cylinder head, camshaft or rocker arm assembly.

INSTALLATION

▶ **Refer to illustration 11.14**

13   Thoroughly clean the camshaft, the bearing surfaces in the head and caps and the rocker arms. Remove all sludge and dirt. Wipe off all components with a clean, lint-free cloth.

14   Lubricate the camshaft bearing surfaces in the head and the bearing journals and lobes on the camshaft with camshaft assembly lubricant (see illustration).

❊❊ CAUTION:

Failure to adequately lubricate the camshaft and related components can cause serious damage to bearing and friction surfaces during the first few seconds after engine start-up, when the oil pressure is low or nonexistent.

15   Carefully lower the camshaft into position. Using an appropriate sized driver, deep socket or section of pipe, install a new camshaft seal with the open (spring) side facing in.

16   Install the rocker arm assembly (see Section 8).

17   Rotate the camshaft as necessary and install the camshaft sprocket with the "UP" mark stamped on the camshaft sprocket at the twelve o'clock position (see illustration 9.24).

18 Install the timing belt and related components as described in Section 10.

19 Rotate the crankshaft counterclockwise slowly by hand through two complete revolutions and recheck the alignment marks on the sprockets. The timing marks should still be aligned. If they're not, remove the timing belt and set all the timing marks again.

20 The remainder of installation is the reverse of removal.

12 Cylinder head - removal and installation

REMOVAL

1 Position the number one piston at Top Dead Center (see Section 3).

2 Disconnect the cable from the negative terminal of the battery (see Chapter 5, Section 1).

3 Drain the cooling system and remove the spark plugs (see Chapter 1).

4 Disconnect the heater hoses, the upper and lower radiator hoses and the bypass hose (see Chapter 3).

5 Remove the air filter housing and intake resonator (see Chapter 4).

6 Remove the drivebelts (see Chapter 1). Unbolt the power steering pump and set it aside without disconnecting any hoses, then remove the power steering pump bracket (see Chapter 10).

7 Disconnect the throttle cable from the throttle body and relieve the fuel system pressure (see Chapter 4).

8 Disconnect the EVAP canister hose, the brake booster vacuum hose, the PCV hose and intake breather hose (Chapters 4 and 6).

9 Disconnect the injector harness, the ECT sensor, the TP sensor, the MAP sensor, oxygen sensor, EGR sensor, the CKP sensor, the CMP sensor, the VTEC solenoid (if equipped) and the IAC control valve connectors. Label each connector to prevent incorrect reassembly.

10 Remove the coolant connector hose from the coolant housing.

11 Remove the power steering pump without disconnecting the hoses (see Chapter 10).

12 Remove the alternator (see Chapter 5).

13 Remove the power steering bracket and the alternator bracket from the cylinder head.

14 Support the engine with a floor jack. Place a wood block between the jack pad and the oil pan to avoid damaging the pan. Remove the left engine mount bracket (see Section 17).

15 Remove the intake manifold brace, the intake manifold (see Section 5) and the exhaust manifold (see Section 6).

16 Remove the valve cover (see Section 4).

17 Remove the timing belt (see Section 9), rocker arm assembly (see Section 8) and the camshaft (see Section 11).

18 Loosen the cylinder head bolts in 1/4-turn increments until they can be removed by hand. Work in a pattern that's the reverse of the tightening sequence to avoid warping the cylinder head (see illustration 12.26). Note where each bolt goes so it can be returned to the same location on installation.

19 Lift the cylinder head off the engine. If resistance is felt, don't pry between the head and block gasket mating surfaces - damage to the mating surfaces will result. Instead, pry between the power steering pump bracket and the engine block. Set the head on blocks of wood to prevent damage to the gasket sealing surfaces.

20 Have an automotive machine shop check the cylinder head for warpage.

INSTALLATION

▶ **Refer to illustration 12.26**

21 The mating surfaces of the cylinder head and block must be perfectly clean when the head is installed.

22 Use a gasket scraper to remove all traces of carbon and old gasket material, then clean the mating surfaces with lacquer thinner or acetone. If there's oil on the mating surfaces when the cylinder head is installed, the gasket may not seal correctly and leaks may develop. When working on the engine block, stuff the cylinders with clean shop rags to keep out debris. Use a vacuum cleaner to remove material that falls into the cylinders. Since the cylinder head and engine block are made of aluminum, aggressive scraping can cause damage. Be extra careful not to nick or gouge the mating surfaces with the scraper.

23 Check the block and cylinder head mating surfaces for nicks, deep scratches and other damage. If damage is slight, it can be removed with a file; if it's excessive, machining may be the only alternative.

24 Use a tap of the correct size to chase the threads in the cylinder head bolt holes. Use a wire brush to remove corrosion and clean the bolt threads. Dirt, corrosion, sealant and damaged threads will affect torque readings.

25 Place a new gasket on the engine block. Check to see if there are any markings (such as "TOP") on the gasket to indicate how it is to be installed. Those identification marks must face UP. Set the cylinder head in position.

26 Lubricate the threads and the seats of the cylinder head bolts with clean engine oil, then install them. Tighten the bolts in the recommended sequence, in four stages, to the torque listed in this Chapter's Specifications (see illustration). Because of the critical function of cylinder head bolts, the manufacturer specifies the following conditions for tightening them:

a) A beam-type or dial-type torque wrench is preferable to a pre-set (click-stop) torque wrench. If you use a pre-set torque wrench, tighten slowly and be careful not to overtighten the bolts.

b) *If a bolt makes any sound while you're tightening it (squeaking, clicking, etc.), loosen it completely and tighten it again in the four specified steps.*

27 Attach the camshaft sprocket to the camshaft and install the timing belt (see Section 9).

28 Rotate the crankshaft counterclockwise slowly by hand through two complete revolutions and recheck the alignment marks on the sprockets.

❊ CAUTION:

If you feel any resistance while turning the engine over, stop and re-check the camshaft timing. The valves may be hitting the pistons.

29 Reinstall the remaining parts in the reverse order of removal.
30 Be sure to refill the cooling system and check all fluid levels.
31 Reconnect the battery (see Chapter 5, Section 1).
32 Start the engine and check the ignition timing (see Chapter 1).

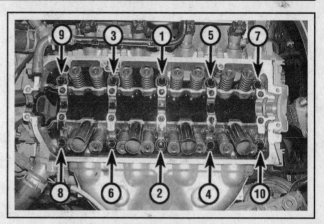

12.26 Cylinder head bolt TIGHTENING sequence

33 Run the engine until normal operating temperature is reached. Check for leaks and proper operation.

13 Oil pan - removal and installation

REMOVAL

▶ **Refer to illustration 13.6**

1 Drain the engine oil and replace the oil filter (see Chapter 1).
2 Disconnect the cable from the negative terminal of the battery.
3 Raise the vehicle and support it securely on jackstands. Remove the splash shield from under the engine.
4 Disconnect the oxygen sensor connectors (see Chapter 6).
5 Disconnect the exhaust pipe (see Chapter 4).

➡**Note: Some models are equipped with an exhaust pipe/muffler assembly (D17A1 engines) or an exhaust pipe/catalytic converter assembly (D17A2 and D17A6 engines).**

6 Remove the bolts securing the oil pan to the engine block (see illustration).
7 Tap on the pan with a soft-face hammer to break the gasket seal and detach the oil pan from the engine. Don't pry between the block and oil pan mating surfaces.

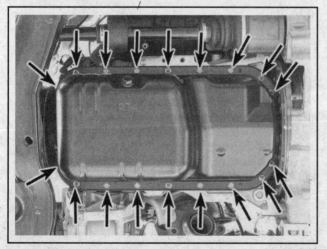

13.6 Remove the oil pan bolts from the oil pan - steel oil pan shown

INSTALLATION

8 Using a gasket scraper, remove all traces of old gasket and/or sealant from the engine block and the oil pan. Also make sure the threaded bolt holes in the block are clean.
9 Clean the oil pan with solvent and dry it thoroughly. Check the gasket flanges for distortion, particularly around the bolt holes. If necessary, place the pan on a wood block and use a hammer to flatten and restore the gasket surface.
10 Clean the mating surfaces on the engine block and the oil pan with lacquer thinner or acetone to remove any oil residue which will prevent the new gasket from sealing properly.

Aluminum oil pans (EX, HX models)

▶ **Refer to illustrations 13.11 and 13.13**

11 Apply a 1/8-inch wide bead of RTV sealant to the perimeter of the oil pan along the inside of the bolt holes (see illustration) then install the gasket onto the oil pan.
12 Carefully place the oil pan in position and install the bolts finger tight.
13 Tighten the oil pan bolts a little at a time, in a criss-cross pattern, to the torque listed in this Chapter's Specifications. Don't overtighten them or leakage may occur.

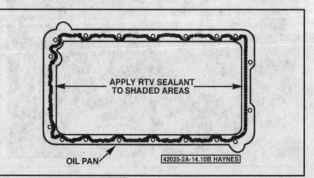

APPLY RTV SEALANT TO SHADED AREAS

OIL PAN

42025-2A-14.10B HAYNES

13.11 On aluminum oil pans, apply a bead of RTV sealant to the perimeter of the oil pan flange, inboard of the bolt holes

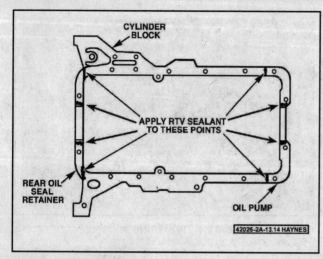

13.14 On LX and DX engine blocks, apply a small amount of RTV sealant to the specified points

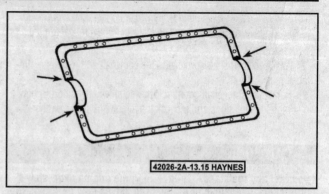

13.15 Apply a small amount of RTV sealant to the oil pan gasket at these points

Steel oil pans (LX/DX models)

▶ Refer to illustrations 13.14, 13.15 and 13.16

14 Apply a 1/8-inch wide bead of RTV sealant to the oil pump cover and rear main seal housing corners where they meet the engine block (see illustration).

15 Apply RTV sealant to the four corners of the recesses on the oil pan gasket (see illustration), then install the gasket onto the oil pan. Carefully place the oil pan in position and install the bolts finger tight.

16 Tighten the oil pan bolts in the correct sequence (see illustration) and to the torque listed in this Chapter's Specifications. Don't overtighten them or leakage may occur.

All models

17 Reconnect the battery (see Chapter 5, Section 1).

18 Wait at least one hour before adding oil (see Chapter 1), then run the engine and check for oil leaks.

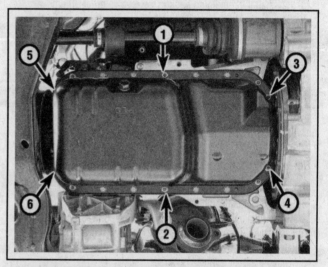

13.16 First tighten the six oil pan nuts finger tight and in sequence to position the oil pan evenly against the engine block - next, tighten all the oil pan bolts and nuts to the torque listed in this Chapter's Specifications

.14 Oil pump - removal, inspection and installation

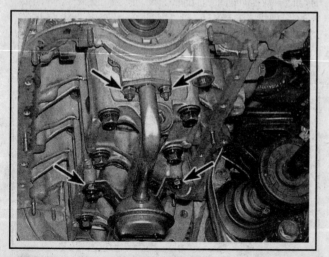

14.3 Remove the oil pick-up tube bolts from the oil pump and main bearing cap bridge

REMOVAL

▶ Refer to illustrations 14.3, 14.4 and 14.5

1 Remove the timing belt (see Section 9).

2 Remove the oil pan (see Section 13).

3 Remove the oil pick-up tube and screen from the pump housing and the main bearing cap bridge (see illustration).

4 Remove the bolts from the oil pump housing and separate the assembly from the engine (see illustration).

5 Remove the screws and disassemble the oil pump (see illustration). You may need to use an impact screwdriver to loosen the pump cover screws without stripping the heads.

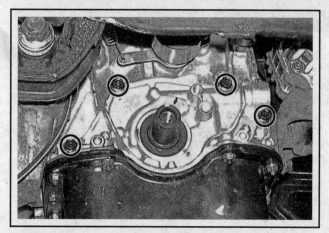

14.4 Remove the oil pump-to-block bolts (circled) and remove the oil pump

14.5 Remove the oil pump cover screws

INSPECTION

▶ **Refer to illustrations 14.6a, 14.6b and 14.6c**

6   Check the oil pump rotor-to-cover clearance, tooth tip clearance and rotor-to-body clearance (see illustrations). Compare your measurements to the figures listed in this Chapter's Specifications. Replace the pump if any of the measurements exceed the specified limits.

7   Remove the pressure relief valve plug and extract the spring and pressure relief valve plunger from the pump housing. Check the spring for distortion and the relief valve plunger for scoring. Replace parts as necessary.

8   Install the pump rotors. Pack the spaces between the rotors with petroleum jelly (this will prime the pump).

9   Apply thread-locking compound to the pump cover screws, install the cover and tighten the screws to the torque listed in this Chapter's Specifications. Install the oil pressure relief valve and spring assembly. Use a new sealing washer on the plug and tighten the plug securely.

INSTALLATION

10   Apply a thin coat of anaerobic sealant to the pump housing-to-block sealing surface and a new O-ring in the pump housing. Install the

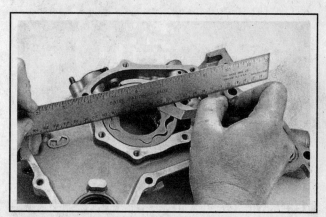

14.6a Use a feeler gauge and straight-edge to check the clearance between the rotors and the cover

pump housing to the engine block and tighten the bolts to the torque listed in this Chapter's Specifications.

11   Install the oil pick-up tube and screen, using a new gasket. Tighten the bolts to the torque listed in this Chapter's Specifications.

12   Install the oil pan (see Section 13).

13   The remainder of installation is the reverse of removal. Add the specified type and quantity of oil and coolant (see Chapter 1), run the engine and check for leaks.

14.6b Use a feeler gauge to check the tooth-tip clearance between the inner and outer rotors

14.6c Use a feeler gauge to check the outer rotor-to-pump body clearance

15 Flywheel/driveplate - removal and installation

REMOVAL

▶ **Refer to illustration 15.3**

1 Raise the vehicle and support it securely on jackstands, then refer to Chapter 7 and remove the transaxle.

2 If the vehicle is equipped with a manual transaxle, remove the pressure plate and clutch disc (see Chapter 8). Now is a good time to check/replace the clutch components and pilot bearing.

3 Remove the bolts that secure the flywheel/driveplate to the crank-

15.3 Remove the flywheel/driveplate bolts from the crankshaft

shaft (see illustration). If the crankshaft turns, wedge a screwdriver in the ring gear teeth (manual transaxle models), or insert a long punch through one of the holes in the driveplate and allow it to rest against a projection on the engine block (automatic transaxle models).

4 Remove the flywheel/driveplate from the crankshaft. Since the flywheel is fairly heavy, be sure to support it while removing the last bolt.

5 Clean the flywheel to remove grease and oil. Inspect the surface for cracks, rivet grooves, burned areas and score marks. Light scoring can be removed with emery cloth. Check for cracked and broken ring gear teeth. Lay the flywheel on a flat surface and use a straightedge to check for warpage.

6 Clean and inspect the mating surfaces of the flywheel/driveplate and the crankshaft. If the rear main oil seal is leaking, replace it before reinstalling the flywheel/driveplate (see Section 16).

INSTALLATION

7 Position the flywheel/driveplate against the crankshaft. Note that some engines have an alignment dowel or staggered bolt holes to ensure correct installation. Before installing the bolts, apply thread-locking compound to the threads.

8 Prevent the flywheel/driveplate from turning by using one of the methods described in Step 3. Using a crossing pattern, tighten the bolts to the torque listed in this Chapter's Specifications.

9 The remainder of installation is the reverse of the removal procedure.

16 Rear main oil seal - replacement

▶ **Refer to illustrations 16.4 and 16.5**

1 The transaxle must be removed from the vehicle for this procedure (see Chapter 7).

2 Remove the flywheel/driveplate (see Section 15).

3 Before removing the seal, it is very important that the clearance between the seal and the outside edge of the retainer is checked. Use a small ruler or caliper and record the distance. The new seal must not be driven in past this measurement.

4 The seal can be replaced without removing the oil pan or seal retainer. Use a screwdriver to carefully pry the seal out of the housing

(see illustration).

5 Apply a film of clean oil to the crankshaft seal journal and the lip of the new seal and carefully tap the seal into place. The lip is stiff so carefully work it onto the seal journal of the crankshaft with a smooth object like the end of a socket extension (see illustration). Tap the seal into the retainer with a seal driver. If a seal driver isn't available, a large socket or piece of pipe, with an outside diameter slightly smaller than that of the seal, can be used. Don't rush it or you may damage the seal.

6 The remaining steps are the reverse of removal.

7 Run the engine and check for oil leaks.

16.4 Carefully pry the oil seal out with a seal removal tool or a screwdriver - don't nick or scratch the crankshaft or the new seal will be damaged and leaks will develop

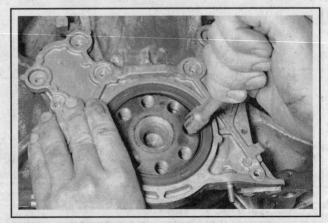

16.5 Lubricate the journal and the seal lip with multi-purpose grease and carefully work the seal over the journal with a smooth, blunt object

17 Engine mounts - check and replacement

1 Engine mounts seldom require attention, but broken or deteriorated mounts should be replaced immediately or the added strain placed on the driveline components may cause damage or wear.

CHECK

2 During the check, the engine must be raised slightly to remove the weight from the mounts.

3 Raise the vehicle and support it securely on jackstands, then position a jack under the engine oil pan. Place a large wood block between the jack head and the oil pan, then carefully raise the engine just enough to take the weight off the mounts.

✷✷ WARNING:

DO NOT place any part of your body under the engine when it's supported only by a jack!

4 Check the mount insulators to see if the rubber is cracked, hardened or separated from the metal in the center of the mount.

5 Check for relative movement between the mount plates and the engine or frame (use a large screwdriver or pry bar to attempt to move the mounts). If movement is noted, lower the engine and tighten the mount fasteners.

6 Rubber preservative should be applied to the insulators to slow deterioration.

REPLACEMENT

▶ **Refer to illustrations 17.9a, 17.9b, 17.9c and 17.9d**

7 Disconnect the cable from the negative terminal of the battery (see Chapter 5, Section 1). Raise the vehicle and support it securely on jackstands (if not already done). Support the engine as described in Step 3.

8 Remove the fasteners, raise the engine with the jack and detach the mount from the frame bracket and engine.

9 Install the new mount, making sure it is correctly positioned in its bracket (see illustrations). Install the fasteners and tighten them securely.

17.9a Left side (driver's side) engine mount bracket fasteners

17.9b Right side transaxle mount through-bolt location

17.9c Rear engine mount bolt locations

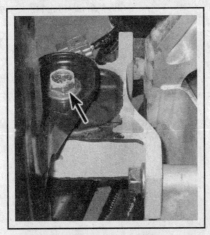

17.9d Front transaxle mount through-bolt

17.9e Rear transaxle mount bolt location

Specifications

General

Firing order	1-3-4-2
Bore	2.95 inches (74.98 mm)
Stroke	3.72 inches (94.40 mm)
Displacement	101.7 cubic inches (1.7 liters)
Oil pressure	See Chapter 2C

④ ③ ② ❶

Front

↓

42026-2A-specs HAYNES

Cylinder locations for the SOHC engines

Valve adjustment

See Chapter 1

Camshaft

Endplay
Standard	0.002 to 0.006 inch (0.05 to 0.15 mm)
Maximum	0.020 inch (0.5 mm)

Lobe height

D17A1
Intake	1.3897 inches (35.299 mm)
Exhaust	1.4678 inches (37.281 mm)

D17A2
Intake	
Primary	1.5198 inches (38.604 mm)
Secondary	1.2932 inches (32.848 mm)
Exhaust	1.5269 inches (38.784 mm)

D17A6
Intake	
Primary	1.5129 inches (38.427 mm)
Secondary	1.2674 inches (32.193 mm)
Exhaust	1.5289 inches (38.784 mm)

Runout
Standard	0.001 inch (0.030 mm)
Service limit	0.002 inch maximum (0.040 mm)

Journal oil clearance
Standard	0.002 to 0.004 inch (0.050 to 0.089 mm)
Service limit	0.006 inch maximum (0.15 mm)

Oil pump

Rotor-to-cover clearance
Standard	0.001 to 0.003 inch (0.02 to 0.07 mm)
Service limit	0.006 inch maximum (0.15 mm)

Tooth tip clearance
Standard	0.002 to 0.007 inch (0.06 to 0.18 mm)
Service limit	0.008 inch maximum (0.20 mm)

Outer rotor-to-pump body clearance
Standard	0.004 to 0.007 inch (0.10 to 0.18 mm)
Service limit	0.008 inch maximum (0.20 mm)

Torque specifications | Ft-lbs (unless otherwise indicated) | Nm

→Note: One foot-pound (ft-lb) of torque is equivalent to 12 inch-pounds (in-lbs) of torque. Torque values below approximately 15 ft-lbs are expressed in inch-pounds, since most foot-pound torque wrenches are not accurate at these smaller values.

	Ft-lbs (unless otherwise indicated)	Nm
Camshaft bearing cap bolts		
6 mm bolts	104 in-lbs	12
8 mm bolts	14	20
Camshaft sprocket bolt	27	37
Crankshaft pulley bolt	181	245
Cylinder head bolts		
Step 1	14	20
Step 2	36	49
Step 3	49	67
Driveplate-to-crankshaft bolts	54	74
Intake manifold bolts/nuts	16	22
Intake manifold brace bolts	104 in-lbs	12
Exhaust manifold-to-cylinder head nuts	23	31
Exhaust manifold heat shield upper bolts		
(manifold bolts)	23	31
Exhaust pipe-to-manifold bolts	16	22
Flywheel-to-crankshaft bolts	87	118
Oil pan drain plug		
D17A1	33	44
D17A2, D17A6	29	39
Oil pan-to-engine bolts	104 in-lbs	12
Oil pump pick-up tube to pump housing nuts	96 in-lbs	11
Oil pump pick-up screen-to-main bearing cap	96 in-lbs	11
Oil pump housing-to-block bolts	96 in-lbs	11
Oil pump cover-to-housing		
Aisin	86 in-lbs	10
Yamada	42 in-lbs	5
Rear main oil seal housing bolts	74 in-lbs	10
Timing belt cover bolts	74 in-lbs	10
Timing belt tensioner mounting bolt	33	44
Valve cover bolts	86 in-lbs	10

Notes

Section

Reference to other Chapters

2B

DOUBLE OVERHEAD CAMSHAFT (DOHC) ENGINES

1 General information

This Part of Chapter 2 is devoted to in-vehicle repair procedures for the 2.0L and 2.4L DOHC (Double Overhead Camshaft), engine as well as procedures such as timing chain and sprocket(s), balance shaft chain and balance shafts and oil pan removal. All information concerning engine removal and installation can be found in Part C of this Chapter.

Two different versions of this engine have been produced by Honda for the CR-V and hatchback models, both of which are covered in this Part of Chapter 2. All versions of this engine utilize a Double Overhead Camshaft (DOHC), with 4 valves per cylinder (16V). This engine incorporates the i-VTEC (intelligent Variable Valve Timing and lift Electronic

Control) system, which electronically alters valve timing to enhance engine performance. For more information on the i-VTEC system, see Section 10 of this Chapter.

Engine designations include:

K20A3 *2.0L 16 valve DOHC i-VTEC 160 horsepower engine*
K24A1 *2.4L 16 valve DOHC i-VTEC 160 horsepower engine*

The Specifications included in this Part of Chapter 2 apply only to the procedures contained in this Part. Part C of Chapter 2 contains the Specifications necessary for certain procedures concerning engine rebuilding.

2 Repair operations possible with the engine in the vehicle

Many major repair operations can be accomplished without removing the engine from the vehicle.

Clean the engine compartment and the exterior of the engine with some type of degreaser before any work is done. It will make the job easier and help keep dirt out of the internal areas of the engine.

Depending on the components involved, it may be helpful to remove the hood to improve access to the engine as repairs are performed (refer to Chapter 11 if necessary). Cover the fenders to prevent damage to the paint. Special pads are available, but an old bedspread or blanket will also work.

If vacuum, exhaust, oil or coolant leaks develop, indicating a need for gasket or seal replacement, the repairs can generally be made with the engine in the vehicle. The intake and exhaust manifold gaskets, oil pan gasket, crankshaft oil seals and cylinder head gasket are all accessible with the engine in place.

Exterior engine components, such as the intake and exhaust manifolds, the oil pan, the oil pump, the water pump, the starter motor, the alternator and the fuel system components can be removed for repair with the engine in place.

Since the cylinder head can be removed without pulling the engine, camshaft and valve component servicing can also be accomplished with the engine in the vehicle. Replacement of the timing chain and sprockets is also possible with the engine in the vehicle.

In extreme cases caused by a lack of necessary equipment, repair or replacement of piston rings, pistons, connecting rods and rod bearings is possible with the engine in the vehicle. However, this practice is not recommended because of the cleaning and preparation work that must be done to the components involved.

3 Top Dead Center (TDC) for number one piston - locating

1   Disable the fuel system (see Chapter 4, Section 2).

2   Remove the spark plugs (see Chapter 1) and install a compression gauge in the number one cylinder. Turn the crankshaft **clockwise** with a socket and breaker bar.

3   When the piston approaches TDC, compression will be noted on the compression gauge. Continue turning the crankshaft until the notch in the crankshaft pulley is aligned with the TDC mark on the front

cover. At this point number one cylinder is at TDC on the compression stroke.

4   After the number one piston has been positioned at TDC on the compression stroke, TDC for any of the remaining pistons can be located by turning the crankshaft clockwise, 180-degrees at a time, and following the firing order.

4 Valve cover - removal and installation

REMOVAL

1   Disconnect the cable from the negative battery terminal (see Chapter 5, Section 1).

2   Remove the intake manifold cover.

3   Remove the ignition coils (see Chapter 5).

4   Remove the bolt attaching the power steering hose bracket to the valve cover.

5   Remove the dipstick and the valve cover breather hose (see Chapter 1).

6   Remove the valve cover nuts (see illustration 4.11). Lift the valve cover off. Tap gently with a soft-face hammer if necessary to break the gasket seal.

INSTALLATION

▶ **Refer to illustration 4.11**

7   Clean the gasket surfaces on the intake manifold, cylinder head and valve cover. Use a shop rag, lacquer thinner or acetone to wipe off

all residue and gasket material from the sealing surfaces.

8   Insert a new valve cover gasket into the grooved recess in the valve cover. Make sure the gasket is positioned properly inside the valve cover groove.

9   Install new seals on the spark plug tubes.

10 Apply a slight amount of RTV sealant to the timing chain cover grooves and the number 5 rocker shaft holder mating areas.

11 Tighten the valve cover nuts in the correct sequence to the torque listed in this Chapter's Specifications (see illustration).

12 The remainder of installation is the reverse of removal.

13 Reconnect the battery (see Chapter 5, Section 1).

4.11 Valve cover nut tightening sequence - CR-V shown, hatchback similar

5   Intake manifold - removal and installation

⁂ WARNING:

Wait until the engine is completely cool before beginning this procedure.

REMOVAL

1   If you're working on a hatchback model, relieve the fuel system pressure (see Chapter 4, Section 2).

2   Disconnect the cable from the negative battery terminal (see Chapter 5, Section 1).

3   Remove the intake manifold cover, then disconnect the breather hose from the valve cover and the intake manifold.

4   Remove the intake duct and the air filter housing (see Chapter 4).

5   Disconnect the accelerator cable and the cruise control cable from the throttle valve (see Chapter 4). Position the cables off to the side.

6   Clamp off the coolant hoses attached to the throttle body, then loosen the clamps and detach the hoses from the throttle body. Be prepared for a little coolant spillage.

CR-V models

7   Disconnect the Intake Manifold Runner Control (IMRC) actuator solenoid connector (see Chapter 6).

8   Disconnect the PCV hose from the intake manifold (see Chapter 1).

9   Remove the IMRC solenoid mounting bolts and remove the actuator solenoid from the intake manifold.

10 Remove the radiator support cover (see Chapter 3).

11 Remove the wiring harness clamps along the radiator support.

12 Remove the mounting brackets and lift the radiator support from the engine compartment.

13 Disconnect the vacuum hoses from the intake manifold. Mark each hose with tape to insure correct reassembly.

14 Disconnect the IAC valve, the TPS, the knock sensor and any other electrical connectors that may interfere with manifold removal.

15 Remove the intake manifold mounting bolts and nuts.

16 Lift the intake manifold from the engine compartment.

Hatchback models

17 Disconnect the inlet line from the fuel rail (see Chapter 4).

18 Remove the intake manifold bracket from below the intake manifold.

19 Disconnect the vacuum hoses from the intake manifold. Mark each hose with tape to insure correct reassembly.

20 Disconnect the IAC valve, the TPS, the knock sensor and any other electrical connectors that may interfere with manifold removal.

21 Disconnect the purge solenoid vacuum hose and the EVAP purge solenoid (see Chapter 6).

22 Remove the intake manifold mounting bolts and nuts.

23 Lift the intake manifold from the engine compartment.

INSTALLATION

24 Clean away all traces of old gasket material. Remove oil and dirt with a cloth and solvent, such as brake system cleaner.

25 Install a new gasket.

26 Install the manifold and mounting fasteners. Tighten the fasteners to the torque listed in this Chapter's Specifications, starting with the center bolts and working towards the ends.

27 The remainder of installation is the reverse of the removal steps.

28 Check the coolant level and add some, if necessary, to bring it to the appropriate level (see Chapter 1).

29 Reconnect the battery (see Chapter 5, Section 1).

30 Run the engine and check for oil, coolant and vacuum leaks.

6 Exhaust manifolds - removal and installation

✳ WARNING:

The engine must be completely cool before beginning this procedure.

REMOVAL

1   Disconnect the cable from the negative battery terminal (see Chapter 5, Section 1).

2   Remove the VTEC solenoid valve (see Chapter 6).

3   Remove the exhaust manifold heat shield.

4   Raise the vehicle and support it on jackstands.

5   Remove the intermediate shaft heat shield.

6   Detach the exhaust pipe from the manifold.

7   Unbolt the exhaust manifold from the cylinder head.

INSTALLATION

8   Using a scraper, thoroughly clean the mating surfaces on the cylinder head, manifold and exhaust pipe. Remove the residue with a solvent such as brake system cleaner.

9   Check that the mating surfaces are perfectly flat and not damaged in any way. Warped or damaged manifolds may require machining. Install the new gasket to the cylinder head studs and place the manifold on the cylinder head. Tighten the bolts evenly to the torque listed in this Chapter's Specifications.

10 Connect the exhaust pipe to the manifold and tighten the nuts evenly to the torque listed in this Chapter's Specifications.

11 The remainder of installation is the reverse of the removal steps.

12 Reconnect the battery (see Chapter 5, Section 1).

13 Run the engine and check for exhaust leaks.

7 Engine front cover - removal and installation

REMOVAL

1   Disconnect the cable from the negative battery terminal (see Chapter 5, Section 1).

2   Remove the VTC oil control solenoid valve from the front cover.

3   Loosen the right front wheel lug nuts. Raise the front of the vehicle and support it securely on jackstands. Remove the right front wheel.

4   Remove the splash shield from below the engine compartment (see Chapter 2, Section 5).

5   Remove the drivebelt (see Chapter 1).

6   Remove the mounting bolts and detach the drivebelt tensioner from the front cover.

7   Remove the crankshaft pulley (see Section 9).

8   Disconnect the crankshaft position sensor harness and other electrical connectors that may interfere with the front cover removal.

9   Drain the engine oil (see Chapter 1).

10 Support the engine with a floor jack. Place a wood block between the jack pad and the oil pan to avoid damaging the pan.

11 Remove the ground cable, the right side engine mount and bracket assembly (see Section 18).

12 Remove the valve cover (see Section 4).

13 Remove the mounting bolts and the front cover.

14 Remove the engine cover-to-block gasket.

INSTALLATION

15 Inspect and clean all sealing surfaces of the engine front cover and the block.

✳ CAUTION:

Be very careful when scraping on aluminum engine parts. Aluminum is soft and gouges easily. Severely gouged parts may require replacement.

16 If necessary, replace the crankshaft seal in the front cover (see Section 9).

17 Apply RTV sealant to the cylinder block mating surfaces on the front cover, the upper surface contact areas and to the oil pan mating surfaces. Also, apply a small amount of RTV sealant to the inner thread holes.

18 Install a new engine front cover O-ring.

19 Install the front cover and fasteners. Make sure the fasteners are in their original locations. Tighten the fasteners by hand until the cover is contacting the block around its entire periphery.

20 Tighten the bolts to the torque listed in this Chapter's Specifications.

21 Install the drivebelt tensioner, tightening the bolts to the torque listed in this Chapter's Specifications.

22 Install the crankshaft pulley (see Section 9).

23 Connect the wiring harness connectors. Secure the wiring harnesses with the clamps.

24 Reinstall the remaining parts in the reverse order of removal.

25 Fill the crankcase with the recommended oil (see Chapter 1).

26 Reconnect the battery (see Chapter 5, Section 1).

27 Start the engine and check for leaks. Check all fluid levels.

8   Timing chain and sprockets - removal, inspection and installation

REMOVAL

▶ **Refer to illustration 8.5**

1   Disconnect the cable from the negative battery terminal (see Chapter 5, Section 1).

2   Set the engine to TDC number 1 (see Section 3).

3   Remove the valve cover (see Section 4).

4   Remove the engine front cover (see Section 7).

5   Rotate the crankshaft counterclockwise slightly to compress the chain tensioner. Install a 0.06 inch (1.5 mm) pin into the alignment holes (see illustration) and rotate the crankshaft slightly clockwise to secure the pin.

6   Remove the mounting bolts and the timing chain tensioner.

7   Remove the upper timing chain guide from between the camshaft sprockets.

8   Remove the camshaft timing chain guide and the tensioner arm (chain guide).

9   Remove the timing chain.

INSPECTION

10   Clean all parts with clean solvent. Dry with compressed air.

11   Inspect the chain tensioner for excessive wear or other damage. Be sure to drain all the oil out of the chain tensioner if it is to be reused.

12   Inspect the timing chain guides for deep grooves, excessive wear, or other damage.

13   Inspect the timing chain for excessive wear or damage.

14   Inspect the crankshaft and camshaft sprockets for chipped or broken teeth, excessive wear, or damage. Replace any component that is in questionable condition.

INSTALLATION

▶ **Refer to illustration 8.16**

15   If the crankshaft has been rotated during this procedure, make sure the number one piston is at the top of its stroke (TDC) (see Section 3). The timing mark (round dot) must align with the pointer on the crankshaft sprocket.

16   Set the alignment marks on the camshaft sprockets. Rotate the sprocket until the chain alignment dot (circular indentation) on the variable valve timing control actuator (VTC) is approximately at the 12 o'clock position. Rotate the sprocket until the exhaust camshaft sprocket chain alignment dot is in the same position. Position the TDC alignment marks on the sprockets opposite each other at the 9 and 3 o'clock positions (see illustration).

17   Install the timing chain around the crankshaft sprocket with the colored link on the chain aligned with the dot (circular indentation) on the crankshaft sprocket (see illustration 8.16).

18   Install the timing chain over the exhaust camshaft sprocket and the VTC actuator (intake camshaft sprocket) with the dots (circular indentations) aligned with each pair of colored chain links. The camshaft sprocket alignment links will be positioned in pairs on the timing chain.

19   Install the camshaft timing chain guide and the tensioner arm. Tighten the bolts to the torque listed in this Chapter's Specifications.

20   Install the timing chain tensioner. Tighten the bolts to the torque

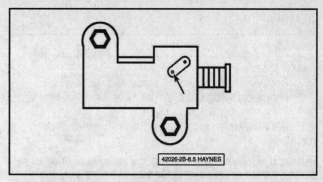

8.5 Align the hole on the lock with the hole in the tensioner, then insert a 0.06 inch (1.5 mm) pin or drill bit through both components to lock the tensioner

listed in this Chapter's Specifications.

21   Install the upper timing chain guide. Tighten the bolts to the torque listed in this Chapter's Specifications.

22   Remove the pin from the timing chain tensioner.

23   Install the valve cover (see Section 4).

24   Install the engine front cover (see Section 7).

25   The remainder of installation is the reverse of the removal Steps.

26   Reconnect the battery (see Chapter 5, Section 1).

27   Run the engine and check for oil or coolant leaks.

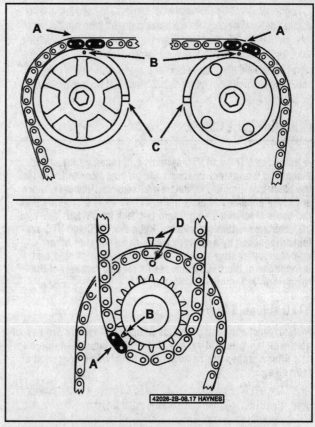

8.16 When the engine is at TDC compression for cylinder no. 1, the bright links (A) on the timing chain must align with the dots (B) on the sprockets. (C) are the camshaft sprocket TDC marks and (D) are the crankshaft sprocket TDC marks

9 Crankshaft pulley and front oil seal - removal and installation

REMOVAL

1 Disconnect the cable from the negative battery terminal (see Chapter 5, Section 1).

2 Raise the vehicle and support it securely on jackstands.

3 Remove the splash shield from below the engine compartment.

4 Remove the drivebelt (see Chapter 1).

5 Use a breaker bar and socket to remove the crankshaft pulley center bolt.

➡**Note: It will be necessary to lock the pulley in position using a strap wrench or special tool. Be sure to wrap a shop rag around the pulley before installing the strap wrench.**

6 Slide the pulley off the crankshaft.

7 Use a seal puller to remove the crankshaft front oil seal. A screwdriver may be used instead, if the tip is wrapped with tape to avoid scratching the crankshaft.

8 Clean the seal bore and check it for nicks or gouges. Also examine the area of the hub that rides in the seal for signs of abnormal wear or scoring. For many popular engines, a repair sleeve is available to restore a smooth finish to the sealing surface. Check with your auto parts store.

INSTALLATION

9 Coat the lip of the new seal with clean engine oil and drive it into the bore with a seal driver or a socket slightly smaller in diameter than the seal. The open side of the seal faces into the engine.

10 Using clean engine oil, lubricate the sealing surface of the hub. Install the crankshaft pulley and tighten the bolt to the torque listed in this Chapter's Specifications.

11 The remainder of the installation is the reverse of the removal procedure.

12 Reconnect the battery (see Chapter 5, Section 1).

10 i-VTEC system - description and component checks

GENERAL DESCRIPTION

1 The i-VTEC system on the DOHC engines is similar to the VTEC system used on the SOHC engine, but with the capability of being able to *continuously* change the intake cam timing - not just above a certain engine speed. Not only does the intake camshaft have two different lobe profiles like on the VTEC system, it is equipped with a Variable valve Timing Control (VTC) actuator, which alters the phasing of the camshaft to yield maximum potential power output for any given engine speed. For more information on the i-VTEC system, see Chapter 6.

COMPONENT CHECKS

➡**Note: The VTEC and VTC systems will require specialized diagnostic equipment to access the on-board computer to test the electrical circuits, actuators and sensors. However, there are some mechanical tests of the VTEC and VTC systems that the home mechanic can perform to check for obvious and simple problems within the system. Have the VTEC and VTC systems diagnosed by a dealer service department or other qualified automotive repair facility. Also, some checks and inspections of the VTEC components require removal of the rocker arm assembly (see Section 11).**

VTEC solenoid valve

➡**Note: Most common problems in the VTEC system are associated with the solenoid valve and its filter. Regular engine oil and filter changes are necessary for trouble-free operation of the valve.**

2 The VTEC solenoid valve is located on the rear of the cylinder head. The VTEC solenoid valve filter is mounted directly behind the VTEC solenoid valve (see Chapter 6).

3 Remove the VTEC solenoid valve (see Chapter 6) and check the filter for clogging. Clean and reinstall. A clogged filter screen is often the cause of system problems.

VTC oil control solenoid valve and strainer

▶ **Refer to illustration 10.5**

➡**Note: Most common problems in the VTC system are associated with the oil control solenoid valve and its strainer. Regular engine oil and filter changes are necessary for trouble-free operation of the valve.**

4 The VTC oil control solenoid valve is located in the cylinder head on the timing chain end of the engine. The VTC oil strainer is located on the right front corner of the cylinder head, near the intake manifold. The strainer cover is retained by two bolts; remove the bolts and cover and check the strainer for clogging, cleaning it as necessary.

5 Remove the VTC oil control solenoid valve (see Chapter 6) and check the strainer for clogging, cleaning it as necessary (if it's too dirty to clean, replace the valve). Look at the position of the valve through the drain port (the port closest to the solenoid portion of the valve); it

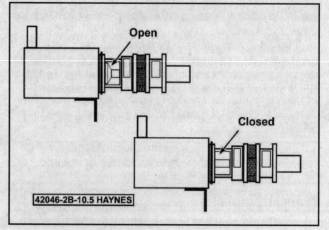

42046-2B-10.5 HAYNES

10.5 Check the position of the VTC solenoid valve - if it's stuck open, replace the valve. Be sure to check the condition of the O-ring, too. Note: *Some models have three strainer screens, while others only have one*

should be closed. If it's open (see illustration), the solenoid valve must be replaced.

Rocker arms

6 Position the number one piston at Top Dead Center (see Section 3). Remove the valve cover (see Section 4).

7 Press on the primary intake rocker arm for cylinder number 1 to see that it moves independently of the secondary intake rockers. Check the rockers for the other cylinders at their own TDC positions.

VTEC synchronizing assembly

8 Once the rocker arm assemblies have been removed and disassembled (see Section 11), separate the rocker arms and synchronizing components.

VTEC components:

  a) *Primary rocker arm*
  b) *Secondary rocker arm*
  c) *Synchronizing pistons*

9 Inspect the timing spring, making sure it's not broken or collapsed. Replace it if necessary.

10 Inspect all other parts (rocker arms and synchronizing pistons) for wear, galling, scoring or signs of overheating (bluish in color). Use your finger to push on the rocker arm pistons to check for smooth movement. Replace any parts, if necessary.

11 Reassemble each cylinder's components and wrap a rubber band around the rocker arms before trying to assemble them on the rocker shaft (see Section 11).

---

11 Camshafts and rocker arms - removal, inspection and installation

➡**Note: The camshaft holders, the camshafts and the rocker arm assembly are bolted to the cylinder head as one complete assembly. After the assembly is removed from the cylinder head, the different components can be separated on the workbench.**

REMOVAL

▶ **Refer to illustration 11.6**

1 Disconnect the cable from the negative battery terminal (see Chapter 5, Section 1).

2 Position the number one piston at Top Dead Center (see Section 3).

3 Remove the valve cover (see Section 4).

4 Remove the timing chain (see Section 7).

5 Loosen all the rocker arm adjusting screws.

6 Remove the camshaft holder bolts. Follow the correct sequence (see illustration).

7 Remove the upper timing chain guide.

8 Lift the camshaft holders and camshafts off the rocker arm assembly. Remove the rocker arm assembly. Install each bolt into the original-camshaft holder for correct reassembly.

※ CAUTION:

If the intake camshaft sprocket (VTC actuator) is removed from the camshaft and reused later, be sure to store the intake sprocket properly. First seal the advance holes and the retard hole on the number 1 camshaft journal with tape. Next, punch a hole in the tape over one of the advance holes and blow compressed air through the opening to release the lock. Double-check that the sprocket moves freely in the advance and retard positions.

INSPECTION

Rocker arm assembly

9 If you wish to disassemble and inspect the rocker arm assembly, (a good idea as long as you have them off), remove the retaining bolts and slip the rocker arms, springs, collars and bearing caps off the shafts. Mark the relationship of the shafts to the bearing caps and keep the components in order. They must be reassembled in the same positions they were removed from.

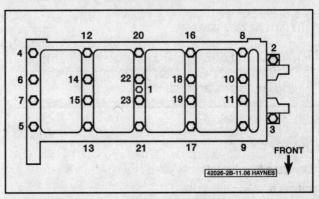

11.6 Camshaft holder bolt loosening sequence

※ CAUTION:

It is a good idea to bundle the intake rocker arms together with rubber bands.

10 Thoroughly clean the components and inspect them for wear and damage. Check the rocker arm faces that contact the camshaft and the rocker arm tips. Check the surfaces of the shafts that the rocker arms ride on, as well as the bearing surfaces inside the rocker arms, for scoring and excessive wear. Replace any parts that are damaged or excessively worn. Also, make sure the oil holes in the shafts are not plugged.

Camshaft endplay and runout

11 To check camshaft endplay:

  a) *Install the rocker arm assembly, the camshafts and the camshaft holders and follow the correct torque sequence (see Step 20).*

  b) *Mount a dial indicator on the cylinder head with the pointer resting on the camshaft nose.*

  c) *Using a large screwdriver as a lever at the opposite end, move the camshaft forward-and-backward and note the dial indicator reading.*

  d) *Compare the reading with the endplay listed in this Chapter's Specifications.*

  e) *If the indicated reading is excessive, either the camshaft or the cylinder head is worn. Replace parts as necessary.*

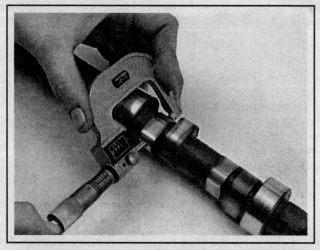

11.14 Measure the camshaft lobe height with a micrometer

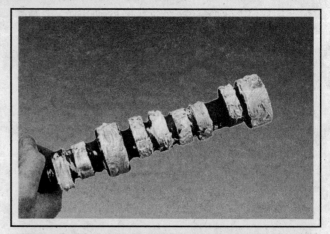

11.18 Be sure to apply camshaft installation lubricant to the lobes and bearing journals before installing the camshaft

12 To check camshaft runout:
  a) *With the camshafts on the workbench, support the camshaft with a pair of V-blocks and set up a dial indicator with the plunger resting against the center bearing journal on the camshaft.*
  b) *Rotate the camshaft and note the indicated runout.*
  c) *Compare the results to the camshaft runout listed in this Chapter's Specifications.*
  d) *If the indicated runout exceeds the specified runout limit, replace the camshaft.*

Camshaft lobe height

▶ **Refer to illustration 11.14**

13 Check the camshaft bearing journals and caps for scoring and signs of wear. If they are worn, replace the camshaft holders and rocker arm assembly with a new or rebuilt assembly.
14 Check the cam lobes for wear:

  a) *Check the toe and ramp areas of each cam lobe for score marks and uneven wear. Also check for flaking and pitting.*
  b) *If there's wear on the toe or the ramp, replace the camshaft, but first try to find the cause of the wear. Look for abrasive substances in the oil and inspect the oil pump and oil passages for blockage. Lobe wear is usually caused by inadequate lubrication or dirty oil.*
  c) *Using a micrometer, measure the cam lobe height (see illustration). If the lobe wear is indicated, replace the camshaft.*

15 If any of the conditions described above are noted, the cylinder head is probably getting insufficient lubrication or dirty oil. Make sure you track down the cause of this problem (low oil level, low oil pump capacity, clogged oil passage, etc.) before installing a new cylinder head, camshaft or rocker arm assembly.

INSTALLATION

▶ **Refer to illustrations 11.18 and 11.20**

16 Lubricate all components with engine assembly lubricant or engine oil and reassemble rocker arms onto the shafts.
17 When installing the rocker arms, shafts and springs, note the markings and the difference between the left and right side components.
18 Coat the camshaft lobes and journals with camshaft installation lubricant (see illustration).
19 Make sure the camshaft sprocket timing marks face up and set the camshafts in the rocker shaft holders.
20 Tighten the camshaft holder bolts a little at a time, in the proper sequence (see illustration) to the torque listed in this Chapter's Specifications.
21 The remainder of installation is the reverse of removal. Adjust the valve clearances (see Chapter 1).
22 Run the engine and check for oil leaks and proper operation.

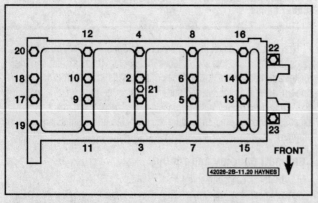

11.20 Camshaft holder bolt tightening sequence

12 Cylinder head - removal and installation

✳✳ WARNING:

Wait until the engine is completely cool before beginning this procedure.

REMOVAL

1   Relieve the fuel system pressure (see Chapter 4). Disconnect the cable from the negative battery terminal (see Chapter 5, Section 1).
2   Drain the cooling system (see Chapter 1).
3   Remove the drivebelt (see Chapter 1) and the drivebelt tensioner.
4   Remove the exhaust manifold (see Section 6).
5   Remove the intake manifold (see Section 5).
6   Remove the timing chain (see Section 8), camshafts and rocker arm assembly (see Section 11).
7   Label and disconnect the electrical connectors from the cylinder head that will interfere with removal. Use tape and mark each connector to insure correct reassembly. Also detach any coolant hoses that would interfere with removal.
8   Remove the cylinder head bolts and discard them, following the reverse of the tightening sequence (see illustration 12.16). Loosen the bolts in sequence 1/4-turn at a time.
9   Lift the cylinder head off the engine. If resistance is felt, place a wood block against the end and strike the wood block with a hammer. If the cylinder head is still stuck, carefully pry on a casting protrusion to break the gasket seal.

✳✳ CAUTION:

Do not pry between the cylinder head and block mating surfaces!

10 Store the cylinder head on wood blocks to prevent damage to the gasket sealing surfaces.
11 Remove the old cylinder head gasket.

INSTALLATION

▶ **Refer to illustration 12.16**

12 The mating surfaces of the cylinder head and block must be perfectly clean when the head is installed. Use a gasket scraper to remove all traces of carbon and old gasket material, then clean the mating surfaces with lacquer thinner or acetone. If there's oil on the mating sur-

faces when the cylinder head is installed, the gasket may not seal correctly and leaks may develop. When working on the engine block, cover the open areas of the engine with shop rags to keep debris out during repair and reassembly. Use a vacuum cleaner to remove any debris that falls into the cylinders.
13 Check the engine block and cylinder head mating surfaces for nicks, deep scratches and other damage. Have an automotive machine shop check the cylinder head for warpage.
14 Use a tap of the correct size to chase the threads in the cylinder head bolt holes. Dirt, corrosion, sealant and damaged threads will affect torque readings.
15 Make sure the new gasket is located on the dowels in the block.
16 Carefully position the cylinder head on the engine block without disturbing the gasket. Install new cylinder head bolts and following the recommended sequence (see illustration), tighten the bolts to the torque listed in this Chapter's Specifications.

➡**Note: The method used for the head bolt tightening procedure is referred to as "torque-angle" or "torque-to-yield" method. A special torque angle gauge (available at most auto parts stores) is available to attach to a breaker bar and socket for better accuracy during the tightening procedure.**

17 Install the rocker arm assembly and camshafts (see Section 11).
18 Install the timing chain (see Section 8).
19 Install the exhaust manifold (see Section 6).
20 Install the intake manifold (see Section 5).
21 The remaining installation steps are the reverse of removal.
22 Reconnect the battery (see Chapter 5, Section 1).
23 Change the engine oil and filter (Chapter 1), refill the cooling system, then start the engine and check carefully for oil and coolant leaks.

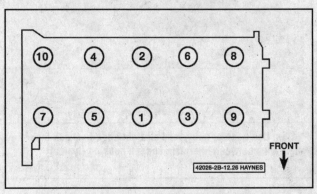

12.16 Cylinder head bolt tightening sequence

13 Oil pan - removal and installation

REMOVAL

1 Remove the subframe (see Chapter 10).
2 Drain the engine oil (see Chapter 1).
3 On manual transaxles, remove the bellhousing brace from the transaxle and the engine block (see Chapter 7A).
4 Remove the oil pan bolts, loosening them a little at a time in a criss-cross pattern.
5 Carefully remove the oil pan from the lower crankcase.

✳✳ CAUTION:

If the oil pan is difficult to separate from the lower crankcase, use a rubber mallet or a block of wood and a hammer to jar it loose. If that doesn't work, an oil pan gasket cutter may be available from your local auto parts store.

INSTALLATION

6 Using a gasket scraper, thoroughly clean all old gasket material from the lower crankcase and oil pan. Remove residue and oil film with a solvent such as acetone or lacquer thinner.
7 Apply a 2 mm bead of RTV sealant to the perimeter of the oil pan, inboard of the bolt holes.
8 Install the oil pan and bolts. Tighten the bolts a little at a time, in a criss-cross pattern beginning with the center bolts and working outward, to the torque listed in this Chapter's Specifications.
9 The remaining installation is the reverse of removal.
10 Change the oil filter and fill the crankcase with the specified engine oil (see Chapter 1).

14 Oil pump - removal, inspection and installation

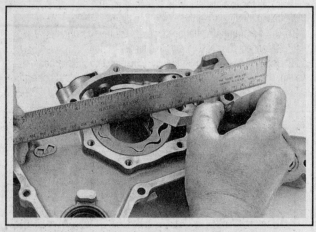

14.6a Use a feeler gauge and straight-edge to check the clearance between the rotors and the housing (typical)

REMOVAL

1 Set the engine to TDC number 1 (see Section 3).
2 Remove the oil pan (see Section 13).
3 Remove the balance shaft assembly (see Section 15).
4 Remove the oil pump housing mounting bolts. Loosen the oil pump mounting bolts one turn. Then, gradually and evenly, loosen each bolt in several steps.
5 When all bolts are loose, remove the bolts and oil pump.

INSPECTION

▶ **Refer to illustrations 14.6a, 14.6b and 14.6c**

6 Check the oil pump rotor-to-housing clearance, tooth tip clear-

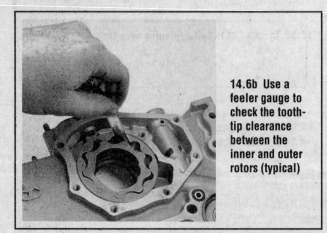

14.6b Use a feeler gauge to check the tooth-tip clearance between the inner and outer rotors (typical)

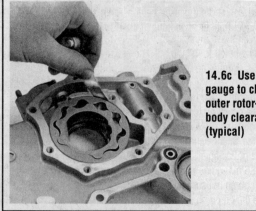

14.6c Use a feeler gauge to check the outer rotor-to-pump body clearance (typical)

ance and rotor-to-body clearance (see illustrations). Compare your measurements to the figures listed in this Chapter's Specifications. Replace the pump if any of the measurements exceed the specified limits.

7   Remove the pressure relief valve plug and extract the spring and pressure relief valve plunger from the pump housing. Check the spring for distortion and the relief valve plunger for scoring. Replace parts as necessary.

8   Install the pump rotors. Pack the spaces between the rotors with petroleum jelly (this will prime the pump).

9   Apply clean engine oil to the pump housing bolts, install the housing and tighten the bolts to the torque listed in this Chapter's Specifications. Install the oil pressure relief valve and spring assembly. Use a new sealing washer on the plug and tighten the plug to the torque listed in this Chapter's Specifications.

INSTALLATION

10   Install the oil pump housing bolts and tighten by hand until snug. Tighten the bolts gradually and evenly to the torque listed in this Chapter's Specifications.

11   Make sure the engine is still set to TDC number 1 (see Section 3).

12   Install the balance shaft assembly (see Section 15).

13   Refer to Chapter 1 and fill the engine with fresh engine oil. Install a new oil filter.

14   Reconnect the battery (See Chapter 5, Section 1).

15   Run the engine and make sure oil pressure comes up to normal quickly. If it doesn't, stop the engine and find out the cause. Severe engine damage can result from running an engine with insufficient oil pressure!

15 Balance shaft assembly and balance shafts - removal, inspection and installation

REMOVAL

1   Remove the oil pan (see Section 13).

2   Remove and discard the oil pump chain tensioner.

3   Remove the oil pump sprocket bolt. To prevent the sprocket from turning, insert a 6 mm guide pin into the maintenance hole directly behind the oil pump housing below the balance shaft assembly.

4   Remove the oil pump sprocket.

5   Remove the balance shaft assembly mounting bolts and separate the assembly from the lower engine block.

INSPECTION

6   Remove the balance shaft assembly mounting bolts and separate the upper and lower cases.

7   Clean all parts with clean solvent. Dry with compressed air.

8   Inspect the balance shaft chain for excessive wear or damage.

9   Inspect the balance shaft chain sprocket for chipped or broken teeth, excessive wear, or damage.

10   Inspect the balance shaft gears for chipping, scoring or missing teeth. Replace the assembly if necessary.

INSTALLATION

▶ **Refer to illustration 15.11 and 15.14**

11   Working on the two balance shafts, align the center punch mark on the rear (drive) balance shaft with the two marks on the front balance shaft (driven) (see illustration).

12   Apply engine oil to the threads and install the balance shaft case mounting bolts. Torque the bolts to the Specifications listed in this Chapter.

13   Install the oil pump housing (see Section 14).

14   Align the dowel pin on the rear balance shaft with the mark on the oil pump housing (see illustration).

15   Install the balance shaft assembly onto the lower engine block and install the bolts finger tight

16   Insert a 6 mm guide pin into the maintenance hole directly behind the oil pump housing (see Step 4).

17   Engage the oil pump sprocket with the chain, then with the balance shaft. Install the oil pump sprocket bolt. Tighten the bolt to the

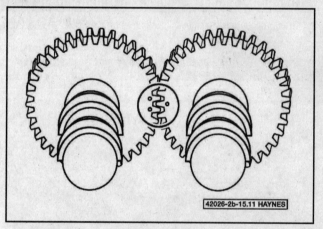

15.11 Align the center punch mark on the rear (drive) balance shaft with the two marks on the front balance shaft (driven)

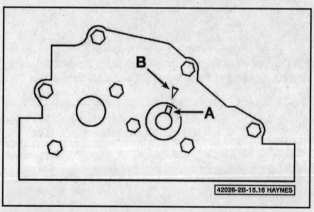

15.14 Align the dowel pin on the rear balance shaft (A) with the mark on the oil pump housing (B)

torque listed in this Chapter's Specifications.

18   Remove the guide pin.

19   Tighten the balancer assembly mounting bolts to the torque listed in this Chapter's Specifications.

20   Working with a new balance shaft chain tensioner, make sure the

tensioner holder clip is installed onto the tensioner and install the tensioner onto the lower engine block.

21 Tighten the balance shaft chain tensioner bolts to the torque listed in this Chapter's Specifications.

22 Remove the holder clip from the tensioner to apply tension to the chain.

23 Install the oil pan (see Section 13).

24 Reconnect the battery (see Chapter 5, Section 1).

25 Run the engine and make sure oil pressure comes up to normal quickly. If it doesn't, stop the engine and find out the cause. Severe engine damage can result from running an engine with insufficient oil pressure!

16 Flywheel/driveplate - removal and installation

This procedure is essentially the same as for the SOHC engine. Refer to Part A and follow the procedure outlined there. However, use the bolt torque listed in this Chapter's Specifications.

17 Rear main oil seal - replacement

This procedure is essentially the same as for the SOHC engine. Refer to Part A and follow the procedure outlined there.

18 Engine mounts - check and replacement

This procedure is essentially the same as for the SOHC engine. Refer to Part A and follow the procedure outlined there.

Specifications

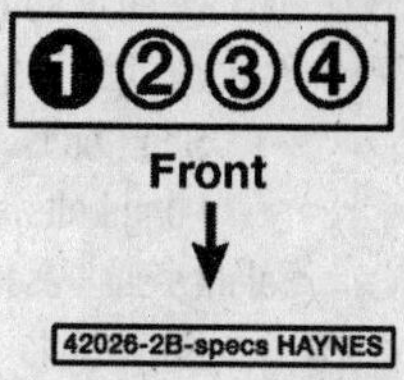

General

Firing order	1-3-4-2
Bore	
CR-V models	3.43 inches (87 mm)
Hatchback models	3.39 inches (86 mm)
Stroke	
CR-V models	3.90 inches (99 mm)
Hatchback models	3.39 inches (86 mm)
Displacement	
CR-V models	144 cubic inches (2.4 liters)
Hatchback models	122 cubic inches (2.0 liters)
Oil pressure	See Chapter 2C

❶ ② ③ ④

Front

↓

42026-2B-specs HAYNES

Cylinder locations for the DOHC engines

Valve adjustment

	See Chapter 1

Camshafts

Lobe height	
Intake	
Primary	1.3356 inches (33.925 mm)
Secondary	1.1668 inches (29.638 mm)
Exhaust	1.3422 inches (34.092 mm)
Endplay	0.002 to 0.008 inch (0.05 to 0.20 mm)
Runout	0.001 inch (0.03 mm)
Journal-to-bearing (oil) clearance	
Journal number 1	0.001 to 0.003 inch (0.030 to 0.069 mm)
Journal number 2, 3, 4, 5	0.002 to 0.004 inch (0.060 to 0.099 mm)

Oil pump

Rotor-to-cover clearance	
2002 and 2003 models	
Standard	0.001 to 0.003 inch (0.020 to 0.070 mm)
Service limit	0.005 inch maximum (0.12 mm)
2004 and later models	
Standard	0.0014 to 0.0027 inch (0.035 to 0.070 mm)
Service limit	0.005 inch maximum (0.12 mm)
Tooth tip clearance	
Standard	0.001 to 0.006 inch (0.02 to 0.16 mm)
Service limit	0.008 inch maximum (0.20 mm)
Outer rotor-to-pump body clearance	
Standard	0.006 to 0.008 inch (0.15 to 0.21 mm)
Service limit	0.009 inch maximum (0.23 mm)

Torque specifications	Ft-lbs (unless otherwise indicated)	Nm

➡ **Note: One foot-pound (ft-lb) of torque is equivalent to 12 inch-pounds (in-lbs) of torque. Torque values below approximately 15 ft-lbs are expressed in inch-pounds, since most foot-pound torque wrenches are not accurate at these smaller values.**

Balance shaft sprocket bolt	33	44
Balance shaft case bolts		
Short bolts	104 in-lbs	12
Long bolts	20	27
Balance shaft assembly-to-engine block bolts		
Short bolts	16	22
Long bolts	33	44
Camshaft sprocket bolts		
Intake camshaft sprocket (VTC actuator)	83	113
Exhaust camshaft sprocket	53	72
Camshaft holder bolts		
6 mm bolts	104 in-lbs	12
8 mm bolts	16	22
Crankshaft pulley bolt		
Step 1	36	49
Step 2	Tighten an additional 90-degrees	
Cylinder head bolts*		
Step 1	29	39
Step 2	Tighten an additional 90-degrees	
Step 3	Tighten an additional 90-degrees	
Step 4	Tighten an additional 90-degrees	
Drivebelt tensioner bolts	16	22
Driveplate bolts	54	74
Flywheel bolts		
2002 through 2005	90	122
2006	76	103
Exhaust manifold bolts/nuts	33	44
Exhaust manifold heat shield bolts	16	22
Exhaust pipe-to-manifold bolts	16	22
Engine front cover bolts	104 in-lbs	12
Intake manifold bolts	16	22
Oil pump housing bolts	104 in-lbs	12
Oil pump pressure relief valve plug	29	39
Oil pan bolts	104 in-lbs	12
Timing chain tensioner bolts	104 in-lbs	12
Timing chain guides		
Camshaft chain guide bolts	104 in-lbs	12
Tensioner arm bolt	16	22
Upper timing chain guide bolts	16	22
Valve cover nuts	104 in-lbs	12
Intake manifold cover bolts	104 in-lbs	12

Bolt(s) must be replaced.

2C

GENERAL ENGINE OVERHAUL PROCEDURES

Section

Reference to other Chapters

1 General information - engine overhaul

▶ **Refer to illustrations 1.1, 1.2, 1.3, 1.4, 1.5 and 1.6**

Included in this portion of Chapter 2 are general information and diagnostic testing procedures for determining the overall mechanical condition of your engine.

The information ranges from advice concerning preparation for an overhaul and the purchase of replacement parts and/or components to detailed, step-by-step procedures covering removal and installation.

The following Sections have been written to help you determine whether your engine needs to be overhauled and how to remove and install it once you've determined it needs to be rebuilt. For information concerning in-vehicle engine repair, see Chapter 2A or 2B.

The Specifications included in this Part are general in nature and include only those necessary for testing the oil pressure and checking the engine compression. Refer to Chapter 2A or 2B for additional engine Specifications.

It's not always easy to determine when, or if, an engine should be completely overhauled, because a number of factors must be considered.

High mileage is not necessarily an indication that an overhaul is needed, while low mileage doesn't preclude the need for an overhaul. Frequency of servicing is probably the most important consideration. An engine that's had regular and frequent oil and filter changes, as well as other required maintenance, will most likely give many thousands of miles of reliable service. Conversely, a neglected engine may require an overhaul very early in its service life.

Excessive oil consumption is an indication that piston rings, valve seals and/or valve guides are in need of attention. Make sure that oil leaks aren't responsible before deciding that the rings and/or guides are bad. Perform a cylinder compression check to determine the extent of the work required (see Section 3). Also check the vacuum readings under various conditions (see Section 4).

Check the oil pressure with a gauge installed in place of the oil pressure sending unit and compare it to this Chapter's Specifications (see Section 2). If it's extremely low, the bearings and/or oil pump are probably worn out.

Loss of power, rough running, knocking or metallic engine noises, excessive valve train noise and high fuel consumption rates may also point to the need for an overhaul, especially if they're all present at the same time. If a complete tune-up doesn't remedy the situation, major mechanical work is the only solution.

An engine overhaul involves restoring the internal parts to the specifications of a new engine. During an overhaul, the piston rings are replaced and the cylinder walls are reconditioned (rebored and/or honed) (see illustrations 1.1 and 1.2). If a rebore is done by an automotive machine shop, new oversize pistons will also be installed. The main bearings, connecting rod bearings and camshaft bearings are generally replaced with new ones and, if necessary, the crankshaft may

1.1 An engine block being bored. An engine rebuilder will use special machinery to recondition the cylinder bores

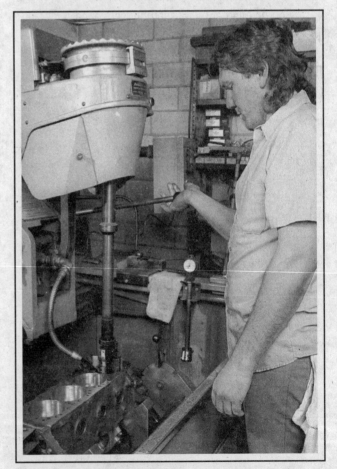

1.2 If the cylinders are bored, the machine shop will normally hone the engine on a machine like this

1.3 A crankshaft having a main bearing journal ground

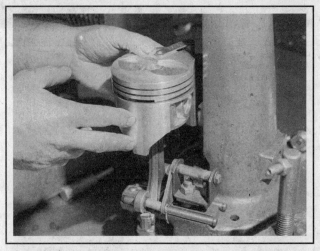

1.4 A machinist checks for a bent connecting rod, using specialized equipment

be reground to restore the journals (see illustration 1.3). Generally, the valves are serviced as well, since they're usually in less-than-perfect condition at this point. While the engine is being overhauled, other components, such as the distributor, starter and alternator, can be rebuilt as well. The end result should be similar to a new engine that will give many trouble free miles.

➡️Note: Critical cooling system components such as the hoses, drivebelts, thermostat and water pump should be replaced with new parts when an engine is overhauled. The radiator should be checked carefully to ensure that it isn't clogged or leaking (see Chapter 3). If you purchase a rebuilt engine or short block, some rebuilders will not warranty their engines unless the radiator has been professionally flushed. Also, we don't recommend overhauling the oil pump - always install a new one when an engine is rebuilt.

Overhauling the internal components on today's engines is a diffi-

cult and time-consuming task which requires a significant amount of specialty tools and is best left to a professional engine rebuilder (see illustrations 1.4, 1.5 and 1.6). A competent engine rebuilder will handle the inspection of your old parts and offer advice concerning the reconditioning or replacement of the original engine; never purchase parts or have machine work done on other components until the block has been thoroughly inspected by a professional machine shop. As a general rule, time is the primary cost of an overhaul, especially since the vehicle may be tied up for a minimum of two weeks or more. Be aware that some engine builders only have the capability to rebuild the engine you bring them while other rebuilders have a large inventory of rebuilt exchange engines in stock. Also be aware that many machine shops could take as much as two weeks time to completely rebuild your engine depending on shop workload. Sometimes it makes more sense to simply exchange your engine for another engine that's already rebuilt to save time.

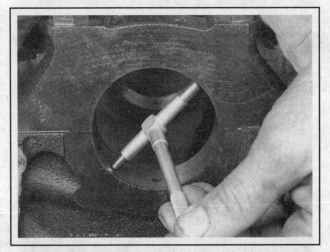

1.5 A bore gauge being used to check the main bearing bore

1.6 Uneven piston wear like this indicates a bent connecting rod

2 Oil pressure check

2.2 Location of the oil pressure sending unit on SOHC models

2.3 Remove the oil pressure sending unit and install an oil pressure gauge

▶ **Refer to illustrations 2.2 and 2.3**

1 Low engine oil pressure can be a sign of an engine in need of rebuilding. A "low oil pressure" indicator (often called an "idiot light") is not a test of the oiling system. Such indicators only come on when the oil pressure is dangerously low. Even a factory oil pressure gauge in the instrument panel is only a relative indication, although much better for driver information than a warning light. A better test is with a mechanical (not electrical) oil pressure gauge.

2 Locate the oil pressure sending unit on the engine block:

 a) *On Single Overhead Camshaft (SOHC) engines, the oil pressure sending unit is located above the oil filter on the rear of the engine block* (see illustration).

 b) *On Double Overhead Camshaft (DOHC) engines, the oil pressure sending unit is located above the oil filter on the front of the engine block.*

3 Unscrew and remove the oil pressure sending unit and screw in the hose for your oil pressure gauge (see illustration). If necessary, install an adapter fitting. Use Teflon tape or thread sealant on the threads of the adapter and/or the fitting on the end of your gauge's hose.

4 Connect an accurate tachometer to the engine, according to the tachometer manufacturer's instructions.

5 Check the oil pressure with the engine running (normal operating temperature) at the specified engine speed, and compare it to this Chapter's Specifications. If it's extremely low, the bearings and/or oil pump are probably worn out.

3 Cylinder compression check

▶ **Refer to illustration 3.6**

1 A compression check will tell you what mechanical condition the upper end of your engine (pistons, rings, valves, head gaskets) is in. Specifically, it can tell you if the compression is down due to leakage caused by worn piston rings, defective valves and seats or a blown head gasket.

➡**Note: The engine must be at normal operating temperature and the battery must be fully charged for this check.**

2 Begin by cleaning the area around the spark plugs before you remove them (compressed air should be used, if available). The idea is to prevent dirt from getting into the cylinders as the compression check is being done.

3 Remove all of the spark plugs from the engine (see Chapter 1).

4 Block the throttle wide open.

5 Disable the fuel system by removing the PGM-FI main relay number 2 (see Chapter 4, Section 2).

6 Install a compression gauge in the spark plug hole (see illustration).

3.6 Use a compression gauge with a threaded fitting for the spark plug hole, not the type that requires hand pressure to maintain the seal

7   Crank the engine over at least seven compression strokes and watch the gauge. The compression should build up quickly in a healthy engine. Low compression on the first stroke, followed by gradually increasing pressure on successive strokes, indicates worn piston rings. A low compression reading on the first stroke, which doesn't build up during successive strokes, indicates leaking valves or a blown head gasket (a cracked head could also be the cause). Deposits on the undersides of the valve heads can also cause low compression. Record the highest gauge reading obtained.

8   Repeat the procedure for the remaining cylinders and compare the results to this Chapter's Specifications.

9   Add some engine oil (about three squirts from a plunger-type oil can) to each cylinder, through the spark plug hole, and repeat the test.

10 If the compression increases after the oil is added, the piston rings are definitely worn. If the compression doesn't increase significantly, the leakage is occurring at the valves or head gasket. Leakage past the valves may be caused by burned valve seats and/or faces or warped, cracked or bent valves.

11 If two adjacent cylinders have equally low compression, there's a strong possibility that the head gasket between them is blown. The appearance of coolant in the combustion chambers or the crankcase would verify this condition.

12 If one cylinder is slightly lower than the others, and the engine has a slightly rough idle, a worn lobe on the camshaft could be the cause.

13 If the compression is unusually high, the combustion chambers are probably coated with carbon deposits. If that's the case, the cylinder head(s) should be removed and decarbonized.

14 If compression is way down or varies greatly between cylinders, it would be a good idea to have a leak-down test performed by an automotive repair shop. This test will pinpoint exactly where the leakage is occurring and how severe it is.

4   Vacuum gauge diagnostic checks

▶ **Refer to illustrations 4.4 and 4.6**

A vacuum gauge provides inexpensive but valuable information about what is going on in the engine. You can check for worn rings or cylinder walls, leaking head or intake manifold gaskets, restricted exhaust, stuck or burned valves, weak valve springs, improper ignition or valve timing and ignition problems.

Unfortunately, vacuum gauge readings are easy to misinterpret, so they should be used in conjunction with other tests to confirm the diagnosis.

Both the absolute readings and the rate of needle movement are important for accurate interpretation. Most gauges measure vacuum in inches of mercury (in-Hg). The following references to vacuum assume the diagnosis is being performed at sea level. As elevation increases (or atmospheric pressure decreases), the reading will decrease. For every 1,000 foot increase in elevation above approximately 2,000 feet, the gauge readings will decrease about one inch of mercury.

Connect the vacuum gauge directly to the intake manifold vacuum, not to ported (throttle body) vacuum (see illustration). Be sure no hoses are left disconnected during the test or false readings will result.

Before you begin the test, allow the engine to warm up completely. Block the wheels and set the parking brake. With the transaxle in Park, start the engine and allow it to run at normal idle speed.

✷✷ WARNING:

Keep your hands and the vacuum gauge clear of the fans.

4.4 A simple vacuum gauge can be handy in diagnosing engine condition and performance

Read the vacuum gauge; an average, healthy engine should normally produce about 17 to 22 in-Hg with a fairly steady needle (see illustration). Refer to the following vacuum gauge readings and what they indicate about the engine's condition:

1   A low steady reading usually indicates a leaking gasket between the intake manifold and cylinder head(s) or throttle body, a leaky vacuum hose, late ignition timing or incorrect camshaft timing. Check ignition timing with a timing light and eliminate all other possible causes, utilizing the tests provided in this Chapter before you remove the timing chain cover to check the timing marks.

2   If the reading is three to eight inches below normal and it fluctuates at that low reading, suspect an intake manifold gasket leak at an intake port or a faulty fuel injector.

3   If the needle has regular drops of about two-to-four inches at a steady rate, the valves are probably leaking. Perform a compression check or leak-down test to confirm this.

4   An irregular drop or down-flick of the needle can be caused by a sticking valve or an ignition misfire. Perform a compression check or leak-down test and read the spark plugs.

5   A rapid vibration of about four in-Hg vibration at idle combined with exhaust smoke indicates worn valve guides. Perform a leak-down test to confirm this. If the rapid vibration occurs with an increase in engine speed, check for a leaking intake manifold gasket or head gasket, weak valve springs, burned valves or ignition misfire.

6   A slight fluctuation, say one inch up and down, may mean igni-

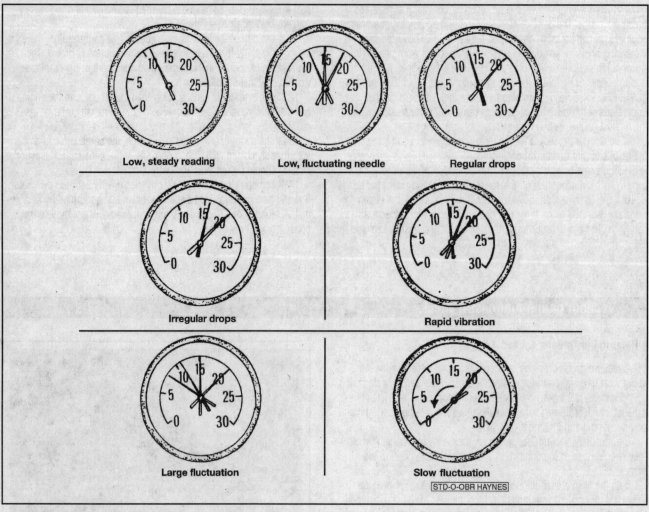

Low, steady reading Low, fluctuating needle Regular drops

Irregular drops Rapid vibration

Large fluctuation Slow fluctuation

STD-O-OBR HAYNES

4.6 Typical vacuum gauge readings

tion problems. Check all the usual tune-up items and, if necessary, run the engine on an ignition analyzer.

7   If there is a large fluctuation, perform a compression or leak-down test to look for a weak or dead cylinder or a blown head gasket.

8   If the needle moves slowly through a wide range, check for a clogged PCV system, incorrect idle fuel mixture, throttle body or intake manifold gasket leaks.

9   Check for a slow return after revving the engine by quickly snap-ping the throttle open until the engine reaches about 2,500 rpm and let it shut. Normally the reading should drop to near zero, rise above nor-mal idle reading (about 5 in-Hg over) and return to the previous idle reading. If the vacuum returns slowly and doesn't peak when the throt-tle is snapped shut, the rings may be worn. If there is a long delay, look for a restricted exhaust system (often the muffler or catalytic con-verter). An easy way to check this is to temporarily disconnect the exhaust ahead of the suspected part and redo the test.

5   Engine rebuilding alternatives

The do-it-yourselfer is faced with a number of options when pur-chasing a rebuilt engine. The major considerations are cost, warranty, parts availability and the time required for the rebuilder to complete the project. The decision to replace the engine block, piston/connecting rod assemblies and crankshaft depends on the final inspection results of your engine. Only then can you make a cost effective decision whether to have your engine overhauled or simply purchase an exchange engine for your vehicle.

Some of the rebuilding alternatives include:

Individual parts - If the inspection procedures reveal that the engine block and most engine components are in reusable condition, purchasing individual parts and having a rebuilder rebuild your engine may be the most economical alternative. The block, crankshaft and pis-ton/connecting rod assemblies should all be inspected carefully by a machine shop first.

Short block - A short block consists of an engine block with a crankshaft and piston/connecting rod assemblies already installed. All new bearings are incorporated and all clearances will be correct. The existing camshafts, valve train components, cylinder head and external parts can be bolted to the short block with little or no machine shop work necessary.

Long block - A long block consists of a short block plus an oil pump, oil pan, cylinder head, valve cover, camshaft and valve train components, timing sprockets and chain or gears and timing cover. All components are installed with new bearings, seals and gaskets incorporated throughout. The installation of manifolds and external parts is all that's necessary.

Low mileage used engines - Some companies now offer low mileage used engines which is a very cost effective way to get your vehicle up and running again. These engines often come from vehicles which have been in totaled in accidents or come from other countries which have a higher vehicle turn over rate. A low mileage used engine also usually has a similar warranty like the newly remanufactured engines.

Give careful thought to which alternative is best for you and discuss the situation with local automotive machine shops, auto parts dealers and experienced rebuilders before ordering or purchasing replacement parts.

6   Engine removal - methods and precautions

▶ **Refer to illustrations 6.1, 6.2, 6.3 and 6.4**

If you've decided that an engine must be removed for overhaul or major repair work, several preliminary steps should be taken. Read all removal and installation procedures carefully prior to committing to this job.

Locating a suitable place to work is extremely important. Adequate work space, along with storage space for the vehicle, will be needed. If a shop or garage isn't available, at the very least a flat, level, clean work surface made of concrete or asphalt is required.

Cleaning the engine compartment and engine before beginning the removal procedure will help keep tools clean and organized (see illustrations 6.1 and 6.2).

An engine hoist will also be necessary. Make sure the hoist is rated in excess of the combined weight of the engine and transaxle. Safety is of primary importance, considering the potential hazards involved in removing the engine from the vehicle.

A vehicle hoist will be necessary for engine removal, since on these models the subframe must be removed and the engine/transaxle assembly must be lowered from the engine compartment, then the vehicle is raised and the powertrain unit is removed from under the vehicle. If the necessary equipment is not available, the engine will have to be removed by a qualified automotive repair facility.

If you're a novice at engine removal, get at least one helper. One person cannot easily do all the things you need to do to remove a big heavy engine and transaxle assembly from the engine compartment. Also helpful is to seek advice and assistance from someone who's experienced in engine removal.

Plan the operation ahead of time. Arrange for or obtain all of the tools and equipment you'll need prior to beginning the job (see illustrations 6.3 and 6.4). Some of the equipment necessary to perform engine removal and installation safely and with relative ease are (in

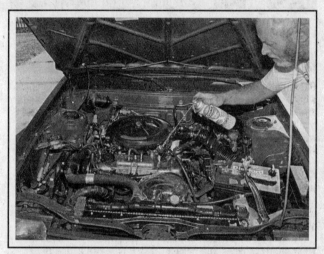

6.1 After tightly wrapping water-vulnerable components, use a spray cleaner on everything, with particular concentration on the greasiest areas, usually around the valve cover and lower edges of the block. If one section dries out, apply more cleaner

6.2 Depending on how dirty the engine is, let the cleaner soak in according to the directions and hose off the grime and cleaner. Get the rinse water down into every area you can get at; then dry important components with a hair dryer or paper towels

6.3 Get an engine stand sturdy enough to firmly support the engine while you're working on it. Stay away from three-wheeled models: they have a tendency to tip over more easily, so get a four-wheeled unit

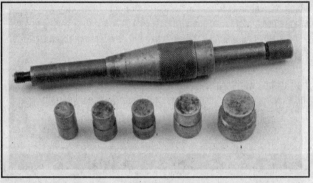

6.4 A clutch alignment tool is necessary if you plan to install a rebuilt engine mated to a manual transaxle

7   Engine - removal and installation

▶ **Refer to illustrations 7.10, 7.35 and 7.40**

✷ WARNING 1:

Gasoline is extremely flammable, so take extra precautions when you work on any part of the fuel system. Don't smoke or allow open flames or bare light bulbs near the work area, and don't work in a garage where a gas-type appliance (such as a water heater or clothes dryer) is present. Since gasoline is carcinogenic, wear fuel-resistant gloves when there's a possibility of being exposed to fuel, and, if you spill any fuel on your skin, rinse it off immediately with soap and water. Mop up any spills immediately and do not store fuel-soaked rags where they could ignite. The fuel system is under constant pressure, so, if any fuel lines are to be disconnected, the fuel pressure in the system must be relieved first (see Chapter 4 for more information). When you perform any kind of work on the fuel system, wear safety glasses and have a Class B type fire extinguisher on hand.

✷ WARNING 2:

The engine must be completely cool before beginning this procedure.

➡**Note 1: Engine removal on these models is a difficult job, especially for the do-it-yourself mechanic working at home.**

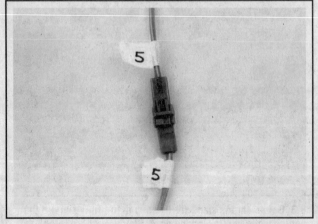

7.10 Label both ends of each wire and hose before disconnecting it

addition to a vehicle hoist and an engine hoist) a heavy duty floor jack (preferably fitted with a transaxle jack head adapter), complete sets of wrenches and sockets as described in the front of this manual, wooden blocks, plenty of rags and cleaning solvent for mopping up spilled oil, coolant and gasoline.

Plan for the vehicle to be out of use for quite a while. A machine shop can do the work that is beyond the scope of the home mechanic. Machine shops often have a busy schedule, so before removing the engine, consult the shop for an estimate of how long it will take to rebuild or repair the components that may need work.

Because of the vehicle's design, the manufacturer states that the engine and transaxle have to be removed as a unit from the bottom of the vehicle, not the top. With a floor jack and jackstands, the vehicle can't be raised high enough or supported safely enough for the engine/transaxle assembly to slide out from underneath. The manufacturer recommends that removal of the engine transaxle assembly only be performed with the use of a frame-contact type vehicle hoist.

➡**Note 2: Read through the entire Section before beginning this procedure. The engine and transaxle are removed as a unit from below, then separated outside the vehicle.**

➡**Note 3: Keep in mind that during this procedure you'll have to adjust the height of the vehicle with the vehicle hoist to perform certain operations.**

REMOVAL

1   Park the vehicle on a frame-contact type vehicle hoist, then engage the arms of the hoist with the jacking points of the vehicle. Raise the hoist arms until they contact the vehicle, but not so much that the wheels come off the ground.

2   Relieve the fuel system pressure (see Chapter 4).

3   Disconnect the cable from the negative battery terminal (see Chapter 5, Section 1).

4   Disconnect the fuel lines from the fuel rail (see Chapter 4).

5   Remove the engine splash shield (see Chapter 2A) and fender splash shields and the hood (see Chapter 11). Cover the fenders and cowl using special pads. An old bedspread or blanket will also work.

6   Remove the accessory drivebelt (see Chapter 1).

7   Remove the intake resonator and the air filter housing (see Chapter 4).

8   Disconnect the accelerator cable, the cruise control cable, if equipped, and bracket from the engine and position them aside (see Chapter 4).

9   Remove the battery and the battery tray (see Chapter 5).

10 Clearly label and disconnect all vacuum lines, emissions hoses, wiring harness connectors and fuel lines. Masking tape and/or a touch up paint applicator work well for marking items (see illustration). Take instant photos or sketch the locations of components and brackets.

11 Disconnect the electrical connectors from the PCM (see Chapter 6). Remove the retaining clip on the engine compartment firewall and remove the wiring harness.

7.35 Attach the chain to the cylinder head using the engine lifting bracket on the front of the cylinder head and the other end of the chain to a transaxle mounting bolt

7.40 The engine/transaxle assembly can be lowered onto the floor using the engine hoist. After the engine/transaxle assembly is resting safely on the floor, the vehicle can be raised using the vehicle hoist to access the powertrain assembly

12 Detach the positive cables and the electrical connectors from the engine compartment fuse/relay box (see Chapter 5) and the ground cable from the vehicle.

13 Detach any other electrical connectors between the engine and the vehicle.

14 Loosen the front wheel lug nuts, then raise the vehicle. Remove the front wheels and tires.

15 Detach the heat shields, exhaust brackets and the exhaust pipes from the exhaust manifold(s) (see Chapter 4).

16 Remove the alternator (see Chapter 5).

17 Remove the power steering pump without disconnecting the power steering hoses (see Chapter 10). Position it off to the side.

18 Remove the exhaust pipe from the exhaust manifold to the catalytic converter (see Chapter 6).

19 Drain the cooling system (see Chapter 1).

20 Drain the engine oil (see Chapter 1).

21 Detach the lower radiator hose from the engine (see Chapter 3).

22 Lower the vehicle and detach the heater hoses at the firewall (see Chapter 3).

23 Remove the upper radiator hose (see Chapter 3).

24 Remove the cooling fan(s) and shroud(s) (see Chapter 3).

25 Remove the radiator (see Chapter 3).

26 Remove the clutch release cylinder and hydraulic line (see Chapter 8).

27 Remove the starter (see Chapter 5).

28 On manual transaxle models, disconnect the shift cable and the select cable from the transaxle (see Chapter 7A). Also disconnect any wiring harness connectors from the transaxle.

29 On automatic transaxle models, disconnect the shift control cable from the transaxle (see Chapter 7B).

30 Disconnect the stabilizer bar links (see Chapter 10).

31 Disconnect the balljoints from the lower control arms (see Chapter 10).

32 Remove the driveaxles (see Chapter 8).

33 Unplug the downstream oxygen sensor electrical connectors.

34 Remove the air conditioning compressor without disconnecting the hoses (see Chapter 3). Use wire to tie the compressor to a bracket or other components mounted on the uni-body structure (not the subframe). It is not necessary to discharge the refrigerant from the system.

35 Attach a lifting sling or chain to the engine, using the lifting

brackets provided. At the transaxle end there should be a lifting eye built into the plate sandwiched between the transaxle and the engine (or secured to the transaxle by two of the mounting bolts). At the drive-belt end of the engine there should be a lifting eye in a bracket attached to the cylinder head. If not, lifting hooks may be available from your local auto parts store. (see illustration). Take up the slack until there is slight tension on the hoist. Remember that the transaxle end of the engine will be heavier, so position the chain on the hoist so it balances the engine and the transaxle level with the vehicle.

➡Note 1: **Depending on the design of the engine hoist, it may be helpful to position the hoist from the side of the vehicle, so that when the engine/transaxle assembly is lowered, it will fit between the legs of the hoist.**

➡Note 2: **The sling or chain must be long enough to allow the engine hoist to lower the engine/transaxle assembly to the ground, without letting the hoist arm contact the vehicle.**

36 Remove the front and rear engine/transaxle mount through-bolts (see Chapter 2A or 2B).

37 Remove the engine mount and the transaxle mount (see Chapter 2A or 2B).

38 Recheck to be sure nothing is still connecting the engine or transaxle to the vehicle. Disconnect and label anything still remaining.

39 Remove the subframe mounting bolts (see Chapter 10). Separate the subframe from the chassis and the engine/transaxle assembly.

40 Lower the engine/transaxle assembly (see illustration). Once the engine/transaxle assembly is on the floor, disconnect the engine lifting hoist and raise the vehicle until it clears the engine/transaxle assembly.

41 Reconnect the chain or sling to support the engine and transaxle.

42 Raise the engine/transaxle assembly, then support the engine with blocks of wood or another floor jack, while leaving the sling or chain attached. Support the transaxle with another floor jack, preferably one with a transaxle jack head adapter. At this point the transaxle can be unbolted and removed from the engine. Be very careful to ensure that the components are supported securely so they won't topple off their supports during disconnection.

43 Reconnect the lifting chain to the engine, then raise the engine and attach it to an engine stand.

INSTALLATION

44 Installation is the reverse of removal, noting the following points:

a) *Check the engine/transaxle mounts. If they're worn or damaged, replace them.*

b) *Attach the transaxle to the engine following the procedure described in Chapter 7.*

c) *When installing the subframe, tighten the subframe mounting bolts to the torque listed in Chapter 10 Specifications. Note the locations of the various size bolts.*

d) *Add coolant, oil, power steering and transaxle fluids as needed (see Chapter 1).*

e) *Reconnect the battery (see Chapter 5, Section 1).*

f) *Run the engine and check for proper operation and leaks. Shut off the engine and recheck fluid levels.*

8   Engine overhaul - disassembly sequence

1   It's much easier to remove the external components if the engine is mounted on a portable engine stand. A stand can often be rented quite cheaply from an equipment rental yard. Before the engine is mounted on a stand, the flywheel/driveplate should be removed from the engine.

2   If a stand isn't available, it's possible to remove the external engine components with it blocked up on the floor. Be extra careful not to tip or drop the engine when working without a stand.

3   If you're going to obtain a rebuilt engine, all external components must come off first, to be transferred to the replacement engine. These components include:

Clutch and flywheel (models with manual transaxle)
Driveplate (models with automatic transaxle)
Ignition system components
Emissions-related components
Engine mounts and mount brackets
Engine rear cover (spacer plate between flywheel/driveplate and engine block)

Intake/exhaust manifolds
Fuel injection components
Oil filter
Ignition coils and spark plugs
Thermostat and housing assembly
Water pump

➡**Note: When removing the external components from the engine, pay close attention to details that may be helpful or important during installation. Note the installed position of gaskets, seals, spacers, pins, brackets, washers, bolts and other small items.**

4   If you're going to obtain a short block (assembled engine block, crankshaft, pistons and connecting rods), then remove the timing chain or belt, cylinder head(s), oil pan, oil pump pick-up tube, oil pump and water pump from your engine so that you can turn in your old short block to the rebuilder as a core. See *Engine rebuilding alternatives* for additional information regarding the different possibilities to be considered.

9   Pistons and connecting rods - removal and installation

REMOVAL

▶ **Refer to illustrations 9.1, 9.3 and 9.4**

➡**Note: Prior to removing the piston/connecting rod assemblies, remove the cylinder head and oil pan (see Chapter 2A).**

1   Use your fingernail to feel if a ridge has formed at the upper limit of ring travel (about 1/4-inch down from the top of each cylinder). If carbon deposits or cylinder wear have produced ridges, they must be completely removed with a special tool (see illustration). Follow the manufacturer's instructions provided with the tool. Failure to remove the ridges before attempting to remove the piston/connecting rod assemblies may result in piston breakage.

2   After the cylinder ridges have been removed, turn the engine so the crankshaft is facing up.

3   Before the connecting rods are removed, check the connecting

9.1 Before you try to remove the pistons, use a ridge reamer to remove the raised material (ridge) from the top of the cylinders

9.3 Checking the connecting rod endplay (side clearance) (typical)

9.4 If the connecting rods and caps are not marked, use paint to mark the caps to the rods by cylinder number (for example, this would be the No. 4 connecting rod)

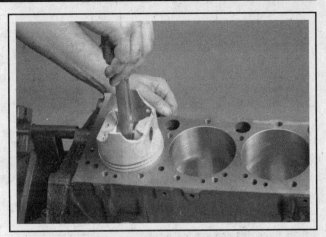

9.13 Install the piston ring into the cylinder then push it down into position using a piston so the ring will be square in the cylinder

rod endplay with feeler gauges. Slide them between the first connecting rod and the crankshaft throw until the play is removed (see illustration). Repeat this procedure for each connecting rod. The endplay is equal to the thickness of the feeler gauge(s). Check with an automotive machine shop for the endplay service limit (a typical endplay limit should measure between 0.005 to 0.015 inch [0.127 to 0.369 mm]). If the play exceeds the service limit, new connecting rods will be required. If new rods (or a new crankshaft) are installed, the endplay may fall under the minimum allowable. If it does, the rods will have to be machined to restore it. If necessary, consult an automotive machine shop for advice.

4   Check the connecting rods and caps for identification marks. If they aren't plainly marked, use paint or marker to clearly identify each rod and cap (1, 2, 3, etc., depending on the cylinder they're associated with) (see illustration).

5   Remove the connecting rod cap bolts from the number one connecting rod.

→ **Note 1: New connecting rod cap bolts must be used when reassembling the engine, but save the old bolts - they'll be required for the bearing oil clearance check during reassembly.**

→ **Note 2: It will be necessary to remove the main bearing bridge to access the connecting rod bearing caps. Refer to Section 10 and remove the main bearing bridge.**

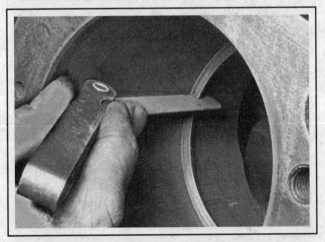

9.14 With the ring square in the cylinder, measure the ring end gap with a feeler gauge

6   Remove the number one connecting rod cap and bearing insert. Don't drop the bearing insert out of the cap.

7   Remove the bearing insert and push the connecting rod/piston assembly out through the top of the engine. Use a wooden dowel to push on the connecting rod. If resistance is felt, double-check to make sure that all of the ridge was removed from the cylinder.

8   Repeat the procedure for the remaining cylinders.

9   After removal, reassemble the connecting rod caps and bearing inserts in their respective connecting rods and install the cap bolts finger tight. Leaving the old bearing inserts in place until reassembly will help prevent the connecting rod bearing surfaces from being accidentally nicked or gouged.

10   The pistons and connecting rods are now ready for inspection and overhaul at an automotive machine shop.

PISTON RING INSTALLATION

▶ **Refer to illustrations 9.13, 9.14, 9.15, 9.19a, 9.19b and 9.22**

11   Before installing the new piston rings, the ring end gaps must be checked. It's assumed that the piston ring side clearance has been checked and verified correct.

12   Lay out the piston/connecting rod assemblies and the new ring sets so the ring sets will be matched with the same piston and cylinder during the end gap measurement and engine assembly.

13   Insert the top (number one) ring into the first cylinder and square it up with the cylinder walls by pushing it in with the top of the piston (see illustration). The ring should be near the bottom of the cylinder, at the lower limit of ring travel.

14   To measure the end gap, slip feeler gauges between the ends of the ring until a gauge equal to the gap width is found (see illustration). The feeler gauge should slide between the ring ends with a slight amount of drag. A typical ring gap should fall between 0.010 and 0.020 inch [0.25 to 0.50 mm] for compression rings and up to 0.030 inch [0.76 mm] for the oil ring steel rails. If the gap is larger or smaller than specified, double-check to make sure you have the correct rings before proceeding.

15   If the gap is too small, it must be enlarged or the ring ends may come in contact with each other during engine operation, which can cause serious damage to the engine. If necessary, increase the end

9.15 If the ring end gap is too small, clamp a file in a vise as shown and file the piston ring ends - be sure to remove all raised material

9.19a Installing the spacer/expander in the oil ring groove

9.19b DO NOT use a piston ring installation tool when installing the oil control side rails

gaps by filing the ring ends very carefully with a fine file. Mount the file in a vise equipped with soft jaws, slip the ring over the file with the ends contacting the file face and slowly move the ring to remove material from the ends. When performing this operation, file only by pushing the ring from the outside end of the file towards the vise (see illustration).

16 Excess end gap isn't critical unless it's greater than 0.040 inch (1.01 mm). Again, double-check to make sure you have the correct ring type.

17 Repeat the procedure for each ring that will be installed in the first cylinder and for each ring in the remaining cylinders. Remember to keep rings, pistons and cylinders matched up.

18 Once the ring end gaps have been checked/corrected, the rings can be installed on the pistons.

19 The oil control ring (lowest one on the piston) is usually installed first. It's composed of three separate components. Slip the spacer/expander into the groove (see illustration). If an anti-rotation tang is used, make sure it's inserted into the drilled hole in the ring groove. Next, install the upper side rail in the same manner (see illustration). Don't use a piston ring installation tool on the oil ring side rails, as they may be damaged. Instead, place one end of the side rail into the groove between the spacer/expander and the ring land, hold it firmly in place and slide a finger around the piston while pushing the rail into the groove. Finally, install the lower side rail.

20 After the three oil ring components have been installed, check to make sure that both the upper and lower side rails can be rotated smoothly inside the ring grooves.

21 The number two (middle) ring is installed next. It's usually stamped with a mark which must face up, toward the top of the piston. Do not mix up the top and middle rings, as they have different cross-sections.

➡**Note: Always follow the instructions printed on the ring package or box - different manufacturers may require different approaches.**

22 Use a piston ring installation tool and make sure the identification mark is facing the top of the piston, then slip the ring into the middle groove on the piston (see illustration). Don't expand the ring any more than necessary to slide it over the piston.

23 Install the number one (top) ring in the same manner. Make sure the mark is facing up. Be careful not to confuse the number one and

number two rings.

24 Repeat the procedure for the remaining pistons and rings.

INSTALLATION

25 Before installing the piston/connecting rod assemblies, the cylinder walls must be perfectly clean, the top edge of each cylinder bore must be chamfered, and the crankshaft must be in place.

26 Remove the cap from the end of the number one connecting rod (refer to the marks made during removal). Remove the original bearing inserts and wipe the bearing surfaces of the connecting rod and cap with a clean, lint-free cloth. They must be kept spotlessly clean.

Connecting rod bearing oil clearance check
▶ **Refer to illustrations 9.30, 9.35, 9.37 and 9.41**

27 Clean the back side of the new upper bearing insert, then lay it in place in the connecting rod.

28 Make sure the tab on the bearing fits into the recess in the rod. Don't hammer the bearing insert into place and be very careful not to nick or gouge the bearing face. Don't lubricate the bearing at this time.

9.22 Use a piston ring installation tool to install the number 2 and the number 1 (top) rings - be sure the directional mark on the piston ring(s) is facing toward the top of the piston

29 Clean the back side of the other bearing insert and install it in the rod cap. Again, make sure the tab on the bearing fits into the recess in the cap, and don't apply any lubricant. It's critically important that the mating surfaces of the bearing and connecting rod are perfectly clean and oil free when they're assembled.

30 Position the piston ring gaps at the specified intervals around the piston as shown (see illustration).

31 Lubricate the piston and rings with clean engine oil and attach a piston ring compressor to the piston. Leave the skirt protruding about 1/4-inch to guide the piston into the cylinder. The rings must be compressed until they're flush with the piston.

32 Rotate the crankshaft until the number one connecting rod journal is at BDC (bottom dead center) and apply a liberal coat of engine oil to the cylinder walls.

33 With the arrow on top of the piston facing the front (timing belt end or timing chain) of the engine, gently insert the piston/connecting rod assembly into the number one cylinder bore and rest the bottom edge of the ring compressor on the engine block. Install the pistons with the cavity mark(s) or arrow facing toward the timing belt or timing chain end of the engine.

34 Tap the top edge of the ring compressor to make sure it's contacting the block around its entire circumference.

35 Gently tap on the top of the piston with the end of a wooden or plastic hammer handle (see illustration) while guiding the end of the connecting rod into place on the crankshaft journal (a pair of wooden dowels would be helpful for this). The piston rings may try to pop out of the ring compressor just before entering the cylinder bore, so keep some downward pressure on the ring compressor. Work slowly, and if any resistance is felt as the piston enters the cylinder, stop immediately. Find out what's hanging up and fix it before proceeding. Do not, for any reason, force the piston into the cylinder - you might break a ring and/or the piston.

36 Once the piston/connecting rod assembly is installed, the connecting rod bearing oil clearance must be checked before the rod cap is permanently installed.

37 Cut a piece of the appropriate size Plastigage slightly shorter than the width of the connecting rod bearing and lay it in place on the number one connecting rod journal, parallel with the journal axis (see illustration).

38 Clean the connecting rod cap bearing face and install the rod

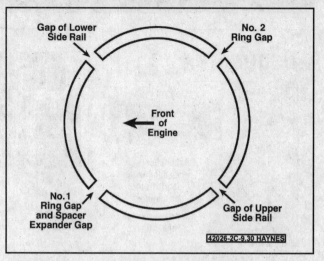

9.30 **Position the piston ring end gaps as shown**

cap. Make sure the mating mark on the cap is on the same side as the mark on the connecting rod (see illustration 9.4).

39 Install the old rod bolts, at this time, and tighten them to the torque listed in this Chapter's Specifications.

➡**Note: Use a thin-wall socket to avoid erroneous torque readings that can result if the socket is wedged between the rod cap and the bolt. If the socket tends to wedge itself between the fastener and the cap, lift up on it slightly until it no longer contacts the cap. DO NOT rotate the crankshaft at any time during this operation.**

40 Remove the fasteners and detach the rod cap, being very careful not to disturb the Plastigage. Discard the cap bolts at this time as they cannot be reused.

➡**Note: You MUST use new connecting rod bolts.**

41 Compare the width of the crushed Plastigage to the scale printed on the Plastigage envelope to obtain the oil clearance (see illustration). The connecting rod oil clearance is usually about 0.001 to 0.002 inch. Consult an automotive machine shop for the clearance specified for the rod bearings on your engine.

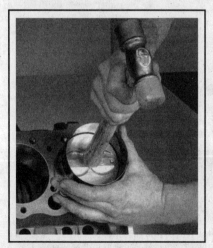

9.35 **Use a plastic or wooden hammer handle to push the piston into the cylinder**

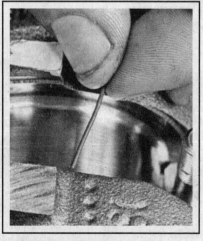

9.37 **Place Plastigage on each connecting rod bearing journal parallel to the crankshaft centerline**

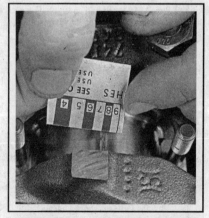

9.41 **Use the scale on the Plastigage package to determine the bearing oil clearance - be sure to measure the widest part of the Plastigage and use the correct scale; it comes with both standard and metric scales**

ENGINE BEARING ANALYSIS

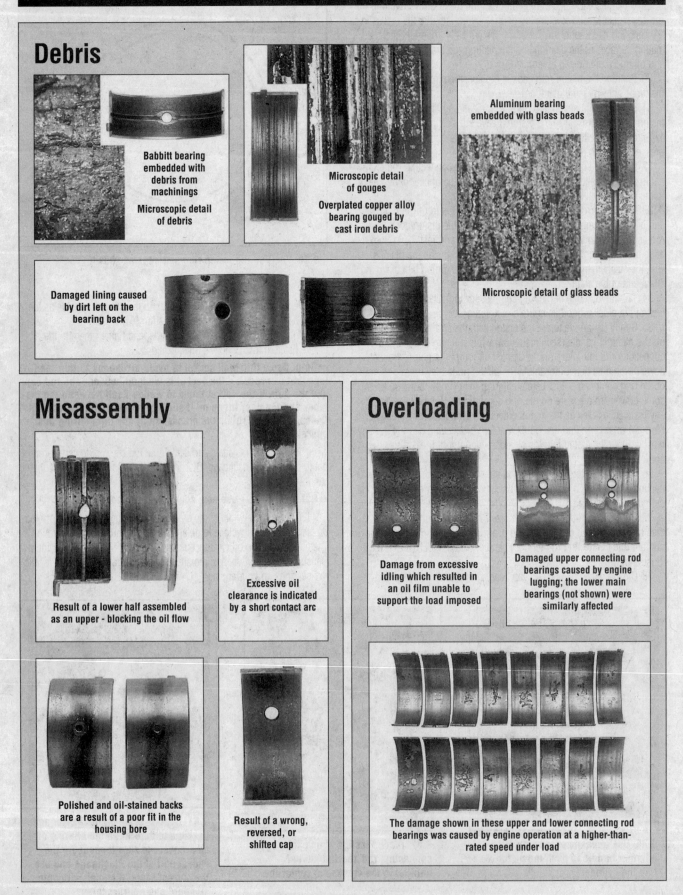

Debris

Babbitt bearing embedded with debris from machinings

Microscopic detail of debris

Microscopic detail of gouges

Overplated copper alloy bearing gouged by cast iron debris

Aluminum bearing embedded with glass beads

Microscopic detail of glass beads

Damaged lining caused by dirt left on the bearing back

Misassembly

Result of a lower half assembled as an upper - blocking the oil flow

Excessive oil clearance is indicated by a short contact arc

Polished and oil-stained backs are a result of a poor fit in the housing bore

Result of a wrong, reversed, or shifted cap

Overloading

Damage from excessive idling which resulted in an oil film unable to support the load imposed

Damaged upper connecting rod bearings caused by engine lugging; the lower main bearings (not shown) were similarly affected

The damage shown in these upper and lower connecting rod bearings was caused by engine operation at a higher-than-rated speed under load

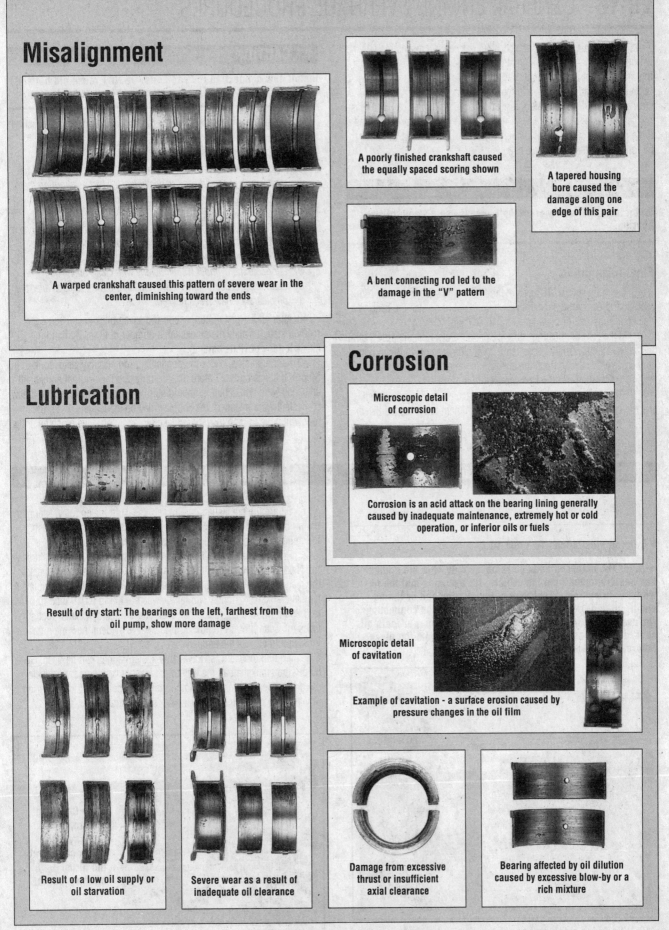

Misalignment

A poorly finished crankshaft caused the equally spaced scoring shown

A tapered housing bore caused the damage along one edge of this pair

A warped crankshaft caused this pattern of severe wear in the center, diminishing toward the ends

A bent connecting rod led to the damage in the "V" pattern

Corrosion

Microscopic detail of corrosion

Corrosion is an acid attack on the bearing lining generally caused by inadequate maintenance, extremely hot or cold operation, or inferior oils or fuels

Lubrication

Result of dry start: The bearings on the left, farthest from the oil pump, show more damage

Microscopic detail of cavitation

Example of cavitation - a surface erosion caused by pressure changes in the oil film

Result of a low oil supply or oil starvation

Severe wear as a result of inadequate oil clearance

Damage from excessive thrust or insufficient axial clearance

Bearing affected by oil dilution caused by excessive blow-by or a rich mixture

42 If the clearance is not as specified, the bearing inserts may be the wrong size (which means different ones will be required). Before deciding that different inserts are needed, make sure that no dirt or oil was between the bearing inserts and the connecting rod or cap when the clearance was measured. Also, recheck the journal diameter. If the Plastigage was wider at one end than the other, the journal may be tapered. If the clearance still exceeds the limit specified, the bearing will have to be replaced with an undersize bearing.

❋❋ CAUTION:

When installing a new crankshaft always use a standard size bearing.

Final installation

43 Carefully scrape all traces of the Plastigage material off the rod journal and/or bearing face. Be very careful not to scratch the bearing - use your fingernail or the edge of a plastic card.

44 Make sure the bearing faces are perfectly clean, then apply a uniform layer of clean moly-base grease or engine assembly lube to both of them. You'll have to push the piston into the cylinder to expose the face of the bearing insert in the connecting rod.

45 Slide the connecting rod back into place on the journal, install the rod cap, install the new bolts and tighten them to the torque listed in this Chapter's Specifications.

❋❋ CAUTION:

Install new connecting rod cap bolts. Do NOT reuse old bolts - they have stretched and cannot be reused (see Step 5).

46 Repeat the entire procedure for the remaining pistons/connecting rods.

47 The important points to remember are:

a) *Keep the back sides of the bearing inserts and the insides of the connecting rods and caps perfectly clean when assembling them.*

b) *Make sure you have the correct piston/rod assembly for each cylinder.*

c) *The arrow or mark on the piston must face the front (timing chain on four-cylinder engines or timing belt on V6 engines) of the engine.*

d) *Lubricate the cylinder walls liberally with clean oil.*

e) *Lubricate the bearing faces when installing the rod caps after the oil clearance has been checked.*

48 After all the piston/connecting rod assemblies have been correctly installed, rotate the crankshaft a number of times by hand to check for any obvious binding.

49 As a final step, check the connecting rod endplay, as described in Step 3. If it was correct before disassembly and the original crankshaft and rods were reinstalled, it should still be correct. If new rods or a new crankshaft were installed, the endplay may be inadequate. If so, the rods will have to be removed and taken to an automotive machine shop for resizing.

10 Crankshaft - removal and installation

REMOVAL

▶ **Refer to illustrations 10.1 and 10.3**

➡**Note: The crankshaft can be removed only after the engine has been removed from the vehicle. It's assumed that the flywheel or driveplate, crankshaft pulley, timing belt or timing chain, oil pan, oil pump body, oil filter and piston/connecting rod assemblies have already been removed. The rear main oil seal retainer must be unbolted and separated from the block before proceeding with crankshaft removal.**

1 Before the crankshaft is removed, measure the endplay. Mount a dial indicator with the indicator in line with the crankshaft and just touching the end of the crankshaft as shown (see illustration).

2 Pry the crankshaft all the way to the rear and zero the dial indicator. Next, pry the crankshaft to the front as far as possible and check the reading on the dial indicator. The distance traveled is the endplay. A typical crankshaft endplay will fall between 0.003 to 0.010 inch (0.076 to 0.254 mm). If it is greater than that, check the crankshaft thrust surfaces for wear after it's removed. If no wear is evident, new main bearings should correct the endplay.

3 If a dial indicator isn't available, feeler gauges can be used. Gently pry the crankshaft all the way to the front of the engine. Slip feeler gauges between the crankshaft and the front face of the thrust bearing or washer to determine the clearance (see illustration).

10.1 Checking crankshaft endplay with a dial indicator

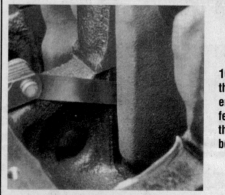

10.3 Checking the crankshaft endplay with feeler gauges at the thrust bearing journal

4   Loosen the main bearing bridge perimeter bolts and the main bearing inner bolts (DOHC engines) or the main bearing bridge bolts (SOHC engines) 1/4-turn at a time each, until they can be removed by hand. Follow the reverse of the tightening sequence (see illustrations 10.19a, 10.19b and 10.19c).

5   Remove the main bearing bridge. Try not to drop the bearing inserts if they come out with the main bearing bridge assembly.

6   Carefully lift the crankshaft out of the engine. It may be a good idea to have an assistant available, since the crankshaft is quite heavy and awkward to handle. With the bearing inserts in place inside the engine block and main bearing bridge, reinstall the bridge or lower crankcase onto the engine block and tighten the bolts finger tight.

INSTALLATION

7   Crankshaft installation is the first step in engine reassembly. It's assumed at this point that the engine block and crankshaft have been cleaned, inspected and repaired or reconditioned.

8   Position the engine block with the bottom facing up.

9   Remove the mounting bolts and lift off the lower crankcase or bearing bridge and main bearing caps.

10 If they're still in place, remove the original bearing inserts from the block and from the main bearing bridge. Wipe the bearing surfaces of the block and main bearing bridge saddle with a clean, lint-free cloth. They must be kept spotlessly clean. This is critical for determining the correct bearing oil clearance.

MAIN BEARING OIL CLEARANCE CHECK

▶ **Refer to illustrations 10.17, 10.19a, 10.19b, 10.19c and 10.21**

11 Without mixing them up, clean the back sides of the new upper main bearing inserts (with grooves and oil holes) and lay one in each main bearing saddle in the engine block. Each upper bearing (engine block) has an oil groove and oil hole in it.

❋❋ CAUTION:

The oil holes in the block must line up with the oil holes in the engine block inserts.

The thrust washer or thrust bearing insert must be installed in the correct location.

➡**Note: The thrust bearing on the SOHC engine is located on the engine block number 5 journal. The thrust washers on the DOHC engine are located on the 4th journal in the engine block (upper).**

Clean the back sides of the lower main bearing inserts and lay them in the corresponding location in the main bearing bridge. Make sure the tab on the bearing insert fits into the recess in the block or main bearing caps.

❋❋ CAUTION:

Do not hammer the bearing insert into place and don't nick or gouge the bearing faces. DO NOT apply any lubrication at this time.

12 Clean the faces of the bearing inserts in the block and the crankshaft main bearing journals with a clean, lint-free cloth.

13 Check or clean the oil holes in the crankshaft, as any dirt here can go only one way - straight through the new bearings.

14 Once you're certain the crankshaft is clean, carefully lay it in position in the cylinder block.

15 Before the crankshaft can be permanently installed, the main bearing oil clearance must be checked.

16 Cut several strips of the appropriate size of Plastigage. They must be slightly shorter than the width of the main bearing journal.

17 Place one piece on each crankshaft main bearing journal, parallel with the journal axis as shown (see illustration).

18 Clean the faces of the bearing inserts in the lower crankcase or main bearing caps. Hold the bearing inserts in place and install the lower crankcase or caps onto the crankshaft and cylinder block. DO NOT disturb the Plastigage.

19 Apply clean engine oil to all bolt threads prior to installation, then install all bolts finger-tight. Tighten the main bearing bridge bolts in the sequence shown (see illustrations) progressing in steps, to the torque listed in this Chapter's Specifications. DO NOT rotate the crankshaft at any time during this operation.

➡**Note: On DOHC engines, be sure to torque the main bearing bridge inner bolts first, followed by the perimeter bolts.**

10.17 Place the Plastigage onto the crankshaft bearing journal as shown

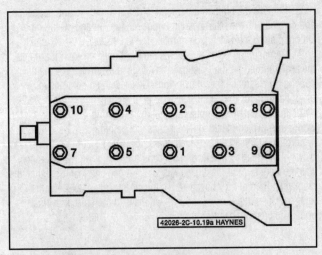

10.19a Main earing cap bolt tightening sequence on SOHC engines

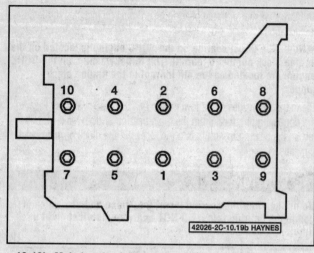

10.19b Main bearing bridge bolt tightening sequence on DOHC engines - inner bolts

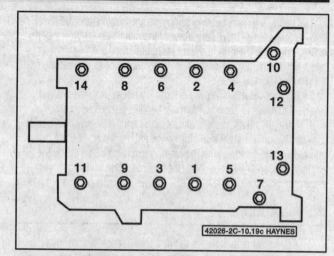

10.19c Main bearing bridge bolt tightening sequence on DOHC engines - outer bolts

10.21 Use the scale on the Plastigage package to determine the bearing oil clearance - be sure to measure the widest part of the Plastigage and use the correct scale; it comes with both standard and metric scales

20 Remove the bolts in the reverse order of the tightening sequence and carefully lift the main bearing bridge straight up and off the block. Do not disturb the Plastigage or rotate the crankshaft.

21 Compare the width of the crushed Plastigage on each journal to the scale printed on the Plastigage envelope to determine the main bearing oil clearance (see illustration). Check with an automotive machine shop for the oil clearance for your engine.

22 If the clearance is not as specified, the bearing inserts may be the wrong size (which means different ones will be required). Before deciding if different inserts are needed, make sure that no dirt or oil was between the bearing inserts and the caps or block when the clearance was measured. If the Plastigage was wider at one end than the other, the crankshaft journal may be tapered. If the clearance still exceeds the limit specified, the bearing insert(s) will have to be replaced with an undersize bearing insert(s).

※※ CAUTION:

When installing a new crankshaft always install a standard bearing insert set.

23 Carefully scrape all traces of the Plastigage material off the main bearing journals and/or the bearing insert faces. Be sure to remove all residue from the oil holes. Use your fingernail or the edge of a plastic card - don't nick or scratch the bearing faces.

FINAL INSTALLATION

24 Carefully lift the crankshaft out of the cylinder block.

25 Clean the bearing insert faces in the cylinder block, then apply a thin, uniform layer of moly-base grease or engine assembly lube to each of the bearing surfaces. Be sure to coat the thrust faces as well as the journal face of the thrust bearing.

26 Make sure the crankshaft journals are clean, then lay the crankshaft back in place in the cylinder block.

27 Clean the bearing insert faces and apply the same lubricant to them. Clean the engine block and the mating surface of the lower crankcase or the bearing caps thoroughly. The surfaces must be free of oil residue. Install the lower main bearing bridge.

28 Prior to installation, apply clean engine oil to all bolt threads, wiping off any excess, then install all bolts finger-tight.

29 Tighten the bolts to the torque listed in this Chapter's Specifications following the correct torque sequence (see illustrations 10.19a, 10.19b and 10.19c).

30 Recheck the crankshaft endplay with a feeler gauge or a dial indicator. The endplay should be correct if the crankshaft thrust faces aren't worn or damaged and if new bearings have been installed.

31 Rotate the crankshaft a number of times by hand to check for any obvious binding. It should rotate with a running torque of 50 in-lbs or less. If the running torque is too high, correct the problem at this time.

32 Install the new rear main oil seal (see Chapter 2A).

11 Engine overhaul - reassembly sequence

1 Before beginning engine reassembly, make sure you have all the necessary new parts, gaskets and seals as well as the following items on hand:

Common hand tools
A 1/2-inch drive torque wrench
New engine oil
Gasket sealant
Thread locking compound

2 If you obtained a short block it will be necessary to install the cylinder head, the oil pump and pick-up tube, the oil pan, the water pump, the timing belt or chain and timing cover, and the valve cover (see Chapter 2A or 2B). In order to save time and avoid problems, the external components must be installed in the following general order:

Thermostat and housing cover
Water pump
Intake and exhaust manifolds
Fuel injection components
Emission control components
Spark plug wires and spark plugs
Ignition coils or coil packs
Oil filter
Engine mounts and mount brackets
Clutch and flywheel (manual transaxle)
Driveplate (automatic transaxle)

12 Initial start-up and break-in after overhaul

✳✳ WARNING:

Have a fire extinguisher handy when starting the engine for the first time.

1 Once the engine has been installed in the vehicle, double-check the engine oil and coolant levels.

2 With the spark plugs out of the engine and the ignition system and fuel pump disabled, crank the engine until oil pressure registers on the gauge or the light goes out.

3 Install the spark plugs, hook up the plug wires and restore the ignition system and fuel pump functions.

4 Start the engine. It may take a few moments for the fuel system to build up pressure, but the engine should start without a great deal of effort.

5 After the engine starts, it should be allowed to warm up to normal operating temperature. While the engine is warming up, make a thorough check for fuel, oil and coolant leaks.

6 Shut the engine off and recheck the engine oil and coolant levels.

7 Drive the vehicle to an area with minimum traffic, accelerate from 30 to 50 mph, then allow the vehicle to slow to 30 mph with the throttle closed. Repeat the procedure 10 or 12 times. This will load the piston rings and cause them to seat properly against the cylinder walls. Check again for oil and coolant leaks.

8 Drive the vehicle gently for the first 500 miles (no sustained high speeds) and keep a constant check on the oil level. It is not unusual for an engine to use oil during the break-in period.

9 At approximately 500 to 600 miles, change the oil and filter.

10 For the next few hundred miles, drive the vehicle normally. Do not pamper it or abuse it.

11 After 2,000 miles, change the oil and filter again and consider the engine broken in.

GLOSSARY

B

Backlash - The amount of play between two parts. Usually refers to how much one gear can be moved back and forth without moving the gear with which it's meshed.

Bearing Caps - The caps held in place by nuts or bolts which, in turn, hold the bearing surface. This space is for lubricating oil to enter.

Bearing clearance - The amount of space left between shaft and bearing surface. This space is for lubricating oil to enter.

Bearing crush - The additional height which is purposely manufactured into each bearing half to ensure complete contact of the bearing back with the housing bore when the engine is assembled.

Bearing knock - The noise created by movement of a part in a loose or worn bearing.

Blueprinting - Dismantling an engine and reassembling it to EXACT specifications.

Bore - An engine cylinder, or any cylindrical hole; also used to describe the process of enlarging or accurately refinishing a hole with a cutting tool, as to bore an engine cylinder. The bore size is the diameter of the hole.

Boring - Renewing the cylinders by cutting them out to a specified size. A boring bar is used to make the cut.

Bottom end - A term which refers collectively to the engine block, crankshaft, main bearings and the big ends of the connecting rods.

Break-in - The period of operation between installation of new or rebuilt parts and time in which parts are worn to the correct fit. Driving at reduced and varying speed for a specified mileage to permit parts to wear to the correct fit.

Bushing - A one-piece sleeve placed in a bore to serve as a bearing surface for shaft, piston pin, etc. Usually replaceable.

C

Camshaft - The shaft in the engine, on which a series of lobes are located for operating the valve mechanisms. The camshaft is driven by gears or sprockets and a timing chain. Usually referred to simply as the cam.

Carbon - Hard, or soft, black deposits found in combustion chamber, on plugs, under rings, on and under valve heads.

Cast iron - An alloy of iron and more than two percent carbon, used for engine blocks and heads because it's relatively inexpensive and easy to mold into complex shapes.

Chamfer - To bevel across (or a bevel on) the sharp edge of an object.

Chase - To repair damaged threads with a tap or die.

Combustion chamber - The space between the piston and the cylinder head, with the piston at top dead center, in which air-fuel mixture is burned.

Compression ratio - The relationship between cylinder volume (clearance volume) when the piston is at top dead center and cylinder volume when the piston is at bottom dead center.

Connecting rod - The rod that connects the crank on the crankshaft with the piston. Sometimes called a con rod.

Connecting rod cap - The part of the connecting rod assembly that attaches the rod to the crankpin.

Core plug - Soft metal plug used to plug the casting holes for the coolant passages in the block.

Crankcase - The lower part of the engine in which the crankshaft rotates; includes the lower section of the cylinder block and the oil pan.

Crank kit - A reground or reconditioned crankshaft and new main and connecting rod bearings.

Crankpin - The part of a crankshaft to which a connecting rod is attached.

Crankshaft - The main rotating member, or shaft, running the length of the crankcase, with offset throws to which the connecting rods are attached; changes the reciprocating motion of the pistons into rotating motion.

Cylinder sleeve - A replaceable sleeve, or liner, pressed into the cylinder block to form the cylinder bore.

D

Deburring - Removing the burrs (rough edges or areas) from a bearing.

Deglazer - A tool, rotated by an electric motor, used to remove glaze from cylinder walls so a new set of rings will seat.

E

Endplay - The amount of lengthwise movement between two parts. As applied to a crankshaft, the distance that the crankshaft can move forward and back in the cylinder block.

F

Face - A machinist's term that refers to removing metal from the end of a shaft or the face of a larger part, such as a flywheel.

Fatigue - A breakdown of material through a large number of loading and unloading cycles. The first signs are cracks followed shortly by breaks.

Feeler gauge - A thin strip of hardened steel, ground to an exact thickness, used to check clearances between parts.

Free height - The unloaded length or height of a spring.

Freeplay - The looseness in a linkage, or an assembly of parts, between the initial application of force and actual movement. Usually perceived as slop or slight delay.

Freeze plug - See Core plug.

G

Gallery - A large passage in the block that forms a reservoir for engine oil pressure.

Glaze - The very smooth, glassy finish that develops on cylinder walls while an engine is in service.

H

Heli-Coil - A rethreading device used when threads are worn or damaged. The device is installed in a retapped hole to reduce the thread size to the original size.

I

Installed height - The spring's measured length or height, as installed on the cylinder head. Installed height is measured from the spring seat to the underside of the spring retainer.

J

Journal - The surface of a rotating shaft which turns in a bearing.

K

Keeper - The split lock that holds the valve spring retainer in position on the valve stem.

Key - A small piece of metal inserted into matching grooves machined into two parts fitted together - such as a gear pressed onto a shaft - which prevents slippage between the two parts.

Knock - The heavy metallic engine sound, produced in the combustion chamber as a result of abnormal combustion - usually detonation. Knock is usually caused by a loose or worn bearing. Also referred to as detonation, pinging and spark knock. Connecting rod or main bearing knocks are created by too much oil clearance or insufficient lubrication.

L

Lands - The portions of metal between the piston ring grooves.

Lapping the valves - Grinding a valve face and its seat together with lapping compound.

Lash - The amount of free motion in a gear train, between gears, or in a mechanical assembly, that occurs before movement can begin. Usually refers to the lash in a valve train.

Lifter - The part that rides against the cam to transfer motion to the rest of the valve train.

M

Machining - The process of using a machine to remove metal from a metal part.

Main bearings - The plain, or babbitt, bearings that support the crankshaft.

Main bearing caps - The cast iron caps, bolted to the bottom of the block, that support the main bearings.

O

O.D. - Outside diameter.

Oil gallery - A pipe or drilled passageway in the engine used to carry engine oil from one area to another.

Oil ring - The lower ring, or rings, of a piston; designed to prevent excessive amounts of oil from working up the cylinder walls and into the combustion chamber. Also called an oil-control ring.

Oil seal - A seal which keeps oil from leaking out of a compartment. Usually refers to a dynamic seal around a rotating shaft or other moving part.

O-ring - A type of sealing ring made of a special rubberlike material; in use, the O-ring is compressed into a groove to provide the sealing action.

Overhaul - To completely disassemble a unit, clean and inspect all parts, reassemble it with the original or new parts and make all adjustments necessary for proper operation.

P

Pilot bearing - A small bearing installed in the center of the flywheel (or the rear end of the crankshaft) to support the front end of the input shaft of the transmission.

Pip mark - A little dot or indentation which indicates the top side of a compression ring.

Piston - The cylindrical part, attached to the connecting rod, that moves up and down in the cylinder as the crankshaft rotates. When the fuel charge is fired, the piston transfers the force of the explosion to the connecting rod, then to the crankshaft.

Piston pin (or wrist pin) - The cylindrical and usually hollow steel pin that passes through the piston. The piston pin fastens the piston to the upper end of the connecting rod.

Piston ring - The split ring fitted to the groove in a piston. The ring contacts the sides of the ring groove and also rubs against the cylinder wall, thus sealing space between piston and wall. There are two types of rings: Compression rings seal the compression pressure in the combustion chamber; oil rings scrape excessive oil off the cylinder wall.

Piston ring groove - The slots or grooves cut in piston heads to hold piston rings in position.

Piston skirt - The portion of the piston below the rings and the piston pin hole.

Plastigage - A thin strip of plastic thread, available in different sizes, used for measuring clearances. For example, a strip of plastigage is laid across a bearing journal and mashed as parts are assembled. Then parts are disassembled and the width of the strip is measured to determine clearance between journal and bearing. Commonly used to measure crankshaft main-bearing and connecting rod bearing clearances.

Press-fit - A tight fit between two parts that requires pressure to force the parts together. Also referred to as drive, or force, fit.

Prussian blue - A blue pigment; in solution, useful in determining the area of contact between two surfaces. Prussian blue is commonly used to determine the width and location of the contact area between the valve face and the valve seat.

R

Race (bearing) - The inner or outer ring that provides a contact surface for balls or rollers in bearing.

Ream - To size, enlarge or smooth a hole by using a round cutting tool with fluted edges.

Ring job - The process of reconditioning the cylinders and installing new rings.

Runout - Wobble. The amount a shaft rotates out-of-true.

S

Saddle - The upper main bearing seat.

Scored - Scratched or grooved, as a cylinder wall may be scored by abrasive particles moved up and down by the piston rings.

Scuffing - A type of wear in which there's a transfer of material between parts moving against each other; shows up as pits or grooves in the mating surfaces.

Seat - The surface upon which another part rests or seats. For example, the valve seat is the matched surface upon which the valve face rests. Also used to refer to wearing into a good fit; for example, piston rings seat after a few miles of driving.

Short block - An engine block complete with crankshaft and piston and, usually, camshaft assemblies.

Static balance - The balance of an object while it's stationary.

Step - The wear on the lower portion of a ring land caused by excessive side and back-clearance. The height of the step indicates the ring's extra side clearance and the length of the step projecting from the back wall of the groove represents the ring's back clearance.

Stroke - The distance the piston moves when traveling from top dead center to bottom dead center, or from bottom dead center to top dead center.

Stud - A metal rod with threads on both ends.

T

Tang - A lip on the end of a plain bearing used to align the bearing during assembly.

Tap - To cut threads in a hole. Also refers to the fluted tool used to cut threads.

Taper - A gradual reduction in the width of a shaft or hole; in an engine cylinder, taper usually takes the form of uneven wear, more pronounced at the top than at the bottom.

Throws - The offset portions of the crankshaft to which the connecting rods are affixed.

Thrust bearing - The main bearing that has thrust faces to prevent excessive endplay, or forward and backward movement of the crankshaft.

Thrust washer - A bronze or hardened steel washer placed between two moving parts. The washer prevents longitudinal movement and provides a bearing surface for thrust surfaces of parts.

Tolerance - The amount of variation permitted from an exact size of measurement. Actual amount from smallest acceptable dimension to largest acceptable dimension.

U

Umbrella - An oil deflector placed near the valve tip to throw oil from the valve stem area.

Undercut - A machined groove below the normal surface.

Undersize bearings - Smaller diameter bearings used with re-ground crankshaft journals.

V

Valve grinding - Refacing a valve in a valve-refacing machine.

Valve train - The valve-operating mechanism of an engine; includes all components from the camshaft to the valve.

Vibration damper - A cylindrical weight attached to the front of the crankshaft to minimize torsional vibration (the twist-untwist actions of the crankshaft caused by the cylinder firing impulses). Also called a harmonic balancer.

W

Water jacket - The spaces around the cylinders, between the inner and outer shells of the cylinder block or head, through which coolant circulates.

Web - A supporting structure across a cavity.

Woodruff key - A key with a radiused backside (viewed from the side).

Specifications

General

Displacement
  SOHC models — 101.7 cubic inches (1.7 liters)
  DOHC models
    CR-V — 144 cubic inches (2.4 liters)
    Hatchback — 122 cubic inches (2.0 liters)

Bore and stroke
  SOHC models — 2.95 x 3.72 inches (75.0 x 94.4 mm)
  DOHC models
    CR-V — 3.43 x 3.90 inches (87.0 x 99.0 mm)
    Hatchback — 3.39 x 3.39 inches (86.0 x 86.0 mm)

Cylinder compression
  Minimum — 135 psi (930 kPa)
  Maximum variation between cylinders — 28 psi (200 kPa)

Oil pressure (engine at operating temperature)
  Idle speed — 10 psi (70 kPa)
  3,000 rpm — 44 psi (300 kPa)

Torque specifications

	Ft-lbs (unless otherwise indicated)	Nm
Subframe mounting bolts	See Chapter 10	
Connecting rod bearing cap nuts		
SOHC models	24	32
DOHC models		
Step 1	14	20
Step 2	Tighten an additional 90 degrees	
Main bearing bridge bolts (SOHC engine) (see illustration 10.19a)		
Step 1	18	25
Step 2	38	51
Main bearing bridge bolts (DOHC engine)		
Main bridge bolts (inner bolts) (see illustration 10.19b)		
Step 1	22	29
Step 2	Tighten an additional 56 degrees	
Perimeter bolts (outer bolts) (see illustration 10.19c)	16	22

* Bolt(s) must be replaced.

3

COOLING, HEATING AND AIR CONDITIONING SYSTEMS

1   General information

▶ **Refer to illustrations 1.1a, 1.1b and 1.2**

ENGINE COOLING SYSTEM

All vehicles covered by this manual employ a pressurized engine cooling system with thermostatically controlled coolant circulation (see illustrations). An impeller-type water pump mounted on the engine block pumps coolant through the engine. The coolant flows around each cylinder and toward the rear of the engine. Cast-in coolant passages direct coolant around the intake and exhaust ports, near the spark plug areas and in close proximity to the exhaust valve guides.

A wax-pellet type thermostat controls engine coolant temperature. During warm up, the closed thermostat prevents coolant from circulating through the radiator. As the engine nears normal operating temperature, the thermostat opens and allows hot coolant to travel through the radiator, where it's cooled before returning to the engine (see illustration).

The cooling system is sealed by a pressure-type radiator cap, which raises the boiling point of the coolant and increases the cooling efficiency of the radiator. If the system pressure exceeds the cap pressure relief value, the excess pressure in the system forces the spring-loaded valve inside the cap off its seat and allows the coolant to escape through the overflow tube into a coolant reservoir. When the system cools the excess coolant is automatically drawn from the reservoir back into the radiator.

The coolant reservoir serves as both the point at which fresh coolant is added to the cooling system to maintain the proper fluid level and as a holding tank for overheated coolant.

This type of cooling system is known as a closed design because coolant that escapes past the pressure cap is saved and reused.

ENGINE COOLING FANS

These models are equipped with two electric cooling fans; a radiator fan and a condenser fan. The fans are controlled by relays, a fan switch and the computer. The fan switch on the coupes and sedans (SOHC engines) is located in the thermostat housing next to the ECT sensor. The fan switch on the CR-V and hatchbacks (DOHC engines) is located in the bottom of the radiator. The radiator fan relay and a condenser fan relay are located in the engine compartment fuse and relay box. The computer uses the information from the fan switch, the air conditioning system and the on-board driveability computer to control the application of the two fans.

1.1a   Cooling, heating and air conditioning components underhood - sedan model shown

1	Air conditioning line service port (high side)	5	Coolant reservoir
2	Air conditioning line service port (low side)	6	Thermostat
3	Radiator (below radiator support cover)	7	Fuse and relay box
4	Radiator cap		

1.1b Cooling, heating and air conditioning components underhood - CR-V model shown

1	Fuse and relay box	4	Coolant reservoir
2	Radiator cap	5	Air conditioning line service port (high side)
3	Thermostat (in housing below intake manifold)	6	Air conditioning line service port (low side)

HEATING SYSTEM

The heating system consists of a blower fan and heater core located in the heater box, the hoses connecting the heater core to the engine cooling system and the heater/air conditioning control head on the dashboard. Hot engine coolant is circulated through the heater core. When the heater mode is activated, a flap door opens to expose the heater box to the passenger compartment. A fan switch on the control head activates the blower motor, which forces air through the core, heating the air.

AIR CONDITIONING SYSTEM

The air conditioning system consists of a condenser mounted in front of the radiator, an evaporator mounted adjacent to the heater core, a compressor mounted on the engine, a receiver-drier next to the condenser and the plumbing connecting all of the above components.

A blower fan forces the warmer air of the passenger compartment through the evaporator core (sort of a radiator-in-reverse), transferring the heat from the air to the refrigerant. The liquid refrigerant boils off into low pressure vapor, taking the heat with it when it leaves the evaporator.

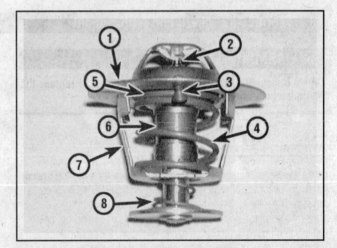

1.2 Typical thermostat for coupes and sedans

1	Flange	5	Valve seat
2	Piston	6	Valve
3	Jiggle valve	7	Frame
4	Main coil spring	8	Secondary coil spring

2 Antifreeze - general information

▶ Refer to illustration 2.5

❄ WARNING:

Do not allow antifreeze to come in contact with your skin or painted surfaces of the vehicle. Rinse off spills immediately with plenty of water. Antifreeze is highly toxic if ingested. Never leave antifreeze lying around in an open container or in puddles on the floor; children and pets are attracted by its sweet smell and may drink it. Check with local authorities about disposing of used antifreeze. Many communities have collection centers which will see that antifreeze is disposed of safely. Never dump used antifreeze on the ground or pour it into drains.

❄ CAUTION:

Use only Honda All Season Antifreeze Type 2 in these vehicles. This antifreeze is already pre-mixed therefore no additional water is necessary. Also, consult the owners manual for additional information.

The cooling system should be filled with a water/ethylene glycol based antifreeze solution, which will prevent freezing down to at least -20-degrees F (even lower in cold climates). It also provides protection against corrosion and increases the coolant boiling point. The engines in these vehicles have aluminum heads. The manufacturer recommends that the correct type of coolant be used and strongly urges that coolant types not be mixed (see the Chapter 1 Specifications).

Drain, flush and refill the cooling system at least every other year (see Chapter 1). The use of antifreeze solutions for periods of longer than two years is likely to cause damage and encourage the formation of rust and scale in the system.

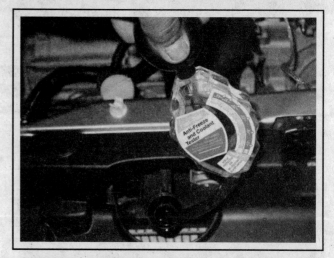

2.5 Use a hydrometer (available at most auto parts stores) to test the condition of your coolant

Before adding antifreeze to the system, inspect all hose connections. Antifreeze can leak through very minute openings.

The exact mixture of antifreeze to water, which you should use, depends on the relative weather conditions. The mixture should contain at least 50-percent antifreeze, but should never contain more than 70-percent antifreeze. Consult the mixture ratio chart on the container before adding coolant.

Hydrometers are available at most auto parts stores to test the coolant (see illustration). Use antifreeze that meets factory specifications for engines with aluminum heads (see Chapter 1).

3 Thermostat - check and replacement

❄ WARNING:

Do not remove the radiator cap, drain the coolant or replace the thermostat until the engine has cooled completely.

❄ CAUTION:

Don't drive the vehicle without a thermostat. The computer may stay in open loop and emissions and fuel economy will suffer.

CHECK

1   Before assuming the thermostat is to blame for a cooling system problem, check the coolant level, drivebelt tension (DOHC engines only, see Chapter 1) and temperature gauge operation.

2   If the engine seems to be taking a long time to warm up, based on heater output or temperature gauge operation, the thermostat is probably stuck open. Replace the thermostat with a new one.

3   If the engine runs hot, use your hand to check the temperature of the lower radiator hose. If the hose isn't hot, but the engine is, the thermostat is probably stuck closed, preventing the coolant inside the engine from escaping to the radiator. Replace the thermostat.

4   If the lower radiator hose is hot, it means that the coolant is flowing and the thermostat is open. Consult the *Troubleshooting* Section at the front of this manual for cooling system diagnosis.

REPLACEMENT

▶ Refer to illustrations 3.9, 3.11, 3.12 and 3.14

5   Disconnect the cable from the negative battery terminal (see Chapter 5, Section 1).

6   Drain the cooling system (see Chapter 1). If the coolant is relatively new or in good condition, save it and reuse it. Read the **Warning** in Section 2.

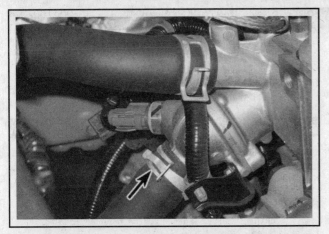

3.9 Use pliers to squeeze the coolant hose clamp and slide the clamp away from the thermostat housing

3.11 Location of the thermostat housing cover bolts - sedan model shown

7   If you're working on a CR-V or Hatchback, access to the thermostat is from the underside of the engine compartment. Raise the front of the vehicle and support it securely on jackstands, then remove the under-vehicle splash shield.

8   Follow the lower radiator hose to the engine to locate the thermostat housing cover.

9   Loosen the hose clamp, then detach the hose from the fitting (see illustration). If it's stuck, grasp it near the end with a pair of adjustable pliers and twist it to break the seal, then pull it off. If the hose is old or deteriorated, cut it off and install a new one.

10   If the outer surface of the large fitting that mates with the hose is deteriorated (corroded, pitted, etc.) it may be damaged further by hose removal. If it is, the thermostat housing cover will have to be replaced.

11   Remove the thermostat cover bolts (see illustration) and detach the housing cover. If the cover is stuck, tap it with a soft-face hammer to jar it loose. Be prepared for some coolant to spill as the gasket seal is broken.

12   On coupe and sedan models, note how it's installed - with the jiggle pin up - then remove the thermostat (see illustration).

→**Note: The thermostat on CR-V and hatchback models is an integral component of the thermostat cover. Replace the cover and thermostat as one complete assembly.**

13   Remove all traces of old gasket material and/or sealant from the

housing and cover.

14   On coupe and sedan models, install a new rubber seal over the thermostat (see illustration). Make sure the cutout is aligned correctly with the jiggle valve.

→**Note: On CR-V and hatchback models, install a new O-ring into the housing before installation.**

15   On coupe and sedan models, install the new thermostat in the housing without using sealant. Make sure the jiggle pin is at the top and the spring end is directed into the engine (see illustration 3.12).

→**Note: On CR-V and hatchback models, the thermostat is positioned correctly by the manufacturer. Make sure the mating surfaces on the thermostat housing are perfectly clean to insure a tight seal before installing the thermostat assembly.**

16   Install the thermostat housing (coupes and sedans) or the thermostat assembly (CR-V and hatchbacks) and bolts. Tighten the bolts to the torque listed in this Chapter's Specifications.

17   Reattach the hose and tighten the hose clamp securely. Install all components that were removed for access.

18   Refill the cooling system (see Chapter 1).

19   Reconnect the battery (see Chapter 5, Section 1).

20   Start the engine and allow it to reach normal operating temperature, then check for leaks and proper thermostat operation (as described in Steps 2 through 4).

3.12 Note the location of the jiggle valve - sedan model shown

3.14 Install a new rubber seal over the thermostat

4   Engine cooling fans and switch - check and replacement

✳✳ WARNING:

To avoid possible injury or damage, DO NOT operate the engine with a damaged fan. Do not attempt to repair fan blades - replace a damaged fan with a new one.

➡ Note: All air conditioned models have two complete fan circuits - one for the condenser fan and one for the radiator fan. The following procedures apply to both.

CHECK

▶ Refer to illustrations 4.1, 4.3 and 4.5

1   If the engine is overheating and the cooling fan is not coming on when the engine temperature rises to an excessive level, unplug the fan motor electrical connector (see illustration) and then connect the motor directly to the battery with a fused jumper cable on terminal B. Use

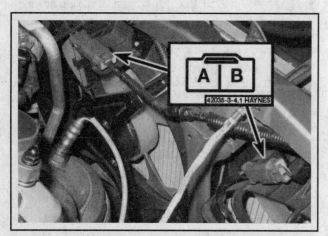

4.1 To test either fan motor, disconnect the electrical connector and use jumper wires to connect the fan directly to the battery (B) and ground (A) - if the fan still doesn't work, replace the motor

4.3 Location of the radiator fan relay (A) and the condenser fan relay (B) (sedan model shown, others similar)

another jumper wire to ground terminal A. If the fan motor doesn't come on, replace the motor. These models are equipped with a separate fan for the condenser. If the radiator fan motor checks out okay, be sure to test the condenser fan motor.

✳✳ CAUTION:

Do not apply battery power to the harness side of the connector.

2   If the radiator fan motor is okay, but it isn't coming on when the engine gets hot, the fan relay(s) might be defective.
3   Locate the fan relays in the engine compartment fuse/relay box (see illustration).
4   Test the relay (see Chapter 12).
5   If the relays are okay, test the radiator fan switch. The radiator fan switch controls the operation of the fans according to the various temperatures of the engine. The fan switch on the coupes and sedans (SOHC engines) is located in the thermostat housing (see illustration). The fan switch on the CR-V and hatchbacks (DOHC engines) is located in the bottom of the radiator. The fan switch activates the fan at 199-degrees F (93 degrees C). The switch can be tested with an ohmmeter. Below 199-degrees there should be no continuity across the terminals of the switch; above 199-degrees there should be continuity.
6   If the relay(s) and the fan switch are okay, check all wiring and connections to the fan motors.

REPLACEMENT

Cooling fans

▶ Refer to illustrations 4.9a, 4.9b, 4.9c, 4.11, 4.14a, 4.14b, 4.15, 4.16a, 4.16b, 4.17 and 4.18

✳✳ WARNING:

Wait until the engine is completely cool before beginning this procedure.

7   Disconnect the cable from the negative battery terminal (see Chapter 5, Section 1).

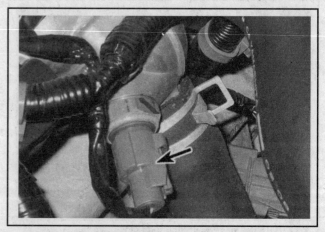

4.5 Location of the radiator fan switch on sedan and coupe models

8   Set the parking brake and block the rear wheels to prevent the vehicle from rolling. Raise the front of the vehicle and support it securely with jackstands. Remove the lower splash pan, if equipped, from under the radiator (see Chapter 2A).

9   Remove the radiator support cover (see illustrations).

➡**Note: The radiator support cover on the coupes and sedans is an integral component of the front bumper cover (see Chapter 11). The radiator support cover on the CR-V and the hatchback can be removed separately by removing the pushpins. If you're just removing the radiator fan (not the condenser fan) from a sedan or coupe model, the bumper cover does not have to be removed.**

10   Drain the cooling system (see Chapter 1). If the coolant is relatively new or in good condition, save it and reuse it. Read the **Warning** in Section 2.

11   Remove the wiring harness clamp and position the harness off to the side (see illustration).

12   Remove the battery, the battery tray and the position the wiring harness off to the side (see Chapter 5).

13   Disconnect the fan wiring connectors (see illustration 4.1).

14   Remove the upper and lower radiator hoses. Loosen the hose clamps, then detach the radiator hoses from the fittings (see illustrations). If they're stuck, grasp each hose near the end with a pair of slip-

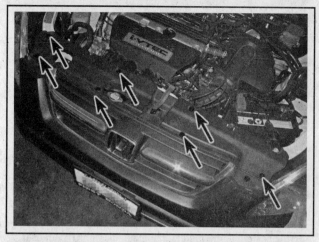

4.9a Location of the radiator cover mounting fasteners on a CR-V model

joint pliers and twist it to break the seal, then pull it off - be careful not to damage the radiator fittings! If the hoses are old or deteriorated, cut them off and install new ones. Also disconnect the small hose to the coolant reservoir.

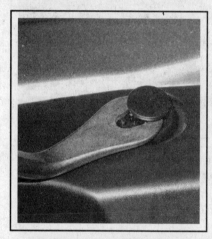

4.9b Lift up on the center release pin . . .

4.9c . . . and remove the push-pin from the body

4.11 Disconnect the radiator fan electrical connector and remove the harness from the fan shroud bracket

4.14a Use pliers to squeeze the hose clamps and slide the clamps off the inlet housing (neck) of the radiator and the coolant housing on the engine block

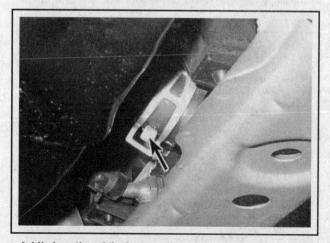

4.14b Location of the lower radiator hose clamp

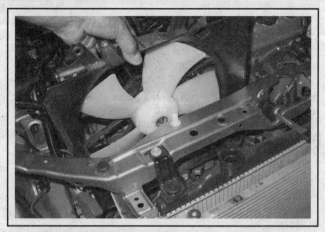

4.16a Lift the radiator fan from the engine compartment - sedan model shown

4.15 Location of the radiator fan mounting bolts (condenser fan similar)

4.16b Remove the radiator and condenser brackets, angle the radiator and condenser toward the front of the vehicle and lift the condenser fan out of the engine compartment (sedan model shown)

➡Note: If you're just removing the radiator fan (not the condenser fan) from a sedan or coupe model, the lower radiator hose does not have to be removed.

15 Unbolt the engine cooling fan(s) from the radiator at the top (see illustration).

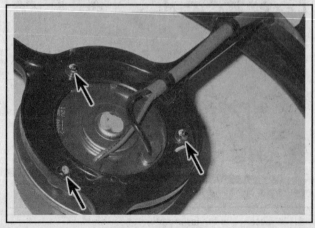

4.18 Location of the engine cooling fan motor mounting screws

4.17 To remove the fan, unscrew the nut in the center, then pull the fan blade from the motor shaft

16 Carefully lift the fan out of the engine compartment (see illustration).

➡Note: It will be necessary to remove the radiator and condenser brackets (see Section 6) and tilt the radiator back slightly to remove one of the cooling fans (see illustration).

17 To detach the fan from the motor, remove the motor shaft nut (see illustration).

18 To detach the fan motor from the shroud, remove the mounting screws (see illustration).

19 Installation is the reverse of removal.

20 Refill the cooling system (see Chapter 1).

21 Reconnect the battery (see Chapter 5, Section 1).

Cooling fan switch

※ WARNING:

Wait until the engine is completely cool before beginning this procedure.

22 Drain the cooling system (see Chapter 1).

23 If you're working on a CR-V or Hatchback, raise the front of the vehicle and support it securely on jackstands. Remove the splash

shield from under the engine compartment.

24 Disconnect the electrical connector, then unscrew the switch from the thermostat housing cover (coupe and sedan models) or from the radiator (CR-V and Hatchback models).

25 Installation is the reverse of removal, noting the following points:

a) *Use a new sealing ring when installing the switch.*
b) *Refill the cooling system (see Chapter 1).*
c) *Start the engine and allow it to reach normal operating temperature, then verify proper operation of the fans.*

5   Coolant reservoir - removal and installation

▶ **Refer to illustration 5.2**

❄ **WARNING:**

Wait until the engine is completely cool before beginning this procedure.

1   Disconnect the reservoir hose from the radiator filler neck. Plug the hose to prevent leakage.

2   Remove the mounting bolts (see illustration).

3   Lift the reservoir out of the engine compartment.

4   Clean out the tank with soapy water and a brush to remove any deposits inside. Inspect the reservoir carefully for cracks. If you find a crack, replace the reservoir.

5   Installation is the reverse of removal.

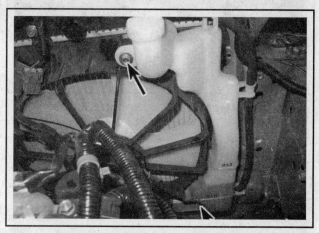

5.2 **Location of the coolant reservoir mounting bolts**

6   Radiator - removal and installation

❄ **WARNING:**

Wait until the engine is completely cool before beginning this procedure.

REMOVAL

▶ **Refer to illustrations 6.5a, 6.5b, 6.6 and 6.10**

1   Disconnect the cable from the negative battery terminal (see Chapter 5, Section 1).

2   Set the parking brake and block the rear wheels. Raise the front of the vehicle and support it securely on jackstands. Remove the splash shield beneath the radiator.

3   Drain the cooling system (see Chapter 1). If the coolant is relatively new or in good condition, save it and reuse it. Read the **Warning** in Section 2.

4   Remove the engine cooling fans (see Section 4).

5   On automatic transaxle models, disconnect the transaxle fluid cooling lines from the radiator lower tank (see illustrations).

6.5a **Location of the transaxle cooling hose on the right side of the radiator . . .**

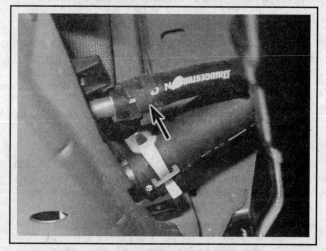

6.5b **. . . and the left side of the radiator**

6.6 Location of the radiator mounting bracket bolts

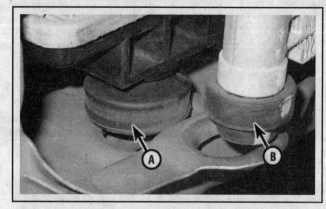

6.10 Location of the radiator (A) and the condenser (B) rubber mounts

6 Remove the radiator brackets (see illustration).

7 Carefully lift out the radiator. Don't spill coolant on the vehicle or scratch the paint.

8 Inspect the radiator for leaks and damage. If it needs repair, have a radiator shop or dealer service department perform the work as special techniques are required.

9 Bugs and dirt can be removed from the radiator by spraying with a garden hose nozzle from the back side. The radiator should be flushed out with a garden hose before reinstallation.

10 Check the radiator mounts (see illustration) for deterioration and replace if necessary.

INSTALLATION

11 Installation is the reverse of the removal procedure. Guide the radiator into the mounts until they seat properly.

12 Tighten the radiator bracket bolts to the torque listed in this Chapter's Specifications.

13 After installation, fill the cooling system with the proper mixture of antifreeze and water (see Chapter 1).

14 Reconnect the battery (see Chapter 5, Section 1).

15 Start the engine and check for leaks. Allow the engine to reach normal operating temperature, indicated by the upper radiator hose becoming hot. Recheck the coolant level and add more if required.

16 Check and add transaxle fluid as needed.

7 Water pump - check

▶ **Refer to illustration 7.3**

1 A failure in the water pump can cause serious engine damage due to overheating.

2 If a failure occurs in the pump seal, coolant will leak from the engine timing belt cover (coupe and sedan models) or the weep hole on the water pump (CR-V and hatchback models).

➡**Note: The water pump on coupes and sedans is mounted behind the timing belt cover and on CR-V and hatchback models, on the engine front cover.**

3 Water pumps are equipped with weep or vent holes. It is possible to check the water pump weep hole using a flashlight. If a failure occurs in the pump seal, coolant will leak from the hole. Use the flashlight to find the vent hole on the water pump and check for leaks.

➡**Note: Because the water pump is mounted behind the timing belt cover on coupes and sedans, use a flashlight and mirror to check the weep hole (see illustration).**

4 If the water pump shaft bearings fail, there may be a howling sound near the water pump while it's running. With the engine off, shaft wear can be felt if the water pump pulley is rocked up-and-down. Don't mistake drivebelt slippage, which causes a squealing sound, for water pump bearing failure.

➡**Note: Because the water pump is mounted behind the timing belt cover on coupes and sedans, it will not be possible to check the water pump shaft and/or pulley without removing the timing belt.**

5 A quick water pump performance check is to put the heater on. If the pump is failing, it won't be able to efficiently circulate hot water all the way to the heater core as it should.

6 Even a pump that exhibits no outward signs of a problem, such as noise or leakage, can still be due for replacement. Removal for close examination is the only sure way to tell. Sometimes the fins on the back of the impeller can corrode to the point that cooling efficiency is hampered.

7.3 On SOHC engines the weep hole passage is at the left rear of the engine, just behind the timing belt cover. In this photo the weep hole (arrow) is visible in the mirror

8 Water pump - replacement

✳✳ WARNING:

Wait until the engine is completely cool before beginning this procedure.

1 Disconnect the cable from the negative battery terminal (see Chapter 5, Section 1).

2 Drain the cooling system (see Chapter 1). If the coolant is relatively new or in good condition, save it and reuse it. Read the **Warning** in Section 2.

3 Remove the drivebelts (see Chapter 1).

COUPE AND SEDAN MODELS

▶ **Refer to illustration 8.5**

4 Remove the timing belt (see Chapter 2A), and remove the timing

8.5 The water pump on coupes and sedans is mounted on the front of the engine and is driven by the timing belt

belt tensioner.

5 Remove the bolts (see illustration) and detach the water pump from the engine. Check the impeller on the backside for evidence of corrosion or missing fins.

CR-V AND HATCHBACK MODELS

6 Remove the crankshaft pulley (see Chapter 2B).

7 Remove the bolts and detach the water pump from the engine. Check the impeller on the backside for evidence of corrosion or missing fins.

ALL MODELS

8 Clean the bolt threads and the threaded holes in the engine to remove corrosion and sealant.

9 Compare the new pump to the old one to make sure they're identical.

10 Remove all traces of old gasket sealant and O-ring from the engine.

11 Clean the engine and new water pump mating surfaces with lacquer thinner or acetone.

12 Apply a thin layer of RTV sealant to the O-ring groove of the new pump, then carefully set a new O-ring in the groove.

13 Carefully attach the pump to the engine and thread the bolts into the holes finger tight. Use a small amount of RTV sealant on the bolt threads, and make sure that the dowel pins are in their original locations.

14 Tighten the bolts to the torque listed in this Chapter's Specifications in 1/4-turn increments. Don't overtighten the bolts or the pump may be distorted.

15 Reinstall all parts removed for access to the pump.

16 Refill the cooling system and check the drivebelt tension (see Chapter 1).

17 Reconnect the battery (see Chapter 5, Section 1). Run the engine and check for leaks.

9 Coolant temperature sending unit - check and replacement

✳✳ WARNING:

Wait until the engine is completely cool before beginning this procedure.

CHECK

▶ **Refer to illustration 9.1**

1 The coolant temperature indicator system consists of a warning light or a temperature gauge on the dash and a coolant temperature sending unit mounted on the engine (see illustration). On the models covered by this manual, the Engine Coolant Temperature (ECT) sensor, which is an information sensor for the Powertrain Control Module (PCM), also functions as the coolant temperature sending unit.

2 If an overheating indication occurs, check the coolant level in the

9.1 The engine coolant temperature (ECT) sensor is mounted on the coolant passage housing on coupes and sedans

system and then make sure all connectors in the wiring harness between the sending unit and the indicator light or gauge are tight.

3   When the ignition switch is turned to START and the starter motor is turning, the indicator light (if equipped) should come on. This doesn't mean the engine is overheated; it just means that the bulb is good.

4   If the light doesn't come on when the ignition key is turned to START, the bulb might be burned out, the ignition switch might be faulty or the circuit might be open.

5   As soon as the engine starts, the indicator light should go out and remain off, unless the engine overheats. If the light doesn't go out, the wire between the sending unit and the light could be grounded; the sending unit might be defective (in which case a trouble code will most likely have been set, turning on the CHECK ENGINE light on the instrument panel - see Chapter 6); or the ignition switch might be faulty (see Chapter 12). Check the coolant to make sure it's correctly mixed; plain water, with no antifreeze, or coolant that's mainly water, might have too low a boiling point to activate the sending unit (see Chapter 1).

REPLACEMENT

6   See Chapter 6.

---

10   Blower motor power transistor and blower motor - replacement

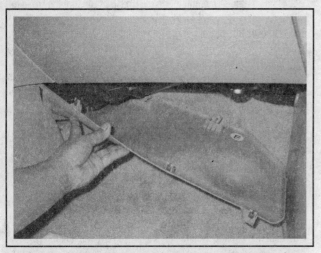

10.2 To remove the lower dash panel, pull it straight down to disengage the retaining clips

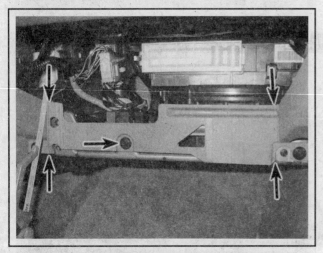

10.4 Cut off the piece of plastic where indicated using a hacksaw or panel cutters, remove the single retaining bolt and discard the plastic (the absence of this plastic cross brace will not weaken the structure) - coupes and sedans shown, CR-V and hatchbacks similar)

✳✳ WARNING:

The models covered by this manual are equipped with Supplemental Restraint systems (SRS), more commonly known as airbags. Always disable the airbag system before working in the vicinity of any airbag system component to avoid the possibility of accidental deployment of the airbag, which could cause personal injury (see Chapter 12).

BLOWER MOTOR POWER TRANSISTOR

▶ **Refer to illustrations 10.2, 10.4, 10.5 and 10.7**

1   Disconnect the cable from the negative battery terminal (see Chapter 5, Section 1).

2   Working in the passenger compartment under the glovebox, remove the lower dash panel (see illustration).

3   Remove the right side kick panel and the glovebox (see Chapter 11).

4   Remove the plastic cross brace from the dash frame structure (see illustration).

5   Detach the relay bracket from the metal cross brace, then remove the cross brace from the dash frame structure (see illustration).

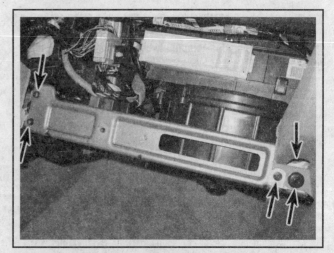

10.5 Remove the metal cross brace mounting screws

6 Remove the PCM (see Chapter 6).

7 Disconnect the electrical connector from the blower motor power transistor (see illustration).

8 Remove the blower motor power transistor mounting screws and remove it from the blower housing.

9 Installation is the reverse of removal.

10 Reconnect the battery (see Chapter 5, Section 1).

BLOWER MOTOR

11 Perform Steps 1 through 6 of this Section.

12 Disconnect the electrical connector from the blower motor (see illustration 10.7).

13 Remove the blower motor mounting screws and then remove the blower motor assembly (see illustration 10.7).

14 Remove the blower motor circlip and remove the blower fan from the motor.

15 Installation is the reverse of removal.

16 Reconnect the battery (see Chapter 5, Section 1).

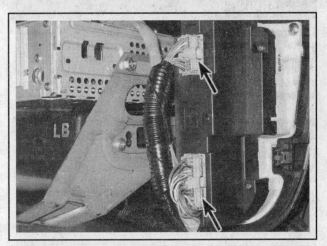

10.7 Location of the power transistor (1) and the blower fan mounting screws (2) - sedan model shown

11 Heater/air conditioning control assembly - removal and installation

◆ Refer to illustrations 11.3a, 11.3b, 11.4a and 11.4b

❋❋ WARNING:

The models covered by this manual are equipped with Supplemental Restraint systems (SRS), more commonly known as airbags. Always disable the airbag system before working in the vicinity of any airbag system component to avoid the possibility of accidental deployment of the airbag, which could cause personal injury (see Chapter 12).

➡Note: The following procedure covers the heater/AC control assembly removal for the sedans and coupes. However, the heater/AC control assembly removal on CR-V and hatchbacks is similar.

1 Disconnect the cable from the negative battery terminal (see Chapter 5, Section 1).

2 Remove the dashboard center trim panel (see Chapter 11). Partially remove the center trim panel to access the electrical connectors.

3 Disconnect the blower motor switches and temperature control

11.3a Disconnect the electrical connectors from the blower motor switches . . .

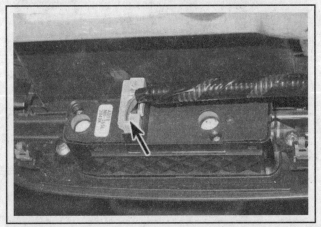

11.3b . . . and the air conditioning selection switch

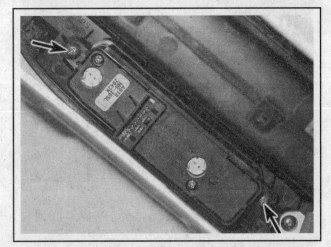

11.4a Location of the air conditioning switch mounting screws

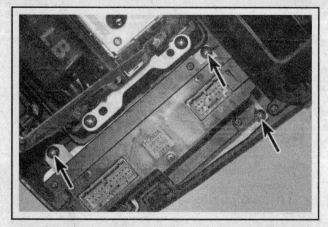

11.4b Location of the blower selection switch mounting screws

module connectors (see illustrations).

4 Remove the heater/air conditioner control assembly retaining screws (see illustrations).

5 Installation is the reverse of removal.

6 Reconnect the battery (see Chapter 5, Section 1).

12 Heater core - replacement

▶ Refer to illustrations 12.5, 12.6, 12.8, 12.11, 12.13a, 12.13b, 12.14, 12.15, 12.16a and 12.16b

❋❋ WARNING 1:

The models covered by this manual are equipped with Supplemental Restraint systems (SRS), more commonly known as airbags. Always disable the airbag system before working in the vicinity of any airbag system component to avoid the possibility of accidental deployment of the airbag, which could cause personal injury (see Chapter 12).

❋❋ WARNING 2:

The air conditioning system is under high pressure. DO NOT loosen any fittings or remove any components until after the system has been discharged. Air conditioning refrigerant must be properly discharged into an EPA-approved container at a dealer service department or an automotive air conditioning repair facility. Always wear eye protection when disconnecting air conditioning system fittings.

❋❋ WARNING 3:

Wait until the engine is completely cool before beginning this procedure.

➡Note: The following procedure covers the heater core removal for the sedans and coupes. However, the heater core removal on CR-V and hatchbacks is similar.

1 If so equipped, have the air conditioning system discharged by a dealer service department or by an automotive air conditioning shop before proceeding (see **Warning** above).

2 Disconnect the cable from the negative battery terminal (see Chapter 5, Section 1).

3 Drain the cooling system (see Chapter 1).

4 Disconnect the air conditioning evaporator lines at the dash inside the engine compartment.

5 Disconnect the heater control valve cable (see illustration).

➡Note: Turn the heater valve to the fully open position after the cable has been disconnected.

6 Disconnect the heater hoses from the heater core inside the engine compartment (see illustration).

12.5 Disconnect the heater control valve and rotate the valve to fully OPEN

12.6 Disconnect the heater hoses from the heater core inside the engine compartment

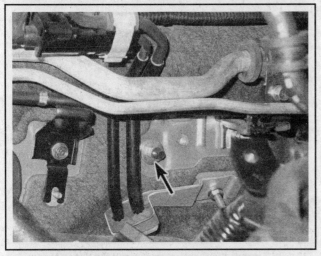

12.8 Working on the inside of the engine compartment, remove the heater control unit mounting nut

12.11 First remove the bolts from the brace (1) and next, remove the blower unit mounting bolts (2)

12.13a First, disconnect the heater control cable from the heater/air conditioning unit . . .

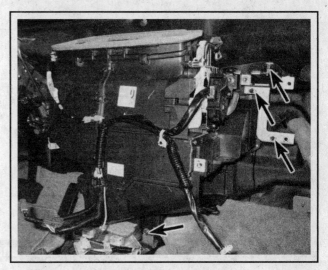

12.13b . . . next, remove the mounting bolts

7   Remove the mounting nut from the heater control valve bracket and position the assembly off to the side.

8   Remove the heater control unit mounting nut on the inside of the engine compartment (see illustration).

9   Remove the PCM (see Chapter 6).

10   Remove the instrument panel (see Chapter 11).

11   Disconnect the blower motor and power transistor electrical connectors. Remove the blower assembly mounting bolts (see illustration) and remove the assembly from the vehicle.

12   Remove the evaporator drain (see Section 13).

13   Disconnect the heater control cable from the heater/air conditioning unit (see illustration), remove the mounting bolts (see illustration) and lift the heater/air conditioning unit from the vehicle.

14   Remove the expansion valve cover (see illustration).

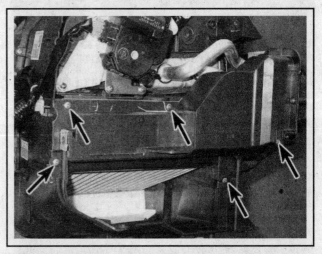

12.14 Remove the screws from the expansion valve cover

12.15 Lift the evaporator from the heater/air conditioning unit

12.16a Remove the rubber grommet and the flange cover mounting screws and separate the flange cover from the heater/AC unit

15 If equipped with air conditioning, remove the evaporator from the heater/air conditioning unit (see illustration).

16 Remove the flange cover (see illustration) and lift the heater cover from the heater/air conditioning unit (see illustration).

17 Installation is the reverse of removal. Don't forget to reconnect the heater core inlet and outlet hoses at the firewall.

18 Reconnect the battery (see Chapter 5, Section 1).

19 Refill the cooling system (see Chapter 1).

20 If equipped, have the air conditioning system evacuated, leak tested and recharged by the shop that discharged it.

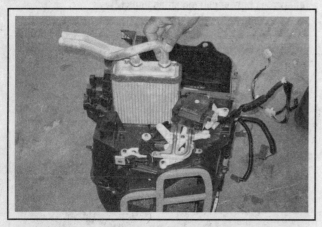

12.16b Lift the heater core from the heater/AC unit

13 Air conditioning and heating system - check and maintenance

▶ Refer to illustration 13.1

✳✳ WARNING:

The air conditioning system is under high pressure. DO NOT loosen any fittings or remove any components until after the system has been discharged. Air conditioning refrigerant must be properly discharged into an EPA-approved container at a dealer service department or an automotive air conditioning repair facility. Always wear eye protection when disconnecting air conditioning system fittings.

1 The following maintenance checks should be performed on a regular basis to ensure the air conditioner continues to operate at peak efficiency.

a) Check the compressor drivebelt. If it's worn or deteriorated, replace it (see Chapter 1).

b) Check the drivebelt tension and, if necessary, adjust it (see Chapter 1).

c) Check the system hoses. Look for cracks, bubbles, hard spots and deterioration. Inspect the hoses and all fittings for oil bubbles and seepage. If there's any evidence of wear, damage or leaks, replace the hose(s).

d) Inspect the condenser fins for leaves, bugs and other debris. Use a "fin comb" or compressed air to clean the condenser.

e) Make sure the system has the correct refrigerant charge.

f) Check the evaporator housing drain tube (see illustration) for blockage.

13.1 Look for the evaporator drain hose on the firewall (viewed from underneath the vehicle) - sedan model shown

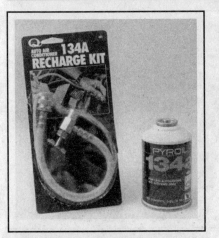

13.9 A basic charging kit for R-134a systems is available at most auto parts stores - it must say R-134a (not R-12) and so should the 12-ounce can of refrigerant

13.12a Cans of R-134A refrigerant (available at auto parts stores) can be added to the low side of the air conditioning system with a simple recharging kit - sedan model shown

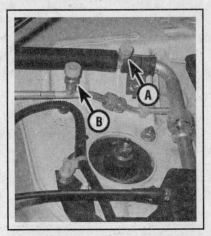

13.12b Location of the low side (suction) service port (A) and the high side (discharge) service port (B) on a CR-V model

2   It's a good idea to operate the system for about 10 minutes at least once a month, particularly during the winter. Long term non-use can cause hardening, and subsequent failure, of the seals.

3   Because of the complexity of the air conditioning system and the special equipment necessary to service it, in-depth troubleshooting and repairs are not included in this manual. However, simple checks and component replacement procedures are provided in this Chapter.

4   The most common cause of poor cooling is simply a low system refrigerant charge. If a noticeable drop in cool air output occurs, the following quick check will help you determine if the refrigerant level is low.

CHECKING THE REFRIGERANT CHARGE

5   Warm the engine up to normal operating temperature.

6   Place the air conditioning temperature selector at the coldest setting and the blower at the highest setting. Open the vehicle doors (to make sure the air conditioning system doesn't cycle off as soon as it cools the passenger compartment).

7   With the compressor engaged - the clutch will make an audible click and the center of the clutch will rotate - feel the evaporator inlet and outlet lines at the firewall. The inlet (small diameter) line should feel somewhat warm and the outlet (large diameter) line should feel cold. If so, the system charge is probably adequate.

8   Place a thermometer in the dashboard vent nearest the evaporator and operate the system until the indicated temperature is around 40 to 45 degrees F. If the ambient (outside) air temperature is very high, say 110 degrees F, the duct air temperature may be as high as 60 degrees F, but generally the air conditioning is 30-40 degrees F cooler than the ambient air.

➡Note: Humidity of the ambient air also affects the cooling capacity of the system. Higher ambient humidity lowers the effectiveness of the air conditioning system.

ADDING REFRIGERANT

♦ Refer to illustrations 13.9, 13.12a, 13.12b and 13.15

9   Buy an automotive charging kit at an auto parts store (see illustration). A charging kit includes a 14-ounce can of refrigerant, a tap

valve and a short section of hose that can be attached between the tap valve and the system low side service valve.

※ CAUTION 1:

Although the system will hold more than one can of refrigerant, don't add more than one can (you could overfill the system).

※ CAUTION 2:

There are two types of refrigerant used in automotive systems; R-12 - which has been widely used on earlier models and the more environmentally-friendly R-134a used in all models covered by this manual. These two refrigerants (and their appropriate refrigerant oils) are not compatible and must never be mixed or components will be damaged. Use only R-134a refrigerant in the models covered by this manual.

10   Hook up the charging kit by following the manufacturer's instructions.

※ WARNING:

DO NOT hook the charging kit hose to the system high side! The fittings on the charging kit are designed to fit only on the low side of the system.

11   Back off the valve handle on the charging kit and screw the kit onto the refrigerant can, making sure first that the O-ring or rubber seal inside the threaded portion of the kit is in place.

※ WARNING:

Wear protective eyewear when dealing with pressurized refrigerant cans.

12   Remove the dust cap from the low-side charging connection and attach the quick-connect fitting on the kit hose (see illustrations).

13   Warm up the engine and turn on the air conditioner. Keep the charging kit hose away from the fan and other moving parts.

13.15 Insert a thermometer in the center vent, turn on the air conditioning system and wait for it to cool down; depending on the humidity, the output air should be 30 to 40 degrees cooler than the ambient air temperature

➡Note: The charging process requires the compressor to be running. Your compressor may cycle off if the pressure is low due to a low charge. If the clutch cycles off, you can pull the low-pressure cycling switch plug and attach a jumper wire across the terminals of the electrical connector (on the harness side). This will keep the compressor ON.

14 Turn the valve handle on the kit until the stem pierces the can, then back the handle out to release the refrigerant. You should be able to hear the rush of gas. Add refrigerant to the low side of the system until the temperature of the evaporator inlet and outlet lines is as described in Step 7. Allow stabilization time between each addition.

15 If you have an accurate thermometer, place it in the center air conditioning vent (see illustration) and note the temperature of the air coming out of the vent. A fully-charged system which is working correctly should cool down to about 40 degrees F. Generally, an air conditioning system will put out air that is 30 to 40 degrees F cooler than the ambient air. For example, if the ambient (outside) air temperature is very high (over 100 degrees F), the temperature of air coming out of the registers should be 60 to 70 degrees F.

16 When the can is empty, turn the valve handle to the closed position and release the connection from the low-side port. Replace the dust cap.

17 Remove the charging kit from the can and store the kit for future use with the piercing valve in the UP position, to prevent inadvertently piercing the can on the next use.

HEATING SYSTEMS

18 If the carpet under the heater core is damp, or if antifreeze vapor or steam is coming through the vents, the heater core is leaking. Remove it (see Section 12) and install a new unit (most radiator shops will not repair a leaking heater core).

19 If the air coming out of the heater vents isn't hot, the problem could stem from any of the following causes:
a) The thermostat is stuck open, preventing the engine coolant from warming up enough to carry heat to the heater core. Replace the thermostat (see Section 3).
b) There is a blockage in the system, preventing the flow of coolant through the heater core. Feel both heater hoses at the firewall. They should be hot. If one of them is cold, there is an obstruction

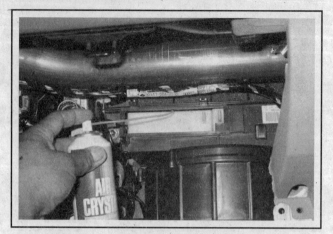

13.23 Remove the glove box (see Chapter 11) and then insert the nozzle of the disinfectant can into the evaporator housing by shoving it through the cabin filter door

in one of the hoses or in the heater core, or the heater control valve is shut. Detach the hoses and back flush the heater core with a water hose. If the heater core is clear but circulation is impeded, remove the two hoses and flush them out with a water hose.
c) If flushing fails to remove the blockage from the heater core, the core must be replaced (see Section 12).

ELIMINATING AIR CONDITIONING ODORS

▶ Refer to illustration 13.23

20 Unpleasant odors that often develop in air conditioning systems are caused by the growth of a fungus, usually on the surface of the evaporator core. The warm, humid environment there is a perfect breeding ground for mildew to develop.

21 The evaporator core on most vehicles is difficult to access, and factory dealerships have a lengthy, expensive process for eliminating the fungus by opening up the evaporator case and using a powerful disinfectant and rinse on the core until the fungus is gone. You can service your own system at home, but it takes something much stronger than basic household germ-killers or deodorizers.

22 Aerosol disinfectants for automotive air conditioning systems are available in most auto parts stores, but remember when shopping for them that the most effective treatments are also the most expensive. The basic procedure for using these sprays is to start by running the system in the RECIRC mode for ten minutes with the blower on its highest speed. Use the highest heat mode to dry out the system and keep the compressor from engaging by disconnecting the wiring connector at the compressor (see Section 14).

23 Make sure that the disinfectant can comes with a long spray hose. Point the nozzle through the cabin filter door so that it protrudes inside the evaporator housing (see illustration), and then spray according to the manufacturer's recommendations. Try to cover the whole surface of the evaporator core, by aiming the spray up, down and sideways. Follow the manufacturer's recommendations for the length of spray and waiting time between applications.

24 Once the evaporator has been cleaned, the best way to prevent the mildew from coming back again is to make sure your evaporator housing drain tube is clear (see illustration 13.1).

14 Air conditioning compressor - removal and installation

♦ Refer to illustrations 14.9 and 14.10

❋❋ WARNING:

The air conditioning system is under high pressure. Do not loosen any hose fittings or remove any components until after the system has been discharged. Air conditioning refrigerant must be properly discharged into an EPA-approved recovery/recycling unit at a dealer service department or an automotive air conditioning repair facility. Always wear eye protection when disconnecting air conditioning system fittings.

❋❋ CAUTION:

When replacing entire components, additional refrigerant oil should be added equal to the amount that is removed with the component being replaced. Be sure to read the can before adding any oil to the system, to make sure it is compatible with the R-134a system.

➡Note: The receiver-drier should be replaced whenever the compressor is replaced.

REMOVAL

1   Have the air conditioning system refrigerant discharged and recovered by an air conditioning technician.

2   Disconnect the cable from the negative battery terminal (see Chapter 5, Section 1).

3   Set the parking brake, block the rear wheels and raise the front of the vehicle, supporting it securely on jackstands.

4   Remove the drivebelt (see Chapter 1).

5   Remove the alternator (see Chapter 5).

6   Remove the splash shield from under the engine compartment (see Chapter 2A).

7   On coupe, sedan and hatchback models, remove the condenser fan (see Section 4).

8   On CR-V models, remove the coolant reservoir (see Section 5).

9   Disconnect the compressor clutch wiring harness (see illustration).

10 Disconnect the refrigerant lines from the compressor. Plug the open fittings to prevent entry of dirt and moisture (see illustration).

11 Remove the compressor mounting bolts from the compressor bracket (see illustration 14.10).

12 Carefully guide the compressor through the opening below the engine compartment.

INSTALLATION

13 The clutch may have to be transferred from the old compressor to the new unit.

14 Add the proper amount of refrigerant oil to the new compressor using the following calculations:

 a) *Drain the refrigerant oil from the old compressor through the suction fitting and measure it in ounces.*

 b) *Subtract this number from 4-1/3 ounces.*

 c) *The difference between these two figures is equal to the amount you should drain from the new compressor.*

15 Installation is the reverse of removal, using new O-rings where the line fittings attach to the compressor.

16 Have the system evacuated, recharged and leak tested by an air conditioning technician.

17 Reconnect the battery (see Chapter 5, Section 1.)

14.9 Location of the compressor clutch electrical connector

14.10 Location of the mounting nuts for the suction line (Low side) (1) and the discharge line (High side) (2) - remove the air conditioning compressor mounting bolts (3)

15 Air conditioning receiver-drier - removal and installation

✱✱ WARNING:

The air conditioning system is under high pressure. Do not loosen any hose fittings or remove any components until after the system has been discharged. Air conditioning refrigerant must be properly discharged into an EPA-approved recovery/recycling unit at a dealer service department or an automotive air conditioning repair facility. Always wear eye protection when disconnecting air conditioning system fittings.

✱✱ CAUTION:

When replacing entire components, additional refrigerant oil should be added equal to the amount that is removed with the component being replaced. Be sure to read the can before adding any oil to the system, to make sure it is compatible with the R-134a system.

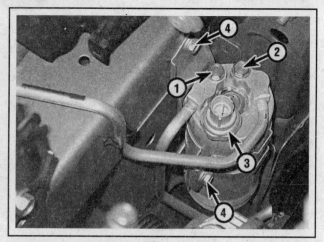

15.3 Receiver-drier mounting details - sedan model shown

1 *Air conditioning line to condenser*
2 *Air conditioning line from compressor*
3 *Air conditioning pressure switch*
4 *Mounting brackets and bolts*

1 Have the refrigerant discharged and recovered by an air conditioning technician.
2 Disconnect the cable from the negative battery terminal (see Chapter 5, Section 1).

SEDAN, COUPE AND HATCHBACK MODELS

▶ **Refer to illustration 15.3**

3 Remove the air conditioning lines from the receiver-drier (see illustration).
4 Disconnect the electrical connector.
5 Remove the bracket bolts from the receiver-drier.
6 Remove the receiver-drier from the engine compartment.
7 Installation is the reverse of removal. Be sure to install new O-rings onto the air conditioning lines.

CR-V MODELS

▶ **Refer to illustrations 15.9, 15.10 and 15.11**

8 Remove the condenser (see Section 16).
9 Remove the cap from the condenser (see illustration).
10 Remove the filter from the condenser (see illustration).
11 Remove the receiver drier desiccant (see illustration).
12 Installation is the reverse of removal. Be sure to install new O-rings onto the receiver-drier cap. Apply a thin layer of refrigerant oil to the desiccant before installing it. If refrigerant oil must be replaced, add it to the condenser (see Section 16).

ALL MODELS

13 Reconnect the battery. Refer to Chapter 5, Section 1.
14 Have the system evacuated, charged and leak tested by an air conditioning technician.

15.9 Remove the cap from the condenser

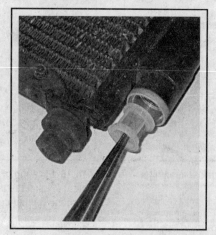

15.10 Remove the filter from the condenser

15.11 Use pliers to remove the desiccant from the condenser

16 Air conditioning condenser - removal and installation

❋❋ WARNING:

The air conditioning system is under high pressure. Do not loosen any hose fittings or remove any components until after the system has been discharged. Air conditioning refrigerant must be properly discharged into an EPA-approved recovery/recycling unit at a dealer service department or an automotive air conditioning repair facility. Always wear eye protection when disconnecting air conditioning system fittings.

❋❋ CAUTION:

When replacing entire components, additional refrigerant oil should be added equal to the amount that is removed with the component being replaced. Be sure to read the can before adding any oil to the system, to make sure it is compatible with the R-134a system.

16.4a Location of the condenser bracket and mounting bolt on the right side

REMOVAL

▶ **Refer to illustrations 16.4a and 16.4b**

1 Have the refrigerant discharged and recovered by an air conditioning technician.
2 Disconnect the cable from the negative battery terminal (see Chapter 5, Section 1).
3 Remove the front bumper (see Chapter 11).
4 Remove the condenser brackets (see illustrations).
5 Disconnect the condenser line and discharge line from the condenser. Cap the fittings on the condenser and lines to prevent entry of dirt or moisture.
6 Remove the condenser by lifting it from its lower mounts.

INSTALLATION

16.4b Location of the condenser bracket and mounting bolt on the left side

7 Installation is the reverse of removal. Assemble all connections with new O-rings, lightly lubricated with R-134a refrigerant oil. If a new condenser was installed, add 1 1/6-ounce of fresh refrigerant oil.

8 Reconnect the battery. Refer to Chapter 5, Section 1.
9 Have the system evacuated, charged and leak tested by an air conditioning technician.

17 Air conditioning pressure switch - replacement

❋❋ WARNING:

The air conditioning system is under high pressure. Do not loosen any hose fittings or remove any components until after the system has been discharged. Air conditioning refrigerant must be properly discharged into an EPA-approved recovery/recycling unit at a dealer service department or an automotive air conditioning repair facility. Always wear eye protection when disconnecting air conditioning system fittings.

➡Note 1: Sedans, coupes and hatchbacks are equipped with an A/C pressure switch mounted on the receiver-drier. CR-V models are equipped with a receiver-drier mounted integrally with the condenser; the A/C pressure switch is mounted in the A/C line going from the condenser to the evaporator.

➡Note 2: The air conditioning pressure switch detects low (28 psi) and high (455 psi) refrigerant line pressure and shuts the system off if the pressure drops below or exceeds these values.

1 Have the refrigerant discharged and recovered by an air conditioning technician.
2 Unplug the electrical connector from the air conditioning pressure switch (see illustration 15.3).
3 Unscrew the pressure switch from the receiver-drier (sedans, coupes and hatchbacks) or the refrigerant line (CR-V models). Use a back-up wrench to prevent damaging the refrigerant line on CR-V models.
4 Lubricate the sensor O-ring with clean refrigerant oil of the correct type.
5 Screw the new sensor onto the refrigerant line or receiver-drier until hand tight, and then tighten it securely.
6 Reconnect the electrical connector.
7 Have the system evacuated, charged and leak tested by an air conditioning technician.

Specifications

General

Radiator cap pressure rating	14 to 18 psi (93 to 123 kPa)
Thermostat rating (opening to fully open temperature range)	169 to 194 degrees F (76 to 90 degrees C)
Cooling system capacity	See Chapter 1
Refrigerant type	R-134a
Refrigerant capacity	Refer to HVAC specification tag

Torque specifications

Note: One foot-pound (ft-lb) of torque is equivalent to 12 inch-pounds (in-lbs) of torque. Torque values below approximately 15 ft-lbs are expressed in inch-pounds, since most foot-pound torque wrenches are not accurate at these smaller values.

	In-lbs	Nm
Condenser inlet and outlet nuts	86 in-lbs	10
Condenser bracket bolts	86 in-lbs	10
Radiator bracket bolts	86 in-lbs	10
Thermostat housing cover bolts		
Coupe and sedan models	104 in-lbs	12
CR-V and hatchback models	86 in-lbs	10
Water pump bolts	104 in-lbs	12

4

FUEL AND EXHAUST SYSTEMS

Section

Reference to other Chapters

1 General information

AIR INDUCTION SYSTEM

The air induction system consists of the air intake duct/resonator, the air filter assembly, the throttle body and the intake manifold.

The throttle body contains a throttle plate that regulates the amount of air entering the intake manifold. The throttle plate is opened and closed by the accelerator cable. The throttle body is also the location of the Throttle Position (TP) sensor, a potentiometer that monitors the opening angle of the throttle plate and sends a variable voltage signal to the Powertrain Control Module (PCM). A Manifold Absolute Pressure (MAP) sensor is located on the throttle body. Another information sensor, the Intake Air Temperature (IAT) sensor, is located at the left rear corner of the intake manifold. All of the air induction components (air filter housing, air intake duct/resonator, accelerator cable and throttle body) are covered in this Chapter except for the intake manifold, which is covered in Chapter 2A (SOHC engines) or 2B (DOHC engines), and the information sensors, which are covered in Chapter 6.

FUEL SYSTEM

The fuel system consists of the fuel tank, an electric fuel pump and fuel pressure regulator (located in the fuel tank), the fuel pulsation damper, the fuel rail and the fuel injectors. Programmed Fuel Injection (PGM-FI) is a "sequential multiport" system, which means that the fuel injectors deliver fuel directly into the intake ports of the cylinders in firing order sequence (1-3-4-2). Sequential multiport systems provide much better control of the air/fuel mixture ratio than earlier fuel injection systems, and are therefore able to produce more power, better mileage and lower emissions. For more information about the PGM-FI system, see Section 12. For more information about the PCM and the information sensors, refer to Chapter 6.

FUEL PUMP AND FUEL LINES

Fuel is pumped from the fuel tank to the fuel injection system through a metal line located on the underside of the vehicle, and a flexible hose connecting the metal line to the fuel rail. An electric fuel pump/fuel gauge sending unit is located inside the fuel tank. The fuel gauge sending unit and the fuel filter are an integral part of the fuel pump. The fuel pump/fuel filter/fuel gauge sending unit can be accessed through a cover plate in the floor of the vehicle, and any of the three components can be replaced separately from the other two. A fuel pulsation damper, which is located at the fuel rail, attenuates the hydraulic and acoustic "noise" produced by the fuel pump when it's operating. A fuel pressure regulator, which is located on the fuel pump/fuel gauge sending unit, maintains the fuel pressure within the specified operating range.

EXHAUST SYSTEM

The exhaust system consists of the exhaust manifold, the catalytic converter(s), the muffler, the tailpipe and various sections of pipe connecting these components. Coupes and sedans with a D17A1 engine have one catalyst, which is an integral part of the exhaust manifold. Coupes and sedans with a D17A2 engine and all CR-Vs and hatchbacks also have one catalyst, but it's located in the exhaust pipe underneath the vehicle. Coupes and sedans with a D17A6 engine have two catalysts: one in the exhaust manifold and one in the exhaust pipe under the vehicle. The exhaust manifolds are covered in Chapter 2A (SOHC engines) and Chapter 2B (DOHC engines), and catalytic converters are in Chapter 6. The information in this Chapter covers maintenance, inspection and service for the rest of the exhaust system.

2 Fuel pressure relief procedure

2.2 On coupes and sedans, you'll find PGM-FI main relay No. 2 on this glove box bracket (on hatchbacks, the PGM-FI main relays are located directly above the PCM)

    A   *PGM-FI main relay No. 2*
    B   *PGM-FI main relay No. 1*
    C   *Automatic transmission reverse relay*

✳✳ WARNING:

Gasoline is extremely flammable, so take extra precautions when you work on any part of the fuel system. Don't smoke or allow open flames or bare light bulbs near the work area, and don't work in a garage where a gas-type appliance (such as a water heater or a clothes dryer) is present. Since gasoline is carcinogenic, wear latex gloves when there's a possibility of being exposed to fuel, and, if you spill any fuel on your skin, rinse it off immediately with soap and water. Mop up any spills immediately and do not store fuel-soaked rags where they could ignite. The fuel system is under constant pressure, so, if any fuel lines are to be disconnected, the fuel pressure in the system must be relieved first. When you perform any kind of work on the fuel system, wear safety glasses and have a Class B type fire extinguisher on hand.

COUPE AND SEDAN

▸ **Refer to illustrations 2.2 and 2.3**

1 Remove the glove box (see Chapter 11).
2 Locate the PGM-FI main relay No. 2. On coupes and sedans, the

two PGM-FI main relays (see illustration) are mounted on the bracket right in front of the Powertrain Control Module (PCM). One way to verify that you have the right relay on coupes and sedans is to look at the wire colors: The No. 1 relay has yellow/black, white/black, white/black and red/yellow wires; the No. 2 relay has yellow/black, yellow/green, yellow/green and green/yellow wires.

3   Once you have identified the PGM-FI relay No. 2, remove it from its mounting bracket (see illustration), then disconnect the electrical connector from the relay.

4   Start the engine. It will cease running immediately. The fuel pressure is now relieved, but there is still fuel in the lines, so be sure to have shop rags handy to mop up any spilled fuel when disconnecting fuel lines.

➡Note: If the Malfunction Indicator Light (MIL) on the instrument cluster comes on while you're cranking the engine, ignore it. The PCM is simply responding to a lean condition and setting the Diagnostic Trouble Code(s) (DTCs) for lean misfires. The DTCs won't remain in the PCM's memory because they'll be erased when you disconnect the battery.

5   Remove the fuel filler neck cap to relieve the pressure inside the fuel tank.

6   Make sure that you have the anti-theft code for the radio and jot down the frequencies for the radio's station's pre-set buttons. Then disconnect the cable from the negative terminal of the battery (see Chapter 5, Section 1). It's now safe to work on the fuel system.

HATCHBACK

7   Remove the passenger side airbag from the dashboard (see "Airbag system - general information" in Chapter 12).

8   Locate the PGM-FI main relay No. 2. On hatchbacks, the two PGM-FI main relays are located above the PCM, to the left of the right side vent. On these models, the PGM-FI main relay No. 2 is the one on the left. To verify that you've got the correct relay, look at the wire colors: The PGM-FI main relay No. 1 relay has yellow/black, white/black, white/black and red/yellow wires; main relay No. 2 relay has yellow/black, yellow/green, yellow/black and green/yellow wires.

9   Once you have identified the PGM-FI relay No. 2, detach it from its mounting bracket and disconnect the electrical connector from the relay.

10   Start the engine. It will cease running immediately. The fuel pressure is now relieved, but there is still fuel in the lines, so be sure to have shop rags handy to mop up any spilled fuel when disconnecting fuel lines.

➡Note: If the Malfunction Indicator Light (MIL) on the instrument cluster comes on while you're cranking the engine, ignore it. The PCM is simply responding to a lean condition and setting the Diagnostic Trouble Code(s) (DTCs) for lean misfires. The DTCs won't remain in the PCM's memory because they'll be erased when you disconnect the battery.

11   Remove the fuel filler neck cap to relieve the pressure inside the fuel tank.

12   Make sure that you have the anti-theft code for the radio and jot down the frequencies for the radio's station's pre-set buttons. Then disconnect the cable from the negative terminal of the battery (see Chapter 5, Section 1). It's now safe to work on the fuel system.

2.3 To disengage the PGM-FI relay No. 2 from its mounting bracket, depress this release tab and pull the relay up, then disconnect the electrical connector from the relay (coupe/sedan model shown)

CR-V

13   Make sure that you have the anti-theft code for the radio and jot down the frequencies for the radio's station's pre-set buttons. Then disconnect the cable from the negative terminal of the battery (see Chapter 5, Section 1).

14   Remove the fuel filler neck cap to relieve the pressure inside the fuel tank.

15   Remove the engine cover (see Chapter 2B).

16   Put a shop rag underneath the fuel pulsation damper to catch any spilled fuel. Then, using a back-up wrench to protect the fuel rail, slowly loosen the pulsation damper one full turn with another wrench to depressurize the fuel system.

※ WARNING:

When performing this procedure, wear a pair of safety goggles to protect your eyes from any fuel that might squirt out under pressure when you loosen the pulsation damper. It's also a good idea to throw a shop rag over the pulsation damper fitting to soak up any fuel that might squirt out.

17   When you're done servicing the fuel system, install the fuel pulsation damper using a new pair of sealing washers, then tighten the pulsation damper to the torque listed in this Chapter's Specifications.

※ WARNING:

To prevent fuel leaks, ALWAYS discard the old sealing washers and use new sealing washers whenever you loosen or remove the fuel pulsation damper.

3 Fuel pump/fuel pressure - check

❊❊ WARNING:

Gasoline is extremely flammable, so take extra precautions when you work on any part of the fuel system. See the *Warning* in Section 2.

GENERAL CHECKS

1 Verify that there is fuel in the fuel tank.

2 Verify that the fuel pump actually runs. Turn the ignition switch to ON - you should hear a brief whirring noise for about two seconds as the pump comes on and pressurizes the system.

➡Note: If you can't hear the pump from inside the vehicle, open the fuel filler neck cap, then have an assistant turn the ignition switch to ON while you listen to the pump through the fuel filler neck.

FUEL PUMP PRESSURE TEST

◆ **Refer to illustrations 3.3, 3.5 and 3.7**

3 To measure the fuel pressure, you'll need a fuel pressure gauge capable of reading at least 60 psi (414 kPa), some fuel hose and an

3.5 Disconnect the fuel supply hose quick-connect fitting (1) from the fuel rail pipe (2), then attach the fuel pressure gauge setup to the fuel line and fuel rail fittings (coupe/sedan model shown)

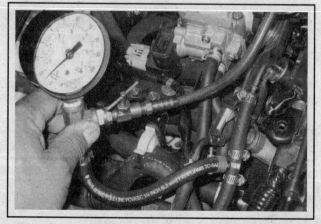

3.7 Here's what your fuel pressure gauge test rig should look like when it's correctly hooked up (coupe/sedan model shown)

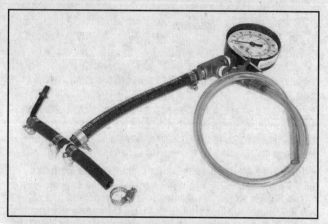

3.3 To measure the fuel pressure, you'll need a fuel pressure gauge, some extra fuel hose and a suitable flare fitting (equivalent to the male side of a quick-connect fitting)

adapter suitable for connecting the gauge to the fuel system. Fuel pressure gauges and hoses are available at most auto parts stores and automotive retailers. Adapters are a little more difficult to find. On coupes, sedans and hatchbacks, you're going to need an adapter suitable for tee-ing the gauge into the fuel system at the quick-connect fitting on the firewall. For CR-Vs, you'll need an adapter suitable for screwing the gauge hose fitting onto the same threaded fitting on the fuel rail to which the fuel pulsation damper is connected.

4 Before disconnecting any fuel line fittings, relieve the system fuel pressure (see Section 2), then disconnect the cable from the negative battery terminal (see Chapter 5, Section 1).

5 On coupes, sedans and hatchbacks, disconnect the fuel supply line from the fuel rail hose at the quick-connect fitting at the fuel rail (see illustration). (If you don't know how to disconnect one of these quick-connect fittings, see Section 4 for help.)

6 On CR-Vs, remove the fuel pulsation damper (see Section 15).

7 Tee your fuel pressure gauge into the fuel system at the connection that you just disconnected (see illustration). If you're working on a CR-V, attach the fuel pressure gauge to the fuel rail using the proper adapter.

8 Reconnect the battery (see Chapter 5, Section 1).

9 Turn the ignition switch to ON (don't start the engine yet) with the air conditioning off. The fuel pump should run for about two seconds - pressure should register on the gauge and should hold steady.

10 Start the engine and let it warm up until it's idling at its normal operating temperature.

11 If the indicated fuel pressure is outside the operating range listed in this Chapter's Specifications, replace the fuel pressure regulator (see Section 6) and the fuel filter (see Section 7), then recheck the fuel pressure.

12 After the test is complete, relieve the system fuel pressure (see Section 2), then disconnect the cable from the negative battery terminal (see Chapter 5, Section 1).

13 Disconnect your fuel pressure testing rig, then - on coupes, sedans and hatchbacks - reconnect the fuel supply line quick-connect fitting (see Section 4), or - on CR-Vs - install the fuel pulsation damper (see Section 15).

14 Reconnect the cable to the negative battery terminal (see Chapter 5, Section 1).

15 Start the engine and check for fuel leaks.

4   Fuel lines and fittings - general information

▶ **Refer to illustration 4.3**

⁂ WARNING:

Gasoline is extremely flammable, so take extra precautions when you work on any part of the fuel system. See the *Warning* in Section 2.

1   Always relieve the fuel pressure before servicing fuel lines or fittings (see Section 2), then disconnect the cable from the negative battery terminal (see Chapter 5, Section 1) before proceeding.

2   The fuel supply lines connect the fuel pump in the fuel tank to the fuel rail on the engine. The Evaporative Emission (EVAP) system vapor lines connect the fuel tank to the EVAP canister and connect the canister to the intake manifold. Whenever you're working under the vehicle, be sure to inspect all fuel and evaporative emission lines for leaks, kinks, dents and other damage. Always replace a damaged fuel or EVAP line immediately. Leaking fuel and EVAP lines will result in loss of fuel and excessive air pollution (the leaking raw fuel emits unburned hydrocarbon vapors into the atmosphere).

3   All lines are secured to the underbody with small plastic or metal brackets that are attached to the vehicle floorpan (see illustration). To detach the metal bracket from the pan, remove both mounting bolts, then squeeze each of the split locator pins together to disengage the lines from the bracket. Each plastic fuel and vapor line bracket is pushed onto a fixed stud protruding downward from the underside of the vehicle pan. To disengage the plastic fuel and EVAP lines from one these plastic brackets, carefully pry each bracket loose, then simply disengage the line(s) that you want to replace from the bracket(s). When you remove one of these brackets, it's a good idea to have some new brackets handy, because once you've detached a bracket it might not fit as tightly onto the stud when you install it again. If any of the brackets feel loose after installation, remove them and replace them with new brackets.

4   If you find signs of dirt in the lines during disassembly, disconnect all lines and blow them out with compressed air. Inspect the fuel strainer on the fuel pump pick-up unit (see Sections 5 and 6) for damage and deterioration. And inspect the fuel filter, which is an integral component of the fuel pump/fuel gauge sending unit module (see Sections 5 and 6). Also inspect the fuel strainers in the fuel injectors (see Section 16).

STEEL TUBING

5   Because fuel lines used on fuel-injected vehicles are under fairly high pressure, it is critical that they be replaced with lines of equivalent specification. If you have to replace a fuel line, use only steel tubing that meets the manufacturer's specifications. Don't use copper or aluminum tubing to replace steel tubing. These materials cannot withstand normal vehicle vibration.

6   Some steel fuel lines have threaded fittings. When loosening these fittings to service or replace components:

a) *Always hold the stationary fitting with a wrench while turning the tube nut (this will prevent the line from twisting).*

b) *If you're going to replace one of these fittings, use original equipment parts or parts that meet original equipment standards.*

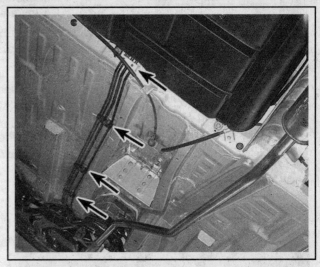

4.3   The fuel and EVAP lines are secured to the underside of the vehicle by several brackets

PLASTIC TUBING

7   Some fuel lines - between the fuel supply and return pipes of the fuel pump and the front of the fuel tank, for example - are plastic. If you ever have to replace either line, use only the original equipment plastic tubing.

⁂ CAUTION:

When removing or installing plastic fuel line tubing, be careful not to bend or twist it too much, which can damage it. And damaged fuel lines MUST be replaced! Also, be aware that the plastic fuel tubing is NOT heat resistant, so keep it away from excessive heat. Nor is it acid-proof, so don't wipe it off with a shop rag that has been used to wipe off battery electrolyte. If you accidentally spill or wipe electrolyte on plastic fuel tubing, replace the tubing.

Flexible hoses

⁂ WARNING:

Use only original equipment replacement hoses or their equivalent. Unapproved hoses might fail when subjected to the high operating pressures of the fuel system.

8   Don't route fuel hoses (or metal lines) within four inches of the exhaust system or within ten inches of the catalytic converter. Make sure that no rubber hoses are installed directly against the vehicle, particularly in places where there is any vibration. If allowed to touch some vibrating part of the vehicle, a hose can easily become chafed and it might start leaking. A good rule of thumb is to maintain a minimum of 1/4-inch clearance around a hose (or metal line) to prevent contact with the vehicle underbody.

Retainer location	Manufacturer	Retainer color
	Coupe and sedan	
Fuel supply line at fuel pump	Sanoh	White
Fuel supply line at fuel rail	Tokai	Green
	CR-V and hatchback	
Fuel supply line at fuel pump	Sanoh	White
Fuel supply line at fuel rail (fuel supply line side)	Tokai	Green
Fuel supply line at fuel rail (fuel rail side)	Tokai	Blue

4.9 Quick-connect fitting color code

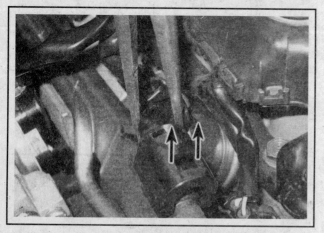

4.11 To remove the protective cover (if equipped) from a quick-connect fitting, simply pull it straight up

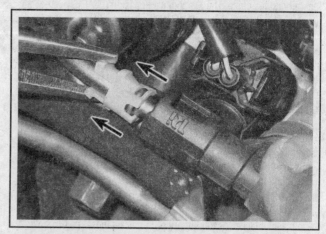

4.12 To disconnect a quick-connect fitting, squeeze the retainer tabs and pull the two halves of the fitting apart until they're separated

DISCONNECTING AND RECONNECTING FUEL SYSTEM FITTINGS

▶ Refer to illustrations 4.9, 4.11, 4.12, 4.13, 4.14 and 4.15

✷✷ CAUTION:

When disconnecting or reconnecting quick-connect fittings, be careful not to bend or twist them excessively, or they will be damaged and will have to be replaced. Also, be aware that the quick-connect fittings are NOT heat resistant, so keep them away from excessive heat. Nor are they acid-proof, so don't wipe them off with a shop rag that has been used to wipe off battery electrolyte. If you accidentally spill or wipe electrolyte on quick-connect fittings, replace them.

9   There are quick-connect fittings at both ends of the fuel supply line, i.e. at the fuel pump and at the fuel rail. You MUST replace the quick-connect fitting *retainers* whenever you disconnect a quick-connect fitting. It is critical that you *use the correct replacement retainer*, which depends on the manufacturer of the tubing and the end of the tube (fuel pump end or fuel rail end) on which you're installing it, because the retainers *are not all the same diameter*. To help you identify the retainer(s) you're replacing, Honda color codes them (see illustration).

10   Relieve the system fuel pressure (see Section 2), then disconnect the cable from the negative battery terminal (see Chapter 5, Section 1).

11   Remove the quick-connect fitting cover (see illustration) if equipped.

12   Holding the black side of the fitting with one hand, squeeze the retainer tabs with a pair of needle nose pliers to release them, then pull the two halves of the fitting apart (see illustrations). Cover the disconnected ends of the fitting with plastic bags to keep out dirt and moisture.

13   Remove the old retainer from the fitting and inspect the contact

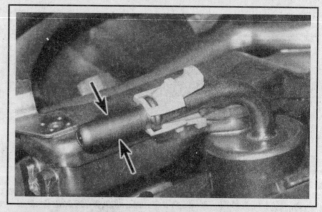

4.13 Spread apart the open side of the old retainer, remove and discard it, then inspect the contact surface of the fuel line for dirt, damage and rust

4.14 Inspect this O-ring inside the fitting; if it's cracked, torn or damaged, replace it

4.15 Insert a new retainer into the female side of the fitting and align the retainer's locking pawls with the grooves in the connector

surface area on the fuel line for dirt and damage (see illustration). If it's dirty, wipe it off with a clean shop rag. If it's rusty, remove and inspect the fuel lines, then remove and inspect the fuel pressure regulator, the fuel pump and the fuel filter (see Section 5). If any of these components are damaged, replace them (see Sections 6 and 7, respectively).

14 Inspect the old O-ring inside the bore of the fitting (see illustration). If it's cracked, torn or otherwise damaged, replace it.

15 Insert a new retainer into the female side of the fitting (see illustration). Be sure to align the locking pawls of the retainer with the grooves in the side of the connector.

16 Press the two halves of the quick-connect fitting together until the ridge on the male end of the fuel pipe is locked into place by the locking pawls on the both retainer tabs. You'll hear a clicking sound

when the pawls snap into place.

17 Verify that the quick-connect fitting is correctly reconnected by trying to pull the two halves of the connector apart.

18 If you're reconnecting the fuel supply line fitting on a coupe or sedan, install the air filter housing. If you're reconnecting the quick-connect fitting at the fuel pump on a coupe, sedan or hatchback, replace the access cover (see Section 5) and install the seat cushion (see Chapter 11). If you're reconnecting the fitting at the pump on a CR-V, install the carpet (see Chapter 11) and put up the seats.

19 Reconnect the cable to the negative battery terminal and perform the PCM idle learn procedure (see Chapter 5, Section 1).

20 Start the engine and check for leaks.

5 Fuel pump/fuel gauge sending unit module - removal and installation

▶ **Refer to illustrations 5.4, 5.5, 5.6, 5.7, 5.8, 5.10 and 5.11**

✲✲ WARNING:

Gasoline is extremely flammable, so take extra precautions when you work on any part of the fuel system. See the *Warning* in Section 2.

1 Relieve the fuel system pressure (see Section 2), then remove the fuel filler neck cap to relieve any pressure inside the fuel tank.

2 Disconnect the cable from the negative battery terminal (see Chapter 5, Section 1).

3 On coupes, sedans and hatchbacks, remove the rear seat cushion (see Chapter 11). On CR-Vs, fold the rear seats forward and pull back the carpet to expose the fuel pump access cover.

4 Remove the fuel pump access cover screws (see illustration) and remove the fuel pump access cover.

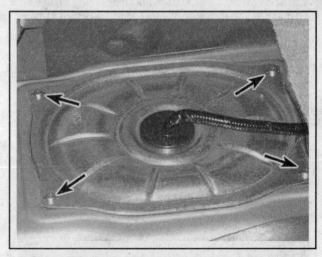

5.4 To detach the fuel pump access cover, remove these screws

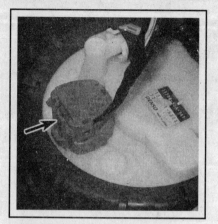

5.5 To disconnect the electrical connector from the fuel pump/fuel gauge sending unit, depress this release tab and pull the connector straight up

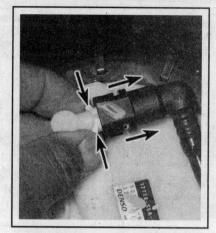

5.6 To disconnect the fuel supply line quick-connect fitting from the fuel pump, depress these two release tabs and pull off the fitting

5.7 This special tool for loosening and tightening the fuel pump/fuel gauge sending unit locknut is available at most auto parts stores

5 Disconnect the fuel pump/fuel gauge sending unit electrical connector (see illustration).

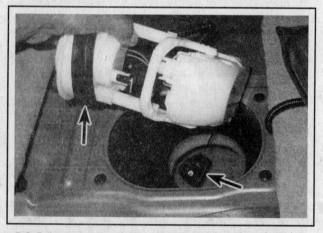

5.8 Being careful not to damage the fuel gauge sending unit float arm and float, remove the fuel pump/fuel gauge sending unit module from the tank. After removing the pump/sending unit, inspect the condition of the seal around the top of the module; if the seal is cracked, torn or deteriorated, replace it

6 Disconnect the quick-connect fitting for the fuel supply line (see illustration) and set the supply line aside.

7 Remove the fuel pump/fuel gauge sending unit locknut (see illustration).

8 Remove the fuel pump/fuel gauge sending unit module from the tank (see illustration). When removing the pump/sending unit from the tank, carefully angle the module as shown in the accompanying illustration to protect the float arm and float from damage. After removing the pump/sending unit module, inspect the seal for cracks, tears and deterioration. If it's damaged, replace it.

9 Before installing the fuel pump/fuel gauge sending unit module in the fuel tank, install the seal in the hole *first. Don't try to install it with the module,* which might cause it to become pinched or distorted.

10 When installing the fuel pump/fuel gauge sending unit module, be sure to align the index mark on top of the module between the two marks on the edge of the hole (see illustration).

11 Before reconnecting the fuel supply line quick-connect fitting, replace the O-ring (see illustration) inside the fitting.

12 Installation is otherwise the reverse of removal. Be sure to tighten the module locknut securely.

13 Reconnect the cable to the negative terminal of the battery, then perform the idle learn procedure (see Chapter 5, Section 1).

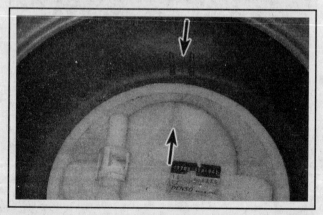

5.10 When installing the fuel pump/fuel gauge sending unit module, be sure to align the index mark on top of the module between the two marks on the edge of the hole

5.11 Before reconnecting the fuel supply line to the fuel pump outlet, replace this O-ring inside the fuel supply line quick-connect fitting

6   Fuel pressure regulator - replacement

♦ **Refer to illustrations 6.4, 6.5, 6.6, 6.7 and 6.8**

⁂ WARNING:

Gasoline is extremely flammable, so take extra precautions when you work on any part of the fuel system. See the *Warning* in Section 2.

1   Relieve the system fuel pressure (see Section 2), then remove the fuel filler neck cap to relieve any pressure inside the fuel tank.

2   Disconnect the cable from the negative battery terminal (see Chapter 5, Section 1).

3   Remove the fuel pump/fuel gauge sending unit module from the fuel tank (see Section 5) and place it on a clean workbench.

4   Disconnect the pressure regulator's return hose fitting from the fuel pump housing (see illustration).

5   Detach the fuel pressure regulator's inlet hose fitting from the fuel pump housing (see illustration).

6   Remove the clip from the fuel pressure regulator (see illustration) and pull the regulator out of the inlet hose fitting.

7   Note the smaller clip (see illustration) that fits inside the larger clip that you just removed. You need *both* clips to reconnect the fuel pressure regulator to its inlet hose fitting, so it's a good idea to store both of them in a plastic bag.

8   Remove the old pressure regulator O-ring (see illustration) and discard it. Be sure to use a new O-ring when you install the pressure regulator (regardless of whether you're installing the old regulator or a new unit).

9   Installation is the reverse of removal.

10   When you're done, reconnect the cable to the negative battery terminal, then perform the idle learn procedure (see Chapter 5, Section 1).

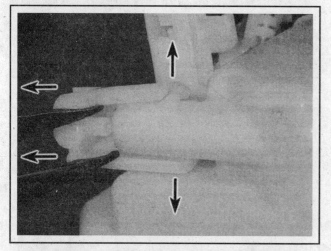

6.4 To disconnect the fuel pressure regulator's return hose fitting from the fuel pump case, spread the locking tabs apart, then pull off the fitting

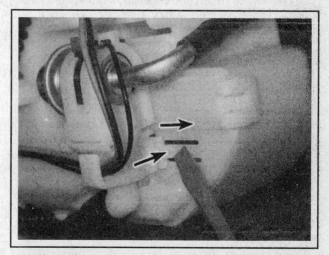

6.5 To detach the fuel pressure regulator's inlet fitting from the fuel pump housing, depress this locking tab with a small screwdriver and slide the fitting to the right

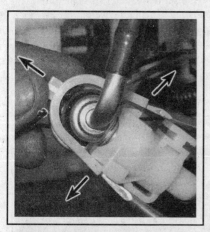

6.6 To detach this clip from the fuel pressure regulator, spread the sides apart with a small screwdriver, then pull the clip straight up and pull the pressure regulator out of the inlet hose fitting

6.7 Remove the smaller clip from the larger clip and store both of them in a plastic bag for reassembly

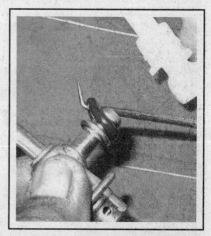

6.8 Remove and discard the old fuel pressure regulator O-ring; be sure to use a new O-ring when installing the regulator (whether you're installing the old regulator or a new unit)

7   Fuel pump/fuel filter/fuel gauge sending unit module - replacement

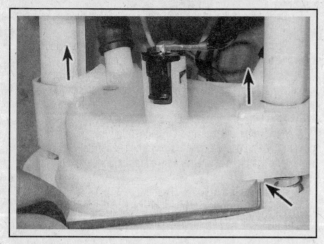

7.5a To remove the fuel filter assembly, turn the filter upside down, disengage the locking tabs for the two stops with a small screwdriver or an awl (left stop has already been released and pushed up) . . .

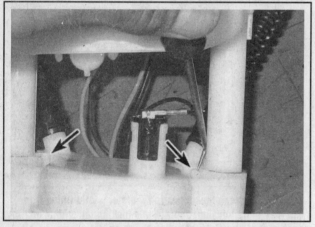

7.5b . . . release these two hooks . . .

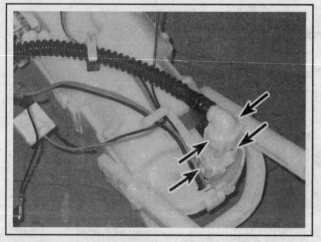

7.6 To disconnect the fuel pump outlet hose fitting, disengage the two tabs on the female side of the fitting from their corresponding slots in the male side of the fitting (fitting already disconnected in this photo for clarity)·

▶ Refer to illustrations 7.5a, 7.5b, 7.5c, 7.6, 7.7, 7.8, 7.9a, 7.9b, 7.10, 7.11a and 7.11b

❊❊ WARNING:

Gasoline is extremely flammable, so take extra precautions when you work on any part of the fuel system. See the *Warning* in Section 2.

1   Relieve the system fuel pressure (see Section 2), then remove the fuel filler neck cap to relieve any pressure inside the fuel tank.
2   Disconnect the cable from the negative battery terminal (see Chapter 5, Section 1).
3   Remove the fuel pump/fuel gauge sending unit module from the fuel tank (see Section 5) and place it on a clean workbench.
4   Disconnect and remove the fuel pressure regulator (see Section 6).
5   Remove the stops, release the hooks and separate the fuel filter assembly from the fuel pump housing (see illustrations).
6   Disconnect the fitting for the hose that connects the fuel pump outlet to the fuel filter (see illustration) and set the fuel filter assembly aside.

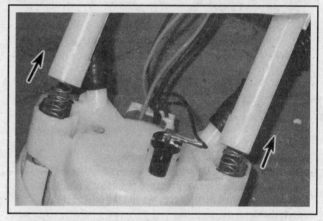

7.5c . . . and separate the spring-loaded legs of the filter assembly from the fuel pump housing, then store the stops and the springs in a plastic bag for reassembly

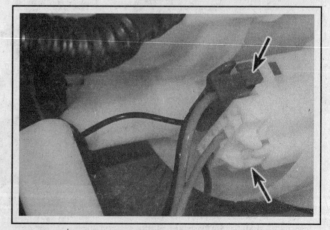

7.7 Depress these two release tabs and disconnect the electrical connectors for the fuel gauge sending unit and for the fuel pump

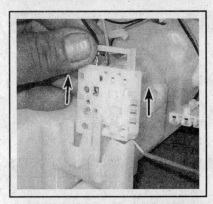

7.8 To detach the fuel gauge sending unit from its mounting bracket on the fuel pump housing, release the locking tab with a small screwdriver, then carefully lift up and remove the sending unit assembly

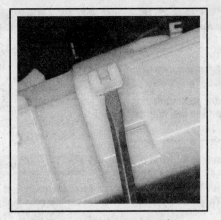

7.9a To separate the upper and lower parts of the housing, release the four locking clips (one on each side of the housing) with a small screwdriver . . .

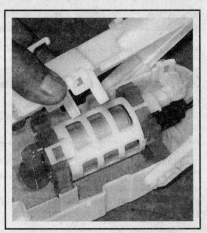

7.9b . . . and lift off the upper half of the housing

7 Disconnect the electrical connectors for the fuel pump and for the fuel gauge sending unit from the fuel filter assembly (see illustration).

8 Remove the fuel gauge sending unit from the fuel pump housing (see illustration).

9 Disassemble the fuel pump housing (see illustrations).

10 Remove the fuel pump from the lower half of the housing (see illustration).

11 Remove the fuel inlet "sock" (strainer) from the fuel pump (see illustrations).

12 Wash the fuel inlet strainer thoroughly in clean solvent, dry it off and inspect it for tears, cracks, clogging and any other damage. If the strainer is damaged or worn, replace it.

13 When installing the fuel pump strainer, be sure to use a new retainer clip.

14 When installing the fuel pump in the housing, make sure that the four tabs on the pump insulators are inserted into their respective slots in the lower half of the housing.

15 Installation is otherwise the reverse of removal, but before installing the fuel pump access cover, be sure to connect the cable to the negative battery terminal (see Chapter 5, Section 1), start the engine and check for fuel leaks at the pump fuel line connection. If there are no

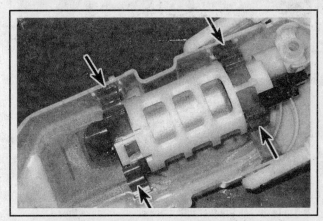

7.10 To remove the fuel pump from the lower half of the housing, note how the four tabs on the fuel pump insulators are seated into their corresponding slots in the housing, then simply depress the fuel pump mounting insulators at these four points and lift out the pump

leaks, install the access cover, the carpet and the rear seat (CR-V) or the seat cushion (coupe, sedan and hatchback).

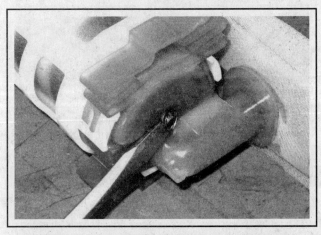

7.11a To detach the fuel inlet strainer from the fuel pump, carefully pry off - and discard - this retainer (always use a new retainer when installing the strainer) . . .

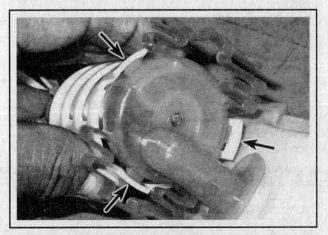

7.11b . . . then disengage these three tabs on the strainer from their corresponding slots in the fuel pump's plastic frame

8 Fuel tank - removal and installation

♦ Refer to illustrations 8.5a, 8.5b and 8.7

❈❈ WARNING:

Gasoline is extremely flammable, so take extra precautions when you work on any part of the fuel system. See the *Warning* in Section 2.

➡Note: The following procedure is much easier to perform if the fuel tank is empty. The tank has no drain plug, so the fuel must be siphoned from the tank with a siphoning kit, which is available at most auto parts stores. NEVER try to start the siphoning action with your mouth!

1   Relieve the fuel system pressure (see Section 2).
2   Disconnect the cable from the negative battery terminal (see Chapter 5, Section 1).
3   Raise the vehicle and place it securely on jackstands.
4   If the fuel tank is empty or nearly empty, it's not necessary to siphon the remaining fuel from the tank. But if there is a lot of fuel in the tank, drain the fuel by removing the fuel pump/fuel gauge sending unit (see Section 5) and siphoning it out through the hole for the pump/sending unit.

❈❈ WARNING:

Always siphon fuel into an approved gasoline container. Also, never start the siphoning action by mouth - use a siphoning pump (available at most auto parts stores).

5   Remove the fuel filler neck cover (see illustration), then disconnect and remove the fuel filler neck hose and the fuel tank vapor hose (see illustration). Inspect these two hoses for cracks, tears and other deterioration. If either hose is damaged or worn, replace it.
6   Support the fuel tank with a transmission jack. If you don't have a transmission jack, use a floor jack. If you're going to use a floor jack, put a piece of plywood between the jack head and the fuel tank to protect the tank.
7   Unbolt the fuel tank retaining straps (see illustration) and remove them.
8   Carefully lower the fuel tank.
9   If you need to remove the fuel pump/fuel gauge sending unit module, but haven't yet done so, refer to Sections 5 and 6. If you're going to have the fuel tank cleaned, refer to Section 9.
10   Installation is the reverse of removal. Be sure to tighten the fuel tank strap bolts to the torque listed in this Chapter's Specifications.
11   When you're done, reconnect the cable to the negative battery terminal and perform the PCM idle learn procedure (see Chapter 5, Section 1), then start the engine and check for fuel leaks.

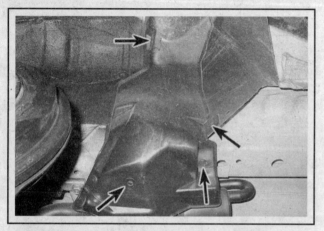

8.5a To detach the fuel filler neck cover, remove these four fasteners

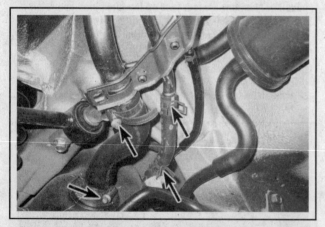

8.5b To disconnect the fuel filler neck hose and the fuel tank vapor hose, loosen these hose clamps and pull off both hoses

8.7 To detach the fuel tank from the underside of the vehicle, remove the fuel tank strap bolts (rear shown, front similar)

9 Fuel tank cleaning and repair - general information

1   The fuel tanks installed in the vehicles covered by this manual are made of plastic and are not repairable. If the fuel tank has been removed for cleaning, this is a job that should be left to a professional who has experience in this critical and potentially dangerous work. Even after cleaning and flushing of the fuel tank, explosive fumes can remain.
2   If the fuel tank is removed from the vehicle, it should not be placed in an area where sparks or open flames could ignite the fumes coming out of the tank. Be especially careful inside garages where a gas-type appliance is located, because it could cause an explosion.

10 Air filter housing - removal and installation

COUPE AND SEDAN

Air intake duct/resonator

▶ Refer to illustrations 10.2 and 10.4

1   Disengage the accelerator cable and cruise control cable from the cable guide at the right rear corner of the valve cover, disengage the accelerator cable from the guide at the right rear corner of the engine compartment (next to the cruise control actuator), then set both cables aside.

2   Detach the fresh air inlet duct from the air intake/resonator (see illustration). (You don't have to detach the fresh air inlet duct from the air intake duct/resonator in order to remove the intake duct/resonator, but you do have detach the harness from the inlet duct and the intake duct/resonator is easier to remove if the fresh air inlet duct is out of the way.) Clearly label all cables and hoses (see illustration) that are attached or connected to the air intake duct, then detach or disconnect them and set them aside.

3   Detach the harness from the bracket at the lower left rear corner of the air intake duct/resonator.

4   Remove the air intake duct/resonator mounting bolts (see illustration) and remove the intake duct/resonator.

5   Installation is the reverse of removal.

Air filter housing

▶ Refer to illustrations 10.7, 10.8, 10.9a and 10.9b

✳✳ WARNING:

Wait until the engine is completely cool before beginning this procedure.

6   Remove the fresh air inlet duct and the air intake duct/resonator assembly (see Steps 1 through 4).

7   Disconnect the electrical connector for the Intake Air Temperature (IAT) sensor (see illustration).

8   Disconnect the Positive Crankcase Ventilation (PCV) fresh air inlet hose from the valve cover (see illustration).

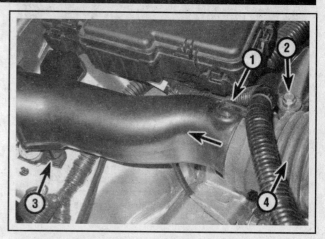

10.2 To detach the fresh air inlet duct from the air intake duct/resonator, detach the harness guide (1) from the top of the inlet duct by pulling it straight up, remove the duct mounting bolt (2), pull the locator pin (3) out of its grommet in the right fender, then pull off the duct to the right (toward the fender); if the pleated rubber boot (4) doesn't come off with the duct, remove it now also

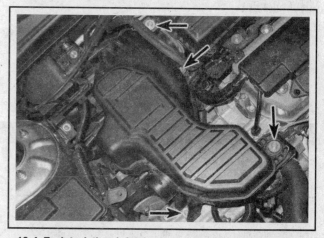

10.4 To detach the air intake duct/resonator from a coupe or sedan, remove these bolts

10.7 To disconnect the electrical connector from the Intake Air Temperature (IAT) sensor, depress this release tab and pull off the connector

10.8 To disconnect the PCV system fresh air inlet hose from the valve cover of a coupe or sedan, loosen this hose clamp and pull off the hose

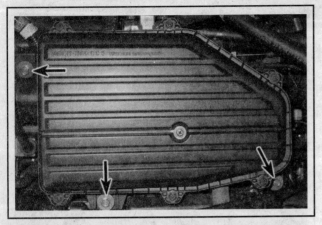

10.9a To remove the air filter housing on a coupe or sedan, remove these bolts . . .

10.9b . . . loosen this hose clamp screw and lift the air filter housing up and off the throttle body

9 Remove the air filter housing mounting bolts, loosen the screw on the hose clamp that secures the filter housing to the throttle body and remove the air filter housing (see illustrations).

10 Installation is the reverse of removal.

CR-V AND HATCHBACK

Air intake duct

CR-V

11 Loosen the hose clamp at the air-filter-housing-end of the duct.
12 Loosen the hose clamp at the throttle-body-end of the duct.
13 Remove the air intake duct.
14 Installation is the reverse of removal.

Hatchback

15 Loosen the hose clamp at the air-filter-housing-end of the duct.
16 Loosen the hose clamp at the throttle-body-end of the duct.
17 Remove the air intake duct.
18 Installation is the reverse of removal.

Air filter housing (CR-V and hatchback)

19 Disconnect the PCV hose (see Chapter 6).
20 Remove the air filter housing mounting nut and bolts.
21 Remove the air filter housing.
22 Installation is the reverse of removal.

---

11 Accelerator cable - removal, installation and adjustment

REMOVAL AND INSTALLATION (CIVIC MODELS AND 2002 THROUGH 2004 CR-V MODELS)

▶ **Refer to illustrations 11.2, 11.3, 11.4, 11.5, 11.6a and 11.6b**

1 Remove the air intake duct and the air filter housing (see Section 10). On CR-Vs, also remove the two throttle lever cover bolts and remove the cover.

2 Rotate the throttle lever cam until the cable is lined up with the slot in the cam, then disengage the cable from the cam (see illustration).

11.2 Rotate the throttle lever cam to put some slack into the accelerator cable, then slide the cable end plug out of its slot in the throttle lever cam (coupe/sedan shown, CR-V and hatchback similar)

11.3 To disengage the accelerator cable from the cable bracket, loosen the locknut and pull out the cable (coupe/sedan shown, CR-V and hatchback similar)

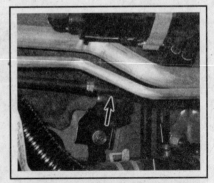

11.4 After noting the routing of the accelerator cable, trace the cable from the cable bracket all the way to the point at which the cable goes through the firewall and disengage the cable from any clips, clamps or cable guides, such as this one on the firewall of a sedan

11.5 Disengage the plastic retainer from the accelerator pedal arm by squeezing these two locking tabs together and pulling the cable to the rear, then separate the cable from the pedal arm

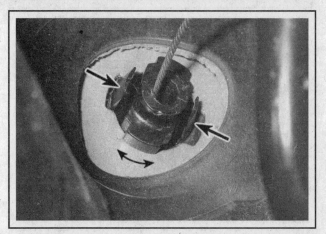

11.6a To unlock the cable ferrule from the firewall, squeeze the two locking tabs and rotate it until the bosses on the ferrule are aligned with their corresponding slots in the firewall . . .

11.6b . . . then pull out the accelerator cable from the engine compartment side (coupe/sedan shown, CR-V and hatchback similar)

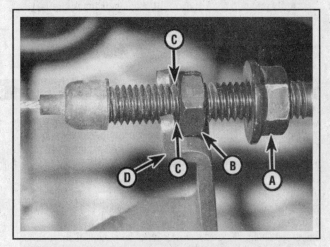

11.17a To adjust the accelerator cable on a coupe or sedan, place the accelerator cable in the cable bracket with the adjusting nut and the locknut on the same side of the bracket (the side facing away from the throttle body), then tighten the adjusting nut until there is zero freeplay between the adjusting nut and the cable bracket (coupe/sedan shown, CR-V and hatchback similar)

A   Locknut
B   Adjusting nut
C   Zero clearance between adjusting nut and cable bracket
D   Accelerator cable bracket

3   Loosen the accelerator cable locknut at the cable bracket (see illustration) and disengage the accelerator cable from its bracket.

➡Note: If the cable bracket has an "L" shape to it, like the bracket in the accompanying illustration, there is no need to use a back-up wrench to hold the other nut (the adjustment nut) because the kink in the bracket prevents the adjustment nut from turning. If, however, the cable bracket does NOT have an L shape, you will need to use a back-up wrench to prevent the adjustment nut from turning when you loosen the locknut.

4   Note the routing of the accelerator cable, then trace the cable from the cable bracket back to the firewall, detaching or disengaging it from any clamps, clips or cable guides (see illustration).

5   Using a flashlight so that you can see underneath the dash, locate the cable connection at the top of the accelerator pedal, push the upper end of the pedal forward and disengage the cable from the pedal arm (see illustration).

6   Unlock the accelerator cable ferrule by turning it counterclockwise until the tabs on the ferrule are aligned with the slots in the firewall (see illustration), then pull the cable out from the engine compartment side (see illustration).

7   Installation is the reverse of removal. When you're done installing the cable, be sure to adjust it.

REMOVAL AND INSTALLATION (2005 AND 2006 CR-V MODELS)

8   Remove the two throttle cable cover bolts and remove the cover from the accelerator pedal position (APP) sensor on the firewall.

9   Loosen the accelerator cable locknut at the cable bracket.

10 Fully open the throttle valve and disengage the throttle cable from the throttle link.

11 Remove the cable housing from the cable bracket.

12 Note the routing of the accelerator cable, then trace the cable from the APP sensor and disengage it from the clamp on the firewall.

13 Using a flashlight so that you can see under the dash, locate the cable connection at the top of the accelerator pedal, push the upper end

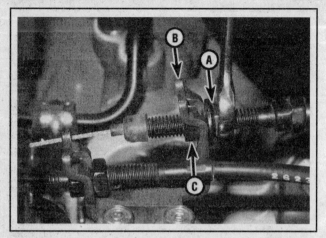

11.17b Once the accelerator cable freeplay is correctly adjusted, lift the cable out of the cable bracket and put the adjusting nut on the other side of the cable bracket (the side facing toward the throttle body), then tighten the locknut securely (coupe/sedan shown, CR-V and hatchback similar)

A   Locknut
B   Accelerator cable bracket
C   Adjusting nut

of the pedal forward and disengage the cable from the pedal arm.

14 Unlock the accelerator cable ferrule by turning it counterclockwise until the tabs on the ferrule align with the slots in the firewall (see illustration 11.6a), then pull the cable out from the engine compartment side (see illustration 11.6b).

15 Installation is the reverse of removal. When you're installing the cable, be sure to adjust it.

ADJUSTMENT (ALL MODELS)

▶ **Refer to illustrations 11.17a and 11.17b**

16 Put the shift lever in Park or Neutral, start the engine, hold it at 3000 rpm until the radiator fan comes on, then allow it to idle.

17 Back off the locknut, then place the accelerator cable in the cable bracket with both the adjusting nut and the locknut on the side of the cable bracket facing away from the throttle body. Then turn the adjusting nut until there is no freeplay between the adjusting nut and the cable bracket (see illustration). When the freeplay is zero, lift up the adjusting nut, place it on the other side of the cable bracket, then tighten the locknut (see illustration).

18 Once the accelerator cable has been installed and adjusted, verify that the throttle valve opens fully when you depress the accelerator pedal and that it returns to its idle position when you release the pedal.

12 Programmed Fuel Injection (PGM-FI) system - general information

The Programmed Fuel Injection (PGM-FI) system is a "sequential multiport" system. This means that there is a fuel injector in each intake port, and that these fuel injectors inject fuel into the intake ports in the cylinder firing order (1-3-4-2). The injectors are turned on and off by the Powertrain Control Module (PCM). When the engine is running, the PCM constantly monitors engine operating conditions with an array of information sensors, calculates the correct amount of fuel, then varies the interval of time during which the injectors are open. Sequential multiport systems provide much better control of the air/fuel mixture ratio than earlier fuel injection systems, and are therefore able to produce more power, better mileage and lower emissions.

The PGM-FI system uses the PCM and an array of information sensors to determine and deliver the correct air/fuel ratio under all operating conditions. The PGM-FI system consists of three sub-systems: air induction, electronic control and fuel delivery. The PGM-FI system is also closely interrelated with PCM-controlled emission control systems. For additional information about the PCM, the information sensors and the emission control systems, refer to Chapter 6.

AIR INDUCTION SYSTEM

The air induction system consists of the air filter assembly, the air intake duct (which is also a resonator on coupes and sedans), the throttle body and the intake manifold. The single-barrel, cast aluminum throttle body contains a throttle plate that regulates the amount of air entering the intake manifold. The throttle plate is opened and closed by the accelerator cable. The lower part of the throttle body is heated by engine coolant to prevent icing in cold weather. The throttle body is also the location of the Throttle Position (TP) sensor, a potentiometer that monitors the opening angle of the throttle plate and sends a variable voltage signal to the Powertrain Control Module (PCM). A Manifold Absolute Pressure (MAP) sensor is also located on the throttle body. The MAP sensor measures intake manifold pressure and vacuum and generates a variable voltage signal that's proportional to the pressure or vacuum. The PCM uses this data to calculate the load on the

engine. Another information sensor, the Intake Air Temperature (IAT) sensor, is located on the intake manifold. The IAT sensor relays a voltage signal to the PCM that varies in accordance with the temperature of the incoming air in the manifold. The PCM uses this data to calculate how rich or lean the air/fuel mixture should be. All of the air induction components (air filter housing, air intake duct and throttle body) are covered in this Chapter, except for the intake manifold, which is covered in Chapter 2A (SOHC engines) or Chapter 2B (DOHC engines), and the information sensors, which are covered in Chapter 6.

When the engine is idling, the Idle Air Control (IAC) system maintains the correct idle speed by regulating the amount of air that bypasses the (closed) throttle plate in response to a command from the Powertrain Control Module (PCM). The IAC system consists of the IAC valve (located on the throttle body), the PCM, and several information sensors, including the Engine Coolant Temperature (ECT) sensor, the Intake Air Temperature (IAT) sensor and the Manifold Absolute Pressure (MAP) sensor. The IAC valve is activated and controlled by the PCM in response to the running conditions of the engine (cold or warm running, power steering pressure high or low, air conditioning system on or off, etc.). As the PCM receives data from the information sensors (vehicle speed, coolant temperature, air conditioning and/or power steering load, etc.) it adjusts the idle according to the demands of the engine and driver.

ELECTRONIC CONTROL SYSTEM

For more information about the electronic control system, i.e. the PCM, its information sensors and output actuators, refer to Chapter 6.

FUEL DELIVERY SYSTEM

The fuel delivery system consists of the fuel pump, the fuel filter, the fuel pressure regulator, the fuel pulsation damper, the fuel rail and fuel injectors, and the lines and fittings that carry fuel between all of these components.

The fuel pump is an in-tank design, and it can be removed from the top of the fuel tank without removing the tank. Fuel is drawn through a "sock" (or strainer) at the pump inlet, then pumped out the other end of the pump and through an integral fuel filter. After the pressurized fuel has been filtered, it's pumped through the supply line to the fuel rail in the engine compartment. Another much shorter line is plumbed into the supply line at the pump. This line leads to a fuel pressure regulator - mounted on the fuel pump assembly - which maintains the fuel pressure within the specified operating range. When the operating pressure exceeds the specified operating range, excess fuel is dumped back into the fuel tank (in other words, there is no fuel "return" line in this system).

Right before the fuel reaches the fuel rail, it's pumped through a fuel pulsation damper, which is located near the fuel rail. The pulsation damper lessens the hydraulic and acoustic "noise" produced by the fuel pump when it's operating. The fuel rail, which is bolted to the intake manifold, functions as a reservoir for pressurized fuel so that there's always enough fuel available for acceleration and high speed operation. The fuel rail also houses the upper end of each fuel injector (the lower end of each injector is inserted into the intake manifold).

Each fuel injector is a solenoid-actuated, pintle-type design consisting of a solenoid, plunger, needle valve and housing. When the engine is running, there is always voltage on the "hot" side of each injector terminal. The PCM turns the injectors on and off by switching their ground paths on and off. When the ground path for an injector is closed by the PCM, current flows through the solenoid coil, the needle valve raises and pressurized fuel inside the injector housing squirts out the nozzle. The quantity of fuel injected each time an injector opens is determined by the "pulse width," which is the interval of time during which the valve is open.

13 Programmed Fuel Injection (PGM-FI) system - check

▶ **Refer to illustrations 13.7 and 13.9**

✳ WARNING:

Gasoline is extremely flammable, so take extra precautions when you work on any part of the fuel system. See the Warning in Section 2.

➡**Note: The following procedure is based on the assumption that the fuel pump is working and the fuel pressure is adequate (see Section 3).**

1   Check all electrical connectors that are related to the system. Check the ground wire connections for tightness. Loose connectors and poor grounds can cause many problems that resemble more serious malfunctions.

2   Verify that the battery is fully charged. The Powertrain Control Module (PCM), information sensors and output actuators (the fuel injectors are output actuators) depend on a stable voltage supply in order to meter fuel correctly.

3   Inspect the air filter element (see Chapter 1). A dirty or partially blocked filter will severely impede performance and economy.

4   Check all fuses related to the fuel system (see Chapter 12). If you find a blown fuse, replace it and see if it blows again. If it does, look for a wire shorted to ground in the circuit(s) protected by that fuse.

5   Check the air induction system between the throttle body and the intake manifold for air leaks, which will cause a lean air/fuel mixture ratio. (When the mixture ratio becomes excessively lean, the engine will misfire.) Also inspect the condition of all vacuum hoses connected to the intake manifold and to the throttle body. A loose or broken vacuum hose will allow "false (unmetered) air" into the intake manifold. The Manifold Absolute Pressure (MAP) sensor and the PCM can compensate for some false air, but if it's excessive, especially at idle and during other high-intake-manifold-vacuum conditions, the engine will misfire.

6   Remove the air intake duct from the throttle body and look for dirt, carbon, varnish, or other residue in the throttle body, particularly around the throttle plate. If it's dirty, clean it with carb cleaner, a toothbrush and a clean shop towel.

7   With the engine running, place an automotive stethoscope against each injector, one at a time, and listen for a clicking sound that indicates operation (see illustration). If you don't have a stethoscope, touch the tip of a long screwdriver against each injector and listen through the handle.

8   If you can hear the injectors operating, but the engine is misfiring, then the electrical circuits are functioning correctly, but the injectors might be dirty or clogged. Try a commercial injector cleaning product (available at auto parts stores). If cleaning the injectors doesn't help, the injectors probably need to be replaced.

9   If an injector is not operating (it makes no clicking sound), disconnect the injector electrical connector and measure the resistance across the injector terminals with an ohmmeter (see illustration). Com-

13.7 Use a stethoscope to listen to each injector; it should make a clicking sound that rises and falls with engine speed

13.9 If an injector isn't working (it's not making a clicking sound), use an ohmmeter to measure the resistance across the two injector terminals

pare your measurement with the resistance value listed in this Chapter's Specifications. Replace any injector whose resistance value does not fall within the specifications.

10 If the injector is not operating, but the resistance reading is within specifications, the PCM or the circuit between the PCM and the injector might be faulty.

14   Throttle body - removal and installation

⁂ WARNING:

Wait until the engine is completely cool before beginning this procedure.

COUPE AND SEDAN

▶ **Refer to illustrations 14.2, 14.6, 14.7 and 14.9**

1 Remove the air intake duct/resonator and the filter housing (see

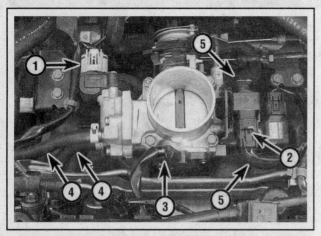

14.2 Throttle body removal (coupe and sedan):

1 *Disconnect the electrical connector from the Idle Air Control (IAC) valve*
2 *Disconnect the electrical connector from the Evaporative Emissions (EVAP) canister purge valve*
3 *Disconnect the electrical connector from the Throttle Position (TP) sensor*
4 *Disconnect the coolant bypass hoses from the throttle body*
5 *Disconnect the vacuum hoses from the EVAP canister purge valve*

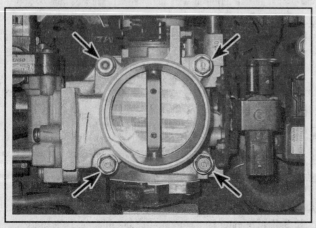

14.6 To detach the throttle body from the intake manifold of a coupe or sedan, remove these fasteners

Section 10).
2 Disconnect the electrical connectors from the Idle Air Control (IAC) valve, the Evaporative Emissions (EVAP) canister purge valve and the Throttle Position (TP) sensor (see illustration).
3 Clamp off the two coolant bypass hoses to the throttle body (see illustration 14.2), then disconnect them. Be prepared for a little coolant spillage.
4 Disconnect the vacuum hoses from the EVAP canister purge valve (see illustration 14.2).
5 Disconnect the cruise control cable from the throttle lever cam. Disconnecting the cruise control cable from the throttle lever cam is the same procedure as disconnecting the accelerator cable (see illustrations 11.2 and 11.3).
6 Remove the three throttle body mounting bolts and the mounting nut (see illustration) and remove the throttle body.
7 Remove the old throttle body gasket (see illustration) and discard it.
8 Remove all traces of old gasket material from the throttle body and the intake manifold.
9 Before installing the old throttle body (if you're installing the old unit), spray the bore with carburetor cleaner or some other suitable solvent and thoroughly clean the bore, particularly the area below the throttle valve, by wiping off the oily residue, varnish and/or carbon deposits with a clean shop rag (see illustration).

⁂ CAUTION:

Unless the throttle body that you're cleaning is stripped of all external components such as the Throttle Position (TP) sensor, EVAP canister purge valve and MAP sensor attached, make sure that you don't spray any of these devices with carb cleaner. Solvent will damage the plastic housings for these units and might even damage the delicate electronics inside them.

10 Installation is the reverse of removal. Be sure to use new gaskets

14.7 After removing the throttle body from the intake manifold, remove and discard the old gasket; always use a new gasket when installing the throttle body to prevent air leaks

14.9 To clean the bore of the throttle body, spray it with carburetor cleaner or some other suitable solvent and wipe out the bore, particularly the area below the throttle valve (shown) with a clean shop rag. Make sure that you remove any oily residue, varnish and/or carbon deposits

and tighten the throttle body mounting bolts and nut to the torque listed in this Chapter's Specifications.

11 When you're done, check the coolant level and top it up if necessary (see Chapter 1).

12 Check the accelerator cable adjustment and adjust it if necessary (see Section 11).

13 Perform the PCM idle learn procedure (see Chapter 5, Section 1).

14 Start the engine and check for air and coolant leaks.

2002 THROUGH 2004 CR-V MODELS

15 On CR-Vs, remove the throttle linkage cover.

16 Loosen the hose clamp and disconnect the air intake duct from the throttle body.

17 Disconnect the electrical connectors from the Evaporative Emission (EVAP) canister purge valve, the Manifold Absolute Pressure (MAP) sensor, the Throttle Position (TP) sensor and the Idle Air Control (IAC) valve.

18 Disconnect the vacuum hoses from the EVAP canister purge valve and from the throttle body.

19 Clamp off the two coolant bypass hoses to the throttle body, then disconnect them. Be prepared for a little coolant spillage.

20 Disconnect the accelerator cable and, if equipped, the cruise control cable from the throttle lever cam (see Section 11).

21 Remove the four throttle body mounting bolts (CR-V) or two mounting bolts and two mounting nuts (hatchback) and remove the throttle body.

22 Remove the old throttle body gasket and discard it.

23 Remove all traces of old gasket material from the throttle body and the intake manifold.

24 Installation is the reverse of removal. Be sure to use new gaskets and tighten the throttle body mounting bolts and nut to the torque listed in this Chapter's Specifications.

25 When you're done, check the coolant level and top it up if necessary (see Chapter 1).

26 Check the accelerator cable adjustment and adjust it if necessary (see Section 11).

27 Perform the PCM idle learn procedure (see Chapter 5, Section 1).

28 Start the engine and check for air and coolant leaks.

2005 AND 2006 CR-V MODELS

29 Loosen the hose clamp and disconnect the air intake duct from the throttle body.

30 Disconnect all electrical connectors from the throttle body.

31 Clamp off the two coolant bypass hoses to the throttle body, then disconnect them. Be prepared for a little coolant spillage. Plug the ends of the hoses.

32 Disconnect the vacuum hose and remove the harness clip from the throttle body.

33 Remove the throttle body mounting bolts and nuts and remove the throttle body.

34 Remove the old throttle body gasket and discard it.

35 Remove all traces of old gasket material from the throttle body and intake manifold.

36 Installation is the reverse of removal. Be sure to use a new gasket and tighten the throttle body mounting bolts and nuts to the torque listed in this Chapter's Specifications.

37 When you're done, check the coolant level and top it up if necessary (see Chapter 1).

38 Perform the PCM Idle learn procedure (see Chapter 5, Section 1).

39 Start the engine and check for vacuum and coolant leaks.

15 Fuel pulsation damper - removal and installation

COUPE AND SEDAN

1 The fuel pulsation damper is an integral part of the fuel rail. It is not available separately. To replace the fuel pulsation damper, you must replace the fuel rail (see Section 16).

CR-V

2 Relieve the system fuel pressure (see Section 2), then disconnect the cable from the negative battery terminal (see Chapter 5, Section 1).

3 Locate the fuel pulsation damper at the left end of the fuel rail.

4 Disconnect the quick-connect fitting (see Section 4) that con-nects the fuel supply line to the fuel pulsation damper.

5 Using a back-up wrench on the big hex at the end of the fuel rail to protect the fuel rail from damage, loosen the pulsation damper with another wrench, then unscrew and remove the damper.

6 Remove and discard the old pulsation damper sealing washer.

7 Installation is the reverse of removal. Be sure to use a new washer when installing the pulsation damper, then tighten the damper to the torque listed in this Chapter's Specifications.

8 Reconnect the cable to the negative battery terminal, then perform the PCM idle learn procedure (see Chapter 5, Section 1).

9 When you're done, start the engine and check for leaks around the pulsation damper.

HATCHBACK

10 Relieve the system fuel pressure (see Section 2), then disconnect the cable from the negative battery terminal (see Chapter 5, Section 1).

11 Remove the engine cover (see Chapter 2B).

12 Locate the fuel pulsation damper on the front of the fuel rail.

13 Remove the fuel rail mounting nuts (see Section 16).

14 Disconnect the ground cable.

15 Raise the fuel rail assembly slightly.

16 Using a back-up wrench on the pulsation damper junction block to protect the fuel rail, loosen the fuel pulsation damper with another wrench. Then unscrew and remove the pulsation damper from the junction block.

17 Remove and discard the old pulsation damper sealing washers.

18 When installing the pulsation damper, make sure that the drain hole on the damper faces *down*. Installation is otherwise the reverse of removal. Be sure to use new sealing washers and tighten the fuel pulsation damper securely.

19 Reconnect the cable to the negative battery cable, then perform the PCM idle learn procedure (see Chapter 5, Section 1).

20 When you're done, start the engine and check the area around the fuel pulsation damper for leaks.

16 Fuel rail and injectors - removal and installation

COUPE AND SEDAN

▶ **Refer to illustrations 16.3, 16.5, 16.7, 16.8, 16.9a, 16.9b and 16.10**

❄ WARNING:

Gasoline is extremely flammable, so take extra precautions when you work on any part of the fuel system. See the Warning in Section 2.

1 Relieve the system fuel pressure (see Section 2), then disconnect the cable from the negative battery terminal (see Chapter 5, Section 1).

2 Remove the air intake duct/resonator and filter housing (see Section 10).

3 Disconnect the electrical connectors from the fuel injectors (see illustration).

4 Disconnect the electrical connectors from the Evaporative Emissions (EVAP) canister purge valve and the Throttle Position (TP) sensor (see illustration 14.2) and disconnect the electrical connector from the Manifold Absolute Pressure (MAP) sensor (see illustration 10.2 in Chapter 6).

5 Disconnect the quick-connect fitting that connects the fuel supply line to the fuel pulsation damper (see illustration). If you're not yet familiar with the disconnection procedure for this type of fitting, refer to Section 4 for help.

6 Disconnect the vacuum hoses from both ends of the pipe that's welded to the fuel rail (see illustration 16.5).

7 Remove the fuel rail mounting nuts (see illustration).

8 Remove the fuel rail and the fuel injectors as a single assembly (see illustration). If any of the injectors are difficult to extract from their bores, carefully pry them loose by wiggling them from side to side and pulling up at the same time. After removing the fuel rail/injector assembly, remove the two spacers and store them in a plastic bag until you need them again for reassembly.

9 To remove each injector from the fuel rail, remove the retainer clip, then pull the injector out of its bore in the fuel rail (see illustrations).

10 Remove and discard the upper and lower O-rings from each injector (see illustration), discard them and install new O-rings. Coat each new O-ring with clean engine oil to make it easier to slide the O-ring into place on the injector. Repeat this procedure for each injector.

16.3 Disconnect the electrical connectors from the four fuel injectors

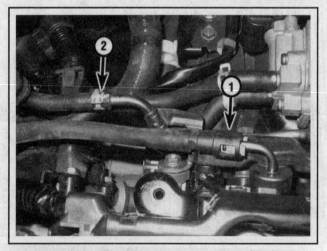

16.5 Disconnect the quick-connect fitting (1) from the fuel pulsation damper (see Section 4 if you don't know how to disconnect this type of fitting), then disconnect the vacuum hoses (2) from both ends of the vacuum pipe that's welded to the fuel rail (left vacuum hose not shown in this photo)

16.7 To detach the fuel rail from the cylinder head, remove these two nuts (coupe sedan shown, others similar)

16.8 Remove the fuel rail and injectors as a single assembly. If any of the injectors stick in their bores, carefully wiggle them from side to side while simultaneously pulling straight up; if that doesn't work, insert a large pry bar between the fuel rail and the valve cover and carefully lever the fuel rail upward to free any stuck injectors

➡ Note: Even if you only removed the fuel rail assembly to replace a single injector or a leaking O-ring, it's a good idea to remove all of the injectors from the fuel rail and replace all the O-rings, cushion rings and seal rings at the same time.

11 Coat the new upper injector O-rings with clean engine oil, then insert each injector into its corresponding bore in the fuel rail.

12 Coat each new lower injector O-ring with clean engine oil and press it into that injector's bore in the intake manifold.

13 Once the fuel rail assembly is in place, with all four injectors fully seated in their respective bores, install the fuel rail mounting nuts and tighten them to the torque listed in this Chapter's Specifications. (Don't forget to install the spacers first!)

14 The remainder of installation is the reverse of removal.

15 When you're done reassembling everything, reconnect the cable to the negative battery terminal, then perform the PCM idle learn procedure (see Chapter 5, Section 1).

16 Turn the ignition switch to ON to activate the fuel pump and build up fuel pressure in the fuel lines and the fuel rail, but DON'T operate the starter yet. Repeat this step two or three times, then check the fuel lines, fuel rails and injectors for fuel leaks.

17 Once you're confident that there are no leaks, start the engine and verify that the injectors are working and there are no fuel leaks.

CR-V AND HATCHBACK

18 Relieve the system fuel pressure (see Section 2), then disconnect the cable from the negative battery terminal (see Chapter 5, Section 1).

19 Disconnect the electrical connectors from the fuel injectors, disconnect the ground cable and remove the harness holder.

20 Disconnect the fuel supply line quick-connect fitting from the fuel pulsation damper (CR-V) or from the left end of the fuel rail (hatchback). Refer to Section 4 if you don't know how to disconnect this type of fitting.

21 Remove the fuel rail mounting nuts.

22 Remove the fuel rail and injectors as a single assembly. After removing the fuel rail/injector assembly, remove the two spacers and store them in a plastic bag until you need them again for reassembly.

23 Remove the injectors from the fuel rail, remove and discard the old injector O-rings, install new O-rings on each injector and reinstall the injectors in the fuel rail (see Steps 9 through 11).

24 Coat each new lower injector O-ring with clean engine oil and press it into that injector's corresponding bore in the intake manifold.

16.9a To detach an injector from the fuel rail, pull off the retainer clip with a pair of pliers . . .

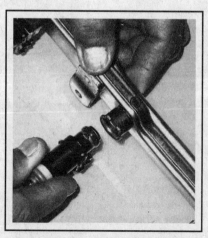

16.9b . . . then carefully work the injector out of its bore in the fuel rail

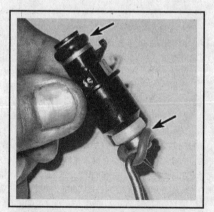

16.10 Be sure to remove both of the old injector O-rings and discard them. Always use new O-rings when installing an injector

25 Once the fuel rail assembly is in place (all four injectors are fully seated in their respective bores), install the fuel rail mounting nuts and tighten them to the torque listed in this Chapter's Specifications. (Don't forget to install the spacers first!)

26 Once the fuel rail assembly is in place, with all four injectors fully seated in their respective bores, install the fuel rail mounting nuts and tighten them to the torque listed in this Chapter's Specifications.

27 The remainder of installation is the reverse of removal.

28 When you're done reassembling everything, reconnect the cable to the negative battery terminal, then perform the PCM idle learn procedure (see Chapter 5, Section 1).

29 Turn the ignition switch to ON to activate the fuel pump and build up fuel pressure in the fuel lines and the fuel rail, but DON'T operate the starter yet. Repeat this step two or three times, then check the fuel lines, fuel rails and injectors for fuel leaks.

30 Once you're confident that there are no leaks, start the engine and verify that the injectors are working and there are no fuel leaks.

17 Electronic throttle components (2005 and 2006 CR-V) - replacement

➡ **Note: 2005 and 2006 CR-V models use an electronically actuated throttle body. On these models, there is no direct cable link between the accelerator pedal and the throttle body. Instead, an electric actuator within the throttle body operates the throttle based on a signal it receives from the Throttle Actuator Control Module (TACM). The Accelerator Pedal Position (APP) sensor provides input to the TACM of the actual position of the accelerator pedal.**

THROTTLE ACTUATOR CONTROL MODULE

1 Open the glove box door.

2 On right side, push on the tab and disconnect the electrical connector from the throttle actuator control module.

3 Remove the throttle actuator control module mounting bolts and remove the throttle actuator control module.

4 Installation is the reverse of removal. Tighten the bolts securely.

Accelerator Pedal Position (APP) sensor

5 The Accelerator Pedal Position (APP) sensor is located in the engine compartment, on the passenger's side of the firewall.

6 Disconnect the accelerator cable from the APP sensor (see Section 11).

7 Disconnect the electrical connnector from the APP sensor.

8 Remove the bolts and remove the APP sensor.

9 Installation is the reverse of removal.

18 Exhaust system servicing - general information

▶ **Refer to illustrations 18.1 and 18.4**

⁕⁕ **WARNING:**

Inspect and repair exhaust system components only after enough time has elapsed after driving the vehicle to allow the system components to cool completely. Also, when working under the vehicle, make sure it is securely supported on jackstands.

1 The exhaust system consists of the exhaust manifolds, the catalytic converter, the muffler, the tailpipe and all connecting pipes, flanges and clamps. The exhaust system is isolated from the vehicle body and from chassis components by a series of rubber hangers (see illustration). Periodically inspect these hangers fr cracks or other signs of deterioration, replacing them as necessary.

2 Conduct regular inspections of the exhaust system to keep it safe and quiet. Look for any damaged or bent parts, open seams, holes, loose connections, excessive corrosion or other defects which could allow exhaust fumes to enter the vehicle. Do not repair deteriorated exhaust system components; replace them with new parts.

3 If the exhaust system components are extremely corroded, or rusted together, you'll need welding equipment and a cutting torch to remove them. The convenient strategy at this point is to have a muffler repair shop remove the corroded sections with a cutting torch. If you want to save money by doing it yourself, but you don't have a welding outfit and cutting torch, simply cut off the old components with a hack-saw. If you have compressed air, there are special pneumatic cutting chisels (available from specialty tool manufacturers) that can also be used. If you decide to tackle the job at home, be sure to wear safety goggles to protect your eyes from metal chips and wear work gloves to protect your hands.

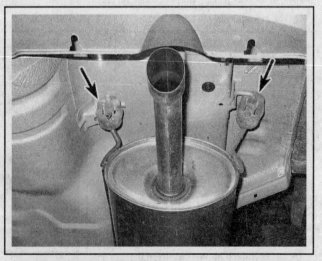

18.1 Inspect the rubber hangers that support the exhaust system every time that you are working underneath the vehicle

4   Here are some simple guidelines to follow when repairing the exhaust system:

a) *Work from the back to the front when removing exhaust system components.*

b) *Apply penetrating oil to the exhaust system component fasteners (see illustration)* to make them easier to remove.

c) *Use new gaskets, hangers and clamps when installing exhaust systems components.*

d) *Apply anti-seize compound to the threads of all exhaust system fasteners during reassembly.*

e) *Be sure to allow sufficient clearance between newly installed parts and all points on the underbody to avoid overheating the floor pan and possibly damaging the interior carpet and insulation. Pay particularly close attention to the catalytic converter and heat shield.*

18.4 Exhaust pipe flange bolts and nuts can be extremely difficult to loosen because they've been subjected to extreme heat for prolonged periods of time. The best way to loosen these fasteners is to apply a liberal dose of penetrant to them, give it plenty of time to loosen them up, *then* unscrew them

Specifications

Accelerator cable deflection	3/8 to 1/2-inch (10 to 12 mm)
Fuel system pressure	
Coupe and sedan	40 to 47 psi
CR-V	48 to 55 psi
Hatchback	47 to 52 psi
Injector resistance	10 to 13 ohms

Torque specifications

Ft-lbs (unless otherwise indicated)   Nm

➡Note: One foot-pound (ft-lb) of torque is equivalent to 12 inch-pounds (in-lbs) of torque. Torque values below approximately 15 ft-lbs are expressed in inch-pounds, since most foot-pound torque wrenches are not accurate at these smaller values.

	Ft-lbs	Nm
Throttle body mounting bolts/nuts (all models)	192 in-lbs	22
Fuel rail mounting nuts		
Coupe and sedan	104.4 in-lbs	12
CR-V and hatchback	192 in-lbs	22
Fuel pulsation damper		
CR-V	192 in-lbs	22

Notes

5

ENGINE ELECTRICAL SYSTEMS

Section

Reference to other Chapters

CHECK ENGINE light on - See Chapter 6

1 General information, precautions and battery disconnection

The engine electrical systems include all ignition, charging and starting components. Because of their engine-related functions, these components are covered separately from body electrical devices such as the lights, the instruments, etc. (which you'll find in Chapter 12).

PRECAUTIONS

Always observe the following precautions when working on the electrical system:

a) *Be extremely careful when servicing engine electrical components. They are easily damaged if checked, connected or handled improperly.*

b) *Never leave the ignition switched on for long periods of time when the engine is not running.*

c) *Never disconnect the battery cables while the engine is running.*

d) *Maintain correct polarity when connecting battery cables from another vehicle during jump starting - see the "Booster battery (jump) starting" Section at the front of this manual.*

e) *Always disconnect the cable from the negative battery terminal before working on the electrical system, but read the following battery disconnection procedure first.*

It's also a good idea to review the safety-related information regarding the engine electrical systems located in the "Safety first!" Section at the front of this manual, before beginning any operation included in this Chapter.

BATTERY DISCONNECTION

Some systems on the vehicle require battery power to be available at all times, either to maintain continuous operation (alarm system, power door locks, etc.), or to maintain control unit memory (radio station presets, Powertrain Control Module and other control units). When the battery is disconnected, the power that maintains these systems is cut. So, before you disconnect the battery, please note the following points to ensure that there are no unforeseen consequences of this action:

a) *The radio in some models is equipped with an anti-theft system; make sure you have the correct anti-theft codes for the radio before disconnecting the battery.*

b) *When the battery, or any of the components listed below, is disconnected, the engine management system's Powertrain Control Module (PCM) will lose some data from its memory regarding the engine idle characteristics. It is imperative that you perform the "PCM idle learn procedure" (see procedure below) after disconnecting any of the components listed below.*

c) *On a vehicle with power door locks, it's a wise precaution to remove the key from the ignition and to keep it with you, so that it does not get locked inside if the power door locks should engage accidentally when the battery is reconnected!*

Devices known as "memory-savers" can be used to avoid some of these problems. Precise details vary according to the device used. The typical memory saver is plugged into the cigarette lighter and is connected to a spare battery. Then the vehicle battery can be disconnected from the electrical system. The memory saver will provide sufficient current to maintain audio unit security codes, PCM memory, etc. and will provide power to "always hot" circuits such as the clock and radio memory circuits.

❄❄ WARNING 1:

Some memory savers deliver a considerable amount of current in order to keep vehicle systems operational after the main battery is disconnected. If you're using a memory saver, make sure that the circuit concerned is actually open before servicing it.

❄❄ WARNING 2:

If you're going to work near any of the airbag system components, the battery MUST be disconnected and a memory saver must NOT be used. If a memory saver is used, power will be supplied to the airbag, which means that it could accidentally deploy and cause serious personal injury.

To disconnect the battery for service procedures requiring power to be cut from the vehicle, loosen the cable clamp nut and disconnect the cable from the negative battery post. Isolate the cable end to prevent it from coming into accidental contact with the battery post.

POWERTRAIN CONTROL MODULE (PCM) IDLE LEARN PROCEDURE

Make sure that the PCM "learns" the engine idle characteristics after you do any of the following procedures:

Disconnect the battery
Replace (or reset) the PCM
Replace the throttle body
Replace the Idle Air Control (IAC) valve
Remove the No. 6 (15 amp) PCM fuse (in the engine compartment fuse and relay box)
Remove the No. 19 (120-amp) BATTERY fuse (in the engine compartment fuse and relay box)
Remove the PGM-FI main relay No. 1
Remove any of the wires from the engine compartment fuse and relay box
Disconnect any of the connectors from the engine compartment fuse and relay box
Disconnect the electrical connector between the engine compartment wire harness and the PCM wire harness
Disconnect the battery ground wire from the transmission housing
Disconnect the ground wire from the body
Disconnect the ground wire from the cylinder head

1   Make sure that all electrical components (air conditioning system, lights, rear window defogger, sound system, etc.) are turned OFF.

2   Start the engine, bring it up to 3000 rpm and hold it there, with no load (in PARK or NEUTRAL), until the radiator fan comes on or until the engine coolant temperature reaches 194-degrees F.

3   Allow the engine to idle for at least five minutes with no load on it and with the throttle fully closed.

➡**Note: If the radiator fan comes on during this five-minute period, don't include the time during which the fan runs as part of the five minutes.**

RESETTING THE POWER WINDOW CONTROL UNIT

On the CR-V and on the 2004 hatchback, you must reset the power window control unit after you do any of the following procedures:

Disconnect the battery
Remove the No. 6 (7.5 amp) and/or the No. 23 (20 amp) fuse from the under-dash fuse and relay box
Disconnect the driver's door wiring harness

4   Turn the ignition switch to OFF, then turn it to ON.

5   Fully open the driver's window by holding the driver's switch in the AUTO DOWN position. After the window reaches its fully open position, hold the driver's switch in the AUTO DOWN position for two seconds.

6   Fully close the driver's window by holding the driver's switch in the AUTO UP position. After the window reaches its fully closed position, hold the driver's switch in the AUTO UP position for two seconds.

7   If the window doesn't operate in AUTO, reset the power window control unit by repeating this entire procedure.

2   Battery - emergency jump starting

Refer to the *Booster battery (jump) starting* procedure at the front of this manual.

3   Battery - check and replacement

✴✴ WARNING:

Always disconnect the cable from the negative battery terminal FIRST and hook it up LAST or the battery may be shorted by the tool being used to loosen the cable clamps.

✴✴ CAUTION:

The radio in some models is equipped with an anti-theft system; make sure you have the correct anti-theft codes for the radio before disconnecting the battery.

CHECK

▶ **Refer to illustrations 3.2 and 3.3**

1   Disconnect the negative battery cable, then the positive cable from the battery.

2   Check the battery state of charge. Visually inspect the indicator eye on the top of the battery; if the indicator eye is black in color charge the battery as described in Chapter 1. Next perform an open voltage circuit test using a digital voltmeter (see illustration).

➡**Note: The battery's surface charge must be removed before accurate voltage measurements can be made. Turn on the high beams for ten seconds, then turn them off and let the vehicle stand for two minutes.**

With the engine and all accessories Off, touch the negative probe of the voltmeter to the negative terminal of the battery and the positive probe to the positive terminal of the battery. The battery voltage should be 11.5 to 12.5 volts or slightly above. If the battery is less than the specified voltage, charge the battery before proceeding to the next test. Do not proceed with the battery load test unless the battery charge is correct.

3   Perform a battery load test. An accurate check of the battery condition can only be performed with a load tester (available at most auto parts stores). This test evaluates the ability of the battery to operate the starter and other accessories during periods of high current draw. Hook up a special load tester to the battery terminals (see illustration). Load test the battery according to the manufacturer's instructions. This tool utilizes a carbon-pile-type variable resistor to increase the load demand (current draw) on the battery. Maintain the load on the battery for 15 seconds or less and observe that the battery voltage does not drop below 9.6 volts. If the battery condition is weak or defective, the tool will indicate this condition immediately.

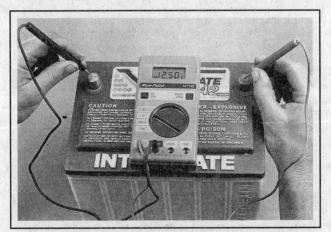

3.2 To test the open circuit voltage of the battery, touch the black probe of the voltmeter to the negative terminal and the red probe to the positive terminal of the battery; a fully charged battery should be about 12.5 volts

3.3 Some battery load testers (like this one) are equipped with an ammeter that allows you to vary the amount of the load on the battery (less expensive testers only have a load switch that puts the battery under a fixed load)

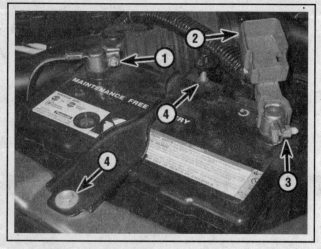

3.4 Battery mounting details

1 *Negative cable clamp (always disconnect this one first, and hook it up last)*
2 *Positive terminal cover*
3 *Positive cable clamp*
4 *Hold-down clamp bolt/nut*

➡Note: Cold temperatures will cause the minimum voltage requirements to drop slightly. Follow the chart given in the manufacturer's instructions to compensate for cold climates. Minimum load voltage for freezing temperatures (32-degrees F) should be approximately 9.1 volts.

REPLACEMENT

▶ Refer to illustrations 3.4, 3.8a and 3.8b

4   Disconnect the cable from the negative battery terminal first, then (and only then!) disconnect the cable from the positive battery terminal (see illustration).
5   Remove the battery hold-down clamp nuts (see illustration 3.4) and remove the hold-down clamp.
6   Lift out the battery. Be careful - it's heavy.
➡Note: Battery straps and handlers are available at most auto parts stores for a reasonable price. They make it easier to remove and carry the battery.
7   While the battery is out, inspect the battery tray for corrosion.

3.8a To remove the battery tray from the engine compartment, remove these two upper mounting bolts . . .

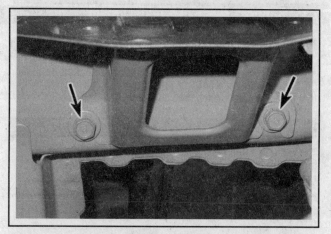

3.8b . . . and remove these two mounting bracket bolts from underneath the tray

8   If there's corrosion on the battery tray, remove the tray's mounting bolts (see illustrations) and remove the tray from the engine compartment. Clean the deposits from the metal to prevent the battery tray from further corrosion.
9   If you are replacing the battery, make sure you get one that's identical, with the same dimensions, amperage rating, cold cranking rating, etc.
10 Installation is the reverse of removal. Be sure to connect the positive cable first and the negative cable last (see Section 1).

4   Battery cables - check and replacement

▶ Refer to illustrations 4.4a, 4.4b, and 4.4c

1   Periodically inspect the entire length of each battery cable for damage, cracked or burned insulation and corrosion. Poor battery cable connections can cause starting problems and decreased engine performance.
2   Inspect the cable-to-terminal connections at the ends of the cables for cracks, loose wire strands and corrosion. The presence of white, fluffy deposits under the insulation at the cable terminal connection means that the cable is corroded and should be replaced. Also inspect the battery posts for distortion and corrosion. If they're corroded, clean them up
3   When removing the cables, always disconnect the cable from the

negative battery terminal first and hook it up last, or you might accidentally short out the battery with the tool you're using to loosen the cable clamps. Even if you're only replacing the cable for the positive terminal, be sure to disconnect the negative cable from the battery first (see Section 1).

✳✳ CAUTION:

The radio on some models is equipped with an anti-theft system. Make sure you have the correct anti-theft codes before disconnecting the battery. You'll also want to write down the frequencies for the radio's preset buttons.

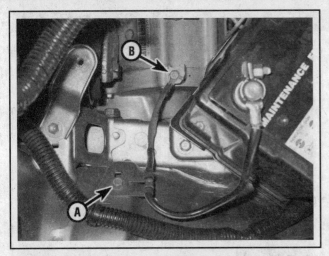

4.4a The battery ground cable is typically secured to the inner fender panel (A) and the transaxle (B)

4.4b One of the positive cables goes from the battery straight to the underhood fuse/relay box (1); the other heavy gauge wire (2) goes to the alternator (coupe/sedan model shown, others similar)

4 Disconnect the old cables from the battery, then trace each cable to its opposite end and disconnect it (see illustrations). Be sure to note the routing of each cable before disconnecting it to ensure correct installation. Starter cable replacement isn't entirely straightforward on the vehicles covered in this manual because the starter cable disappears into a thicket of harnesses and emerges from the other end down at the starter solenoid. What you must do is carefully remove all of the old electrical tape, remove the conduit surrounding each harness, then separate the starter cable from the other wiring. Then, after you've installed the new starter cable, carefully bunch the wiring - including the starter cable - back together again, tape it to hold it together tightly, re-cover it with the conduit, then finish taping all exposed wiring.

5 When purchasing battery cables, *take the old one(s) with you when buying new cables.* It is vitally important that you replace the cables with identical parts.

6 Clean the threads of the solenoid or ground connection with a wire brush to remove rust and corrosion. Apply a light coat of battery terminal corrosion inhibitor or petroleum jelly to the threads to prevent future corrosion.

7 Attach the cable to the solenoid or ground connection and tighten the mounting nut/bolt securely.

8 Before connecting a new cable to the battery make sure that it reaches the battery post without having to be stretched.

4.4c The positive battery cable to the starter disappears into a conduit and is secured along its length by tape and clips

9 Connect the cable to the positive battery terminal first, then connect the ground cable to the negative battery terminal (see Section 1).

5 Ignition system - general information

❊❊ WARNING:

Because of the high voltage generated by the ignition system, be extremely careful when performing any procedure involving ignition components.

1 The electronic ignition system consists of the Powertrain Control Module (PCM), the ignition switch, the battery, the four ignition coils and the spark plugs.

2 The PCM alters ignition timing in accordance with the engine speed, the manifold absolute pressure and the engine coolant temperature. The PCM uses data from the Camshaft Position (Top Dead Center) [CMP (TDC)] sensors to determine ignition timing during start-ups, and anytime that the crank angle is abnormal. The PCM calculates engine speed based on the data that it receives from the Crankshaft Position (CKP) sensor. It uses a Manifold Absolute Pressure (MAP) sensor to determine manifold absolute pressure. For more information about the CMP (TDC), CKP and MAP sensors, refer to Chapter 6.

6 Ignition system - check

▶ Refer to illustration 6.2

⁂ WARNING:

Because of the high voltage generated by the ignition system, use extreme care when performing a procedure involving ignition components.

1   If a malfunction occurs in the ignition system, check the following items:

a) *Make sure that the cable clamps at the battery terminals are clean and tight.*

b) *Test the condition of the battery (see Section 3). If it doesn't pass all the tests, replace it.*

c) *Check the ignition coil connections.*

d) *Check any relevant fuses in the engine compartment fuse and relay box (see Chapter 12). If they're burned, determine the cause and repair the circuit.*

2   Check the ignition spark from each coil. If the engine turns over but won't start, disconnect the ignition coil (see Section 7) from any spark plug and install a calibrated spark tester (available at most auto parts stores) inline between the coil high-tension terminal and the spark plug (see illustration). Then crank the engine and see if the tester flashes.

3   If sparks occur during cranking, sufficient voltage is reaching the plug to fire it (repeat the check for each cylinder to verify that the other coils are OK). However, be aware that even if all four ignition coils are able to fire the spark tester the plugs themselves might be fouled, so remove and inspect the plugs too (see Chapter 1).

4   If no sparks occur during cranking at one cylinder, inspect the primary wire connection at the coil. Make sure that it's clean and tight.

5   If no sparks or intermittent sparks occur during cranking at all

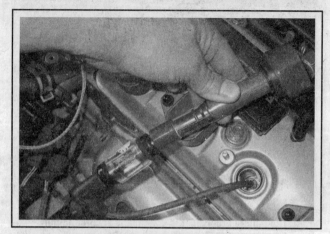

6.2 To use a calibrated spark tester, remove a coil, insert the tester into the coil, push the boot on the other end of the tester onto the spark plug and crank the engine; if the coil is generating enough voltage to fire the plug, filament inside the tester housing will flash

cylinders, the PCM is probably defective. Have the PCM checked out by a dealer service department or other qualified repair shop (testing the PCM is beyond the scope of the do-it-yourselfer because it requires expensive special tools).

6   If the spark plug is in good shape, the coil might be defective. Have it checked out by a dealer service department or other qualified repair shop (again, this procedure is beyond the scope of the home mechanic because it requires special tools).

7   Any additional testing of the ignition system must be done by a dealer service department or other qualified repair shop with the right tools.

7 Ignition coils - replacement

▶ Refer to illustrations 7.1a, 7.1b, 7.2 and 7.3

1   Remove the ignition coil cover (see illustrations).

2   Disconnect the electrical connector from the ignition coil (see illustration).

7.1a To access an ignition coil, rotate the two coil cover fasteners counterclockwise a quarter-turn and remove the cover . . .

7.1b . . . then remove the fasteners that secure the ignition coil harness to the valve cover so that you can push the harness aside as necessary in order to disconnect the electrical connector(s) from the ignition coil(s)

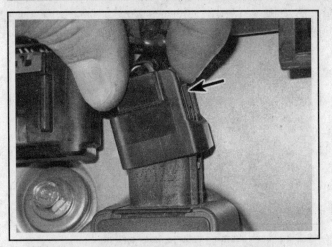

7.2 To disconnect the electrical connector from the ignition coil, depress the locking tab on the side of the connector and pull

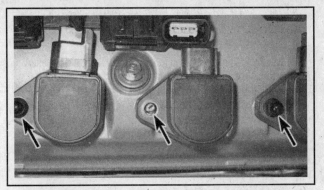

7.3 To detach an ignition coil from the valve cover, remove the mounting nut (nut already removed from one coil)

3   Remove the ignition coil mounting nut (see illustration).
4   Remove the ignition coil from the spark plug.
5   Installation is the reverse of removal. Be sure to tighten the ignition coil mounting nut securely.

8   Charging system - general information and precautions

The charging system includes the alternator (with an integral voltage regulator inside), the battery, an Electrical Load Detector (ELD) unit (in the engine compartment fuse and relay box), a charge indicator light (on the instrument cluster) and the wiring connecting all of these components. The charging system supplies electrical power for the ignition system, the lights, the radio, etc. The alternator is driven by a drivebelt at the one end of the engine. The alternator's voltage output is controlled by a conventional internal voltage regulator, which keeps charging output within a range of about 13.5 to 14.5 volts. The ELD unit, which is located in the engine compartment fuse and relay box, sends a variable voltage signal to the Powertrain Control Module (PCM) that varies in accordance with the total power demand imposed on the charging system by the electrical devices and systems in operation. The PCM uses this variable voltage signal to calculate the actual level of charging voltage needed and alters the charging voltage output accordingly.

The charging system doesn't ordinarily require periodic maintenance. However, the drivebelt, battery and wires and connections should be inspected at the intervals outlined in Chapter 1.

The dashboard warning light should come on when the ignition key

is turned to ON, but it should go off immediately after the engine is started. If it remains on, there is a malfunction in the charging system (see Section 9).

Be very careful when making electrical circuit connections to a vehicle equipped with an alternator and note the following:

a) *When reconnecting wires to the alternator from the battery, be sure to note the polarity.*
b) *Before using arc-welding equipment to repair any part of the vehicle, disconnect the wires from the alternator and the battery terminals.*
c) *Never start the engine with a battery charger connected.*
d) *Always disconnect both battery leads before using a battery charger.*
e) *The alternator is turned by an engine drivebelt that could cause serious injury if your hands, hair or clothes become entangled in it with the engine running.*
f) *Because the alternator is connected directly to the battery, it could arc or cause a fire if overloaded or shorted out.*
g) *Wrap a plastic bag over the alternator and secure it with rubber bands before steam cleaning the engine.*

9   Charging system - check

▶ **Refer to illustration 9.3**

1   If a malfunction occurs in the charging circuit, do not immediately assume that the alternator is causing the problem. First, check the following items:

a) *Make sure the battery cable clamps, where they connect to the battery, are clean and tight.*
b) *Test the condition of the battery (see Section 3). If it does not pass all the tests, replace it with a new battery.*
c) *Check the external alternator wiring and connections.*
d) *Check the drivebelt condition and tension (see Chapter 1).*
e) *Check the alternator mounting bolts for tightness.*
f) *Run the engine and check the alternator for abnormal noise.*

g) *Check the 120-amp fuse in the engine compartment fuse and relay box (see Chapter 12). If it's burned, determine the cause and repair the circuit.*
h) *Check the charge light on the dash. It should illuminate when the ignition key is turned ON (engine not running). If it doesn't come on, disconnect the electrical connector and the ground wire from the alternator. The charge light should now come on (because by opening the charging circuit, you have eliminated all charging voltage. If the light still doesn't illuminate, check fuse number 10 (7.5 amp), which is located in the left (driver's side) passenger compartment fuse and relay box. If the fuse is blown, troubleshoot and repair the charge light circuit and then replace the fuse. If the charge light still doesn't come on, check the bulb (see Chapter 12). If it's blown, replace it.*

i) Make sure that the PCM hasn't stored any diagnostic trouble codes for the Electronic Load Detector (ELD) system (see Chapter 6 for more information about the ELD).

2   With the ignition key turned to the OFF position, check battery voltage with all electrical accessories (blower fan, radio, cigarette lighter, cooling fan, etc.) turned off. It should be about 12.5 volts (it might be slightly higher if the engine has been turned off for less than an hour).

3   Check the charging voltage with the engine running. Start the engine, raise the engine rpm to 1500 and check the battery voltage again. It should now be approximately 13.8 to 14.8 volts (see illustration).

4   Load the battery and observe the charging voltage. Turn on the high beam headlights, the A/C blower on HIGH, the windshield wipers and the radio. The voltage should drop and then come back up as each accessory is selected. If the charging system is working properly the voltage should stay above 13.5 volts. If the voltage drops below 13 volts, the charging system is defective.

5   Lower the engine rpm back to idle and observe the charging voltage. The charging voltage should not drop below 13 volts with the decrease in engine rpm. Apply the brakes and observe the charging voltage at idle. It should remain above 13 volts.

6   Turn off all the electrical loads (high beam headlights, the A/C blower on HIGH, the windshield wipers and the radio), run the engine at 1600 rpm and watch the charging voltage rise. It should not rise

9.3 To check charging voltage, hook up a multimeter to the battery terminals and note the indicated voltage with the engine running, which should be about 13.5 volts

above 15 volts.

7   If the charging voltage does not exhibit distinct changes when engine rpm increases and accessory loads are added, the voltage regulator is defective. If the charging voltages are low and the drivebelts and battery are all in good condition, the alternator is defective. In this situation, replace the alternator and voltage regulator as a single unit.

10 Alternator - removal and installation

ALL MODELS

1   Disconnect the cable from the negative battery terminal (see Section 1).

> ✳ **CAUTION:**
>
> **The radio on some models is equipped with an anti-theft system. So make sure that you have the correct anti-theft codes before disconnecting the battery. You'll also want to write down the frequencies for the radio's preset buttons.**

COUPE AND SEDAN

▶ **Refer to illustrations 10.3, 10.6a and 10.6b**

2   Remove the power steering pump belt (see Chapter 1), then remove the power steering pump (see Chapter 10) and set the pump aside.

➡**Note: Do NOT disconnect any of the power steering hoses.**

3   Disconnect the harness clip that secures the harness to the alternator, remove the nut that attaches the alternator output cable to the stud on the backside of the alternator and disconnect the electrical connector from the alternator (see illustration). Set the alternator output cable aside.

4   Remove the alternator/air conditioning compressor drivebelt (see Chapter 1).

5   Loosen the lug nuts on the left front wheel, raise the front of the vehicle, place it securely on jackstands and remove the left front wheel.

6   Remove the lock bolt and adjusting bolt (see illustration) from the bracket between the alternator and the air conditioning compressor,

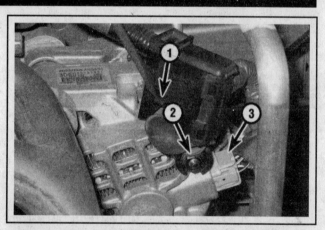

10.3 To detach the alternator output cable clip from the alternator, depress this lock button (1), remove the nut (2) that attaches the alternator output cable to the stud terminal on the backside of the alternator, set the output cable aside, then disconnect the alternator electrical connector (3)

then remove the upper alternator mounting bolt (see illustration) and remove the alternator.

7   If you're replacing the alternator, take the old one with you when purchasing the replacement unit. Make sure that the new/rebuilt unit looks identical to the old alternator. Look at the terminals - they should be the same in number, size and location as the terminals on the old alternator. Finally, look at the identification numbers - they will be stamped into the housing or printed on a tag attached to the housing. Make sure the numbers are the same on both alternators.

8   Many new/rebuilt alternators DO NOT have a pulley installed, so you might have to swap the pulley from the old unit to the new/rebuilt one. When buying an alternator, find out the store's policy regarding

10.6a To detach the alternator from its lower mounting bracket, remove the lock bolt (1) and the adjusting bolt (2)

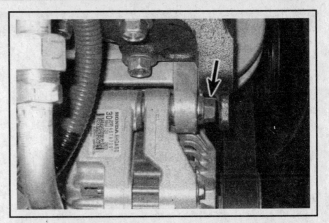

10.6b To detach the alternator from its upper mounting point, remove this bolt

pulley swaps. Some stores perform this service free of charge. If your local auto parts store doesn't offer this service, you'll have to purchase a puller for removing the pulley and do it yourself.

9   Installation is the reverse of removal. Be sure to tighten the alternator adjusting and mounting bolts securely. Tighten the wheel lug nuts to the torque listed in the Chapter 1 Specifications.

10 Reconnect the cable to the negative terminal of the battery, then perform the PCM idle learn procedure (see Section 1). When you're done, check the charging voltage (see Section 9) to verify that the alternator is operating correctly.

CR-V

11 Unscrew the battery ground strap bolt from the radiator crossmember, remove the cover from the radiator crossmember and remove the upper radiator mounting brackets and rubber insulators (see "Radiator - removal and installation" in Chapter 3).

12 Remove the three alternator mounting bolts (removing the mounting bolts first will give you a little "wiggle room" for disconnecting the electrical connections).

13 Disconnect the electrical connector and the black wire from the alternator (the black wire goes to the ELD unit in the engine compartment fuse and relay box). Then detach the harness clip from the alternator and set the electrical harness aside. Remove the alternator.

14 Refer to Steps 7 and 8.

15 Installation is the reverse of removal. Tighten the alternator mounting bolts to the torque listed in this Chapter's Specifications.

16 After reconnecting the cable to the negative terminal of the battery, perform the PCM idle learn procedure (see Section 1). When you're done, check the charging voltage (see Section 9) to verify that the alternator is operating correctly.

HATCHBACK

17 Remove the front bumper cover (see Chapter 11).

18 Remove the right headlight housing (see Chapter 12).

19 Remove the coolant reservoir (see Chapter 3).

20 Remove the accessory drivebelt (see Chapter 1).

21 Remove the three alternator mounting bolts.

22 Disconnect the electrical connector and the black wire from the alternator (the black wire goes to the ELD unit in the engine compartment fuse and relay box). Then detach the harness clip from the alternator and set the electrical harness aside. Remove the alternator.

23 Refer to Steps 7 and 8.

24 Installation is the reverse of removal. Tighten the alternator mounting bolts to the torque listed in this Chapter's Specifications.

25 After reconnecting the cable to the negative terminal of the battery, perform the PCM idle learn procedure (see Section 1). When you're done, check the charging voltage (see Section 9) to verify that the alternator is operating correctly.

11 Starting system - general information and precautions

The starting system consists of the battery, the 80 amp fuse, the ELD, the 40 amp fuse (all three of which are located in the engine compartment fuse and relay box), the ignition switch, the starter cut relay (in the under-dash fuse and relay box), the starter control relay and the starter solenoid and starter motor, and the wires connecting these components. The solenoid is mounted directly on the starter motor. The solenoid/starter motor assembly is installed on top of the transaxle on coupes and sedans, and on the front of the engine block on CR-Vs and hatchbacks.

When the ignition key is turned to the START position, the starter solenoid is actuated through the starter control circuit. The starter solenoid then connects the battery to the starter. The battery supplies the electrical energy to the starter motor, which does the actual work of cranking the engine.

On models with a manual transaxle, the starter can only be operated when the clutch pedal is depressed. On models with an automatic transaxle, the starter can only be operated when the shift lever is in PARK or NEUTRAL.

Always observe the following precautions when working on the starting system:

a) *Excessive cranking of the starter motor can overheat it and cause serious damage. Never operate the starter motor for more than 15 seconds at a time without pausing to allow it to cool for at least two minutes.*

b) *The starter is connected directly to the battery and could arc or cause a fire if mishandled, overloaded or shorted out.*

c) *Always detach the cable from the negative terminal of the battery before working on the starting system.*

12 Starter motor and circuit - check

▶ **Refer to illustrations 12.3 and 12.4**

1   If a malfunction occurs in the starting circuit, do not immediately assume that the starter is causing the problem. First, check the following items:

a) *Make sure the battery cable clamps, where they connect to the battery, are clean and tight.*

b) *Check the condition of the battery cables* (see Section 4). *Replace any defective battery cables with new ones.*

c) *Test the condition of the battery* (see Section 3). *If it does not pass all the tests, replace it with a new battery.*

d) *Check the starter solenoid wiring and connections. Refer to the wiring diagrams at the end of Chapter 12.*

e) *Check the starter mounting bolts for tightness.*

f) *Check the fuses in the engine compartment fuse and relay box* (see Chapter 12). *If they're burned, determine the cause and repair the circuit. Also, check the ignition switch circuit for correct operation (see the wiring diagrams at the end of Chapter 12).*

g) *Check the operation of the gear position switch (automatic transaxle) or clutch start circuit (manual transaxle). Make sure the shift lever is in PARK or NEUTRAL (automatic transaxle) or the clutch pedal is pressed (manual transaxle). Refer to Chapter 7 for the gear position switch check and adjustment procedure. Refer to Chapter 12 wiring diagrams for the necessary circuit checks for the clutch activation system. These systems must operate correctly to provide battery voltage to the starter solenoid.*

h) *Check the operation of the starter cut relay. The starter cut relay is located in the fuse/relay box under the driver's side of the dash. Refer to Chapter 12 for relay testing procedures.*

2   If the starter does not activate when the ignition switch is turned to the start position, check for battery voltage to the solenoid. This will determine if the solenoid is receiving the correct voltage signal from the ignition switch. Connect a voltmeter to the starter solenoid "S" terminal. Then note the indicated voltage when an assistant turns the ignition switch to the START position. It should be about the same as battery voltage. If there's no voltage at the S terminal, refer to the wiring diagrams at the end of Chapter 12 and check the starting system fuses. The two starting system fuses are located inside the engine compart-

ment fuse and relay box. Also check the starter cut relay for correct operation. The starter cut relay is located inside the left (driver's side) fuse/relay panel. Refer to Chapter 12 for help with testing relays. If voltage is available but the starter motor doesn't engage and spin the driveplate ring gear, remove the starter from the engine (see Section 13) and bench test the starter (see Step 4).

3   If the starter turns over slowly, check the starter cranking voltage and the current draw from the battery. This test must be performed with the starter assembly on the engine. Crank the engine over (for 10 seconds or less) and observe the battery voltage. It should not drop below 8.5 volts. Also, observe the current draw using an ammeter (see illustration). It should not exceed 380 amps. If the starter motor exceeds these values, replace it. Several conditions might affect the starter's cranking power. The battery must be in good condition and the battery cold-cranking rating must not be under-rated for the application. Be sure to check the battery specifications carefully. The battery terminals and cables must be clean and not corroded. Also, in cases of extremely cold temperatures, make sure the battery and/or engine block is warmed before performing the tests.

4   If the starter is receiving voltage but does not activate, remove and check the starter/solenoid assembly on the bench. Most likely the solenoid is defective. In some rare cases, the engine may be seized, so be sure to try and rotate the crankshaft pulley (see Chapter 2) before proceeding. With the starter/solenoid assembly mounted in a vise on the bench, install one jumper cable from the negative terminal (-) to the body of the starter. Install another jumper cable from the positive terminal (+) on the battery to the B+ terminal on the starter (see illustration). Install a starter switch and apply battery voltage to the solenoid S terminal (for 10 seconds or less) and observe the solenoid plunger, shift lever and overrunning clutch extend and rotate the pinion drive. If the pinion drive extends but does not rotate, the solenoid is operating but the starter motor is defective. If there is no movement but the solenoid clicks, the solenoid and/or the starter motor is defective. If the solenoid plunger extends and rotates the pinion drive, the starter/solenoid assembly is working properly.

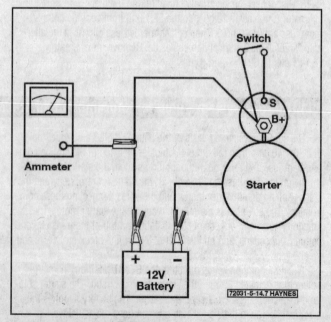

12.3 To use an inductive ammeter, simply hold the ammeter over the positive or negative battery cable (whichever cable has better clearance)

12.4 Starter motor bench testing details

13 Starter motor - removal and installation

ALL MODELS

1   Detach the cable from the negative terminal of the battery (see Section 1).

✻✻ CAUTION:

The radio on some models is equipped with an anti-theft system. Make sure that you have the correct anti-theft codes before disconnecting the battery. You'll also want to write down the frequencies for the radio's preset buttons.

COUPE AND SEDAN

▸ **Refer to illustration 13.3**

2   Remove the air intake resonator (see "Air filter housing - removal and installation" in Chapter 4).

3   Clearly label, then disconnect the wires from the terminals on the starter motor solenoid (see illustration). Also disconnect any clips that attach the wiring to the starter assembly.

4   Remove the starter mounting bolts (see illustration) and detach the starter.

5   Installation is the reverse of removal. Be sure to tighten the starter mounting bolts to the torque listed in this Chapter's Specifications, then reconnect the cable to the negative terminal of the battery (see Section 1).

6   When you're done, perform the PCM idle learn procedure (see Section 1).

CR-V AND HATCHBACK

7   Disconnect the knock sensor electrical connector (see "Knock sensor - replacement" in Chapter 6).

8   On hatchbacks, remove the bolt that attaches the harness bracket

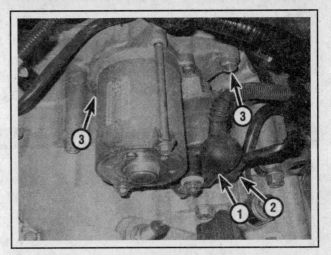

13.3 To remove the solenoid/starter assembly, disconnect the starter cable from the B terminal (1) and the wire from the S terminal (2) on the solenoid, then remove the two mounting bolts (3) (coupe/sedan shown, CR-V and hatchback similar)

and the intake manifold bracket, then remove the intake manifold bracket.

9   Clearly label, then disconnect the wires from the terminals on the starter motor solenoid. Also disconnect any clips that attach the wiring to the starter assembly.

10 Remove the two starter mounting bolts and remove the starter motor.

11 Installation is the reverse of removal. Be sure to tighten the starter mounting bolts to the torque listed in this Chapter's Specifications, then reconnect the cable to the negative terminal of the battery (see Section 1).

12 When you're done, perform the PCM idle learn procedure (see Section 1).

Specifications

General

Battery voltage
    Engine off   12 to 12.5 volts
    Engine running   Approximately 13.5 volts
Firing order   1-3-4-2

Torque specifications	Ft-lbs	Nm
Starter mounting bolts		
Coupe and sedan (both bolts)	33	44
CR-V and hatchback		
Smaller (10 x 1.25 mm) bolt	33	44
Larger (12 x 1.25 mm) bolt	47	64
Alternator mounting bolts		
Coupe and sedan		
Upper (pivot) bolt	33	44
Adjuster lock bolt	17	24
CR-V and hatchback	16	22

6

EMISSIONS AND ENGINE CONTROL SYSTEMS

1 General information

◗ Refer to illustration 1.4

To prevent pollution of the atmosphere from incompletely burned and evaporating gases, and to maintain good driveability and fuel economy, a number of emission control systems are incorporated. They include the:

Catalytic converter
Electrical Load Detector (ELD)
Evaporative Emissions Control (EVAP) system
Exhaust Gas Recirculation (EGR) system
Intake Manifold Runner Control (IMRC) system (CR-V only)
On-Board Diagnostic-II (OBD-II) system
Positive Crankcase Ventilation (PCV) system
Programmed Fuel Injection (PGM-FI) system (the electronic engine control system)

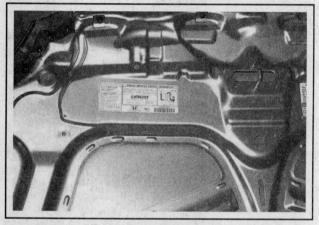

1.4 The Vehicle Emission Control Information (VECI) label specifies the emission-control systems on your vehicle, and includes important tune-up specifications and a vacuum hose routing diagram

Variable Valve Timing and Lift Electronic Control (VTEC) system (optional, on some coupes and sedans)
"intelligent" Variable Valve Timing and Lift Electronic Control/Variable Valve Timing Control (i-VTEC/VTC) system (CR-V and hatchback)

This Chapter includes general descriptions of these and other emissions-related devices and component replacement procedures (when possible) for each of the systems listed above. Before assuming that an emissions control system is malfunctioning, check the fuel and ignition systems carefully. The diagnosis of some emission control devices requires specialized tools, equipment and training. If a procedure is beyond your ability, consult a dealer service department or other repair shop. Remember, the most frequent cause of emissions problems is simply a loose or broken wire or vacuum hose, so always check all hose and wiring connections first.

➡Note: Because of a Federally mandated extended warranty which covers the emissions control system components, check with your dealer about warranty coverage before working on any emissions-related systems. Once the warranty has expired, you may wish to perform some of the component checks and/or replacement procedures in this Chapter to save money.

Pay close attention to any special precautions outlined in this Chapter. It should be noted that the illustrations of the various systems might not exactly match the system installed on your vehicle because of annual changes made by the manufacturer during production and because of "running changes" made during a model year.

A Vehicle Emissions Control Information (VECI) label (see illustration) is located in the engine compartment, either on the underside of the hood or attached to the radiator support or one of the strut towers. This label specifies the important emissions systems on the vehicle and it provides the important specifications for tune-ups. Part of the VECI label, the Vacuum Hose Routing Diagram, provides a vacuum hose schematic with emissions components identified. When servicing the engine or emissions systems, the VECI label and the vacuum hose routing diagram should always be checked for up-to-date information.

2 On Board Diagnostic (OBD) system and trouble codes

SCAN TOOL INFORMATION

◗ Refer to illustration 2.1

1   Hand-held scanners are the most powerful and versatile tools for analyzing engine management systems used on later model vehicles (see illustration). Early model scanners handle codes and some diagnostics for many systems. Each brand scan tool must be examined carefully to match the year, make and model of the vehicle you are working on. Often, interchangeable cartridges are available to access the particular manufacturer (Chrysler, Ford, GM, Honda, Toyota etc.). Some manufacturers will specify by continent (Asia, Europe, USA, etc.).

➡Note: An aftermarket generic scanner should work with any model covered by this manual. Before purchasing a generic scan tool, contact the manufacturer of the scanner you're planning to buy and verify that it will work properly with the OBD-II system you want to scan. If necessary, of course, you can always have the codes extracted by a dealer service department or an independent repair shop with a professional scan tool.

2.1 Scanners like these from Actron and AutoXray are powerful diagnostic aids - programmed with comprehensive diagnostic information, they can tell you just about anything you want to know about your engine management system

OBD SYSTEM GENERAL DESCRIPTION

2   All models are equipped with the second generation OBD-II system. This system consists of an on-board computer known as the Powertrain Control Module (PCM), and information sensors, which monitor various functions of the engine and send data to the PCM. This system incorporates a series of diagnostic monitors that detect and identify fuel injection and emissions control systems faults and store the information in the computer memory. This updated system also tests sensors and output actuators, diagnoses drive cycles, freezes data and clears codes.

3   This powerful diagnostic computer must be accessed using an OBD-II scan tool and 16-pin Data Link Connector (DLC) located under the driver's dash area. The PCM is located below the center of the instrument panel, mounted to the firewall. The PCM is the "brain" of the electronically controlled fuel and emissions system. It receives data from a number of sensors and other electronic components (switches, relays, etc.). Based on the information it receives, the PCM generates output signals to control various relays, solenoids (i.e. fuel injectors) and other actuators. The PCM is specifically calibrated to optimize the emissions, fuel economy and driveability of the vehicle.

4   It isn't a good idea to attempt diagnosis or replacement of the PCM or emission control components at home while the vehicle is under warranty. Because of a Federally mandated warranty which covers the emissions system components and because any owner-induced damage to the PCM, the sensors and/or the control devices may void this warranty, take the vehicle to a dealer service department if the PCM or a system component malfunctions.

INFORMATION SENSORS

5   **Brake Pedal Position (BPP) switch** - The BPP switch is located at the top of the brake pedal. It's a normally open switch that closes when the brake pedal is applied and sends a signal to the PCM, which interprets this signal as its cue to disengage the torque converter clutch. The BPP switch is also used to disengage the brake shift interlock. For information regarding the replacement and adjustment of the BPP switch, refer to Chapter 9.

6   **Camshaft Position (CMP) sensor** - The CMP sensor produces a signal that the PCM uses to identify the number 1 cylinder and to time the firing sequence of the fuel injectors. On coupes and sedans, the CMP sensor is located on the left (timing belt) end of the cylinder head, under the timing belt cover, near the camshaft timing belt sprocket. On the CR-V and hatchback, there are two CMP sensors: CMP sensor A and CMP sensor B (TDC sensor). CMP sensor A is located at the left end of the cylinder head, near the intake camshaft. CMP sensor B (TDC sensor) is located at the left end of the cylinder head, near the exhaust camshaft. On these models, CMP sensor A monitors the position of the camshaft for the VTEC system. CMP sensor B fulfills the same function as the CMP sensor on coupe and sedan engines.

7   **Crankshaft Position (CKP) sensor** - The CKP sensor produces a signal that the PCM uses to determine the position of the crankshaft. On coupes and sedans, the CKP sensor is located on the left (timing belt) end of the engine, under the timing belt cover, near the crankshaft timing belt sprocket. On CR-Vs and hatchbacks, the CKP sensor is located on the rear side of the engine, near the right (timing chain) end of the block.

8   **Electrical Load Detector (ELD)** - The ELD monitors the electrical load on the system and keeps the PCM informed. The PCM controls the voltage output of the alternator in response to the data conveyed by this signal. The ELD unit is located inside the engine compartment fuse and relay box.

9   **Engine Coolant Temperature (ECT) sensor** - The ECT sensor is a thermistor (temperature-sensitive variable resistor) that sends a voltage signal to the PCM, which uses this data to determine the temperature of the engine coolant. The ECT sensor helps the PCM control the air/fuel mixture ratio and ignition timing, and it also helps the PCM determine when to turn the Exhaust Gas Recirculation (EGR) system on and off. On coupes and sedans, the ECT sensor is located at the right end of the cylinder head, near the EGR valve. On CR-Vs and hatchbacks, the ECT sensor is located at the left end of the cylinder head.

10   **Fuel tank pressure sensor** - The fuel tank pressure sensor measures the fuel tank pressure when the PCM tests the EVAP system, and it's also used to control fuel tank pressure by signaling the EVAP system to purge the tank when the pressure becomes excessive. The fuel tank pressure sensor is located to the left of EVAP canister, right above the two-way/bypass solenoid valve.

11   **Input shaft (mainshaft) speed sensor** - The input shaft (or mainshaft) speed sensor is a magnetic pick-up coil located on the front of the automatic transaxle (coupe and sedan) or on the rear side of the transaxle (CR-V). On OBD-II vehicles, the PCM compares the signal from the input shaft (mainshaft) speed sensor with the signal from the output shaft (countershaft) speed sensor to calculate whether slippage (i.e. wear) is occurring inside the transaxle.

12   **Intake Air Temperature (IAT) sensor** - The IAT sensor monitors the temperature of the air entering the engine and sends a signal to the PCM. On coupes and sedans, the IAT sensor is located at the left end of the intake manifold. On CR-Vs and hatchbacks, the IAT sensor is located on the air intake duct.

13   **Knock sensor** - The knock sensor is a "piezoelectric" crystal that oscillates in proportion to engine vibration. (The term piezoelectric refers to the property of certain crystals that produce a voltage when subjected to a mechanical stress.) The oscillation of the piezoelectric crystal produces a voltage output that is monitored by the PCM, which retards the ignition timing when the oscillation exceeds a certain threshold. When the engine is operating normally, the knock sensor oscillates consistently and its voltage signal is steady. When detonation occurs, engine vibration increases, and the oscillation of the knock sensor exceeds a design threshold. (Detonation is an uncontrolled explosion, after the spark occurs at the spark plug, which spontaneously combusts the remaining air/fuel mixture, resulting in a "pinging" or "slapping" sound.) If allowed to continue, detonation is annoying, and engine performance is diminished. On coupes and sedans, the knock sensor is located on the backside of the engine block, near the oil filter. On CR-Vs and hatchbacks, the knock sensor is located on the front side of the block.

14   **Manifold Absolute Pressure (MAP) sensor** - The MAP sensor, which is located on the throttle body on all models, monitors the pressure or vacuum downstream from the throttle plate, inside the intake manifold. The MAP sensor measures intake manifold pressure and vacuum on the absolute scale, i.e. from zero instead of from sea-level atmospheric pressure (14.7 psi). The MAP sensor converts the absolute pressure into a variable voltage signal that changes with the pressure. The PCM uses this data to determine engine load so that it can alter the ignition advance and fuel enrichment.

15   **Output shaft (countershaft) speed sensor** - The output shaft (or countershaft) speed sensor is a magnetic pick-up coil, which is located on top of the transaxle. The output shaft speed sensor provides the Powertrain Control Module (PCM) with information about the rotational speed of the output shaft in the transmission. The PCM uses this information to control the torque converter and to calculate speed

scheduling and the correct operating pressure for the transaxle. On OBD-II vehicles, the PCM compares the signal from the input shaft (mainshaft) speed sensor with the signal from the output shaft (countershaft) speed sensor to calculate whether slippage (i.e. wear) is occurring inside the transaxle.

16 **Oxygen sensors** - An oxygen sensor is a galvanic battery that generates a small variable voltage signal in proportion to the difference between the oxygen content in the exhaust stream and the oxygen content in the ambient air. The PCM uses the voltage signal from the upstream oxygen sensor to maintain a "stoichiometric" air/fuel ratio of 14.7:1 by constantly adjusting the "on-time" of the fuel injectors. There are two oxygen sensors: one upstream sensor (ahead of the catalytic converter) and a downstream oxygen sensor (at the catalyst). On coupes and sedans with non-VTEC engines, there are two oxygen sensors; the upstream oxygen sensor is located above the catalytic converter (which is a part of the exhaust manifold) and the downstream sensor is located below the catalyst. On coupes and sedans with VTEC engines, there are either two or three oxygen sensors.

a) *VTEC coupes and sedans with a catalyst in the exhaust manifold (same manifold/catalyst assembly as non-VTEC engines), the upstream sensor is located right above the catalyst and the downstream sensor is located right below the catalyst. There is also a third oxygen sensor at the second catalyst, which is located underneath the vehicle.*

b) *VTEC coupes and sedans without a catalyst in the exhaust manifold have only a single catalytic converter under the vehicle, with an upstream oxygen sensor right below the mounting flange at the forward end of the pipe that contains the catalyst, and the downstream sensor installed at the rear end of the catalyst.*

All CR-Vs and hatchbacks have two oxygen sensors (and a single catalytic converter, which is located under the vehicle). The upstream oxygen sensor (Honda refers to it as an air/fuel ratio sensor) is installed in the front end of the catalyst. The downstream sensor is installed in the rear end of the catalyst.

17 **Power Steering Pressure (PSP) switch** - The PSP switch monitors the pressure inside the power steering system. When the pressure exceeds a certain threshold at idle or during low speed maneuvers, the switch sends a voltage signal to the PCM, which raises the idle slightly to compensate for the extra load on the engine. On coupes and sedans, the PSP switch is located on the power steering pressure line, right above the pressure line connection to the steering rack assembly. On CR-Vs, the PSP switch is located in the "feed hose" (pressure line), right above the steering rack. (There's no PSP switch on hatchbacks. They have Electrical Power Steering).

18 **Throttle Position (TP) sensor** - The TP sensor is a potentiometer that receives a constant voltage input from the PCM and sends back a voltage signal that varies in relation to the opening angle of the throttle plate inside the throttle body. This voltage signal tells the PCM when the throttle is closed, half-open, wide open or anywhere in between. The PCM uses this data, along with information from other sensors, to calculate injector "pulse width" (the interval of time during which an injector solenoid is energized by the PCM). The TP sensor is located on the throttle body, on the end of the throttle plate shaft. The TP sensor is not removable on any model. If it's defective, replace the throttle body.

19 **Transmission range switch** - The transmission range switch, which is used only on automatics, functions like a conventional Park/Neutral Position (PNP) switch: it prevents the engine from starting in any gear other than Park or Neutral, and it closes the circuit for the back-up lights when the shift lever is moved to Reverse. The PCM also sends a voltage signal to the transmission range switch, which uses a series of step-down resistors that act as a voltage divider. The PCM monitors the voltage output signal from the switch, which corresponds to the position of the manual lever. Thus the PCM is able to determine the gear selected and is able to determine the correct pressure for the electronic pressure control system of the transaxle. On coupes and sedans, the transmission range switch is located on the right end of the transaxle, under a small cover. On CR-Vs, it's located on the left end of the transaxle, under a small cover. (Hatchbacks are not available with an automatic transaxle.)

20 **Vehicle Speed Sensor (VSS)** - The VSS is a Hall Effect type switch that is driven by the differential. The VSS receives a 5-volt reference signal from the PCM and generates a pulsed output that the PCM uses to determine vehicle speed (the number of pulses per minute rises and falls in proportion to the speed). The VSS is used on all manual transaxles and on some automatics (coupes and sedans, but not CR-Vs) The VSS is located on top of the transaxle, right above the differential.

OUTPUT ACTUATORS

21 **EVAP canister purge valve** - The EVAP canister purge valve is located on the throttle body. The purge valve is normally closed. But when ordered to do so by the PCM, it allows the fuel vapors that are stored in the EVAP canister to be drawn into the intake manifold, where they're mixed with intake air, then burned along with the normal air/fuel mixture, under certain operating conditions.

22 **EVAP canister vent shut valve** - The EVAP canister vent shut valve is located on the EVAP canister, which is located underneath the vehicle. The canister vent shut valve is normally open, but it closes and seals off the EVAP system for inspection and maintenance tests and for OBD-II leak and pressure tests.

23 **EVAP two-way valve/bypass solenoid valve** - The EVAP two-way valve is located at the EVAP canister, underneath the vehicle. It sends fuel vapors to the EVAP canister in proportion to the pressure inside the fuel tank, and prevents excessive vacuum in the fuel tank by drawing in fresh air through the EVAP canister. The bypass solenoid valve opens to bypass the two-way valve during EVAP leak checks.

24 **Exhaust Gas Recirculation (EGR) valve** - When the engine is put under a load (hard acceleration, passing, going up a steep hill, pulling a trailer, etc.), combustion chamber temperature increases. When combustion chamber temperature exceeds 2500 degrees, excessive amounts of oxides of nitrogen (NOx) are produced. NOx is a precursor of photochemical smog. When combined with hydrocarbons (HC), other "reactive organic compounds" (ROCs) and sunlight, it forms ozone, nitrogen dioxide and nitrogen nitrate and other nasty stuff. The PCM-controlled EGR valve allows exhaust gases to be recirculated back to the intake manifold where they dilute the incoming air/fuel mixture, which lowers the combustion chamber temperature and decreases the amount of NOx produced during high-load conditions. Coupes and sedans (except for pre-2004 non-VTEC models) are equipped with an EGR system. (CR-Vs and hatchbacks don't use an EGR system.)

25 **Fuel injectors** - The fuel injectors, which spray a fine mist of fuel into the intake ports, where it is mixed with incoming air, are inductive coils under PCM control. For more information about the injectors, see Chapter 4.

26 **Idle Air Control (IAC) valve** - The IAC valve controls the amount of air allowed to bypass the throttle plate when the throttle plate is at its (nearly closed) idle position. The IAC valve is controlled by the PCM. When the engine is placed under an additional load at idle (high power steering pressure or running the air conditioning com-

pressor during low-speed maneuvers, for example), the engine can run roughly, stumble and even stall. To prevent this from happening, the PCM opens the IAC valve to increase the idle speed enough to overcome the extra load imposed on the engine. The IAC valve is mounted on the underside of the throttle body.

27 **Ignition coils** - There is one ignition coil per spark plug. The coils are located directly on top of the valve cover, directly over the spark plugs. The ignition coils are under the control of the Powertrain Control Module (PCM). There is no separate ignition control module. Instead, "coil drivers" inside the PCM turn the primary side of the coils on and off. For more information about the ignition coils, see Chapter 5.

28 **Variable Valve Timing and Lift Electronic Control (VTEC) solenoid valve** - On VTEC-equipped models, the VTEC system changes valve lift and timing by using more than one cam lobe profile. It changes cam profiles by altering the hydraulic pressure in a special circuit that circulates through the rocker arms. The VTEC solenoid valve is the device that the VTEC system uses to control the oil pressure that locks and unlocks each adjacent pair of intake rocker arms in response to engine speed. On SOHC engines (D17A2 and D17A6), the VTEC solenoid valve is located at the right rear corner of the cylinder head. For more information about the VTEC solenoid valve and the VTEC system, see Section 24.

29 **Variable Valve Timing Control (VTC) oil control solenoid valve** - CR-Vs and hatchbacks are equipped with a newer type of VTEC system known as "intelligent" Variable Valve Timing and Lift Electronic Control (i-VETEC). Besides the usual VTEC components, these models are also equipped with Variable Valve Timing Control (VTC), which changes the phase of the intake camshaft. The VTC actuator is inside the camshaft timing chain sprocket. The VTC oil control solenoid valve is the PCM-controlled device that controls the oil pressure to the actuator. For more information about the VTC oil control solenoid valve and the VTEC system, refer to Section 24.

OBTAINING AND CLEARING DIAGNOSTIC TROUBLE CODES (DTCS)

30 All models covered by this manual are equipped with on-board diagnostics. When the PCM recognizes a malfunction in a monitored emission control system, component or circuit, it turns on the Malfunction Indicator Light (MIL) on the dash. The PCM will continue to display the MIL until the problem is fixed and the Diagnostic Trouble Code (DTC) is cleared from the PCM's memory. You'll need a scan tool to access any DTCs stored in the PCM.

31 Before outputting any DTCs stored in the PCM, thoroughly inspect ALL electrical connectors and hoses. Make sure that all electrical connections are tight, clean and free of corrosion. And make sure that all hoses are correctly connected, fit tightly and are in good condition (no cracks or tears). Also, make sure that the engine is tuned up. A poorly running engine is probably one of the biggest causes of emission-related malfunctions. Often, simply giving the engine a good tune-up will correct the problem.

Accessing the DTCs

♦ **Refer to illustration 2.32**

32 On these models, all of which are equipped with On-Board Diagnostic II (OBD-II) systems, the Diagnostic Trouble Codes (DTCs) can only be accessed with a scan tool. Professional scan tools are expensive, but relatively inexpensive generic scan tools (see illustration 2.1) are available at most auto parts stores. Simply plug the connector of the scan tool into the diagnostic connector (see illustration), which is located under the lower edge of the dash, just to the right of the steering column. Then follow the instructions included with the scan tool to extract the DTCs.

33 Once you have outputted all of the stored DTCs, look them up on the accompanying DTC chart.

34 After troubleshooting the source of each DTC make any necessary repairs or replace the defective component(s).

Clearing the DTCs

35 Clear the DTCs with the scan tool in accordance with the instructions provided by the scan tool's manufacturer.

DIAGNOSTIC TROUBLE CODES

36 The accompanying tables are a list of the Diagnostic Trouble Codes (DTCs) that can be accessed by a do-it-yourselfer working at home (there are many, many more DTCs available to professional mechanics with proprietary scan tools and software, but those codes cannot be accessed by a generic scan tool). If, after you have checked and repaired the connectors, wire harness and vacuum hoses (if applicable) for an emission-related system, component or circuit, the problem persists, have the vehicle checked by a dealer service department or other qualified repair shop.

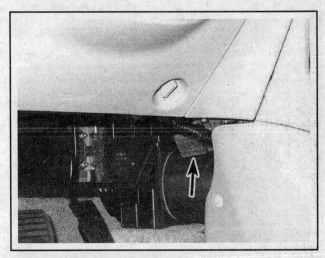

2.32 The Data Link Connector (DLC) is located under the dash, to the right of the steering column

OBD-II TROUBLE CODES

➡**Note: Not all trouble codes apply to all models.**

Code	Probable cause
P0010	Variable Valve Timing Control (VTC) oil control solenoid valve malfunction
P0011	Variable Valve Timing Control (VTC) system malfunction
P0107	Manifold Absolute Pressure (MAP) sensor circuit, low voltage
P0108	Manifold Absolute Pressure (MAP) sensor circuit, high voltage
P0111	Intake Air Temperature (IAT) sensor circuit, range performance problem
P0112	Intake Air Temperature (IAT) sensor circuit, low voltage
P0113	Intake Air Temperature (IAT) sensor circuit, high voltage
P0116	Engine Coolant Temperature (ECT) sensor range/performance problem
P0117	Engine Coolant Temperature (ECT) sensor circuit, low voltage
P0118	Engine Coolant Temperature (ECT) sensor circuit, high voltage
P0122	Throttle Position (TP) sensor circuit, low voltage
P0123	Throttle Position (TP) sensor circuit, high voltage
P0125	Engine Coolant Temperature (ECT) sensor, slow response
P0128	Cooling system malfunction
P0131	Upstream oxygen sensor circuit, low voltage
P0132	Upstream oxygen sensor circuit, high voltage
P0133	Upstream oxygen sensor circuit, slow response
P0133	Air/Fuel (A/F) ratio sensor circuit, slow response
P0134	Air/Fuel (A/F) ratio sensor circuit, no activity detected
P0135	Upstream oxygen sensor, heater circuit malfunction
P0135	Air/Fuel (A/F) ratio sensor, heater circuit malfunction
P0137	Downstream oxygen sensor circuit, low voltage
P0138	Downstream oxygen sensor circuit, high voltage
P0139	Downstream oxygen sensor circuit, slow response
P0141	Downstream oxygen sensor, heater circuit malfunction
P0143	Third oxygen sensor circuit, low voltage
P0144	Third oxygen sensor circuit, high voltage
P0145	Third oxygen sensor circuit, slow response
P0147	Third oxygen sensor, heater circuit malfunction
P0171	Fuel system too lean
P0172	Fuel system too rich
P0222	Throttle Position Sensor (TP) sensor circuit, low voltage
P0223	Throttle Position Sensor (TP) sensor circuit, high voltage
P0300	Random misfire detected

Code	Probable cause
P0301	Cylinder no. 1 misfire detected
P0302	Cylinder no. 2 misfire detected
P0303	Cylinder no. 3 misfire detected
P0304	Cylinder no. 4 misfire detected
P0325	Knock sensor circuit malfunction
P0335	Crankshaft Position (CKP) sensor circuit, no signal
P0336	Crankshaft Position (CKP) sensor circuit, intermittent interruption
P0339	Crankshaft Position (CKP) sensor circuit, intermittent interruption
P0340	Camshaft Position (CMP) sensor, no signal
P0340	Camshaft Position (CMP) sensor A, no signal
P0341	Variable Valve Timing Control (VTC) phase gap
P0344	Camshaft Position (CMP) sensor, intermittent interruption
P0344	Camshaft Position (CMP) sensor A, intermittent interruption
P0365	Camshaft Position (CMP) sensor B, no signal
P0369	Camshaft Position (CMP) sensor B, intermittent interruption
P0401	Exhaust Gas Recirculation (EGR) system, insufficient flow
P0404	Exhaust Gas Recirculation (EGR) valve, insufficient lift
P0406	Exhaust Gas Recirculation (EGR) valve position sensor circuit, high voltage
P0420	Catalyst system efficiency below threshold
P0451	Fuel tank pressure sensor, range or performance problem
P0452	Fuel tank pressure sensor circuit, low voltage
P0453	Fuel tank pressure sensor circuit, high voltage
P0497	Evaporative Emission (EVAP) system, low purge flow
P0500	Vehicle Speed Sensor (VSS), circuit malfunction
P0501	Vehicle Speed Sensor (VSS), range or performance problem
P0502	Vehicle Speed Sensor (VSS), no signal
P0505	Idle control system malfunction
P0506	Idle control system, rpm lower than expected
P0507	Idle control system, rpm higher than expected
P0511	Idle Air Control (IAC) valve, circuit malfunction
P0563	Powertrain Control Module (PCM) power source circuit, unexpected voltage
P0600	Serial communication link malfunction
P0602	Engine Control Module (ECM), programming error
P0603	Engine Control Module (ECM), internal circuit malfunction
P0606	Engine Control Module (ECM), processor malfunction
P0607	Powertrain Control Module (PCM) internal circuit malfunction

Automatic transmission diagnostic trouble codes

Code	Probable cause
P0630	VIN not programmed, or mismatched
P0661	Intake Manifold Runner Control (IMRC) valve position sensor circuit, low voltage
P0662	Intake Manifold Runner Control (IMRC) valve position sensor circuit, high voltage
P0705	Transmission Range (TR) switch, multiple shift position input
P0706	Transmission Range (TR) switch, open circuit
P0710	Automatic Transmission Fluid (ATF) temperature sensor
P0715	Input shaft (mainshaft) speed sensor
P0716	Input shaft (mainshaft) speed sensor, range or performance problem
P0717	Input shaft (mainshaft) speed sensor, no signal input
P0720	Output shaft (countershaft) speed sensor
P0721	Output shaft (countershaft) speed sensor, range or performance problem
P0722	Output shaft (countershaft) speed sensor, no signal input
P0730	Shift control system
P0740	Lock-up control system
P0741	Lock-up control system
P0745	Mechanical problem in hydraulic system
P0748	Automatic transmission clutch pressure control solenoid valve A
P0750	Mechanical problem in hydraulic system
P0753	Shift control solenoid valve A
P0758	Shift control solenoid valve B
P0778	Automatic transmission clutch pressure control solenoid valve B
P0780	Mechanical problem in hydraulic system
P0795	Mechanical problem in hydraulic system
P0798	Automatic transmission clutch pressure control solenoid valve C
P0840	2nd clutch transmission fluid pressure switch
P0845	3rd clutch transmission fluid pressure switch
P0962	Clutch pressure control solenoid valve A, short or open circuit
P0963	Clutch pressure control solenoid valve A
P0966	Clutch pressure control solenoid valve B
P0967	Clutch pressure control solenoid valve C
P0973	Shift solenoid valve A, short circuit
P0974	Shift solenoid valve A, open circuit
P0976	Shift solenoid valve B, short circuit
P0977	Shift solenoid valve B, open circuit

3   Camshaft Position (CMP) sensor - replacement

▶ **Refer to illustrations 3.2 and 3.4**

1   Disconnect the cable from the negative battery terminal (see Chapter 5, Section 1).

2   Disconnect the CMP sensor electrical connector (see illustration).

3   Remove the upper timing belt cover (see Chapter 2A).

4   Remove the CMP sensor mounting bolts (see illustration) and remove the CMP sensor.

5   Installation is the reverse of removal. Be sure to tighten the CMP sensor mounting bolts to the torque listed in this Chapter's Specifications.

6   When you're done, reconnect the cable to the negative battery terminal and perform the PCM idle learn procedure (see Chapter 5, Section 1).

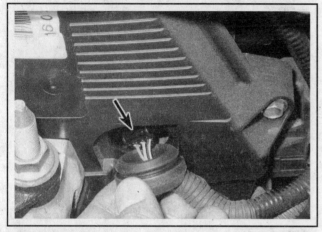

3.2 To disconnect the CMP sensor electrical connector, remove this rubber grommet from the timing belt cover (coupe and sedan)

3.4 To detach the CMP sensor from the cylinder head, remove this mounting bolt (coupe and sedan)

4   Crankshaft Position (CKP) sensor - replacement

▶ **Refer to illustrations 4.3 and 4.5**

1   Disconnect the cable from the negative battery terminal (see Chapter 5, Section 1).

2   Raise the front of the vehicle and place it securely on jackstands.

3   Disconnect the CKP sensor electrical connector (see illustration).

4   Remove the timing belt cover and the timing belt (see Chapter 2A or 2B).

5   Remove the CKP sensor mounting bolt (see illustration) and remove the CKP sensor.

6   Installation is the reverse of removal. Be sure to tighten the CKP sensor mounting bolt to the torque listed in this Chapter's Specifications.

7   When you're done reconnect the cable to the negative battery terminal (see Chapter 5, Section 1).

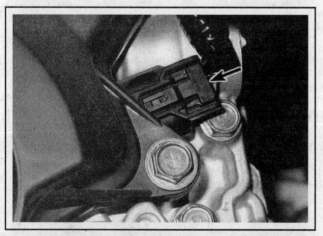

4.3 The CKP sensor electrical connector is located at the left end of the engine, behind the lower timing belt cover, near the crankshaft. To release the connector, depress this tab and pull off the connector

4.5 To detach the CKP sensor from the engine, remove this mounting bolt. When installing the CKP sensor, make sure that the rubber weather seal is correctly seated to prevent moisture from entering the timing belt area

5   Electrical Load Detector (ELD) unit - replacement

▶ Refer to illustrations 5.3, 5.5a, 5.5b, 5.5c, 5.6 and 5.7

1   Disconnect the cable from the negative battery terminal (see Chapter 5, Section 1).

2   Remove the cover from the engine compartment fuse and relay box (see Chapter 12 if necessary).

3   Locate the ELD (see illustration) in the fuse and relay box.

4   Remove the mounting screws for the 80-amp fuse and the 40-amp fuse (see illustration 5.3), then remove both fuses and their contact bars. (The ELD cannot be removed until the contact bars for the two fuses are out of the way.)

5   Detach the fuse and relay box from its mounting brackets (see illustration), turn it over and remove the cover from the underside of the box (see illustrations).

6   Locate the electrical connector for the ELD and disconnect it (see illustration).

7   Remove the ELD (see illustration).

8   Remove the contact plate from the ELD, inspect it for corrosion, clean it off as necessary, then install it in the new ELD. Note that the contact plate must be oriented exactly the same way it was in the old ELD. It won't fit into the fuse and relay box if it's incorrectly oriented.

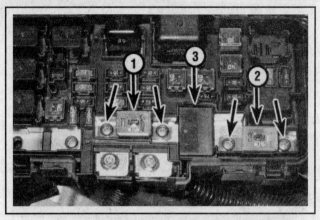

5.3 The Electrical Load Detector (ELD) unit is located inside the engine compartment fuse and relay box, between the 80-amp and 40-amp fuses, both of which must be removed before you can remove the ELD

1	80-amp fuse	3	ELD unit
2	40-amp fuse		

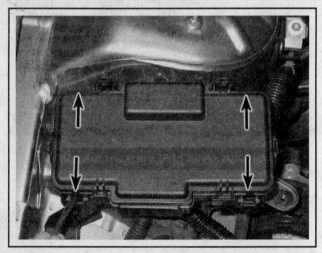

5.5a To detach the engine compartment fuse and relay box, pry loose the retaining clips

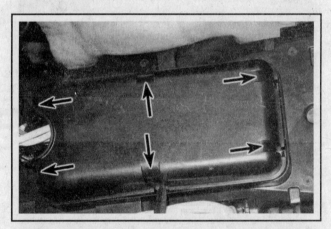

5.5b To remove the cover from the underside of the fuse and relay box, carefully pry it loose at these six spots with a flat blade screwdriver . . .

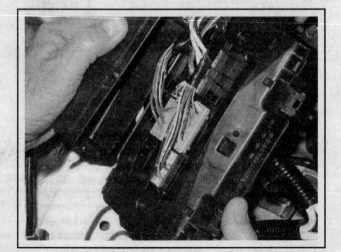

5.5c . . . and remove the cover

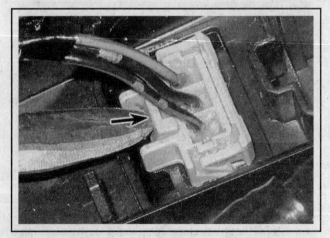

5.6 To disconnect the electrical connector from the ELD, depress this locking tab with a screwdriver and unplug the connector

5.7 Carefully remove the ELD from the fuse and relay box, then remove the contact bar from the ELD and inspect it for corrosion (before removing the contact plate from the old ELD, note how it's oriented in relation to the ELD and to the fuse box and be sure to install it exactly the same way in the new unit)

9 Installation is the reverse of removal. Reconnect the cable to the negative battery terminal and perform the PCM idle learn procedure (see Chapter 5, Section 1).

6 Engine Coolant Temperature (ECT) sensor - replacement

▶ Refer to illustrations 6.1, 6.3 and 6.5

✳✳ WARNING:

Wait until the engine has cooled completely before beginning this procedure.

1 The ECT sensor is located at the right end of the cylinder head on coupes and sedans and at the left end of the cylinder head on CR-Vs and hatchbacks (see illustration).

2 Drain the engine coolant (see Chapter 1). (If you don't drain the coolant, some coolant will run out when you remove the ECT sensor, so install the new sensor as quickly as possible.)

3 Disconnect the electrical connector from the ECT sensor (see illustration).

4 Unscrew the ECT sensor.

✳✳ CAUTION:

If you're planning to reuse the old ECT sensor, handle it with care. Damage to the ECT sensor will adversely affect the operation of the PGM-FI system.

5 Remove and discard the old ECT sensor O-ring (see illustration). Whether you're planning to reuse the old ECT sensor or install a new unit, be sure to use a new O-ring.

6 Installation is the reverse of removal. Be sure to tighten the ECT sensor securely.

7 Refill the cooling system (see Chapter 1).

6.1 The ECT sensor is located at the right end of the cylinder head on coupes and sedans (shown) and on the left end of the cylinder head on CR-Vs and hatchbacks

6.3 To disconnect the electrical connector from the ECT sensor, depress this locking tab and pull straight up

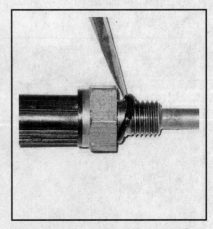

6.5 Be sure to remove and discard the old O-ring from the ECT sensor; always use a new O-ring when installing the ECT sensor

7 Input shaft (mainshaft) speed sensor - replacement

◆ **Refer to illustrations 7.1, 7.4, 7.6 and 7.7**

➡**Note: This section applies only to models with an automatic transaxle.**

1　Locate the input shaft (mainshaft) speed sensor (see illustration) on the front side of the transaxle on coupes and sedans, or on the backside of the transaxle on CR-Vs and hatchbacks.

2　On coupes and sedans remove the air intake resonator (see *Air filter housing - removal and installation* in Chapter 4) and remove the battery (see Chapter 5). (For even more working room, you might want to remove the battery tray as well, but it's not absolutely necessary to do so.)

3　On CR-Vs and hatchbacks, raise the vehicle and place it securely on jackstands, then remove the splash shield, if equipped, from underneath the engine/transaxle assembly.

4　Disconnect the electrical connector from the input shaft speed sensor (see illustration).

5　Remove the input shaft speed sensor mounting bolt (see illustration 7.4) and remove the sensor.

6　On models with an SLXA (not a BMXA) transaxle, remove the special spacer washer from the input shaft sensor (see illustration) and save it for reassembly. (If you don't know whether your vehicle has an SLXA or a BMXA transaxle, look at the tag on top of the transaxle.)

7　Remove and discard the sensor O-ring (see illustration).

8　Installation is the reverse of removal. Be sure to use a new O-ring and, if you're installing the sensor on an SLXA transaxle, make sure you install the special spacer washer, then tighten the sensor mounting bolt to the torque listed in this Chapter's Specifications.

9　If you're servicing a coupe or sedan, install the battery tray (if removed) and the battery (see Chapter 5) and the air intake resonator (see *Air filter housing - removal and installation* in Chapter 4).

10　If you're servicing a CR-V or a hatchback, lower the vehicle when you're done.

7.1 The input shaft (mainshaft) speed sensor is located on the front of the transaxle on coupes and sedans (shown) or on the backside of the transaxle on CR-Vs and hatchbacks

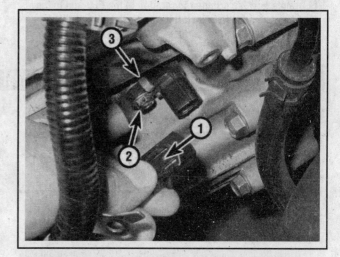

7.4 To remove the input shaft (mainshaft) speed sensor, depress the tab and disconnect the electrical connector (1), remove the mounting bolt (2), remove the sensor and, on SLXA transaxles, remove and bag the special spacer washer (3)

7.6 On models with an SLXA (not a BMXA) automatic transaxle, the input shaft (mainshaft) speed sensor uses a special spacer washer that you'll need when installing the sensor again

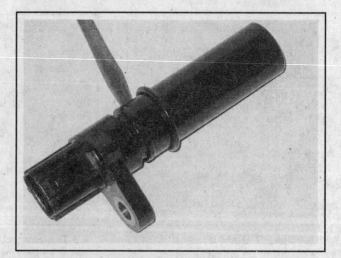

7.7 Be sure to remove and discard the old O-ring from the input shaft sensor; even if you plan to reuse the old input shaft speed sensor, be sure to use a new O-ring

8   Intake Air Temperature (IAT) sensor - replacement

▶ **Refer to illustrations 8.1 and 8.4**

1   Locate the IAT sensor (see illustration), which is on the left end of the air filter housing on coupes and sedans and on the air intake duct on CR-Vs and hatchbacks.

2   Disconnect the electrical connector from the IAT sensor.

3   Pull the IAT sensor out of its mounting grommet.

4   Remove the IAT sensor mounting grommet (see illustration) and inspect it for cracks, tears and other deterioration. If the grommet is damaged or worn, replace it.

5   Installation is the reverse of removal.

8.1 On coupes and sedans, the IAT sensor is located on the left end of the air filter housing

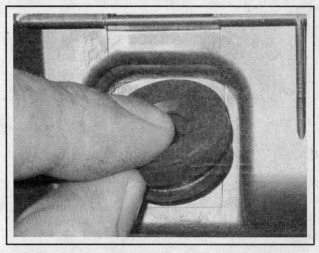

8.4 Remove the old IAT sensor mounting grommet and inspect it for cracks, tears and other deterioration; if the grommet is damaged or worn, replace it

9   Knock sensor - replacement

▶ **Refer to illustrations 9.4 and 9.5**

1   Locate the knock sensor, which is located on the backside of the engine block on coupes and sedans, and on the front side of the block on CR-Vs and hatchbacks.

2   Raise the vehicle and place it securely on jackstands.

3   Remove the under-engine splash shield, if equipped (see Chapter 2).

4   Disconnect the knock sensor electrical connector (see illustration).

5   On SOHC engines, remove the knock sensor retaining bolt and detach the sensor (see illustration). On DOHC engines, unscrew the sensor.

6   Installation is the reverse of removal. Be sure to tighten the knock sensor retaining bolt or sensor to the torque listed in this Chapter's Specifications.

9.4 To disconnect the knock sensor electrical connector (A), depress this release button (B) with your finger or with a flat-blade screwdriver (coupe/sedan shown)

9.5 Knock sensor retaining bolt (oil filter removed for clarity) (coupe/sedan shown)

10 Manifold Absolute Pressure (MAP) sensor - replacement

▶ **Refer to illustration 10.2**

1   Remove the air filter housing (see Chapter 4).

2   Disconnect the electrical connector from the MAP sensor (see illustration).

3   Remove the MAP sensor retaining screw (see illustration 10.2) and remove the MAP sensor.

4   Remove the old MAP sensor O-ring and discard it.

5   Installation is the reverse of removal. Be sure to use a new O-ring and tighten the MAP sensor mounting screw securely.

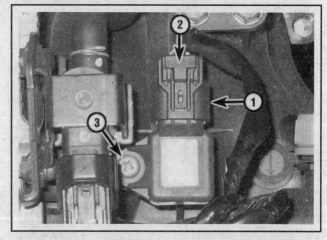

10.2 To remove the MAP sensor, disconnect the electrical connector (1) by depressing the release tab (2), then remove the sensor mounting screw (3). After removing the MAP sensor, be sure to remove and discard the old O-ring; always use a new O-ring when installing the MAP sensor

11 Output shaft (countershaft) speed sensor - replacement

▶ **Refer to illustration 11.3**

➡**Note: This procedure applies only to models with an automatic transaxle.**

1   Locate the output shaft (countershaft) speed sensor on top of the transaxle, near the transaxle fluid level dipstick, on coupes and sedans, or on the backside of the transaxle on CR-Vs.

2   If you're replacing the output shaft sensor on a coupe or sedan, remove the air intake resonator (see *Air filter housing - removal and installation* in Chapter 4). If you're replacing the output shaft sensor on a CR-V, raise the vehicle and place it securely on jackstands, then remove any splash shield, if equipped, that's in the way.

3   Disconnect the electrical connector from the output shaft (countershaft) speed sensor (see illustration).

4   Remove the output shaft sensor mounting bolt and remove the sensor.

5   Remove and discard the sensor O-ring (see illustration 7.7).

6   Installation is the reverse of removal. Be sure to use a new

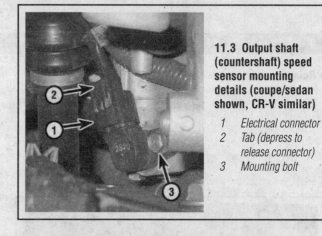

11.3 Output shaft (countershaft) speed sensor mounting details (coupe/sedan shown, CR-V similar)

1   *Electrical connector*
2   *Tab (depress to release connector)*
3   *Mounting bolt*

O-ring and tighten the sensor mounting bolt to the torque listed in this Chapter's Specifications.

12 Oxygen sensors - replacement

➡**Note: Because it is installed in the exhaust manifold or pipe, both of which contract when cool, an oxygen sensor might be very difficult to loosen when the engine is cold. Rather than risk damage to the sensor or its mounting threads, start and run the engine for a minute or two, then shut it off. Be careful not to burn yourself during the following procedure.**

1   Remove the key from the ignition key lock cylinder. Raise the vehicle and place it securely on jackstands.

2   Special care must be taken whenever a sensor is serviced.

a) *Oxygen sensors have a permanently attached pigtail and an elec-*

trical connector that cannot be removed. Damaging or removing the pigtail or electrical connector will render the sensor useless.

b) *Keep grease, dirt and other contaminants away from the electrical connector and the louvered end of the sensor.*

c) *Do not use cleaning solvents of any kind on an oxygen sensor.*

d) *Oxygen sensors are extremely delicate. Do not drop a sensor, throw it around or handle it roughly.*

e) *Make sure the silicone boot on the sensor is installed in the correct position. Otherwise, the boot might melt and it might prevent the sensor from operating correctly.*

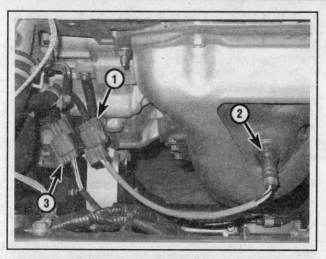

12.4 If you're removing the upstream oxygen sensor on a coupe or sedan with a D17A1 (non-VTEC) or a D17A6 (VTEC) engine, disconnect the electrical connector (1) and unscrew the sensor (2). If you're removing the downstream oxygen sensor, disconnect the electrical connector (3) for that sensor (the upstream sensor for a D17A2 engine is located just below the exhaust manifold-to-exhaust pipe flange)

12.10 If you're removing the downstream oxygen sensor on a coupe or sedan with a D17A1 (non-VTEC) or a D17A6 (VTEC) engine, you'll find the sensor right above the exhaust manifold-to-exhaust pipe flange. The downstream oxygen sensor of a D17A2 VTEC engine is at the rear end of the catalytic converter

COUPE AND SEDAN

3   On coupes and sedans with non-VTEC (D17A1) engines, there are two oxygen sensors. The upstream oxygen sensor - also referred to by Honda as the "Air/Fuel (A/F) ratio sensor" - is located above the catalytic converter (which is an integral part of the exhaust manifold) and the downstream sensor is located right below the catalyst. On coupes and sedans with VTEC engines, there are either two oxygen sensors (D17A2 engines) or three oxygen sensors (D17A6 engines). On VTEC models with two oxygen sensors, the sensors are located ahead of and on the catalyst, which is located underneath the vehicle (these models do not use the integral exhaust manifold/catalyst assembly). VTEC models with three oxygen sensors use the same integral exhaust manifold/catalyst as non-VTEC models, and their upstream and downstream oxygen sensors are installed at the same locations as the upstream and downstream sensors on non-VTEC models. But these models have a third oxygen sensor, which is located at the second catalyst, which is in the same location, i.e. underneath the vehicle, as the catalyst on VTEC models with only two sensors.

Upstream oxygen sensor

▶ Refer to illustration 12.4

4   Disconnect the upstream oxygen sensor electrical connector (see illustration).
5   Remove the upstream oxygen sensor.
6   If you're going to install the old sensor, apply anti-seize compound to the threads of the sensor to facilitate future removal. If you're going to install a new oxygen sensor, it's not necessary to apply anti-seize compound to the threads. The threads on new sensors already have anti-seize compound on them.
7   Installation is the reverse of removal. Be sure to tighten the upstream oxygen sensor to the torque listed in this Chapter's Specifications.

Downstream oxygen sensor

▶ Refer to illustration 12.10

8   Disconnect the electrical connector (see illustration 12.4).
9   Raise the front of the vehicle and place it securely on jackstands.
10 Locate the upstream oxygen sensor at the lower end of the exhaust manifold (see illustration).
11 Remove the downstream oxygen sensor from the exhaust manifold.
12 If you're going to install the old sensor, apply anti-seize compound to the threads of the sensor to facilitate future removal. If you're going to install a new oxygen sensor, it's not necessary to apply anti-seize compound to the threads. The threads on new sensors already have anti-seize compound on them.
13 Installation is the reverse of removal. Be sure to tighten the oxygen sensor to the torque listed in this Chapter's Specifications.

Third oxygen sensor (D17A6 engine only)

14 Raise the vehicle and place it securely on jackstands.
15 Disconnect the oxygen sensor electrical connector.
16 Unscrew the oxygen sensor from the catalytic converter.
17 If you're going to install the old sensor, apply anti-seize compound to the threads of the sensor to facilitate future removal. If you're going to install a new oxygen sensor, it's not necessary to apply anti-seize compound to the threads. The threads on new sensors already have anti-seize compound on them.
18 Installation is the reverse of removal. Be sure to tighten the oxygen sensor to the torque listed in this Chapter's Specifications.

CR-V AND HATCHBACK

19 The upstream oxygen sensor - also referred to by Honda as the "Air/Fuel (A/F) ratio sensor" - is located at the upstream end of the catalytic converter. The downstream oxygen sensor is located at the middle of the catalyst. The catalyst is located underneath the vehicle.

20 Raise the vehicle and place it securely on jackstands.

21 Disconnect the electrical connector for the upstream or downstream oxygen sensor.

22 Unscrew and remove the upstream or downstream oxygen sensor.

23 If you're going to install the old sensor, apply anti-seize compound to the threads of the sensor to facilitate future removal. If you're going to install a new oxygen sensor, it's not necessary to apply anti-seize compound to the threads. The threads on new sensors already have anti-seize compound on them.

24 Installation is the reverse of removal. Be sure to tighten the oxygen sensor to the torque listed in this Chapter's Specifications.

13 Power Steering Pressure (PSP) switch - replacement

▶ **Refer to illustrations 13.3 and 13.5**

➡**Note: This procedure does not apply to hatchbacks, which are equipped with Electrical Power Steering.**

1 On coupes and sedans, remove the air filter housing (see Chapter 4).

2 On CR-Vs raise the front end of the vehicle and place it securely on jackstands.

3 Find the power steering pressure switch (see illustration), which is located in the pressure line for the power steering system, right above the steering rack.

4 Disconnect the electrical connector from the PSP switch.

5 Using a back-up wrench unscrew the PSP switch (see illustration).

6 Installation is the reverse of removal. Be sure to tighten the PSP switch to the torque listed in this Chapter's Specifications.

7 When you're done lower the vehicle and check the power steering fluid level, adding fluid of the proper type if necessary (see Chapter 1).

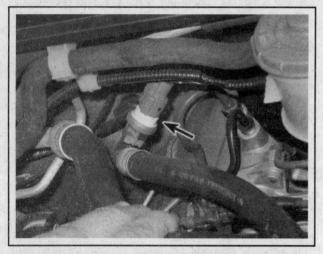

13.3 The Power Steering Pressure (PSP) switch is located on the pressure line for the power steering system, right above the steering rack (coupe/sedan shown, CR-V similar)

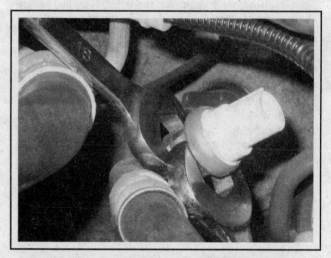

13.5 To remove the PSP switch from the power steering pressure line, put a back-up wrench on the junction block to prevent kinking the pressure line when you loosen the switch (use the back-up wrench when you install the switch too)

14 Throttle Position (TP) sensor - replacement

The TP sensor is not removable. If it's defective, replace the throttle body (see Chapter 4).

15 Transmission range switch - replacement and adjustment

▶ **Refer to illustrations 15.4, 15.5, 15.6 and 15.8**

1 On coupes and sedans, loosen the lug nuts for the right front wheel. On CR-Vs, loosen the lug nuts for the left front wheel. Raise the vehicle and place it securely on jackstands, then remove the right front wheel (coupes and sedans) or the left front wheel (CR-Vs).

2 Remove the inner fender splash shield from the right front wheel well (coupes and sedans) or from the left front wheel well (CR-Vs) (see Chapter 11).

3 Put the shift lever inside the vehicle in the Neutral position.

4 Remove the cover from the transmission range switch (see illustration).

5 Disconnect the electrical connector from the transmission range switch (see illustration).

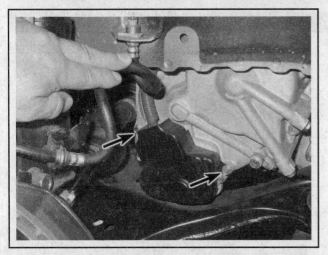

15.4 To detach the transmission range switch cover, remove these two bolts (coupe/sedan shown, CR-Vs similar)

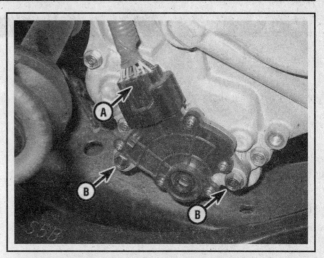

15.5 To disconnect the electrical connector from the transmission range switch, depress the locking tab (A) and pull off the connector; to detach the transmission range switch from the transaxle, remove the two bolts (B) (coupe/sedan shown, CR-Vs similar)

6   Remove the transmission range switch mounting bolts (see illustration 15.5) and remove the switch.

✳✳ CAUTION:

While the transmission range switch is removed, do NOT rotate the control shaft (see illustration) on the transaxle.

7   Before installing the transmission range switch, make sure that the switch is in the Neutral position. (You'll hear/feel a click when you put the switch into Neutral.) Also make sure that the control shaft is in the Neutral position (see illustration 15.6) before installing the transmission range switch. To do so, rotate the control shaft in a clockwise direction until it stops. As you rotate the shaft, it clicks into each gear position. Rotate it counterclockwise to the third position (third click), which is Neutral.

8   Install the transmission range switch and loosely install the switch mounting bolts. Then use a long, thin drill bit or a metal rod to align the control shaft with the rotary frame (see illustration) and to lock them together while you tighten the switch mounting bolts to the torque listed in this Chapter's Specifications.

➡**Note: Be careful not to move the transmission range switch while tightening the switch mounting bolts.**

9   The remainder of installation is the reverse of removal.

10 When you're done, turn the ignition switch to ON, move the shift lever through all the gears and verify that the transmission range switch is correctly synchronized with the gear position indicator on the instrument cluster. Then verify that the engine will NOT start in any gear position other than Park or Neutral, and that the back-up lights come on when the shift lever is in the Reverse position. If the vehicle fails to meet any of these criteria, readjust the transmission range switch.

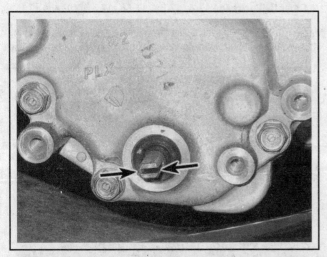

15.6 Once you have removed the transmission range switch from the transaxle, do NOT move the control shaft from the Neutral position (shown)

15.8 When installing the transmission range switch, align the slot in the control shaft with the cutouts in the rotary frame and the switch housing

16 Vehicle Speed Sensor (VSS) - replacement

◆ Refer to illustration 16.2

1   On coupes, sedans and hatchbacks, remove the air intake resonator (see *Air filter housing - removal and installation* in Chapter 4). On CR-Vs, remove the air filter housing (see Chapter 4).

2   Locate the VSS on top of the transaxle (see illustration).

3   Disconnect the electrical connector from the VSS.

4   Remove the VSS mounting bolt and remove the VSS.

5   Installation is the reverse of removal.

16.2 The VSS is located on top of the rear part of the transaxle, right above the differential, where the inner CV joints are connected to the transaxle (coupe/sedan shown, CR-V and hatchback similar)

17 Powertrain Control Module (PCM) - removal and installation

※ WARNING:

All models covered by this manual are equipped with a Supplemental Restraint System (SRS), more commonly known as airbags. Always disarm the airbag system before working in the vicinity of any airbag system component to avoid the possibility of accidental deployment of the airbag, which could cause personal injury (see Chapter 12).

※ CAUTION:

To avoid electrostatic discharge damage to the PCM, handle the PCM only by its case. Do not touch the electrical terminals during removal and installation. If available, ground yourself to the vehicle with a anti-static ground strap, available at computer supply stores.

➡ Note: The PCM is a component of the "immobilizer" (vehicle security) system. If a new PCM is installed in the vehicle, the immobilizer code must be programmed into the new PCM by a dealership service department before the engine will start. The dealer will need the vehicle, the new PCM unit and all of the vehicle keys to program the new PCM unit. So if you're planning to replace the old PCM with a new unit, a dealer service department must perform the following procedure (unless you want to have the vehicle towed to the dealer after you have installed the new PCM!).

1   Disconnect the cable from the negative battery terminal (see Chapter 5, Section 1).

2   Disable the airbag system (see Chapter 12).

3   On coupes, sedans and hatchbacks, remove the passenger's dashboard lower cover (see *Dashboard trim panels - removal and installation* in Chapter 11). On all models, remove the glove box (see same section in Chapter 11).

COUPE, SEDAN AND CR-V

◆ Refer to illustration 17.4, 17.5a, 17.5b, 17.6, 17.7 and 17.8

4   On coupes and sedans, cut off and unbolt the section of plastic that covers up the glove box frame (see illustration). (The manufacturer

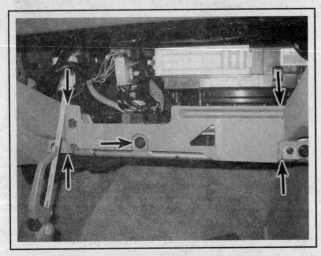

17.4 On coupes and sedans, cut off this piece of plastic where indicated, remove the single retaining bolt and discard the plastic

17.5a On coupes and sedans, unbolt and remove the glove box frame . . .

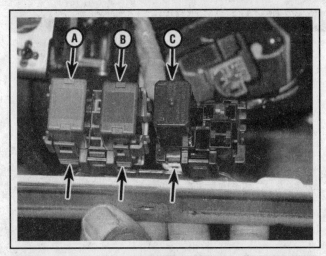

17.5b . . . depress the relay release tabs, detach the relays from the frame and set it aside (unlike the plastic that was covering it, the frame is structural, so you will need to install it after you have replaced the PCM)

A   PGM-FI main relay No. 2
B   PGM-FI main relay No. 1
C   Automatic transmission reverse relay

leaves this piece of plastic intact when the dash is assembled, but it's not structural, so you're not weakening the dash when you remove it.)

5   On coupes and sedans, unbolt the glove box frame (see illustration), detach the relays from it (see illustration) and remove the frame. (Unlike the plastic piece that was covering it, this frame is structural, so you will have to install it again after replacing the PCM.)

6   Detach the big electrical connector from the PCM mounting bracket (see illustration).

7   Disconnect the electrical connectors from the PCM (see illustration).

8   Remove the PCM mounting bolt and the two mounting nuts (see illustration) and remove the PCM.

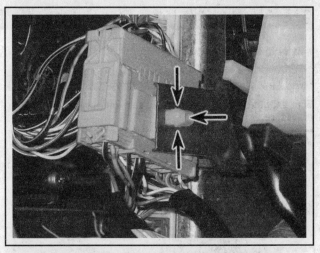

17.6 Detach this big electrical connector from the PCM mounting bracket by squeezing the two release tabs together (into the locator pin) and pushing the locator pin from the bracket

✳✳ CAUTION:

Avoid any static electricity damage to the computer by grounding yourself to the body before touching the PCM and using a special anti-static pad to store the PCM on once it is removed.

9   Installation is the reverse of removal.

10 When you're done, reconnect the cable to the negative battery terminal and perform the PCM idle learn procedure (see Chapter 5, Section 1).

HATCHBACK

11 Disconnect the electrical connectors from the underside of the PCM.

12 Remove the three PCM mounting bolts and remove the PCM.

13 Installation is the reverse of removal.

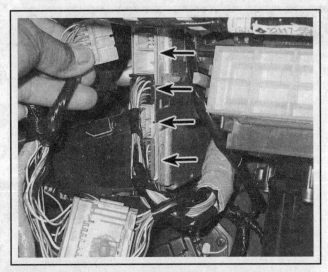

17.7 Disconnect the four electrical connectors from the PCM (coupe/sedan shown; CR-V similar)

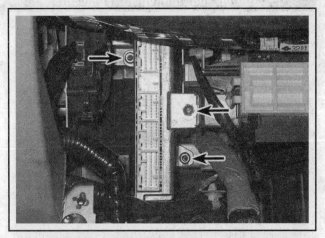

17.8 To detach the PCM from a coupe, sedan or CR-V, remove these fasteners

18 Idle Air Control (IAC) valve (all except 2005 and 2006 CR-V) - replacement

▶ **Refer to illustrations 18.4 and 18.5**

☀ WARNING:

Wait until the engine is completely cool before beginning this procedure.

1 Remove the air filter housing (see Chapter 4).

2 Clamp off the coolant hoses to the IAC valve, then detach the hoses from the valve. Be prepared for a little coolant spillage.

3 On CR-Vs and hatchbacks, remove the throttle body from the intake manifold (see Chapter 4). (On coupes and sedans, the IAC valve

is on the front side of the throttle body, so it's not necessary to remove the throttle body in order to remove the IAC valve. On CR-Vs and hatchbacks, the IAC valve is mounted on the underside of the throttle body, so you must first remove the throttle body before you can remove the IAC valve from it.)

4 Remove the IAC valve mounting screws (see illustration) and remove the IAC valve.

5 Remove the old IAC valve gasket (see illustration) and discard it.

6 When installing the IAC valve, be sure to use a new gasket and tighten the IAC valve mounting screws securely.

7 Installation is otherwise the reverse of removal.

8 Check the coolant level and add some, if necessary, to bring it to the appropriate level (see Chapter 1).

18.4 IAC valve mounting screws (coupe/sedan shown, CR-V and hatchback IAC valve similar, except that it's on the underside of the throttle body and has two screws instead of three)

18.5 After removing the IAC valve from the throttle body, remove this gasket and replace it

19 Intake Manifold Runner Control (IMRC) or Intake Manifold Tuning (IMT) system - description and component replacement

DESCRIPTION

1 The Intake Manifold Runner Control (IMRC) system, which is used only on CR-V engines, produces improved torque at all engine speeds. On later CR-V models, the system is known as the Intake Manifold Tuning (IMT) system. These systems use a rotating barrel-shaped valve located inside the intake manifold assembly. When the valve is closed, the intake manifold runners are lengthened and there is more torque at low engine speeds. When the valve is open, the runners are shortened and there is more torque at high engine speeds. Here's why: When intake air is drawn into the cylinders at idle or at low engine speeds, less air is needed because the cylinders don't need to be filled so often or so quickly. So at idle and at low engine speeds, the air drawn into an engine with longer intake runners will have a higher velocity than one with shorter intake runners. However, at higher engine speeds, longer intake runners would prevent the cylinders from filling quickly enough and would therefore limit power. Most intake manifold designs are a compromise between the conflicting demands of low and high engine speeds.

2 The IMRC/IMT system helps to maintain a uniformly higher intake air velocity throughout the engine's operating range. Higher intake air velocity promotes better vaporization of the fuel sprayed into the stream of incoming air by the fuel injectors, which means more complete combustion, more power, better fuel economy and less emissions.

3 The IMRC/IMT system consists of the PCM, a PCM-controlled solenoid valve, a special intake manifold with a barrel-type valve inside, a vacuum-controlled actuator mounted on the manifold and a valve position sensor mounted on the actuator. The PCM-controlled solenoid valve controls the vacuum signal to the actuator. The actuator is a vacuum diaphragm that rotates the barrel valve inside the manifold. When the engine is idling or operating below 4300 rpm the vacuum path through the solenoid valve is closed. When the vacuum path through the solenoid is closed, the barrel valve inside the manifold directs incoming air through a longer path. Directing incoming air through a longer intake path at low engine speeds promotes higher intake air velocities because the incoming air can move more quickly through the intake manifold to fill the cylinders. When engine speed reaches 4300 rpm, the PCM energizes the solenoid valve, which allows intake vacuum to reach the actuator. When the diaphragm inside the

actuator moves, it turns the barrel valve inside the intake manifold. When the barrel valve turns, it sends the incoming air through a shorter intake path designed to handle a larger volume of air. At that point, the volume of air drawn into the cylinders is sufficient to promote good velocity even through the shorter intake path. And the shorter intake path enhances performance during heavy acceleration or high cruising speeds. The PCM monitors the position (angle) of the barrel valve with a valve position sensor, which is a potentiometer (three-terminal variable resistor with an adjustable center connection) mounted on the side of the actuator. The valve position sensor is connected to the barrel-valve shaft. As the position of the valve changes, the valve position sensor varies the signal voltage to the PCM.

COMPONENT REPLACEMENT

IMRC/IMT valve position sensor

4   Disconnect the electrical connector from the IMRC/IMT valve position sensor.
5   Remove the two valve position sensor mounting screws and remove the sensor.
6   Remove and discard the old sensor O-ring.

7   Install a new O-ring.
8   When installing the valve position sensor, make sure that the projection inside the IMRC/IMT valve is aligned with the groove in the sensor.
9   Installation is otherwise the reverse of removal. Be sure to tighten the IMRC/IMT valve position sensor mounting screws to the torque listed in this Chapter's Specifications.

IMRC/IMT actuator/valve assembly

10 Remove the intake manifold (see Chapter 2B).
11 Remove the three IMRC/IMT actuator/valve assembly mounting bolts.
12 Remove the actuator/valve assembly.
13 Remove and discard the old O-rings and install new O-rings.
14 When installing the actuator/valve assembly, make sure that the pilot bearing is in place.
15 Also, when installing the actuator/valve assembly, make sure that the hole is visible.
16 Installation is otherwise the reverse of removal. Be sure to tighten the actuator/valve assembly mounting bolts to the torque listed in this Chapter's Specifications.

20 Catalytic converter - general description, check and replacement

➡Note: Because of a Federally mandated extended warranty which covers emissions-related components like the catalytic converter, check with a dealer service department before replacing the converter at your own expense.

GENERAL DESCRIPTION

1   A catalytic converter (or catalyst) is an emission control device in the exhaust system that reduces certain pollutants in the exhaust gas stream. There are two types of converters: oxidation converters and reduction converters.
2   Oxidation converters contain a "monolithic substrate" (a ceramic honeycomb) coated with the semi-precious metals platinum and palladium. An oxidation catalyst reduces unburned hydrocarbons (HC) and carbon monoxide (CO) by adding oxygen to the exhaust stream as it passes through the substrate, which in the presence of high temperature and the catalyst materials converts the HC and CO to water vapor (H_2O) and carbon dioxide (CO_2).
3   Reduction converters contain a monolithic substrate coated with platinum and rhodium. A reduction catalyst reduces oxides of nitrogen (NOx) by removing oxygen, which in the presence of high temperature and the catalyst material produces nitrogen (N) and carbon dioxide (CO_2).
4   Catalytic converters that combine both types of catalysts in one assembly are known as "three-way catalysts" or TWCs. A TWC can reduce all three pollutants. All catalysts used by the vehicles covered in this manual are equipped with three-way catalysts.
5   On coupes and sedans with a non-VTEC (D17A1) engine, the catalytic converter is an integral component of the exhaust manifold. The engine codes - D17A1, D17A2, D17A6, etc. - for coupes and sedans are stamped onto a flat machined surface located at the right front corner of the engine block. On these models, you must remove or replace the exhaust manifold to remove or replace the catalyst (see *Exhaust manifold - removal and installation* in Chapter 2A). Coupes

and sedans with a VTEC (D17A6) engine have two catalysts. The first catalyst is identical the exhaust manifold catalyst used on non-VTEC engines. The second catalyst is located in the exhaust pipe, underneath the vehicle. Coupes and sedans with a VTEC (D17A2) engine and all CR-Vs and hatchbacks have a single catalyst in the exhaust pipe underneath the vehicle.

CHECK

6   The test equipment for a catalytic converter (a "loaded-mode" dynamometer and a 5-gas analyzer) is expensive. If you suspect that the converter on your vehicle is malfunctioning, take it to a dealer or authorized emission inspection facility for diagnosis and repair.
7   Whenever you raise the vehicle to service underbody components, inspect the converter assembly for leaks, corrosion, dents and other damage. Carefully inspect the welds and/or flange bolts and nuts that attach the front and rear ends of the converter to the exhaust system. If you note any damage, replace the converter.
8   Although catalytic converters don't break too often, they can become clogged or even plugged up. The easiest way to check for a restricted converter is to use a vacuum gauge to diagnose the effect of a blocked exhaust on intake vacuum.

  a) *Connect a vacuum gauge to any intake manifold vacuum source (any pipe on the intake manifold with a vacuum hose connected to it will provide the necessary intake manifold vacuum).*
  b) *Warm the engine to operating temperature, place the transaxle in Park (automatic models) or Neutral (manual models) and apply the parking brake.*
  c) *Note the vacuum reading at idle and jot it down.*
  d) *Quickly open the throttle to near its wide-open position and then quickly get off the throttle and allow it to close. Note the vacuum reading and jot it down.*
  e) *Do this test three more times, recording your measurement after each test.*

f) If your fourth reading is more than one in-Hg lower than the reading that you noted at idle, the exhaust system might be restricted (the catalytic converter could be plugged, OR an exhaust pipe or muffler could be restricted).

REPLACEMENT

Integral exhaust manifold/catalytic converter assembly (coupes and sedans with D17A1 or D17A6 engines only)

9   Remove the upstream and downstream oxygen sensors (see Section 12).

10 Remove the exhaust manifold (see Chapter 2A). (The catalyst is an integral part of the exhaust manifold.)

11 Installation is the reverse of removal.

Under-vehicle catalytic converter (coupe and sedan with D17A2 and D17A6 engines and all CR-Vs and hatchbacks)

12 Raise the vehicle and place it securely on jackstands.

13 On models with a D17A2 engine, remove the upstream and downstream oxygen sensors (see Section 12). On models with a D17A6 engine, remove the third oxygen sensor (see Section 12).

14 Remove the spring-loaded bolts from the front mounting flange and the nuts from the rear flange and remove the catalytic converter.

15 If you're planning to replace (rather than just remove) the catalytic converter, remove the heat shield bolts and remove the heat shield, then install the heat shield on the new unit.

16 Installation is the reverse of removal. Be sure to replace any rusted or damaged fasteners and to tighten all fasteners to the torque listed in this Chapter's Specifications.

21 Evaporative Emissions Control (EVAP) system - general description and component replacement

GENERAL DESCRIPTION

▶ **Refer to illustration 21.2**

1   The Evaporative Emissions Control (EVAP) system prevents fuel system vapors (which contain unburned hydrocarbons) from escaping into the atmosphere. On warm days, vapors trapped inside the fuel tank expand until the pressure reaches a certain threshold. Then the fuel vapors are routed from the fuel tank through the EVAP two-way valve to the EVAP canister, where they're stored temporarily until the next time the vehicle is operated. When the conditions are right (engine warmed up, vehicle up to speed, moderate or heavy load on the engine, etc.) the PCM opens the canister purge valve, which allows fuel vapors to be drawn from the canister into the intake manifold. Once in the intake manifold, the fuel vapors mix with incoming air before drawn through the intake ports into the combustion chambers where they're burned up with the rest of the air/fuel mixture. The EVAP system is complex and virtually impossible to troubleshoot without the right tools and training. However, the following description should give you a good idea of how it works:

2   The **EVAP canister** (see illustration) is located under the vehicle, behind the fuel tank. The canister, which contains activated carbon, is a repository for storing fuel vapors. You'll have to raise the vehicle to inspect or replace the canister, or any other part of the EVAP system, except for the canister purge valve (which is located in the engine compartment). But the canister is designed to be maintenance-free and should last the life of the vehicle. There are several other important components located on or near the canister: the air filter, the canister vent shut valve, the two-way valve/bypass solenoid valve assembly and the fuel tank pressure sensor.

3   The **EVAP canister filter** is located near the canister vent shut valve. When the canister is purged, fresh air is drawn through the filter before passing through the canister. The filter prevents dust and dirt particles from entering the EVAP canister and the EVAP system.

4   The **canister vent shut valve** is located on the front of the EVAP canister. The canister vent shut valve is normally closed, but it opens to allow fresh air from the filter to enter the EVAP canister when the canister is being purged.

5   The **fuel tank pressure sensor** is located behind the upper rear edge of the EVAP canister, above the EVAP bypass solenoid valve. The fuel tank pressure sensor monitors the pressure inside the fuel tank, converts fuel tank absolute pressure into a variable voltage signal and transmits this data to the PCM.

6   The **EVAP two-way valve** is located at the left end of the EVAP canister, right below the fuel tank pressure sensor. When the pressure of the fuel vapors inside the fuel tank exceeds the preset value of the two-way valve, the valve opens and regulates the flow of excess vapors to the canister. The two-way valve also prevents excessive vacuum in the fuel tank by drawing in fresh air through the EVAP canister.

7   The **EVAP bypass solenoid valve** is also located at the left end of the EVAP canister, below the fuel tank pressure sensor. The bypass solenoid valve opens to bypass the two-way valve when the PCM does an EVAP system leak check. (The two-way valve and the

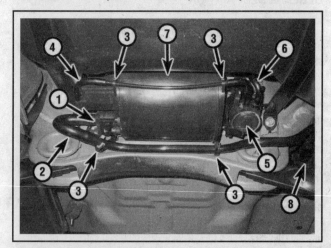

21.2 A typical EVAP canister installation (coupe/sedan shown, other models similar)

1   Vent shut valve
2   Vent shut valve-to-air filter hose
3   Hose guides
4   EVAP canister-to-two-way valve hose
5   Two-way valve/bypass solenoid valve assembly (bypass solenoid, on top of two-way valve, not visible in this photo)
6   Two-way valve-to-EVAP valve (EVAP valve, on top of fuel tank, not visible in this photo)
7   EVAP canister
8   Air filter

21.13 The EVAP canister purge valve is located on the side of the throttle body (coupe and sedan)

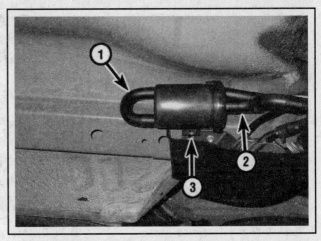

21.26 To remove the EVAP canister air filter:

1   Disconnect the fresh air inlet hose
2   Disconnect the outlet hose (goes to the vent shut valve on the EVAP canister)
3   Remove the air filter mounting bolt

bypass solenoid valve are connected together and look like a single assembly, but they can be separated, and they're available as separate components.)

8   The **EVAP canister purge control valve**, which is under the control of the Powertrain Control Module (PCM), regulates the flow of vapors being purged from the EVAP canister into the intake manifold. The canister purge valve is always closed when engine coolant temperature is below 147-degrees F (64-degrees C), which cuts off intake manifold vacuum to the EVAP canister. Above that threshold - 158 degrees F (70 degrees C) on coupes and sedans, 149 degrees F (65 degrees C) on CR-Vs and hatchbacks - the PCM opens or closes the purge valve in accordance with data from various information sensor inputs. The interval of time during which the purge valve is opened by the PCM is known as its "duty cycle." The purge valve is located on the throttle body.

General system checks

9   The most common symptom of a faulty EVAP system is a strong fuel odor (particularly during hot weather). If you smell fuel while driving or (more likely) right after you park the vehicle and turn off the engine, check the fuel filler cap first. Make sure that it's screwed onto the fuel filler neck all the way. If the odor persists, inspect all EVAP hose connections, both in the engine compartment and under the vehicle. You'll have to raise the vehicle and place it securely on jackstands to inspect most of the EVAP system, since it's located under the vehicle. Be sure to inspect each hose attached to the canister for damage and leakage along its entire length. Repair or replace as necessary. Inspect the canister for damage and look for fuel leaking from the bottom. If fuel is leaking or the canister is otherwise damaged, replace it.

10   Poor idle, stalling, and poor driveability can be caused by a defective fuel vapor vent valve or canister purge valve, a damaged canister, cracked hoses, or hoses connected to the wrong tubes. Fuel loss or fuel odor can be caused by fuel leaking from fuel lines or hoses, a cracked or damaged canister, or a defective vapor valve.

11   To check for excessive fuel vapor pressure in the fuel tank, remove the gas cap and listen for the sound of pressure release. If the fuel tank emits a "whooshing" sound when you open the filler cap, fuel tank vapor pressure is excessive. Inspect the canister vapor hoses and the canister inlet port for blockage or collapsed hoses. Also inspect the vapor vent valve. A complete test can only be done with a proprietary OBD-II scan tool (see Section 2), which will run a series of checks using the fuel tank pressure sensor and other output actuators to detect excessive pressure. You'll have to take the vehicle to a dealer service

department or other qualified repair shop to have the EVAP system professionally diagnosed.

COMPONENT REPLACEMENT

EVAP canister purge valve

Coupe and sedan

▶ **Refer to illustration 21.13**

12   Remove the air filter housing (see Chapter 4).
13   Locate the EVAP purge control valve on the side of the throttle body (see illustration).
14   Disconnect the electrical connector from the purge control valve.
15   Disconnect the vacuum hoses from the purge control valve.
16   Remove the purge control valve mounting screws and remove the purge control valve.
17   Installation is the reverse of removal.

CR-V and hatchback

18   Disconnect the electrical connector from the EVAP canister purge valve.
19   Disconnect the vacuum hose from the EVAP canister purge valve.
20   Remove the EVAP canister purge valve mounting screws.
21   Remove the EVAP canister purge valve.
22   Remove and discard the EVAP canister purge valve O-ring.
23   Using a new O-ring, install the EVAP canister purge valve and tighten the mounting screws to the torque listed in this Chapter's Specifications.
24   Installation is otherwise the reverse of removal.

EVAP canister air filter

▶ **Refer to illustration 21.26**

25   Raise the vehicle and place it securely on jackstands.
26   Clearly label the two hoses connected to the EVAP canister air filter (see illustration), then disconnect them.
27   Remove the canister air filter mounting bolt (see illustration 21.26) and remove the air filter from its mounting bracket.
28   Installation is the reverse of removal.

21.30 Disconnect the vapor hose from the EVAP canister vent shut valve and disengage it from this hose clip

21.31 Disconnect the electrical connector from the EVAP canister vent shut valve, then remove the vent shut valve mounting screws and remove the valve from the EVAP canister

21.33 Remove and discard this O-ring from the EVAP canister vent shut valve; whether you're planning to install the old vent shut valve or a new unit, always use a new O-ring when installing the valve

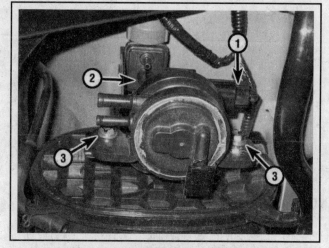

21.36 Clearly label and then disconnect the two vapor hoses from the two-way valve

    A   Goes to the EVAP canister
    B   Goes to the EVAP valve on top of the fuel tank

21.37 EVAP two-way/bypass solenoid valve installation details

    1   Disconnect the electrical connector from the bypass solenoid
    2   Disconnect the vapor hose that connects the fuel tank pressure sensor to the two-way valve
    3   Remove the two-way valve mounting screws

EVAP canister vent shut valve

▶ Refer to illustrations 21.30, 21.31 and 21.33

29 Raise the vehicle and place it securely on jackstands.
30 Disconnect the vapor hose from the EVAP canister vent shut valve (see illustration).
31 Disconnect the electrical connector from the EVAP canister vent shut valve (see illustration).
32 Remove the EVAP canister vent shut valve mounting screws (see illustration 21.31) and remove the shut valve from the EVAP canister.
33 Replace the O-ring on the vent shut valve (see illustration).
34 Installation is the reverse of removal.

EVAP two-way valve/bypass solenoid valve

▶ Refer to illustrations 21.36 and 21.37

35 Raise the vehicle and place it securely on jackstands.

36 Disconnect the vapor hoses from the two-way valve (see illustration).
37 Disconnect the electrical connector from the bypass solenoid valve (see illustration).
38 Disconnect the vapor hose that connects the fuel tank pressure sensor to the two-way valve (see illustration 21.37).
39 Remove the two-way valve mounting screws (see illustration 21.37) and remove the two-way valve/bypass solenoid valve assembly.
40 Installation is the reverse of removal.

EVAP fuel tank pressure sensor

▶ Refer to illustration 21.42

41 Remove the EVAP two-way valve/bypass solenoid valve assembly (see Steps 36 through 39).

21.42 EVAP fuel tank pressure sensor installation details

1   *Disconnect the hose that connects the fuel tank pressure sensor to the two-way valve*
2   *Disconnect the vent hose*
3   *Disconnect the electrical connector*
4   *Push the sensor straight up to detach it from its mounting bracket*

42 Disconnect the vapor hoses from the fuel tank pressure sensor (see illustration).
43 Disconnect the electrical connector from the fuel tank pressure sensor (see illustration 21.42).
44 Remove the fuel tank pressure sensor from its mounting bracket by pushing it straight up.
45 Installation is the reverse of removal.

EVAP canister

▶ **Refer to illustrations 21.47**

46 Raise the vehicle and place it securely on jackstands.
47 Disconnect the vapor hose and the electrical connector from the vent shut valve and disconnect the two vapor hoses from the right end of the EVAP canister (see illustration).
48 Detach the two-way valve/bypass solenoid valve assembly from

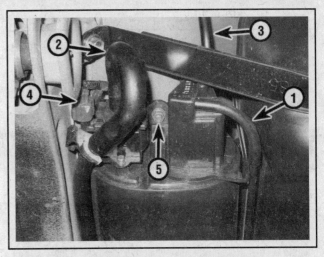

21.47 EVAP canister installation details (right end)

1   *Disconnect the hose that connects the EVAP canister to the two-way valve*
2   *Disconnect the hose that connects the vent shut valve to the air filter*
3   *Disconnect the hose that connects the EVAP canister to the canister purge valve in the engine compartment*
4   *Disconnect the vent shut valve electrical connector*
5   *Remove the EVAP canister mounting bolt*

the left end of the EVAP canister (see illustration 21.37). (It's not necessary to actually remove the two-way valve/bypass solenoid assembly - just remove the two bracket mounting screws and pull the bracket away from the canister.)
49 Disengage any vapor hoses that are attached to the sides of the canister.
50 Remove the EVAP canister mounting bolt (see illustration 21.47), then remove the canister.
51 If you're planning to replace the EVAP canister, be sure to remove the vent shut valve (see illustration 21.31), and any other EVAP system components attached to the canister, and install them on the new canister.
52 Installation is the reverse of removal.

22 Exhaust Gas Recirculation (EGR) system - general description and component replacement

GENERAL DESCRIPTION

1   Oxides of nitrogen (or simply NOx) is a compound that is formed in the combustion chambers when the oxygen and nitrogen in the incoming air mix together. NOx is a natural by product of high combustion chamber temperatures. When NOx is emitted from the tailpipe, it mixes with reactive organic compounds (ROCs), hydrocarbons (HC) and sunlight to form ozone and photochemical smog. The Exhaust Gas Recirculation (EGR) system reduces oxides of nitrogen by recirculating exhaust gases from the exhaust manifold, through the EGR valve and intake manifold, then back to the combustion chambers, where it mixes with the incoming air/fuel mixture before being consumed. These recirculated exhaust gases "dilute" the incoming air/fuel mixture, which cools the combustion chambers, thereby reducing NOx emissions.
2   2001 through 2003 coupes and sedans with VTEC engines and all 2004 coupes and sedans are equipped with an EGR system. CR-Vs

and hatchbacks do not use EGR systems.
3   The EGR system consists of the Powertrain Control Module (PCM), the EGR valve, the EGR valve position sensor (an integral part of the EGR valve) and various other information sensors that the PCM uses to determine when to open the EGR valve. The EGR valve is located on the coolant housing at the right end of the engine. The degree to which the EGR valve is opened is referred to as "EGR valve lift." The PCM is programmed to produce the ideal EGR valve lift for varying operating conditions. The EGR valve position sensor, which is an integral part of the EGR valve, detects the amount of EGR valve lift and sends this information to the PCM. The PCM then compares it with the appropriate EGR valve lift for the operating conditions. The PCM increases current flow to the EGR valve to increase valve lift and reduces the current to reduce the amount of lift. If EGR flow is inappropriate to the operating conditions (idle, cold engine, etc.) the PCM simply cuts the current to the EGR valve and the valve closes.

EGR VALVE REPLACEMENT

4   Locate the EGR valve on the coolant housing at the right end of the engine.

5   Disconnect the electrical connector from the EGR valve.

6   Remove the EGR valve mounting nuts and remove the EGR valve from the coolant housing.

7   Remove and discard the old EGR valve gasket.

8   Installation is the reverse of removal. Be sure to use a new EGR valve gasket, and tighten the EGR valve mounting nuts securely.

23   Positive Crankcase Ventilation (PCV) system - general description, check and component replacement

GENERAL DESCRIPTION

1   The Positive Crankcase Ventilation (PCV) system reduces hydrocarbon emissions by scavenging crankcase vapors. It does this by circulating fresh air from the air intake duct into and through the crankcase, where it mixes with blow-by gases before being drawn by intake manifold vacuum through a PCV valve to the intake manifold.

2   The main components of the PCV system are the PCV valve and a pair of hoses, and, on coupes and sedans only, an air/oil separator (baffle), which is located on the backside of the engine block. The fresh air inlet hose draws fresh air from the air filter housing into the crankcase, where it mixes with blow-by gases. This mixture of fresh air and crankcase vapors is drawn into the intake manifold by intake manifold vacuum through the PCV valve and the crankcase ventilation hose, which connects the crankcase to the intake manifold.

3   On coupes and sedans, the fresh air inlet hose connects the air filter housing to a pipe on the rear edge of the valve cover. After mixing with blow-by bases in the crankcase, the fresh air-and-crankcase-vapor mixture is drawn from the crankcase by manifold vacuum through the PCV valve and the crankcase ventilation hose, which connects the crankcase, via an air/oil separator (baffle) located on the backside of the block, to the intake manifold.

4   On CR-Vs and hatchbacks, the fresh air inlet hose connects the air filter housing to a pipe on the left end of the valve cover. After mixing with blow-by gases in the crankcase, the fresh air-and-crankcase vapor mixture is drawn from the crankcase by manifold vacuum through the PCV valve, which is located on the right front side of the block, and the crankcase ventilation hose, which connects the

crankcase to the intake manifold.

5   To maintain idle quality, the PCV valve restricts the flow of crankcase vapors into the intake manifold when intake manifold vacuum is high, and allows full flow when intake manifold decreases.

CHECK

▶ **Refer to illustration 23.6a, 23.6b and 23.7**

6   Inspect the fresh air inlet hose (see illustration) and the PCV valve and crankcase ventilation hose (see illustration). Inspect the two PCV system hoses for cracks, tears and deterioration. If either hose is damaged or worn, replace it.

7   Start the engine and allow it to warm up. With the engine idling, pinch off the crankcase ventilation hose (see illustration) and verify that the PCV valve makes a clicking sound. If there is no clicking sound, the crankcase ventilation hose might be clogged or punctured. Remove the crankcase ventilation hose, blow it out with compressed air, then inspect it for damage.

8   If the hose is damaged or clogged, replace it, then retest the PCV valve. If the valve still doesn't click, replace it.

COMPONENT REPLACEMENT

Fresh air inlet hose

9   On coupes and sedans, remove the air filter housing (see Chapter 4).

  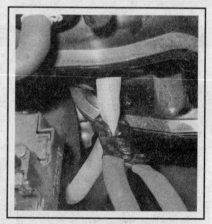

23.6a Inspect the PCV system's fresh air inlet hose for cracks, tears and deterioration; if it's damaged or worn, replace it (coupe/sedan shown)

23.6b Inspect the PCV system's crankcase ventilation hose for cracks, tears and deterioration; if it's damaged or worn, replace it (couple/sedan shown)

23.7 To check the PCV valve, start the engine and allow it to idle, then pinch off the crankcase ventilation hose with a pair of pliers and verify that the PCV valve makes a clicking sound (coupe/sedan shown)

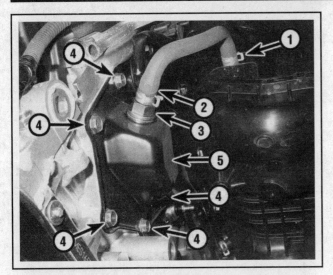

23.13 PCV system crankcase ventilation hose, PCV valve and air/oil separator installation details (coupe/sedan)

1   Hose clamp at air filter housing
2   Hose clamp at PCV valve
3   PCV valve
4   Air/oil separator mounting bolts (upper bolt is not visible in this photo)
5   Air/oil separator

10 Simply loosen the hose clamps at both ends of the hose, slide them back and disconnect the hose from the valve cover and from the air filter housing.

11 Installation is the reverse of removal. Make sure that both hose clamps are in good shape. If either one is loose, replace it.

Crankcase ventilation hose

Coupe and sedan

▶ **Refer to illustration 23.13**

12 Raise the front of the vehicle and place it securely on jackstands.

13 Loosen the hose clamps at both ends of the crankcase ventilation hose (see illustration), then disconnect the hose from the PCV valve and from the intake manifold.

14 Installation is the reverse of removal. Make sure that both hose clamps are in good shape. If either one is loose, replace it.

CR-V and hatchback

15 On CR-Vs, remove the intake manifold cover (see Chapter 2B). (On these models, the crankcase ventilation hose is routed across the top of the intake manifold.)

16 Loosen the hose clamps at both ends of the crankcase ventilation hose, then disconnect the hose from the PCV valve and from the intake manifold.

17 Installation is the reverse of removal. Make sure that both hose clamps are in good shape. If either one is loose, replace it.

PCV valve

Coupe and sedan

18 Raise the front of the vehicle and place it securely on jackstands.

19 Disconnect the crankcase ventilation hose from the PCV valve (see illustration 23.13).

20 Unscrew the PCV valve from the air/oil separator.

21 Installation is the reverse of removal. Be sure to tighten the PCV valve to the torque listed in this Chapter's Specifications.

CR-V and hatchback

22 Disconnect the crankcase ventilation hose from the PCV valve.

23 Unscrew and remove the PCV valve.

24 Installation is the reverse of removal. Be sure to tighten the PCV valve to the torque listed in this Chapter's Specifications.

Air/oil separator (coupe and sedan only)

25 Raise the front of the vehicle and place it securely on jackstands.

26 Remove the crankcase ventilation hose and the PCV valve (see illustration 23.13).

27 Unbolt the air/oil separator and remove it.

28 Using solvent and a gasket scraper, remove all residual liquid gasket material from the gasket mating surfaces of the separator and the block, then blow dry with compressed air.

29 Apply a fresh coat of liquid gasket to the mating surface of the separator and to the inner threads of the bolt holes in the block, then install the separator within the interval of time specified by the manufacturer of the liquid gasket. (If you wait too long - more than four minutes, for example - some liquid gaskets will not seal correctly.)

30 Installation is otherwise the reverse of removal. Be sure to tighten the air/oil separator mounting bolts to the torque listed in this Chapter's Specifications.

24 Variable Valve Timing and Lift Electronic Control (VTEC) system - description and component replacement

DESCRIPTION

1   A low-lift, short-duration camshaft intake lobe produces good torque, quick response, good fuel economy and low emissions at lower engine speeds, but can't deliver sufficient air/fuel mixture to the combustion chamber at higher engine speeds. A high-lift, long-duration intake cam lobe produces good power at high engine speeds, but produces a lumpy idle and poor driveability, wastes fuel and produces unacceptable emissions at lower engine speeds. That's why camshaft intake lobe profiles are always a compromise between economy and performance. But Honda's Variable Valve Timing and Lift Electronic Control (VTEC) system allows an engine to operate economically and make good power at the same time.

2   The VTEC system is used on some coupe and sedan engines (D17A2 and D17A6) and on all CR-V and hatchback engines. The principal differences between VTEC and non-VTEC engines are in the cylinder head, the camshaft(s) and the rocker arms. The block, the lubrication and cooling systems and most other components are identical on VTEC and non-VTEC engines. For more information about the cylinder head, the camshaft(s) and the rocker arms, refer to Chapter 2.

This Section is intended to familiarize you with how VTEC works and to show you how to replace the PCM-controlled components (the VTEC solenoid valve and the VTC oil control solenoid valve) in the VTEC system. If you don't know whether your vehicle is equipped with VTEC, look for the letters "VTEC" on top of the valve cover.

VTEC system on SOHC models (coupes and sedans)

3   There are two cam lobes for each pair of intake valves on D17A2 and D17A6 SOHC engines (D17A1 SOHC engines do not use VTEC). These "primary" and "secondary" lobe profiles differ in lift and duration: the secondary lobe has lower lift and less duration (it opens later and closes sooner), while the primary lobe has higher lift and more duration (opens sooner and closes later). Each lobe operates its own rocker arm, which in turn pushes on its own valve. At low speeds, the secondary camshaft lobe operates one intake valve and the primary cam lobe operates the other valve. The low-lift, short-duration lobe produces good low-end torque and responsiveness.

4   When more power is needed at higher engine speeds, the PCM activates the VTEC solenoid valve, which allows higher oil pressure to a hydraulically-operated, spring-loaded pin inside the primary rocker arm. When hydraulic pressure overcomes spring pressure the pin slides sideways and locks the secondary rocker arm to the primary rocker arm. The two rocker arms are both activated by the primary cam lobe; the secondary rocker arm no longer contacts its own camshaft lobe again until the system is disengaged. So both valves are now opened by the primary camshaft lobe with its higher lift and longer duration, increasing performance.

5   The PCM turns the VTEC solenoid on and off in accordance with engine rpm, vehicle speed, throttle opening angle, engine load and coolant temperature. Although diagnosis of the VTEC system is beyond the scope of the home mechanic, it's not difficult to replace the VTEC solenoid valve or to clean the filter for the system, both of which are outlined below.

Intelligent Variable Valve Timing and Lift Electronic Control (i-VTEC) system on DOHC models (CR-Vs and hatchbacks)

6   The "intelligent" VTEC (i-VTEC) system used on the DOHC engines in these two models is similar in operation to the SOHC VTEC system used on coupes and sedans, except that they also employ Variable Valve Timing Control (VTC).

Variable Valve Timing Control (VTC)

7   The VTEC system changes the valve lift and duration of the intake camshaft by using two different cam profiles. The VTC system, which is employed only on i-VTEC systems, changes the phase of the intake camshaft, which is another way of saying that it changes the cam timing, except that it does so continuously, not just when engine speed exceeds a certain threshold, as with the VTEC system. The VTC system, which is also operated by hydraulic (oil) pressure, improves fuel efficiency even more than VTEC alone, and it reduces exhaust emissions at all combinations of engine speed, vehicle speed and engine load.

8   When the engine is under a light load, the VTC control actuator (located inside the intake cam timing chain sprocket) is at its "base" position. The angle of the intake cam lobes is retarded to reduce the entry of exhaust gases into the intake ports and to achieve stable fuel consumption during lean burn.

9   When the engine is under a medium-to-high load, the VTC control actuator is at its "advance control" position. Cam angle is advanced slightly to reduce the effect of a diluted charge when the EGR system is operating by reducing the accompanying pumping loss. The intake

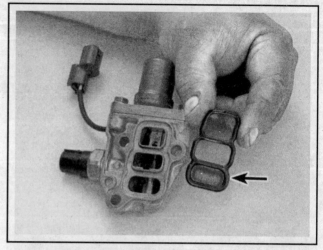

24.23 Check the VTEC solenoid valve filter screens; clean or replace the screens as necessary

valve is closed quickly to help reduce the entry of air/fuel mixture into the intake port and to improve the charging effect.

10   When the engine is operating at higher speeds, the VTC control actuator is at its "advance-base" position. The cam phase angle is controlled for maximum valve timing and maximum engine power.

COMPONENT REPLACEMENT

Coupe and sedan

VTEC solenoid valve

11   Remove the air intake resonator (see *Air filter housing - removal and installation* in Chapter 4).

12   The VTEC solenoid valve is located at the right rear corner of the cylinder head.

13   Disconnect the electrical connector from the VTEC solenoid valve.

14   Remove the VTEC solenoid valve mounting bolts and remove the VTEC solenoid valve from the cylinder head.

15   Remove the VTEC solenoid valve filter.

16   Inspect the filter for clogging and, if necessary, clean it with fresh solvent. If the filter is too dirty to be cleaned, replace it, and replace the engine oil and the engine oil filter (see Chapter 1).

17   Remove the three solenoid mounting bolts and separate the solenoid from the valve.

18   Remove the old O-ring between the solenoid and the valve and discard it. Always install a new O-ring when you disassemble the solenoid and the valve.

19   Using a new O-ring and, if necessary, a new filter, install the VTEC solenoid valve.

20   Installation is otherwise the reverse of removal. Be sure to tighten the solenoid-to-valve bolts and the VTEC solenoid valve mounting bolts to the torque listed in this Chapter's Specifications.

CR-V and hatchback

VTEC solenoid valve

▶ **Refer to illustrations 24.23 and 24.24**

21   Locate the VTEC solenoid valve at the right rear corner of the cylinder head and disconnect the electrical connector.

22   Remove the VTEC solenoid valve mounting bolts, remove the

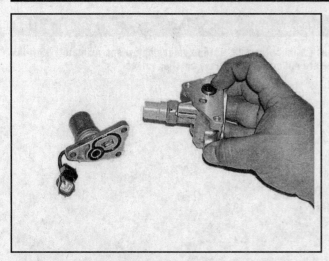

24.24 The plunger in the solenoid should move freely

solenoid valve heat shield and remove the VTEC solenoid from the cylinder head.

23 Remove the VTEC solenoid valve filter (see illustration). Inspect the filter for clogging and, if necessary, clean it with fresh solvent. If the filter is too dirty to be cleaned, replace it, and replace the engine oil and the engine oil filter (see Chapter 1).

24 Remove the solenoid-to-valve mounting bolts and separate the solenoid from the valve. Depress the plunger into the valve with your finger (see illustration). It should move freely in its bore in the valve. If it doesn't, replace the VTEC solenoid valve.

25 Installation is the reverse of removal. Be sure to tighten the VTEC solenoid valve mounting bolts to the torque listed in this Chapter's Specifications.

VTC oil control solenoid valve

26 Locate the VTC oil control solenoid valve on the right end of the cylinder head.

27 Disconnect the electrical connector from the VTC oil control solenoid valve.

28 Remove the VTC oil control solenoid mounting bolt and remove the solenoid valve.

29 Remove and discard the old VTC oil control solenoid valve O-ring.

30 Inspect the VTC oil control solenoid valve for clogging. If the oil control solenoid valve is clogged, replace it and inspect the VTC oil strainer (see Step 32).

31 Using a new O-ring, install the VTC oil control solenoid valve and tighten the mounting bolt to the torque listed in this Chapter's Specifications and plug in the electrical connector.

VTC oil strainer

32 Locate the VTC oil control solenoid oil strainer on the right front corner of the cylinder head.

33 Remove the VTC oil strainer cover bolts and remove the cover.

34 Remove the VTC oil strainer and inspect it for clogging. If the strainer is clogged, clean it in fresh solvent. If the strainer is too dirty to clean, replace it, then replace the engine oil and the oil filter (see Chapter 1).

35 Installation is the reverse of removal. Be sure to tighten the VTC oil strainer cover bolts securely.

Torque specifications   Ft-lbs (unless otherwise indicated)   Nm

➡**Note: One foot-pound (ft-lb) of torque is equivalent to 12 inch-pounds (in-lbs) of torque. Torque values below approximately 15 ft-lbs are expressed in inch-pounds, since most foot-pound torque wrenches are not accurate at these smaller values.**

	Ft-lbs (unless otherwise indicated)	Nm
Air/oil separator mounting bolts		
(coupe and sedan only)	86.4 in-lbs	9.8
Camshaft Position (CMP) sensor mounting bolt		
Coupe and sedan	86.4 in-lbs	9.8
CR-V and hatchback	104.4 in-lbs	12
Coolant outlet bolts	105 in-lbs	12
Crankshaft Position (CKP) sensor mounting bolt	104.4 in-lbs	12
IMRC actuator/valve assembly mounting bolts	86.4 in-lbs	9.8
IMRC valve position sensor mounting screws	30 in-lbs	3.5
Input shaft (mainshaft) speed sensor mounting bolt	104.4 in-lbs	12
Knock sensor		
Coupe and sedan	16	22
CR-V and hatchback	23	31
Output shaft (countershaft) speed sensor		
mounting bolt	104.4 in-lbs	12
Oxygen sensors	33	44
Positive Crankcase Ventilation (PCV) valve	33	44
Power Steering Pressure (PSP) switch	104.4 in-lbs	12
Transmission range switch mounting bolts	104.4 in-lbs	12
VTEC system (coupe and sedan)		
VTEC solenoid valve mounting bolts	86.4 in-lbs	9.8
Solenoid-to-valve mounting bolts	86.4 in-lbs	9.8
i-VTEC system (CRV and hatchback)		
VTEC solenoid valve mounting bolts	86.4 in-lbs	9.8
VTC oil control solenoid mounting bolt	104.4 in-lbs	12
VTC strainer cover bolts	N/A	

Section

Reference to other Chapters

7A

MANUAL
TRANSAXLE

1 General information

Vehicles covered by this manual are equipped with a five-speed manual transaxle, a four-speed automatic transaxle or a Continuously Variable Transaxle (CVT).

All information on the manual transaxle is included in this Part of Chapter 7. Service procedures for the four-speed automatic transaxle and Continuously Variable Transaxle (CVT) can be found in Chapter 7, Part B. You'll also find certain procedures common to both transaxles - such as oil seal replacement - in this Chapter.

Depending on the expense involved in having a transaxle overhauled, it might be a better idea to consider replacing it with either a new or rebuilt unit. Your local dealer or transaxle shop should be able to supply information concerning cost, availability and exchange policy. Regardless of how you decide to remedy a transaxle problem, you can still save a lot of money by removing and installing the unit yourself.

2 Driveaxle oil seals - replacement

♦ **Refer to illustrations 2.4 and 2.6**

1 Oil leaks frequently occur due to wear of the driveaxle oil seals. Replacement of these seals is relatively easy, since the repair can usually be performed without removing the transaxle from the vehicle.

2 Driveaxle oil seals are located at the sides of the transaxle, where the driveaxles are attached. If leakage at the seal is suspected, raise the vehicle and support it securely on jackstands. If the seal is leaking, lubricant will be found on the sides of the transaxle, below the seals.

3 Refer to Chapter 8 and remove the driveaxles.

4 Use a screwdriver or prybar to carefully pry the oil seal out of the transaxle bore (see illustration).

5 If the oil seal cannot be removed with a screwdriver or prybar, a special oil seal removal tool (available at auto parts stores) will be required.

6 Using a large section of pipe or a large deep socket (slightly smaller than the outside diameter of the seal) as a drift, install the new oil seal (see illustration). Drive it into the bore squarely and make sure it's completely seated. Coat the seal lip with transaxle lubricant.

7 Install the driveaxle(s). Be careful not to damage the lip of the new seal.

2.4 Insert the tip of a large screwdriver or prybar behind the oil seal and very carefully pry it out

2.6 Using a large socket or a section of pipe, drive the new seal squarely into the bore

3 Transaxle mount - check and replacement

1 Raise the front of the vehicle and place it securely on jackstands.

2 Insert a large screwdriver or prybar between the mount support arm and the frame and try to lever the support arm.

3 The transaxle support arm should not move up more than about 1/2 to 3/4-inch within the mount. If it does, replace the mount.

4 To replace the mount, support the transaxle with a jack, remove the nuts and bolts and remove the mount.

❋❋ WARNING:

Do not place any part of your body under the transaxle when it's supported only by a jack.

5 Installation is the reverse of removal.

4   Shift cables - removal and installation

1   Remove the center console (see Chapter 11).
2   Remove the cotter pins and detach the cable ends from the lock pins on the shift lever.

➡**Note: Hatchback models are equipped with clamps that snap fit over the cable ends while coupes and sedans are equipped with cotter pins.**

3   Pry off the spring clips and detach the cables from the shift lever housing. Rotate the cables until the squared edge aligns with the slot in the shift lever housing cutout.
4   Pull back the carpet and dislodge the grommet from the floorpan.

5   Raise the front of the vehicle and support it securely on jackstands.
6   Unscrew the nut and detach the cable bracket from the floorpan.
7   Remove the clip(s) and washer(s) and detach the cable(s) from the shift lever(s) on the transaxle.
8   Pry off the spring clip(s) and detach the cable(s) from the bracket on the transaxle.
9   Guide the cable(s) through the floorpan.
10   Installation is the reverse of removal

5   Back-up light switch - check and replacement

CHECK

1   Before testing the back-up light switch, check the fuse in the engine compartment fuse/relay box. Refer to the wiring diagrams at the end of Chapter 12.
2   Put the shift lever in Reverse and turn the ignition switch to the On position. The back-up lights should go on. Turn off the ignition switch.
3   If the back-up lights don't go on, check the back-up light bulbs in the tail light assembly.
4   If the fuse and bulbs are both okay, locate the back-up light switch on top of the transaxle, trace the leads back to the electrical connector, unplug the connector and hook up an ohmmeter or continuity tester across the terminals of the back-up light switch.
5   With the shift lever in Reverse, there should be continuity; with

the shifter in any other gear, there should be no continuity.
6   If the switch fails this test, replace it (see below).
7   If the switch is OK, but the back-up lights aren't coming on, check for power to the switch. If voltage is not available, trace the circuit between the switch and the fuse block. If power is present, trace the circuit between the switch and the back-up lights for an open circuit condition.

REPLACEMENT

8   Unplug the back-up light switch electrical connector.
9   Unscrew the back-up light switch.
10   Discard the old washer.
11   Using a new washer, install the new switch.
12   Plug in the connector.

6   Manual transaxle - removal and installation

REMOVAL

1   Remove the air intake duct and the air filter housing (see Chapter 4).
2   Remove the battery and the battery tray (see Chapter 5).
3   Remove the clutch release cylinder and hydraulic line, without disconnecting any fittings. Support the cylinder out of the way with a length of wire or rope.

❄ CAUTION:

Don't depress the clutch pedal while the release cylinder is removed.

4   Remove the starter (see Chapter 5).
5   Clearly label and disconnect all vacuum lines, emissions hoses, electrical connectors and wiring harness clamps/brackets that may interfere with transaxle removal. Masking tape and/or a touch up paint applicator work well for marking items. Take instant photos or sketch the locations of components and brackets.
6   Support the engine with an engine support fixture or an engine

hoist (an engine support fixture is recommended, as it doesn't have legs that extend under the vehicle that would get in the way). Connect the sling or chain to the lifting hook at the end of the engine near the transaxle, not to the lifting eye on the transaxle. If no lifting hook is provided, use the threaded hole(s) in the cylinder head to attach the sling or chain.
7   Loosen the front wheel lug nuts, then raise the vehicle and support it securely on jackstands. Remove the wheels.
8   Remove the engine splash shield (see Chapter 2A, Section 5) and the inner fender splash shields (see Chapter 11, Section 12). Cover the fenders and cowl using special pads. An old bedspread or blanket will also work.
9   Drain the transaxle fluid (see Chapter 1).
10   Remove the front section of the exhaust pipe, between the exhaust manifold(s) and the downstream catalytic converter.
11   Remove the driveaxles and, on 4WD CR-V models, the driveshaft (see Chapter 8).
12   Disconnect the shift cables from the transaxle (see Section 4).
13   Remove all of the powertrain mounts except the mount at the timing belt (or chain) end of the engine (see Chapter 2A).
14   Remove the subframe (see Chapter 10).
15   Support the transaxle with a jack, preferably one made for this

purpose. Secure the transaxle to the jack with straps or chains.

16 Remove the transaxle-to-engine bolts.

17 Move the transaxle away from the engine to disengage the transaxle input shaft from the clutch disc, and far enough to clear the pressure plate. Lower the transaxle from the vehicle.

➡**Note: It may be necessary to slowly lower the engine a slight amount while the jack supporting the transaxle is being lowered. This will provide more clearance between the transaxle and the body.**

INSTALLATION

18 If removed, install the clutch components (see Chapter 8).

19 Make sure the dowel pins are installed in the engine block. With the transaxle secured to the jack with a chain, raise it into position behind the engine, then carefully slide it forward, engaging the two dowel pins on the transaxle with the corresponding holes in the block and the input shaft with the clutch plate hub splines. Do not use excessive force to install the transaxle - if the input shaft does not slide into place, readjust the angle of the transaxle so it is level and/or turn the input shaft so the splines engage properly with the clutch plate hub.

20 Install the transaxle-to-engine bolts and tighten them to the torque listed in this Chapter's Specifications.

21 The remainder of installation is the reverse of removal, noting the following points:

a) *Refill the transaxle with the specified type of lubricant (see Chapter 1).*

b) *Tighten the driveaxle/hub nuts to the torque listed in the Chapter 8 Specifications.*

c) *Tighten the wheel lug nuts to the torque listed in the Chapter 1 Specifications.*

d) *Road test the vehicle for proper operation and check for leaks.*

7   Manual transaxle overhaul - general information

1   Overhauling a manual transaxle is a difficult job for the do-it-yourselfer. It involves the disassembly and reassembly of many small parts. Numerous clearances must be precisely measured and, if necessary, changed with select fit spacers and snap-rings. As a result, if transaxle problems arise, it can be removed and installed by a competent do-it-yourselfer, but overhaul should be left to a transaxle repair shop. Rebuilt transaxles may be available - check with your dealer parts department and auto parts stores. At any rate, the time and money involved in an overhaul is almost sure to exceed the cost of a rebuilt unit.

2   Nevertheless, it's not impossible for an inexperienced mechanic to rebuild a transaxle if the special tools are available and the job is done in a deliberate step-by-step manner so nothing is overlooked.

3   The tools necessary for an overhaul include internal and external snap-ring pliers, a bearing puller, a slide hammer, a set of pin punches, a dial indicator and possibly a hydraulic press. In addition, a large, sturdy workbench and a vise or transaxle stand will be required.

4   During disassembly of the transaxle, make careful notes of how each piece comes off, where it fits in relation to other pieces and what holds it in place. Noting how the parts are installed when you remove them will make it much easier to get the transaxle back together.

5   Before taking the transaxle apart for repair, it will help if you have some idea what area of the transaxle is malfunctioning. Certain problems can be closely tied to specific areas in the transaxle, which can make component examination and replacement easier. Refer to the *Troubleshooting* Section at the front of this manual for information regarding possible sources of trouble.

Torque specifications	Ft-lbs (unless otherwise indicated)	Nm
Transaxle mounting bolts	47	64
Starter bolts	See Chapter 5	

Section

7B

AUTOMATIC
TRANSAXLE

1   General information

The vehicles covered by this manual are equipped with a five-speed manual, a four-speed automatic transaxle or a Continuously Variable Transaxle (CVT). All information on automatic transaxles and the Continuously Variable Transaxle is included in this Part of Chapter 7. Information for the manual transaxle can be found in Part A of this Chapter. Information related to the transfer case on 4WD CR-V models can be found in Chapter 8.

Due to the complexity of the automatic transaxles and Continuously Variable Transaxles covered in this manual and to the specialized equipment necessary to perform most service operations, this Chapter contains only those procedures related to general diagnosis, routine maintenance, adjustment and removal and installation.

If the transaxle requires major repair work, this should be left to a dealer service department or an automotive or transmission repair shop. You can, however, remove and install the transaxle yourself and save the expense, even if a transmission shop does the repair work (but be sure a proper diagnosis has been made before removing the transaxle).

2   Diagnosis - general

1   Automatic transaxle malfunctions may be caused by five general conditions:

    a) Poor engine performance
    b) Improper adjustments
    c) Hydraulic malfunctions
    d) Mechanical malfunctions
    e) Malfunctions in the computer or its signal network

2   Diagnosis of these problems should always begin with a check of the easily repaired items: fluid level and condition (see Chapter 1), shift cable adjustment and shift lever installation. Next, perform a road test to determine if the problem has been corrected or if more diagnosis is necessary. If the problem persists after the preliminary tests and corrections are completed, additional diagnosis should be performed by a dealer service department or other qualified transmission repair shop. Refer to the *Troubleshooting* Section at the front of this manual for information on symptoms of transaxle problems.

PRELIMINARY CHECKS

3   Drive the vehicle to warm the transaxle to normal operating temperature.

4   Check the fluid level as described in Chapter 1:

    a) If the fluid level is unusually low, add enough fluid to bring the level within the designated area of the dipstick, then check for external leaks (see below).
    b) If the fluid level is abnormally high, drain off the excess, then check the drained fluid for contamination by coolant. The presence of engine coolant in the automatic transmission fluid indicates that a failure has occurred in the internal radiator walls that separate the coolant from the transmission fluid (see Chapter 3).
    c) If the fluid is foaming, drain it and refill the transaxle, then check for coolant in the fluid, or a high fluid level.

5   Make sure the engine idle speed is correct. If the idle speed is incorrect, have it adjusted by a dealer service department or other qualified repair shop before proceeding.

6   Inspect the shift cable. Make sure that it's properly adjusted and operates smoothly (see Section 4).

FLUID LEAK DIAGNOSIS

7   Most fluid leaks are easy to locate visually. Repair usually consists of replacing a seal or gasket. If a leak is difficult to find, the following procedure may help.

8   Identify the fluid. Make sure it's transmission fluid and not engine oil or brake fluid (automatic transmission fluid is a deep red color).

9   Try to pinpoint the source of the leak. Drive the vehicle several miles, then park it over a large sheet of cardboard. After a minute or two, you should be able to locate the leak by determining the source of the fluid dripping onto the cardboard.

10   Make a careful visual inspection of the suspected component and the area immediately around it. Pay particular attention to gasket mating surfaces. A mirror is often helpful for finding leaks in areas that are hard to see.

11   If the leak still cannot be found, clean the suspected area thoroughly with a degreaser or solvent, then dry it.

12   Drive the vehicle for several miles at normal operating temperature and varying speeds. After driving the vehicle, visually inspect the suspected component again.

13   Once the leak has been located, the cause must be determined before it can be properly repaired. If a gasket is replaced but the sealing flange is bent, the new gasket will not stop the leak. The bent flange must be straightened.

14   Before attempting to repair a leak, check to make sure that the following conditions are corrected or they may cause another leak.

➡**Note: Some of the following conditions cannot be fixed without highly specialized tools and expertise. Such problems must be referred to a transmission shop or a dealer service department.**

SEAL LEAKS

15   If a transaxle seal is leaking, the fluid level or pressure may be too high, the vent may be plugged, the seal bore may be damaged, the seal itself may be damaged or improperly installed, the surface of the shaft protruding through the seal may be damaged or a loose bearing may be causing excessive shaft movement.

16   Make sure the dipstick tube seal is in good condition and the tube is properly seated. Periodically check the area around the speedometer gear or sensor for leakage. If transmission fluid is evident, check the O-ring for damage.

CASE LEAKS

17   If the case itself appears to be leaking, the casting is porous and will have to be repaired or replaced.

18   Make sure the oil cooler hose fittings are tight and in good condition.

FLUID COMES OUT VENT PIPE OR FILL TUBE

19   If this condition occurs, the transaxle is overfilled, there is coolant in the fluid, the case is porous, the dipstick is incorrect, the vent is plugged or the drain-back holes are plugged.

3 Shift cable - replacement and adjustment

❋❋ WARNING 1:

These models are equipped with a Supplemental Restraint System (SRS), more commonly known as airbags. Always disable the airbag system before working in the vicinity of any airbag system component to avoid the possibility of accidental deployment of the airbag(s), which could cause personal injury (see Chapter 12).

❋❋ WARNING 2:

Do not use a memory saving device to preserve the PCM or radio memory when working on or near airbag system components

1 Raise the vehicle and support it securely on jackstands.

SEDAN AND COUPE MODELS

Replacement

▶ Refer to illustrations 3.4, 3.5, 3.6, 3.7a, 3.7b, 3.8a and 3.8b

2 Set the parking brake, then place the shift lever in the Neutral position.

3 Remove the center console panels. Remove the center console (see Chapter 11).

4 Remove the nut that secures the shift cable end (see illustration).

5 Rotate the socket holder 1/4 turn until the flattened edge of the cable grommet guide aligns with the base and slide the assembly out of the slotted recess (see illustration).

6 Remove the shift cable guide bracket and mounting bolts (see illustration) and separate it from the vehicle body.

7 Remove the shift cable holder (see illustrations).

8 Remove the lock washer and lock bolt and the control lever from the transaxle control shaft and remove the shift cable together with the control lever (see illustrations).

9 Pull the rubber grommet and shift cable out of the vehicle.

10 Installation is the reverse of the removal procedure, noting the following points:

a) Install a new lock washer, then bend the locking tang against the bolt head.

b) Be sure to adjust the cable before reattaching it to the shift lever (see below).

Adjustment

▶ Refer to illustrations 3.12, 3.13 and 3.14

11 Shift to the Neutral position, then remove the lock nut from the cable and disconnect it from the mounting bracket (see Step 4).

12 Push the shift cable until it stops and release your hand. Pull back two clicks until the cable stops (locks-in) in position (see illustration). This is the NEUTRAL position.

13 Insert a 0.24 inch (6.0 mm) pin into the positioning hole on the shift lever bracket base (see illustration). Once the pin is slid through the positioning hole on the shift lever bracket base, align the shift lever and slide the pin into the shift lever positioning hole to lock the assembly into place.

14 Install the shift cable into the mounting bracket, then install the cable end to the shift lever mounting bolt and align the square surface with the alignment casting on the mounting bolt.

➡Note: It will be necessary to rotate the shift cable socket holder 1/4 turn to align it with the slotted recess (see illustration).

15 Install the lock nut on the cable and tighten the cable in this position.

16 Remove the alignment pin from the shift lever bracket base.

3.4 Remove the nut from the shift cable end

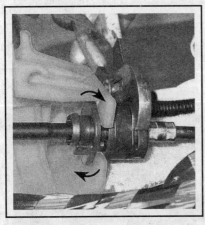

3.5 Rotate the socket holder 1/4 turn until the flattened edge of the cable grommet guide aligns with the base

3.6 Remove the shift cable guide bracket bolts and the rubber grommet

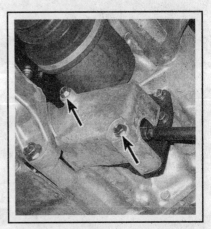

3.7a First, remove the shift cable holder cover bolts . . .

3.7b . . . then remove the holder bolts and separate the assembly from the transaxle

3.8a Bend back the metal tab and remove the lock bolt from the control shaft

3.8b After the lock bolt is removed from the control shaft (C), the shift cable (A) and the control lever (B) will be removed as one unit

17 Start the engine and check the shift lever in all gears. If any gear doesn't work properly, refer to Section 2.

CR-V MODELS

Replacement

18 Set the parking brake, then place the shift lever in the Reverse position.

19 Remove the dashboard lower cover on the driver's side and the instrument panel (see Chapter 11).

20 Slide the lock tab down over the shift cable end holder.

21 Use needlenose pliers to grasp the middle of the lock tab and lift the lock tab off the shift cable end holder. Be sure to replace the lock tab with a new part on reassembly.

22 Remove the shift cable end from the cable holder.

23 Rotate the socket holder 1/4 turn until the flattened edge of the cable grommet guide aligns with the base and slide the assembly out of the slotted recess.

24 Remove the shift cable guide bracket and mounting bolts and separate it from the vehicle body.

25 Remove the shift cable cover, remove the spring clip and separate the shift cable from the control lever.

26 Pull the rubber grommet and shift cable out of the vehicle.

27 Installation is the reverse of the removal procedure, noting the following points:

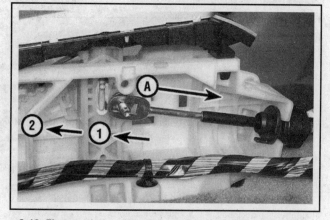

3.12 First, push the shift cable until it stops (A), pull back two clicks until the cable locks-in the Neutral position

a) Install a new lock tab on the shift cable end holder.
b) Be sure to adjust the cable before reattaching it to the shift lever (see below).

Adjustment

28 Shift to the Reverse position.

29 Push the shift cable until it stops and release your hand. Pull

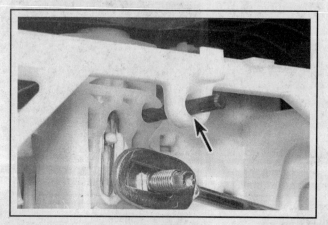

3.13 Insert a 0.24 inch (6.0 mm) pin into the positioning hole on the shift lever bracket base

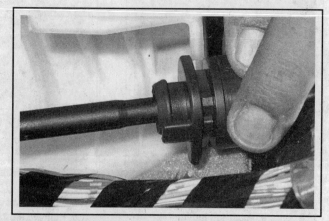

3.14 Rotate the shift cable socket holder 1/4 turn to align it with the slotted recess

back one click until the cable stops (locks-in) in position. This is the REVERSE position.

30 Insert a 0.24 inch (6.0 mm) pin into the positioning hole on the shift lever bracket base. Once the pin is slid through the positioning hole on the shift lever bracket base, align the shift lever and slide the pin into the shift lever positioning hole to lock the assembly into place.

31 Install the shift cable into the slotted recess of the cable base.

➡Note: It will be necessary to rotate the shift cable socket holder 1/4 turn to align it with the slotted recess.

32 Install a new shift cable lock to secure the shift cable end in the shift cable holder.

33 Remove the alignment pin from the shift lever bracket base.

34 Start the engine and check the shift lever in all gears. If any gear doesn't work properly, refer to Section 2.

4 Shift lever - replacement

✳✳ WARNING 1:

These models are equipped with a Supplemental Restraint System (SRS), more commonly known as airbags. Always disable the airbag system before working in the vicinity of any airbag system component to avoid the possibility of accidental deployment of the airbag(s), which could cause personal injury (see Chapter 12).

✳✳ WARNING 2:

Do not use a memory saving device to preserve the PCM or radio memory when working on or near airbag system components

SEDAN AND COUPE MODELS

▶ **Refer to illustrations 4.5, 4.6a and 4.6b**

1 Set the parking brake, then place the shift lever in the Neutral position.

2 Remove the center console panels. Remove the center console (see Chapter 11).

3 Remove the nut that secures the shift cable end (see illustration 3.4).

4 Rotate the socket holder 1/4 turn until the flattened edge of the cable grommet guide aligns with the base and slide the assembly out of the slotted recess (see illustration 3.5).

5 Disconnect the shift lock solenoid electrical connector (see illus-

tration) and park pin electrical connector.

6 Remove the four bolts and remove the shift lever assembly from the floor (see illustrations).

7 Installation is the reverse of the removal procedure, but note the following points:
   a) *Verify the indicator for the neutral position lights with the ignition switch on.*
   b) *Adjust the shift cable, if necessary* (see Section 3).

CR-V MODELS

8 Set the parking brake, then place the shift lever in the Reverse position.

9 Remove the dashboard lower cover on the driver's side and the instrument panel (see Chapter 11).

10 Disconnect the O/D switch electrical connector.

11 Use needlenose pliers to grasp the middle of the lock tab and lift the lock tab off the shift cable end holder. Be sure to replace the lock tab with a new part on reassembly.

12 Remove the shift cable end from the cable holder.

13 Rotate the socket holder 1/4 turn until the flattened edge of the cable grommet guide aligns with the base and slide the assembly out of the slotted recess.

14 Remove the bolts and remove the shift lever assembly.

15 Installation is the reverse of the removal procedure, but note the following points:
   a) *Verify the indicator for the neutral position lights with the ignition switch on.*
   b) *Adjust the shift cable, if necessary* (see Section 3).

4.5 Disconnect the shift lock solenoid electrical connector

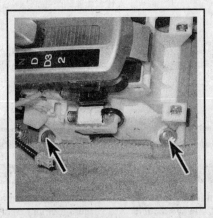

4.6a Remove the shift lever assembly mounting bolts from the left side and . . .

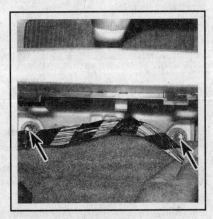

4.6b . . . the right side

5 Interlock system - description and solenoid replacement

❄❄ WARNING 1:

These models are equipped with a Supplemental Restraint System (SRS), more commonly known as airbags. Always disable the airbag system before working in the vicinity of any airbag system component to avoid the possibility of accidental deployment of the airbag(s), which could cause personal injury (see Chapter 12).

❄❄ WARNING 2:

Do not use a memory saving device to preserve the PCM or radio memory when working on or near airbag system components

DESCRIPTION

1 Vehicles equipped with an automatic transaxle have an interlock system to prevent unintentional shifting. The interlock system consists of two subsystems: a shift lock system and a key interlock system.

Key interlock system

2 The key interlock system prevents the ignition key from being removed from the ignition switch unless the shift lever is in the Park position.

Shift lock system

3 The shift lock system prevents the shift lever from moving from the Park position unless the brake pedal is depressed. Nor can the shift lever be shifted when the brake pedal and the accelerator pedal are depressed at the same time. In the event of a system malfunction, you can release the shift lever by inserting a screwdriver into the release slot near the shift lever (sedans/coupes) or into the slot in the upper steering column cover (CR-V).

SOLENOID REPLACEMENT

➡Note: The following procedure pertains only to the shift lock solenoid. For information on how to replace the key interlock solenoid, refer to the "Ignition switch/key lock cylinder replacement" Section in Chapter 12. The key interlock solenoid isn't available separately.

Coupe and sedan models

4 Remove the center console panels. Remove the center console (see Chapter 11).
5 Disconnect the shift lock solenoid electrical connector.

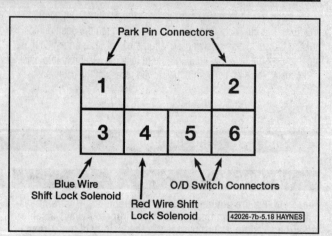

5.18 Terminal designations for the O/D switch/shift lock solenoid/park pin switch connector

6 Pry the plastic lock tabs and slide the shift lock solenoid, clear the tabs and remove the solenoid.
7 Installation is the reverse of removal. Install the plunger and plunger spring into the new shift lock solenoid.
8 Align the shift lock solenoid plunger with the tip of the shift lock stop.
9 Connect the shift lock solenoid electrical connector.

CR-V models

▸ **Refer to illustration 5.18**

10 Remove the lower instrument panel, knee bolster and the steering column covers (see Chapter 11).
11 Remove the shift lever assembly (see Section 4).
12 Remove the harness band clamp from the shift lever bracket base.
13 Disconnect the O/D switch/shift lock solenoid/park pin switch connector.
14 Remove each terminal connector by pushing the lock tab connector inside the housing using a thin-bladed screwdriver. Label each terminal correctly and remove all six terminals.
15 Remove the cover and the shift lock solenoid.
16 Installation is the reverse of removal. Install the plunger and plunger spring into the new shift lock solenoid.
17 Align the shift lock solenoid plunger with the tip of the shift lock stop.
18 Connect all the terminal connectors into the new shift lock harness connector (see illustration).
19 Installation is the reverse of the removal.

6 Automatic transaxle and Continuously Variable transaxle (CVT) - removal and installation

❄❄ WARNING 1:

These models are equipped with a Supplemental Restraint System (SRS), more commonly known as airbags. Always disable the airbag system before working in the vicinity of any airbag system component to avoid the possibility of accidental deployment of the airbag(s), which could cause personal injury (see Chapter 12).

❄❄ WARNING 2:

Do not use a memory saving device to preserve the PCM or radio memory when working on or near airbag system components

➡Note: Read through the entire Section before beginning this

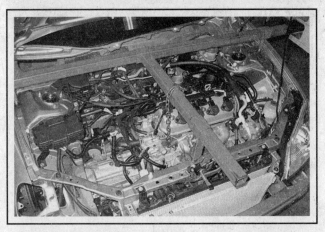

6.6 Install an engine support fixture to support the engine while the transaxle is removed

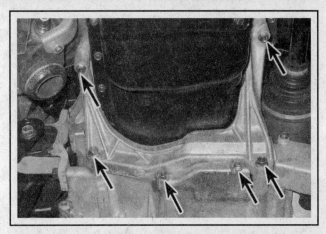

6.13a Remove the transaxle brace mounting bolts and . . .

procedure. The engine and transaxle are removed as a unit from below, then separated outside the vehicle.

REMOVAL

▶ **Refer to illustrations 6.6, 6.13a, 6.13b, 6.14 and 6.15**

1   Open the hood and cover the fenders and cowl using special pads. An old bedspread or blanket will also work. Remove the air intake duct and the air filter housing (see Chapter 4).

2   Remove the battery and the battery tray (see Chapter 5).

3   Remove the starter (see Chapter 5).

4   Clearly label and disconnect all vacuum lines, emissions hoses, electrical connectors and wiring harness clamps/brackets that may interfere with transaxle removal. Masking tape and/or a touch up paint applicator work well for marking items. Take instant photos or sketch the locations of components and brackets.

5   Disconnect the automatic transaxle fluid cooler lines from the transaxle. Be sure to position a pan to catch excess fluid. Plug the lines to prevent leakage.

6   Support the engine with an engine support fixture or an engine hoist (an engine support fixture is recommended, as it doesn't have legs that extend under the vehicle that would get in the way) (see illustration). Connect the sling or chain to the lifting hook at the end of the

engine near the transaxle, not to the lifting eye on the transaxle. If no lifting hook is provided, use the threaded hole(s) in the cylinder head to attach the sling or chain.

7   Loosen the front wheel lug nuts, then raise the vehicle and support it securely on jackstands. Remove the wheels.

8   Remove the engine splash shield (see Chapter 2A, Section 5) and the inner fender splash shields (see Chapter 11, Section 12).

9   Disconnect the shift cable from the transaxle (see Section 3).

10   Drain the transaxle fluid (see Chapter 1). Be sure to use a new sealing washer when you reinstall the drain plug.

11   Remove the front section of the exhaust pipe, between the exhaust manifold and the downstream catalytic converter.

12   Remove the driveaxles and, on 4WD CR-V models, the driveshaft (see Chapter 8).

13   Remove the transaxle brace and the torque converter cover (see illustrations).

14   Mark the relationship of the torque converter (conventional transaxle) or the flywheel (CVT) to the driveplate so that they can be reinstalled in the same relationship to one another (see illustration).

15   Remove the torque converter-to-driveplate bolts (see illustration) one at a time by rotating the crankshaft pulley for access to each bolt.

16   Remove all of the powertrain mounts except the mount at the timing belt (or chain) end of the engine (see Chapter 2A).

17   Remove the subframe (see Chapter 10).

18   Support the transaxle with a jack, preferably one made for this

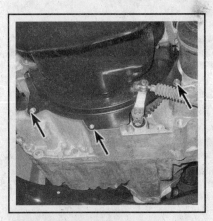

6.13b . . . the torque converter driveplate cover - note several bolts have been removed along with the transaxle brace

6.14 Mark the relationship of the torque converter to the driveplate - sedan model shown

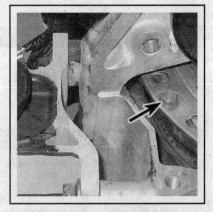

6.15 Location of one of the torque converter bolts

purpose. Secure the transaxle to the jack with straps or chains.

19 Remove the transaxle-to-engine bolts.

20 Move the transaxle back to disengage it from the engine block dowel pins and make sure the torque converter is detached from the driveplate. Secure the torque converter to the transaxle so it will not fall out during removal. Lower the transaxle from the vehicle.

➡Note: It may be necessary to slowly lower the engine a slight amount while the jack supporting the transaxle is being lowered. This will provide more clearance between the transaxle and the body.

INSTALLATION

21 Honda recommends flushing the transaxle cooler and the cooler hoses and lines with solvent whenever the transaxle is removed from the vehicle. Flush the lines and fluid cooler thoroughly and make sure no solvent remains in the lines or cooler after flushing. It's a good idea to repeat the flushing procedure with clean automatic transaxle fluid to ensure that no solvent remains in the lines or cooler.

22 Prior to installation, make sure that the torque converter hub is securely engaged in the transaxle pump. With the transaxle secured to the jack, raise it into position. Be sure to keep it level so the torque converter does not slide out.

23 Line-up the marks you made on the torque converter and driveplate.

24 Make sure the dowel pins are still installed, then move the transaxle forward carefully until the dowel pins are engaged with the holes in the engine block.

25 Install the transaxle-to-engine bolts and tighten them to the torque listed in this Chapter's Specifications.

⁜⁜ CAUTION:

Don't use the bolts to force the transaxle and engine together. If the transaxle doesn't slide easily up against the engine, find out why before you tighten the bolts

26 The remainder of installation is the reverse of the removal procedure, noting the following points:

a) *Tighten the transaxle mounting bolts to the torque listed in this Chapter's Specifications.*

b) *Install all of the driveplate bolts before tightening any of them. Tighten the driveplate bolts to the torque listed in this Chapter's Specifications.*

c) *Tighten the driveaxle/hub nuts to the torque listed in the Chapter 8 Specifications.*

d) *Tighten the wheel lug nuts to the torque listed in the Chapter 1 Specifications.*

e) *Refill the transaxle with the specified type and amount of lubricant (see Chapter 1). Note that the transaxle may require more fluid than in a normal fluid and filter change, since the torque converter may be empty (the converter is not drained during a fluid change).*

f) *Start the engine, set the parking brake and shift the transaxle through all gears three times. Make sure the shift cable is adjusted properly (see Section 3).*

g) *Allow the engine to reach its proper operating temperature with the transaxle in Park or Neutral, then turn it off and check the fluid level again.*

h) *Road test the vehicle and check for fluid leaks.*

7 Automatic transmission overhaul - general information

In the event of a problem occurring, it will be necessary to establish whether the fault is electrical, mechanical or hydraulic in nature, before repair work can be contemplated. Diagnosis requires detailed knowledge of the transmission's operation and construction, as well as access to specialized test equipment, and so is deemed to be beyond the scope of this manual. It is therefore essential that problems with the automatic transmission are referred to a dealer service department or other qualified repair facility for assessment.

Note that a faulty transmission should not be removed before the vehicle has been diagnosed by a knowledgeable technician equipped with the proper tools, as troubleshooting must be performed with the transmission installed in the vehicle.

Specifications

General

Fluid type and capacity	See Chapter 1

Torque specifications

➡Note: One foot-pound (ft-lb) of torque is equivalent to 12 inch-pounds (in-lbs) of torque. Torque values below approximately 15 ft-lbs are expressed in inch-pounds, since most foot-pound torque wrenches are not accurate at these smaller values.

	Ft-lbs (unless otherwise indicated)	Nm
Driveplate-to-torque converter bolts	108 in-lbs	12
Flywheel-to-driveplate bolts (Continuously Variable Transaxle)	108 in-lbs	12
Transaxle mounting bolts	47	64

Section

8

CLUTCH AND DRIVELINE

1   General information

The information in this Chapter deals with the components from the rear of the engine to the front wheels, except for the transaxle, which is dealt with in the previous Chapter. For the purposes of this Chapter, these components are grouped into two categories - clutch and driveaxles. Separate Sections within this Chapter offer general descriptions and checking procedures for components in each of the two groups.

Since nearly all the procedures covered in this Chapter involve working under the vehicle, make sure it's securely supported on sturdy jackstands or on a hoist where the vehicle can be easily raised and lowered.

2   Clutch - description and check

1   All vehicles with a manual transaxle use a single dry-plate, diaphragm-spring type clutch. The clutch disc has a splined hub which allows it to slide along the splines of the transaxle input shaft. The clutch and pressure plate are held in contact by spring pressure exerted by the diaphragm in the pressure plate.

2   The clutch release system is operated by hydraulic pressure. The hydraulic release system consists of the clutch pedal, a master cylinder and fluid reservoir, the hydraulic line, a release (or slave) cylinder which actuates the clutch release lever and the clutch release (or throwout) bearing.

3   When pressure is applied to the clutch pedal to release the clutch, hydraulic pressure is exerted against the outer end of the clutch release lever. As the lever pivots the shaft fingers push against the release bearing. The bearing pushes against the fingers of the diaphragm spring of the pressure plate assembly, which in turn releases the clutch plate.

4   Terminology can be a problem when discussing the clutch components because common names are in some cases different from those used by the manufacturer. For example, the driven plate is also called the clutch plate or disc, the clutch release bearing is sometimes called a throwout bearing, the release cylinder is sometimes called the operating or slave cylinder.

5   Other than to replace components with obvious damage, some preliminary checks should be performed to diagnose clutch problems.

These checks assume that the transaxle is in good working condition.

a) The first check should be of the fluid level in the clutch master cylinder (see Chapter 1). If the fluid level is low, add fluid as necessary and inspect the hydraulic system for leaks. If the master cylinder reservoir has run dry, bleed the system as described in Section 5 and retest the clutch operation.

b) To check "clutch spin-down time," run the engine at normal idle speed with the transaxle in Neutral (clutch pedal up - engaged). Disengage the clutch (pedal down), wait several seconds and shift the transaxle into Reverse. No grinding noise should be heard. A grinding noise would most likely indicate a problem in the pressure plate or the clutch disc.

c) To check for complete clutch release, run the engine (with the parking brake applied to prevent movement) and hold the clutch pedal approximately 1/2-inch from the floor. Shift the transaxle between 1st gear and Reverse several times. If the shift is rough, component failure is indicated. Check the release cylinder pushrod travel. With the clutch pedal depressed completely, the release cylinder pushrod should extend substantially. If it doesn't, check the fluid level in the clutch master cylinder.

d) Visually inspect the pivot bushing at the top of the clutch pedal to make sure there is no binding or excessive play.

e) Crawl under the vehicle and make sure the clutch release lever is solidly mounted on the ball stud.

3   Clutch master cylinder - removal and installation

REMOVAL

1   If you're working on a hatchback model, remove the air filter housing (see Chapter 4).

2   Working inside the engine compartment, clamp a pair of locking pliers onto the clutch fluid feed hose, a couple of inches downstream of the reservoir. The pliers should be just tight enough to prevent fluid flow when the hose is disconnected.

3   Remove the hydraulic line retaining clip holder and retaining clip, then disconnect the hydraulic line at the cylinder. Loosen the fluid feed hose clamp and detach the hose from the cylinder. Have rags handy as some fluid will be lost as the line is removed. Cap or plug the ends of the lines (and/or hose) to prevent fluid leakage and the entry of contaminants.

✳✳ CAUTION:

Don't allow brake fluid to come into contact with the paint as it will damage the finish.

4   Working under the dashboard, remove the cotter pin or spring clip from the master cylinder pushrod clevis. Pull out the clevis pin to disconnect the pushrod from the pedal. Unscrew the two clutch master cylinder retaining nuts and remove the cylinder.

INSTALLATION

5   Installation is the reverse of removal, noting the following points:

a) Use new gasket between the master cylinder and the firewall. Tighten the master cylinder mounting nuts to the torque listed in this Chapter's Specifications.

b) Install a new o-ring seal on the hydraulic line fitting at the master cylinder.

c) Fill the clutch master cylinder reservoir with brake fluid conforming to DOT 3 specifications and bleed the clutch system as outlined in Section 5.

4   Clutch release cylinder - removal and installation

REMOVAL

1   If you're working on a CR-V or hatchback model, remove the battery and battery tray (see Chapter 5), then remove the air filter housing and intake duct (see Chapter 4). Disconnect the hydraulic line mounting bracket.

2   Remove the roll pins securing the hydraulic line to the release cylinder, then disconnect the line. Have a small can and rags handy - some fluid will be spilled as the line is removed. Plug the line to prevent excessive fluid loss.

3   Remove the two release cylinder mounting bolts and remove the release cylinder.

INSTALLATION

4   Lightly lubricate the release cylinder pushrod and the release fork pocket with high temperature grease. Install the release cylinder on the clutch housing. Make sure the pushrod is seated in the release fork pocket, then tighten the mounting bolts to the torque listed in this Chapter's Specifications.

5   Install a new O-ring on the hydraulic line, then connect the hydraulic line to the release cylinder and install the roll pins.

6   The remainder of installation is the reverse of removal, noting the following points:

   a)   *Fill the clutch master cylinder with brake fluid conforming to DOT 3 specifications.*

   b)   *Bleed the system as described in Section 5.*

   c)   *If you're working on a CR-V or hatchback model, before reconnecting the battery, refer to Chapter 5, Section 1.*

5   Clutch hydraulic system - bleeding

1   Bleed the hydraulic system whenever any part of the system has been removed or the fluid level has fallen so low that air has been drawn into the master cylinder. The bleeding procedure is very similar to bleeding a brake system.

2   Fill the master cylinder with new brake fluid conforming to DOT 3 specifications.

✳ CAUTION:

Do not re-use any of the fluid coming from the system during the bleeding operation or use fluid which has been inside an open container for an extended period of time.

3   If you're working on a CR-V or hatchback model, remove the battery and battery tray (see Chapter 5), then remove the air filter housing and intake duct (see Chapter 4).

4   Remove the dust cap which fits over the bleeder valve and push a length of plastic hose over the valve. Place the other end of the hose into a clear container with about two inches of brake fluid. The hose end must be in the fluid at the bottom of the container.

5   Have an assistant depress the clutch pedal and hold it. Open the bleeder valve on the release cylinder, allowing fluid to flow through the hose. Close the bleeder valve when the flow of fluid (and bubbles) ceases. Once closed, have your assistant release the pedal.

6   Continue this process until all air is evacuated from the system, indicated by a solid stream of fluid being ejected from the bleeder valve each time with no air bubbles in the hose or container. Keep a close watch on the fluid level inside the clutch master cylinder reservoir - if the level drops too far, air will get into the system and you'll have to start all over again.

7   Check carefully for proper operation before placing the vehicle into normal service.

8   If you're working on a CR-V or hatchback model, before reconnecting the battery, refer to Chapter 5, Section 1.

6   Clutch components - removal, inspection and installation

✳ WARNING:

Dust produced by clutch wear is hazardous to your health. DO NOT blow it out with compressed air and DO NOT inhale it. DO NOT use gasoline or petroleum-based solvents to remove the dust. Brake system cleaner should be used to flush the dust into a drain pan. After the clutch components are wiped clean with a rag, dispose of the contaminated rags and cleaner in a covered, marked container.

REMOVAL

▸ **Refer to illustration 6.5**

1   Access to the clutch components is normally accomplished by removing the transaxle, leaving the engine in the vehicle. If the engine is being removed for major overhaul, check the clutch for wear and replace worn components as necessary. However, the relatively low cost of the clutch components compared to the time and trouble spent gaining access to them warrants their replacement anytime the engine or transaxle is removed, unless they are new or in near-perfect condition. The following procedures are based on the assumption the engine will stay in place.

2   Remove the transaxle from the vehicle (see Chapter 7, Part A). Support the engine while the transaxle is out. Preferably, an engine support fixture or a hoist should be used to support it from above.

3   The clutch fork and release bearing can remain attached to the transaxle housing for the time being.

4   To support the clutch disc during removal, install a clutch alignment tool through the clutch disc hub.

5   Carefully inspect the flywheel and pressure plate for indexing marks. The marks are usually an X, an O or a white letter. If they cannot

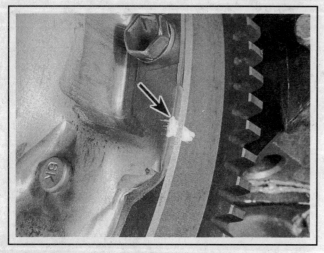

6.5 Mark the relationship of the pressure plate to the flywheel (if you're planning to re-use the old pressure plate)

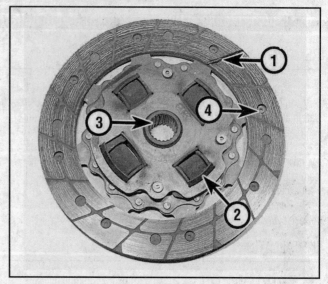

6.9 The clutch disc
1 **Lining** - *this will wear down in use*
2 **Springs or dampers** - *check for cracking and deformation*
3 **Splined hub** - *the splines must not be worn and should slide smoothly on the transaxle input shaft splines*
4 **Rivets** - *these secure the lining and will damage the flywheel or pressure plate if allowed to contact the surfaces*

be found, scribe or paint marks yourself so the pressure plate and the flywheel will be in the same alignment during installation (see illustration).

6 Turning each bolt a little at a time, loosen the pressure plate-to-flywheel bolts. Work in a criss-cross pattern until all spring pressure is relieved. Then hold the pressure plate securely and completely remove the bolts, followed by the pressure plate and clutch disc.

INSPECTION

▶ **Refer to illustrations 6.9, 6.11a and 6.11b**

7 Ordinarily, when a problem occurs in the clutch, it can be attributed to wear of the clutch driven plate assembly (clutch disc). However, all components should be inspected at this time.

8 Inspect the flywheel for cracks, heat checking, grooves and other obvious defects. If the imperfections are slight, a machine shop can machine the surface flat and smooth, which is highly recommended regardless of the surface appearance. Refer to Chapter 2 for the flywheel removal and installation procedure.

9 Inspect the lining on the clutch disc. There should be at least 1/16-inch of lining above the rivet heads. Check for loose rivets, distortion, cracks, broken springs and other obvious damage (see illustration). As mentioned above, ordinarily the clutch disc is routinely replaced, so if in doubt about the condition, replace it with a new one.

10 The release bearing should also be replaced along with the clutch disc (see Section 7).

11 Check the machined surfaces and the diaphragm spring fingers of the pressure plate (see illustrations). If the surface is grooved or otherwise damaged, replace the pressure plate. Also check for obvious damage, distortion, cracking, etc. Light glazing can be removed with emery cloth or sandpaper. If a new pressure plate is required, new and re-manufactured units are available.

INSTALLATION

▶ **Refer to illustration 6.13**

12 Before installation, clean the flywheel and pressure plate machined surfaces with brake cleaner, lacquer thinner or acetone. It's important that no oil or grease is on these surfaces or the lining of the clutch disc. Handle the parts only with clean hands.

13 Position the clutch disc and pressure plate against the flywheel with the clutch held in place with an alignment tool (see illustration). Make sure the disc is installed properly (most replacement clutch discs will be marked "flywheel side" or something similar - if not marked, install the clutch disc with the damper springs toward the transaxle).

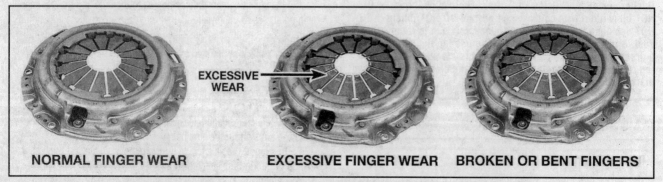

NORMAL FINGER WEAR   EXCESSIVE FINGER WEAR   BROKEN OR BENT FINGERS

6.11a Replace the pressure plate if excessive wear or damage are noted

6.11b Inspect the pressure plate surface for excessive score marks, cracks and signs of overheating

6.13 Center the clutch disc in the pressure plate with a clutch alignment tool

14 Tighten the pressure plate-to-flywheel bolts only finger tight, working around the pressure plate.

15 Center the clutch disc by ensuring the alignment tool extends through the splined hub and into the pilot bearing in the crankshaft. Wiggle the tool up, down or side-to-side as needed to center the disc. Tighten the pressure plate-to-flywheel bolts a little at a time, working in a criss-cross pattern to prevent distorting the cover. After all of the bolts are snug, tighten them to the torque listed in this Chapter's Specifica-

tions. Remove the alignment tool.

16 Using high-temperature grease, lubricate the inner groove of the release bearing (see Section 7). Also place a small amount of grease on the release lever contact areas and the transaxle input shaft bearing retainer.

17 Install the clutch release bearing (see Section 7).

18 Install the transaxle and all components removed previously.

7   Clutch release bearing and lever - removal, inspection and installation

✳✳ WARNING:

Dust produced by clutch wear is hazardous to your health. DO NOT blow it out with compressed air and DO NOT inhale it. DO NOT use gasoline or petroleum-based solvents to remove the dust. Brake system cleaner should be used to flush the dust into a drain pan. After the clutch components are wiped clean with a rag, dispose of the contaminated rags and cleaner in a covered, marked container.

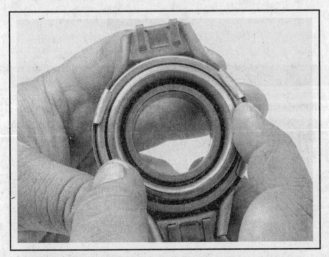

7.4 Hold the bearing by the outer race and rotate the inner race while applying pressure - if the bearing doesn't turn smoothly or if it's noisy, replace the bearing

REMOVAL

1   Remove the transaxle (see Chapter 7A).

2   Pull the clutch release fork off the ballstud and slide the release bearing off the input shaft along with the release fork.

INSPECTION

▶ **Refer to illustration 7.4**

3   Wipe off the bearing with a clean rag and inspect it for damage, wear and cracks. Don't immerse the bearing in solvent - it's sealed for life and immersion in solvent will ruin it.

4   Hold the center of the bearing and rotate the outer portion while applying pressure (see illustration). If the bearing doesn't turn smoothly or if it's noisy or rough, replace it.

➡**Note: Considering the difficulty involved with replacing the release bearing, we recommend replacing the release bearing whenever the clutch components are replaced.**

INSTALLATION

5   Lightly lubricate the friction surfaces of the release bearing, ballstud and the input shaft bearing retainer with high-temperature grease.

6   Install the release lever and bearing onto the input shaft.

7   The remainder of installation is the reverse of removal.

8 Clutch pedal adjustment

PEDAL HEIGHT

▶ **Refer to illustration 8.1**

1   The height of the clutch pedal is the distance the pedal sits off the floor with the carpet pulled back (see illustration). If the pedal height is not within the specified range, it must be adjusted.

2   To adjust the clutch pedal, loosen the locknut on the clutch start switch or adjusting bolt and back the switch out until it no longer touches the pedal, then loosen the locknut on the clutch pushrod. Turn the pushrod to adjust the pedal height, then tighten the locknut.

3   Turn the switch or bolt clockwise until it just contacts the pedal arm, then turn it in an additional 3/4 to 1 turn. Tighten the locknut.

4   Adjust the clutch start switch as described in Section 9.

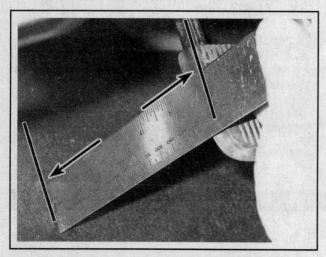

8.1 Pedal height is the distance between the pedal and the floor

PEDAL FREEPLAY

▶ **Refer to illustration 8.5**

5   The freeplay is the pedal slack, or the distance the pedal can be depressed before it begins to have any effect on the clutch system (see illustration). If the pedal freeplay is not within the specified range, it must be adjusted.

6   To adjust the pedal freeplay, loosen the locknut on the clutch pushrod. Then back off the pushrod to adjust the pedal freeplay to the specified range and retighten the locknut.

7   Check and, if necessary, adjust the clutch start switch (see Section 9).

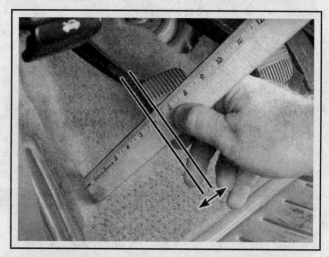

8.5 Pedal freeplay is the distance the pedal travels before resistance is felt

9 Clutch start switch - check and replacement

CHECK

1   Verify that the engine will not start when the clutch pedal is released.

2   Verify that the engine will start when the clutch pedal is depressed all the way.

3   If the engine won't start with the pedal depressed, or starts with the pedal released, unplug the electrical connector to the switch. The clutch start switch is located near the top of the clutch pedal. Check continuity between the connector terminals with the clutch pedal depressed.

4   If there's continuity between the terminals with the pedal depressed, the switch is okay; if there's no continuity between the ter-minals with the pedal depressed, replace the switch. If there's continuity between the terminals when the clutch pedal is released, replace the switch.

REPLACEMENT

5   Unplug the switch electrical connector, if you haven't already done so.

6   Loosen the locknut and unscrew the switch from the clutch pedal bracket.

7   Installation is the reverse of removal. To adjust the switch, loosen the locknut and turn the switch in or out, as necessary, to provide continuity through the switch when the clutch pedal is depressed.

10 Driveaxles - removal and installation

FRONT

Removal

▶ **Refer to illustrations 10.2, 10.3, 10.6a and 10.6b**

1   Loosen the front wheel lug nuts, raise the vehicle and support it securely on jackstands. Remove the wheel.

2   Unstake the driveaxle/hub nut with a punch or chisel (see illustration).

3   Loosen the driveaxle/hub nut with a large socket and breaker bar (see illustration), then remove the driveaxle/hub nut from the axle and discard it.

4   Separate the lower control arm from the steering knuckle (see Chapter 10).

5   Swing the knuckle/hub assembly out (away from the vehicle) until the end of the driveaxle is free of the hub.

➡**Note: If the driveaxle splines stick in the hub, tap on the end of the driveaxle with a plastic hammer.**

Support the outer end of the driveaxle with a piece of wire to avoid unnecessary strain on the inner CV joint.

6   Pry the inner CV joint out of the transaxle - or, on models so equipped, the intermediate shaft, using a large screwdriver or prybar (see illustrations).

7   Support the CV joints and carefully remove the driveaxle from the vehicle.

Installation

▶ **Refer to illustrations 10.8a and 10.8b**

8   Pry the old spring clip from the inner end of the driveaxle - or, on models so equipped, the outer end of the intermediate shaft and install a new one (see illustrations).

9   Installation is the reverse of removal, but with the following addi-

10.2 Use a punch or chisel and unstake the driveaxle/hub nut

10.3 To prevent the hub from turning while you're loosening the driveaxle/hub nut, wedge a prybar between two of the wheel studs

10.6a Use a large screwdriver or a prybar to pop the inner end of the driveaxle from the transaxle, or . . .

10.6b . . . if you're removing a driveaxle from a vehicle equipped with an intermediate shaft, insert the prybar between the intermediate shaft bearing and the driveaxle to pop it loose

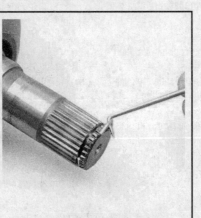

10.8a Pry the old spring clip from the inner end of the driveaxle with a small screwdriver or awl

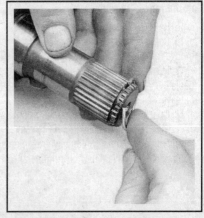

10.8b To install the new spring clip, start one end in the groove and work the clip over the shaft end, into the groove

tional points:

a) *Remove the old set-ring from the driveaxle or intermediate shaft (depending on which model you're working on) and install a new one.*

b) *Apply a film of multi-purpose grease around the splines of the joints.*

c) *When installing the driveaxle, hold the driveaxle straight out, then push it in sharply to seat the driveaxle set-ring.*

d) *Clean all foreign matter from the driveaxle outer CV joint threads and coat the splines with multi-purpose grease. Guide the driveaxle into the hub splines and install the new driveaxle/hub nut. Tighten the nut securely but not to the specified torque at this time.*

e) *Reconnect the control arm, then tighten the suspension fasteners to the torque listed in the Chapter 10 Specifications.*

f) *Install the wheel and lug nuts, then lower the vehicle.*

g) *Tighten the driveaxle/hub nut to the torque listed in this Chapter's Specifications.*

h) *Tighten the wheel lug nuts to the torque listed in the Chapter 1 Specifications.*

i) *Add transaxle lubricant if it was drained or if any fluid spilled out (see Chapter 1).*

INTERMEDIATE SHAFT

Removal

10 Loosen the right front wheel lug nuts, raise the vehicle and support it securely on jackstands. Remove the wheel.

11 Unstake the driveaxle/hub nut with a punch or chisel (see illustration 10.2).

12 Loosen the driveaxle/hub nut with a large socket and breaker bar (see illustration 10.3), then remove the driveaxle/hub nut from the axle and discard it.

13 Separate the lower control arm from the steering knuckle (see Chapter 10).

14 Swing the knuckle/hub assembly out (away from the vehicle) until the end of the driveaxle is free of the hub.

→**Note: If the driveaxle splines stick in the hub, tap on the end of the driveaxle with a plastic hammer. Support the outer end of the driveaxle with a piece of wire to avoid unnecessary strain on the inner CV joint.**

15 Remove the driveaxle (see Step 6).

16 Remove the intermediate shaft heat shield mounting bolts, then remove the heat shield.

17 Remove the bearing support mounting bolts and slide the intermediate shaft out of the transaxle. Be careful not to damage the transaxle seal when pulling the shaft out.

18 Check the support bearing for smooth operation by turning the shaft while holding the bearing. If you feel any roughness, take the intermediate shaft to an automotive machine shop or other qualified repair facility to have a new bearing installed.

Installation

19 Lubricate the lips of the transaxle seal with multi-purpose grease. Carefully guide the intermediate shaft into the transaxle side gear then install the mounting nuts for the bearing support. Tighten the nuts to the torque listed in this Chapter's Specifications.

20 The remainder of installation is the reverse of removal.

REAR (4WD CR-V MODELS)

Removal

21 Remove the wheel cover or hub cap. Unstake the driveaxle/hub nut with a punch or chisel (see illustration 10.2), then break the hub nut loose with a socket and large breaker bar.

22 Block the front wheels to prevent the vehicle from rolling. Loosen the wheel lug nuts, raise the rear of the vehicle and support it securely on jackstands. Remove the wheel.

23 Remove the driveaxle/hub nut from the axle and discard it.

24 Detach the trailing arm from the knuckle (see Chapter 10), then pry the knuckle outward and remove the outer end of the driveaxle from the hub.

❊❊ CAUTION:

Don't let the driveaxle hang by the inner CV joint.

25 Place a drain pan under the rear differential. Pry the inner end of the driveaxle out of the differential and remove it from the vehicle.

Installation

26 Pry the old spring clip from the inner end of the driveaxle and install a new one (see illustrations 10.8a and 10.8b).

27 Apply a light film of grease to the area on the inner CV joint stub shaft where the seal rides, then insert the splined end of the inner CV joint into the differential. Make sure the spring clip locks in its groove.

28 Apply a light film of grease to the outer CV joint splines, pry the trailing arm outward and insert the outer end of the driveaxle into the hub.

29 Connect the trailing arm to the knuckle and install the bolts. Using a floor jack, raise the trailing arm to simulate normal ride height, then tighten the bolt to the torque listed in the Chapter 10 Specifications.

30 Install a new driveaxle/hub nut. Tighten the hub nut securely, but don't try to tighten it to the actual torque specification until you've lowered the vehicle to the ground.

31 Install the wheel and lug nuts, then lower the vehicle. Tighten the lug nuts to the torque listed in the Chapter 1 Specifications.

32 Tighten the driveaxle/hub nut to the torque listed in this Chapter's Specifications, then, using a hammer and a punch, stake the collar of the nut into the slot in the driveaxle. Install the wheel cover or hub cap.

33 Check the differential lubricant, adding as necessary to bring it to the appropriate level (see Chapter 1).

11 Driveaxle boot - replacement

➡ **Note 1:** If the CV joints are worn, indicating the need for an overhaul (usually due to torn boots), explore all options before beginning the job. Complete rebuilt driveaxles are available on an exchange basis, which eliminates much time and work. If you decide to rebuild a CV joint, check on the cost and availability of parts before disassembling the driveaxle.

➡ **Note 2:** Some auto parts stores carry "split" type replacement boots, which can be installed without removing the driveaxle from the vehicle. This is a convenient alternative; however, the driveaxle should be removed and the CV joint disassembled and cleaned to ensure the joint is free from contaminants such as moisture and dirt which will accelerate CV joint wear.

1   Remove the driveaxle from the vehicle (see Section 10).
2   Mount the driveaxle in a vise. The jaws of the vise should be lined with wood or rags to prevent damage to the driveaxle.

INNER CV JOINT AND BOOT (FRONT DRIVEAXLE) OR INNER AND OUTER CV JOINT AND BOOT (REAR DRIVEAXLE)

Disassembly

▶ **Refer to illustrations 11.3a, 11.3b and 11.6**

3   If you have any doubts about the condition of the outer boot this would be a good time to replace it as well. Cut off both boot clamps and slide the boot towards the center of the driveaxle (see illustrations).
4   Scribe or paint alignment marks on the outer race and the tri-pot bearing assembly so they can be returned to their original position, then slide the outer race off the tri-pot bearing assembly.
5   Remove the snap-ring from the end of the axleshaft.
6   Secure the bearing rollers with tape, then remove the tri-pot bearing assembly from the axleshaft with a brass drift and a hammer (see illustration). Remove the tape, but don't let the rollers fall off and get mixed up.
7   Remove the stop-ring (if equipped), slide the old boot off the driveaxle and discard it.

Inspection

8   Clean the old grease from the outer race and the tri-pot bearing assembly. Carefully disassemble each section of the tri-pot assembly, one at a time so as not to mix up the parts, and clean the needle bearings with solvent.
9   Inspect the rollers, tri-pot, bearings and outer race for scoring, pitting or other signs of abnormal wear, which will warrant the replacement of the inner CV joint.

Reassembly

▶ **Refer to illustrations 11.10a, 11.10b, 11.12, 11.13, 11.14, 11.16, 11.17a, 11.17b 11.17c, 11.17d and 11.17e**

10   Wrap the splines of the axleshaft with tape to avoid damaging the new boot, then slide the boot onto the axleshaft (see illustration). Remove the tape and slide the inner stop-ring (if equipped) into place (see illustration).
11   Slide the tri-pot assembly onto the axleshaft.
12   Install the outer snap-ring (see illustration).

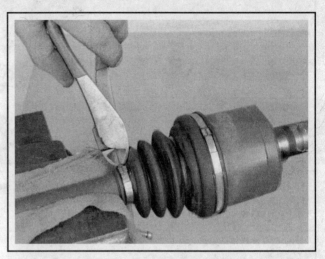

11.3a Cut off the boot clamps and discard them - don't try to re-use old clamps

11.3b Slide the boot down the driveaxle, out of the way

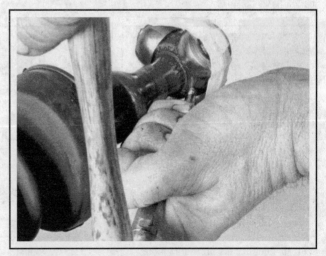

11.6 Secure the bearing rollers with tape and drive the tripot off the shaft with a hammer and brass drift, then remove the stop-ring

11.10a Wrap the splined area of the axleshaft with tape to prevent damage to the boot when installing it

11.10b Install the stop-ring on the axleshaft, making sure it seats in its groove

11.12 Install the tri-pot assembly on the axleshaft, then install the snap-ring

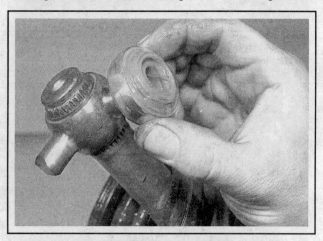

11.13 Use plenty of CV joint grease to hold the needle bearings in place when you install the roller assemblies on the tri-pot, and make sure you put each roller in its original position

13 Apply a coat of CV joint grease to the inner bearing surfaces to hold the needle bearings in place when reassembling the tri-pot assembly (see illustration). Make sure each roller is installed on the same post as before.

11.14 Pack the outer race with grease and slide it over the tri-pot assembly - make sure the match marks on the outer race and tri-pot line up

➡️**Note: If the rollers are equipped with a flat, rectangular shaped surface, make sure the flat sides are positioned closest to the driveaxle.**

14 Pack the outer race with half of the grease furnished with the new boot and place the remainder in the boot. Install the outer race (see

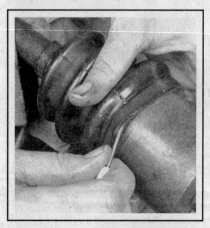

11.16 Equalize the pressure inside the boot by inserting a small, dull screwdriver between the boot and the outer race

11.17a To install fold-over type clamps, bend the tang down . . .

11.17b . . . and flatten the tabs to hold it in place

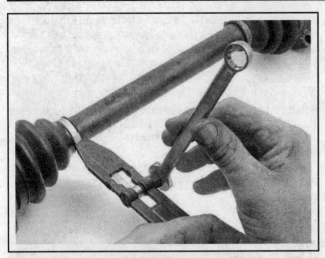

11.17c You'll need a special tightening tool to install "band" type boot clamps: Install the band with its end pointing in the direction of axle rotation and tighten it securely . . .

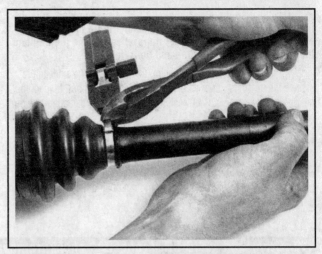

11.17d . . . bend back the end of the clamp, cut off the excess, then place a dimple in the center of the folded-over portion with a hammer and center punch

illustration). Make sure the marks you made on the tri-pot assembly and the outer race are aligned.

15 Seat the boot in the grooves in the outer race and the axleshaft, then position the driveaxle (front) or CV joint (rear) midway through its travel.

16 With the driveaxle (front) or CV joint (rear) set to the proper length, equalize the pressure in the boot by inserting a blunt screwdriver between the boot and the outer race (see illustration). Don't damage the boot with the tool.

17 Install and tighten the new boot clamps (see illustrations).

18 Install the driveaxle assembly (see Section 10).

OUTER CV JOINT AND BOOT (FRONT DRIVEAXLE)

Disassembly

19 Following Steps 3 through 7, remove the inner CV joint from the driveaxle and disassemble it.

20 If the driveaxle is equipped with a dynamic damper, scribe or paint a location mark on the axleshaft along the outer edge of the damper (the side facing the outer CV joint), cut the retaining clamp and slide the damper off.

➡Note: If you're planning to replace the axleshaft and outer CV joint assembly, measure the distance between the inner CV joint boot and the dynamic damper so the damper can be placed in the proper position on the new driveaxle.

21 Cut the boot clamps from the outer CV joint. Slide the boot off the shaft.

➡Note: The outer CV joint can't be disassembled or removed from the shaft.

Inspection

◗ Refer to illustration 11.23

22 Thoroughly wash the inner and outer CV joints in clean solvent and blow them dry with compressed air, if available.

✳✳ WARNING:

Wear eye protection when using compressed air.

11.17e If you're installing crimp-type boot clamps, you'll need a pair of special crimping pliers (available at most auto parts stores)

11.23 After the old grease has been rinsed away and the solvent has been blown out with compressed air, rotate the outer joint assembly through its full range of motion and inspect the bearing surfaces for wear and damage - if any of the ball bearings, the race or the cage look damaged, replace the driveaxle and outer joint assembly

➡Note: Because the outer joint can't be disassembled, it is difficult to wash away all the old grease and to rid the bearing of solvent once it's clean. But it is imperative that the job be done thoroughly, so take your time and do it right.

23 Bend the outer CV joint housing at an angle to the axleshaft to expose the bearings, inner race and cage (see illustration). Inspect the bearing surfaces for signs of wear. If the bearings are damaged or worn, replace the driveaxle.

Reassembly

24 Slide the new outer boot onto the axleshaft. It's a good idea to wrap tape around the splines of the shaft to prevent damage to the boot (see illustration 11.10a). When the boot is in position, add the specified amount of grease (included in the boot replacement kit) to the outer joint and the boot (pack the joint with as much grease as it will hold and put the rest into the boot). Slide the boot on the rest of the way and install the new clamps (see illustrations 11.17a through 11.17e).

25 Slide the dynamic damper, if equipped, onto the shaft. Make sure its outer edge is aligned with the previously applied mark.

➡Note: If you're using a new axleshaft and outer CV joint assembly, install the damper on the shaft to the distance from the inner CV joint boot measured in Step 20. Install a new retaining clamp.

26 Clean and reassemble the inner CV joint by following Steps 8 through 17, then install the driveaxle as outlined in Section 10.

---

12 Driveshaft (4WD CR-V models) - check, removal and installation

CHECK

▸ **Refer to illustration 12.6**

1 Raise the rear of the vehicle and support it securely on jackstands. Block the front wheels to keep the vehicle from rolling off the stands. Release the parking brake and place the transaxle in Neutral.

2 Crawl under the vehicle and visually inspect the driveshaft. Look for any dents or cracks in the tubing. If any are found, the driveshaft must be replaced.

3 Check for oil leakage at the front and rear of the driveshaft. Leakage where the driveshaft connects to the transfer case indicates a defective transfer case seal. Leakage where the driveshaft connects to the differential indicates a defective pinion seal.

4 While under the vehicle, have an assistant rotate a rear wheel so the driveshaft will rotate. As it does, make sure the universal joints are operating properly without binding, noise or looseness. Listen for any noise from the center bearing, indicating it's worn or damaged. Also check the rubber portion of the center bearing for cracking or separation, which will necessitate replacement of the driveshaft assembly.

5 The universal joints can also be checked with the driveshaft motionless, by gripping your hands on either side of the joint and attempting to twist the joint. Any movement at all in the joint is a sign of considerable wear. Lifting up on the shaft will also indicate movement in the universal joints. If the joints are worn, the driveshaft must be replaced as an assembly.

6 Mount a dial indicator with its plunger touching the center of either the front or rear driveshaft section (see illustration). Slowly turn the driveshaft and measure the runout, comparing your findings with the runout limit listed in this Chapter's Specifications. Repeat the check on the other driveshaft section. If runout exceeds the maximum allowable limit on either shaft section, replace the driveshaft as an assembly.

7 Finally, check the driveshaft mounting bolts at the ends to make sure they're tight.

REMOVAL AND INSTALLATION

▸ **Refer to illustrations 12.9, 12.10, 12.11 and 12.12**

8 Raise the rear of the vehicle and support it securely on jackstands. Place the transaxle in Neutral with the parking brake off. Block the front wheels to prevent the vehicle from rolling.

9 Make reference marks on the driveshaft flanges, the differential pinion flange and the transfer case pinion flange in line with each other (see illustration). This is to make sure the driveshaft is reinstalled in the same position to preserve the balance.

10 Remove the rear universal joint bolts. Turn the driveshaft (or wheels) as necessary to bring the bolts into the most accessible position. Insert a screwdriver into the joint while loosening the bolts to pre-

12.6 Checking driveshaft runout with a dial indicator

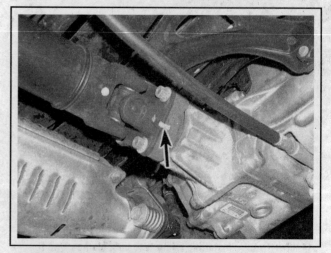

12.9 Mark the relationship of the driveshaft to the differential pinion flange and the transfer case flange

12.10 Immobilize the driveshaft by placing a screwdriver into the universal joint while loosening the bolts

12.11 Remove the driveshaft safety loops

12.12 The driveshaft center support bearing is retained by two bolts

vent the shaft from turning (see illustration).

11 Unbolt the driveshaft safety loops from the floorpan (see illustration).

12 Unbolt the center support bearing from the floorpan (see illustration).

13 Unbolt the front of the driveshaft from the transfer case flange and remove the driveshaft assembly.

14 Installation is the reverse of the removal procedure. Be sure to align the marks on the flanges and tighten all fasteners to the torque values listed in this Chapter's Specifications.

13 Differential oil seals (4WD CR-V models) - replacement

PINION OIL SEAL

▶ **Refer to illustrations 13.3, 13.4, 13.7, 13.8 and 13.9**

1 Raise the rear of the vehicle and support it securely on jackstands. Place the transaxle in Neutral with the parking brake off. Block the front wheels to prevent the vehicle from rolling.

2 Mark the relationship of the driveshaft to the pinion flange, then unbolt the driveshaft from the flange (see Section 12). Suspend the driveshaft with a piece of wire (don't let it hang by the center support bearing).

3 Using a hammer and a punch, unstake the pinion flange nut

(see illustration).

4 A flange holding tool will be required to keep the companion flange from moving while the self-locking pinion nut is loosened. A chain wrench will also work (see illustration).

5 Remove the pinion nut, spring washer, back-up ring and O-ring.

6 Withdraw the flange. It may be necessary to use a two-jaw puller engaged behind the flange to draw it off. Do not attempt to pry or hammer behind the flange or hammer on the end of the pinion shaft.

7 Pry out the old seal and discard it (see illustration).

8 Lubricate the lips of the new seal and fill the space between the seal lips with wheel bearing grease, then tap it evenly into position with a seal installation tool or a large socket (see illustration). Make sure it

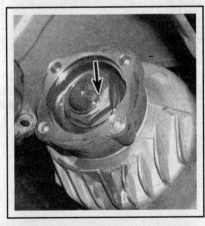

13.3 Insert a punch into the slot and unstake the pinion flange nut before unscrewing it

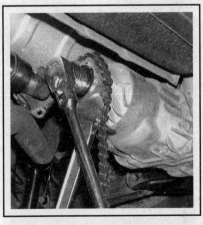

13.4 A chain wrench can be used to prevent the pinion flange from turning when loosening the nut

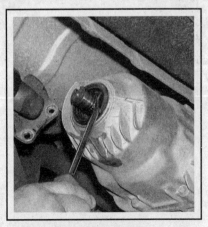

13.7 Carefully pry out the old seal . . .

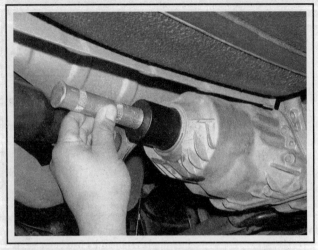

13.8 . . . and drive the new one in with a seal installation tool or a socket with an outside diameter slightly smaller than that of the seal

enters the housing squarely and is tapped in to its full depth.

9   Install the pinion flange, a new O-ring (lubricated with clean differential lubricant), the back-up ring, spring washer (with the concave side facing the flange), and a new nut (see illustration). If necessary, tighten the pinion nut to draw the flange into place. Do not try to hammer the flange into position.

10 Tighten the nut to the torque listed in this Chapter's Specifications, then stake the collar of the nut into the slot in the pinion shaft.

11 Reconnect the driveshaft to the pinion flange (see Section 12).

12 Check the differential lubricant level and add some, if necessary, to bring it to the appropriate level (see Chapter 1).

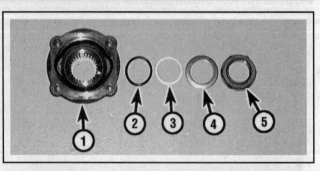

13.9 Differential pinion flange details (4WD CR-V models)

1	*Pinion flange*	*4*	*Spring washer*
2	*O-ring*	*5*	*Nut*
3	*Back-up ring*		

DRIVEAXLE OIL SEALS

▶ **Refer to illustrations 13.15 and 13.16**

13 Raise the rear of the vehicle and support it securely on jackstands. Place the transaxle in Neutral with the parking brake off. Block the front wheels to prevent the vehicle from rolling.

14 Remove the driveaxle(s) (see Section 10).

15 Pry the seal from the differential housing (see illustration).

16 Using a seal installer or a large deep socket as a drift, install the new oil seal. Drive it into the bore squarely and make sure it's completely seated (see illustration).

17 Lubricate the lip of the new seal with multi-purpose grease, then install the driveaxle. Be careful not to damage the lip of the new seal.

18 Check the differential lubricant level and add some, if necessary, to bring it to the appropriate level (see Chapter 1).

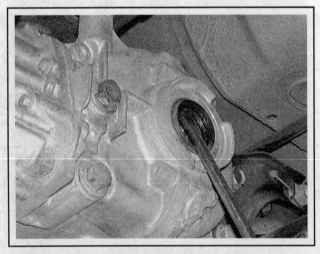

13.15 Carefully pry out the driveaxle oil seal with a seal removal tool or a large screwdriver; make sure you don't scratch the seal bore

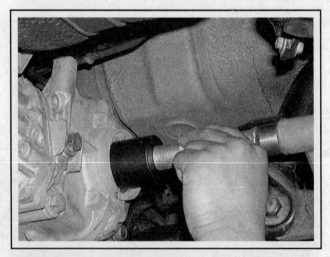

13.16 Use a seal installer or a large socket to install the new seal - whatever type of tool you use, make sure it doesn't contact the raised seal lip

14 Differential (4WD CR-V models) - removal and installation

▶ **Refer to illustrations 14.8 and 14.9**

1   Raise the rear of the vehicle and support it securely on jack-stands. Place the transaxle in Neutral with the parking brake off. Block the front wheels to prevent the vehicle from rolling.

2   Drain the differential lubricant (see Chapter 1).

3   Remove the driveaxles (see Section 10).

4   Mark the relationship of the driveshaft to the pinion flange, then unbolt the driveshaft from the flange (see Section 12). Suspend the driveshaft with a piece of wire (don't let it hang by the center support bearing).

5   Remove the EVAP canister and mounting bracket (see Chapter 6).

6   Unbolt the damper weight from the differential.

7   Detach the breather tube from the fitting on the floorpan.

8   Support the differential with a floor jack. Remove the nuts and bolts from the mounting bracket at the rear of the differential (see illustration).

9   Remove the differential-to-floorpan bolts (see illustration). Slowly lower the jack and remove the differential out from under the vehicle.

10 Installation is the reverse of the removal procedure. Tighten all fasteners to the torque values listed in this Chapter's Specifications. Fill the differential with the proper lubricant (see Chapter 1).

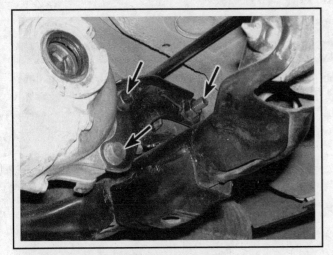

14.8 Differential mounting bracket bolts

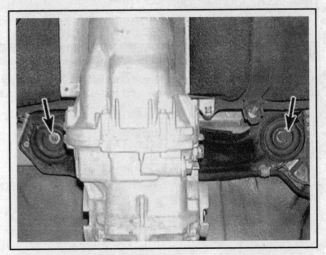

14.9 Differential-to-floorpan bolts

15 Transfer case (4WD CR-V models) - removal and installation

1   Raise the front of the vehicle and support it securely on jack-stands.

2   Mark the relationship of the driveshaft to the transfer case flange, then unbolt the driveshaft from the flange (see Section 12). Suspend the driveshaft with a piece of wire (don't let it hang by the center support bearing).

3   Drain the transaxle lubricant (see Chapter 1).

4   Remove the bolts securing the transfer case to the transaxle, then

carefully remove the transfer case from the transaxle.

5   Installation is the reverse of removal, noting the following points:

a) *Install a new O-ring to the case.*

b) *Tighten the mounting bolts to the torque listed in this Chapter's Specifications.*

c) *Refill the transaxle with the proper type and amount of lubricant (see Chapter 1).*

Specifications

Clutch fluid type	See Chapter 1
Driveshaft runout limit (4WD CR-V models)	0.06 inch (1.5 mm)
Clutch pedal	
Pedal height	
Coupe and sedan models	7.8 inch (198 mm)
Hatchback models	7.6 inch (193 mm)
CR-V models	7.87 inch (200 mm)
Pedal freeplay	
Hatchback models	0.39 to 0.63 inch (10 to 16 mm)
CR-V models	0.24 to 0.67 inch (6 to 17 mm)

Torque specifications

➡**Note: One foot-pound (ft-lb) of torque is equivalent to 12 inch-pounds (in-lbs) of torque. Torque values below approximately 15 ft-lbs are expressed in inch-pounds, since most foot-pound torque wrenches are not accurate at these smaller values.**

	Ft-lbs (unless otherwise indicated)	Nm
Clutch master cylinder mounting nuts	108 in-lbs	13
Clutch pressure plate-to-flywheel bolts	19	25
Clutch release cylinder mounting fasteners	16	22
Differential mounting bracket-to-floorpan mounting bolts (4WD CR-V models)	36	49
Differential pinion flange nut (4WD CR-V models)	87	118
Driveshaft center support bearing mounting bolts (4WD CR-V models)	29	39
Driveshaft-to-differential pinion flange mounting bolts (4WD CR-V models)	24	32
Driveshaft-to-transfer case pinion flange mounting bolts (4WD CR-V models)	24	24
Driveaxle hub/nut		
Coupe, sedan and hatchback models	134	181
CR-V models		
Front	181	245
Rear (4WD CR-V models)	134	181
Intermediate shaft bearing support mounting bolts	29	39
Transfer case mounting bolts	33	44
Wheel lug nuts	See Chapter 1	

Section

9

BRAKES

1 General information

The vehicles covered by this manual are equipped with hydraulically operated front and rear brake systems. The front brakes are disc type and the rear brakes are disc or drum type. Both the front and rear brakes are self adjusting. The disc brakes automatically compensate for pad wear, while the drum brakes incorporate an adjustment mechanism which is activated as the parking brake is applied.

HYDRAULIC SYSTEM

The hydraulic system consists of two separate circuits. The master cylinder has separate reservoir chambers for the two circuits, and, in the event of a leak or failure in one hydraulic circuit, the other circuit will remain operative. A dual proportioning valve on the firewall provides brake balance between the front and rear brakes.

POWER BRAKE BOOSTER

The power brake booster, utilizing engine manifold vacuum and atmospheric pressure to provide assistance to the hydraulically operated brakes, is mounted on the firewall in the engine compartment.

PARKING BRAKE

The parking brake operates the rear brakes only, through cable actuation. It's activated by a lever mounted in the center console.

SERVICE

After completing any operation involving disassembly of any part of the brake system, always test drive the vehicle to check for proper braking performance before resuming normal driving. When testing the brakes, perform the tests on a clean, dry, flat surface. Conditions other than these can lead to inaccurate test results.

Test the brakes at various speeds with both light and heavy pedal pressure. The vehicle should stop evenly without pulling to one side or the other. Avoid locking the brakes, because this slides the tires and diminishes braking efficiency and control of the vehicle.

Tires, vehicle load and wheel alignment are factors which also affect braking performance.

PRECAUTIONS

There are some general cautions and warnings involving the brake system on this vehicle:

a) *Use only brake fluid conforming to DOT 3 specifications.*
b) *The brake pads and linings contain fibers which are hazardous to your health if inhaled. Whenever you work on brake system components, clean all parts with brake system cleaner. Do not allow the fine dust to become airborne. Also, wear an approved filtering mask.*
c) *Safety should be paramount whenever any servicing of the brake components is performed. Do not use parts or fasteners which are not in perfect condition, and be sure that all clearances and torque specifications are adhered to. If you are at all unsure about a certain procedure, seek professional advice. Upon completion of any brake system work, test the brakes carefully in a controlled area before putting the vehicle into normal service. If a problem is suspected in the brake system, don't drive the vehicle until it's fixed.*

2 Anti-lock Brake System (ABS) and Vehicle Stability Assist (VSA) system - general information

GENERAL INFORMATION

1 Some models are equipped with an Anti-lock Brake System (ABS). Beginning in 2005, CR-V models are equipped with a combined ABS/VSA system. These systems are designed to maintain vehicle steerability, directional stability and optimum deceleration under severe braking and handling conditions. It does so by monitoring the rotational speed of each wheel and controlling the brake line pressure to each wheel during braking. This prevents the wheels from locking up.

2 The ABS or VSA systems have three main components - the wheel speed sensors, the electronic control (ECU) and the hydraulic unit. On 2006 and later CR-V models, the hydraulic unit is called the Modulator Control Unit (MCU). Four wheel speed sensors - one at each wheel - send a variable voltage signal to the control unit, which monitors these signals, compares them to its program and determines whether a wheel is about to lock up. When a wheel is about to lock up, the control unit signals the hydraulic unit to reduce hydraulic pressure (or not increase it further) at that wheel's brake caliper. Pressure modulation is handled by electrically-operated solenoid valves.

3 If a problem develops within the system, an "ABS" or "VSA" warning light will glow on the dashboard. Sometimes, a visual inspection of the ABS or VSA can help you locate the problem. Carefully inspect the ABS or VSA wiring harness. Pay particularly close attention to the harness and connections near each wheel. Look for signs of chafing and other damage caused by incorrectly routed wires. If a wheel sensor harness is damaged, the sensor must be replaced.

✳✳ WARNING:

Do NOT try to repair an ABS/VSA wiring harness. The ABS/VSA system is sensitive to even the smallest changes in resistance. Repairing the harness could alter resistance values and cause the system to malfunction. If the ABS/VSA wiring harness is damaged in any way, it must be replaced.

✳✳ CAUTION:

Make sure the ignition is turned off before unplugging or reattaching any electrical connections.

DIAGNOSIS AND REPAIR

4 If the dashboard warning light comes on and stays on while the vehicle is in operation, the ABS or VSA system requires attention. Although special electronic ABS or VSA diagnostic testing tools are necessary to properly diagnose the system, you can perform a few pre-

liminary checks before taking the vehicle to a dealer service department.

- a) *Check the brake fluid level in the reservoir.*
- b) *Verify that the computer electrical connectors are securely connected.*
- c) *Check the electrical connectors at the hydraulic control unit.*
- d) *Check the fuses.*
- e) *Follow the wiring harness to each wheel and verify that all connections are secure and that the wiring is undamaged.*

5   If the above preliminary checks do not rectify the problem, the vehicle should be diagnosed by a dealer service department or other qualified repair shop. Due to the complex nature of this system, all actual repair work must be done by a qualified automotive technician.

WHEEL SPEED SENSOR - REMOVAL AND INSTALLATION

6   Loosen the wheel lug nuts, raise the vehicle and support it securely on jackstands. Remove the wheel.

7   Make sure the ignition key is turned to the Off position.

8   Trace the wiring back from the sensor, detaching all brackets and clips while noting its correct routing, then disconnect the electrical connector.

9   Remove the mounting bolt and carefully pull the sensor out from the knuckle or brake backing plate.

10   Installation is the reverse of the removal procedure. Tighten the mounting bolt securely.

11   Install the wheel and lug nuts, tightening them securely. Lower the vehicle and tighten the lug nuts to the torque listed in the Chapter 1 Specifications.

3   Disc brake pads - replacement

✳✳ WARNING:

Disc brake pads must be replaced on both front and rear wheels at the same time - never replace the pads on only one side. Also, the dust created by the brake system is harmful to your health. Never blow it out with compressed air and don't inhale any of it. An approved filtering mask should be worn when working on the brakes. Do not, under any circumstances, use petroleum-based solvents to clean brake parts. Use brake system cleaner only!

➥Note: This procedure applies to front and rear disc brakes.

1   Remove the cap from the brake fluid reservoir.

2   Loosen the wheel lug nuts, raise the front, or rear, of the vehicle and support it securely on jackstands.

3   Remove the front, or rear, wheels. Work on one brake assembly at a time, using the assembled brake for reference if necessary.

4   Inspect the brake disc carefully as outlined in Section 5. If machining is necessary, follow the information in that Section to remove the disc, at which time the calipers and pads can be removed as well.

FRONT PADS

▶ Refer to illustrations 3.5 and 3.6a through 3.6n

5   Push the piston back into the bore to provide room for the new brake pads. A C-clamp can be used to accomplish this (see illustration). As the piston is depressed to the bottom of the caliper bore, the fluid in the master cylinder will rise. Make sure it doesn't overflow. If necessary, siphon off some of the fluid.

6   Follow the accompanying illustrations, beginning with 3.6a, for the actual pad replacement procedure. Be sure to stay in order and read the caption under each illustration. Once you have installed the new pads, proceed to Step 20.

3.5 Using a large C-clamp, push the piston back into the caliper - note that one end of the clamp is on the back side of the caliper and the other end (screw end) is pressing on the outer brake pad (front caliper shown - CR-V rear calipers similar)

3.6a Before removing anything, spray the assembly with brake system cleaner to remove the dust produced by brake pad wear - DO NOT blow the dust off with compressed air!

3.6b Remove the lower caliper mounting bolt . . .

3.6c . . . then swing the caliper up and secure it to the strut with a piece of wire

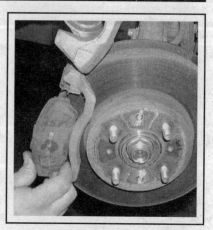

3.6d Remove the outer brake pad and shim

3.6e Remove the inner brake pad (some models don't have a shim on the inner pad)

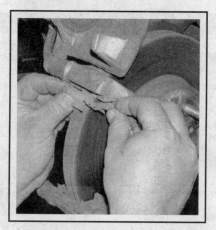

3.6f Remove and inspect the upper and lower brake pad retainer clips

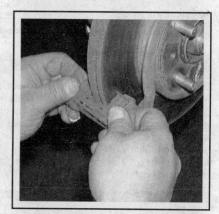

3.6g The pad retainer clips should fit snugly into their respective grooves in the caliper mounting bracket; if they don't, replace them

REAR PADS

▶ Refer to illustrations 3.10, 3.11 and 3.18

7 If you're working on a hatchback model, disconnect the brake line from its mounting bracket.

8 If you're working on a CR-V model, push the piston back into the bore to provide room for the new brake pads. A C-clamp can be used to accomplish this (see illustration 3.5).

9 Remove the caliper mounting bolts while holding the caliper pins with a second wrench, then remove the caliper from its mounting bracket and hang the caliper out of the way with a piece of wire. Don't

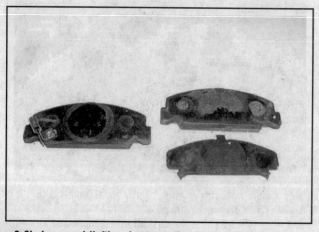

3.6h Inner pad (left) and outer pad and shim layout - some models have inner pad shims

3.6i Apply anti-squeal compound to the back of the pads, then install the shim(s)

3.6j Install the new inner pad; make sure the "ears" on the upper and lower ends of the pad are fully engaged with their respective grooves and the pad retainer clips

3.6k Install the new outer pad and shim (if the new pad has no shim, take the old shim off the old pad and install it on the new outer pad)

3.6l Before installing the caliper, remove the caliper pin dust boots and inspect them for tears and cracks; if they're damaged, replace them. If you're using the same ones, clean off the caliper sliding pins and coat them with high-temperature grease

3.6m Swing the caliper down over the disc and new pads (if the piston hits the inner pad, depress the piston further into the caliper bore with your C-clamp)

let the caliper hang by the brake hose.
10 Remove the outer brake pad and shim (see illustration).

11 Remove the inner brake pad and shim(s) (see illustration).
12 Remove and inspect the upper and lower pad retainer clips.
➡**Note: On 2004 CR-V models, the upper and lower pad retainers are different. Make note of the position before removing.**

3.6n Install the lower bolt and tighten it to the torque listed in this Chapter's Specifications

3.10 Remove the outer pad and shim

3.11 Remove the inner pad and shim

13 Install the pad retainer clips. They should fit snugly in the caliper mounting bracket; if they don't, replace them. Apply a thin film of high-temperature grease to the retainer.

14 Apply a small amount of high-temperature grease to both sides of the shims.

15 Install the new inner pad and shim(s). Make sure the "ears" on the upper and lower ends of the pad are fully engaged with their respective grooves and the pad retainer clips

3.18 To provide clearance for the new brake pads, back the piston into the caliper bore by rotating it with a pair of needle-nose pliers

16 Install the new outer pad and shim.

17 Before installing the caliper, remove the caliper pin dust boots and inspect them for tears and cracks; if they're damaged, replace them.

18 If you're working on a hatchback model, retract the piston by engaging the tips of a pair of needle-nose pliers with two of the grooves in the face of the piston and turning it clockwise until it bottoms in the bore (see illustration). Now, rotate the piston out until one of its grooves is aligned with the tab on the inner brake pad when you install the caliper. You may have to adjust the piston position by turning it back and forth to fit the tab in the groove. If the piston dust boot becomes distorted when the piston is turned, turn the piston in the opposite direction to restore the shape of the boot, but make sure the groove is aligned properly.

19 Install the caliper mounting bolts while holding the caliper pins with a second wrench. Tighten them to the torque listed in this Chapter's Specifications. If the brake line was disconnected from its mounting bracket, reconnect the line and tighten the bolt securely.

FRONT OR REAR PADS

20 Install the wheel and lug nuts, lower the vehicle and tighten the lug nuts to the torque specified in Chapter 1.

21 Apply and release the brake pedal several times to bring the pads into contact with the brake discs. Check the brake fluid level and add fluid, if necessary (see Chapter 1).

22 Check the operation of the brakes in an isolated area before driving the vehicle in traffic.

4 Disc brake caliper - removal and installation

✳✳ WARNING:

The dust created by the brake system is harmful to your health. Never blow it out with compressed air and don't inhale any of it. An approved filtering mask should be worn when working on the brakes. Do not, under any circumstances, use petroleum-based solvents to clean brake parts. Use brake system cleaner only!

➡Note: Always replace the calipers in pairs - never replace just one of them.

FRONT

Removal

▸ Refer to illustrations 4.2a and 4.2b

1 Loosen - but don't remove - the lug nuts on the front wheels. Raise the front of the vehicle and place it securely on jackstands. Remove the front wheels.

2 Disconnect the brake line from the caliper and plug it to keep contaminants out of the brake system and to prevent losing any more brake fluid than is necessary (see illustrations).

➡Note: If you're simply removing the caliper for access to other components, don't disconnect the hose.

3 Remove the caliper mounting bolts while holding the caliper

pins with a second wrench.

4 Detach the caliper from its mounting bracket.

Installation

5 Install the caliper by reversing the removal procedure. Remember to replace the sealing washers on either side of the brake line fitting with new ones. Tighten the caliper mounting bolts and the banjo bolt to the torque listed in this Chapter's Specifications.

6 Bleed the brake system (see Section 10).

4.2a Remove the brake hose banjo bolt

7 Install the wheels and lug nuts and lower the vehicle. Tighten the wheel lug nuts to the torque listed in the Chapter 1 Specifications.

REAR

Removal

8 Loosen - but don't remove - the lug nuts on the rear wheels. Raise the rear of the vehicle and place it securely on jackstands. Remove the rear wheels.

9 Unscrew the banjo bolt and detach the brake line from the caliper. Plug the fitting to prevent fluid loss and contamination (see illustration 4.2b).

➡Note: **If you're simply removing the caliper for access to other components, don't disconnect the hose.**

10 Remove the caliper mounting bolts while holding the caliper pins with a second wrench.

11 If you're working on a hatchback model, remove the clip securing the parking brake cable to the calipers parking brake lever, then separate the cable from the caliper.

12 Detach the caliper from its mounting bracket.

Installation

13 Install the caliper by reversing the removal procedure. Remember to replace the sealing washers on either side of the brake line fitting

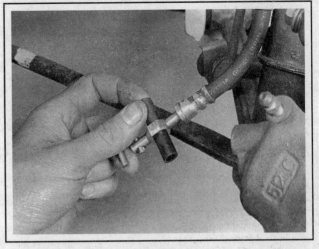

4.2b Using a short piece of rubber hose of the appropriate diameter, plug the brake line banjo fitting

with new ones. Tighten the caliper mounting bolts and the banjo bolt to the torque listed in this Chapter's Specifications.

14 Bleed the brake system (see Section 10).

15 Install the wheels and lug nuts. Lower the vehicle and tighten the lug nuts to the torque listed in the Chapter 1 Specifications.

---

5 Brake disc - inspection, removal and installation

✳✳ WARNING:

The dust created by the brake system is harmful to your health. Never blow it out with compressed air and don't inhale any of it. An approved filtering mask should be worn when working on the brakes. Do not, under any circumstances, use petroleum-based solvents to clean brake parts. Use brake system cleaner only!

INSPECTION

▶ **Refer to illustrations 5.2, 5.3, 5.4a, 5.4b and 5.5**

1 Loosen the wheel lug nuts, raise the vehicle and support it securely on jackstands. Remove the wheel and install the lug nuts to hold the disc in place against the hub flange.

➡Note: **If the lug nuts don't contact the disc when screwed on all the way, install washers under them. If you're checking the rear disc, release the parking brake.**

2 Remove the brake caliper as outlined in Section 4. It isn't necessary to disconnect the brake hose. After removing the caliper bolts, suspend the caliper out of the way with a piece of wire. Remove the two caliper mounting bracket-to-steering knuckle bolts (see illustration) or, on rear calipers, the bracket-to-knuckle bolts and remove the mounting bracket.

5.2 Caliper mounting bracket-to-steering knuckle bolts

5.3 The brake pads on this vehicle were obviously neglected, as they wore down completely and cut deep grooves into the disc - wear this severe means the disc must be replaced

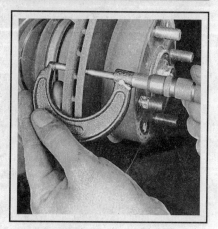

5.4a To check disc runout, mount a dial indicator as shown and rotate the disc

5.4b Using a swirling motion, remove the glaze from the disc surface with sandpaper or emery cloth

5.5 Use a micrometer to measure disc thickness

3   Visually inspect the disc surface for score marks and other damage. Light scratches and shallow grooves are normal after use and may not always be detrimental to brake operation, but deep scoring requires disc removal and refinishing by an automotive machine shop. Be sure to check both sides of the disc (see illustration). If pulsating has been noticed during application of the brakes, suspect disc runout.

4   To check disc runout, place a dial indicator at a point about 1/2-inch from the outer edge of the disc (see illustration). Set the indicator to zero and turn the disc. The indicator reading should not exceed the specified allowable runout limit. If it does, the disc should be refinished by an automotive machine shop.

➡Note: The discs should be resurfaced regardless of the dial indicator reading, as this will impart a smooth finish and ensure a perfectly flat surface, eliminating any brake pedal pulsation or other undesirable symptoms related to questionable discs. At the very least, if you elect not to have the discs resurfaced, remove the glaze from the surface with emery cloth or sandpaper, using a swirling motion (see illustration).

5   It's absolutely critical that the disc not be machined to a thickness under the specified minimum thickness. The minimum (or discard) thickness is cast or stamped into the disc. The disc thickness can be checked with a micrometer (see illustration).

REMOVAL

▶ **Refer to illustrations 5.6a and 5.6b**

6   Remove the lug nuts which were installed to hold the disc in place, or remove the two disc retaining screws (see illustration) and remove the disc from the hub. If the disc is stuck to the hub and won't come off, thread two bolts into the holes provided (see illustration) and tighten them. Alternate between the bolts, turning them a couple of turns at a time, until the disc is free. Remove the disc from the hub.

INSTALLATION

7   Place the disc in position over the threaded studs. Install the disc retaining screws and tighten them securely.

8   Install the caliper mounting bracket and caliper, tightening the bolts to the torque values listed in this Chapter's Specifications.

9   Install the wheel, then lower the vehicle to the ground. Tighten the lug nuts to the torque listed in the Chapter 1 Specifications. Depress the brake pedal a few times to bring the brake pads into contact with the disc. Bleeding won't be necessary unless the brake hose was disconnected from the caliper. Check the operation of the brakes carefully before driving the vehicle.

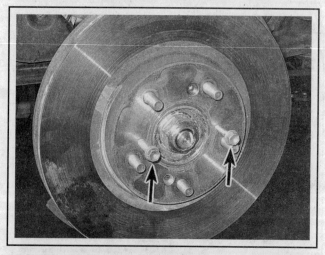

5.6a If the disc retaining screws are stuck, use an impact screwdriver to loosen them

5.6b If the disc is stuck, thread two bolts into the disc and tighten to force the disc off the hub

6 Drum brake shoes/parking brake shoes - replacement

▸ Refer to illustrations 6.4, 6.5, 6.6a through 6.6p and 6.7

✶✶ WARNING:

Drum brake shoes must be replaced on both wheels at the same time - never replace the shoes on only one wheel. Also, the dust created by the brake system is harmful to your health. Never blow it out with compressed air and don't inhale any of it. An approved filtering mask should be worn when working on the brakes. Do not, under any circumstances, use petroleum-based solvents to clean brake parts. Use brake system cleaner only!

✶✶ CAUTION:

Whenever the brake shoes are replaced, the return and hold-down springs should also be replaced. Due to the continuous heating/cooling cycle the springs are subjected to, they can lose tension over a period of time and may allow the shoes to drag on the drum and wear at a much faster rate than normal.

1 Loosen the wheel lug nuts, raise the rear of the vehicle and support it securely on jackstands. Block the front wheels to keep the vehicle from rolling.

2 Release the parking brake.
3 Remove the wheel.

➡Note: All four rear brake shoes must be replaced at the same time, but to avoid mixing up parts, work on only one brake assembly at a time.

4 Remove the brake drum.

➡Note: If the brake drum cannot be easily pulled off the axle and shoe assembly, make sure the parking brake is completely released. If the drum still cannot be pulled off, the brake shoes will have to be retracted. This is done by first removing the plug from the backing plate (see illustration). With the plug removed, push the lever off the adjuster star wheel with a screwdriver while turning the adjuster wheel with another screwdriver, moving the shoes away from the drum. The drum should now come off.

5 Clean the brake shoe assembly with brake system cleaner before beginning work (see illustration).
6 Follow the accompanying illustrations for the brake shoe replacement procedure (see illustrations 6.6a through 6.6p). Be sure to stay in order and read the caption under each illustration.

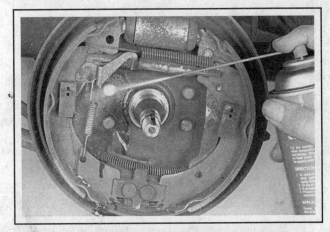

6.5 Before removing anything, clean the brake assembly with brake cleaner and allow it to dry - position a drain pan under the brake to catch the residue - DO NOT USE COMPRESSED AIR TO BLOW BRAKE DUST OFF THE PARTS!

6.4 Remove this plug for access to the adjuster star wheel

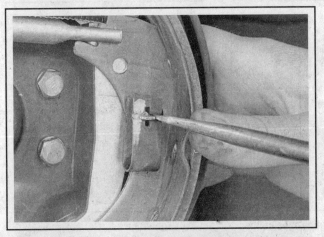

6.6a Push down on the retainer spring with a screwdriver, then turn the tension pin to align its blade with the slot in the retainer spring - the spring should pop off (repeat this on the other spring)

6.6b Pull the shoe assembly away from the backing plate (hub removed for clarity) . . .

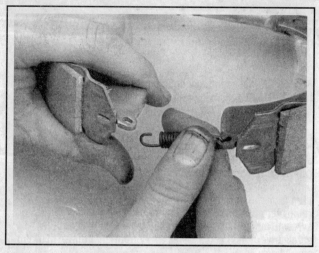

6.6c . . . and unhook the return spring

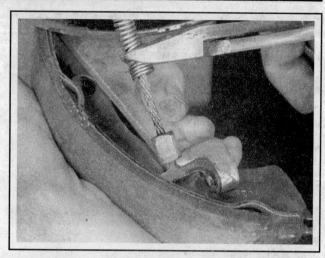

6.6d Pull back on the parking brake cable spring and squeeze the pliers just enough to grip the cable, holding the spring in the compressed position (diagonal cutting pliers are being used because they grip the cable well - be careful not to cut the cable); unhook the cable end from the parking brake lever

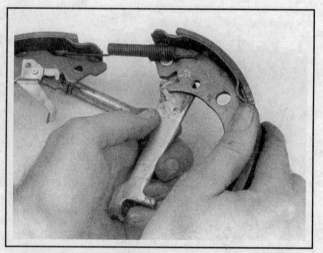

6.6e Swing the parking brake lever away from the trailing shoe, which will force the adjuster bolt clevis out of its groove in the shoe; the two shoes can now be separated

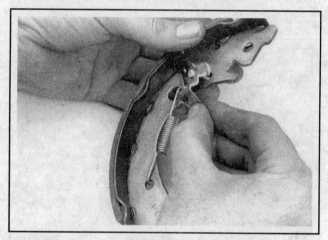

6.6f Remove the self-adjuster lever and spring from the leading shoe

6.6g Pry open the parking brake lever retaining clip and separate the lever from the shoe; be careful not to lose the wave washer that is under the clip

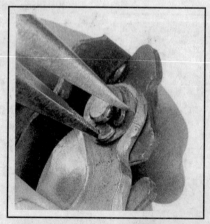

6.6h Put the new trailing shoe on the lever, place the wave washer over the pin, then install the retaining clip; crimp the ends of the clip together with a pair of needle-nose pliers

6.6i Clean the adjuster bolt and clevis, then lubricate the threads and ends with high-temperature grease

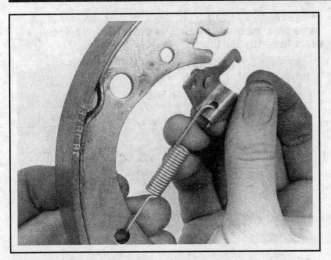

6.6j Connect the self-adjuster lever spring to the leading brake shoe, then insert the pin on the lever into its hole in the shoe

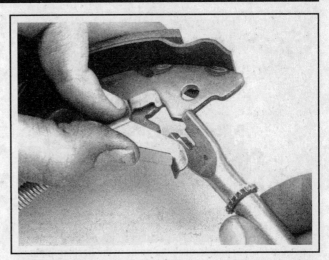

6.6k Insert the short clevis of the adjuster bolt into its slot in the leading shoe, making sure it catches the self-adjuster lever

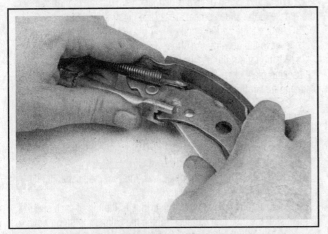

6.6l Connect the upper return spring between the two shoes, pry the lower ends of the shoes apart and insert the clevis at the other end of the adjuster bolt into the slot in the shoe; note the position of the stepped portion of the clevis opening

6.6m Lubricate the brake shoe contact areas on the backing plate with high-temperature grease

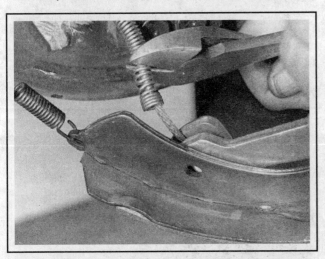

6.6n Compress the parking brake cable spring, hold it in position and connect the cable end to the parking brake lever (again, if you use diagonal cutting pliers, be careful not to cut or nick the cable)

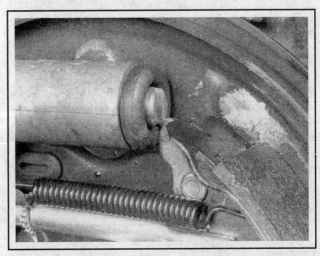

6.6o Place the brake shoe assembly against the backing plate, engaging the upper ends of the shoes in the slots in the wheel cylinder pistons. Connect the lower return spring between the shoes

6.6p With the brake shoes in position on the backing plate, pass the tension pins through the holes in the backing plate and brake shoes, then install the retainer springs (see illustration 6.6a) - make sure the parking brake cable spring and the lower return spring are seated behind the anchor plate, as shown here

7   Before reinstalling the drum, it should be checked for cracks, score marks, deep scratches and hard spots, which will appear as small discolored areas. If the hard spots cannot be removed with fine emery cloth or if any of the other conditions listed above exist, the drum must be taken to an automotive machine shop to have it resurfaced.

➥Note: Professionals recommend resurfacing the drums each time a brake job is done. Resurfacing will eliminate the possibility of out-of-round drums. If the drums are worn so much that they can't be resurfaced without exceeding the maximum allowable diameter (see illustration), then new ones will be required. At the very least, if you elect not to have the drums resurfaced, remove the glaze from the surface with emery cloth using a swirling motion.

8   Install the brake drum on the hub flange. Using a screwdriver inserted through the adjusting hole in the brake backing plate (see illustration 6.4), turn the adjuster star wheel until the brake shoes drag on the drum as the drum is rotated, then back off the star wheel until the shoes don't drag. Reinstall the plug in the backing plate.

9   Mount the wheel and install the lug nuts. Lower the vehicle and tighten the lug nuts to the torque listed in the Chapter 1 Specifications.

10   Make a number of forward and reverse stops and operate the parking brake to adjust the brakes until satisfactory pedal action is obtained.

11   Check the operation of the brakes carefully before driving the vehicle.

PARKING BRAKE SHOES (CR-V MODELS)

✳✳ WARNING:

The dust created by the brake system is harmful to your health. Never blow it out with compressed air and don't inhale any of it. An approved filtering mask should be worn when working on the brakes. Do not, under any circumstances, use petroleum-based solvents to clean brake parts. Use brake system cleaner only!

Removal

12   Loosen the rear wheel lug nuts, raise the rear of the vehicle and support it securely on jackstands. Block the front wheels and remove the rear wheels. Release the parking brake.

➥Note: All four parking brake shoes must be replaced at the same time, but to avoid mixing up parts, work on only one brake assembly at a time.

13   Remove the rear calipers (see Section 4). Support the caliper assemblies with a coat hanger or heavy wire and don't disconnect the brake line from the caliper.

14   Remove the rear discs (see Section 5).

15   Clean the parking brake assembly with brake system cleaner.

16   Remove the two upper return springs.

17   Push the hold-down clips on the shoes and turn the pins 90-degrees, then remove the clips.

18   Remove the connecting rod and rod spring.

19   Remove the lower return spring, then pull the leading shoe back and remove the adjuster screw.

20   On the backing plate side of the trailing shoe, use diagonal cutters to pry the U-clip and washer from the top of the shoe.

21   Remove the parking brake lever from the trailing shoe and remove the shoe.

Installation

22   With the backing plate cleaned, apply light dabs of high-temperature grease to the shoe contact areas (see illustration 6.6m).

23   Lubricate the parking brake lever pin, then assemble the parking brake lever to the new trailing shoe.

24   Position the trailing shoe against the stationary stop at the top of the backing plate, then insert the hold-down pin through the backing plate and install the hold-down clip.

25   Clean the adjuster bolt and clevis, then lubricate the threads and ends with high-temperature grease.

26   Install the adjuster and lower return spring on each shoe, then position the leading shoe and insert the hold-down pin through the backing plate and install the hold-down clip.

27   Place the rod spring on the connecting rod, then separate the shoes and install the connecting rod.

28   Connect the two upper return springs to the top of each shoe.

29   Install the disc and caliper. Tighten the caliper mounting bolts to the torque listed in this Chapter's Specifications.

30   Using a screwdriver inserted through the adjusting hole in the disc, turn the adjuster star wheel until the brake shoes drag on the drum as the drum is rotated, then back off the star wheel until the shoes don't drag.

31   Mount the wheel and install the lug nuts. Lower the vehicle and tighten the lug nuts to the torque listed in the Chapter 1 Specifications.

32   Make a number of forward and reverse stops and operate the parking brake to adjust the brakes until satisfactory pedal action is obtained.

33   Check the operation of the brakes carefully before driving the vehicle.

6.7 The maximum allowable drum diameter is cast into the drum (typical)

7 Wheel cylinder - removal and installation

⁎⁕ WARNING:

The dust created by the brake system is harmful to your health. Never blow it out with compressed air and don't inhale any of it. An approved filtering mask should be worn when working on the brakes. Do not, under any circumstances, use petroleum-based solvents to clean brake parts. Use brake system cleaner only!

➡Note: If replacement is indicated (usually because of fluid leakage or sticky operation), it is recommended that the wheel

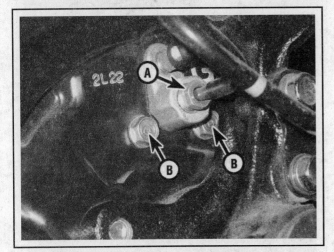

7.4 Disconnect the brake line (A), then remove the wheel cylinder mounting bolts (B)

cylinders be replaced, not overhauled. Always replace the wheel cylinders in pairs - never replace just one of them.

REMOVAL

▶ **Refer to illustration 7.4**

1 Raise the rear of the vehicle and support it securely on jackstands. Block the front wheels to keep the vehicle from rolling.

2 Remove the brake shoe assembly (see Section 6).

3 Remove all dirt and foreign material from around the wheel cylinder.

4 Disconnect the brake line (see illustration). Don't pull the brake line away from the wheel cylinder.

5 Remove the wheel cylinder mounting bolts.

6 Detach the wheel cylinder from the brake backing plate and immediately plug the brake line to prevent fluid loss and contamination.

INSTALLATION

7 Apply a small amount of RTV sealant between the backing plate and wheel cylinder, then place the wheel cylinder in position and install the bolts finger tight. Connect the brake line to the cylinder, being careful not to cross thread the fitting. Tighten the wheel cylinder mounting bolts to the torque listed in this Chapter's Specifications. Now tighten the brake line fitting securely.

8 Install the brake shoe assembly (see Section 6).

9 Bleed the brakes (see Section 10).

10 Check the operation of the brakes carefully before driving the vehicle.

8 Master cylinder - removal and installation

REMOVAL

▶ **Refer to illustrations 8.2 and 8.6**

1 The master cylinder is located in the engine compartment, mounted to the power brake booster.

2 If you're working on a hatchback model, remove the air filter housing (see Chapter 4). If you're working on a CR-V model, remove the strut bar (see illustration).

3 Disconnect the electrical connector from the fluid level warning switch.

4 Using a syringe or equivalent, siphon the brake fluid from the master cylinder reservoir and dispose of it properly.

⁎⁕ CAUTION:

Brake fluid will damage paint. Cover all painted surfaces and avoid spilling fluid during this procedure.

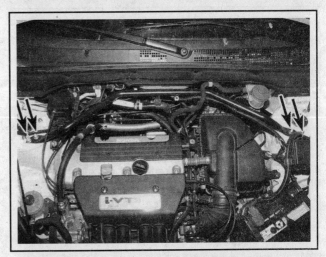

8.2 Remove the fasteners securing the strut bar, then remove the bar

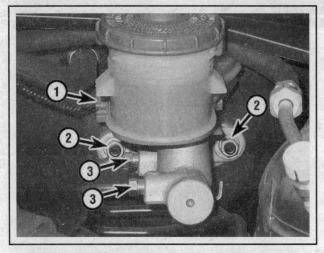

8.6 Master cylinder mounting details

1	Electrical connector	3	Brake line fittings
2	Mounting nuts		

5   If you're working on a hatchback model, separate the clutch master cylinder reservoir and the engine wire harness clip from the master cylinder mounting base. Remove the bolt attaching the brake reservoir to the mounting base.

6   Place rags under the fluid fittings and prepare caps or plastic bags to cover the ends of the lines once they are disconnected. Loosen the fittings at the ends of the brake lines where they enter the master cylinder (see illustration). To prevent rounding off the corners on these nuts, the use of a flare-nut wrench, which wraps around the nut, is preferred. Pull the brake lines slightly away from the master cylinder and plug the ends to prevent contamination.

7   Remove the nuts attaching the master cylinder to the power booster. Pull the master cylinder off the studs and out of the engine compartment. Again, be careful not to spill the fluid as this is done.

8   If a new master cylinder is being installed, remove the reservoir from the master cylinder and transfer it to the new master cylinder.

➡ Note: On coupes, sedans and CR-V models, be sure to install new seals when transferring the reservoir.

INSTALLATION

◆ Refer to illustration 8.10

9   Bench bleed the new master cylinder before installing it. Mount the master cylinder in a vise, with the jaws of the vise clamping on the mounting flange.

10   Attach a pair of master cylinder bleeder tubes to the outlet ports of the master cylinder (see illustration).

11   Fill the reservoir with brake fluid of the recommended type (see Chapter 1).

12   Slowly push the pistons into the master cylinder (a large Phillips screwdriver can be used for this) - air will be expelled from the pressure chambers and into the reservoir. Because the tubes are submerged in fluid, air can't be drawn back into the master cylinder when you release the pistons.

13   Repeat the procedure until no more air bubbles are present.

14   Remove the bleed tubes, one at a time, and install plugs in the open ports to prevent fluid leakage and air from entering. Install the

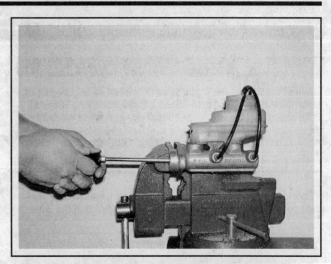

8.10 The best way to bleed air from the master cylinder before installing it on the vehicle is with a pair of bleeder tubes that direct brake fluid into the reservoir during bleeding

reservoir cap.

15   Install the master cylinder over the studs on the power brake booster and tighten the attaching nuts only finger tight at this time.

➡ Note: Be sure to install a new rod seal on the master cylinder.

16   Thread the brake line fittings into the master cylinder. Since the master cylinder is still a bit loose, it can be moved slightly in order for the fittings to thread in easily. Do not strip the threads as the fittings are tightened.

17   Fully tighten the mounting nuts, then the brake line fittings. Tighten the nuts to the torque listed in this Chapter's Specifications.

18   Fill the master cylinder reservoir with fluid, then bleed the master cylinder and the brake system as described in Section 10. To bleed the cylinder on the vehicle, have an assistant depress the brake pedal and hold the pedal to the floor. Loosen the fitting to allow air and fluid to escape. Repeat this procedure on both fittings until the fluid is clear of air bubbles.

❊❊ CAUTION:

Have plenty of rags on hand to catch the fluid - brake fluid will ruin painted surfaces. After the bleeding procedure is completed, rinse the area under the master cylinder with clean water.

19   The remainder of installation is the reverse of removal. Test the operation of the brake system carefully before placing the vehicle into normal service.

❊❊ WARNING:

Do not operate the vehicle if you are in doubt about the effectiveness of the brake system. On models equipped with ABS, it is possible for air to become trapped in the anti-lock brake system hydraulic control unit, so, if the pedal continues to feel spongy after repeated bleedings or the BRAKE or ANTI-LOCK light stays on, have the vehicle towed to a dealer service department or other qualified shop to be bled with the aid of a scan tool.

9   Brake hoses and lines - inspection and replacement

1   About every six months, with the vehicle raised and placed securely on jackstands, the flexible hoses which connect the steel brake lines with the front and rear brake assemblies should be inspected for cracks, chafing of the outer cover, leaks, blisters and other damage. These are important and vulnerable parts of the brake system and inspection should be complete. A light and mirror will be needed for a thorough check. If a hose exhibits any of the above defects, replace it with a new one.

FLEXIBLE HOSES

▶ **Refer to illustration 9.3**

2   Clean all dirt away from the ends of the hose.
3   To disconnect a brake hose from the brake line, unscrew the metal tube nut with a flare nut wrench, then remove the U-clip from the female fitting at the bracket and remove the hose from the bracket (see illustration).
4   Disconnect the hose from the caliper, discarding the sealing washers on either side of the fitting.
5   Using new sealing washers, attach the new brake hose to the caliper.
6   To reattach a brake hose to the metal line, insert the end of the hose through the frame bracket, make sure the hose isn't twisted, then attach the metal line by tightening the tube nut fitting securely. Install the U-clip at the frame bracket.
7   Carefully check to make sure the suspension or steering components don't make contact with the hose. Have an assistant push down on the vehicle and also turn the steering wheel lock-to-lock during inspection.
8   Bleed the brake system (see Section 10).

METAL BRAKE LINES

9   When replacing brake lines, be sure to use the correct parts.

9.3 Unscrew the brake line threaded fitting with a flare-nut wrench to protect the fitting corners from being rounded off (A), then pull off the U-clip (B) with a pair of pliers and remove the brake line mounting bolt (C)

Don't use copper tubing for any brake system components. Purchase steel brake lines from a dealer parts department or auto parts store.
10 Prefabricated brake line, with the tube ends already flared and fittings installed, is available at auto parts stores and dealer parts departments. These lines can be bent to the proper shapes using a tubing bender.
11 When installing the new line make sure it's well supported in the brackets and has plenty of clearance between moving or hot components.
12 After installation, check the master cylinder fluid level and add fluid as necessary. Bleed the brake system as outlined in Section 10 and test the brakes carefully before placing the vehicle into normal operation.

10   Brake hydraulic system - bleeding

▶ **Refer to illustration 10.8**

※※ WARNING 1:

If air has found its way into the hydraulic control unit on models with ABS, the system must be bled with the use of a scan tool. If the brake pedal feels "spongy" even after bleeding the brakes, or the ABS light on the instrument panel does not go off, or if you have any doubts whatsoever about the effectiveness of the brake system, have the vehicle towed to a dealer service department or other repair shop equipped with the necessary tools for bleeding the system.

※※ WARNING 2:

Wear eye protection when bleeding the brake system. If the fluid comes in contact with your eyes, immediately rinse them with water and seek medical attention.

➡Note: Bleeding the brake system is necessary to remove any air that's trapped in the system when it's opened during removal and installation of a hose, line, caliper, wheel cylinder or master cylinder.

1   It will probably be necessary to bleed the system at all four brakes if air has entered the system due to low fluid level, or if the brake lines have been disconnected at the master cylinder.
2   If a brake line was disconnected only at a wheel, then only that caliper or wheel cylinder must be bled.
3   If a brake line is disconnected at a fitting located between the master cylinder and any of the brakes, that part of the system served by the disconnected line must be bled.
4   Remove any residual vacuum (or hydraulic pressure) from the brake power booster by applying the brake several times with the engine off.
5   Remove the master cylinder reservoir cap and fill the reservoir with brake fluid. Reinstall the cap.

→Note: Check the fluid level often during the bleeding operation and add fluid as necessary to prevent the fluid level from falling low enough to allow air bubbles into the master cylinder.

6   Have an assistant on hand, as well as a supply of new brake fluid, an empty clear plastic container, a length of plastic, rubber or vinyl tubing to fit over the bleeder valve and a wrench to open and close the bleeder valve.

7   Beginning at the front left wheel, loosen the bleeder screw slightly, then tighten it to a point where it's snug but can still be loosened quickly and easily.

8   Place one end of the tubing over the bleeder screw fitting and submerge the other end in brake fluid in the container (see illustration).

9   Have the assistant slowly depress the brake pedal and hold it in the depressed position.

10   While the pedal is held depressed, open the bleeder screw just enough to allow a flow of fluid to leave the valve. Watch for air bubbles to exit the submerged end of the tube. When the fluid flow slows after a couple of seconds, tighten the screw and have your assistant release the pedal.

11   Repeat Steps 9 and 10 until no more air is seen leaving the tube, then tighten the bleeder screw and proceed to the right front wheel, the right rear wheel and the left rear wheel, in that order, and perform the same procedure. Be sure to check the fluid in the master cylinder reservoir frequently.

12   Never use old brake fluid. It contains moisture which can boil, rendering the brake system inoperative.

13   Refill the master cylinder with fluid at the end of the operation.

14   Check the operation of the brakes. The pedal should feel solid when depressed, with no sponginess. If necessary, repeat the entire process.

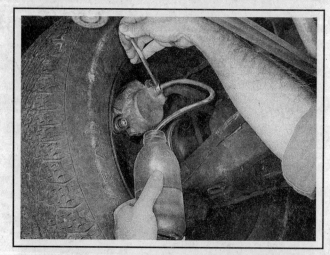

10.8 When bleeding the brakes, a hose is connected to the bleed screw at the caliper and submerged in brake fluid - air will be seen as bubbles in the tube and container (all air must be expelled before moving to the next wheel)

✷✷ WARNING:

Do not operate the vehicle if you are in doubt about the effectiveness of the brake system. On models equipped with ABS, it's possible for air to become trapped in the anti-lock brake system hydraulic control unit, so, if the pedal continues to feel spongy after repeated bleedings or the BRAKE or ANTI-LOCK light stays on, have the vehicle towed to a dealer service department or other qualified shop to be bled with the aid of a scan tool.

11   Power brake booster - removal and installation

OPERATING CHECK

1   Depress the brake pedal several times with the engine off and make sure there is no change in the pedal reserve distance.

2   Depress the pedal and start the engine. If the pedal goes down slightly, operation is normal.

AIRTIGHTNESS CHECK

3   Start the engine and turn it off after one or two minutes. Depress the brake pedal several times slowly. If the pedal goes down farther the first time but gradually rises after the second or third depression, the booster is airtight.

4   Depress the brake pedal while the engine is running, then stop the engine with the pedal depressed. If there is no change in the pedal reserve travel after holding the pedal for 30 seconds, the booster is airtight.

REMOVAL

▶ **Refer to illustrations 11.8, 11.9 and 11.10**

5   Power brake booster units should not be disassembled. They require special tools not normally found in most automotive repair stations or shops. They are fairly complex and because of their critical relationship to brake performance it is best to replace a defective booster unit with a new or rebuilt one.

6   To remove the booster, first remove the brake master cylinder as described in Section 8. On coupe or sedan models equipped with ABS, remove the master cylinder brake lines from the ABS hydraulic unit.

7   Disconnect the hose leading from the engine to the booster. Be careful not to damage the hose when removing it from the booster fitting.

8   If you're working on a coupe or sedan model, remove the bolts securing the throttle cable bracket, then remove the power steering and

11.8 Remove the bolts securing the throttle cable bracket

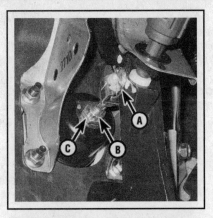

11.9 Remove the clevis pin retaining clip (A) and clevis pin and disconnect the pushrod from the pedal - (B) is the star locknut and (C) is the adjuster mentioned in Step 15

11.10 Remove the four booster mounting nuts

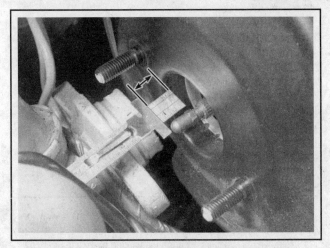

11.14a Measure the distance that the pushrod protrudes from the brake booster at the master cylinder mounting surface (including the gasket, if equipped)

air conditioning lines from their holders (see illustration).

9   Locate the pushrod clevis pin connecting the booster to the brake pedal (see illustration). Remove the clevis pin retaining clip with pliers and pull out the pin.

10 Remove the four nuts (see illustration) holding the brake booster to the firewall.

11 Slide the booster straight out from the firewall until the studs clear the holes and pull the booster, brackets and gaskets from the engine compartment area.

INSTALLATION

▶ **Refer to illustrations 11.14a, 11.14b and 11.14c**

12 If a new booster is being installed, measure the length of the input rod, from the booster mounting surface to the hole in the clevis; it should be as listed in this Chapter's Specifications. If it isn't, loosen the locknut and turn the clevis one way or the other until the length is correct.

13 Installation procedures are the reverse of those for removal. Tighten the booster mounting nuts to the torque listed in this Chapter's Specifications. Also, be sure to use a new cotter pin on the clevis pin.

14 If a new power brake booster unit is being installed, the booster pushrod-to-master cylinder clearance must be as specified - if there is interference between the two, the brakes may drag; if there is too much clearance, there will be excessive brake pedal travel. Check the pushrod

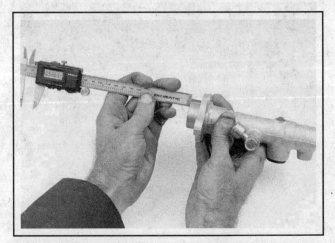

11.14b Measure the distance from the mounting flange to the end of the master cylinder

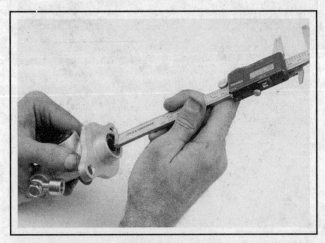

11.14c Measure the distance from the piston pocket to the end of the master cylinder

clearance as follows:

a) Using a hand-held vacuum pump, apply a vacuum of 20 in-Hg to the booster. Measure the distance that the pushrod protrudes from the master cylinder mounting surface on the front of the power brake booster, including the gasket (if used). Write down this measurement (see illustration). This is "dimension A."

b) Measure the distance from the mounting flange to the end of the master cylinder (see illustration). Write down this measurement. This is "dimension B."

c) Measure the distance from the end of the master cylinder to the bottom of the pocket in the piston (see illustration). Write down this measurement. This is "dimension C."

d) Subtract measurement B from measurement C, then subtract mea-

surement A from the difference between B and C. This the pushrod clearance.

e) Compare your calculated pushrod clearance to the pushrod clearance listed in this Chapter's Specifications. If necessary, adjust the pushrod length to achieve the correct clearance (see the next Step).

15 If the clearance is more or less than specified, loosen the star locknut (see illustration 11.9) and turn the adjuster on the power booster pushrod until the clearance is within the specified limit. After adjustment, tighten the locknut. Recheck the clearance. Repeat this step as often as necessary until the clearance is correct.

16 After the final installation of the master cylinder and brake hoses and lines, bleed the brakes as described in Section 10.

12 Parking brake - adjustment

▶ **Refer to illustrations 12.1 and 12.3**

COUPE AND SEDAN MODELS

1 Remove the center console rear cover (see illustration).

2 Block the front wheels, raise the rear of the vehicle and support it securely on jackstands. Apply the parking brake lever until you hear one click.

3 Tighten the adjusting nut on the equalizer while rotating the rear wheels (see illustration). Stop turning the nut when the brakes just start to drag on the rear wheels.

4 Release the parking brake lever and check to see that the brakes don't drag when the rear wheels are turned. The travel on the parking brake lever should be as listed in the Chapter 1 Specifications when properly adjusted.

5 Lower the vehicle and reinstall the center console rear cover.

HATCHBACK MODELS

6 Remove the center console (see Chapter 11).

7 Release the parking brake lever and loosen the parking brake lever adjusting nut.

8 Start the engine, then set the self-adjusting brake by depressing the brake several times. Turn off the engine.

9 Block the front wheels, raise the rear of the vehicle and support it securely on jackstands.

10 At the rear caliper, be sure the parking brake arm is contacting the brake caliper pin.

11 Apply the parking brake lever until you hear one click. Tighten the adjusting nut on the equalizer while rotating the rear wheels. Stop turning the nut when the brakes just start to drag on the rear wheels.

12 Release the parking brake lever and check to see that the brakes don't drag when the rear wheels are turned. The travel on the parking brake lever should be as listed in the Chapter 1 Specifications when properly adjusted.

13 Lower the vehicle and reinstall the center console.

CR-V MODELS

14 Working inside the vehicle, pull the driver's seat all the way forward and pull back the carpet under the seat.

15 Remove the fasteners securing the parking brake equalizer cover, then remove the cover.

16 With the parking brake lever fully released, remove the return spring from the parking brake equalizer.

17 Block the front wheels, raise the rear of the vehicle and support it securely on jackstands. Apply the parking brake lever until you hear one click.

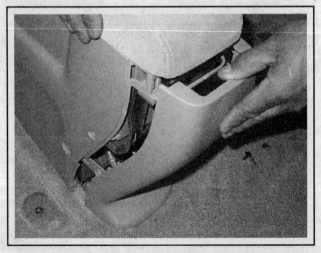

12.1 Remove the fasteners securing the center console rear cover, then detach the rear cover

12.3 The parking brake adjusting nut is on the equalizer assembly

18 Tighten the adjusting nut on the equalizer while rotating the rear wheels. Stop turning the nut when the brakes just start to drag on the rear wheels.

19 Release the parking brake lever and check to see that the brakes don't drag when the rear wheels are turned. The travel on the parking brake lever should be as listed in the Chapter 1 Specifications when properly adjusted.

20 Lower the vehicle and reinstall the equalizer return spring and cover.

13 Brake light switch - replacement

▶ **Refer to illustration 13.1**

1 Disconnect the electrical connector from the brake light switch (see illustration).

2 Rotate the switch counterclockwise slightly, so it unlocks from its holder, then pull it out of the holder.

3 To install the switch, insert it into its holder (canted slightly counterclockwise as during removal) and push it in until the switch body contacts the bracket on the brake pedal. Rotate the switch 45-degrees clockwise to lock it into place.

4 Plug the electrical connector into the switch.

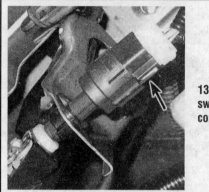

13.1 Brake light switch electrical connector

14 Brake pedal - adjustment

BRAKE PEDAL HEIGHT

▶ **Refer to illustration 14.2**

1 Disconnect the brake light switch electrical connector, then remove the brake light switch (see Section 13).

2 Pull the carpet back and find the insulator cutout, then with the brake pedal fully released, measure the distance from the top of the pad to the floor (see illustration).

3 If the height is not as listed in the Specifications at the end of this Chapter it must be adjusted.

4 Loosen the locknut just in front of the clevis on the power brake booster pushrod.

5 Turn the booster pushrod until the pedal height is correct.

6 Tighten the locknut.

7 After adjusting the pedal height, check the freeplay, then install the brake light switch (see Section 13).

BRAKE PEDAL FREEPLAY

▶ **Refer to illustration 14.8**

8 Press down lightly on the brake pedal and measure the distance that it moves freely before resistance is felt (see illustration). The freeplay should be within the specified limits. If it isn't, check the clevis, clevis pin and the hole in the brake pedal arm for excessive wear. Also make sure the brake light switch is properly adjusted (see Section 13).

14.2 With the brake pedal fully released, measure the distance from the top of the pedal pad to the floor

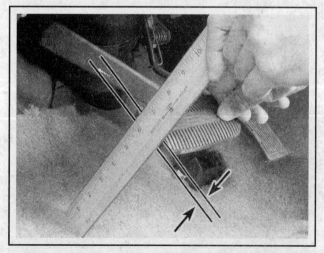

14.8 To measure brake pedal freeplay, press down lightly on the pedal and measure the distance that it moves freely before resistance is felt

Specifications

General

Brake fluid type	See Chapter 1
Power brake booster pushrod-to-master cylinder piston clearance (with 20 in-Hg of vacuum applied to the booster)	0.0 to 0.020 inch (0.0 to 0.5 mm)

Disc brakes

Brake pad minimum thickness	See Chapter 1
Disc lateral runout limit	0.004 inch (0.10 mm)
Disc minimum thickness	Cast into disc
Parallelism (thickness variation) limit	0.0006 inch (0.015 mm)

Drum brakes

Maximum drum diameter	Cast into drum
Shoe lining minimum thickness	See Chapter 1

Torque specifications   Ft-lbs (unless otherwise indicated)   Nm

➡Note: One foot-pound (ft-lb) of torque is equivalent to 12 inch-pounds (in-lbs) of torque. Torque values below approximately 15 ft-lbs are expressed in inch-pounds, since most foot-pound torque wrenches are not accurate at these smaller values.

	Ft-lbs (unless otherwise indicated)	Nm
Caliper mounting bracket bolts		
Front	80	108
Rear	41	55
Caliper mounting guide pins/bolts		
Front	25	34
Rear	17	23
Master cylinder mounting nuts	11	15
Power brake booster mounting bolts	108 in-lbs	13
Wheel cylinder mounting bolt	11	15
Wheel lug nuts	See Chapter 1	

Section

10

SUSPENSION AND STEERING SYSTEMS

1   General information

▶ **Refer to illustrations 1.1 and 1.2**

The front suspension is a MacPherson strut design. The upper end of each strut is attached to the vehicle's body strut support. The lower end of the strut is connected to the upper end of the steering knuckle. The steering knuckle is attached by a balljoint mounted to the outer end of the suspension control arm. A stabilizer bar connected to each control arm and mounted to the suspension crossmember reduces body roll during cornering (see illustration).

The rear suspension employs a trailing arm, upper control arms, and shock absorbers with coil springs (see illustration). A stabilizer bar is clamped to a suspension support and connected to the trailing arms by two links.

The power-assisted rack-and-pinion steering gear is attached to the front suspension subframe. On Coupe, Sedan and CR-V models, power assist comes from an engine-mounted hydraulic pump. Hatchback models are equipped with an electrically assisted power steering gear. The steering gear actuates the tie-rods, which are attached to the steering knuckles. The steering column is designed to collapse in the event of an accident.

Frequently, when working on the suspension or steering system components, you may come across fasteners that seem impossible to loosen. These fasteners on the underside of the vehicle are continually subjected to water, road grime, mud, etc., and can become rusted or "frozen," making them extremely difficult to remove. In order to unscrew these stubborn fasteners without damaging them (or other components), be sure to use lots of penetrating oil and allow it to soak in for a while. Using a wire brush to clean exposed threads will also ease removal of the nut or bolt and prevent damage to the threads. Sometimes a sharp blow with a hammer and punch will break the bond between a nut and bolt threads, but care must be taken to prevent the punch from slipping off the fastener and ruining the threads. Heating the stuck fastener and surrounding area with a torch sometimes helps too, but isn't recommended because of the obvious dangers associated with fire. Long breaker bars and extension, or "cheater," pipes will increase leverage, but never use an extension pipe on a ratchet - the ratcheting mechanism could be damaged. Sometimes tightening the nut or bolt first will help to break it loose. Fasteners that require drastic measures to remove should always be replaced with new ones.

Since most of the procedures dealt with in this Chapter involve jacking up the vehicle and working underneath it, a good pair of jack-stands will be needed. A hydraulic floor jack is the preferred type of jack to lift the vehicle, and it can also be used to support certain components during various operations.

✲✲ WARNING:

Never, under any circumstances, rely on a jack to support the vehicle while working on it. Whenever any of the suspension or steering fasteners are loosened or removed they must be inspected and, if necessary, replaced with new ones of the same part number or of original equipment quality and design. Torque specifications must be followed for proper reassembly and component retention. Never attempt to heat or straighten any suspension or steering components. Instead, replace any bent or damaged part with a new one.

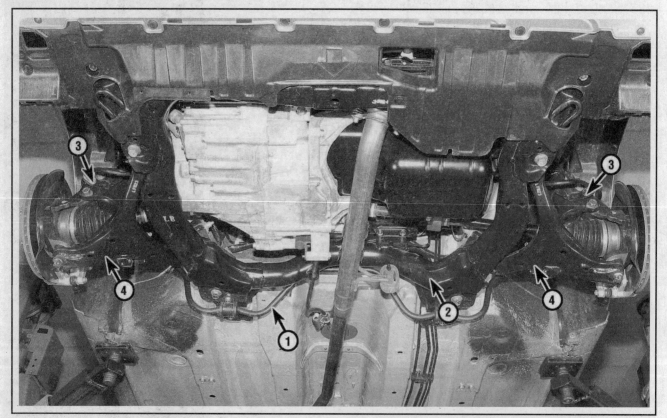

1.1 Front suspension components (Civic model shown)

1 Stabilizer bar	*2 Subframe*	*3 Strut/coil spring assembly*	*4 Control arm*

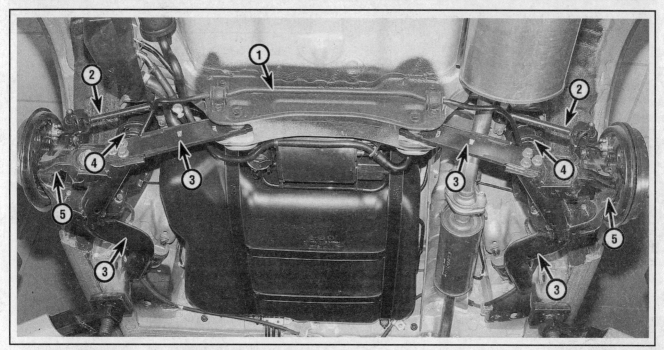

1.2 Rear suspension components (Civic model shown)

1	*Stabilizer bar*	*3*	*Trailing arm*	*5*	*Rear knuckle (hub and bearing)*
2	*Upper arm*	*4*	*Shock absorber/coil spring assembly*		

2   Stabilizer bar and bushings (front) - removal, inspection and installation

REMOVAL

▶ **Refer to illustrations 2.2 and 2.3**

1   Loosen the front wheel lug nuts, raise the front of the vehicle and support it securely on jackstands. Apply the parking brake and block the rear wheels to keep the vehicle from rolling off the stands. Remove the front wheels.

2   Remove the nuts and the stabilizer bar attaching link assemblies from the lower control arms (see illustration).

➡**Note: Use an Allen wrench to prevent the ballstud from turning when removing the attaching link nut.**

3   Remove the stabilizer bar bushing retainer bolts (see illustration).

4   Remove the stabilizer bar from the vehicle.

INSPECTION

5   Inspect for cracked, torn, or distorted stabilizer bar bushings, bushing retainers, and worn or damaged stabilizer bar links.

2.2 Stabilizer bar link attaching nuts

2.3 Stabilizer bar bushing clamps

6   To replace damaged stabilizer bar bushings, remove the retainer, open the bushing slit and peel the bushing from the stabilizer bar. On some models it will be necessary to bend back the tabs holding the retainer together.

✳✳ CAUTION:

Install the new bushings with the slits facing the same way that the original bushing slits faced.

INSTALLATION

7   Guide the stabilizer bar into position. Install the retainer bolts, tightening them to the torque listed in this Chapter's Specifications.
8   Connect the stabilizer bar links to the lower control arms. Tighten the nuts to the torque listed in this Chapter's Specifications.
9   Install the wheels and lug nuts. Lower the vehicle and tighten the lug nuts to the torque listed in the Chapter 1 Specifications.

3   Strut assembly (front) - removal, inspection and installation

REMOVAL

▶ **Refer to illustrations 3.4 and 3.6**

➡**Note: If both strut assemblies are going to be removed, mark the assemblies Right and Left so they will be reinstalled on the correct side.**

1   Loosen the wheel lug nuts, raise the vehicle and support it securely on jackstands. Remove the wheels.
2   Unbolt the brake hose bracket from the strut. If the vehicle is equipped with ABS, detach the speed sensor wiring harness from the strut by removing the clamp bracket bolt.
3   Disconnect the tie-rod end from the steering arm on the strut (see Section 14).
4   Mark the position of the strut to the steering knuckle (see illustration).

➡**Note: This is only necessary if special camber adjusting bolts have been installed in place of the regular strut-to-knuckle bolts. Remove the strut-to-knuckle nuts, then knock the bolts out with a hammer and punch.**

5   Separate the strut from the steering knuckle. Be careful not to overextend the inner CV joint. Also, don't let the steering knuckle fall outward and strain the brake hose.
6   Support the strut and spring assembly with one hand and remove the three strut-to-body nuts (see illustration). Remove the assembly out from the fenderwell.

INSPECTION

7   Check the strut body for leaking fluid, dents, cracks and other obvious damage which would warrant repair or replacement.
8   Check the coil spring for chips or cracks in the spring coating (this will cause premature spring failure due to corrosion). Inspect the spring seat for cuts, hardness and general deterioration.
9   If any undesirable conditions exist, proceed to the strut disassembly procedure (see Section 4).

INSTALLATION

▶ **Refer to illustration 3.10**

10 Guide the strut assembly up into the fenderwell and insert the upper mounting studs through the holes in the body (see illustration). Once the studs protrude, install the nuts so the strut won't fall back through. This is most easily accomplished with the help of an assistant, as the strut is quite heavy and awkward.
11 Slide the steering knuckle into the strut flange and insert the two bolts. Install the nuts, align the previously made matchmarks and tighten them to the torque listed in this Chapter's Specifications.
12 Connect the brake hose bracket to the strut and tighten the bolt securely. If the vehicle is equipped with ABS, install the speed sensor wiring harness bracket.
13 Connect the stabilizer bar link to the control arm. Tighten the nut to the torque listed in this Chapter's Specifications.

3.4 Mark the position of the strut to the steering knuckle, around the bolt heads and where the strut meets the knuckle

3.6 Support the strut and remove the upper mounting nuts (DON'T remove the nut in the center

3.10 Carefully guide the strut assembly up into the fenderwell

14 Connect the tie-rod end to the steering arm on the strut. Tighten the nut to the torque listed in this Chapter's Specifications.

15 Install the wheel and lug nuts, then lower the vehicle and tighten the lug nuts to the torque listed in the Chapter 1 Specifications.

16 Tighten the upper mounting nuts to the torque listed in this Chapter's Specifications.

17 Drive the vehicle to an alignment shop to have the front end alignment checked, and if necessary, adjusted.

4 Strut/spring assembly - replacement

✳✳ WARNING:

Struts and/or coil springs must be replaced in pairs - never replace just one of them.

1 If the struts or coil springs exhibit the telltale signs of wear (leaking fluid, loss of damping capability, chipped, sagging or cracked coil springs) explore all options before beginning any work. The strut/shock absorber assemblies are not serviceable and must be replaced if a problem develops. However, strut assemblies complete with springs may be available on an exchange basis, which eliminates much time and work. Whichever route you choose to take, check on the cost and availability of parts before disassembling your vehicle.

✳✳ WARNING:

Disassembling a strut is potentially dangerous and utmost attention must be directed to the job, or serious injury may result. Use only a high-quality spring compressor and carefully follow the manufacturer's instructions furnished with the tool. After removing the coil spring from the strut assembly, set it aside in a safe, isolated area.

DISASSEMBLY

▶ **Refer to illustrations 4.3, 4.5, 4.6 and 4.7**

2 Remove the strut and spring assembly (see Section 3). Mount the strut assembly in a vise. Line the vise jaws with wood or rags to prevent damage to the unit and don't tighten the vise excessively.

3 Following the tool manufacturer's instructions, install the spring compressor (which can be obtained at most auto parts stores or equipment yards on a daily rental basis) on the spring and compress it sufficiently to relieve all pressure from the upper spring seat (see

4.3 Install the spring compressor following the tool manufacturer's instructions; compress the spring until all pressure is relieved from the upper spring seat (you can verify the spring is loose by wiggling it)

illustration). This can be verified by wiggling the spring.

4 Hold the damper rod with an Allen wrench, and unscrew the damper rod nut with a box-end wrench.

5 Remove the nut and upper mount (see illustration). Lay the parts out in the exact order in which they are removed. Inspect the bearing in the suspension support for smooth operation. If it doesn't turn smoothly, replace the upper mount. Check the rubber portion of the upper mount for cracking and general deterioration. If there is any separation of the rubber, replace it.

6 Remove the upper spring seat from the damper rod (see illustration). Check the spring seat for cracking and hardness; replace it if necessary. Remove the upper insulator from the damper shaft.

4.5 Lift the upper mount off the damper rod

4.6 Remove the upper spring seat and insulator from the damper rod

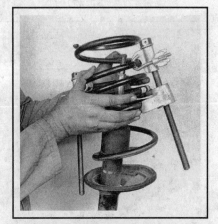

4.7 Remove the compressed spring from the strut/shock absorber assembly - keep the ends of the spring pointed away from your body

7   Carefully lift the compressed spring from the assembly (see illustration) and set it in a safe place.

✳ WARNING:

When removing the compressed spring, lift it off carefully and set it in a safe place. Keep the ends of the spring away from your body.

➡**Note: If you are disassembling both struts, mark the springs LEFT and RIGHT so you don't mix them up (they're different).**

8   Remove the dust cover plate and dust cover.
9   Slide the rubber bump stop off the damper rod. Check the bump stop for cracking and general deterioration. If there is any deterioration of the rubber, replace it.

REASSEMBLY

▸ **Refer to illustration 4.11**

10 Extend the damper rod to its full length and install the rubber bump stop, dust cover and dust cover plate.
11 Carefully place the compressed coil spring onto the lower seat of the damper, with the end of the spring resting in the lowest part of the seat (see illustration).

4.11 When installing the spring, make sure the end fits into the recessed portion of the lower seat

12 Install the upper insulator and spring seat.
13 Install the bearing and suspension support.
14 Install the washer and damper rod nut and tighten it to the torque listed in this Chapter's Specifications. Remove the spring compressor tool.
15 Install the strut/spring assembly (see Section 3).

5   Control arm (front) - removal and installation

▸ **Refer to illustrations 5.4 and 5.6**

1   Loosen the wheel lug nuts, raise the vehicle and support it securely on jackstands. Remove the wheel.
2   Detach the stabilizer bar link from the control arm (see Section 2).
3   Remove the lock-pin from the castle nut on the balljoint stud. Loosen the nut, but don't remove it yet. Using a puller, separate the control arm from the balljoint in the steering knuckle. Remove the nut.
4   Remove the control arm-to-subframe mounting bolts (see illustration).
5   Remove the control arm.
6   Installation is the reverse of removal, noting the following points:

  a) Raise the control arm with a floor jack to simulate normal ride height before tightening the fasteners to the specified torque. Do not place the jack in a position so that it interferes with the tightening of the balljoint nut.
  b) Position the lock-pin so that it's facing the specified direction (see illustration).

➡**Note: If necessary, tighten the nut a little more to allow lock pin insertion. Never loosen the nut in order to align the hole in the balljoint with the castellations in the nut.**

  c) Install the wheel and lug nuts, lower the vehicle and tighten the lug nuts to the torque listed in the Chapter 1 Specifications.

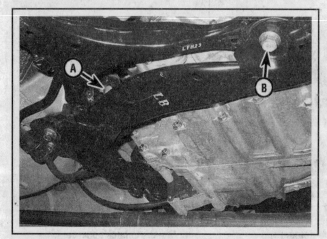

5.4 Remove the control arm rear pivot bolt (A) and the front mounting bolt (B)

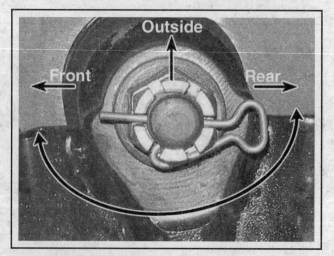

5.6 Install the lock pin from the inside of the vehicle to the outside. Be sure the closed end of the pin is within the range shown

6 Steering knuckle and hub - removal and installation

✳✳ WARNING:

Dust created by the brake system is harmful to your health. Never blow it out with compressed air and don't inhale any of it. Do not, under any circumstances, use petroleum-based solvents to clean brake parts. Use brake system cleaner only.

REMOVAL

1   Loosen the driveaxle/hub nut (see Chapter 8). Loosen the wheel lug nuts, raise the vehicle and support it securely on jackstands. Remove the wheel.

2   Remove the brake caliper and support it with a piece of wire as described in Chapter 9. Remove the caliper mounting bracket, then remove the brake disc from the hub.

3   Mark the strut to the steering knuckle, then loosen, but do not remove the strut-to-steering knuckle bolts (see illustration 3.4).

4   If the vehicle is equipped with ABS, remove the speed sensor (see Chapter 8).

5   Separate the balljoint from the control arm (see Section 5).

6   Disconnect the stabilizer bar attaching link from the lower control arm (see Section 2). The strut-to-knuckle bolts can now be removed.

7   Push the driveaxle from the hub as described in Chapter 8. Support the end of the driveaxle with a piece of wire.

8   Separate the steering knuckle from the strut.

INSTALLATION

9   Guide the knuckle and hub assembly into position, inserting the driveaxle into the hub.

10 Push the knuckle into the strut flange and install the bolts and nuts, but don't tighten them yet.

11 Connect the balljoint to the control arm and install the nut (don't tighten it yet).

12 Tighten the strut bolt nuts, the balljoint-to-control arm nut and the tie-rod nut to the torque values listed in this Chapter's Specifications.

13 Place the brake disc on the hub and install the caliper mounting bracket and caliper as outlined in Chapter 9.

14 Install the driveaxle/hub nut and tighten it securely (final tightening will be carried out when the vehicle is lowered). Install the wheel and lug nuts.

15 Lower the vehicle and tighten the lug nuts to the torque listed in the Chapter 1 Specifications. Tighten the driveaxle/hub nut to the torque listed in the Chapter 8 Specifications.

16 Have the front wheel alignment checked and, if necessary, adjusted.

7 Hub and bearing assembly (front) - replacement

Due to the special tools and expertise required to press the hub and bearing from the steering knuckle, this job should be left to a professional mechanic. However, the steering knuckle and hub may be removed and the assembly taken to an automotive machine shop or other qualified repair facility equipped with the necessary tools. See Section 6 for the steering knuckle and hub removal procedure.

8 Shock absorber/coil spring assembly (rear) - removal, component replacement and installation

REMOVAL

⏵ **Refer to illustrations 8.2 and 8.3**

1   Loosen the rear wheel lug nuts. Raise the rear of the vehicle and support it securely on jackstands. Block the front wheels to prevent the vehicle from rolling. Remove the wheel.

2   Remove the side trim panels from the trunk (Coupe and Sedan models) or from the cargo area (CR-V and Hatchback models). Remove the shock absorber upper mounting nuts (see illustration).

3   Remove the shock absorber lower mounting bolt (see illustration), then remove the shock absorber/coil spring assembly.

4   Check the shock body for leaking fluid, dents, cracks and other obvious damage which would warrant repair or replacement.

5   Check the coil spring for chips or cracks in the spring coating (this will cause premature spring failure due to corrosion). Inspect the spring seat for cuts, hardness and general deterioration.

6   If any undesirable conditions exist, proceed to the component replacement procedure.

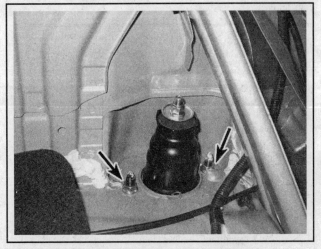

8.2 Remove the nuts from the shock absorber mounting studs - don't remove the larger nut in the center

COMPONENT REPLACEMENT

➡Note: if the shocks or coil springs exhibit the telltale signs of wear (leaking fluid, loss of damping capability, chipped, sagging or cracked coil springs) explore all options before beginning any work. The shock absorber/coil spring assemblies are not serviceable and must be replaced if a problem develops. However, assemblies complete with springs may be available on an exchange basis, which eliminates much time and work. Whichever route you choose to take, check on the cost and availability of parts before disassembling your vehicle.

❉❉ WARNING:

Disassembling a shock/coil spring is potentially dangerous and utmost attention must be directed to the job, or serious injury may result. Use only a high-quality spring compressor and carefully follow the manufacturer's instructions furnished with the tool. After removing the coil spring from the shock assembly, set it aside in a safe, isolated area.

7   Mount the shock/coil spring assembly in a vise. Line the vise jaws with wood or rags to prevent damage to the unit and don't tighten the vise excessively.

8   Following the tool manufacturer's instructions, install the spring compressor (which can be obtained at most auto parts stores or equipment yards on a daily rental basis) on the spring and compress it sufficiently to relieve all pressure from the upper spring seat. This can be verified by wiggling the spring.

➡Note: Note the orientation of the upper mount in relation to the lower mounting eye (when reassembling the unit the mount will have to be in the same position). Make a sketch or some matchmarks to help you get the mount positioned properly when reinstalling it.

9   Hold the shock damper rod with an Allen wrench, and unscrew the retaining nut with a box-end wrench.

10   Disassemble the parts from the damper, taking care to lay the parts out in the exact order in which they are removed.

❉❉ WARNING:

When removing the compressed spring, lift it off carefully and set it in a safe place. Keep the ends of the spring away from your body

8.3 Rear shock absorber lower mounting bolt

11   Reassembly is the reverse of removal, noting the following points:
  a) Carefully place the spring onto the shock absorber body, with the end of the spring resting in the lowest part of the seat.
  b) Use a new self-locking nut, then tighten the nut to the torque listed in this Chapter's Specifications.
  c) Before releasing the spring compressor, make sure the upper mount is oriented as it was before removal in Step 8.

INSTALLATION

12   Guide the shock absorber/coil spring assembly up into the fenderwell and insert the upper mounting studs through the holes in the body. Once the studs protrude from the holes, install the nuts so the assembly won't fall back through, but don't tighten the nuts completely yet. The shock absorber is heavy and awkward, so get an assistant to help you, if possible.

13   Connect the shock to the trailing arm. Raise the trailing arm with the floor jack to simulate normal ride height, Tighten the shock absorber lower mounting bolt to the torque listed in this Chapter's Specifications.

14   Install the wheel and lug nuts, lower the vehicle and tighten the lug nuts to the torque listed in the Chapter 1 Specifications.

15   Tighten the upper mounting nuts to the torque listed in this Chapter's Specifications.

9   Suspension arms (rear) - removal and installation

1   Loosen the rear wheel lug nuts. Raise the rear of the vehicle and support it securely on jackstands. Block the front wheels to prevent the vehicle from rolling. Remove the wheel.

UPPER ARM

▸ Refer to illustration 9.4

2   On models with ABS, remove the ABS wheel speed sensor and unbolt the harness bracket from the upper arm.

3   Support the trailing arm with a floor jack.

❉❉ WARNING:

The jack must remain in this position until the new arm is installed.

4   Remove the upper arm-to-knuckle bolt, then remove the mounting/pivot bolt(s) from the inner end of the arm (see illustration).

5   Installation is the reverse of removal, noting the following points:
  a) Before fully tightening the fasteners, raise the trailing arm with the floor jack to simulate normal ride height.

9.4 Upper arm pivot and mounting bolts

9.6 Mark the relationship of the toe adjusting cam to the trailing arm

b) *Tighten all fasteners to the proper torque specifications.*
c) *Tighten the wheel lug nuts to the torque listed in the Chapter 1 Specifications.*
d) *Have the rear wheel alignment checked and, if necessary, adjusted.*

TRAILING ARM

▶ **Refer to illustrations 9.6, 9.9, 9.10a and 9.10b**

6   Mark the relationship of the toe adjusting cam to the trailing arm (see illustration), then support the trailing arm with a floor jack.

7   Remove the trailing arm-to-knuckle bolts, then disconnect the arm from the knuckle (see illustration).

➡**Note: Suspend the knuckle with a bungee cord or piece of wire.**

8   Disconnect the stabilizer bar link from the trailing arm (see Sec-

tion 11).

9   Remove the shock absorber lower mounting bolt and disconnect the shock from the trailing arm (see illustration 8.3).

10   Remove the trailing arm-to-chassis front mounting bolts, then remove the trailing arm-to-chassis pivot bolt (see illustrations).

11   Remove the trailing arm.

12   Installation is the reverse of removal, noting the following points:

a) *Align the mark you made on the adjuster cam with the mark on the trailing arm.*
b) *Before fully tightening the fasteners, raise the trailing arm with the floor jack to simulate normal ride height.*
c) *Tighten all fasteners to the proper torque specifications.*
d) *Tighten the wheel lug nuts to the torque listed in the Chapter 1 Specifications.*
e) *Have the rear wheel alignment checked and, if necessary, adjusted.*

9.7 Remove the knuckle-to-trailing arm bolts

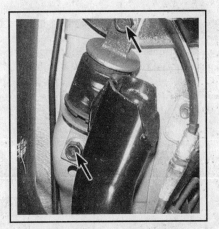

9.10a Remove the trailing arm-to-chassis front mounting bolts . . .

9.10b . . . and the trailing arm-to-chassis pivot bolt

10 Hub and bearing assembly (rear) - removal and installation

❋ WARNING:

Dust created by the brake system is harmful to your health. Never blow it out with compressed air and don't inhale any of it. Do not, under any circumstances, use petroleum-based solvents to clean brake parts. Use brake system cleaner only.

COUPE, SEDAN AND HATCHBACK MODELS

▶ **Refer to illustrations 10.3a, 10.3b and 10.5**

➡**Note: The rear hub and bearing are combined into a single assembly. The bearing is sealed for life and requires no lubrication or attention. If the bearing is worn or damaged, replace the entire hub and bearing assembly.**

1   Loosen the rear wheel lug nuts, raise the rear of the vehicle, support it securely on jackstands. Block the front wheels to prevent the vehicle from rolling. Remove the wheels.

2   Remove the brake drum or disc (see Chapter 9).

3   Remove the dust cover then unstake and remove the hub retaining nut (see illustrations).

4   Remove the hub and bearing assembly from the spindle.

5   Installation is the reverse of removal, noting the following points:

   a) *Install a new hub retaining nut and tighten it to the torque listed in this Chapter's Specifications. Stake the new hub nut in place (see illustration).*

➡**Note: Apply a little clean engine oil to the seating surface of the hub retaining nut before installing it.**

   b) *Install the dust cover by tapping lightly around the edge until it is seated.*

   c) *On models with rear disc brakes, tighten the caliper mounting bolts to the torque listed in the Chapter 9 Specifications.*

   d) *Install the wheel and lug nuts. Lower the vehicle and tighten the lug nuts to the torque listed in the Chapter 1 Specifications.*

CR-V MODELS

➡**Note: Due to the special tools and expertise required to press the hub and bearing from the knuckle, this job should be left to a professional mechanic. However, the knuckle and hub may be removed and the assembly taken to an automotive machine shop or other qualified repair facility equipped with the necessary tools.**

6   If you're working on a 4WD model, loosen the rear driveaxle/hub nut (see Chapter 8).

7   Loosen the rear wheel lug nuts, raise the rear of the vehicle, support it securely on jackstands and remove the wheels.

8   Remove the brake caliper and disc (see Chapter 9).

9   If you're working on a 2WD model, unstake and remove the hub retaining nut.

10 Remove the parking brake shoes, wheel speed sensor and parking brake cable (see Chapter 9).

11 Support the trailing arm with a floor jack, then disconnect the suspension arms from the knuckle (see Section 9).

12 On 4WD models, carefully separate the driveaxle from the knuckle and hub assembly as described in Chapter 8. Support the end of the driveaxle with a piece of wire.

13 Remove the knuckle along with the brake backing plate from the vehicle.

10.3a Using a hammer and chisel, remove the dust cover

10.3b Unstake the hub nut

10.5 Stake the hub nut back into place

14 Installation is the reverse of removal, noting the following points:

a) *Before fully tightening the suspension arm fasteners, raise the trailing arm with a floor jack to simulate normal ride height.*

b) *Align the matchmarks on the toe adjusting cam (see Section 9).*

c) *Tighten all fasteners to the proper torque specifications.*

d) *Install a new hub retaining or driveaxle nut and tighten it to the torque listed in this Chapter's Specifications. Stake the new hub nut in place.*

➡**Note: Apply a little clean engine oil to the seating surface of the hub retaining nut before installing it.**

e) *Tighten the caliper mounting bolts to the torque listed in the Chapter 9 Specifications.*

f) *It won't be necessary to bleed the brakes unless a hydraulic fitting was loosened.*

g) *Have the rear wheel alignment checked and, if necessary, adjusted.*

11 Stabilizer bar and bushings (rear) - removal, inspection and installation

▶ **Refer to illustrations 11.2a and 11.2b**

1 Loosen the rear wheel lug nuts. Raise the rear of the vehicle and place securely on jackstands. Block the front wheels to prevent the vehicle from rolling. Remove the rear wheels.

2 Remove the stabilizer bar-to-link nuts and the stabilizer bar-to-body clamp bolts and remove the stabilizer bar (see illustrations).

3 Pull the brackets off the stabilizer bar and inspect the bushings for cracks, hardness and other signs of deterioration. If the bushings are damaged, replace them.

4 Installation is the reverse of removal.

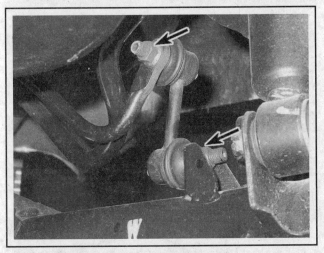

11.2a Stabilizer bar link attaching nuts

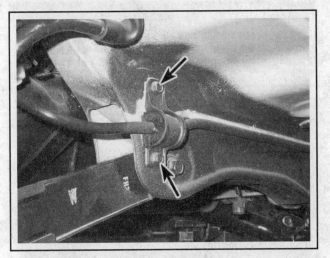

11.2b Stabilizer bar bracket bolts

12 Steering wheel - removal and installation

❋❋ WARNING 1:

These models are equipped with a Supplemental Restraint System (SRS), more commonly known as airbags. Always disable the airbag system before working in the vicinity of any airbag system component to avoid the possibility of accidental deployment of the airbag(s), which could cause personal injury (see Chapter 12).

❋❋ WARNING 2:

Do not use a memory saving device to preserve the PCM or radio memory when working on or near airbag system components.

REMOVAL

▶ **Refer to illustrations 12.2, 12.3, 12.4, 12.6 and 12.8**

1 Make sure the front wheels are pointed straight ahead, then disconnect the cable from the negative terminal of the battery (see Chapter 5, Section 1). Wait at least three minutes before proceeding.

12.2 Remove the panel from the underside of the steering wheel

2 Remove the airbag connector access panel from the bottom of the steering wheel (see illustration).

3 Unplug the airbag module connector (see illustration).

4 On each side of the steering wheel, remove the fasteners retaining the airbag module to the steering wheel (see illustration).

5 Pull off the airbag module, then carefully set it in a safe location.

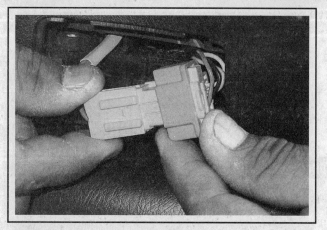

12.3 Disconnect the electrical connector for the airbag module

6   Disconnect the connectors for the horn and the cruise control switch (see illustration).

12.6 Disconnect the electrical connectors for the cruise control and horn

12.8 Use a steering wheel puller to remove the steering wheel

12.4 Remove the airbag fasteners on each side of the steering wheel

7   Loosen the steering wheel retaining bolt until about 1/2-inch of threads are showing between the bolt head and the steering wheel.

8   Remove the steering wheel using a steering wheel puller (see illustration). The puller screw must be contacting the steering wheel bolt or shaft.

Once the steering wheel has been released from the shaft, remove the puller and retaining bolt, make a mark indicating the relationship of the steering wheel hub to the steering shaft, then pull the steering wheel off the shaft.

9   If it is necessary to remove the clockspring, remove the steering column covers (see Chapter 11).

10 Unplug the clockspring electrical connectors, then release the locking tabs and detach it from the column.

INSTALLATION

11 With the front wheels pointed straight ahead, make sure that the airbag clockspring is centered with the arrow on the clockspring pointing up. This shouldn't be a problem as long as you have not turned the steering shaft while the wheel was removed. If for some reason the shaft was turned, center the clockspring as follows:

 a) *Rotate the clockspring clockwise until it stops.*
 b) *Rotate the clockspring counterclockwise about 2-1/2 turns until the arrow on the clockspring points straight up.*

12 Be sure to align the index mark on the steering wheel hub with the mark on the shaft when you slip the wheel onto the shaft. Make sure the locating pins on the clockspring engage the holes in the backside of the steering wheel, and the notches in the steering wheel hub engage the tabs on the turn signal canceling cam. Install a NEW steering wheel bolt and tighten it to the torque listed in this Chapter's Specifications.

13 Connect the horn and the cruise control switch connectors.

14 Reattach the airbag module using NEW fasteners and tighten them to the torque listed in this Chapter's Specifications.

15 Plug in the electrical connector for the airbag module.

16 Reconnect the negative battery cable (see Chapter 5, Section 1).

13 Steering column - removal and installation

❋❋ WARNING 1:

These models are equipped with a Supplemental Restraint System (SRS), more commonly known as airbags. Always disable the airbag system before working in the vicinity of any airbag system component to avoid the possibility of accidental deployment of the airbag(s), which could cause personal injury (see Chapter 12).

❋❋ WARNING 2:

Do not use a memory saving device to preserve the PCM or radio memory when working on or near airbag system components.

REMOVAL

▶ Refer to illustration 13.7

1   Park the vehicle with the wheels pointing straight ahead. Disconnect the cable from the negative terminal of the battery (see Chapter 5, Section 1).
2   Adjust the steering wheel tilt to the Neutral position, approximately 8 mm down from the uppermost position.
3   Remove the steering wheel (see Section 12). Prevent the steering shaft from turning.

❋❋ CAUTION:

If this is not done, the airbag clockspring could be damaged.

4   Remove the steering column covers (see Chapter 11).
5   Remove the clockspring (see Section 12).
6   Remove the steering column switches (see Chapter 12).
7   Mark the relationship of the intermediate shaft to the steering

13.7 Mark the relationship of the intermediate shaft to the steering gear U-joint (A), then remove the pinch bolt (B)

gear U-joint, then remove the pinch bolt (see illustration).
8   Remove the steering column mounting fasteners, lower the column and pull it to the rear, making sure nothing is still connected, then remove the column.

INSTALLATION

9   Guide the steering column into position, then install the steering column mounting fasteners and tighten them to the torque listed in this Chapter's Specifications.
10 Connect the U-joint to the intermediate shaft. Install the intermediate shaft pinch bolt and nut, tightening it to the torque listed in this Chapter's Specifications.
11 The remainder of installation is the reverse of removal. Reconnect the negative battery cable (see Chapter 5, Section 1).

14 Tie-rod ends - removal and installation

REMOVAL

▶ Refer to illustrations 14.2, 14.3 and 14.4

1   Loosen the wheel lug nuts, raise the front of the vehicle and support it securely on jackstands. Apply the parking brake and block the rear wheels to keep the vehicle from rolling off the jackstands. Remove the wheel.
2   Loosen the tie-rod end jam nut (see illustration).
3   Mark the relationship of the tie-rod end to the threaded portion of the tie-rod. This will ensure the toe-in setting is restored when reassembled (see illustration).

14.2 Using a back-up wrench to prevent the tie-rod end from turning, loosen the jam nut

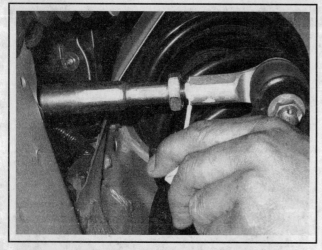

14.3 Back off the jam nut and mark the exposed threads to ensure that the new tie-rod end is threaded on the same number of turns

4   Remove the cotter pin and loosen the nut from the tie-rod end ballstud a few turns. Disconnect the tie-rod end ballstud from the steering arm with a puller (see illustration).

5   Remove the nut from the ballstud, separate the tie-rod end from the steering knuckle, and then unscrew the tie-rod end from the tie-rod.

INSTALLATION

6   Thread the tie-rod end onto the tie-rod to the marked position

14.4 Use a two-jaw puller or balljoint separator to push the tie-rod end out of the steering arm

and connect the tie-rod end to the steering arm. Install the nut on the ballstud and tighten it to the torque listed in this Chapter's Specifications. Install a new cotter pin.

➡**Note: If necessary, tighten the nut a little more to allow insertion of the cotter pin. Never loosen the nut to align the cotter pin holes.**

7   Tighten the jam nut securely and install the wheel. Lower the vehicle and tighten the lug nuts to the torque listed in the Chapter 1 Specifications.

8   Have the front end alignment checked and, if necessary, adjusted.

15   Steering gear - removal and installation

✳✳ WARNING:

Make sure the steering shaft is not turned while the steering gear is removed or you could damage the clockspring for the airbag system. To prevent the shaft from turning, place the ignition key in the lock position or thread the seat belt through the steering wheel and clip it into place.

15.3 Mark the relationship of the intermediate shaft and the steering gear output shaft to the steering gear U-joint (A), then remove the pinch bolts (B)

REMOVAL

1   Park the vehicle with the front wheels pointing straight ahead. Loosen the front wheel lug nuts, raise the front of the vehicle and support it securely on jackstands. Apply the parking brake and remove the wheels.

2   Disconnect the cable from the negative terminal of the battery (see Chapter 5, Section 1).

Coupe, Sedan and CR-V models

▶ **Refer to illustrations 15.3, 15.5, 15.6, 15.9a and 15.9b**

3   Mark the relationship of the universal joint to the steering gear input shaft and the intermediate shaft. Remove the universal joint pinch bolts and separate the shafts from joint (see illustration).

4   Remove the air filter housing assembly (see Chapter 4).

5   Separate the heater valve from the firewall (see illustration).

6   Place a drain pan under the steering gear. Detach the power steering pressure and return lines (see illustration) and cap the ends to prevent excessive fluid loss and contamination.

7   Separate the tie-rod ends from the steering arms (see Section 14).

8   Disconnect the pressure line clamp and engine harness from the steering gear.

9   Remove the steering gear mounting nuts and bolts (see illustration), then pull on the steering gear to release it from the right-side mounting stud.

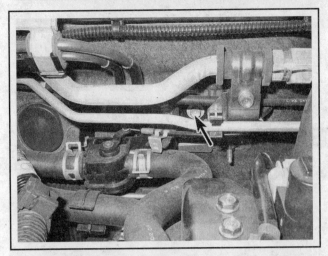

15.5 Remove the fastener securing the clamp and release the heater valve from the firewall

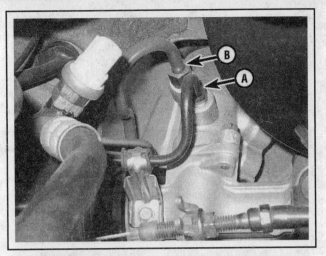

15.6 Disconnect the pressure (A) and return (B) lines from the steering gear (Sedan model shown, other models similar)

10 Remove the bolts securing the right-side bracket, then remove the bracket.

11 Lower the steering gearbox, then rotate the steering gear so that the input shaft is pointing upward. Carefully guide the steering gear assembly through the right wheel opening and remove it from the vehicle.

Hatchback models

12 Mark the relationship of the universal joint to the steering gear input shaft and the intermediate shaft. Remove the universal joint pinch bolts and separate the shafts from the joint (see illustration 15.3).

13 Remove the air filter housing assembly (see Chapter 4).

14 Working at the steering gear, remove the bracket securing the power steering motor electrical connector, then disconnect the connector.

15 Remove the fasteners securing the power steering motor, then remove the motor.

16 Separate the tie-rod ends from the steering arms (see Section 14).

17 Remove the exhaust heat shield from the floor pan and let it rest on the exhaust pipe.

18 Disconnect the electrical connector for the steering gear, then separate the connector mounting bracket. Remove the ground connec-

tion at the steering gear.

19 Working in the engine compartment, separate the engine wire harness from the mounting brackets securing it to the firewall.

20 Separate the heater valve from the firewall (see illustration 15.5).

21 Remove the fasteners securing the body stiffener, then remove the stiffener.

22 Remove the steering gear mounting nuts and bolts, then pull on the steering gear to release it from the right-side mounting stud.

23 Lower the steering gearbox, then rotate the steering gear so that the input shaft is pointing upward. Carefully guide the steering gear assembly through the right wheel opening, then raise the left side of the steering gear up through the engine compartment and remove it from the vehicle.

INSTALLATION

24 Installation is the reverse of removal, noting the following points:

a) *Raise the steering gear into position and connect the U-joint, aligning the marks.*

b) *Install the mounting bolts and nuts and tighten them to the torque listed in this Chapter's Specifications.*

15.9a Remove the steering gear mounting nuts . . .

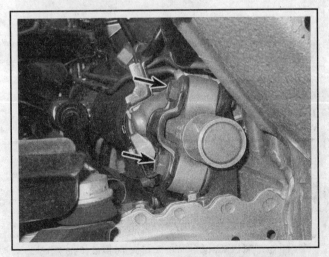

15.9b . . . and bolts

c) Install the U-joint pinch bolts and tighten them to the torque listed in this Chapter's Specifications.
d) If you're working on a Hatchback model, be sure to use a new O-ring when installing the power steering motor.
e) Install the wheels and lug nuts. Lower the vehicle, then tighten the lug nuts to the torque listed in the Chapter 1 Specifications.

f) If you're working on a Coupe, Sedan or CR-V model, fill the power steering pump reservoir with the recommended fluid (see Chapter 1). Then bleed the steering system (see Section 17).
g) Have the front wheel alignment checked and, if necessary, adjusted.

16 Power steering pump - removal and installation

▶ **Refer to illustration 16.2**

1 Disconnect the cable from the negative battery terminal (see Chapter 5, Section 1).

2 Clamp the power steering feed hose shut so fluid loss will be minimized when the hose is disconnected, then disconnect the fluid hoses at the pump (see illustration). Note the difference between the pressure and the return hoses; the return hose is held to the pump with a spring type clamp, and the pressure line has two bolts holding it to the pump body. Cap or plug both hoses to prevent leakage or contamination. Install a new O-ring on the end of the pressure line.

3 Remove the pump adjusting bolt.

4 Remove the pump mounting nuts/bolts and remove the pump from the engine.

5 Installation is the reverse of removal. Be sure to adjust the drivebelt tension (see Chapter 1) and bleed the power steering system (see Section 17).

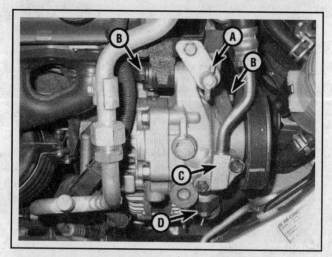

16.2 Power steering pump details (Coupe and Sedan models shown, CR-V similar)

A)	Adjusting bolt	C)	Pressure line
B)	Mounting nuts	D)	Feed hose and clamp

17 Power steering system - bleeding

1 The power steering system must be bled whenever a line is disconnected. Bubbles can be seen in power steering fluid that has air in it and the fluid will often have a tan or milky appearance. Low fluid level can cause air to mix with the fluid, resulting in a noisy pump as well as foaming of the fluid.

2 Open the hood and check the fluid level in the reservoir, adding the specified fluid necessary to bring it up to the proper level (see Chapter 1).

3 Start the engine and slowly turn the steering wheel several times from left-to-right and back again. Do not turn the wheel completely from lock-to-lock. Check the fluid level, topping it up as necessary until it remains steady and no more bubbles are visible.

18 Subframe - removal and installation

✸✸ WARNING:

The manufacturer recommends replacing the subframe bolts with new ones whenever they are removed.

REMOVAL

▶ **Refer to illustrations 18.12**

1 Disconnect the cable from the negative battery terminal (see Chapter 5, Section 1).

2 Loosen the front wheel lug nuts, raise the front of the vehicle and support it securely on jackstands. Remove both front wheels.

➡**Note: The jackstands must be behind the front suspension subframe, not supporting the vehicle by the subframe.**

3 Remove the engine splash shield (see Chapter 2A).

4 Remove the exhaust pipe from the exhaust manifold to the catalytic converter (see Chapter 6).

5 Disconnect the stabilizer bar links from the control arms (see Section 2).

6 Disconnect the control arms from the steering knuckles (see Section 5).

7 On automatic transaxle models, disconnect the shift control cable from the transaxle (see Chapter 7B).

8 Carefully mark the position of the subframe in relation to the vehicle chassis.

18.12 Subframe details (Coupe and Sedan models shown, CR-V and Hatchback similar)

A)   Subframe mounting bolts   *B)   Alignment reference holes*

9   Using two floor jacks, support the subframe. Position one jack on each side of the subframe, midway between the front and rear mounting points.

10 Roll an engine hoist into position and attach it to the engine with a couple pieces of heavy-duty chain. If the engine is equipped with lifting brackets, use them. If not, you'll have to fasten the chain to some substantial part of the engine - one that is strong enough to take the weight, but in a location that will provide good balance. If you're attaching the chain to a stud on the engine, or are using a bolt passing through the chain and into a threaded hole, place a washer between the nut or bolt head and the chain, and tighten the nut or bolt securely. Take up the slack in the chain, but don't lift the engine.

⁂ WARNING:

DO NOT place any part of your body under the engine when it's supported only by a hoist or other lifting device.

11 Remove the engine mount and the transaxle mount (see Chapter 2A or 2B).

12 Make alignment marks from each corner of the subframe to the vehicle body. With the jacks sufficiently supporting the subframe, remove the four subframe-to-chassis mounting bolts (see illustration).

13 Lower the jacks until the subframe is resting on the ground.

INSTALLATION

14 Installation is the reverse of removal, noting the following points:

a) *Replace the subframe bolts with new ones. Align the reference marks on the subframe then tighten the subframe mounting bolts to the torque listed in this Chapter's Specifications.*

b) *Reconnect the negative battery cable (see Chapter 5, Section 1).*

c) *Have the front end alignment checked and, if necessary, adjusted.*

19 Wheels and tires - general information

▶ **Refer to illustration 19.1**

1   All vehicles covered by this manual are equipped with metric-sized fiberglass or steel belted radial tires (see illustration). Use of other size or type of tires may affect the ride and handling of the vehicle. Don't mix different types of tires, such as radials and bias belted, on the same vehicle as handling may be seriously affected. It's recommended that tires be replaced in pairs on the same axle, but if only one tire is being replaced, be sure it's the same size, structure and tread design as the other.

2   Because tire pressure has a substantial effect on handling and wear, the pressure on all tires should be checked at least once a month or before any extended trips (see Chapter 1).

3   Wheels must be replaced if they are bent, dented, leak air, have elongated bolt holes, are heavily rusted, out of vertical symmetry or if the lug nuts won't stay tight. Wheel repairs that use welding or peening are not recommended.

4   Tire and wheel balance is important in the overall handling, braking and performance of the vehicle. Unbalanced wheels can adversely affect handling and ride characteristics as well as tire life. Whenever a tire is installed on a wheel, the tire and wheel should be balanced by a shop with the proper equipment.

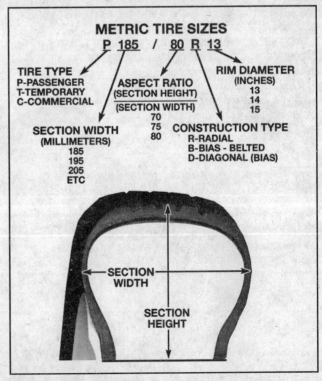

19.1 Metric tire size code

20 Wheel alignment - general information

▶ **Refer to illustration 20.1**

A wheel alignment refers to the adjustments made to the wheels so they are in proper angular relationship to the suspension and the ground. Wheels that are out of proper alignment not only affect vehicle control, but also increase tire wear. The front end angles normally measured are camber, caster and toe-in (see illustration). Toe-in is the only routine adjustment made; camber on the front end is adjustable, but only after installing special strut-to-knuckle bolts. If the caster is not correct, check for bent components.

Getting the proper wheel alignment is a very exacting process, one in which complicated and expensive machines are necessary to perform the job properly. Because of this, you should have a technician with the proper equipment perform these tasks. We will, however, use this space to give you a basic idea of what is involved with a wheel alignment so you can better understand the process and deal intelligently with the shop that does the work.

Toe-in is the turning in of the wheels. The purpose of a toe specification is to ensure parallel rolling of the wheels. In a vehicle with zero toe-in, the distance between the front edges of the wheels will be the same as the distance between the rear edges of the wheels. The actual amount of toe-in is normally only a fraction of an inch. At the front end, toe-in is controlled by the tie-rod end position on the tie-rod. At the rear, it's adjusted by a cam bolt at the inner end of control arm B. Incorrect toe-in will cause the tires to wear improperly by making them scrub against the road surface.

Camber is the tilting of the wheels from vertical when viewed from one end of the vehicle. When the wheels tilt out at the top, the camber is said to be positive (+). When the wheels tilt in at the top the camber is negative (-). The amount of tilt is measured in degrees from vertical and this measurement is called the camber angle. This angle affects the amount of tire tread which contacts the road and compensates for changes in the suspension geometry when the vehicle is cornering or traveling over an undulating surface. On the front end it is adjusted using special camber adjusting bolts, which alter the relationship between the strut and the steering knuckle. At the rear end camber is not adjustable.

Caster is the tilting of the front steering axis from vertical. A tilt toward the rear is positive caster and a tilt toward the front is negative caster.

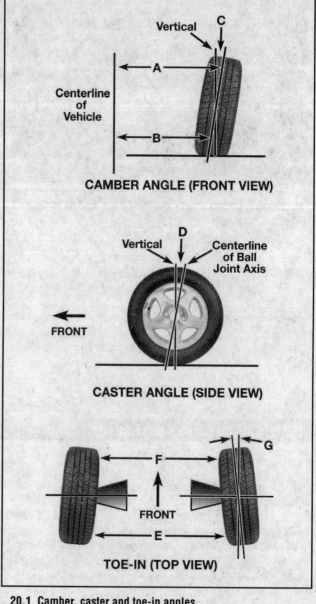

CAMBER ANGLE (FRONT VIEW)

CASTER ANGLE (SIDE VIEW)

TOE-IN (TOP VIEW)

20.1 Camber, caster and toe-in angles

A minus B = C (degrees camber)
D = degrees caster
E minus F = toe-in (measured in inches)
G = toe-in (expressed in degrees)

Specifications

General

Power steering fluid type	See Chapter 1

Torque specifications	Ft-lbs (unless otherwise indicated)	Nm
Front suspension		
Strut		
Damper rod nut	33	44
Strut upper mounting nuts	33	44
Strut-to-steering knuckle bolts/nuts		
Coupe and Sedan models		
2002 and earlier models	76	103
2003 and later models	116	157
Hatchback and CR-V models	116	157
Stabilizer bar		
Stabilizer bar link-to-control arm nut	29	39
Stabilizer bar link-to-stabilizer bar	28	38
Stabilizer bar bracket bolts	29	39
Control arm		
Arm-to-subframe	61	83
Balljoint-to-control arm nut	43 to 51	59 to 69
Driveaxle/hub nut	See Chapter 8	
Rear suspension		
Rear hub retaining nut	134	181
Shock absorber		
Upper mounting nuts		
Coupe, Sedan and Hatchback models	43	59
CR-V models	54	74
Lower mounting bolt		
Coupe, Sedan and Hatchback models	45	61
CR-V models	69	93
Damper rod nut	22	29
Stabilizer bar		
Clamp bolts	16	22
Link-to-trailing arm nuts	29	39
Link-to-stabilizer bar nuts		
Coupe, Sedan and Hatchback models	28	38
CR-V models	22	29
Trailing arm-to-chassis mounting bolts		
Coupe, Sedan and Hatchback models	80	108
CR-V models	85	115
Trailing arm-to-chassis pivot bolt	43	59
Trailing arm-to-knuckle bolts	43	59
Upper arm-to-knuckle pivot bolt	43	59
Upper arm-to-chassis mounting bolts		
Coupe, Sedan and Hatchback models	80	108
Upper arm-to-chassis pivot bolt (CR-V models)	69	93

| Torque specifications | Ft-lbs (unless otherwise indicated) | Nm |

➡**Note: One foot-pound (ft-lb) of torque is equivalent to 12 inch-pounds (in-lbs) of torque. Torque values below approximately 15 ft-lbs are expressed in inch-pounds, since most foot-pound torque wrenches are not accurate at these smaller values.**

Steering system

	Ft-lbs	Nm
Airbag module-to-steering wheel fasteners	86 in-lbs	9.8
Power steering pump-to-engine bracket		
mounting fasteners	14	20
Coupe and Sedan models	17	24
CR-V models	16	22
Power steering motor bolts (Hatchback models)	14	20
Steering gear mounting bolts/nuts	45	61
Tie-rod end-to-steering knuckle nut	32	43
Intermediate shaft-to-universal joint pinch-bolt		
Coupe and Sedan models	22	29
Hatchback and CR-V models	21	28
Steering gear input shaft-to-universal joint pinch-bolt		
Coupe and Sedan models	22	29
Hatchback and CR-V models	21	28
Steering column mounting fasteners	12	16
Steering wheel mounting bolt/nut	29	39

Section

11

BODY

1 General information

These models feature a "unibody" layout, using a floor pan with front and rear frame side rails which support the body components, and front and rear subframes which support suspension systems and other mechanical components.

Certain components are particularly vulnerable to accident damage and can be unbolted and repaired or replaced. Among these parts are the body moldings, bumpers, front fenders, the hood and trunk lid (or liftgate) and all glass.

Only general body maintenance practices and body panel repair procedures within the scope of the do-it-yourselfer are included in this Chapter.

2 Body - maintenance

1 The condition of your vehicle's body is very important, because the resale value depends a great deal on it. It's much more difficult to repair a neglected or damaged body than it is to repair mechanical components. The hidden areas of the body, such as the wheel wells, the frame and the engine compartment, are equally important, although they don't require as frequent attention as the rest of the body.

2 Once a year, or every 12,000 miles, it's a good idea to have the underside of the body steam cleaned. All traces of dirt and oil will be removed and the area can then be inspected carefully for rust, damaged brake lines, frayed electrical wires, damaged cables and other problems.

3 At the same time, clean the engine and the engine compartment with a steam cleaner or water soluble degreaser.

4 The wheel wells should be given close attention, since under-coating can peel away and stones and dirt thrown up by the tires can cause the paint to chip and flake, allowing rust to set in. If rust is found, clean down to the bare metal and apply an anti-rust paint.

5 The body should be washed about once a week. Wet the vehicle thoroughly to soften the dirt, then wash it down with a soft sponge and plenty of clean soapy water. If the surplus dirt is not washed off very carefully, it can wear down the paint.

6 Spots of tar or asphalt thrown up from the road should be removed with a cloth soaked in solvent.

7 Once every six months, wax the body and chrome trim. If a chrome cleaner is used to remove rust from any of the vehicle's plated parts, remember that the cleaner also removes part of the chrome, so use it sparingly.

3 Vinyl trim - maintenance

Don't clean vinyl trim with detergents, caustic soap or petroleum based cleaners. Plain soap and water works just fine, with a soft brush to clean dirt that may be ingrained. Wash the vinyl as frequently as the rest of the vehicle.

After cleaning, application of a high quality rubber and vinyl protectant will help prevent oxidation and cracks. The protectant can also be applied to weather-stripping, vacuum lines and rubber hoses, which often fail as a result of chemical degradation, and to the tires.

4 Upholstery and carpets - maintenance

1 Every three months remove the carpets or mats and clean the interior of the vehicle (more frequently if necessary). Vacuum the upholstery and carpets to remove loose dirt and dust.

2 Leather upholstery requires special care. Stains should be removed with warm water and a very mild soap solution. Use a clean, damp cloth to remove the soap, then wipe again with a dry cloth. Never use alcohol, gasoline, nail polish remover or thinner to clean leather upholstery.

3 After cleaning, regularly treat leather upholstery with a leather wax. Never use car wax on leather upholstery.

4 In areas where the interior of the vehicle is subject to bright sunlight, cover leather seats with a sheet if the vehicle is to be left out for any length of time.

5 Body repair - minor damage

PLASTIC BODY PANELS

The following repair procedures are for minor scratches and gouges. Repair of more serious damage should be left to a dealer service department or qualified auto body shop. Below is a list of the equipment and materials necessary to perform the following repair procedures on plastic body panels. Although a specific brand of material may be mentioned, it should be noted that equivalent products from other manufacturers may be used instead.

Wax, grease and silicone removing solvent
Cloth-backed body tape
Sanding discs
Drill motor with three-inch disc holder
Hand sanding block

Rubber squeegees
Sandpaper
Non-porous mixing palette
Wood paddle or putty knife
Curved tooth body file
Flexible parts repair material

FLEXIBLE PANELS (FRONT AND REAR BUMPER FASCIA)

1 Remove the damaged panel, if necessary or desirable. In most cases, repairs can be carried out with the panel installed.

2 Clean the area(s) to be repaired with a wax, grease and silicone removing solvent applied with a water-dampened cloth.

3 If the damage is structural, that is, if it extends through the panel, clean the backside of the panel area to be repaired as well. Wipe dry.

4 Sand the rear surface about 1-1/2 inches beyond the break.

5 Cut two pieces of fiberglass cloth large enough to overlap the break by about 1-1/2 inches. Cut only to the required length.

6 Mix the adhesive from the repair kit according to the instructions included with the kit, and apply a layer of the mixture approximately 1/8-inch thick on the backside of the panel. Overlap the break by at least 1-1/2 inches.

7 Apply one piece of fiberglass cloth to the adhesive and cover the cloth with additional adhesive. Apply a second piece of fiberglass cloth to the adhesive and immediately cover the cloth with additional adhesive insufficient quantity to fill the weave.

8 Allow the repair to cure for 20 to 30 minutes at 60-degrees to 80-degrees F.

9 If necessary, trim the excess repair material at the edge.

10 Remove all of the paint film over and around the area(s) to be repaired. The repair material should not overlap the painted surface.

11 With a drill motor and a sanding disc (or a rotary file), cut a "V" along the break line approximately 1/2-inch wide. Remove all dust and loose particles from the repair area.

12 Mix and apply the repair material. Apply a light coat first over the damaged area; then continue applying material until it reaches a level slightly higher than the surrounding finish.

13 Cure the mixture for 20 to 30 minutes at 60-degrees to 80-degrees F.

14 Roughly establish the contour of the area being repaired with a body file. If low areas or pits remain, mix and apply additional adhesive.

15 Block sand the damaged area with sandpaper to establish the actual contour of the surrounding surface.

16 If desired, the repaired area can be temporarily protected with several light coats of primer. Because of the special paints and techniques required for flexible body panels, it is recommended that the vehicle be taken to a paint shop for completion of the body repair.

STEEL BODY PANELS

See photo sequence

Repair of minor scratches

17 If the scratch is superficial and does not penetrate to the metal of the body, repair is very simple. Lightly rub the scratched area with a fine rubbing compound to remove loose paint and built-up wax. Rinse the area with clean water.

18 Apply touch-up paint to the scratch, using a small brush. Continue to apply thin layers of paint until the surface of the paint in the scratch is level with the surrounding paint. Allow the new paint at least two weeks to harden, then blend it into the surrounding paint by rubbing with a very fine rubbing compound. Finally, apply a coat of wax to the scratch area.

19 If the scratch has penetrated the paint and exposed the metal of the body, causing the metal to rust, a different repair technique is required. Remove all loose rust from the bottom of the scratch with a pocket knife, then apply rust inhibiting paint to prevent the formation of rust in the future. Using a rubber or nylon applicator, coat the scratched area with glaze-type filler. If required, the filler can be mixed with thinner to provide a very thin paste, which is ideal for filling narrow scratches. Before the glaze filler in the scratch hardens, wrap a piece of smooth cotton cloth around the tip of a finger. Dip the cloth in thinner and then quickly wipe it along the surface of the scratch. This will ensure that the surface of the filler is slightly hollow. The scratch can now be painted over as described earlier in this section.

Repair of dents

20 When repairing dents, the first job is to pull the dent out until the affected area is as close as possible to its original shape. There is no point in trying to restore the original shape completely as the metal in the damaged area will have stretched on impact and cannot be restored to its original contours. It is better to bring the level of the dent up to a point, which is about 1/8-inch below the level of the surrounding metal. In cases where the dent is very shallow, it is not worth trying to pull it out at all.

21 If the back side of the dent is accessible, it can be hammered out gently from behind using a soft-face hammer. While doing this, hold a block of wood firmly against the opposite side of the metal to absorb the hammer blows and prevent the metal from being stretched.

22 If the dent is in a section of the body which has double layers, or some other factor makes it inaccessible from behind, a different technique is required. Drill several small holes through the metal inside the damaged area, particularly in the deeper sections. Screw long, self-tapping screws into the holes just enough for them to get a good grip in the metal. Now the dent can be pulled out by pulling on the protruding heads of the screws with locking pliers.

23 The next stage of repair is the removal of paint from the damaged area and from an inch or so of the surrounding metal. This is done with a wire brush or sanding disk in a drill motor, although it can be done just as effectively by hand with sandpaper. To complete the preparation for filling, score the surface of the bare metal with a screwdriver or the tang of a file, or drill small holes in the affected area. This will provide a good grip for the filler material. To complete the repair, see the subsection on filling and painting later in this Section.

Repair of rust holes or gashes

24 Remove all paint from the affected area and from an inch or so of the surrounding metal using a sanding disk or wire brush mounted in a drill motor. If these are not available, a few sheets of sandpaper will do the job just as effectively.

25 With the paint removed, you will be able to determine the severity of the corrosion and decide whether to replace the whole panel, if possible, or repair the affected area. New body panels are not as expensive as most people think and it is often quicker to install a new panel than to repair large areas of rust.

26 Remove all trim pieces from the affected area except those which will act as a guide to the original shape of the damaged body, such as headlight shells, etc. Using metal snips or a hacksaw blade, remove all loose metal and any other metal that is badly affected by rust. Hammer the edges of the hole in to create a slight depression for the filler material.

These photos illustrate a method of repairing simple dents. They are intended to supplement Body repair - minor damage in this Chapter and should not be used as the sole instructions for body repair on these vehicles.

1   If you can't access the backside of the body panel to hammer out the dent, pull it out with a slide-hammer-type dent puller. In the deepest portion of the dent or along the crease line, drill or punch hole(s) at least one inch apart . . .

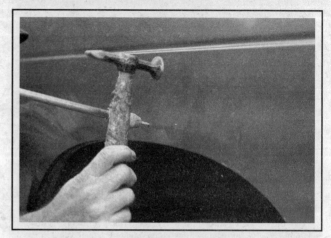

2   . . . then screw the slide-hammer into the hole and operate it. Tap with a hammer near the edge of the dent to help 'pop' the metal back to its original shape. When you're finished, the dent area should be close to its original contour and about 1/8-inch below the surface of the surrounding metal

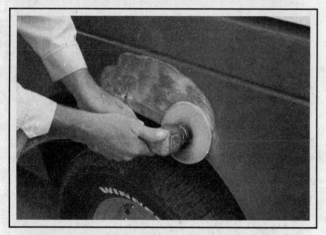

3   Using coarse-grit sandpaper, remove the paint down to the bare metal. Hand sanding works fine, but the disc sander shown here makes the job faster. Use finer (about 320-grit) sandpaper to feather-edge the paint at least one inch around the dent area

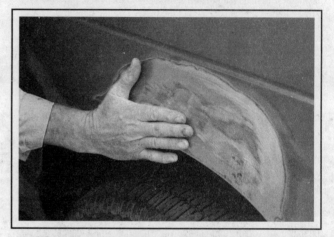

4   When the paint is removed, touch will probably be more helpful than sight for telling if the metal is straight. Hammer down the high spots or raise the low spots as necessary. Clean the repair area with wax/silicone remover

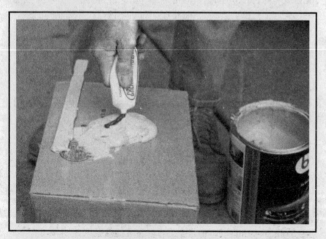

5   Following label instructions, mix up a batch of plastic filler and hardener. The ratio of filler to hardener is critical, and, if you mix it incorrectly, it will either not cure properly or cure too quickly (you won't have time to file and sand it into shape)

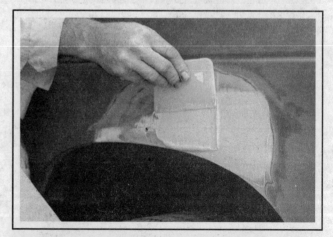

6   Working quickly so the filler doesn't harden, use a plastic applicator to press the body filler firmly into the metal, assuring it bonds completely. Work the filler until it matches the original contour and is slightly above the surrounding metal

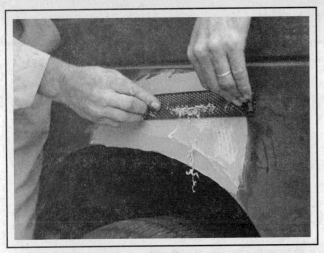

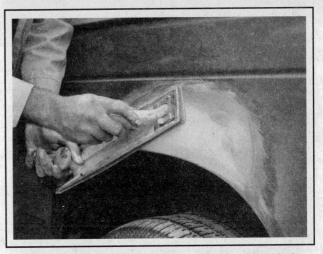

7   Let the filler harden until you can just dent it with your fingernail. Use a body file or Surform tool (shown here) to rough-shape the filler

8   Use coarse-grit sandpaper and a sanding board or block to work the filler down until it's smooth and even. Work down to finer grits of sandpaper - always using a board or block - ending up with 360 or 400 grit

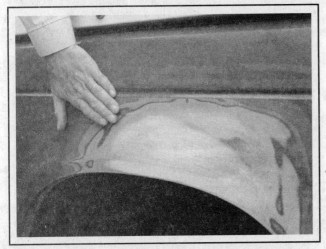

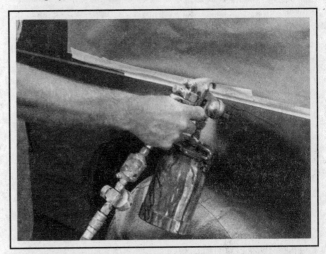

9   You shouldn't be able to feel any ridge at the transition from the filler to the bare metal or from the bare metal to the old paint. As soon as the repair is flat and uniform, remove the dust and mask off the adjacent panels or trim pieces

10   Apply several layers of primer to the area. Don't spray the primer on too heavy, so it sags or runs, and make sure each coat is dry before you spray on the next one. A professional-type spray gun is being used here, but aerosol spray primer is available inexpensively from auto parts stores

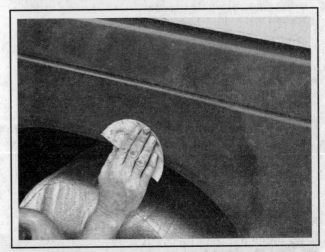

11   The primer will help reveal imperfections or scratches. Fill these with glazing compound. Follow the label instructions and sand it with 360 or 400-grit sandpaper until it's smooth. Repeat the glazing, sanding and respraying until the primer reveals a perfectly smooth surface

12   Finish sand the primer with very fine sandpaper (400 or 600-grit) to remove the primer overspray. Clean the area with water and allow it to dry. Use a tack rag to remove any dust, then apply the finish coat. Don't attempt to rub out or wax the repair area until the paint has dried completely (at least two weeks)

27 Wire brush the affected area to remove the powdery rust from the surface of the metal. If the back of the rusted area is accessible, treat it with rust inhibiting paint.

28 Before filling is done, block the hole in some way. This can be done with sheet metal riveted or screwed into place, or by stuffing the hole with wire mesh.

29 Once the hole is blocked off, the affected area can be filled and painted. See the following subsection on filling and painting.

Filling and painting

30 Many types of body fillers are available, but generally speaking, body repair kits which contain filler paste and a tube of resin hardener are best for this type of repair work. A wide, flexible plastic or nylon applicator will be necessary for imparting a smooth and contoured finish to the surface of the filler material. Mix up a small amount of filler on a clean piece of wood or cardboard (use the hardener sparingly). Follow the manufacturer's instructions on the package, otherwise the filler will set incorrectly.

31 Using the applicator, apply the filler paste to the prepared area. Draw the applicator across the surface of the filler to achieve the desired contour and to level the filler surface. As soon as a contour that approximates the original one is achieved, stop working the paste. If you continue, the paste will begin to stick to the applicator. Continue to add thin layers of paste at 20-minute intervals until the level of the filler is just above the surrounding metal.

32 Once the filler has hardened, the excess can be removed with a body file. From then on, progressively finer grades of sandpaper should be used, starting with a 180-grit paper and finishing with 600-grit wet-or-dry paper. Always wrap the sandpaper around a flat rubber or wooden block, otherwise the surface of the filler will not be completely flat. During the sanding of the filler surface, the wet-or-dry paper should be periodically rinsed in water. This will ensure that a very smooth finish is produced in the final stage.

33 At this point, the repair area should be surrounded by a ring of bare metal, which in turn should be encircled by the finely feathered edge of good paint. Rinse the repair area with clean water until all of the dust produced by the sanding operation is gone.

34 Spray the entire area with a light coat of primer. This will reveal any imperfections in the surface of the filler. Repair the imperfections with fresh filler paste or glaze filler and once more smooth the surface with sandpaper. Repeat this spray-and-repair procedure until you are satisfied that the surface of the filler and the feathered edge of the paint are perfect. Rinse the area with clean water and allow it to dry completely.

35 The repair area is now ready for painting. Spray painting must be carried out in a warm, dry, windless and dust free atmosphere. These conditions can be created if you have access to a large indoor work area, but if you are forced to work in the open, you will have to pick the day very carefully. If you are working indoors, dousing the floor in the work area with water will help settle the dust, which would otherwise be in the air. If the repair area is confined to one body panel, mask off the surrounding panels. This will help minimize the effects of a slight mismatch in paint color. Trim pieces such as chrome strips, door handles, etc., will also need to be masked off or removed. Use masking tape and several thickness of newspaper for the masking operations.

36 Before spraying, shake the paint can thoroughly, then spray a test area until the spray painting technique is mastered. Cover the repair area with a thick coat of primer. The thickness should be built up using several thin layers of primer rather than one thick one. Using 600-grit wet-or-dry sandpaper, rub down the surface of the primer until it is very smooth. While doing this, the work area should be thoroughly rinsed with water and the wet-or-dry sandpaper periodically rinsed as well. Allow the primer to dry before spraying additional coats.

37 Spray on the top coat, again building up the thickness by using several thin layers of paint. Begin spraying in the center of the repair area and then, using a circular motion, work out until the whole repair area and about two inches of the surrounding original paint is covered. Remove all masking material 10 to 15 minutes after spraying on the final coat of paint. Allow the new paint at least two weeks to harden, then use a very fine rubbing compound to blend the edges of the new paint into the existing paint. Finally, apply a coat of wax.

6 Body repair - major damage

1 Major damage must be repaired by an auto body shop specifically equipped to perform unibody repairs. These shops have the specialized equipment required to do the job properly.

2 If the damage is extensive, the body must be checked for proper alignment or the vehicle's handling characteristics may be adversely affected and other components may wear at an accelerated rate.

3 Due to the fact that all of the major body components (hood, fenders, etc.) are separate and replaceable units, any seriously damaged components should be replaced rather than repaired. Sometimes the components can be found in a wrecking yard that specializes in used vehicle components, often at considerable savings over the cost of new parts.

7 Hinges and locks - maintenance

Once every 3000 miles, or every three months, the hinges and latch assemblies on the doors, hood and trunk (or liftgate) should be given a few drops of light oil or lock lubricant. The door latch strikers should also be lubricated with a thin coat of grease to reduce wear and ensure free movement. Lubricate the door and trunk (or liftgate) locks with spray-on graphite lubricant.

8 Windshield and fixed glass - replacement

Replacement of the windshield and fixed glass requires the use of special fast-setting adhesive/caulk materials and some specialized tools and techniques. These operations should be left to a dealer service department or a shop specializing in glass work.

9   Hood - removal, installation and adjustment

REMOVAL AND INSTALLATION

▶ **Refer to illustration 9.2**

➡**Note: The hood is heavy and somewhat awkward to remove and install - at least two people should perform this procedure.**

1   Use blankets or pads to cover the fenders and cowl areas. This will protect the body and paint as the hood is lifted off.

2   Scribe or draw alignment marks around the bolt heads to ensure proper alignment during installation (see illustration).

3   Disconnect any cables or wire harnesses, which will interfere with removal.

4   Have an assistant support the weight of the hood. Remove the hinge-to-hood bolts.

5   Lift off the hood.

6   Installation is the reverse of removal. If you position the hood so that the hinges fit within the scribe marks you made before loosening the bolts, in the same location they were in prior to removal, then the hood should still be aligned. Of course, if you're installing a new hood, or forgot to scribe the hinge positions, then you'll need to readjust the hood position.

ADJUSTMENT

▶ **Refer to illustrations 9.10 and 9.11**

7   You can adjust the hood fore-and-aft and right-and-left by means of the elongated holes in the hinges.

8   Scribe a line around the entire hinge plate so you can judge the amount of movement.

9   Loosen the bolts and move the hood into correct alignment. Move it only a little at a time. Tighten the hinge bolts or nuts and carefully lower the hood to check the alignment.

10 If necessary after installation, the entire hood latch assembly can

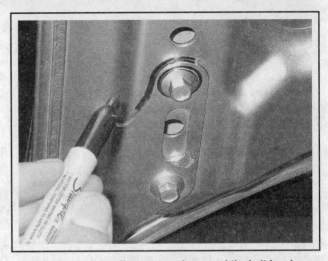

9.2 Scribe or draw alignment marks around the bolt heads and the hood hinges to ensure proper alignment of the hood when it's reinstalled

be adjusted up-and-down as well as from side-to-side on the upper radiator support so the hood closes securely and is flush with the fenders (see illustration). To do this, scribe a line around the hood latch mounting bolts to provide a reference point. Then loosen the bolts and reposition the latch assembly as necessary. Following adjustment, retighten the mounting bolts.

11 Adjust the vertical height of the leading edge of the hood by screwing the edge cushions in or out so that the hood, when closed, is flush with the fenders (see illustration).

12 The hood latch assembly, as well as the hinges, should be periodically lubricated with white lithium-base grease to prevent sticking and wear.

9.10 Scribe a line around the hood latch so you can judge the movement, then loosen the bolts and adjust the latch position

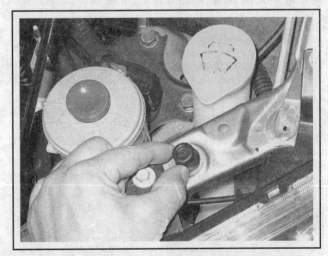

9.11 To adjust the vertical height of the leading edge of the hood so it's flush with the fenders, turn each edge cushion clockwise (to lower the hood) or counterclockwise (to raise the hood)

10 Hood release latch and cable - removal and installation

LATCH

▶ **Refer to illustration 10.2**

1   Remove the radiator grille opening cover (if equipped), then scribe a line around the latch to aid alignment when installing, detach the latch retaining bolts from the radiator support (see illustration 9.10) and remove the latch.

2   Disconnect the hood release cable by disengaging the cable from the latch assembly (see illustration).

3   Installation is reverse of the removal.

➡**Note: Adjust the latch so the hood engages securely when closed and the hood bumpers are slightly compressed.**

CABLE

▶ **Refer to illustration 10.6**

4   Disconnect the hood release cable from the latch assembly (see illustration 10.2), then detach cable from any retaining clips securing it to the radiator support.

5   Attach a piece of wire or string to the latch end of the cable.

6   Working in the passenger's compartment, remove the driver's side kick panel. Then remove the release lever mounting bolts and detach the hood release lever (see illustration).

7   Remove the left side inner fender splash shield (see Section 12). Detach the cable from the retaining clip.

8   Push the grommet through the body and pull the cable into the passenger compartment. Ensure that the new cable has a grommet attached, then remove the old cable from the wire and replace it with the new cable.

9   Pull the wire back through the body.

10 Installation is the reverse of the removal

➡**Note: Push on the grommet to seat it in the body completely.**

10.2 Detach the cable (A) then unhook the end from the latch (B)

10.6 Remove the release lever bolts and detach the cable and lever

11 Bumper covers - removal and installation

FRONT

▶ **Refer to illustrations 11.2, 11.3, 11.4a and 11.4b**

1   Raise the vehicle and support it securely on jackstands.

2   Working under the vehicle, detach the bolts or screws securing the lower edges of the bumper cover (see illustration).

3   Working in the front wheel opening, remove the retaining screw securing the bumper cover to the fenderwell (see illustration).

4   Remove the fasteners securing the upper portion of the bumper cover (see illustrations) and pull the bumper cover out and away from the vehicle.

5   Installation is the reverse of removal.

REAR

▶ **Refer to illustrations 11.7, 11.8 and 11.9**

6   Raise the vehicle and support it securely on jackstands.

11.2 Bumper cover lower retaining bolts

11.3 Remove the outer bolt securing the bumper cover to the inner fender (sedan model shown)

7   Working under the vehicle, detach the plastic clips and screws securing the lower edge of the bumper cover (see illustration).

8   Remove the screws securing the bumper cover in the rear wheel openings (see illustration).

9   Open the trunk or rear liftgate and remove the screws and clips

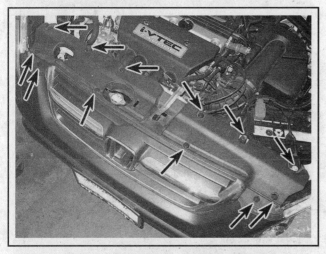

11.4b Bumper cover upper fasteners (CR-V models)

11.8 The ends of the bumper cover are retained by screws

11.4a Bumper cover upper fasteners (CR-V models)

securing the upper edge of the bumper cover (see illustration). Pull the bumper cover out and away from the vehicle.

10 Installation is the reverse of removal.

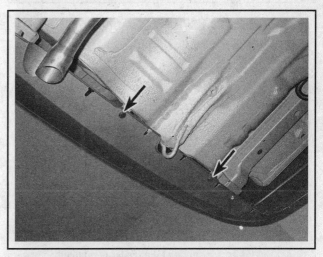

11.7 Remove the push-pins from the lower section of the bumper cover

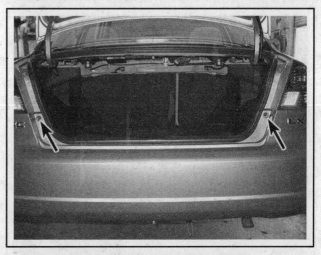

11.9 Remove the clips along the upper edge of the bumper cover

12 Front fender - removal and installation

▶ **Refer to illustrations 12.3, 12.4a, 12.4b, 12.4c and 12.4d**

1 Loosen the wheel lug nuts, raise the front of the vehicle and support it securely on jackstands. Remove the wheel.

2 Remove the front bumper cover (see Section 11).

3 Remove the fasteners securing the inner fender splash shield and detach the shield (see illustration).

4 Remove the fender mounting bolts (see illustrations).

5 Detach the fender. It's a good idea to have an assistant support the fender while it's being moved away from the vehicle to prevent damage to the surrounding body panels.

6 Installation is the reverse of removal.

12.3 Remove the fasteners retaining the inner fender splash shield

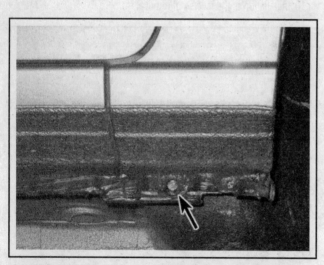

12.4a The lower rear corner of the fender is retained by a bolt

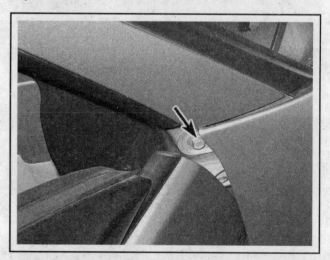

12.4b The upper rear corner of the fender is retained to the A-pillar with a bolt

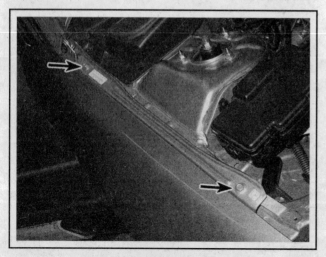

12.4c Remove the bolts along the top of the fender

12.4d Remove the bolt and detach the bracket behind the headlight

13 Liftgate handle, latch and lock cylinder (hatchback models) - removal and installation

1 Open the liftgate.
2 On the inside of the liftgate, remove the liftgate lower trim cover (see Section 18).

HANDLE

3 Remove the fasteners securing the hatch lock cylinder and rear license trim panel.
4 Remove the clips securing the license trim panel, then remove the trim panel.
5 Remove the rear window wiper motor (see Chapter 12).
6 Detach the liftgate release cable from the liftgate handle.
7 Remove the liftgate handle retaining nuts and remove the handle.
8 Installation is the reverse of removal.

LATCH

9 Disconnect the liftgate release cable and lock cylinder rod from the latch.
10 Disconnect the liftgate latch electrical connectors.
11 Remove the bolts securing the liftgate latch and remove the latch.
12 Installation is the reverse of removal.

LOCK CYLINDER

13 Remove the rear license trim panel (see Step 3).
14 Disconnect the lock cylinder rod from the cylinder.
15 Working outside of the liftgate, remove the bolt securing the lock cylinder.
16 Working inside the liftgate, remove the lock cylinder from inside of the liftgate.
17 Installation is the reverse of removal.

14 Liftgate (hatchback models) - removal, installation and adjustment

→Note: The liftgate is heavy and somewhat awkward to hold - at least two people should perform this procedure.

REMOVAL AND INSTALLATION

▶ Refer to illustration 14.3

1 Open the liftgate and support it securely.
2 Remove the upper trim molding from the liftgate opening and disconnect all wiring harness connectors leading to the liftgate.
3 While an assistant supports the liftgate, detach both ends of the support struts (see illustration).
4 Remove the C-pillar trim panels, then carefully pull down the rear portion of the headliner.
5 Detach the liftgate hinge-to-body bolts and remove the liftgate from the vehicle.
6 Installation is the reverse of removal.

ADJUSTMENT

▶ Refer to illustrations 14.8 and 14.9

7 Adjustments are made by loosening the liftgate hinge-to-body bolts and moving the liftgate. Proper alignment is achieved when the edges of the liftgate are parallel with the rear quarter panels and the roof panel.
8 Remove the rear trim panel and adjust the latch striker assembly as necessary to provide positive engagement with the latch mechanism (see illustration).
9 Finally, adjust the height of the liftgate in relation to the body by screwing the rubber bumpers in-or-out (see illustration).

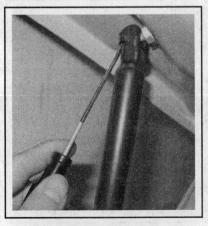

14.3 Release the strut support clip and detach it from the ballstud

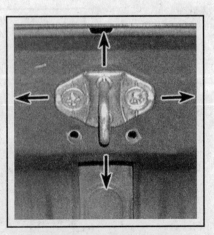

14.8 To adjust the liftgate striker, loosen the screws and move the striker as necessary

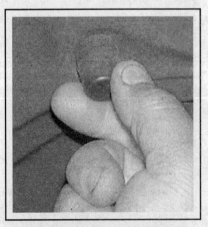

14.9 Screw the bumpers in-or-out to make final adjustments to the liftgate

15   Trunk lid latch, lock cylinder and support struts (coupe and sedan models) - removal and installation

TRUNK LID LATCH

▶ **Refer to illustrations 15.2 and 15.3**

1   Open the trunk and scribe a line around the trunk lid latch assembly for a reference point to aid the installation procedure.

2   Disconnect the latch cable from the latch (see illustration).

3   Disconnect the electrical connector, then remove the bolts retaining the trunk lid latch (see illustration).

4   Installation is the reverse of removal.

TRUNK LOCK CYLINDER

▶ **Refer to illustration 15.5**

5   Open the trunk. Look upward through the trunk lid access hole and detach the rod from the lock cylinder (see illustration).

6   Remove the mounting bolts and remove it from the trunk lid.

7   Installation is the reverse of removal.

15.2 Detach the cable and unhook the end from the latch

15.3 Trunk lid latch retaining bolts

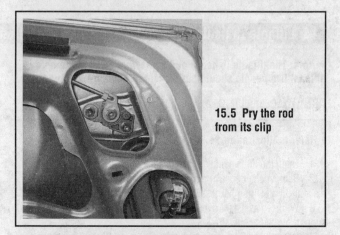

15.5 Pry the rod from its clip

16   Trunk lid (coupe and sedan models) - removal, installation and adjustment

➡**Note:** *The trunk lid is heavy and somewhat awkward to remove and install - at least two people should perform this procedure.*

REMOVAL AND INSTALLATION

▶ **Refer to illustrations 16.3 and 16.4**

1   Open the trunk lid and cover the edges of the trunk compartment with pads or cloths to protect the painted surfaces when the lid is removed.

2   Disconnect any cables or wire harness connectors attached to the trunk lid that would interfere with removal.

3   Make alignment marks around the hinge (see illustration).

4   While an assistant supports the trunk lid, remove the lid-to-hinge bolts on both sides and lift it off (see illustration).

5   Installation is the reverse of removal.

➡**Note:** *When reinstalling the trunk lid, align the lid-to-hinge bolts with the marks made during removal.*

16.3 Draw around the hinge with a marking pen before loosening the bolts to ensure proper alignment of the trunk lid when it's reinstalled

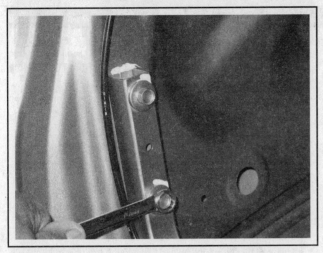

16.4 With an assistant holding the trunk lid, remove the four trunk lid retaining bolts

ADJUSTMENT

6   Fore-and-aft and side-to-side adjustment of the trunk lid is accomplished by moving the lid in relation to the hinge after loosening the bolts or nuts.

7   Scribe a line around the hinge plate as described earlier in this Section so you can determine the amount of movement.

8   Loosen the bolts and move the trunk lid into correct alignment. Move it only a little at a time. Tighten the hinge bolts or nuts and carefully lower the trunk lid to check the alignment.

9   If necessary after installation, the entire trunk lid striker assembly can be adjusted up and down as well as from side to side on the trunk lid so the lid closes securely and is flush with the rear quarter panels. To do this, scribe a line around the trunk lid striker assembly to provide a reference point. Then loosen the bolts and reposition the striker as necessary. Following adjustment, retighten the mounting bolts.

10 The trunk lid latch assembly, as well as the hinges, should be periodically lubricated with white lithium-base grease to prevent sticking and wear.

11 Finally, adjust the height of the trunk lid in relation to the body by screwing the rubber bumpers in-or-out.

17 Trunk release and fuel door cables - removal and installation

RELEASE LEVER (COUPE, SEDAN AND HATCHBACK MODELS)

▶ **Refer to illustrations 17.1a and 17.1b**

1   Detach the lower trim panel for access to the release cable and lever, then remove the lever retaining bolt (see illustrations). Detach the cable from the release assembly.

2   Installation is the reverse of removal.

CABLES

▶ **Refer to illustration 17.5**

3   If you're working on a CR-V model, remove the driver's side kick panel, then remove the fasteners securing the release handle.

4   Working in the trunk or rear compartment, remove the plastic clips securing the driver's side and rear inside finishing panels to allow access to the fuel door assembly.

5   Twist the cable 90-degrees to align the tabs on the striker assembly with the slots in the body and withdraw it into the rear compartment (see illustration). Detach the trunk release cable from the trunk lid latch (see Section 15).

6   Remove the left door sill plate, the rear seat and the left rear quarter trim panel. Pull the carpet back and detach all the cable retaining clips.

7   Working in the trunk or rear compartment, pull the cable assembly towards the rear of the vehicle.

8   Installation is the reverse of removal.

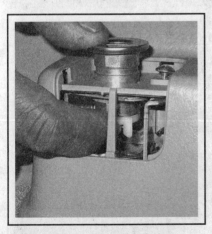

17.1a Remove the lock cylinder, then remove the trim panel

17.1b Remove the fastener and detach the release lever assembly

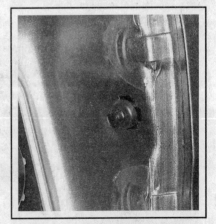

17.5 From inside the trunk or hatch area, rotate the fuel door release cable 90-degrees so the tabs line up with the slots in the body, then withdraw it

18 Door trim panels - removal and installation

REMOVAL

Front doors

Coupe, Sedan and Hatchback models

▶ Refer to illustrations 18.1, 18.2a, 18.2b, 18.2c, 18.3a, 18.3b and 18.5

1   On manual window regulator equipped models, remove the window crank (see illustration).

2   On Coupe and Sedan models, remove the inside door handle trim cover. Remove the mounting screws, then detach the handle rod and electrical connector (see illustrations).

3   Remove the pull handle trim cover, then remove the pull handle retaining screws (see illustrations). If equipped with power windows, disconnect the electrical connector from the window switch.

4   Remove the mirror trim cover (see Section 23).

5   Remove the door trim panel using a door panel removal tool (see illustration). Start from the bottom of the trim panel and work around the perimeter until all the fasteners have been released from the door.

6   Lift the trim panel up to disengage the panel from the upper door ridge, unplug any electrical connectors, and remove the panel.

7   For access to the door outside handle or the door window regulator inside the door, raise the window fully, then carefully peel back the plastic watershield.

CR-V models

▶ Refer to illustration 18.9

8   Remove the inside door handle trim cover. Remove the mounting screws, then detach the handle rod and electrical connector (see illustrations 18.2a, 18.2b and 18.2c).

9   Remove the armrest mounting screws (see illustration).

10 If you're working on a passenger door panel, remove the window switch.

11 Remove the mirror trim cover (see Section 23).

12 Remove the door trim panel using a door panel removal tool (see illustration 18.5). Start from the bottom of the trim panel and work around the perimeter until all the fasteners have been released from the door. If equipped with power windows, disconnect the electrical connector from the window switch.

13 For access to the door outside handle or the door window regulator inside the door, raise the window fully, then carefully peel back the plastic watershield.

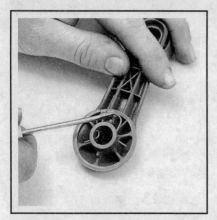

18.1 Remove the window crank by pulling this clip off with a wire hook or a special tool made for this purpose (handle removed for clarity)

18.2a Remove the door handle trim cover . . .

18.2b . . . then remove the screw(s) from the inside pull handle area

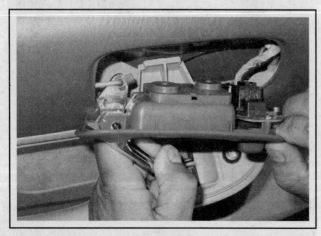

18.2c Pull the handle outward to access the door lock switch electrical connector and the door handle actuating rod

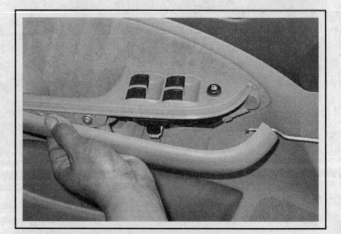

18.3a Carefully remove the pull handle trim cover . . .

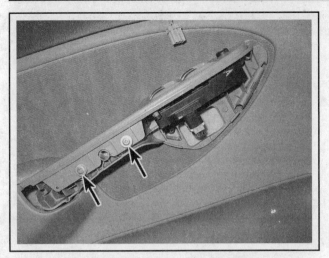

18.3b . . . to gain access to the pull handle retaining screws

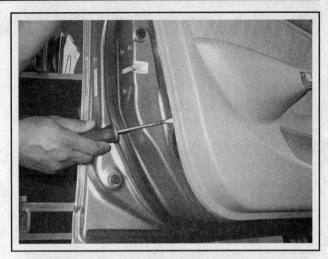

18.5 Carefully pry the clips free so the door trim panel can be removed

Rear doors

Sedan and CR-V models

14 On manual window regulator equipped models, remove the window crank (see illustration 18.1).

15 Remove the inside door handle trim cover. Remove the mounting screws, then detach the handle rod and electrical connector (see illustrations 18.2a, 18.2b and 18.2c).

16 On Sedan models, remove the pull handle trim cover, then remove the pull handle retaining screws. If equipped with power windows, disconnect the electrical connector from the window switch.

17 If you're working on a CR-V model, remove the armrest mounting screws, then remove the window switch and disconnect the electrical connector.

18 On CR-V models remove the door quarter trim panel, then remove the door trim panel upper push-pin.

19 Remove the door trim panel using a door panel removal tool (see illustration 18.5). Start from the bottom of the trim panel and work around the perimeter until all the fasteners have been released from the door.

20 For access to the door outside handle or the door window regulator inside the door, raise the window fully, then carefully peel back the plastic watershield.

Tailgate

▶ **Refer to illustration 18.21**

21 Remove the tailgate upper trim panel and the left and right trim panels by carefully releasing the clips (see illustration).

22 Remove the screw securing the cargo hook and remove the hook.

23 Remove the door trim panel using a door panel removal tool. Start from the bottom of the trim panel and work around the perimeter until all the fasteners have been released from the door.

INSTALLATION

24 Prior to installation of the door trim panels and/or the tailgate trim panel, be sure to reinstall any clips in the panel which may have come out when you removed the panel.

25 Position the wire harness connectors for the power door lock switch and the power window switch (if equipped) on the back of the panel, then place the panel in position in the door. Press the door panel into place until the clips are seated.

26 The remainder of the installation is the reverse of removal.

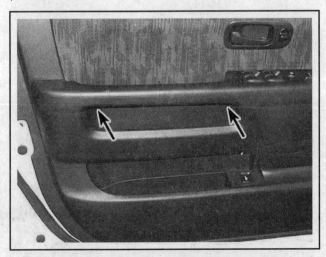

18.9 Remove the two fasteners securing the armrest

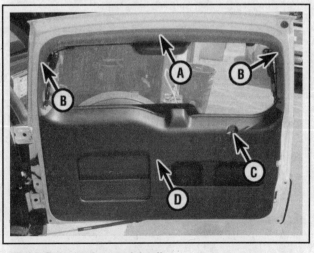

18.21 Tailgate trim panel details

A Upper trim panel	C Cargo hook
B Left and right trim panels	D Tailgate trim panel

19 Door - removal, installation and adjustment

➡ **Note 1: On CR-V and 2004 hatchback models, you must reset the power window control unit after you disconnect the driver's door wiring harness (see Chapter 5, Section 1).**

➡ **Note 2: The door is heavy and somewhat awkward to remove and install - at least two people should perform this procedure.**

REMOVAL AND INSTALLATION

▸ **Refer to illustrations 19.6 and 19.8**

1 Lower the window completely in the door, then disconnect the cable from the negative battery terminal (see Chapter 5, Section 1).

2 Open the door all the way and support it on jacks or blocks covered with rags to prevent damaging the paint.

3 Remove the door trim panel and water deflector as described in Section 18.

4 Disconnect all electrical connections, ground wires and harness retaining clips from the door.

➡ **Note: It is a good idea to label all connections to aid the reassembly process.**

5 From the door side, detach the rubber conduit between the body and the door. Then pull the wiring harness through the conduit hole and remove it from the door.

6 Remove the door stop strut (see illustration).

7 Mark around the door hinges with a pen or a scribe to facilitate realignment during reassembly.

8 With an assistant holding the door, remove the hinge-to-door bolts (see illustration) and lift the door off.

9 Installation is the reverse of removal.

ADJUSTMENT

▸ **Refer to illustrations 19.11 and 19.13**

10 Having proper door-to-body alignment is a critical part of a well functioning door assembly. First check the door hinge pins for excessive play. Fully open the door and lift up and down on the door without lifting the body. If a door has 1/16-inch or more excessive play, the hinges should be replaced.

11 Door-to-body alignment adjustments are made by loosening the hinge-to-body bolts (see illustration) or hinge-to-door bolts and mov-

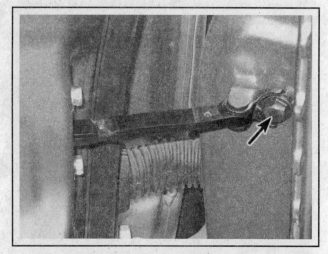

19.6 Remove the door strut retaining bolt

19.8 Remove the door hinge bolts

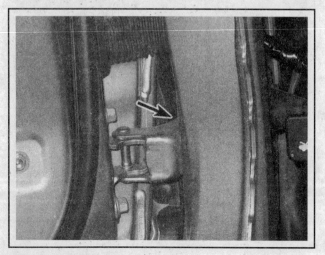

19.11 Loosen the hinge-to-body bolts to adjust the doors

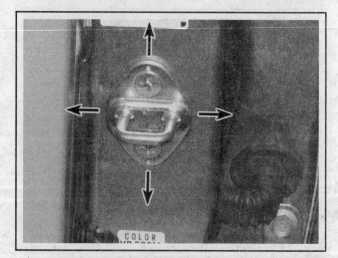

19.13 Adjust the door lock striker by loosening the mounting screws and gently tapping the striker in the desired direction

ing the door. Proper body alignment is achieved when the top of the doors are parallel with the roof section, the front door is flush with the fender, the rear door is flush with the rear quarter panel and the bottom of the doors are aligned with the lower rocker panel. If these goals can't be reached by adjusting the hinge-to-body or hinge-to-door bolts, body alignment shims may have to be purchased and inserted behind the hinges to achieve correct alignment.

12 To adjust the door closed position, scribe a line or mark around the striker plate to provide a reference point, then check that the door latch is contacting the center of the latch striker. If not adjust the up and down position first.

13 Finally adjust the latch striker sideways position, so that the door panel is flush with the center pillar or rear quarter panel and provides positive engagement with the latch mechanism (see illustration).

20 Door latch, lock cylinder and handles - removal and installation

✳✳ CAUTION:

Wear gloves when working inside the door openings to protect against cuts from sharp metal edges.

DOOR LATCH

▶ Refer to illustrations 20.2 and 20.3

1   Raise the window, then remove the door trim panel and water-shield (see Section 18).

2   Working through the large access hole, remove the lock rod protector and glass run channel (see illustration).

3   Remove the screws securing the latch to the door (see illustration).

4   Disengage the outside door handle-to-latch rod, outside door lock-to-latch rod, the inside handle-to-latch rod, and the lock solenoid-to-latch rod.

5   All door lock rods are attached by plastic clips. The plastic clips can be removed by unsnapping the portion engaging the connecting rod and then pulling the rod out of its locating hole. On models with power door locks, disconnect the electrical connectors at the latch. Remove the latch assembly from the door.

6   Installation is the reverse of removal.

OUTSIDE HANDLE AND DOOR LOCK CYLINDER

▶ Refer to illustration 20.8

7   To remove the outside handle and lock cylinder assembly, raise the window and remove the door trim panel and watershield (see Section 18).

8   Working through the access hole, disengage the plastic clips that secure the outside handle-to-latch rod, the outside door lock-to-latch rod (see illustration).

9   The lock cylinder can be removed from the handle assembly by

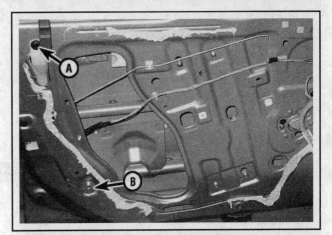

20.2 Remove the plastic pin to release the lock rod protector (A) then remove the fastener securing the glass run channel (B)

removing a clip.

10 Remove the outside handle retaining nuts, then remove the handle from the vehicle.

11 Installation is the reverse of removal.

INSIDE HANDLE

12 Remove the inside door handle trim cover. Remove the mounting screws, then detach the handle rod and electrical connector (see illustrations 18.2a, 18.2b and 18.2c).

13 Installation is the reverse of removal.

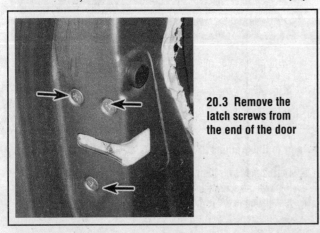

20.3 Remove the latch screws from the end of the door

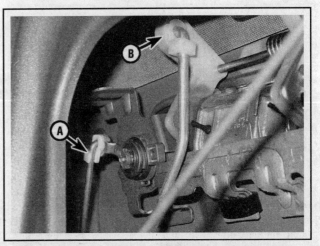

20.8 Detach the lock actuating rod (A) and handle-to-latch rod (B)

21 Door window glass - removal and installation

▶ Refer to illustration 21.2

※※ **CAUTION:**

Wear gloves when working inside the door openings to protect against cuts from sharp metal edges.

1 Remove the door trim panel and the plastic watershield (see Section 18).

2 Raise the window glass just enough to access the window retaining bolts through the holes in the door frame (see illustration).

3 Place a rag over the glass to help prevent scratching the glass and remove the two glass mounting bolts.

4 Remove the glass by tilting it slightly, pulling it up and out.

5 Installation is the reverse of removal.

21.2 Raise the window just enough to access the glass retaining bolts through the holes in the door frame - remove the bolts securing the glass to the equalizer arm

22 Door window glass regulator - removal and installation

▶ Refer to illustration 22.4

※※ **CAUTION:**

Wear gloves when working inside the door openings to protect against cuts from sharp metal edges.

1 Remove the door trim panel and the plastic watershield (see Section 18).

2 Remove the window glass assembly (see Section 21).

3 On power operated windows, disconnect the electrical connector from the window regulator motor.

4 Remove the regulator mounting bolts (see illustration), then slide the regulator assembly out of the service hole in the door frame to remove it.

5 Installation is the reverse of removal.

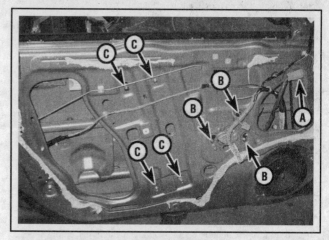

22.4 Door window glass regulator details

A   Regulator motor electrical connector
B   Regulator motor mounting bolts
C   Window regulator mounting bolts

23 Rearview mirrors - removal and installation

OUTSIDE MIRRORS

▶ Refer to illustrations 23.1 and 23.3

1 Pry off the mirror trim cover (see illustration).

2 Disconnect the electrical connector from the mirror (if equipped).

➡Note: On some models the electrical connector plugs right into the mirror and can be unplugged without removing the door panel. On other models the electrical connector is located in the wiring harness, behind the door panel. See Section 18 for door panel removal, if necessary.

3 Remove the three mirror retaining nuts and detach the mirror from the vehicle (see illustration).

4 Installation is the reverse of removal.

INSIDE MIRROR

▶ Refer to illustrations 23.5 and 23.6

5 Detach the cover from the retaining bracket (see illustration).

6 Remove the screws and lower the mirror (see illustration).

7 Installation is the reverse of removal.

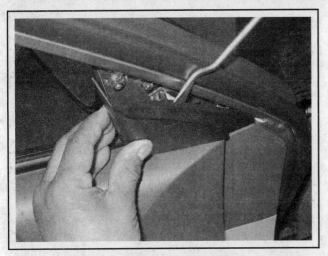

23.1 Use a small screwdriver or trim removal tool to pry off the mirror cover

23.3 To remove the mirror, remove these three nuts - if the vehicle has power mirrors, unplug the electrical connector too

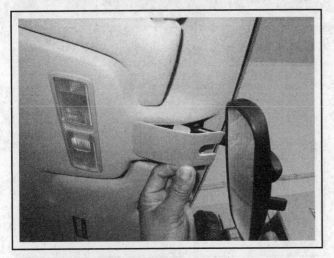

23.5 Remove the mirror cover

23.6 Remove the three screws and detach the mirror

24 Center console - removal and installation

✳✳ WARNING:

Models covered by this manual are equipped with a Supplemental Restraint System (SRS), more commonly known as airbags. Always disable the airbag system before working in the vicinity of any airbag system component to avoid the possibility of accidental deployment of the airbag, which could cause personal injury (see Chapter 12).

1 Disconnect the cable from the negative terminal of the battery, see Chapter 5, Section 1.

HATCHBACK MODELS

Rear console

2 Slide the front seats all the way to the forward position.

3 At the rear of the console, remove the fasteners from each side.

4 Slide the front seats all the way to the rear, then carefully pull up on the front of the rear console to release the clips.

5 Remove the rear half of the console by lifting it up and toward the rear.

Front console

6 Pry out the dashboard center lower cover, remove the two console fasteners and disconnect the electrical connector.

7 Remove the mat from the console box, then remove the two fasteners from the bottom of the box.

8 At the front of the console, remove the fasteners along both sides of console, then gently lift the console up and toward the rear to remove it from the vehicle.

9 Installation is the reverse of removal.

COUPE AND SEDAN MODELS

Console with armrest

▶ Refer to illustrations 24.10a, 24.10b, 24.11a, 24.11b, 24.12a, 24.12b and 24.13

10 If you're working on automatic transaxle model, pry off the gear selector trim bezel and center console trim (see illustrations). On manual transaxle models, unscrew the shift lever knob.

11 Remove the dashboard center lower cover and disconnect any electrical connectors, then detach the parking brake lever trim panel (see illustrations).

12 Remove the console retaining screws and surrounding fasteners (see illustrations).

13 Disconnect any electrical connections and remove the console from the vehicle (see illustration).

14 Installation is the reverse of removal.

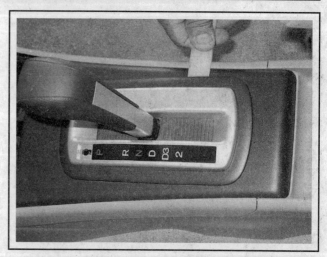

24.10a Carefully detach the clips and remove the trim ring from around the shifter (automatic transaxle)

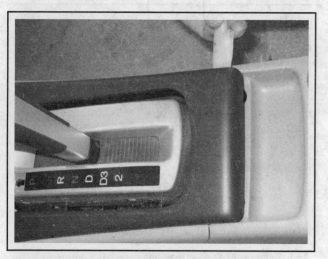

24.10b Carefully detach the clips and remove the trim panel (automatic transaxle model shown, manual transaxle model similar)

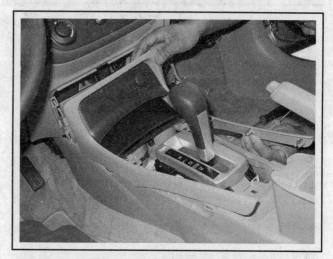

24.11a Pry off the dashboard center lower cover

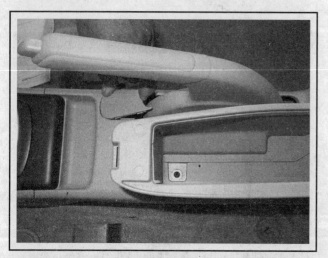

24.11b Pull up and remove the brake lever trim panel

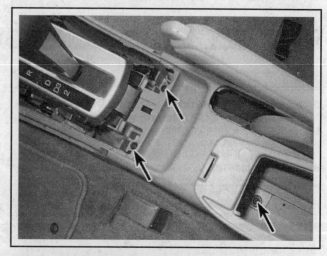

24.12a Remove the console mounting fasteners . . .

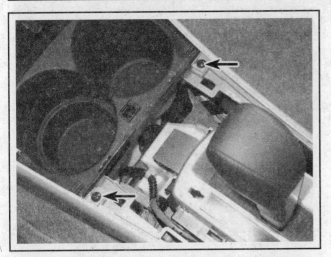

24.12b . . . from the top of the center console. Don't forget the fasteners securing the sides of the console

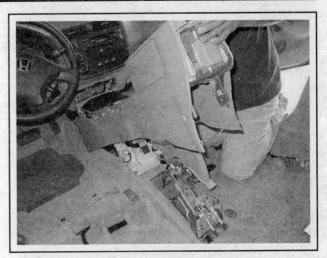

24.13 Lift the rear of the console up, then pull it out

25 Dashboard trim panels - removal and installation

✳ WARNING:

Models covered by this manual are equipped with a Supplemental Restraint System (SRS), more commonly known as airbags. Always disable the airbag system before working in the vicinity of any airbag system component to avoid the possibility of accidental deployment of the airbag, which could cause personal injury (see Chapter 12).

1   Disconnect the cable from the negative battery terminal (see Chapter 5, Section 1).

PASSENGER'S LOWER DASHBOARD COVER

▶ **Refer to illustration 25.2**

2   Pull the edge of the panel down until the clips are disengaged

and remove the panel (see illustration).

3   Installation is the reverse of removal.

DRIVER'S INSTRUMENT PANEL UNDER COVER

▶ **Refer to illustration 25.4**

4   Turn the locking knob and remove the panel (see illustration).

5   Installation is the reverse of removal.

GLOVE BOX

▶ **Refer to illustration 25.6**

6   Open the glove box door and remove the glove box stops, then close the glove box (see illustration).

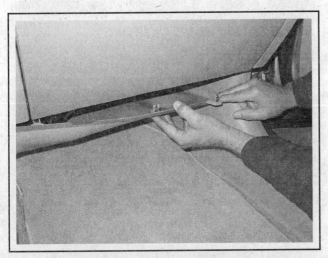

25.2 Carefully pull the panel down to release the clips (sedan model shown, other models similar)

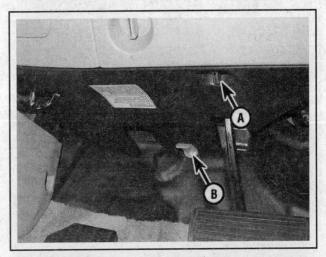

25.4 Turn the locking knob (A) and pull down the front of the panel and release the rear part from the clip (B) (sedan model shown, other models similar)

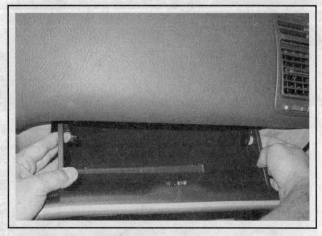

25.6 Remove the glovebox stops

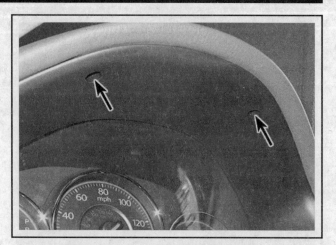

25.11 Remove the cluster bezel retaining screws

7 At the bottom of the glove box, remove the screws from the hinges.

8 Open the glove box door and lower the glove box from the instrument panel.

9 Installation is the reverse of removal.

INSTRUMENT CLUSTER BEZEL

Coupe and sedan models

▶ **Refer to illustration 25.11**

10 Remove the steering column upper cover (see Section 26).

11 Remove the screws (see illustration), then grasp the bezel securely and pull back to detach the clips from the instrument panel.

12 Installation is the reverse of removal.

CR-V models

13 Remove the driver's instrument panel lower cover (see Steps 23 through 26).

14 Remove the steering column upper cover (see Section 26).

15 Grasp the bezel securely and gently pull back to detach the clips from the instrument panel.

16 Installation is the reverse of removal.

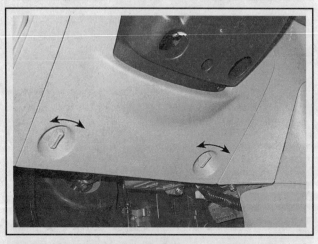

25.21 Give these two knobs a 1/2-turn either way, then remove the driver's dashboard lower cover and carefully pull down to release the clips

Hatchback models

17 Tilt the steering wheel down to the lowest position, then remove the steering column upper cover (see Section 26).

18 Grasp the bezel securely and gently pull back to detach the clips from the instrument panel.

19 Installation is the reverse of removal.

DRIVER'S INSTRUMENT PANEL LOWER COVER

Coupe and sedan models

▶ **Refer to illustration 25.21**

20 Tilt the steering wheel up to the highest position.

21 Turn the locking knobs and remove the panel (see illustration).

22 Installation is the reverse of removal.

CR-V models

23 Open the access door for the under-dash fuse/relay box, and remove the fastener located in the opening.

24 Open the driver's side pocket and remove the fastener located in the opening.

25 Grasp the bottom of the instrument panel lower cover securely and gently pull back to detach the bottom clips from the instrument panel. Repeat the same for the upper clips. Unplug any electrical connectors, then remove the panel.

26 Installation is the reverse of removal.

Hatchback models

27 Tilt the steering wheel up to the highest position.

28 Turn the locking knob a 1/2-turn either way, then grasp the side of the panel and gently pull back to remove the panel.

29 Installation is the reverse of removal.

CENTER TRIM PANEL

Coupe and sedan models

▶ **Refer to illustration 25.31**

30 Remove the dashboard center lower cover (see Section 24).

31 Remove the center trim panel mounting bolts, then release the trim panel clips (see illustration).

32 Carefully slide the trim panel out far enough to unplug any elec-

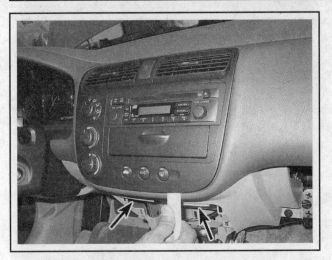

25.31 Remove the center trim panel mounting bolts (arrows), then carefully pry the panel using a trim stick

trical connectors that interfere with removal, then remove the trim panel from the dashboard.

33 Installation is the reverse of removal.

CR-V models

34 Remove the screws securing the lower edge of the center trim panel.

35 Lift the lower edge of the panel and work your way upward along the edges to detach the clips. Unplug any electrical connectors, then remove the panel.

36 Installation is the reverse of removal.

Hatchback models

37 Remove the driver's instrument panel lower cover (see Steps 27 through 29).

38 Remove the passenger's lower dashboard cover (see illustration 25.2).

39 Remove the glove box (see Steps 6 through 9).

40 Using a ratchet wrench with an 11-inch extension or a long screwdriver, wrap the end with a towel, then carefully insert the end through the glove box opening and gently release the clips by pushing from under the shift lever trim.

41 Remove the center panel fasteners from the driver's lower cover and glove box openings.

42 Carefully slide the trim panel out far enough to unplug any electrical connectors that interfere with removal, then remove the trim panel from the dashboard.

26 Steering column covers - removal and installation

▶ Refer to illustration 26.4

> ❋❋ **WARNING:**
>
> Models covered by this manual are equipped with a Supplemental Restraint System (SRS), more commonly known as airbags. Always disable the airbag system before working in the vicinity of any airbag system component to avoid the possibility of accidental deployment of the airbag, which could cause personal injury (see Chapter 12).

1 Disconnect the cable from the negative battery terminal (see Chapter 5, Section 1).

2 Remove the driver's instrument panel lower cover (see Section 25).

3 On tilt steering columns, move the column to the lowest position.

4 Remove the retaining screws, then separate the halves and remove the covers (see illustration).

5 Installation is the reverse of the removal procedure.

26.4 Steering column cover retaining screws (Sedan model shown, other models similar)

27 Instrument panel - removal and installation

▶ Refer to illustrations 27.7, 27.9, 27.11, 27.16, 27.17a and 27.17b

> ❋❋ **WARNING:**
>
> Models covered by this manual are equipped with a Supplemental Restraint System (SRS), more commonly known as airbags. Always disable the airbag system before working in the vicinity of any airbag system component to avoid the possibility of accidental deployment of the airbag, which could cause personal injury (see Chapter 12).

➡ **Note 1:** This is a difficult procedure for the home mechanic. There are many hidden fasteners, difficult angles to work in and many electrical connectors to tag and disconnect/connect. We recommend that this procedure be done only by an experienced do-it-yourselfer.

➡ **Note 2:** During removal of the instrument panel, make careful notes of how each piece comes off, where it fits in relation to other pieces and what holds it in place. If you note how each part is installed before removing it, getting the instrument panel back together again will be much easier.

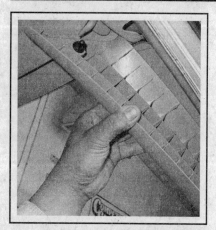

27.7 Remove the front pillar trim by carefully releasing the clips

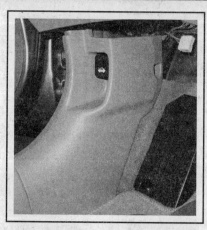

27.9 Carefully detach both side kick panels

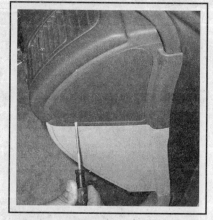

27.11 Carefully pry off both dashboard side covers

➡**Note 3: It is not necessary, but it is suggested to remove both front seats to allow additional working space and lessen the chance of damage to the seats during this procedure.**

1 Disconnect the cable from the negative battery terminal (see Chapter 5, Section 1).

2 Remove the steering wheel (see Chapter 10).

3 If equipped, remove the center floor console (see Section 24).

4 Remove the instrument cluster bezel (see Section 25).

5 Remove the instrument cluster (see Chapter 12).

6 Remove all of the dashboard trim panels described in Section 25.

7 Remove the front pillar trim (see illustration).

8 Remove the nuts and lower the steering column (see Chapter 10).

9 Remove the side kick panels (see illustration).

10 On CR-V models, remove the passenger's side vent.

11 Remove the dashboard side covers (see illustration).

12 Remove the glove box (see Section 25).

13 Remove the radio (see Chapter 12) and the heater control assembly (see Chapter 3).

14 Remove the rear vent duct.

15 Disconnect the instrument panel electrical connectors.

➡**Note: A number of electrical connectors must be disconnected in order to remove the instrument panel. Most are designed so that they will only fit on the matching connector (male or female), but if there is any doubt, mark the connectors with masking tape and a marking pen before disconnecting them.**

16 Remove the fasteners securing the lower center part of the instrument panel (see illustration).

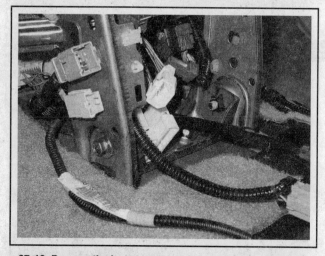

27.16 Remove the instrument panel center brace mounting bolts (sedan model shown, other models similar)

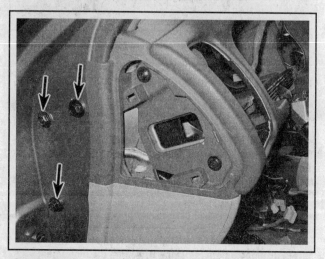

27.17a Remove the bolts from the support structure on the left . . .

27.17b . . . and the right side of the instrument panel (sedan model shown, other models similar)

17 Remove the fasteners from each end of the instrument panel (see illustrations).

18 Pull the instrument panel towards the rear of the vehicle and detach any electrical connectors interfering with removal.

19 Once all the electrical connectors are detached, lift the instrument panel then pull it away from the windshield and take it out through the driver's door opening.

➡ **Note: This is a two-person job.**

20 Installation is the reverse of removal.

21 Reconnect the battery. Refer to Chapter 5, Section 1.

28 Cowl cover - removal and installation

▸ **Refer to illustrations 28.2a and 28.2b**

1 Remove the windshield wiper arms (see Chapter 12).

2 Remove the hood seal and the push-pin fasteners securing the cowl cover (see illustrations).

3 Installation is the reverse of removal.

28.2a **Using a fastener removal tool, remove the hood seal . . .**

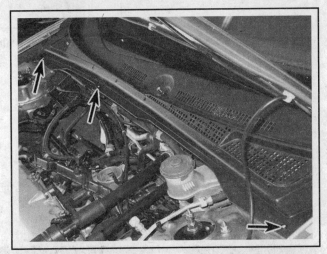

28.2b **. . . then detach the plastic fasteners and remove the cowl (sedan model shown, other models similar)**

29 Seats - removal and installation

❋❋ WARNING 1:

The front seat belts on some models are equipped with pre-tensioners, which are pyrotechnic (explosive) devices designed to retract the seat belts in the event of a collision. On models equipped with pre-tensioners, do not remove the front seat belt retractor assemblies, and do not disconnect the electrical connectors leading to the assemblies. Problems with the pre-tensioners will turn on the SRS (airbag) warning light on the dash. If any pre-tensioner problems are suspected, take the vehicle to a dealer service department.

❋❋ WARNING 2:

On models with side-impact airbags, be sure to disarm the airbag system before beginning this procedure (see Chapter 12).

FRONT SEAT

▸ **Refer to illustrations 29.2a and 29.2b**

1 Disconnect the cable from the negative battery terminal (see Chapter 5, Section 1).

2 Position the seat all the way forward, then all the way to the rear to access the seat retaining bolts (see illustrations).

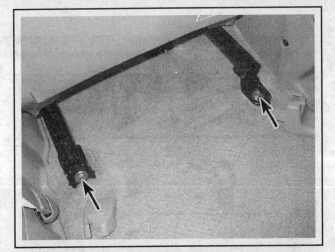

29.2a **Move the front seat all the way forward to access the rear retaining bolts . . .**

3 Detach any bolt trim covers and remove the retaining bolts.

4 Tilt the seat upward to access the underneath, then disconnect any electrical connectors and lift the seat from the vehicle.

5 Installation is the reverse of removal.

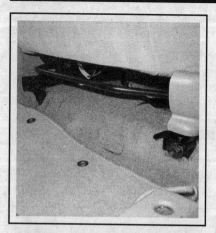

29.2b ... then move the seat all the way to the rear to access the front retaining bolts

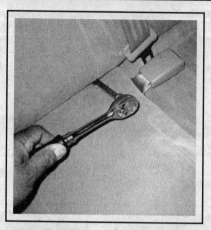

29.6a Remove the rear seat cushion retaining bolt

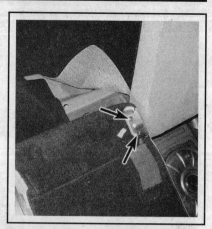

29.6b Remove the fasteners securing the seat hinge

REAR SEAT

▶ **Refer to illustrations 29.6a and 29.6b**

6   On Coupe, Sedan and Hatchback models, remove the seat cushion bolt and remove the cushion (see illustration). Pull back the seat

back trim cover, then remove the fasteners securing the seat hinge and remove the seat backs (see illustration).

7   On CR-V models, tilt the seat forward and remove the retaining bolts at the front of the seat. Remove the seat from the vehicle.

8   Installation is the reverse of removal.

30 Radiator grille - removal and installation

1   Remove the front bumper cover (see Section 11).

2   Remove the fasteners securing the edges of the grille to the bumper cover.

3   Pull the grille forward to disengage it from the bumper.

4   Installation is the reverse of removal.

31 Tailgate latch, lock cylinder and handle (CR-V models) - removal and installation

✳✳ CAUTION:

Wear gloves when working inside the door openings to protect against cuts from sharp metal edges.

1   Open the tailgate and remove the tailgate trim panel (see Section 18).

LATCH

2   Reaching through the access hole, detach the tailgate rod and cylinder rod then disconnect the actuator connector from the latch.

3   Remove latch mounting screws and remove the latch from the tailgate.

4   Installation is the reverse of removal.

LOCK CYLINDER

5   Reaching through the access hole, detach the actuating rod from the rear of the lock cylinder.

6   Remove the lock cylinder retaining clip and pull it outward to remove it from the tailgate handle.

7   Installation is the reverse of removal.

HANDLE

8   Reaching through the access hole, remove the lock cylinder (see Steps 5 and 6).

9   Remove the bolt securing the lock cylinder protector and handle to the tailgate. Release the clip and remove the protector.

10 Remove the bolt securing the handle and spacer handle to the tailgate.

11 Carefully remove the handle from the tailgate.

12 Installation is the reverse of removal.

32 Tailgate and assist strut (CR-V models) - removal, installation and adjustment

→Note: The tailgate is heavy and somewhat awkward to hold - at least two people should perform this procedure.

REMOVAL AND INSTALLATION

♦ Refer to illustrations 32.5 and 32.6

1   Remove the spare tire from the tailgate if equipped. Open the tailgate and support it securely with several jack stands. Place pads or cloths between the jack stands and the tailgate to protect the paint.

2   Remove the tailgate trim panel (see Section 31).

3   Working through the openings in the tailgate frame, disconnect all wiring harness connectors leading to the tailgate.

4   From the tailgate side, detach the rubber conduit between the body and the tailgate. Then pull the wiring harness through conduit hole and remove it from the tailgate.

5   Remove the tailgate assist strut (see illustration).

6   While an assistant supports the tailgate, detach the hinge-to-tailgate bolts (see illustration) and remove the tailgate from the vehicle.

7   Installation is the reverse of removal.

ADJUSTMENT

8   Adjustments are made by loosening the hinge-to-body bolts or the hinge-to-tailgate bolts and moving the tailgate (see illustration 32.6). Proper alignment is achieved when the edges of the tailgate are parallel with the rear quarter panels and the lower door sill.

9   Adjust the latch striker assembly as necessary (up and down) to provide positive engagement with the latch mechanism.

10 Finally, adjust the tailgate wedge by slightly loosening the bolts and centering the wedge between the holes in the adjustment slots. While holding the tailgate handle open, close the tailgate until it is flush with the body and the latch mechanism engages. Tighten the wedge bolts and recheck the adjustment, making sure the tailgate is flush with the body when closed.

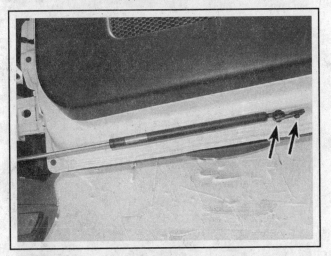

32.5 Remove the bolts securing the assist strut to the tailgate

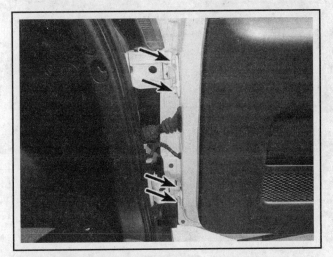

32.6 Tailgate hinge-to-tailgate bolts

33 Rear hatch glass and support struts (CR-V models) - removal, installation and adjustment

✳✳ WARNING:

The rear hatch glass is heavy and awkward to hold. At least two people should perform this procedure.

REMOVAL AND INSTALLATION

1   Open the rear hatch glass and support it fully in this position. If you're just replacing the glass support struts proceed to Step 4.

2   Remove the tailgate upper trim panel and the left and right trim panels by carefully releasing the clips.

3   Remove the screws and detach the rear windshield wiper motor cover. Also remove the high mount brake light cover by pushing inward on the tabs at the side. Disconnect the electrical connector and remove the mounting nuts then remove the high mount brake light.

4   Detach the support struts at the rear hatch glass. If you're replacing the glass support struts, detach the strut from the body in the same manner as you detached the strut from the glass.

5   Remove the rear hatch glass mounting nuts, while at least one assistant, preferably two, helps you hold the rear hatch glass.

6   Installation is the reverse of the removal procedure. Be extremely careful not to overtighten the fasteners.

ADJUSTMENT

7   Adjustments are made by loosening the hinge-to-body bolts or the hinge-to-glass bolts and moving the glass. Proper alignment is achieved when the edges of the glass are parallel with the rear quarter panel pillars and the top of the tailgate.

8   Adjust the latch striker assembly as necessary (up and down) to provide positive engagement with the latch mechanism.

34 Rear shelf trim panel - removal and installation

◆ **Refer to illustrations 34.3a, 34.3b and 34.3c**

1 Remove the rear seat cushion and seat back (see Section 29).
2 Open the trunk and disconnect the high mounted brake light
3 Detach the roof pillar trim pieces on both sides, then remove the lock cylinder trim ring and detach the shelf trim panel (see illustrations).
4 Installation is the reverse of the removal procedure.

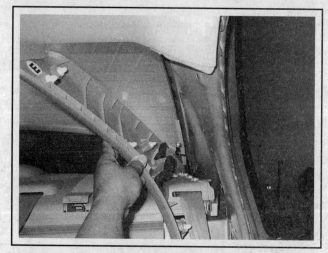

34.3a Carefully pull on the roof pillar trim pieces to detach the clips

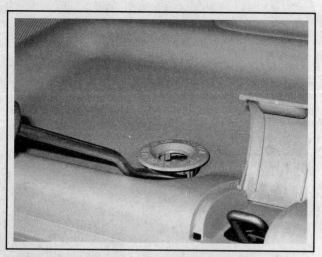

34.3b Pry or pull the plastic trim ring from around the lock cylinder

34.3c Carefully pull up on the shelf trim panel to release the clips

Section

12

CHASSIS ELECTRICAL SYSTEM

1   General information

The electrical system is a 12-volt, negative ground type. Power for the lights and all electrical accessories is supplied by a lead/acid-type battery, which is charged by the alternator.

This Chapter covers repair and service procedures for the various electrical components not associated with the engine. Information on the battery, ignition system, alternator and starter motor can be found in Chapter 5.

It should be noted that when portions of the electrical system are serviced, the negative battery cable should be disconnected from the battery to prevent electrical shorts and/or fires.

2   Electrical troubleshooting - general information

▶ **Refer to illustrations 2.5a and 2.5b**

1   A typical electrical circuit consists of an electrical component, any switches, relays, motors, fuses, fusible links or circuit breakers related to that component and the wiring and connectors that link the component to both the battery and the chassis. Wiring diagrams are included at the end of this Chapter to help you pinpoint an electrical circuit problem.

2   Before tackling any troublesome electrical circuit, study the appropriate wiring diagrams to get a complete understanding of what makes up that individual circuit. Noting if other components related to the circuit are operating correctly, for instance, can often narrow trouble spots, down. If several components or circuits fail at one time, chances are the problem is in a fuse or ground connection, because several circuits are often routed through the same fuse and ground connections.

3   Electrical problems usually stem from simple causes, such as loose or corroded connections, a blown fuse, a melted fusible link or a failed relay. Visually inspect the condition of all fuses, wires and connections in a problem circuit before troubleshooting the circuit.

4   If test equipment and instruments are going to be utilized, use the diagrams to plan ahead of time where you will make the necessary connections in order to accurately pinpoint the trouble spot.

5   Basic electrical troubleshooting tools include a circuit tester, test light or voltmeter, a continuity tester, a set of test leads and a jumper wire (preferably with a circuit breaker), which can be used to bypass electrical components (see illustrations). Before attempting to locate a problem with test instruments, use the wiring diagram(s) to decide where to make the connections.

VOLTAGE CHECKS

▶ **Refer to illustration 2.6**

6   Voltage checks should be performed if a circuit is not functioning correctly. Connect one lead of a circuit tester to either the negative battery terminal or a known good ground. Connect the other lead to a

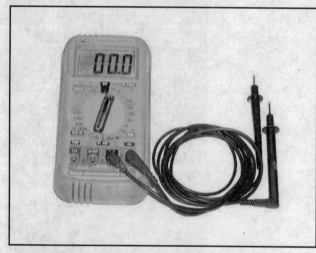

2.5a The most useful tool for electrical troubleshooting is a digital multimeter that can check volts, amps, and test continuity

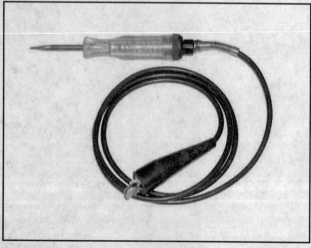

2.5b A simple test light is a very handy tool for testing voltage

2.6 In use, a basic test light's lead is clipped to a known good ground, then the pointed probe can test connectors, wires or electrical sockets - if the bulb lights, the circuit being tested has battery voltage

connector in the circuit being tested, preferably nearest to the battery or fuse (see illustration). If the bulb of the tester lights, voltage is present, which means that the part of the circuit between the connector and the battery is problem free. Continue checking the rest of the circuit in the same fashion. When you reach a point at which no voltage is present, the problem lies between that point and the last test point with voltage. Most of the time the problem can be traced to a loose connection.

→Note: Keep in mind that some circuits receive voltage only when the ignition key is in the ACC or ON position.

FINDING A SHORT

7   One method of finding shorts in a live circuit is to remove the fuse and connect a test light in place of the fuse terminals (fabricate two jumper wires with small spade terminals, plug the jumper wires into the fuse box and connect the test light). There should be no voltage present in the circuit. Move the suspected wiring harness from side-to-side while watching the test light. If the bulb goes on, there is a short to ground somewhere in that area, probably where the insulation has rubbed through.

GROUND CHECK

8   Perform a ground test to check whether a component is correctly grounded. Disconnect the battery and connect one lead of a continuity tester or multimeter (set to the ohm scale), to a known good ground. Connect the other lead to the wire or ground connection being tested. If the resistance is low (less than 5 ohms), the ground is good. If the bulb on a self-powered test light does not go on, the ground is not good.

CONTINUITY CHECK

▸ **Refer to illustration 2.9**

9   Do a continuity check to verify that there are no opens in a circuit. With the circuit off (no power in the circuit), a self-powered continuity tester or multimeter can be used to check the circuit. Connect the test leads to both ends of the circuit (or to the "power" end and a good ground), and if the test light comes on the circuit is passing current correctly (see illustration). If the resistance is low (less than 5 ohms), there is continuity; if the reading is 10,000 ohms or higher, there is a break somewhere in the circuit. The same procedure can be used to test a switch, by connecting the continuity tester to the switch terminals. With the switch turned to ON, the test light should come on (or low resistance should be indicated on a meter).

FINDING AN OPEN CIRCUIT

10 When diagnosing for possible open circuits, it is often difficult to locate them by sight because the connectors hide oxidation or terminal misalignment. Merely wiggling a connector on a sensor or in the wiring harness may correct the open circuit condition. Remember this when an open circuit is indicated when troubleshooting a circuit. Intermittent problems may also be caused by oxidized or loose connections.

11 Electrical troubleshooting is simple if you keep in mind that all electrical circuits are basically electricity running from the battery,

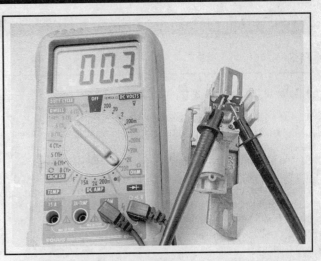

2.9 With a multimeter set to the ohm scale, resistance can be checked across two terminals - when checking for continuity, a low reading indicates continuity, a high reading or infinity indicates high resistance or lack of continuity

through the wires, switches, relays, fuses and fusible links to each electrical component (light bulb, motor, etc.) and to ground, from which it is passed back to the battery. Any electrical problem is an interruption in the flow of electricity to and from the battery.

CONNECTORS

12 Most electrical connections on these vehicles consist of multiple-terminal plastic connectors. The two halves of most connectors are locked together by tabs molded into the plastic connector shells. So always look for the release tab(s) or locking tab(s) on a connector and release it/them before trying to disconnect the connector. If the connector is too dirty to find the release or locking tab(s), wipe it off. If a connector is in a dark area, use a flashlight. You might have to look closely (very closely!) at some connectors before you figure out how to separate the two halves, because the locking or release tabs are engaged in a way that is not immediately clear. And many connectors have not one but two sets of release or locking tabs.

13 Connectors are usually locked together by release tabs that you simply depress to release, or by locking tabs that you spread apart or pry loose from some projection on the other half of the connector. Once you have figured out how to release a connector with locking or release tabs, carefully depress the release tabs or pry the locking tabs apart with a small screwdriver, then separate the connector halves. Pull only on the connector halves. Never pull on the wires or the wiring harness, because you might damage the wires and terminals inside the connector.

14 Each pair of connector terminals has a "male" half and a "female" half. This is particularly important to remember when you look at a connector terminal guide in a wiring diagram or wiring schematic, because you need to know whether you're looking at the wiring harness side or the component side of the connector. Connector halves are mirror images of each other, and a terminal that is shown on the right side end-view of one half will be on the left side end view of the other half. In other words, the terminal locations - and terminal numbering, if applicable - will be "flipped").

3 Fuses - general information

FUSES

▶ **Refer to illustrations 3.1a, 3.1b, 3.1c and 3.2**

The electrical circuits of the vehicle are protected by a combination of fuses, circuit breakers and relays (for more information about circuit breakers, refer to Section 4; for more information about relays, refer to Section 5). Fuse and relay boxes are located in the engine compartment and underneath the dashboard (see illustrations). A wide array of mini and maxi-style fuses is used to protect various circuits. These fuses, which employ a blade terminal design, can be removed and installed without special tools. Each fuse protects a specific circuit or circuits, and the protected circuits are identified on the fuse panel cover. If the fuse panel cover is difficult to read, or missing, you can also refer to your owner's manual, which includes a complete guide to all fuses and relays in all three fuse/relay boxes.

If an electrical component fails, always check the fuse first. The best way to check a fuse is with a test light. Check for power at the exposed terminal tips of each fuse. If power is present on one side of the fuse but not the other, the fuse is blown. A blown fuse can also be confirmed by visually inspecting it (see illustration).

Be sure to replace blown fuses with the correct type. Fuses of different ratings are physically interchangeable, but only fuses of the correct rating should be used. Replacing a fuse with one of a higher or lower value than specified is not recommended. Each electrical circuit needs a specific amount of protection. The amperage value of each fuse is molded into the fuse body.

If the replacement fuse immediately fails, don't replace it again until the cause of the problem is isolated and corrected. In most cases, this will be a short circuit in the wiring caused by a broken or deteriorated wire.

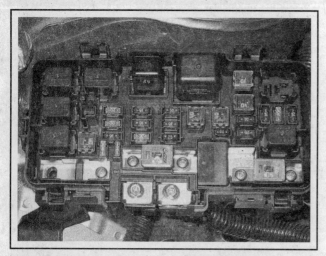

3.1a On coupes and sedans, the engine compartment fuse/relay box is located on the right side of the engine compartment. The functions and locations of the various fuses and relays are listed on the fuse/relay box cover (on CR-Vs and hatchbacks, this fuse/relay box is located on the *left* side of the engine compartment)

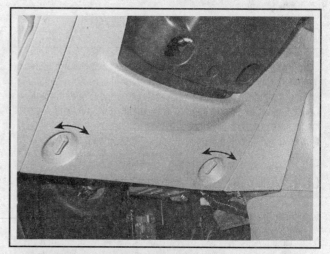

3.1b To access the fuse/relay box inside the passenger compartment of a coupe, sedan or hatchback, give these two fasteners a 1/2-turn either way, then remove the driver's dashboard lower cover . . .

3.1c . . . to expose the under-dash fuse and relay box (on CR-Vs, the under-dash fuse/relay box is located in the same spot but has an access door in the driver's dashboard lower cover, so you don't have to remove the cover)

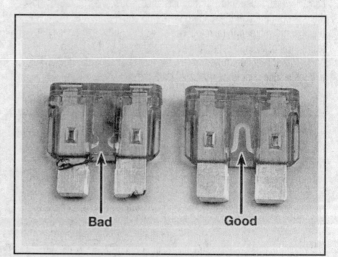

3.2 When a fuse blows, the element between the terminals melts - the fuse on the left is blown, the fuse on the right is good

4   Circuit breakers - general information

Circuit breakers protect certain circuits, such as the power windows or heated seats. The number of circuit breakers employed on your vehicle depends on its electrical accessories. Some circuit breakers are located in a fuse/relay box; others are located as stand-alone units under the dash and in other locations throughout the vehicle.

Because a circuit breaker resets automatically, a temporary or intermittent electrical overload in a circuit-breaker-protected system will cause the circuit to open momentarily, then close again. If a circuit-breaker-protected circuit does not close, or constantly opens and closes, check it immediately. There's probably an intermittent short or ground somewhere in the circuit that's causing the current overload, which causes the circuit breaker to cycle the circuit on and off.

For a basic check, pull the circuit breaker up out of its socket on the fuse panel, but just far enough to probe with a voltmeter. The breaker should still contact the sockets.

With the voltmeter negative lead on a good chassis ground, touch each end prong of the circuit breaker with the positive meter probe. There should be battery voltage at each end. If there is battery voltage only at one end, the circuit breaker must be replaced.

Some circuit breakers must be reset manually.

5   Relays - general information and testing

GENERAL INFORMATION

1   Many electrical accessories - the fuel injection system, horns, starter, and fog lamps, for example - use relays to control current to components. A relay allows a low-current circuit (the control circuit) to be used to open and close a high-current circuit (the power circuit). If a relay is defective, the component(s) powered by the high-current circuit controlled by the relay will not operate. Relays are located in the engine compartment fuse/relay box and in or near the fuse and relay boxes under the dash (see illustrations 3.1a and 3.1c). If a relay is suspect, test it using the procedure below, or have it tested by a dealer service department or a repair shop. If a relay is defective, replace it. Relays cannot be repaired.

TESTING

2   There are three basic types of relays used in these vehicles: normally-open Type A, normally-open Type B and the five-terminal type. Type A and Type B relays have similar internal circuitry, but their external spade terminals are arranged differently and they're numbered differently. Five-terminal relays have different internal circuitry and one more external spade terminal than Type A and Type B relays. To test a relay, remove it from the vehicle and use an ohmmeter to check for continuity.

Normally-open Type A relays
▶ Refer to illustration 5.4

3   Normally-open type A relays are used for:
Air-conditioning clutch relay
Air/fuel (A/F) ratio sensor relay
Condenser fan relay
Headlight relay No. 1 (2001 models)
Headlight relay No. 2 (2001 models)
Headlight relay (2002 and later models)
Horn relay
Power window relay
Radiator fan relay
Reverse relay
Starter cut relay
Taillight relay
Daytime Running Lights (DRL) relay (Canadian models)
PGM-FI main relay No. 1
PGM-FI main relay No. 2

4   Type A relays (see illustration) have four external spade terminals: two horizontal terminals, one on top of the other, with two vertical terminals, side-by-side, below them. In other words, the two horizontal terminals are perpendicular to the two vertical terminals. So an easy way to determine whether you're dealing with a Type A relay is to place the relay you want to test on a table top or workbench, with the spade terminals facing toward you. Then position it so that its two horizontal terminals are on top and its two vertical terminals are on the bottom. If that's what it looks like, it's a Type A relay. If it has four terminals, but they're all parallel to each other, it's a Type B relay. Some Type A relays have numbered terminals (1,2, 3. 4) and some don't. If the Type A relay that you want to test doesn't have numbered terminals, how do you know which terminal is No. 1, which is No. 2, etc.? Here's a simple way to determine terminal numbering: All Type A relays are numbered from top-to-bottom and from left-to-right, so once you have your Type A relay positioned with the two horizontal terminals at the top, those are terminal Nos. 1 and 2, respectively. And the two vertical terminals below them are numbered from left to right, so those two lower terminals are Nos. 3 and 4.

5   To test a normally-open Type A relay verify that there is no continuity between terminal No. 1 and No. 2 when the power is disconnected. Then verify that there is continuity between terminal No. 1 and No. 2 when the No. 3 and No. 4 terminals are connected to power and ground, respectively.

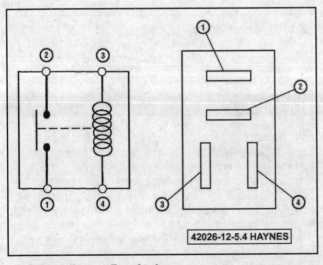

42026-12-5.4 HAYNES

5.4 Normally-open Type A relay

Normally-open Type B relays

▶ **Refer to illustration 5.7**

6   Normally-open Type B relays are used for:
Blower motor relay
Rear window defogger relay

7   Type B relays also have four external spade terminals (see illustration), but they're arranged in two parallel rows, with two terminals per row. So to identify a Type B relay, lay it flat with the four terminals horizontal (NOT vertical!). If two of the terminals are closer together, position the relay so that those two terminals are on your right. Then the terminal in the upper left corner is No. 1, the terminal in the upper right corner is No. 2, the terminal in the lower left corner is No. 3 and the terminal in the lower right corner is No. 4. This method of identification works well on Type B relays like the type 1 and type 2 blower motor relays because they each have a set of terminals that are closer together (Nos. 2 and 4). But on Type B relays such as the rear window defogger relay, where both terminals in each row are parallel (i.e. the two on the right - Nos. 2 and 4 - are the same distance apart as terminal Nos. 1 and 3), there's no way to be sure that you have placed the relay "right side up" because it looks the same right side up or upside down. On these Type Bs, look for the number 1 next to the No. 1 terminal. If the No. 1 terminal isn't numbered, you'll have to take a guess and then see what happens when you power up the relay. If it works as

it's supposed to (closes the other circuit when you power up the control circuit) then you got it right. If it doesn't, flip it over and retest it.

8   To test a normally-open Type B relay verify that there is no continuity between terminal No. 1 and No. 3 when the power is disconnected. Then verify that there is continuity between terminal No. 1 and No. 3 when the No. 2 and No. 4 terminals are connected to power and ground, respectively.

Five-terminal type relays

▶ **Refer to illustration 5.10**

9   Five-terminal relays are used for:
Moonroof-closing relay
Moonroof-opening relay
Low-beam cut relay (Canadian models)

10   Five-terminal relays are easy to identify because they have five terminals (see illustration) instead of four. To determine the terminal numbering, place a five-terminal relay with its two terminals at the top and parallel to the table top, and with the other three vertical terminals underneath the two upper horizontal ones. The top terminal is No. 1, the one below it is No. 2 and the three terminals below No. 2 are, from left to right, Nos. 3, 4 and 5.

11   To test a five-terminal relay verify that there is continuity between terminal No. 1 and No. 4 when the power is disconnected. Then verify that there is continuity between terminal No. 1 and No. 2 when power and ground are connected to the No. 3 and No. 5 terminals.

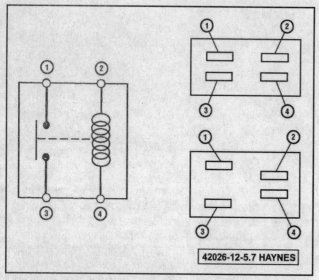

5.7   Normally-open Type B relay

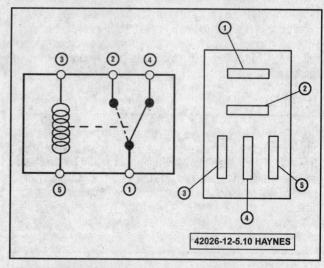

5.10   Five-terminal relay

6   Turn signal and hazard flasher relay - check and replacement

▶ **Refer to illustration 6.1**

❋❋❋ **WARNING:**

The models covered by this manual are equipped with a Supplemental Restraint System (SRS), commonly referred to as airbags. Always disable the airbag system before working in the vicinity of any airbag system component to avoid the possibility of accidental deployment of the airbag, which could cause personal injury (see Section 25).

1   The turn signal and hazard flashers are controlled by the turn signal and hazard flasher relay, which is located on the under-dash fuse and relay box under the left side of the dash (see illustration).

2   If the flasher unit is functioning correctly, you'll hear an audible click when it's operating. If one of the turn signal indicator lights on the instrument cluster flashes more rapidly than normal, a turn signal bulb for that side has a blown filament.

3   If neither turn signal indicator blinks, the problem might be a blown fuse, a faulty turn signal and hazard flasher relay, a broken switch or a loose or open connection. If the left or right turn signal fuse

has blown, check the wiring for a short before installing a new fuse.

4   To access the under-dash fuse and relay box, remove the driver's dashboard lower cover (see illustration 3.1b).

5   Pull the turn signal and hazard flasher relay straight out to remove it.

6   If the turn signal and hazard flasher relay is bad, take it with you when buying a replacement unit. Make sure that the replacement unit is identical to the original.

7   Installation is the reverse of removal.

6.1 The turn signal and hazard flasher unit is located on the under-dash fuse/relay box

7   Steering column switches - replacement

❄❄ WARNING:

The models covered by this manual are equipped with a Supplemental Restraint System (SRS), more commonly known as airbags. Always disable the airbag system before working in the vicinity of any airbag system component to avoid the possibility of accidental deployment of the airbag, which could cause personal injury (see Section 25).

1   Disconnect the cable from the negative battery terminal (see Chapter 5, Section 1), then wait at least three minutes before proceeding.

2   Remove the driver's dashboard lower cover (see illustration 3.1b) and the steering column covers (see Chapter 11).

MULTI-FUNCTION SWITCH

♦ **Refer to illustrations 7.3, 7.4 and 7.5**

3   Disconnect the electrical connector from the multi-function switch (see illustration).

4   Remove the multi-function switch retaining screws (see illustration).

5   Remove the multi-function switch (see illustration).

6   Installation is the reverse of removal.

7.3 To disconnect the electrical connector from the multi-function switch, depress this release tab

7   After you're done, reconnect the cable to the negative battery terminal (see Chapter 5, Section 1).

7.4 To detach the multi-function switch, remove these two screws

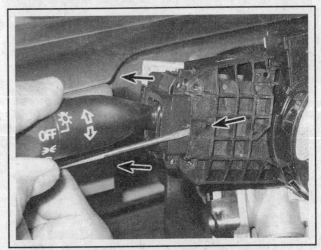

7.5 To remove the multi-function switch, carefully pry the combination switch housing off the small lug on the multi-function switch housing with a small screwdriver, then pull the multi-function switch straight out to the side

7.8 Disconnect the electrical connector from the windshield wiper/washer switch

7.9 To detach the windshield wiper/washer switch, remove these two screws

7.10 To remove the windshield wiper/washer switch, carefully pry the combination switch housing off the small lug on the wiper switch housing with a small screwdriver, then pull the switch straight out to the right

WINDSHIELD WIPER/WASHER SWITCH

▶ **Refer to illustrations 7.8, 7.9 and 7.10**

8 Disconnect the electrical connector from the windshield wiper/washer switch (see illustration).

9 Remove the windshield wiper/washer switch retaining screws (see illustration).

10 Remove the windshield wiper/washer switch (see illustration).

11 Installation is the reverse of removal.

12 After you're done, reconnect the cable to the negative battery terminal (see Chapter 5, Section 1).

8 Ignition switch and key lock cylinder - replacement

✷✷ WARNING:

All models covered by this manual are equipped with a Supplemental Restraint System (SRS), more commonly known as airbags. Always disable the airbag system before working in the vicinity of any airbag system component to avoid the possibility of accidental deployment of the airbag, which could cause personal injury (see Section 25).

1 Disconnect the cable from the negative battery terminal (see Chapter 5, Section 1), then wait at least three minutes before proceeding.

2 Remove the driver's dashboard lower cover (see illustration 3.1b) and the steering column covers (see Chapter 11).

IGNITION SWITCH

▶ **Refer to illustrations 8.3 and 8.4**

3 Disconnect the electrical connector from the ignition switch (see illustration).

4 Remove the ignition switch mounting screws (see illustration) and remove the switch.

5 Installation is the reverse of removal. When you're done, recon-

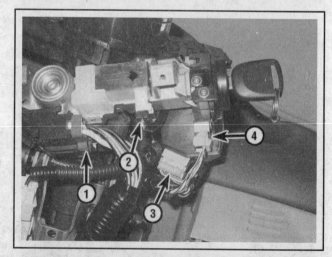

8.3 Ignition switch and key lock cylinder electrical connectors

1 *Ignition switch electrical connector*
2 *Ignition key lock cylinder electrical connector*
3 *Immobilizer control unit/receiver electrical connector*
4 *Ignition key lock cylinder/key light electrical connector*

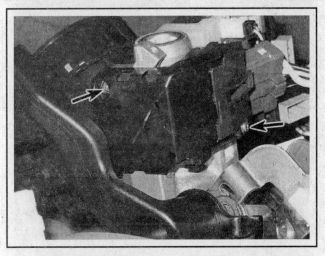

8.4 To detach the ignition switch, remove these two screws

8.7 To detach the key lock cylinder housing from the steering column, drill out the bolts with a 3/16-inch (5 mm) drill bit and remove the bolts with a screw extractor

nect the cable to the negative battery terminal and perform the PCM idle learn procedure (see Chapter 5, Section 1), then verify that the ignition switch operates correctly in the LOCK, ACC, ON and START positions.

KEY LOCK CYLINDER

▶ **Refer to illustration 8.7**

6   Disconnect the ignition switch electrical connector and the connectors for the ignition key lock cylinder, the immobilizer control unit/receiver and the ignition key lock cylinder/key light (see illustration 8.3).

7   Center-punch the shear-head bolts that secure the key lock cylin-

der housing to the steering column, then drill a hole in the center of each bolt with a 3/16-inch (5 mm) drill bit (see illustration) and unscrew them with a screw extractor.

8   Remove the key lock cylinder assembly from the steering column.

9   Before tightening the new shear-head bolts, insert the ignition key and verify that the steering wheel lock mechanism functions correctly and that the ignition key turns freely in the key lock cylinder. Then tighten the shear-head bolts until the heads break off.

10 Installation is otherwise the reverse of removal. When you're done, reconnect the cable to the negative battery terminal and perform the PCM idle learn procedure (see Chapter 5, Section 1).

| 9 | **Dashboard switches - replacement** |

✳✳ WARNING:

The models covered by this manual are equipped with a Supplemental Restraint System (SRS), more commonly known as airbags. Always disable the airbag system before working in the vicinity of any airbag system component to avoid the possibility of accidental deployment of the airbag, which could cause personal injury (see Section 25).

COUPE AND SEDAN

Switches in driver's pocket (cruise control, moonroof and power mirrors)

▶ **Refer to illustrations 9.3a, 9.3b and 9.4**

1   Disconnect the cable from the negative battery terminal (see Chapter 5, Section 1), then wait at least three minutes before proceeding.

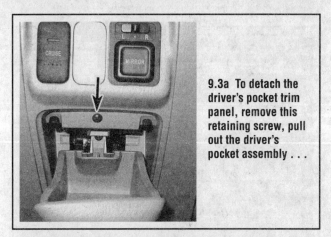

9.3a To detach the driver's pocket trim panel, remove this retaining screw, pull out the driver's pocket assembly . . .

2   Remove the driver's dashboard under cover (see *Dashboard trim panels - removal and installation* in Chapter 11).

3   Open the "driver's pocket," remove the retaining screw and remove the driver's pocket assembly (see illustrations).

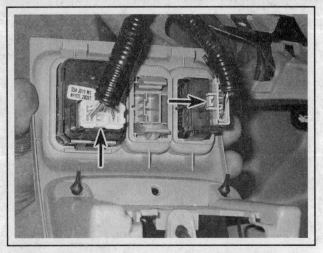

9.3b ... then depress the release tab on each electrical connector and pull out the connectors

4   To remove the cruise control, moonroof or power mirror switch, simply depress the release tab on top and push the switch out from the backside of the trim piece (see illustration).

5   Installation is the reverse of removal. When you're done, reconnect the cable to the negative battery terminal, then perform the PCM idle learn procedure (see Chapter 5, Section 1). Finally, be sure to verify that the switch that you replaced works correctly.

Hazard flasher switch

▶ Refer to illustrations 9.8 and 9.9

6   Disconnect the cable from the negative battery terminal (see Chapter 5, Section 1) and wait at least three minutes.

7   Remove the center trim panel from the dashboard (see Chapter 11).

8   Disconnect the electrical connector from the hazard flasher switch (see illustration).

9   Remove the hazard flasher switch (see illustration).

10 Installation is the reverse of removal. When you're done, reconnect the cable to the negative battery terminal, then perform the PCM idle learn procedure (see Chapter 5, Section 1). Finally, be sure to verify that the hazard flasher switch works correctly.

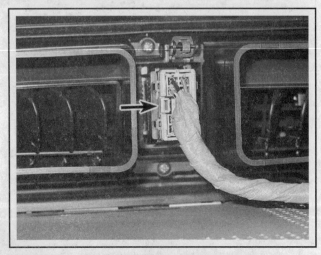

9.8 To disconnect the electrical connector from the hazard flasher switch, depress this release tab and pull off the connector

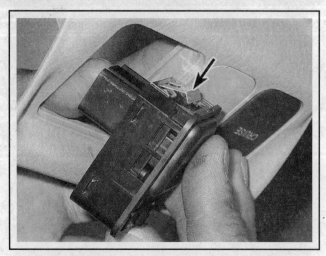

9.4 To release a switch from the driver's pocket trim panel, depress the locking spring or tab with a small screwdriver from the backside of the trim panel, then push out the switch through the front side of the panel

Rear window defogger switch

11 The rear window defogger switch is an integral part of the heater and air conditioning control assembly. To replace the rear window defogger switch, you must replace the heater and air conditioning control assembly (see Chapter 3).

CR-V

Cruise control switch or moonroof switch

12 Disconnect the cable from the negative battery terminal (see Chapter 5, Section 1), then wait at least three minutes before proceeding.

13 Remove the driver's dashboard lower cover (see Chapter 11).

14 Depress the release tabs on the cruise control switch or moonroof switch and push the switch out of the trim panel (see illustration 9.4), then disconnect the electrical connector from the switch.

15 Installation is the reverse of removal. When you're done, reconnect the cable to the negative battery terminal, then perform the PCM idle learn procedure (see Chapter 5, Section 1). Finally, be sure to verify that the cruise control switch or moonroof switch works correctly.

9.9 To separate the hazard flasher switch from the center trim panel, depress these two locking tabs with a small screwdriver from the backside of the trim panel and push out the switch through the front of the trim panel

Hazard flasher switch

16 Disconnect the cable from the negative battery terminal (see Chapter 5, Section 1), then wait at least three minutes before proceeding.

17 Remove the center trim panel (see Chapter 11).

18 Disconnect the electrical connector from the hazard flasher switch (see illustration 9.8).

19 Depress the release tabs, then push out the hazard flasher switch from behind the center trim panel (see illustration 9.9).

20 Installation is the reverse of removal. When you're done, reconnect the cable to the negative battery terminal, then perform the PCM idle learn procedure (see Chapter 5, Section 1). Finally, be sure to verify that the hazard flasher switch works correctly.

Seat heater switches

21 Disconnect the cable from the negative battery terminal (see Chapter 5, Section 1), then wait at least three minutes before proceeding.

22 Remove the driver's dashboard lower cover (see Chapter 11).

23 Reach underneath the dash and disconnect the electrical connector from the seat heater switch.

24 Depress the seat heater switch release tabs with a small screwdriver and push the switch out of the dashboard from the backside of the dash.

25 Installation is the reverse of removal. When you're done, reconnect the cable to the negative battery terminal, then perform the PCM idle learn procedure (see Chapter 5, Section 1). Finally, be sure to verify that the seat heater switch works correctly.

HATCHBACK

Hazard flasher switch

26 Disconnect the cable from the negative battery terminal (see Chapter 5, Section 1), then wait at least three minutes before proceeding.

27 Remove the center trim panel (see Chapter 11).

28 Disconnect the electrical connector from the hazard warning switch (see illustration 9.8).

29 Remove the two hazard warning switch mounting screws, then push out the hazard warning switch from behind the center trim panel (see illustration 9.9).

30 Installation is the reverse of removal. When you're done, reconnect the cable to the negative battery terminal, then perform the PCM idle learn procedure (see Chapter 5, Section 1). Finally, be sure to verify that the hazard flasher switch works correctly.

Rear window defogger switch

31 The rear window defogger switch is an integral part of the heater and air conditioning control assembly. To replace the defogger switch, you must replace the heater and air conditioning control assembly (see Chapter 3).

Cruise control main switch

32 Disconnect the cable from the negative battery terminal (see Chapter 5, Section 1), then wait at least three minutes before proceeding.

33 Remove the driver's dashboard lower cover (see Chapter 11).

34 Reach underneath the dash and disconnect the electrical connector from the cruise control main switch.

35 Depress the cruise control main switch release tabs with a small screwdriver and push the switch out of the dashboard from the backside of the dash.

36 Installation is the reverse of removal. When you're done, reconnect the cable to the negative battery terminal, then perform the PCM idle learn procedure (see Chapter 5, Section 1). Finally, be sure to verify that the cruise control main switch works correctly.

Power mirror switch

37 Disconnect the cable from the negative battery terminal (see Chapter 5, Section 1), then wait at least three minutes before proceeding.

38 Remove the driver's pocket.

39 Reach through the opening for the driver's pocket, depress the release tabs on the power mirror switch and push the switch out of the dash from the backside.

40 Disconnect the electrical connector from the power mirror switch.

41 Installation is the reverse of removal. When you're done, reconnect the cable to the negative battery terminal, then perform the PCM idle learn procedure (see Chapter 5, Section 1). Finally, be sure to verify that the cruise control main switch works correctly.

Moonroof switch

42 Disconnect the cable from the negative battery terminal (see Chapter 5, Section 1), then wait at least three minutes before proceeding.

43 Pry the moonroof switch out of the headliner.

44 Disconnect the electrical connector from the moonroof switch and remove the switch.

45 Installation is the reverse of removal. When you're done, reconnect the cable to the negative battery terminal, then perform the PCM idle learn procedure (see Chapter 5, Section 1). Finally, be sure to verify that the cruise control main switch works correctly.

10 Instrument cluster - removal and installation

▶ Refer to illustrations 10.3a and 10.3b

☀☀ WARNING:

The models covered by this manual are equipped with a Supplemental Restraint System (SRS), more commonly known as airbags. Always disable the airbag system before working in the vicinity of any airbag system component to avoid the possibility of accidental deployment of the airbag, which could cause personal injury (see Section 25).

1   Disconnect the cable from the negative battery terminal and wait at least three minutes before proceeding (see Chapter 5, Section 1).

2   Remove the instrument cluster trim panel (see Chapter 11).

3   Remove the instrument cluster retaining screws (see illustration), then pull out the cluster and disconnect the electrical connectors from the backside (see illustration).

4   Installation is the reverse of removal.

5   Reconnect the cable to the negative battery terminal and perform the PCM idle learn procedure (see Chapter 5, Section 1). When you're done, verify that the instrument cluster functions correctly.

10.3a To detach the instrument cluster from the dashboard, remove these three screws . . .

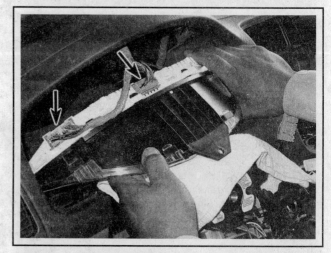

10.3b . . . then pull out the cluster and disconnect the electrical connectors (coupe/sedan shown, CR-V and hatchback similar)

11 Wiper motor - check and replacement

WIPER MOTOR CIRCUIT CHECK

➡Note: Refer to the wiring diagrams for wire colors in the following checks. When checking for voltage, probe a grounded 12-volt test light to each terminal at a connector until it lights; this verifies voltage (power) at the terminal. If the following checks fail to locate the problem, have the system diagnosed by a dealer service department or other properly equipped repair facility.

1   If the wipers work slowly, make sure the battery is fully charged and in good condition (see Chapter 5). If the battery is in good shape, remove the wiper motor (see below) and operate the wiper arms by hand. Check for binding linkage and pivots. Lubricate or repair the linkage or pivots as necessary. Reinstall the wiper motor. If the wipers still operate slowly, check for loose or corroded connections, especially the ground connection. If all connections look OK, replace the motor.

2   If the wipers fail to operate when activated, check the fuse (see Section 3). If the fuse is OK, connect a jumper wire between the wiper motor's ground terminal and ground, then retest. If the motor works now, repair the ground connection. If the motor still doesn't work, turn the wiper switch to the HI position and check for voltage at the motor.

➡Note: Remove the hood seal and cowl covers (see Step 7) and disconnect the electrical connector (see Step 8).

3   If there's voltage at the connector, remove the motor and check it off the vehicle with fused jumper wires from the battery. If the motor now works, check for binding linkage (see Step 1). If the motor still doesn't work, replace it. If there's no voltage to the motor, check for voltage at the wiper control relays. If there's voltage at the wiper control relays and no voltage at the wiper motor, have the switch tested. If the switch is OK, the wiper control relay is probably bad. See Section 5 for relay testing.

4   If the interval (delay) function is inoperative, check the continuity of all the wiring between the switch and the wiper control module.

5   If the wipers fail to "park" (if they stop at the position that they're in when the switch is turned off instead of returning to their normal "off" position), turn the wiper switch to OFF and the ignition switch to ON, then check for voltage at the park feed wire of the wiper motor connector. If no voltage is present, check for an open circuit between the wiper motor and the fuse panel.

WIPER MOTOR REPLACEMENT

Windshield wiper motor

▶ **Refer to illustrations 11.6, 11.8, 11.9a, 11.9b, 11.9c, 11.9d and 11.10**

6   Remove the windshield wiper arm retaining nut covers and then remove the nuts. Be sure to mark the position of each wiper arm in relation to its splined shaft (see illustration), then remove the wiper arms.

7   Remove the hood seal and cowl covers (see Chapter 11).

8   Remove the windshield wiper linkage/motor assembly mounting bolts (see illustration), then disconnect the electrical connector from the windshield wiper motor.

9   Separate the windshield wiper linkage from the wiper motor (see illustrations).

10   Remove the windshield wiper motor mounting bolts (see illustration) and separate the motor from its mounting bracket.

11   Before installing the windshield wiper linkage (especially if you're installing the old linkage), be sure to grease the moving parts.

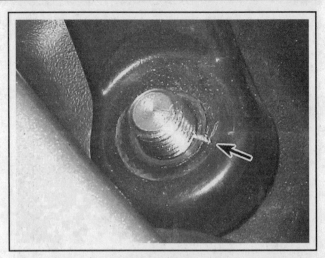

11.6 Pry off the trim caps and remove the windshield wiper arm retaining nuts, then mark the relationship of each wiper arm to its splined shaft before removing the arm

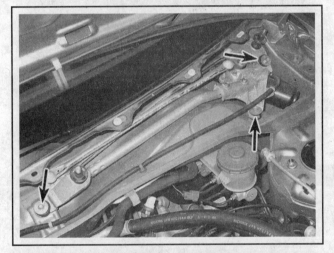

11.8 To detach the windshield wiper linkage/motor assembly from the cowl area, remove these three bolts

11.9a Mark the relationship of the linkage arm and the motor mounting bracket to ensure that the arm is correctly realigned during reassembly

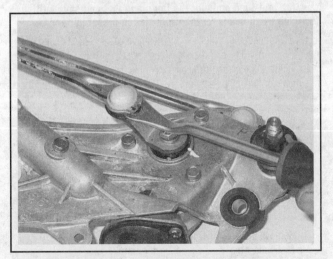

11.9b To separate the windshield wiper linkage from the linkage arm, pry the two halves of the spherical bearing apart

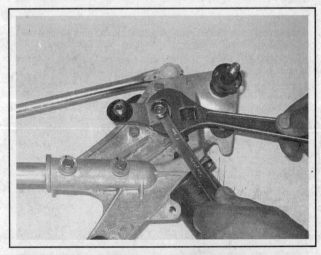

11.9c Using an adjustable wrench (shown) or a pair of large adjustable pliers to immobilize the linkage arm, loosen the arm retaining nut and remove the arm from the motor shaft

11.9d Mark the relationship of the linkage arm to the motor shaft, then remove the arm from the shaft

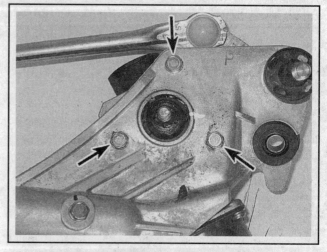

11.10 To detach the windshield wiper motor from its mounting bracket, remove these three bolts

12 Installation is otherwise the reverse of removal. Be sure to align the marks you made between the linkage arm and the motor mounting bracket and between the windshield wiper arm and the motor shaft.

13 Reconnect the cable to the negative battery terminal, then perform the PCM idle learn procedure (see Chapter 5, Section 1).

14 Turn on the windshield wipers and verify that the wiper motor operates correctly in all modes (see your owner's manual if necessary).

Rear window wiper motor

15 Open the hatch. Remove the hatch trim panel (see Chapter 11).

16 Remove the windshield wiper arm retaining nut cover, then remove the nut. Be sure to mark the position of the wiper arm in relation to its splined shaft (see illustration 11.6), then remove the wiper arm.

17 Disconnect the electrical connector from the rear window wiper motor.

18 Remove the three wiper motor mounting bolts.

19 Remove the rear window wiper motor.

20 Installation is the reverse of removal.

12 Radio and speakers - removal and installation

❈❈ WARNING:

The models covered by this manual are equipped with a Supplemental Restraint System (SRS), more commonly known as airbags. Always disable the airbag system before working in the vicinity of any airbag system component to avoid the possibility of accidental deployment of the airbag, which could cause personal injury (see Section 25).

12.2 Pull out the center trim panel and disconnect the electrical connector and antenna cable from the backside of the radio

COUPE AND SEDAN

Radio

▶ **Refer to illustration 12.2 and 12.3**

➡**Note: Before beginning this procedure, make sure that you have the anti-theft code for the radio and that you have written down the frequencies for the radio station preset buttons.**

1 Disconnect the cable from the negative battery terminal and wait at least three minutes before proceeding (see Chapter 5, Section 1).

2 Remove the center trim panel from the dashboard (see Chapter 11), then disconnect the antenna and the electrical connector from the back of the radio (see illustration).

3 Remove the radio mounting bolts (see illustration) and remove the radio from its mounting bracket.

4 Installation is the reverse of removal.

5 Reconnect the cable to the negative battery terminal and perform the PCM idle learn procedure (see Chapter 5, Section 1).

Speakers

Tweeters

6 Remove the front door trim panel (see Chapter 11).

7 Disconnect the electrical connector from the tweeter.

8 Remove the mirror mount cover (see Chapter 11).

9 Remove the tweeter retaining screw and remove the tweeter.

10 Installation is the reverse of removal.

12.3 To detach the radio unit from its mounting bracket, remove the two bolts from each side

12.12 Carefully pry the front door speaker out of the door with a panel removal tool (shown) or with a large screwdriver (pry only at the top)

12.13 Disconnect the electrical connector from the front door speaker and remove the speaker

Front door speakers

▶ Refer to illustrations 12.12 and 12.13

11 Remove the front door trim panel (see Chapter 11).
12 Working from the top, carefully pry the speaker out of door (see illustration).
13 Disconnect the electrical connector (see illustration) and remove the speaker from the vehicle.
14 Installation is the reverse of removal.

Rear speakers

▶ Refer to illustrations 12.16 and 12.17

15 Remove the rear shelf trim panel (see Chapter 11).
16 Open the trunk and disconnect the electrical connector from the speaker (see illustration).
17 Remove the speaker mounting screws (see illustration) and pull the speaker out of its receptacle.
18 Installation is the reverse of removal.

CR-V

Radio

➡Note: Before beginning this procedure, make sure that you have the anti-theft code for the radio and that you have written down the frequencies for the radio station preset buttons.

19 Remove the dashboard center panel (see *Dashboard trim panels - removal and installation* in Chapter 11).
20 Remove the four radio mounting bolts and pull out the radio.
21 Disconnect the electrical connector and the antenna lead from the radio.
22 If you're planning to replace the radio with a new unit, remove all four mounting bracket bolts from the left and right radio mounting brackets and remove the mounting brackets from both sides of the radio. Install these brackets on the new unit.
23 Installation is the reverse of removal.

Speakers

Door speakers

24 Remove the door trim panel (see Chapter 11).
25 Push down on the upper release tab and pull out the top of the

12.16 To disconnect the electrical connector from a rear speaker, open the trunk, locate the speaker connector at the front of the trunk right behind the rear seat, then depress the release tabs and pull off the connector

speaker just enough to release the upper tab (if you pull out the speaker too far, you will damage the two lower mounting tabs). Then pull the speaker straight up to disengage its two lower mounting tabs.

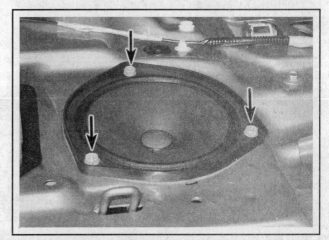

12.17 To detach a rear speaker from the rear shelf area, remove these three screws

26 Disconnect the electrical connector from the speaker and remove the speaker.

27 Installation is the reverse of removal.

Tweeters

28 Carefully pry the tweeter speaker grille loose from the dashboard, then remove the tweeter speaker grille and the tweeter as a single assembly.

29 Disconnect the electrical connector from the tweeter and remove the tweeter.

30 Installation is the reverse of removal.

HATCHBACK

Radio

→Note: Before beginning this procedure, make sure that you have the anti-theft code for the radio and that you have written down the frequencies for the radio station preset buttons.

31 Remove the driver's dashboard lower cover (see *Dashboard trim panels - removal and installation* in Chapter 11).

32 Open the glove box, remove the glove "stops" (see *Glove box - removal and installation* in Chapter 11) and let the glove box hang down.

33 Remove the two center panel mounting bolts, then pull out the center panel.

34 Disconnect the electrical connector and the antenna lead from the radio, disconnect the electrical connectors from the heater/air condi-tioner control assembly and remove the center panel, the radio and the heater/air conditioner control panel as a single assembly.

35 Remove the heater/air conditioner control panel from the center panel (see Chapter 3).

36 Remove the four radio mounting bolts and detach the radio from its mounting brackets.

37 Installation is the reverse of removal.

Speakers

Door speakers

38 Remove the door trim panel (see Chapter 11).

39 Pull the top of the speaker straight out, just enough to release the upper retaining tab, then pull the speaker straight up to disengage the two lower mounting tabs and remove the speaker from the door and disconnect the speaker electrical connector.

40 Installation is the reverse of removal.

Tweeters

41 Carefully pry the tweeter out of the mirror mounting trim cover.

42 Disconnect the electrical connector from the tweeter.

43 Installation is the reverse of removal.

Rear speakers

44 Carefully pry off the speaker cover.

45 Remove the three speaker mounting screws.

46 Pull out the speaker and disconnect the electrical connector.

47 Installation is the reverse of removal.

13 Antenna - removal and installation

COUPE AND SEDAN (REPAIR ONLY)

1 Coupes and sedans use a rear window-mounted antenna grid, which is similar to the defogger grid on the rear window. To replace the antenna, you have to replace the rear window. However, you can easily repair the antenna grid as long as the broken part is no more than one inch long. The procedure for repairing the antenna grid is identical to repairing the rear window defogger grid (see Section 14).

CR-V

2 Unscrew and remove the antenna mast from its mounting base. (If you're simply replacing the antenna mast, stop here. If you're replacing the entire antenna assembly, keep going.)

3 Unscrew the antenna nut, the mounting base and the rubber bushing.

4 Disconnect the antenna lead electrical connector.

5 Remove the right inner fender housing panel (see *Front fender - removal and installation* in Chapter 11).

6 Pull the antenna lead and weatherseal grommet out of the A-pillar.

7 Remove the antenna housing bracket mounting nut and remove the antenna mounting bracket assembly.

8 Installation is the reverse of removal.

HATCHBACK

9 Carefully remove the rear part of the headliner.

10 Disconnect the electrical connector from the antenna.

11 Remove the antenna mounting nut.

12 Remove the antenna.

13 Installation is the reverse of removal.

14 Rear window defogger - check and repair

1 The rear window defogger consists of a number of horizontal elements baked onto the glass surface.

2 Small breaks in the element can be repaired without removing the rear window.

CHECK

▶ **Refer to illustrations 14.4, 14.5 and 14.7**

3 Turn the ignition switch and defogger system switches to the ON position. Using a voltmeter, place the positive probe against the defogger grid positive terminal and the negative probe against the ground terminal. If battery voltage is not indicated, check the fuse, defogger switch and related wiring. If voltage is indicated, but all or part of the defogger doesn't heat, proceed with the following tests.

4 When measuring voltage during the next two tests, wrap a piece of aluminum foil around the tip of the voltmeter positive probe and press the foil against the heating element with your finger (see illustration). Place the negative probe on the defogger grid ground terminal.

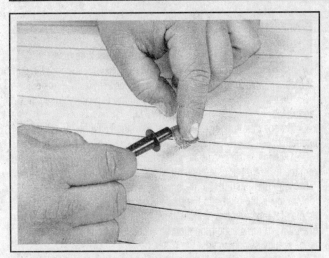

14.4 When measuring the voltage at the rear window defogger grid, wrap a piece of aluminum foil around the positive probe of the voltmeter and press the foil against the wire with your finger

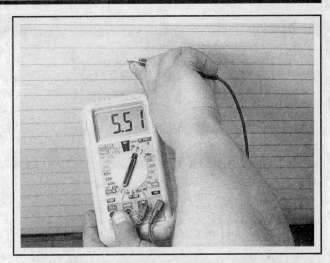

14.5 To determine if a heating element has broken, check the voltage at the center of each element; if the voltage is 5 or 6-volts, the element is unbroken, but if the voltage is 10 or 12-volts, the element is broken between the center and the ground side. If there is no voltage, the element is broken between the center and the positive side

5   Check the voltage at the center of each heating element (see illustration). If the voltage is 5 or 6-volts, the element is okay (there is no break). If the voltage is zero, the element is broken between the center of the element and the positive end. If the voltage is 10 to 12-volts the element is broken between the center of the element and ground. Check each heating element.

6   Connect the negative lead to a good body ground. The reading should stay the same. If it doesn't, the ground connection is bad.

7   To find the break, place the voltmeter negative probe against the defogger ground terminal. Place the voltmeter positive probe with the foil strip against the heating element at the positive terminal end and slide it toward the negative terminal end. The point at which the voltmeter deflects from several volts to zero is the point at which the heating element is broken (see illustration).

REPAIR

▶ **Refer to illustration 14.13**

8   Repair the break in the element using a repair kit for this purpose (available at most auto parts stores). Make sure that the repair kit includes plastic conductive epoxy.

9   Prior to repairing a break, turn off the system and allow it to cool off for a few minutes.

10 Lightly buff the element area with fine steel wool, then clean it thoroughly with rubbing alcohol.

11 Use masking tape to mask off the area being repaired.

12 Thoroughly mix the epoxy, following the instructions provided with the repair kit.

13 Apply the epoxy material to the slit in the masking tape, overlapping the undamaged area about 3/4-inch on either end (see illustration).

14 Allow the repair to cure for 24 hours before removing the tape and using the system.

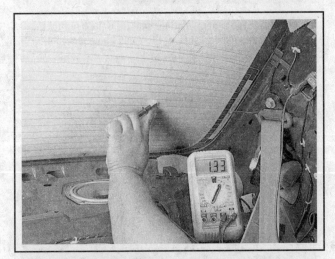

14.7 To find the break, place the voltmeter negative lead against the defogger ground terminal, place the voltmeter positive lead with the foil strip against the heating element at the positive terminal end and slide it toward the negative terminal end. The point at which the voltmeter reading changes abruptly is the point at which the element is broken

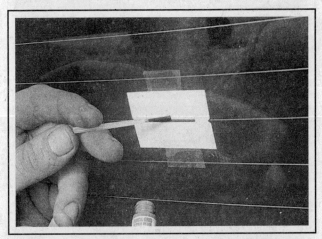

14.13 To use a defogger repair kit, apply masking tape to the inside of the window at the damaged area, then brush on the special conductive coating

15 Headlight bulb - replacement

2001 THROUGH 2003 COUPE AND SEDAN, 2002 THROUGH 2004 CR-V AND 2002 AND 2003 HATCHBACK

► Refer to illustrations 15.3, 15.4, 15.5a and 15.5b

✳✳ WARNING:

Halogen gas filled bulbs are under pressure and can shatter if the surface is scratched or the bulb is dropped. Wear eye protection and handle the bulbs carefully, grasping only the base whenever possible. Do not touch the surface of the bulb with your fingers because the oil from your skin could cause it to overheat and fail prematurely. If you do touch the bulb surface, clean it with rubbing alcohol.

1   Make sure that the headlight switch and the ignition switch are both turned off, then open the hood.

2   If you're going to replace the left headlight bulb, remove the power steering reservoir from its mounting bracket by pulling it straight up, then set it aside (do NOT disconnect any power steering hoses!).

3   Disconnect the electrical connector from the headlight (see illustration).

4   Remove the rubber weather seal from the headlight housing (see illustration).

5   Disengage the headlight bulb retainer wire, then remove the bulb from the headlight housing (see illustrations).

6   Without touching the glass part of the new bulb with your bare fingers, insert the bulb into the headlight assembly. Make sure that the three metal tabs on the bulb (see illustration 15.5a) are aligned with the three slots in the plastic mounting base and that the bulb mounting flange is fully seated against the base.

7   Swing the bulb retainer wire back into place and engage the end with its slot.

8   Install the rubber weather seal on the back of the headlight assembly (see illustration).

9   Plug in the electrical connector.

10 Verify that the new headlight bulb operates correctly.

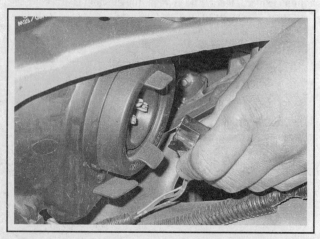

15.3 Disconnect the electrical connector from the headlight assembly (coupe/sedan shown, CR-V and hatchback similar)

15.4 Remove the rubber weather seal from the headlight assembly (coupe/sedan shown, CR-V and hatchback similar)

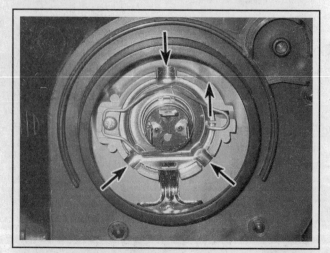

15.5a Before removing the old headlight bulb, note how the three metal tabs on the bulb mounting flange are aligned with their respective slots in the headlight mounting base. To disengage the headlight bulb retainer wire from the headlight assembly, lift the right end of the wire up and out of its slot . . .

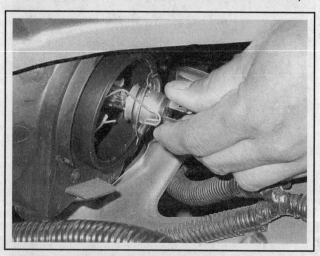

15.5b . . . then swing the wire retainer to the left (don't try to remove the retainer - it's hinged on the left side) and pull the headlight bulb out of the headlight assembly

2004 COUPE, SEDAN AND HATCHBACK

11 Make sure that the headlight switch and the ignition switch are both turned off, then open the hood.

12 Disconnect the electrical connector from the headlight bulb socket.

13 Rotate the bulb socket counterclockwise 45-degrees and pull it out.

14 Installation is the reverse of removal.

16 Headlights - adjustment

▶ **Refer to illustrations 16.1 and 16.3**

※※ CAUTION:

The headlights must be aimed correctly. If adjusted incorrectly they could blind the driver of an oncoming vehicle and cause a serious accident or seriously reduce your ability to see the road. The headlights should be checked for correct aim every 12 months and any time a new headlight is installed or front end body work is performed. It should be emphasized that the following procedure is only an interim step that will provide temporary adjustment until a properly equipped shop can adjust the headlights.

1 The vertical adjuster (see illustration) is located on the upper backside of each headlight housing. Use a Phillips screwdriver to turn the adjusters. (There are no horizontal adjustment screws.)

2 There are several methods for adjusting the headlights. The simplest method requires masking tape, a blank wall and a level floor.

3 Position masking tape vertically on the wall in relation to the vehicle centerline and in relation to the centerlines of both headlights (see illustration).

4 Position a horizontal tape line in reference to the centerline of all the headlights.

➡**Note: It might be easier to position the tape on the wall with the vehicle parked only a few inches away.**

5 Adjustment should be made with the vehicle parked 25 feet from the wall, sitting level, the gas tank half-full and no heavy load in the vehicle.

6 With the low beams turned on, position the high intensity zone so it is two inches below the horizontal line.

7 With the high beams on, the high intensity zone should be vertically centered with the exact center just below the horizontal line.

➡**Note: It might not be possible to position the headlight aim exactly for both high and low beams. If a compromise must be made, keep in mind that the low beams are the most used and have the greatest effect on safety.**

8 If you have any difficulty adjusting the headlights, have them adjusted by a dealer service department as soon as possible.

16.1 The vertical adjuster is located on the upper backside of each headlight housing (coupe/sedan shown, CR-V and hatchback similar)

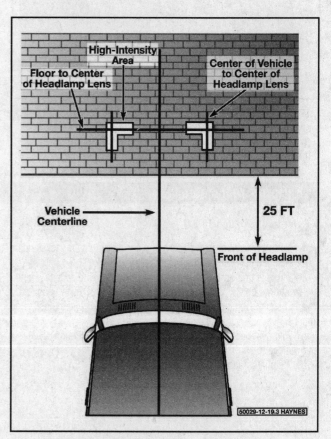

16.3 Headlight adjustment details

17 Headlight housing - replacement

▶ **Refer to illustrations 17.3a, 17.3b and 17.5**

1   Make sure that the headlight switch and the ignition switch are turned off.

2   Remove the front bumper cover (see Chapter 11).

3   Remove the headlight housing mounting bolts (see illustrations).

4   Disconnect the electrical connectors from the headlight, turn signal and parking light bulbs.

5   If you're replacing the headlight housing, detach the corner bumper beam (the small black metal piece that's attached to the underside of the headlight housing (see illustration) and install it on the new headlight housing unit.

6   Installation is the reverse of removal.

17.3a To detach the headlight housing assembly, remove the two upper mounting bolts . . .

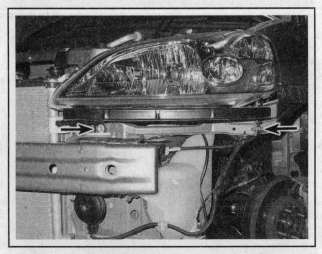

17.3b . . . and the two lower mounting bolts (coupe/sedan shown, CR-V and hatchback similar, except that CR-V has *two* mounting bolts at the outer end of the corner upper beam instead of one bolt as shown here)

17.6 To detach the corner bumper beam from the underside of the headlight housing, remove this bolt (coupe/sedan shown, CR-V and hatchback similar)

18 Horn - replacement

▶ **Refer to illustration 18.3**

1   Raise the front of the vehicle and place it securely on jackstands.

2   Remove the front bumper cover (see Chapter 11).

3   There is one horn (see illustration) on coupes and sedans. There are two horns on CR-Vs and on hatchbacks, one below each headlight.

4   Disconnect the electrical connector from the horn (see illustration 18.3).

5   Remove the horn mounting bracket bolt (see illustration 18.3) and remove the horn.

6   Installation is the reverse of removal.

18.3 On coupes and sedans (shown), the horn is located below the left headlight. To remove the horn, simply disconnect the electrical connector and remove the mounting bracket bolt (on CR-Vs and hatchbacks there are two horns, one below each headlight, and they're virtually identical to this unit)

19 Bulb replacement

COUPE AND SEDAN

Exterior light bulbs

Front turn signal/side marker and parking light bulb(s)

▶ **Refer to illustrations 19.3a, 19.3b, 19.3c and 19.4**

1 Loosen the left or right front wheel lug nuts. Raise the front of the vehicle and place it securely on jackstands. Remove the left or right front wheel.

2 Remove the front part of the left or right inner fender liner (see *Front fender - removal and installation* in Chapter 11).

3 Locate the front turn signal bulb holder and the front parking light bulb holder (see illustration). Disconnect the electrical connector from the front turn signal bulb holder (see illustration) or from the front parking light bulb holder. To remove the bulb holder, simply turn it counterclockwise (see illustration) and pull it out of the housing.

4 Remove the turn signal bulb from the bulb holder. On 2001 through 2003 models, simply pull the bulb straight out of its holder (see illustration). To install a new bulb, push it straight into the bulb holder. 2004 models have a single bayonet-type bulb for everything. To remove the bulb from the holder on a 2004 model, push it into the holder, rotate it counterclockwise, then pull it out of the holder. To install a new bulb, push it into the bulb holder until it's seated, then give it a clockwise turn to lock it into place in the holder.

5 Installation is the reverse of removal.

High-mount brake light

▶ **Refer to illustration 19.6**

6 Open the trunk and look for the electrical connector for the high-mount brake light, which is located in the underside of the rear shelf area, just ahead of the trunk light (see illustration).

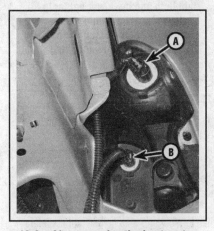

19.3a After removing the front part of the inner fender liner, locate the electrical connector for the front turn signal light bulb (A) or for the front parking light bulb (B) (2001 through 2003 coupe/sedan shown; 2004 coupe/sedan uses a single bulb for everything)

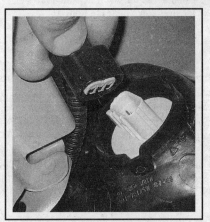

19.3b Disconnect the electrical connector from the front turn signal light/side marker bulb holder (shown) or from the parking light bulb holder

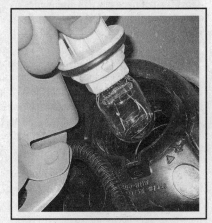

19.3c To remove the bulb holder for the turn signal/side marker bulb holder (shown) or for the parking light bulb holder from the headlight housing, turn it counterclockwise and pull it out of the housing

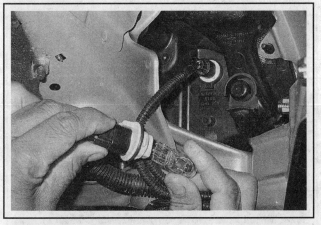

19.4 To remove the front turn signal/side marker bulb or the front parking light bulb from its holder on a 2001 through 2003 coupe or sedan, grasp the holder firmly and pull the bulb straight out

19.6 Disconnect the electrical connector from the high-mount brake light bulb holder, then turn the bulb holder counter-clockwise to remove it from the high-mount brake light housing

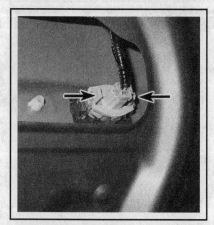

19.11 To remove the bulb holder for either license plate light, depress these two release tabs and pull the holder out of the license plate light lens (it's not necessary to disconnect the electrical connector)

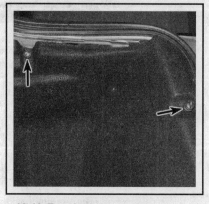

19.16 To gain access to the outer taillight bulbs, remove these two screws and carefully peel back the molded carpeting (if you have difficulty pulling back the carpeting, remove the third screw, which is located down near the floor of the trunk)

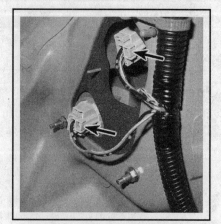

19.17 When you peel back the carpeting in the trunk, you'll see two bulb holders: the upper bulb holder is for the brake/tail/rear side marker light bulb and the lower holder is for the turn signal light bulb. To remove either bulb holder, simply turn it counterclockwise and pull it out

7   Disconnect the electrical connector from the bulb holder.

8   To remove the bulb holder from the high-mount brake light assembly rotate the bulb holder counterclockwise and pull it out.

9   To remove the old bulb from the bulb holder simply pull it straight out of the holder. To install a new bulb, push it straight into the bulb holder.

10   Installation is the reverse of removal.

License plate light

▶ **Refer to illustration 19.11**

11   Open the trunk and locate the electrical connector for the license plate bulb you wish to replace (see illustration).

12   To remove the bulb holder depress the release tabs on the sides of the holder (see illustration 19.11) and pull it out. (It's not necessary to disconnect the electrical connector from the bulb holder in order to remove the holder.)

13   To remove the bulb from the socket, pull it straight out.

14   To install a new bulb in the holder push it straight into the holder.

15   Installation is the reverse of removal.

Taillight bulbs (in rear fender)

▶ **Refer to illustrations 19.16 and 19.17**

16   To access the outer taillight bulbs (in the vehicle's rear fender), detach and peel back the trunk carpeting (see illustration).

17   After peeling back the carpeting, you'll see two bulb holders (see illustration). The upper bulb holder is for the brake/tail/rear side marker light bulb; the lower bulb holder is for the turn signal light bulb. To remove a bulb holder from an inner taillight, rotate the holder counterclockwise and pull it out.

18   To remove an inner taillight bulb from its holder, pull it straight out.

19   To install a bulb in its socket, push it straight into the socket.

20   Installation is the reverse of removal.

Taillight bulbs (in trunk lid)

▶ **Refer to illustration 19.21**

21   Open the trunk lid and locate the bulb holders for the taillight and back-up light bulbs (see illustration).

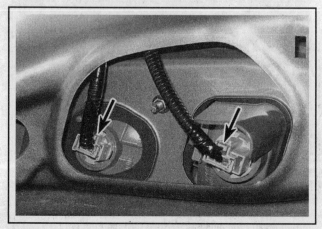

19.21 The bulb holders for the taillight and back-up light bulbs are in the trunk lid

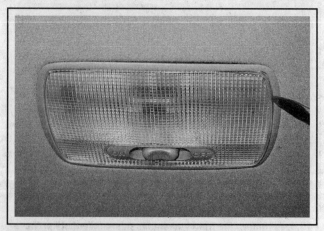

19.25 To remove the lens from the ceiling light, simply pry it off with a small screwdriver. Be careful not to damage the plastic trim around the edge of the lens

19.26 To remove the old bulb from the ceiling light, simply pull it straight out of the two metal clips

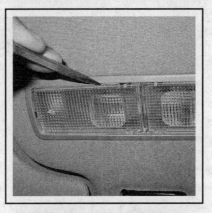

19.29 To remove the lens for the spotlight or the lens for the ceiling light/spotlight, carefully pry it loose with a fingernail file or with a small screwdriver

19.30 To remove a bulb from a spotlight assembly, pull it out of the two metal clips

22 To remove either bulb holder, turn it counterclockwise and pull it out.

23 To remove either bulb from its bulb holder, simply pull it straight out of the holder.

24 To install either bulb in its bulb holder, push it straight into the holder.

Interior lights

Ceiling light (dome light)

▶ **Refer to illustrations 19.25 and 19.26**

25 Using a fingernail file or a small screwdriver, pry off the lens (see illustration). Be careful not to damage the plastic trim around the edge of the lens.

26 Remove the old bulb from the two metal clips (see illustration).

27 Install the new bulb. Make sure that it's fully seated between the two metal clips.

28 Install the lens. Make sure that it snaps back into place.

Spotlight or ceiling light/spotlight

▶ **Refer to illustrations 19.29 and 19.30**

➡**Note: Models without a moonroof (as shown here) are equipped with a spotlight, which has two bulbs that look like a**

conventional "dome light." Models with a moonroof are equipped with a combination ceiling light/spotlight, which has three bulbs. Although the lenses are removed the same way on both types of lights, they don't use the same types of bulbs. Models with a moonroof use bulbs of a later design that are easier to remove and install (simply pull out the old bulb and push in the new one).

29 Carefully pry off the lens with a fingernail file or with a small screwdriver (see illustration).

30 Remove the old bulb. On models without a moonroof, pull the bulb out from the two metal retaining clips (see illustration). On models with a moonroof, simply pull the bulb straight down from its receptacle.

31 Install a new bulb. On models without a moonroof, make sure that the bulb is fully seated in the two metal clips (see illustration 19.26). If the vehicle is equipped with a moonroof, insert the bulb into its receptacle and push it straight up until it stops.

32 Install the lens. Make sure that it snaps into place.

Hazard flasher switch light bulb

▶ **Refer to illustrations 19.34a and 19.34b**

33 Remove the hazard flasher switch (see Section 9).

34 Unscrew and remove the light bulb from the left side of the hazard flasher switch (see illustrations).

35 Installation is the reverse of removal.

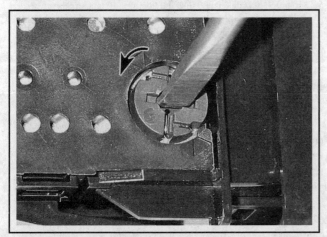

19.34a To remove the illumination bulb from the hazard flasher switch, unscrew it . . .

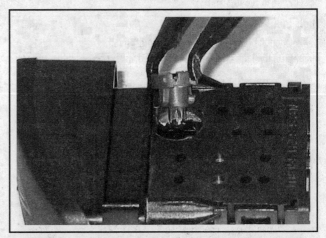

19.34b . . . and pull it out with a pair of tweezers or with a pair of small needle-nose pliers

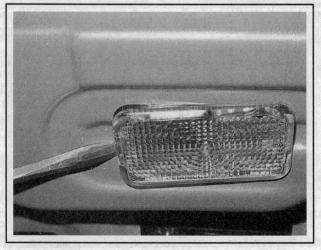

19.36 To remove the trunk light lens, carefully pry it loose from the trunk

19.37 To remove the old bulb from the trunk light lens assembly, pull it straight out; to install a new bulb, push it in until it stops

Trunk light bulb

▶ Refer to illustrations 19.36 and 19.37

36 Open the trunk. Remove the trunk light lens (see illustration).
37 To remove the old bulb pull it straight out (see illustration).
38 To install a new bulb, push it straight in until it stops.
39 Install the trunk light lens. Make sure that it snaps into place.

CR-V

Exterior lights

Front side marker/turn signal light bulb

40 The electrical connector for the front side marker/turn signal light bulb is located near the headlight bulb connector. The procedure for replacing the bulb is similar to the procedure for doing so on a coupe or sedan (see Steps 3 and 4).

Front parking light bulbs

41 Remove the radiator cover.
42 The electrical connector for the front side marker/turn signal light bulb is located near the outer edge of the grille. The procedure for replacing the bulb is similar to the procedure for doing so on a coupe or sedan (see Steps 3 and 4).

High-mount brake light bulb

43 Open the tailgate. To remove the high-mount brake light housing, push in on the tabs on the ends of the housing and pull off the housing.
44 To remove the bulb holder, turn it counterclockwise and pull it out.
45 To remove the bulb from the holder, pull it straight out.
46 To install the new bulb in the holder, push it straight in.
47 To install the housing place it in position and push it on until it snaps into place.

License plate light bulb

48 Pry off the lens by inserting a small flat-tipped screwdriver between the right edge of the lens and the housing. To protect the lens from scratches, put a clean shop rag over the tip of the screwdriver or put a piece of duct tape on the tip.

49 Pull the license plate light bulb straight out of its socket.
50 Push the new bulb into the socket until it's fully seated.
51 Place the lens in position, left end first, then push on the right end until it snaps into place.

Taillight bulbs

52 Open the tailgate. Each of the two mounting screws for each taillight assembly is hidden by a trim cover. To remove the two trim covers, carefully pry off each of them with a small flat-tipped screwdriver. Put a piece of tape or a clean shop rag over the tip to protect the finish on the trim covers, then use the slot provided in each cover to pry it off.
53 Remove the two taillight assembly mounting screws and remove the taillight assembly.
54 There are four bulbs in the taillight assembly. They are, from top to bottom, the turn signal light bulb, the brake light bulb, the side marker/running light bulb and the back-up light bulb. To remove any of the bulb sockets, simply turn it counterclockwise and pull it out.
55 To remove a bulb from its socket simply pull it straight out of the socket.
56 To install a new bulb in its socket simply push it straight into the socket.
57 To install a bulb socket into the taillight assembly insert the socket into its receptacle and give it a quarter-turn clockwise.
58 When installing the taillight assembly make sure the locator pins on the taillight assembly are aligned with their respective holes in the pillar.
59 Installation is otherwise the reverse of removal.

Interior lights

Ceiling light and cargo area light bulbs

60 If you're replacing a ceiling light (dome light) bulb, carefully pry on the rear edge of the lens with a small flat-tipped screwdriver and remove the lens. (Don't pry on the housing around the lens.) If you're replacing a cargo area light bulb, pry on the front edge of the lens.
61 The ceiling light and cargo area light bulbs are identical. To remove an old bulb, pull it straight down.
62 To install a new bulb push it straight up until it's fully seated in the two metal tabs.
63 Install the lens. Make sure that it snaps into place.

Spotlight bulbs

64 Pry on the front edge of the lens with a small flat-tipped screwdriver (right in front of the two spotlight bulbs).

65 Pull the bad spotlight bulb straight down to remove it.

66 Push the new spotlight bulb straight up until it's fully seated.

67 Install the lens. Make sure that it snaps into place.

Hazard switch light bulb

68 Remove the center panel and pull out the hazard flasher switch (see Section 9).

69 Remove the illumination bulb from the side of the hazard flasher switch.

70 Install a new illumination bulb in the switch.

71 Install the hazard flasher switch (see Section 9).

Glove box light bulb

72 Open the glove box and locate the glove box light in the upper front part of the glove box ceiling.

73 Remove the bulb by pulling it straight out of the two metal mounting tabs.

74 To install the new bulb simply push it into the two metal tabs until it's fully seated.

HATCHBACK

Exterior lights

Front turn signal bulbs

75 Using a flat-tipped screwdriver remove the holding clip from the inner fender cover (see *Fender - removal and installation* in Chapter 11 if necessary).

76 Pull back the inner fender cover.

77 To remove the bulb socket from the headlight housing, turn it counterclockwise and pull it out.

78 To remove the old bulb from the socket, push it in and turn it counterclockwise until it unlocks, then pull it out.

79 To install the new bulb in the socket push it in and turn it clockwise until it stops.

Front parking light bulbs

80 Open the hood and locate the electrical connector for the front parking light bulb, which is next to the headlight bulb connector.

81 To remove the bulb socket from the housing, turn it counterclockwise and pull it out of the housing.

82 To remove the old bulb from the socket pull it straight out of the socket.

83 To install a new bulb in the socket push it straight into the socket until it stops.

84 Insert the bulb socket into the parking light housing and turn it clockwise to lock it into place.

Front side marker bulbs

85 Push the front edge of the side marker lens toward the rear of the vehicle until the front edge of the lens pops out of the bumper cover.

86 To remove the bulb socket from the lens, turn the bulb socket counterclockwise and pull it out.

87 To remove the old bulb from the socket pull it straight out of the socket.

88 To install a new bulb in the socket push it straight into the socket until it stops.

89 Insert the bulb socket into the lens assembly and turn it clockwise until it stops.

90 Insert the tabbed end of the side marker assembly into the hole first, then the looped end, then press on the looped end until the assembly snaps into place.

High-mount brake light bulbs

91 Open the hatch. To remove the trim covering the high-mount brake light assembly, put your fingers between the trim and the hatch glass, then carefully pull down on the trim to unsnap the trim retaining clips from the hatch.

92 To remove the bulb holder from the high-mount brake light assembly push the tabs on both sides and pull down the bulb holder.

93 To remove an old bulb from the holder pull it straight out of the holder.

94 To install a new bulb in the holder push it straight into the holder until it stops.

95 Push the bulb holder into the high-mount brake light assembly until it locks into place.

96 Align the clips on the trim with their corresponding holes in the hatch then push the trim until the clips snap into place.

License plate light bulbs

97 To remove the license plate light assembly, slide the lens to the right until the left end pops out of the body, then pull out the license plate light assembly.

98 To remove the lens from the bulb socket pull on the lens and squeeze the tabs on both sides of the socket at the same time.

99 To remove the old bulb from the bulb socket pull the bulb straight out of the socket.

100 To install a new bulb in the socket push it straight into the socket until it stops.

101 To install the lens on the bulb socket push it into place until it latches.

102 To install the license plate light assembly slide the right end of the assembly into the hole and push on the left end until the assembly snaps into place.

Side turn signal bulbs

103 Push the front of the side turn signal assembly toward the rear of the vehicle until it pops out of the body.

104 To remove the bulb socket from the lens, turn the socket counterclockwise.

105 To remove the old bulb from the bulb socket, pull it straight out.

106 To install a new bulb in the socket push it straight into the socket until it stops.

107 To install the bulb socket into the lens insert it into the hole in the lens and turn it clockwise until it stops.

108 To install the side turn signal assembly in the body insert it into the hole rear end first. Then push on the front end until it snaps into place.

Taillight bulbs

109 Open the hatch. Locate the trim cover in the corner of the cargo area. To remove the trim cover, carefully pry on the upper front edge with a small flat-tipped screwdriver.

110 You'll see three bulb sockets. The upper socket is for the turn signal light bulb, the middle socket is for the back-up light bulb and the lower one is for the brake light/taillight bulb. All three sockets are removed the same way.

111 To remove a bulb socket, turn it counterclockwise and pull it out.

112 To remove an old bulb from its socket, push it in and turn it counterclockwise until it unlocks.

113 To install a new bulb into a socket push it in and turn it clockwise until it stops.

114 Insert the bulb socket into the taillight assembly and turn it clockwise until it locks into place.

115 Install the trim cover.

Interior lights

Front ceiling light/spotlight bulbs

116 To remove the lens for the front ceiling light/spotlight pry on the middle of the front edge of the lens.

117 To remove one of the old bulbs pull it straight down.

118 To install a new bulb push it straight up until it stops.

119 To install the lens, place the side with the tabs in position, then push the other side into place until it snaps into position.

Center ceiling light bulb

120 To remove the lens for the center ceiling light pry on the middle of the side edge of the lens.

121 To remove the old bulb pull it straight down from the two metal tabs.

122 To install a new bulb, insert it into the metal tabs until it snaps into place.

123 To install the lens, place the edge with the tabs in position, then push the other edge into place until it snaps into position.

Cargo area light bulb

124 Open the hatch. To remove the lens for the cargo area light, carefully pry on the front edge of the lens with a small screwdriver. Put a shop towel or a piece of tape on the tip of the screwdriver to protect the trim.

125 To remove the old bulb pull it straight out of the bulb holder.

126 To install a new bulb push it straight into the holder until it's fully seated.

127 To install the lens, insert it into the mounting hole rear side first, then push on the front side until it snaps into place.

20 Electric side view mirrors - general information

1   Most electric rear view mirrors use two motors to move the glass; one for up-and-down adjustments and one for left-right adjustments.

2   During mirror adjustment, the power mirror adjustment switch sends voltage to the left or right side mirror. With the ignition key turned to ON (engine not running), operate the mirror adjustment switch through all of its functions (left-right and up-down) for both the left and right side mirrors.

3   Listen carefully for the sound of the electric motors running in the mirrors.

4   If you can hear the motors but the mirror glass doesn't move, there's a problem with the drive mechanism inside the mirror.

5   If the mirrors do not operate and no sound comes from the mirrors, check the fuse (see Section 3).

6   If the fuse is OK, remove the power mirror adjustment switch (see Section 9). Have the switch continuity checked by a dealership service department or other qualified automobile repair facility.

7   Test the ground connections.

8   If the mirror still doesn't work, remove the mirror and check the wires at the mirror for voltage.

9   If there is no voltage in any switch position, check the circuit between the mirror and the adjustment switch for opens and shorts.

10 If there's voltage, remove the mirror and test it off the vehicle with jumper wires. Replace the mirror if it fails this test.

21 Cruise control system - general information

1   The cruise control system maintains vehicle speed with an electrically operated motor located in the engine compartment, which is connected to the throttle body by a cable. The system consists of the Powertrain Control Module, the speed control actuator, the speed control cable, the speed control indicator light, the speed control actuator switches, the Brake Pedal Position (BPP) switch and the transmission range switch. The cruise control system requires diagnostic procedures that are beyond the scope of this manual, but there are some general procedures that will help you identify common problems.

2   Check the fuses (see Section 3).

3   Have an assistant operate the brake lights while you check their operation (voltage from the brake light switch deactivates the cruise control).

4   If the brake lights don't come on or stay on all the time, correct the problem and retest the cruise control system.

5   Visually inspect the control cable between the cruise control motor and the throttle linkage for free movement. Replace it if necessary.

6   Test drive the vehicle to determine if the cruise control is now working. If it isn't, take it to a dealer service department or an automotive electrical specialist for further diagnosis.

22 Power window system - general information

1   The power window system operates electric motors, mounted in the doors, which lower and raise the windows. The system consists of the control switches, the motors, regulators, glass mechanisms and associated wiring.

2   The power windows can be lowered and raised from the master control switch by the driver or by remote switches located at the individual windows. Each window has a separate motor, which is reversible. The position of the control switch determines the polarity and therefore the direction of operation.

3   The circuit is protected by a fuse and a circuit breaker. Each motor is also equipped with an internal circuit breaker, this prevents one stuck window from disabling the whole system.

4   The power window system will only operate when the ignition switch is turned to ON. There's also a main switch at the master power window control panel (in the driver's door) which, when activated, disables the switches at the rear windows and the switch at the passenger's window. So if there's a problem with the passenger window or with either of the rear windows, make sure that it's not simply a matter of flipping the main switch before proceeding.

5   The procedures listed below are general in nature, so if you can't find the problem using them, take the vehicle to a dealer service department.

6   If the power windows won't operate, always check the fuses and relays first (see Sections 3 and 5, respectively). Also verify that there's voltage to the relay and that the relay is well grounded.

7   If only the rear windows are inoperative, or if the windows only operate from the master control switch, check the main switch for continuity in the unlocked position. Replace it if it doesn't have continuity (see *Door trim panel - removal and installation* in Chapter 11).

8   Check the wiring between the switches and the fuse and relay box for continuity. Repair the wiring, if necessary.

9   If only one window is inoperative from the main switch, try the other control switch at the window.

→Note: This doesn't apply to the driver's door window.

10 If the same window works from one switch, but not the other, check the switch for continuity.

11 If the switch tests OK, check for a short or open in the circuit between the affected switch and the window motor.

12 If one window is inoperative from both switches, remove the trim panel from the affected door (see *Door trim panel - removal and installation* in Chapter 11) and check for voltage at the switch and at the motor while the switch is operated.

13 If voltage is reaching the motor, disconnect the glass from the regulator (see Chapter 11). Move the window up-and-down by hand while checking for binding and damage. Also check for binding and damage to the regulator. If the regulator is not damaged and the window moves up and down smoothly, replace the motor. If there's binding or damage, lubricate, repair or replace parts, as necessary.

14 If voltage isn't reaching the motor, check the wiring in the circuit for continuity between the switches and motors. You'll need to consult the wiring diagram for the vehicle.

23 Power door lock system - general information

1   A power door lock system operates the door lock actuators mounted in each door. The system consists of the switches, actuators, a control unit and associated wiring. On some models, the power door lock system is part of the security alarm system. On these models, the power door lock system is more complex, and more difficult to diagnose. Therefore, home troubleshooting is limited to simple checks of the wiring connections and actuators for minor faults that can be easily repaired.

2   Power door lock systems are operated by bi-directional solenoids located in the doors. The lock switches have two operating positions: LOCK and UNLOCK. When activated, the switch sends a ground signal to the door lock control unit to lock or unlock the doors. Depending on which way the switch is activated, the control unit reverses polarity to the solenoids, allowing the two sides of the circuit to be used alternately as the feed (positive) and ground side.

3   The following general guidelines should help you quickly identify and repair typical problems. If you're unable to locate the trouble using these guidelines, consult a dealer service department.

4   Always check the fuses first (see Section 3 and your owners' manual).

5   Operate the door lock switches in both directions (LOCK and UNLOCK) with the engine off. Listen for the click of the solenoids operating.

6   Test the switches for continuity. Remove the switches and have them checked by a dealer service department.

7   Check the wiring between the switches, control unit and solenoids for continuity. Repair the wiring if there's no continuity.

8   Check for a bad ground at the switches and at the control unit.

9   If only one lock solenoid doesn't operate, remove the trim panel from the door with the bad solenoid (see *Door trim panel - removal and installation* in Chapter 11) and check for voltage at the solenoid while the lock switch is operated. One of the wires should have voltage in the Lock position; the other should have voltage in the Unlock position.

10 If the inoperative solenoid is receiving voltage, replace the solenoid.

11 If the inoperative solenoid isn't receiving voltage, check for an open or short in the wire between the lock solenoid and the control unit.

→Note: Wire harnesses typically break between the body and door, because repeatedly opening and closing the door fatigues and eventually breaks the wires.

24 Daytime Running Lights (DRL) - general information

The Daytime Running Lights (DRL) system illuminates the headlights whenever the engine is running. The only exception is with the engine running and the parking brake engaged. Once the parking brake is released, the lights will remain on as long as the ignition switch is on, even if the parking brake is later applied. The DRL system supplies reduced power to the headlights during daylight operation to prolonging headlight life.

25 Airbag system - general information

GENERAL INFORMATION

1   All models are equipped with a Supplemental Restraint System (SRS), more commonly known as airbags. This system is designed to protect the driver, and the front seat passenger, from serious injury in the event of a head-on or frontal collision. It uses an SRS control unit mounted under the center of the dash, a pair of crash sensors mounted along the base of the inner fender panels. The airbag assemblies are mounted on the steering wheel and inside the passenger's end of the dash. Some models are also equipped with side-impact airbags mounted in the backs of the front seats.

These models are also equipped with seat belt pre-tensioners. These are pyrotechnic devices that reduce the slack in the seat belts during an impact of sufficient force to trigger the airbags.

AIRBAG MODULE

Driver's side airbag

2   The airbag inflator module contains a housing incorporating the cushion (airbag) and inflator unit, mounted in the center of the steering wheel. The inflator assembly is mounted on the back of the housing over a hole through which gas is expelled, inflating the bag almost instantaneously when an electrical signal is sent from the system. A "clockspring" on the steering column under the steering wheel carries this signal to the module. This clockspring assembly can transmit an electrical signal regardless of steering wheel position. The igniter in the airbag converts the electrical signal to heat and ignites the powder, which inflates the bag.

3   For information on how to remove and install the driver's side airbag, refer to *Steering wheel - removal and installation* in Chapter 10.

Passenger's side airbag

4   The airbag is mounted at the top of the passenger's side of the instrument panel. It consists of an inflator containing an igniter, a reaction housing/airbag assembly and a trim cover.

5   The passenger's side airbag is considerably larger than the steering wheel-mounted unit and is mounted inside the dash, above the glove box. The airbag trim cover on top of the dash is textured and painted to match the instrument panel and has a molded seam, which splits when the bag inflates.

SRS CONTROL UNIT

6   This unit supplies the current to the airbag system (and seat belt pre-tensioners, on models so equipped) in the event of the collision, even if battery power is cut off. It checks this system every time the vehicle is started, causing the "SRS" light to go on, then off, if the system is operating correctly. If there is a fault in the system, the light will go on and stay on, or it will flash or the dash will make a beeping sound. If this happens, take the vehicle to your dealer immediately for service.

DISARMING THE SYSTEM AND OTHER PRECAUTIONS

✳ WARNING:

Failure to follow these precautions could result in accidental deployment of the airbag and personal injury.

7   Whenever working in the vicinity of the steering wheel, instrument panel or any of the other SRS system components, the system must be disarmed. To disarm the system:

   a) *Point the wheels straight ahead and turn the key to the Lock position.*
   b) *Disconnect the cable from the negative battery terminal(s). Refer to Chapter 5, Section 1 for the disconnecting procedure.*
   c) *Wait at least three minutes for the back-up power supply to be depleted.*

8   Whenever handling an airbag module, always keep the airbag opening side (the trim, or upholstered side) pointed away from your body. Never place the airbag module on a workbench or other surface with the airbag opening facing the surface. Always place the airbag module in a safe location with the airbag opening facing up.

9   Never measure the resistance of any SRS component or use any electrical test equipment on any of the wiring or components. An ohmmeter has a built-in battery supply that could accidentally deploy the airbag.

10 Never use electrical welding equipment on a vehicle equipped with an airbag without first disconnecting the airbag electrical connectors. The connector for the driver's side airbag is located near the bottom of the steering column (see *Steering wheel - removal and installation* in Chapter 10); the connector for the passenger's side airbag is located inside the dash, near the glove box (see below). The seat belt pre-tensioner electrical connectors are located behind the B-pillar trim panels. The electrical connectors for the side impact airbags, on models so equipped, are located under the front seats.

11 Never dispose of a live airbag module or seat belt pre-tensioner. Return it to a dealer service department or other qualified repair shop for safe deployment and disposal.

AIRBAG MODULE REMOVAL AND INSTALLATION

Driver's side airbag module and clockspring

12 Refer to Chapter 10, *Steering wheel - removal and installation*, for the driver's side airbag module and clockspring removal and installation procedures.

Passenger's side airbag module

Coupe, sedan and hatchback

▶ **Refer to illustrations 25.15, 25.16 and 25.17**

13 Disarm the airbag system as described previously in this Section.

14 Remove the glove box (see Chapter 11).

15 Disconnect the passenger side airbag module electrical connector (see illustration).

16 Remove the airbag module mounting nuts (see illustration).

17 Working from above, carefully pry the trim cover in the dash loose (see illustration), then lift the airbag trim cover and airbag module out of the dash as a single assembly. If necessary (and only if necessary), carefully separate the airbag module from the trim cover. Be sure to heed the precautions outlined previously in this Section.

18 Installation is the reverse of removal. Tighten the airbag module mounting nuts securely.

19 Reconnect the cable to the negative battery terminal (see Chapter 5, Section 1).

20 Perform the idle learn procedure (see Chapter 5, Section 1).

CR-V

21 Disarm the airbag system as described previously in this Section.

22 Right above the glove box, you'll find a small access panel. Removing this panel provides access to the airbag module electrical connector. Carefully pry the access panel from the dashboard with a small screwdriver. Tape the end of the screwdriver to protect the dash trim.

23 Disconnect the passenger-side airbag module electrical connector.

24 Remove the three passenger-side airbag module mounting bracket nuts.

25 Working from above, carefully pry the trim cover in the dash loose (see illustration 25.17), then lift the airbag trim cover and airbag module out of the dash as a single assembly. If necessary (and only if necessary), carefully separate the airbag module from the trim cover. Be sure to heed the precautions outlined previously in this Section.

26 Installation is the reverse of removal. Tighten the airbag module mounting nuts securely.

27 Reconnect the cable to the negative battery terminal (see Chapter 5, Section 1).

28 Perform the idle learn procedure (see Chapter 5, Section 1).

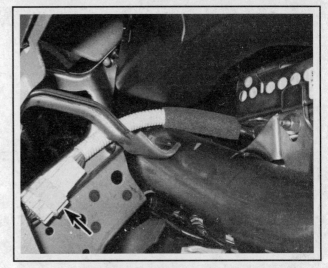

25.15 Before removing the passenger-side airbag module, be sure to disconnect the electrical connector (coupe, sedan and hatchback)

25.16 To detach the passenger-side airbag module, remove these three nuts (coupe, sedan and hatchback)

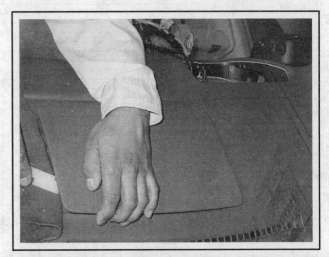

25.17 Using a shop towel to protect the dashboard, carefully pry loose the trim cover in the top of the dash, then lift out the cover and airbag module as a single assembly

26 Wiring diagrams - general information

Since it isn't possible to include all wiring diagrams for every year covered by this manual, the following diagrams are those that are typical and most commonly needed.

Prior to troubleshooting any circuits, check the fuses and relays to ensure that they're in good condition. Make sure that the battery is correctly charged and check the cable connections (see Chapters 1 and 5).

When checking a circuit, make sure that all connections are clean and tight, with no broken or loose terminals. If an electrical connector is difficult to disconnect, it's probably because the two halves of the

connector are locked together on one or two sides of the connector. So stop and look for the locks, which are usually small plastic tabs that must either be depressed to unlock them, or must be released with a small screwdriver. If you have a problem finding the lock(s), clean off the connector with electronic parts cleaner, then look again. If you're trying to unplug a connector that's located in a dark area, use a flashlight to find the locks. When disconnecting an electrical connector, do NOT pull on the wires; pull on the two halves of the connector itself.

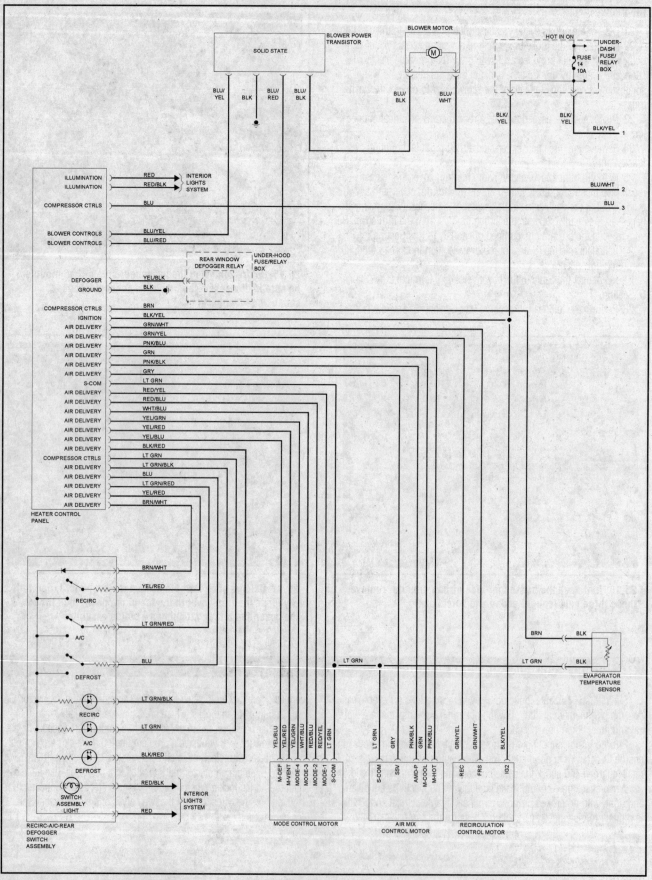

Air conditioning and engine cooling systems - coupe/sedan (1 of 2)

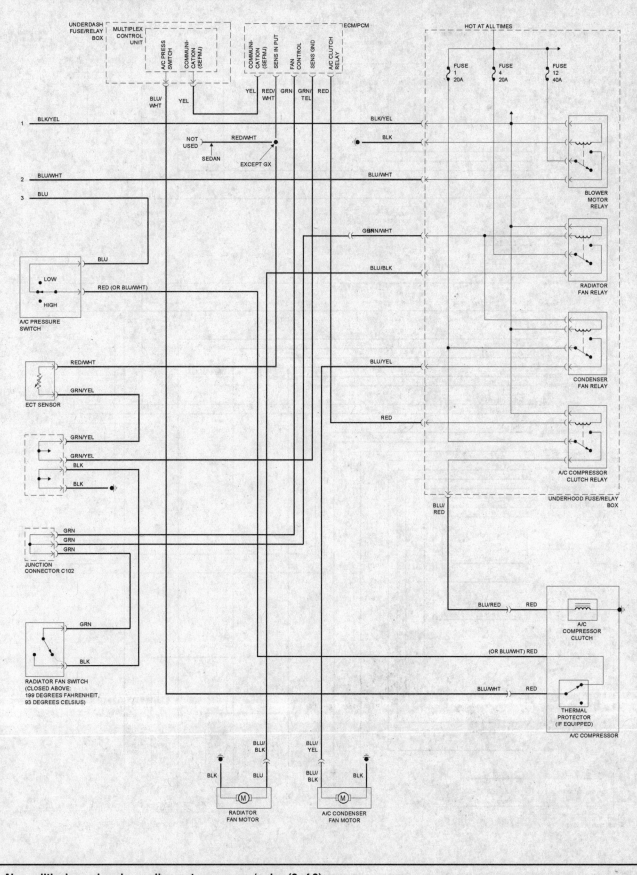

Air conditioning and engine cooling systems - coupe/sedan (2 of 2)

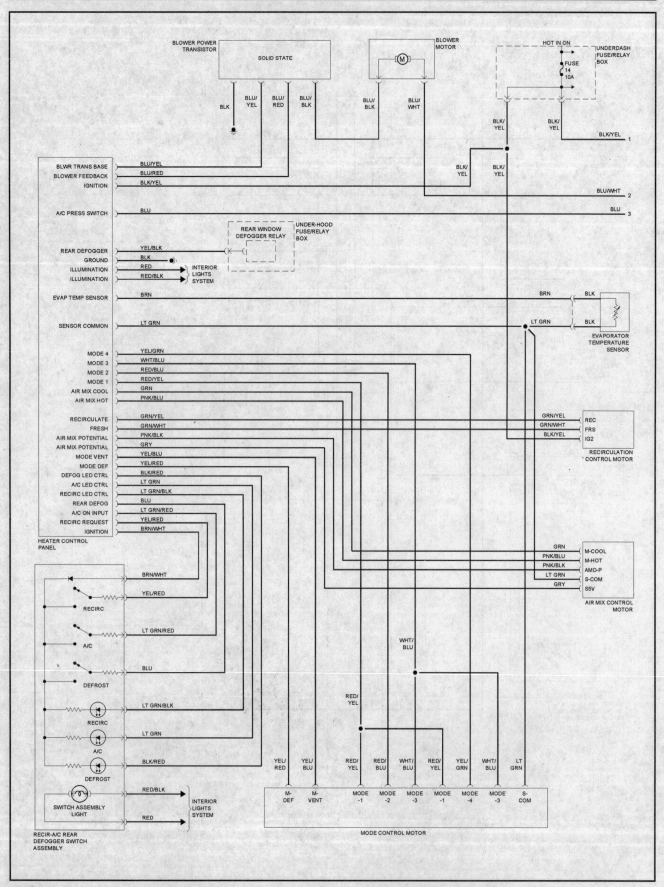

Air conditioning and engine cooling systems - hatchback (1 of 2)

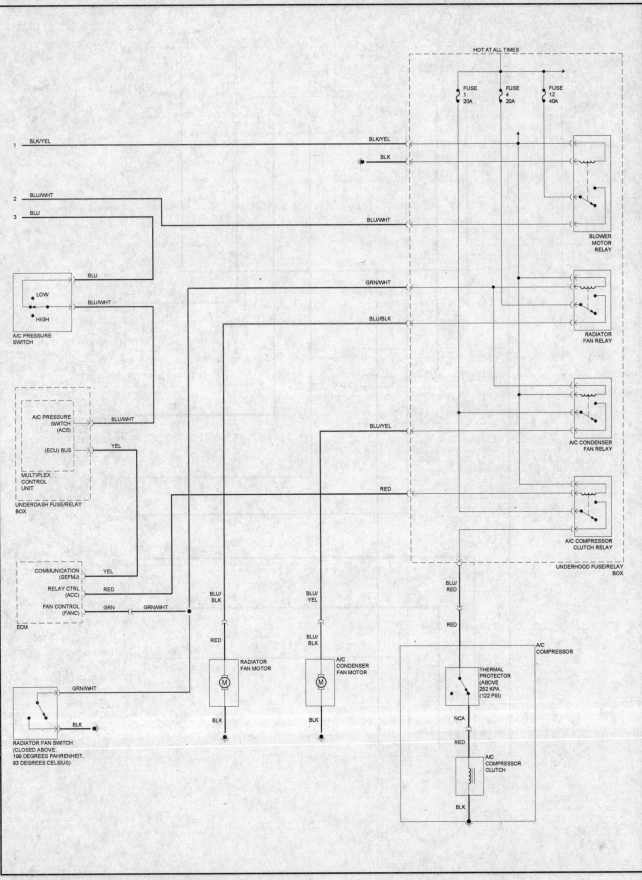

Air conditioning and engine cooling systems - hatchback (2 of 2)

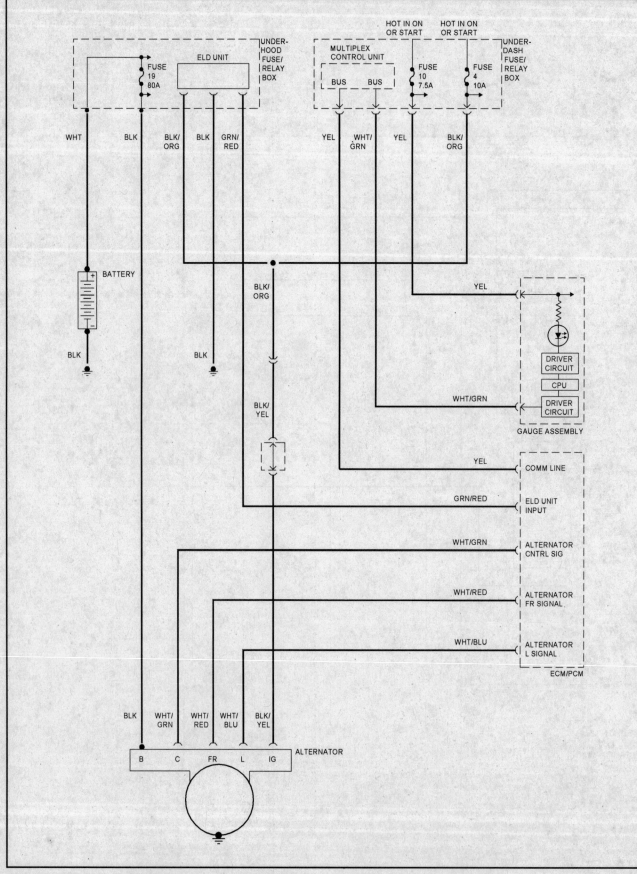

Starting and charging systems (coupe/sedan and hatchback)

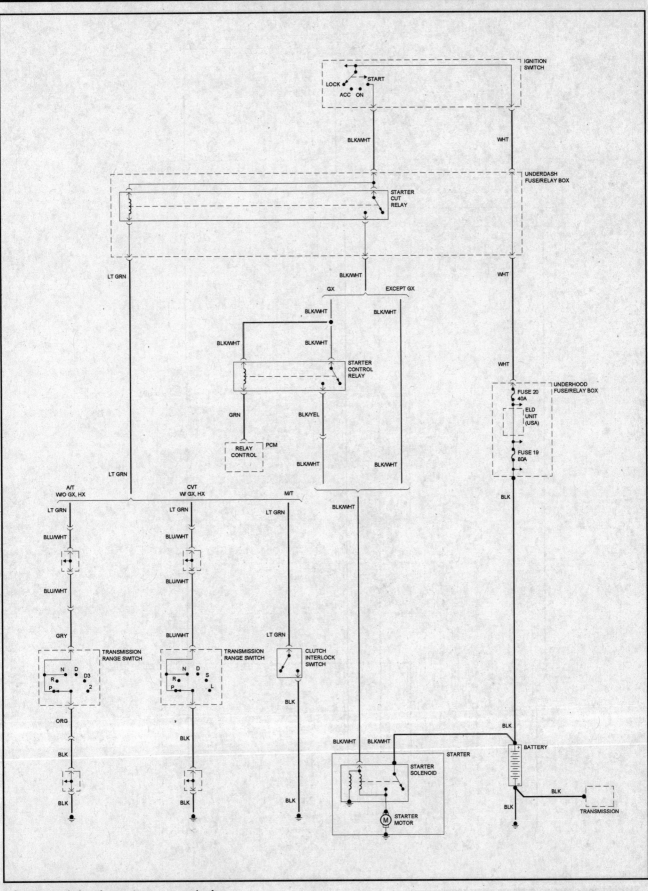

Starting and charging systems - coupe/sedan

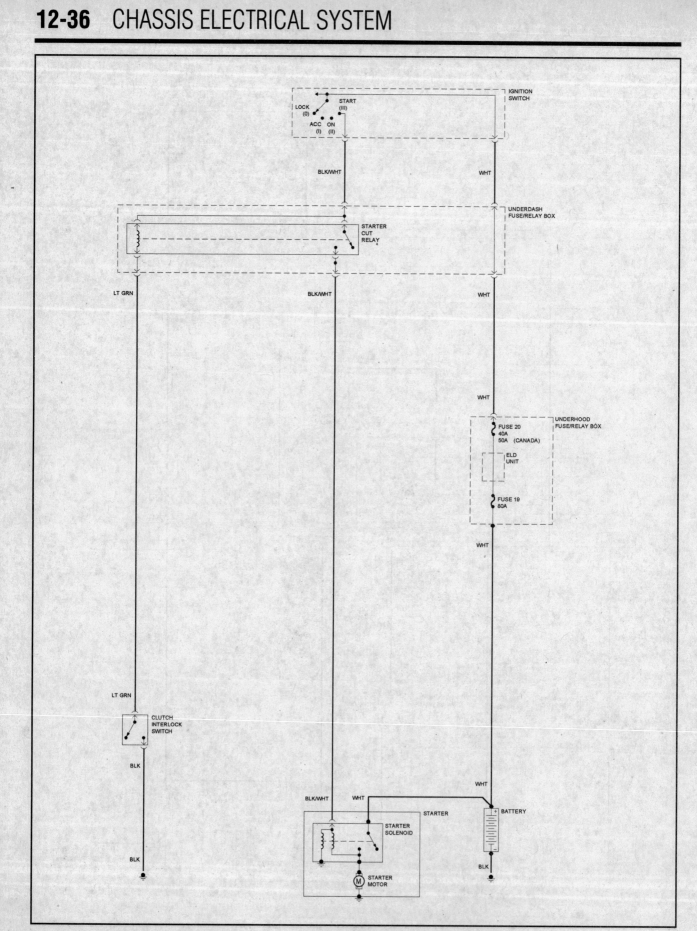

Starting and charging systems - hatchback

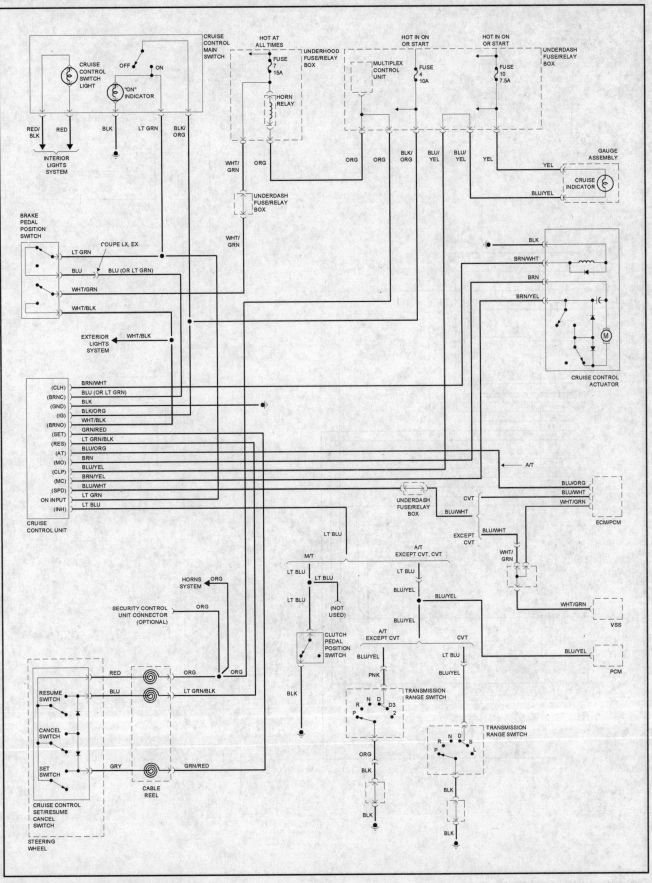

Cruise control system - coupe/sedan

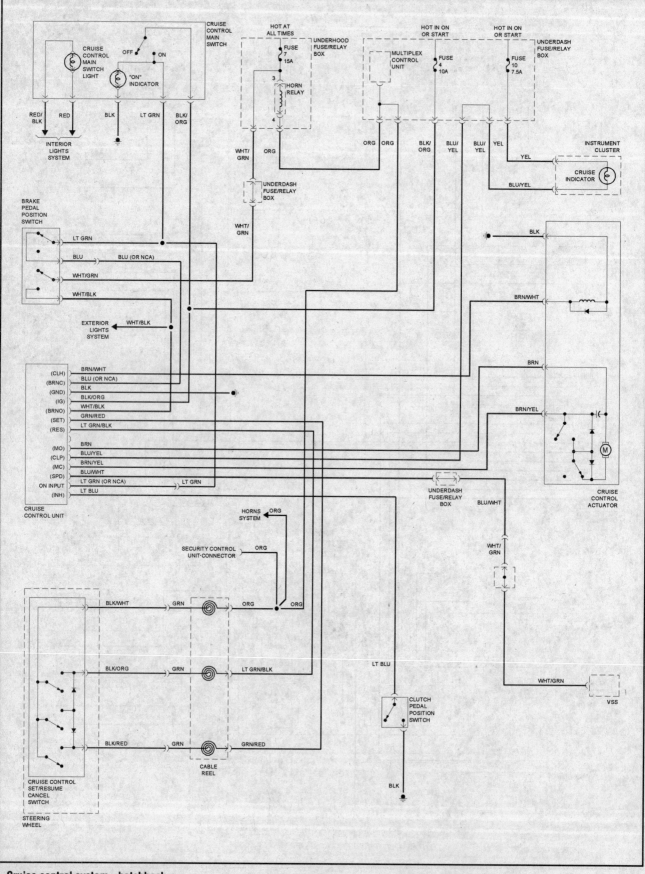

Cruise control system - hatchback

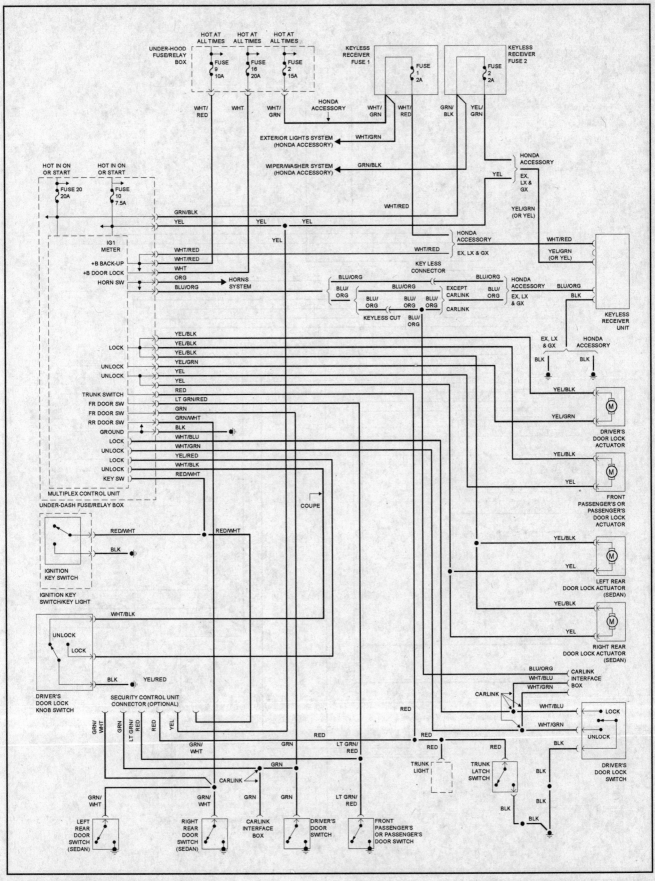

Power door lock system - coupe/sedan

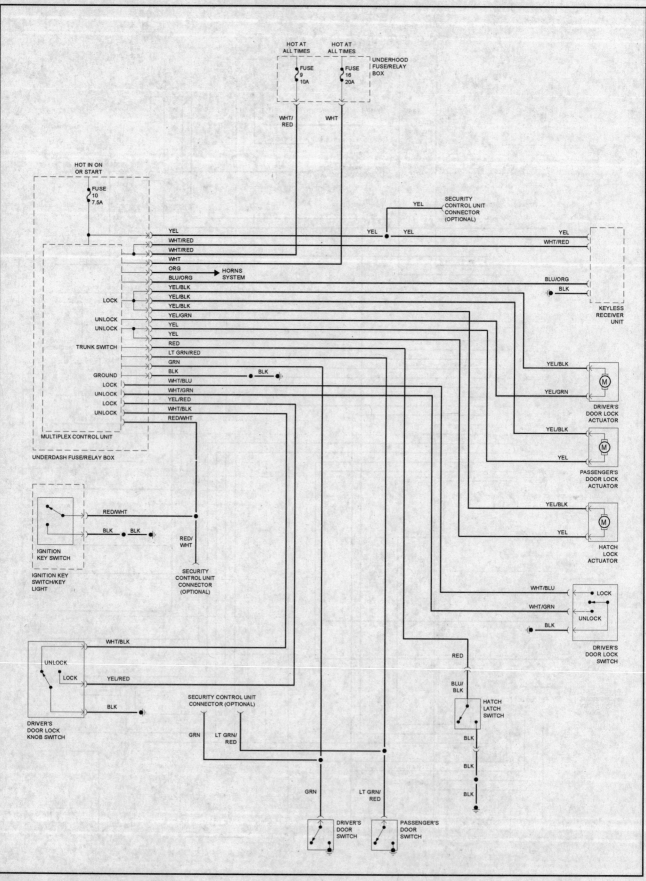

Power door lock system - hatchback

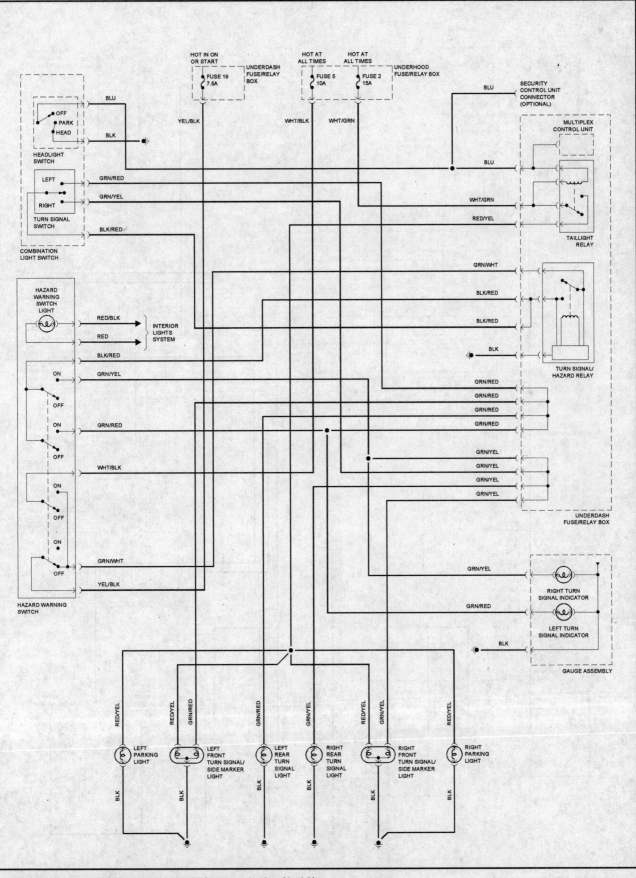

Exterior lighting system (except headlights) - coupe/sedan (1 of 2)

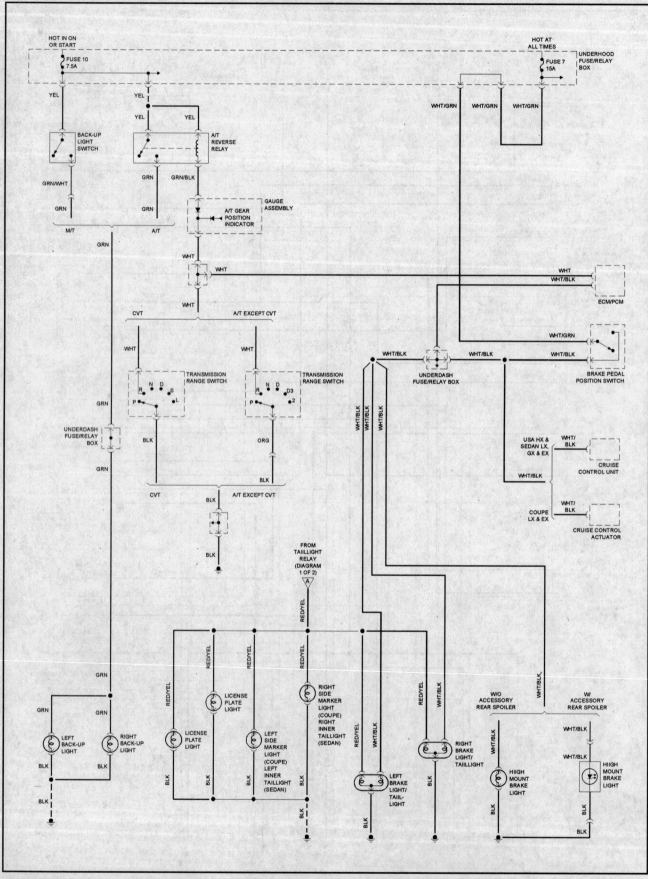

Exterior lighting system (except headlights) - coupe/sedan (2 of 2)

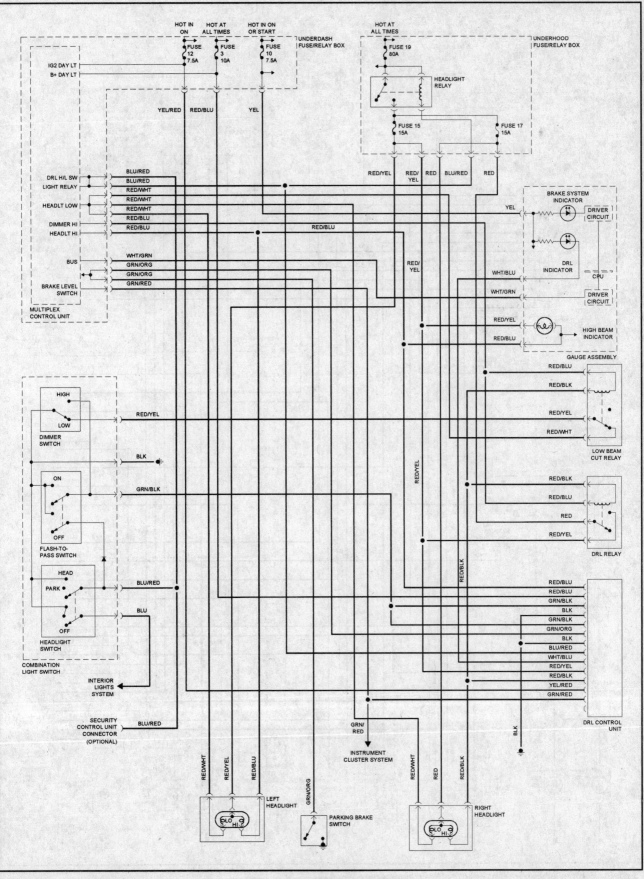

Headlight system (with Daytime Running Lights) - 2001 through 2003 coupe/sedan

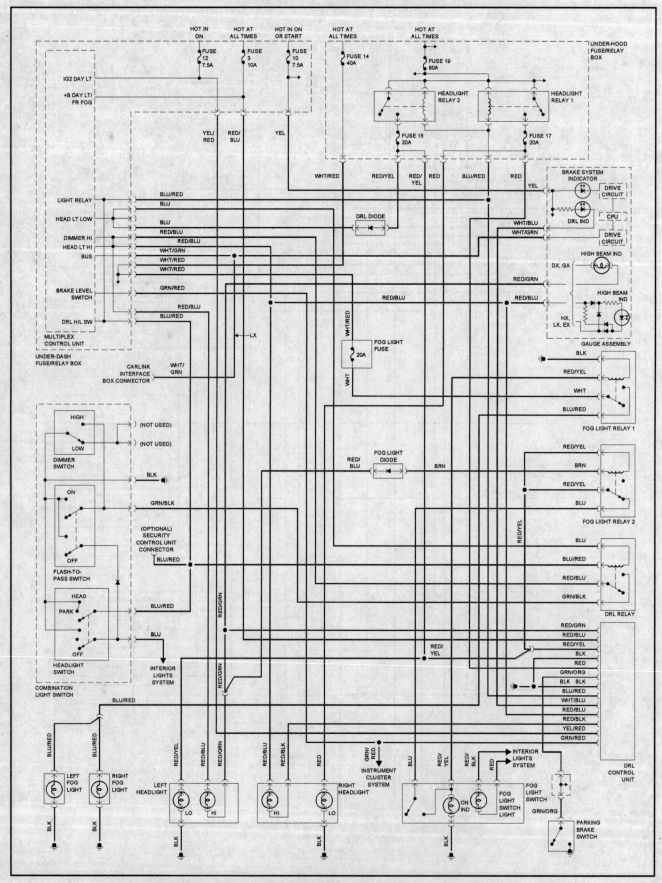

Headlight system (with Daytime Running Lights) - 2004 coupe/sedan

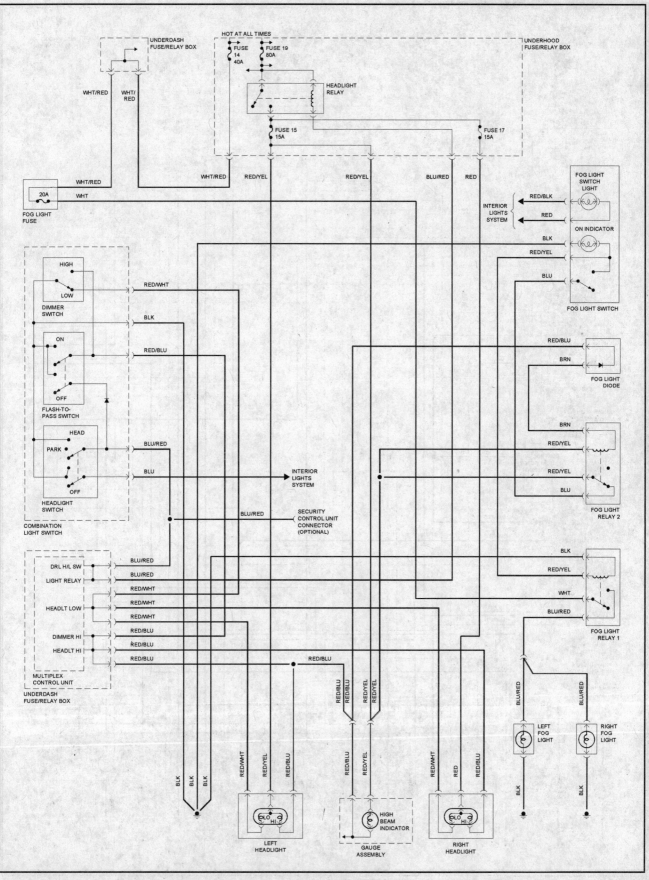

Headlight system (without Daytime Running Lights) - 2001 through 2003 coupe/sedan

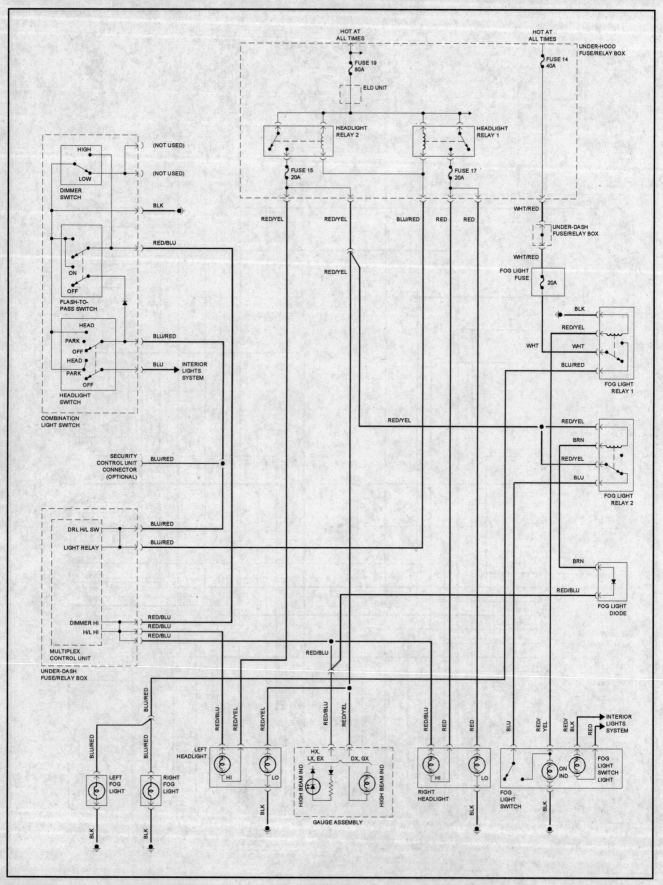

Headlight system (without Daytime Running Lights) - 2004 coupe/sedan

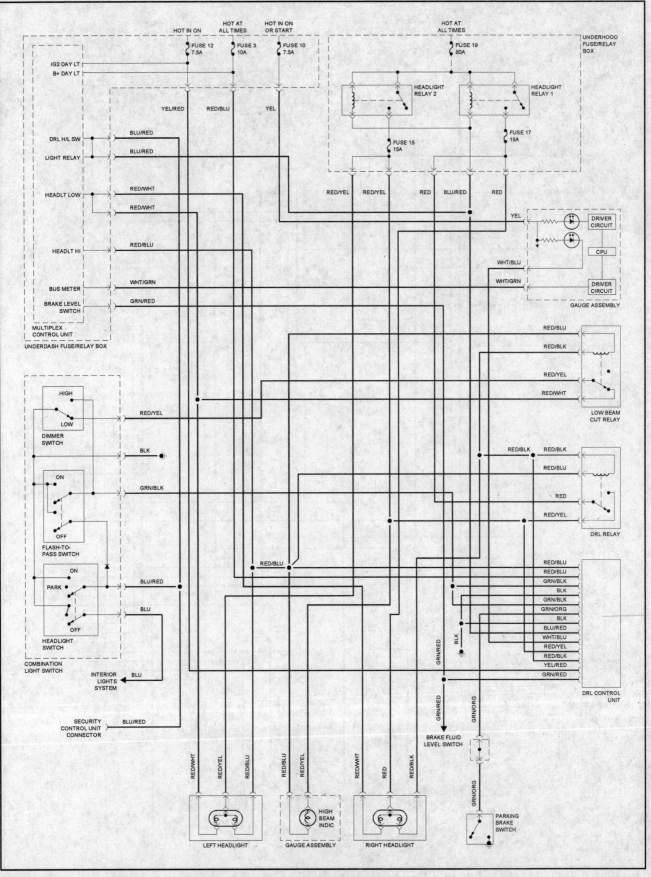

Headlight system (with Daytime Running Lights) - 2002 through 2003 hatchback

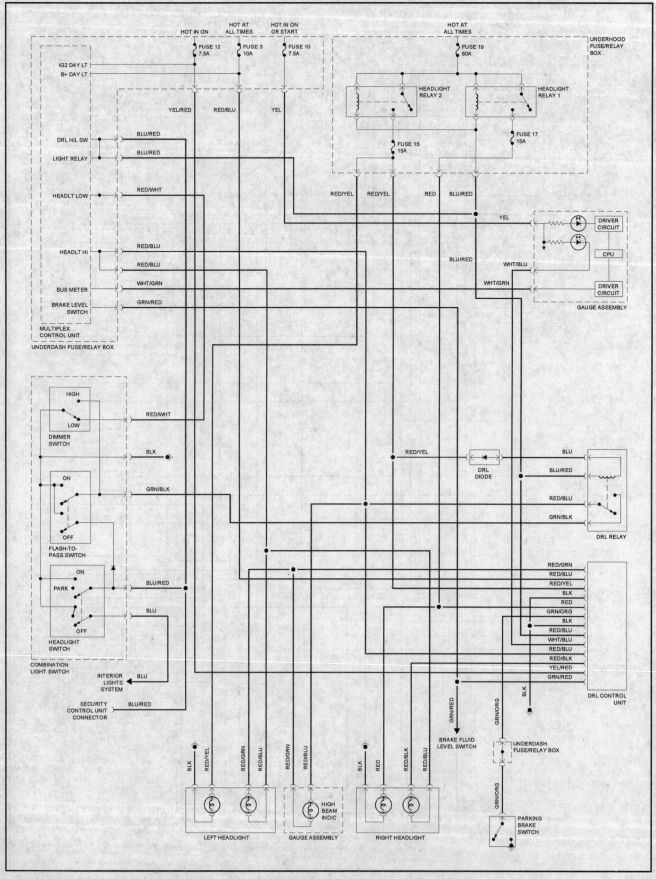

Headlight system (with Daytime Running Lights) - 2004 hatchback

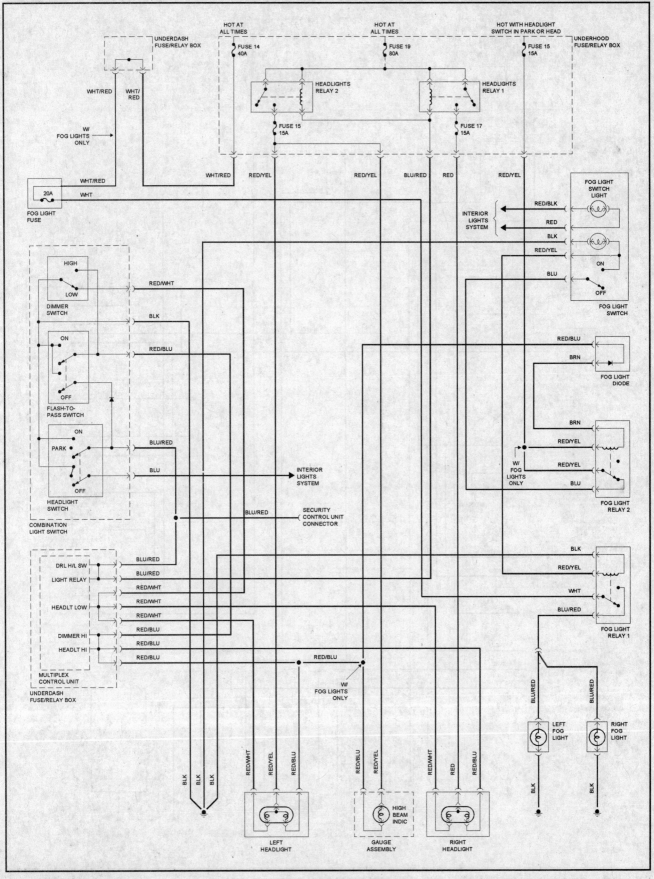

Headlight system (without Daytime Running Lights) - 2002 through 2003 hatchback

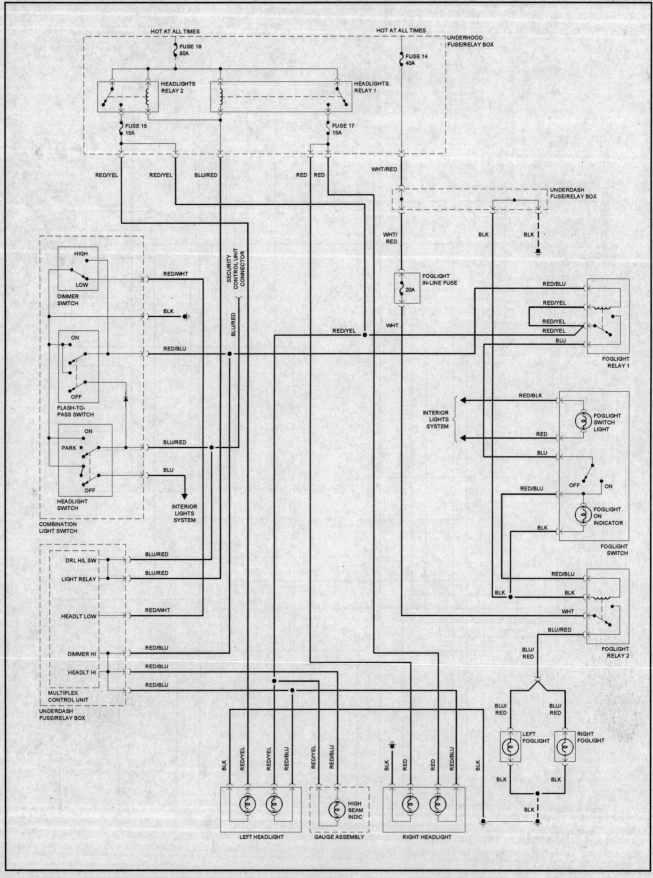

Headlight system (without Daytime Running Lights) - 2004 hatchback

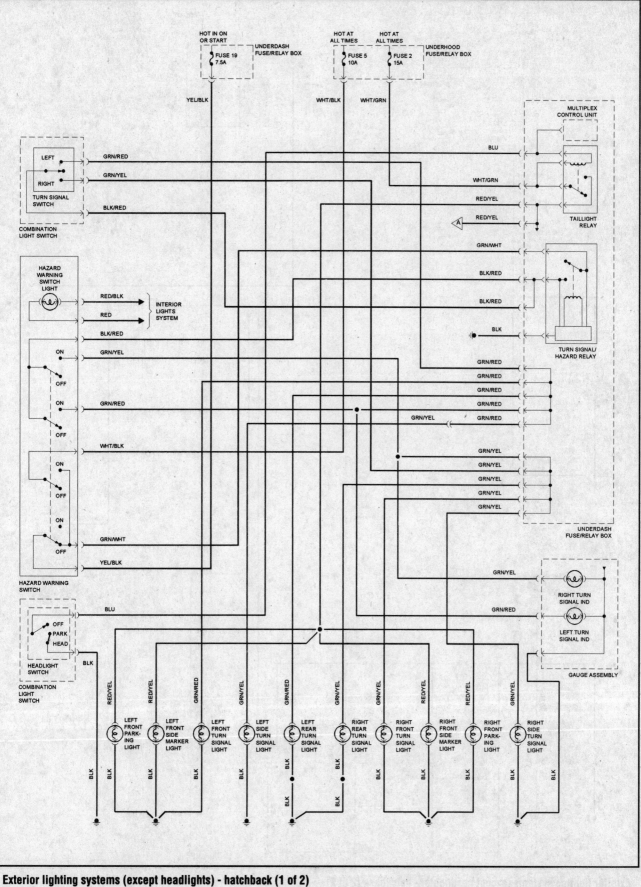

Exterior lighting systems (except headlights) - hatchback (1 of 2)

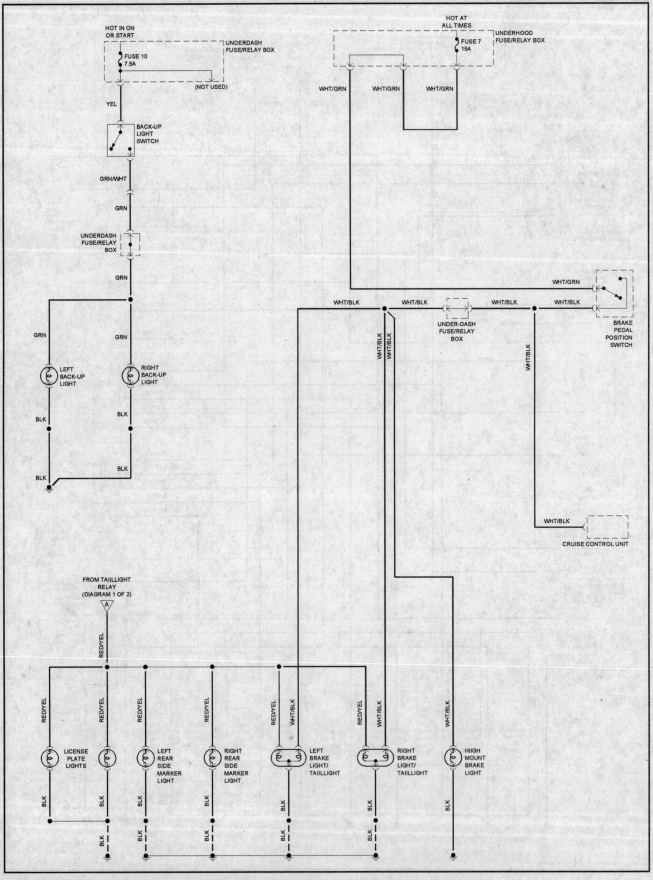

Exterior lighting systems (except headlights) - hatchback (2 of 2)

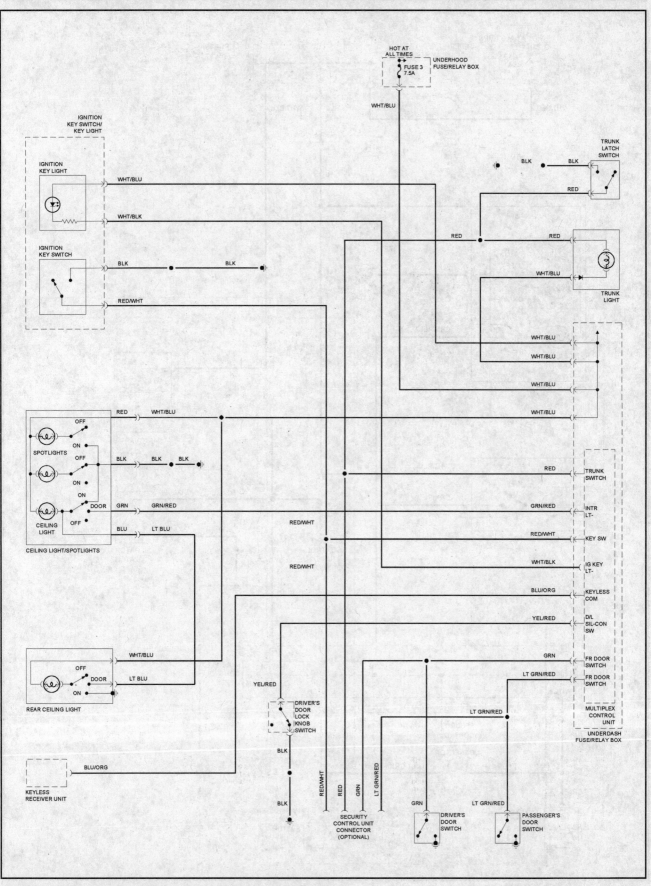

Interior lighting systems, including courtesy lights (coupe with sunroof)

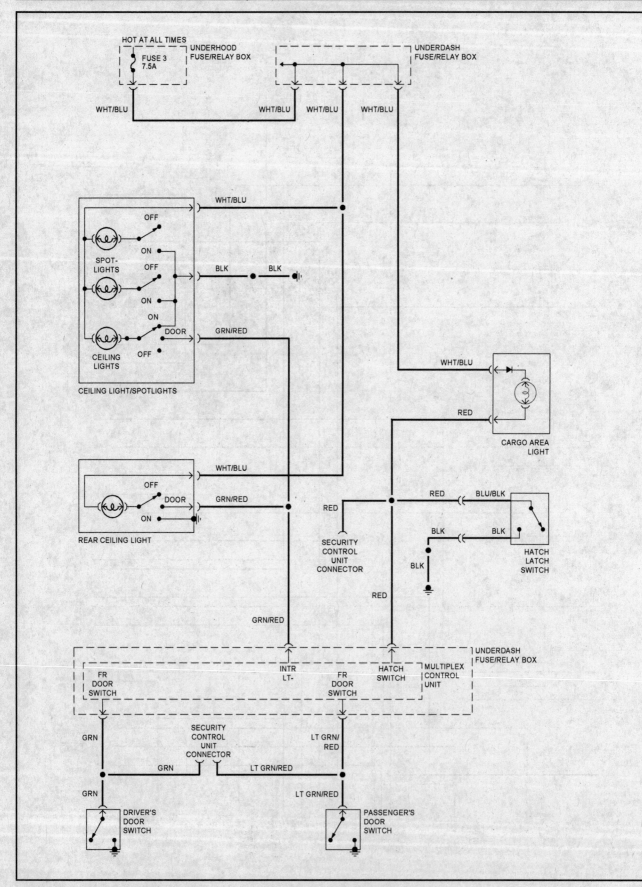

Interior lighting systems, including courtesy lights (hatchback without sunroof)

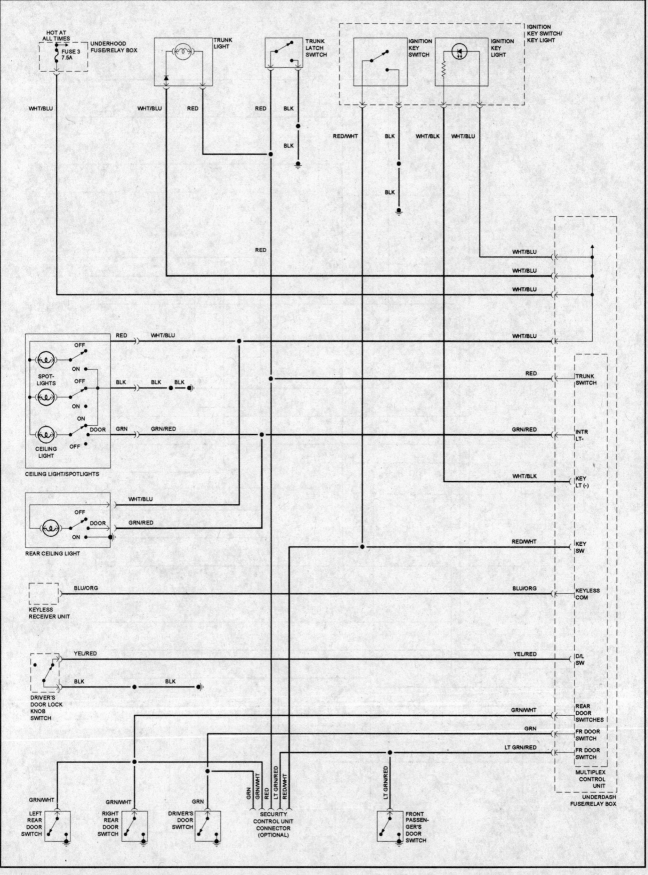

Interior lighting systems, including courtesy lights (sedan with sunroof)

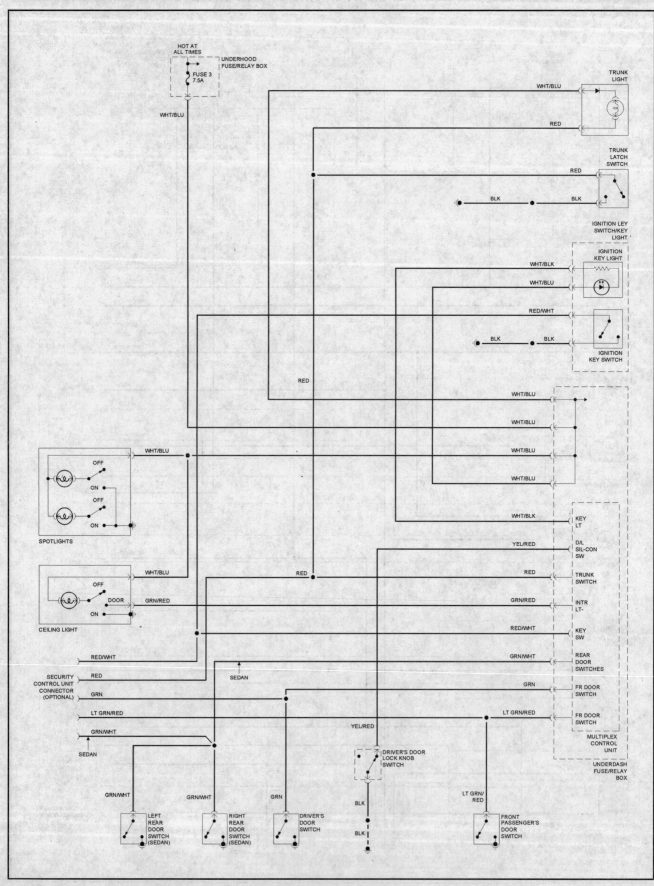

Interior lighting systems, including courtesy lights (coupe/sedan without sunroof)

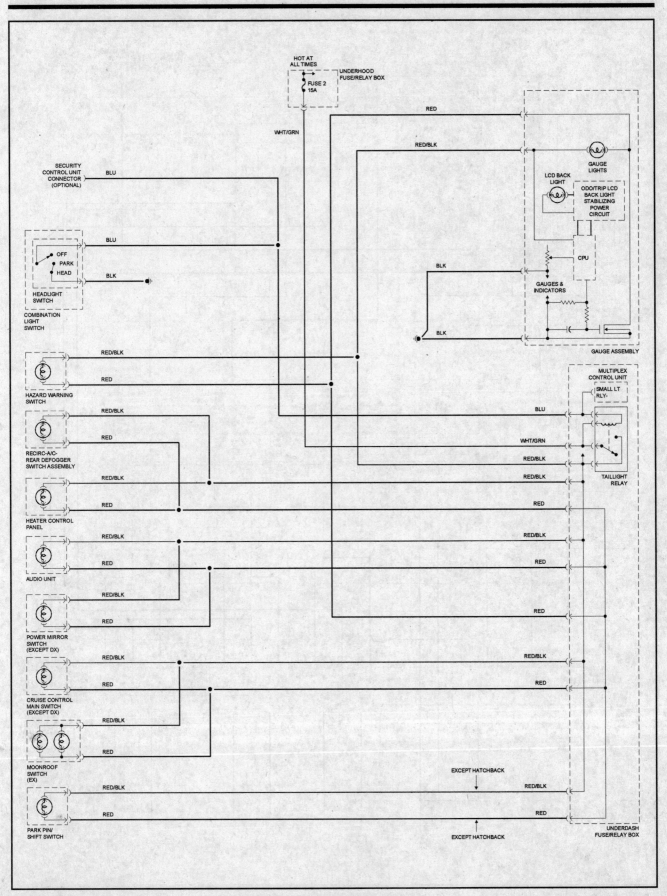

Interior lighting systems, including illumination lights (coupe, sedan and hatchback)

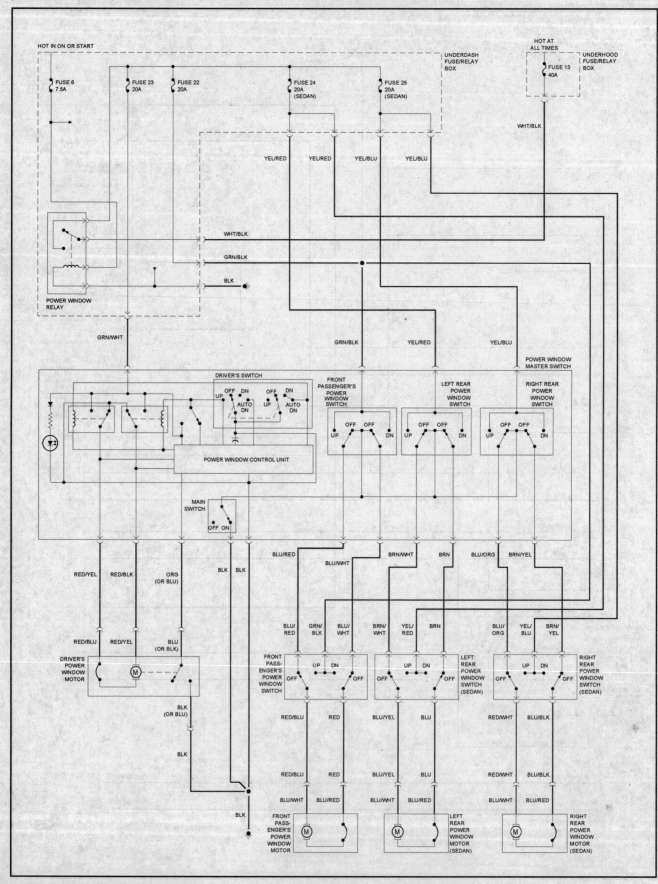

Power window systems (coupe/sedan)

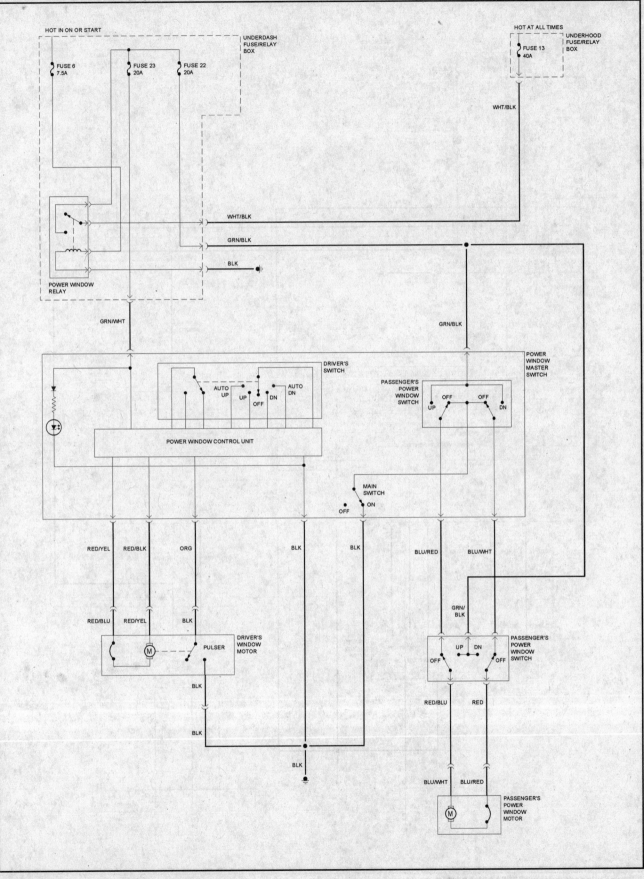

Power window systems (2002 and 2003 hatchback)

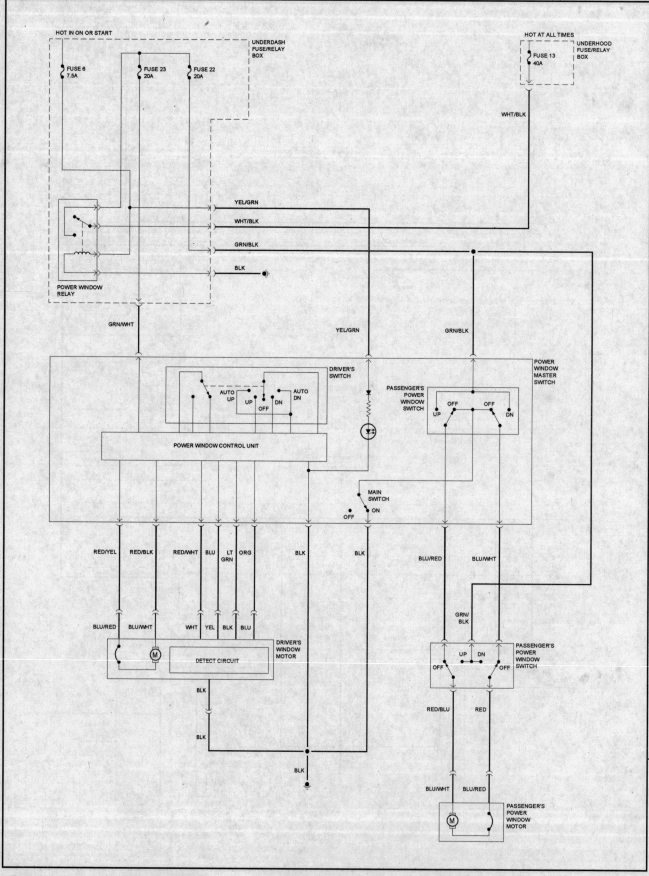

Power window systems (2004 hatchback)

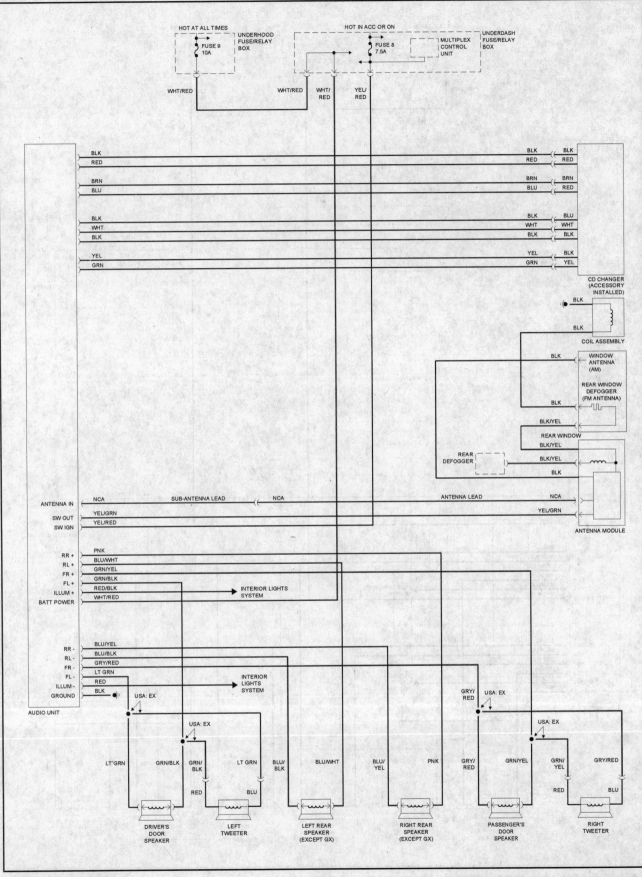

Sound system (coupe)

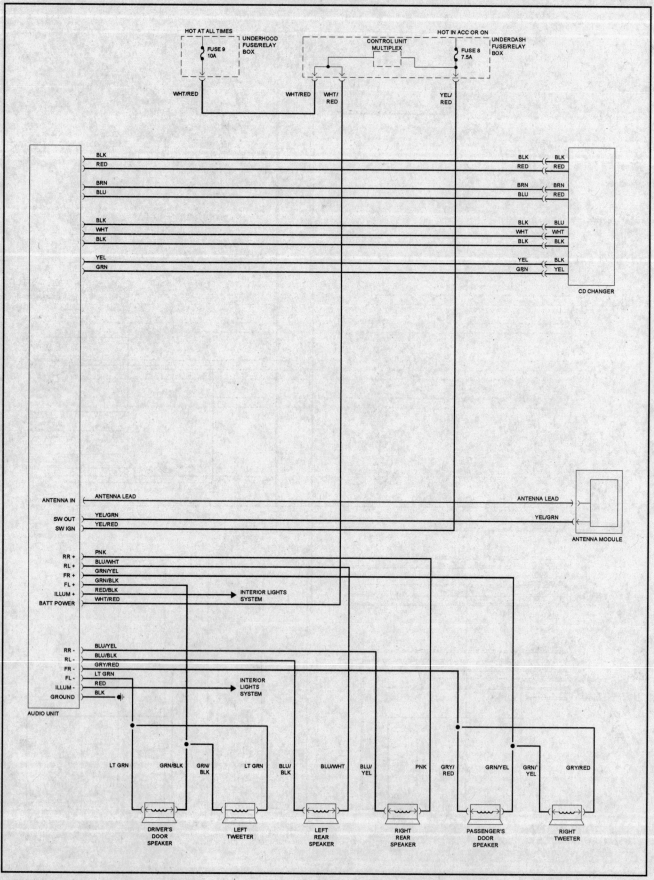

Sound system (hatchback)

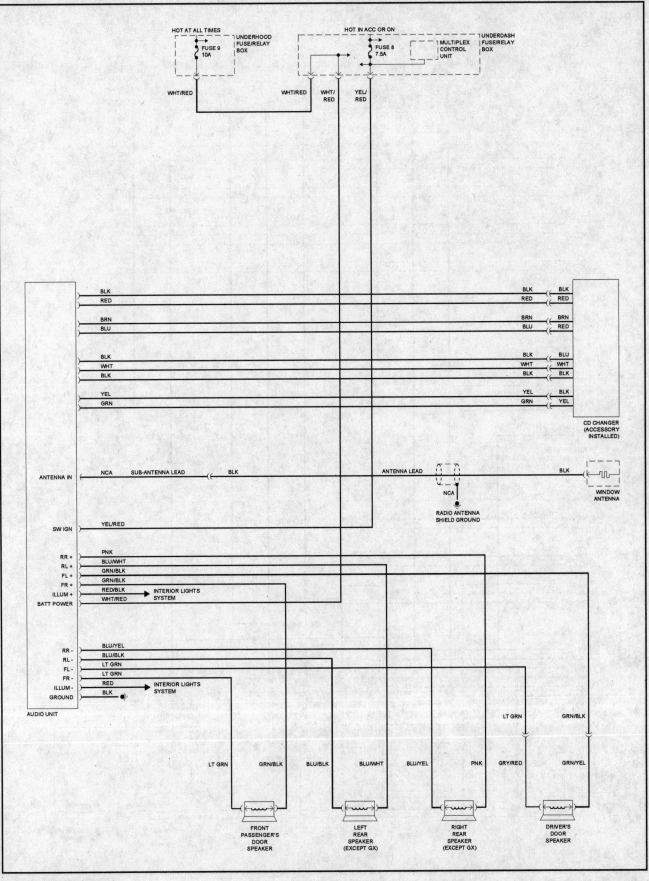

Sound system (sedan)

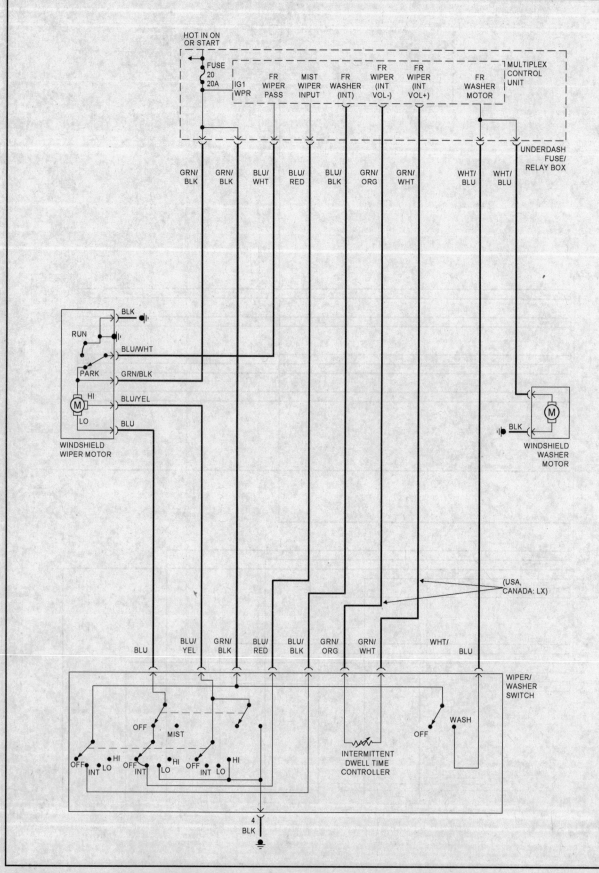

Windshield wiper/washer system (coupe/sedan)

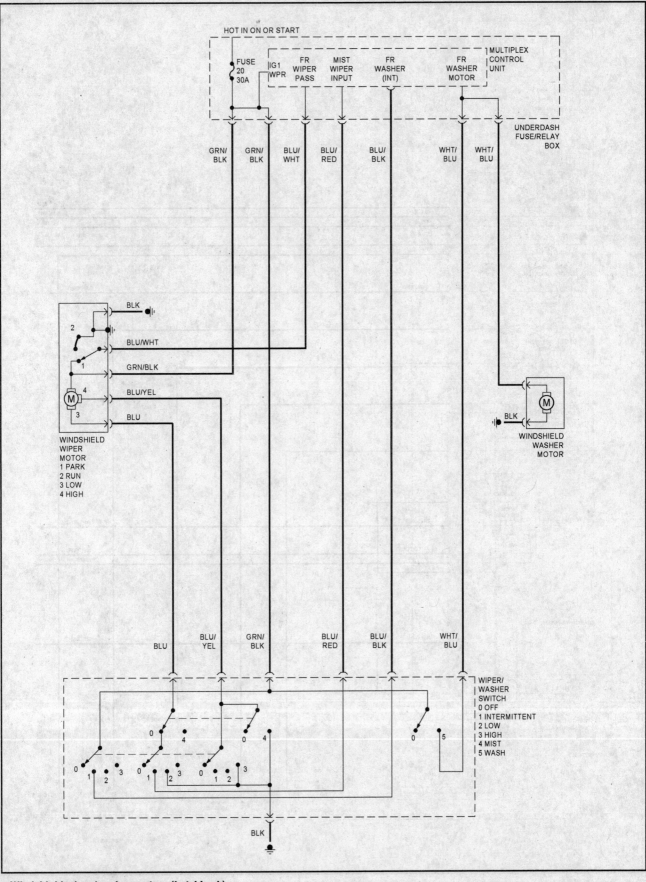

Windshield wiper/washer system (hatchback)

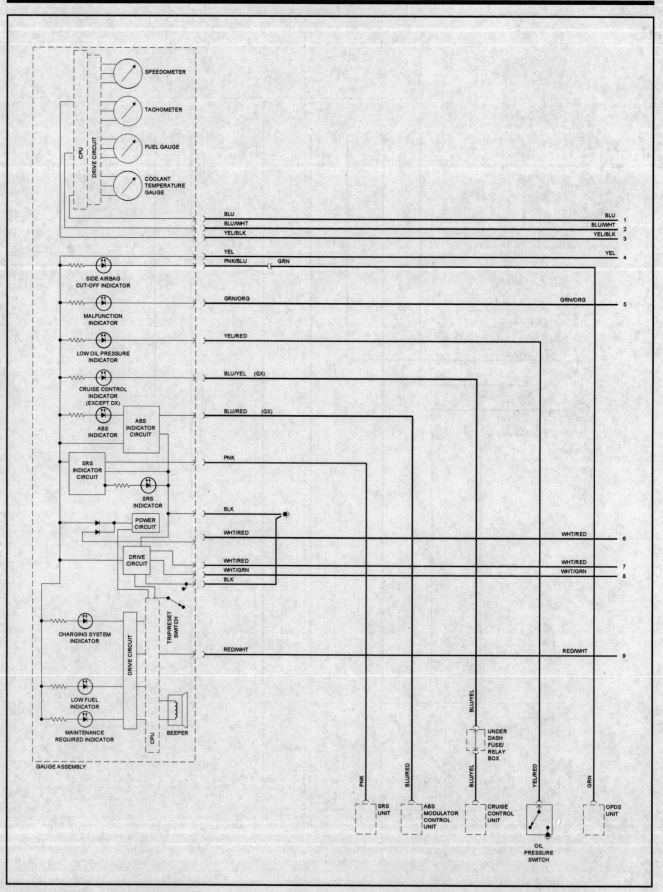

Warning systems - coupe/sedan (1 of 2)

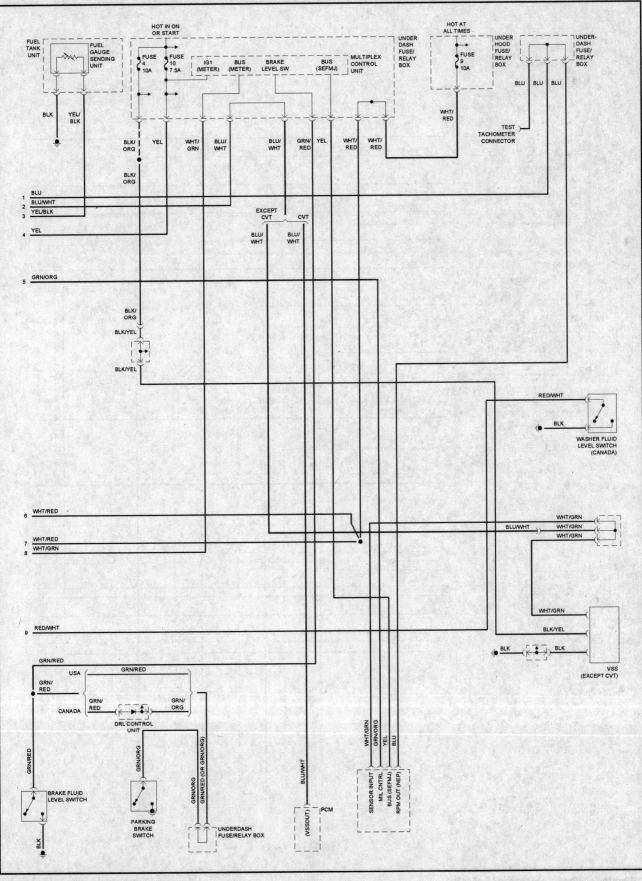

Warning systems - coupe/sedan (2 of 2)

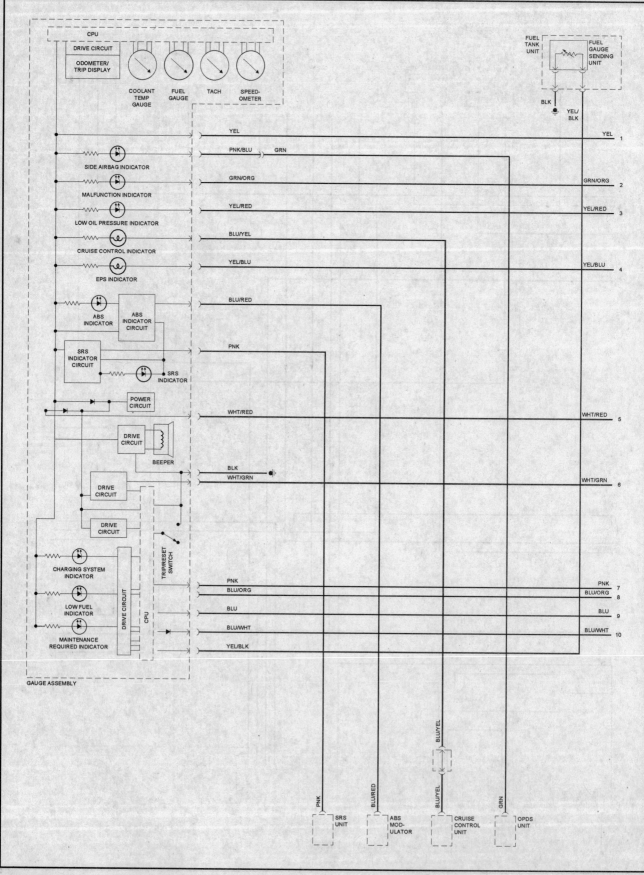

Warning systems - hatchback (1 of 2)

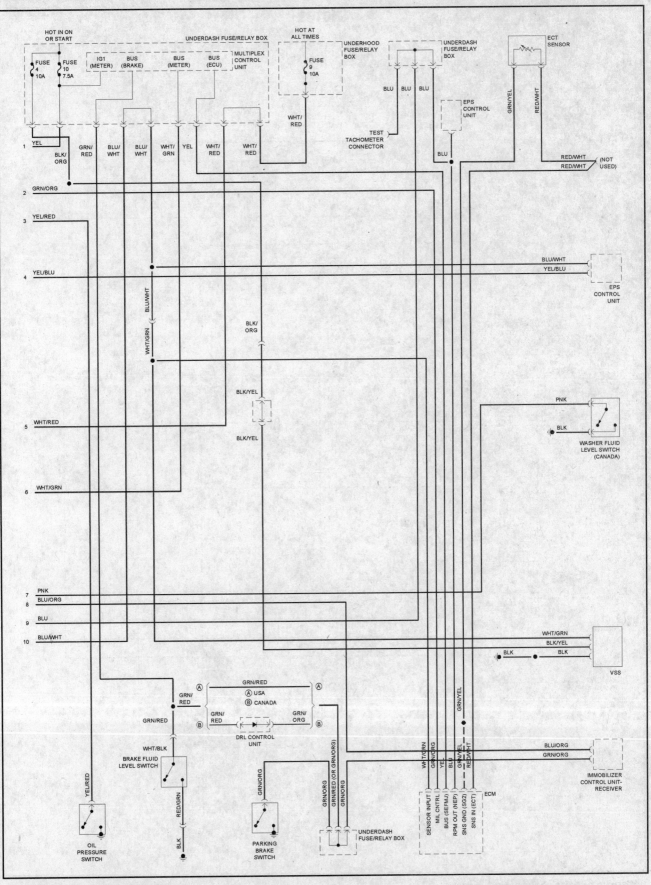

Warning systems - hatchback (2 of 2)

Notes

GLOSSARY

AIR/FUEL RATIO: The ratio of air-to-gasoline by weight in the fuel mixture drawn into the engine.

AIR INJECTION: One method of reducing harmful exhaust emissions by injecting air into each of the exhaust ports of an engine. The fresh air entering the hot exhaust manifold causes any remaining fuel to be burned before it can exit the tailpipe.

ALTERNATOR: A device used for converting mechanical energy into electrical energy.

AMMETER: An instrument, calibrated in amperes, used to measure the flow of an electrical current in a circuit. Ammeters are always connected in series with the circuit being tested.

AMPERE: The rate of flow of electrical current present when one volt of electrical pressure is applied against one ohm of electrical resistance.

ANALOG COMPUTER: Any microprocessor that uses similar (analogous) electrical signals to make its calculations.

ARMATURE: A laminated, soft iron core wrapped by a wire that converts electrical energy to mechanical energy as in a motor or relay. When rotated in a magnetic field, it changes mechanical energy into electrical energy as in a generator.

ATMOSPHERIC PRESSURE: The pressure on the Earth's surface caused by the weight of the air in the atmosphere. At sea level, this pressure is 14.7 psi at 32°F (101 kPa at 0°C).

ATOMIZATION: The breaking down of a liquid into a fine mist that can be suspended in air.

AXIAL PLAY: Movement parallel to a shaft or bearing bore.

BACKFIRE: The sudden combustion of gases in the intake or exhaust system that results in a loud explosion.

BACKLASH: The clearance or play between two parts, such as meshed gears.

BACKPRESSURE: Restrictions in the exhaust system that slow the exit of exhaust gases from the combustion chamber.

BAKELITE: A heat resistant, plastic insulator material commonly used in printed circuit boards and transistorized components.

BALL BEARING: A bearing made up of hardened inner and outer races between which hardened steel balls roll.

BALLAST RESISTOR: A resistor in the primary ignition circuit that lowers voltage after the engine is started to reduce wear on ignition components.

BEARING: A friction reducing, supportive device usually located between a stationary part and a moving part.

BIMETAL TEMPERATURE SENSOR: Any sensor or switch made of two dissimilar types of metal that bend when heated or cooled due to the different expansion rates of the alloys. These types of sensors usually function as an on/off switch.

BLOWBY: Combustion gases, composed of water vapor and unburned fuel, that leak past the piston rings into the crankcase during normal engine operation. These gases are removed by the PCV system to prevent the buildup of harmful acids in the crankcase.

BRAKE PAD: A brake shoe and lining assembly used with disc brakes.

BRAKE SHOE: The backing for the brake lining. The term is, however, usually applied to the assembly of the brake backing and lining.

BUSHING: A liner, usually removable, for a bearing; an anti-friction liner used in place of a bearing.

CALIPER: A hydraulically activated device in a disc brake system, which is mounted straddling the brake rotor (disc). The caliper contains at least one piston and two brake pads. Hydraulic pressure on the piston(s) forces the pads against the rotor.

CAMSHAFT: A shaft in the engine on which are the lobes (cams) which operate the valves. The camshaft is driven by the crankshaft, via a belt, chain or gears, at one half the crankshaft speed.

CAPACITOR: A device which stores an electrical charge.

CARBON MONOXIDE (CO): A colorless, odorless gas given off as a normal byproduct of combustion. It is poisonous and extremely dangerous in confined areas, building up slowly to toxic levels without warning if adequate ventilation is not available.

CARBURETOR: A device, usually mounted on the intake manifold of an engine, which mixes the air and fuel in the proper proportion to allow even combustion.

CATALYTIC CONVERTER: A device installed in the exhaust system, like a muffler, that converts harmful byproducts of combustion into carbon dioxide and water vapor by means of a heat-producing chemical reaction.

CENTRIFUGAL ADVANCE: A mechanical method of advancing the spark timing by using flyweights in the distributor that react to centrifugal force generated by the distributor shaft rotation.

CHECK VALVE: Any one-way valve installed to permit the flow of air, fuel or vacuum in one direction only.

CHOKE: A device, usually a moveable valve, placed in the intake path of a carburetor to restrict the flow of air.

CIRCUIT: Any unbroken path through which an electrical current can flow. Also used to describe fuel flow in some instances.

CIRCUIT BREAKER: A switch which protects an electrical circuit from overload by opening the circuit when the current flow exceeds a predetermined level. Some circuit breakers must be reset manually, while most reset automatically.

COIL (IGNITION): A transformer in the ignition circuit which steps up the voltage provided to the spark plugs.

COMBINATION MANIFOLD: An assembly which includes both the intake and exhaust manifolds in one casting.

COMBINATION VALVE: A device used in some fuel systems that routes fuel vapors to a charcoal storage canister instead of venting them into the atmosphere. The valve relieves fuel tank pressure and allows fresh air into the tank as the fuel level drops to prevent a vapor lock situation.

COMPRESSION RATIO: The comparison of the total volume of the cylinder and combustion chamber with the piston at BDC and the piston at TDC.

CONDENSER: 1. An electrical device which acts to store an electrical charge, preventing voltage surges. 2. A radiator-like device in the air conditioning system in which refrigerant gas condenses into a liquid, giving off heat.

CONDUCTOR: Any material through which an electrical current can be transmitted easily.

CONTINUITY: Continuous or complete circuit. Can be checked with an ohmmeter.

COUNTERSHAFT: An intermediate shaft which is rotated by a mainshaft and transmits, in turn, that rotation to a working part.

CRANKCASE: The lower part of an engine in which the crankshaft and related parts operate.

CRANKSHAFT: The main driving shaft of an engine which receives reciprocating motion from the pistons and converts it to rotary motion.

CYLINDER: In an engine, the round hole in the engine block in which the piston(s) ride.

CYLINDER BLOCK: The main structural member of an engine in which is found the cylinders, crankshaft and other principal parts.

CYLINDER HEAD: The detachable portion of the engine, usually fastened to the top of the cylinder block and containing all or most of the combustion chambers. On overhead valve engines, it contains the valves and their operating parts. On overhead cam engines, it contains the camshaft as well.

DEAD CENTER: The extreme top or bottom of the piston stroke.

DETONATION: An unwanted explosion of the air/fuel mixture in the combustion chamber caused by excess heat and compression, advanced timing, or an overly lean mixture. Also referred to as "ping".

DIAPHRAGM: A thin, flexible wall separating two cavities, such as in a vacuum advance unit.

DIESELING: A condition in which hot spots in the combustion chamber cause the engine to run on after the key is turned off.

DIFFERENTIAL: A geared assembly which allows the transmission of motion between drive axles, giving one axle the ability to turn faster than the other.

DIODE: An electrical device that will allow current to flow in one direction only.

DISC BRAKE: A hydraulic braking assembly consisting of a brake disc, or rotor, mounted on an axle, and a caliper assembly containing, usually two brake pads which are activated by hydraulic pressure. The pads are forced against the sides of the disc, creating friction which slows the vehicle.

DISTRIBUTOR: A mechanically driven device on an engine which is responsible for electrically firing the spark plug at a predetermined point of the piston stroke.

DOWEL PIN: A pin, inserted in mating holes in two different parts allowing those parts to maintain a fixed relationship.

DRUM BRAKE: A braking system which consists of two brake shoes and one or two wheel cylinders, mounted on a fixed backing plate, and a brake drum, mounted on an axle, which revolves around the assembly.

DWELL: The rate, measured in degrees of shaft rotation, at which an electrical circuit cycles on and off.

ELECTRONIC CONTROL UNIT (ECU): Ignition module, module, amplifier or igniter. See Module for definition.

ELECTRONIC IGNITION: A system in which the timing and firing of the spark plugs is controlled by an electronic control unit, usually called a module. These systems have no points or condenser.

END-PLAY: The measured amount of axial movement in a shaft.

ENGINE: A device that converts heat into mechanical energy.

EXHAUST MANIFOLD: A set of cast passages or pipes which conduct exhaust gases from the engine.

FEELER GAUGE: A blade, usually metal, of precisely predetermined thickness, used to measure the clearance between two parts.

FIRING ORDER: The order in which combustion occurs in the cylinders of an engine. Also the order in which spark is distributed to the plugs by the distributor.

FLOODING: The presence of too much fuel in the intake manifold and combustion chamber which prevents the air/fuel mixture from firing, thereby causing a no-start situation.

FLYWHEEL: A disc shaped part bolted to the rear end of the crankshaft. Around the outer perimeter is affixed the ring gear. The starter drive engages the ring gear, turning the flywheel, which rotates the crankshaft, imparting the initial starting motion to the engine.

FOOT POUND (ft. lbs. or sometimes, ft.lb.): The amount of energy or work needed to raise an item weighing one pound, a distance of one foot.

FUSE: A protective device in a circuit which prevents circuit overload by breaking the circuit when a specific amperage is present. The device is constructed around a strip or wire of a lower amperage rating than the circuit it is designed to protect. When an amperage higher than that stamped on the fuse is present in the circuit, the strip or wire melts, opening the circuit.

GEAR RATIO: The ratio between the number of teeth on meshing gears.

GENERATOR: A device which converts mechanical energy into electrical energy.

HEAT RANGE: The measure of a spark plug's ability to dissipate heat from its firing end. The higher the heat range, the hotter the plug fires.

HUB: The center part of a wheel or gear.

HYDROCARBON (HC): Any chemical compound made up of hydrogen and carbon. A major pollutant formed by the engine as a byproduct of combustion.

HYDROMETER: An instrument used to measure the specific gravity of a solution.

INCH POUND (inch lbs.; sometimes in.lb. or in. lbs.): One twelfth of a foot pound.

INDUCTION: A means of transferring electrical energy in the form of a magnetic field. Principle used in the ignition coil to increase voltage.

INJECTOR: A device which receives metered fuel under relatively low pressure and is activated to inject the fuel into the engine under relatively high pressure at a predetermined time.

INPUT SHAFT: The shaft to which torque is applied, usually carrying the driving gear or gears.

INTAKE MANIFOLD: A casting of passages or pipes used to conduct air or a fuel/air mixture to the cylinders.

JOURNAL: The bearing surface within which a shaft operates.

KEY: A small block usually fitted in a notch between a shaft and a hub to prevent slippage of the two parts.

MANIFOLD: A casting of passages or set of pipes which connect the cylinders to an inlet or outlet source.

MANIFOLD VACUUM: Low pressure in an engine intake manifold formed just below the throttle plates. Manifold vacuum is highest at idle and drops under acceleration.

MASTER CYLINDER: The primary fluid pressurizing device in a hydraulic system. In automotive use, it is found in brake and hydraulic clutch systems and is pedal activated, either directly or, in a power brake system, through the power booster.

MODULE: Electronic control unit, amplifier or igniter of solid state or integrated design which controls the current flow in the ignition primary circuit based on input from the pick-up coil. When the module opens the primary circuit, high secondary voltage is induced in the coil.

NEEDLE BEARING: A bearing which consists of a number (usually a large number) of long, thin rollers.

OHM: (Ω) The unit used to measure the resistance of conductor-to-electrical flow. One ohm is the amount of resistance that limits current flow to one ampere in a circuit with one volt of pressure.

OHMMETER: An instrument used for measuring the resistance, in ohms, in an electrical circuit.

OUTPUT SHAFT: The shaft which transmits torque from a device, such as a transmission.

OVERDRIVE: A gear assembly which produces more shaft revolutions than that transmitted to it.

OVERHEAD CAMSHAFT (OHC): An engine configuration in which the camshaft is mounted on top of the cylinder head and operates the valve either directly or by means of rocker arms.

OVERHEAD VALVE (OHV): An engine configuration in which all of the valves are located in the cylinder head and the camshaft is located in the cylinder block. The camshaft operates the valves via lifters and pushrods.

OXIDES OF NITROGEN (NOx): Chemical compounds of nitrogen produced as a byproduct of combustion. They combine with hydrocarbons to produce smog.

OXYGEN SENSOR: Use with the feedback system to sense the presence of oxygen in the exhaust gas and signal the computer which can reference the voltage signal to an air/fuel ratio.

PINION: The smaller of two meshing gears.

PISTON RING: An open-ended ring with fits into a groove on the outer diameter of the piston. Its chief function is to form a seal between the piston and cylinder wall. Most automotive pistons have three rings: two for compression sealing; one for oil sealing.

PRELOAD: A predetermined load placed on a bearing during assembly or by adjustment.

PRIMARY CIRCUIT: the low voltage side of the ignition system which consists of the ignition switch, ballast resistor or resistance wire, bypass, coil, electronic control unit and pick-up coil as well as the connecting wires and harnesses.

PRESS FIT: The mating of two parts under pressure, due to the inner diameter of one being smaller than the outer diameter of the other, or vice versa; an interference fit.

RACE: The surface on the inner or outer ring of a bearing on which the balls, needles or rollers move.

REGULATOR: A device which maintains the amperage and/or voltage levels of a circuit at predetermined values.

RELAY: A switch which automatically opens and/or closes a circuit.

RESISTANCE: The opposition to the flow of current through a circuit or electrical device, and is measured in ohms. Resistance is equal to the voltage divided by the amperage.

RESISTOR: A device, usually made of wire, which offers a preset amount of resistance in an electrical circuit.

RING GEAR: The name given to a ring-shaped gear attached to a differential case, or affixed to a flywheel or as part of a planetary gear set.

ROLLER BEARING: A bearing made up of hardened inner and outer races between which hardened steel rollers move.

ROTOR: 1. The disc-shaped part of a disc brake assembly, upon which the brake pads bear; also called, brake disc. 2. The device mounted atop the distributor shaft, which passes current to the distributor cap tower contacts.

SECONDARY CIRCUIT: The high voltage side of the ignition system, usually above 20,000 volts. The secondary includes the ignition coil, coil wire, distributor cap and rotor, spark plug wires and spark plugs.

SENDING UNIT: A mechanical, electrical, hydraulic or electro-magnetic device which transmits information to a gauge.

SENSOR: Any device designed to measure engine operating conditions or ambient pressures and temperatures. Usually electronic in nature and designed to send a voltage signal to an on-board computer, some sensors may operate as a simple on/off switch or they may provide a variable voltage signal (like a potentiometer) as conditions or measured parameters change.

SHIM: Spacers of precise, predetermined thickness used between parts to establish a proper working relationship.

SLAVE CYLINDER: In automotive use, a device in the hydraulic clutch system which is activated by hydraulic force, disengaging the clutch.

SOLENOID: A coil used to produce a magnetic field, the effect of which is to produce work.

SPARK PLUG: A device screwed into the combustion chamber of a spark ignition engine. The basic construction is a conductive core inside of a ceramic insulator, mounted in an outer conductive base. An electrical charge from the spark plug wire travels along the conductive core and jumps a preset air gap to a grounding point or points at the end of the conductive base. The resultant spark ignites the fuel/air mixture in the combustion chamber.

SPLINES: Ridges machined or cast onto the outer diameter of a shaft or inner diameter of a bore to enable parts to mate without rotation.

TACHOMETER: A device used to measure the rotary speed of an engine, shaft, gear, etc., usually in rotations per minute.

THERMOSTAT: A valve, located in the cooling system of an engine, which is closed when cold and opens gradually in response to engine heating, controlling the temperature of the coolant and rate of coolant flow.

TOP DEAD CENTER (TDC): The point at which the piston reaches the top of its travel on the compression stroke.

TORQUE: The twisting force applied to an object.

TORQUE CONVERTER: A turbine used to transmit power from a driving member to a driven member via hydraulic action, providing changes in drive ratio and torque. In automotive use, it links the driveplate at the rear of the engine to the automatic transmission.

TRANSDUCER: A device used to change a force into an electrical signal.

TRANSISTOR: A semi-conductor component which can be actuated by a small voltage to perform an electrical switching function.

TUNE-UP: A regular maintenance function, usually associated with the replacement and adjustment of parts and components in the electrical and fuel systems of a vehicle for the purpose of attaining optimum performance.

TURBOCHARGER: An exhaust driven pump which compresses intake air and forces it into the combustion chambers at higher than atmospheric pressures. The increased air pressure allows more fuel to be burned and results in increased horsepower being produced.

VACUUM ADVANCE: A device which advances the ignition timing in response to increased engine vacuum.

VACUUM GAUGE: An instrument used to measure the presence of vacuum in a chamber.

VALVE: A device which control the pressure, direction of flow or rate of flow of a liquid or gas.

VALVE CLEARANCE: The measured gap between the end of the valve stem and the rocker arm, cam lobe or follower that activates the valve.

VISCOSITY: The rating of a liquid's internal resistance to flow.

VOLTMETER: An instrument used for measuring electrical force in units called volts. Voltmeters are always connected parallel with the circuit being tested.

WHEEL CYLINDER: Found in the automotive drum brake assembly, it is a device, actuated by hydraulic pressure, which, through internal pistons, pushes the brake shoes outward against the drums.

A

B

MASTER INDEX